THE GROWTH OF THE
AMERICAN REPUBLIC

Thomas Jefferson
Portrait by Sully in the American Philosophical
Society, Philadelphia

THE *GROWTH* OF THE

AMERICAN REPUBLIC

SAMUEL ELIOT MORISON

JONATHAN TRUMBULL PROFESSOR OF AMERICAN HISTORY
IN HARVARD UNIVERSITY

AND

HENRY STEELE COMMAGER

PROFESSOR OF HISTORY, COLUMBIA UNIVERSITY

Volume One

OXFORD UNIVERSITY PRESS · *New York*

LONDON · TORONTO · BOMBAY · MELBOURNE

1942

Printed in the United States of America
by the Plimpton Press, Norwood, Mass.

PREFACE

The Growth of the American Republic appeared in 1930 as a single volume, beginning the story in 1763 and terminating it in 1917. In 1936–7 we rewrote the entire book, greatly enlarging the period since the Civil War, and carrying the story down to the second inauguration of President Franklin D. Roosevelt.

Our sincere thanks are extended to the many readers who have notified us of errors in earlier editions; to our colleagues who have read parts of the copy; to authors and publishers severally mentioned in the footnotes, who have allowed us to quote passages from prose and poetry; to the Carnegie Institution of Washington and the House of Harper for permitting us to use maps from the *Atlas of Historical Geography* and *Harper's Atlas of American History*.

We write for young men and women of all ages, for whom economy in truth-telling is neither necessary nor appropriate. We believe that history embraces the whole of a people's activity: economic and social, literary and spiritual, as well as political. We have endeavored therefore to give such stress to these different aspects that our story will be that of American civilization.

In this, the third edition, we have extended the story backward to the origin of man in America and forward to cover America's entry into the Second World War; being neither geologists nor prophets we can go no further. The new survey of the colonial period has made it possible to eliminate some of the descriptive matter in Volume I, so that the third edition is not substantially longer than the second. Otherwise the text has been revised only where fresh researches have convinced us that we were incorrect.

This new edition is dedicated to our fellow Americans in the fighting forces. They are furthering the most marvellous movement in the history of mankind, the Growth of the American Republic!

SAMUEL ELIOT MORISON

HENRY STEELE COMMAGER

May 1942

CONTENTS

VOLUME I

school. 5. Humanitarianism and Abolition: insane and blind, peace, temperance, Colonization Society, Garrison, Liberty Party, the Under Ground, J. Q. Adams.

LIST OF ILLUSTRATIONS

VOLUME I

THE GROWTH OF THE AMERICAN REPUBLIC

Now Praise to God's oft-granted grace,
Now Praise to Man's undaunted face,
Despite the land, despite the sea,
I was: I am: and I shall be —
How long, Good Angel, O how long?
Sing me from Heaven a man's own song!

'Long as thine Art shall love true love,
Long as thy Science truth shall know,
Long as thine Eagle harms no Dove,
Long as thy Law by law shall grow,
Long as thy God is God above,
Thy brother every man below,
So long, dear Land of all my love,
Thy name shall shine, thy fame shall glow!'

— SIDNEY LANIER, *Centennial Cantata* (1876)

THE GROWTH OF THE
AMERICAN REPUBLIC

I

ISOLATED AMERICA

?–1492

1. *The First Discovery*

ONE summer day somewhat over twenty-five thousand and less than forty thousand years ago, a tribe of Mongolian savages stood on lofty Cape Dejneva, the easternmost promontory of Siberia, about thirty miles south of the Arctic Circle. They or their parents had abandoned their old home in what is now the Gobi Desert, because that area was beginning to dry up. They had had a long, hard trek of at least three thousand miles, living off the country and fighting the natives all along the way for several years. Perhaps only the magic of their medicine man, his promise of a new world toward the rising sun, had kept them going. Food was scarce, the latest enemy to resent their intrusion followed hard at their heels, and their skin garments were in tatters; in fact they were a tough-looking lot, even according to Siberian standards of that very unrefined era. Looking southeastward over Bering Strait, our hard-pressed savages saw clearly, only twenty-three miles away, a dome-shaped island over seventeen hundred feet high rising above the sea. They had no experience in navigation, but something had to be done quickly. So, either by fastening together whatever logs and driftwood they could procure, or (more likely) by stealing native kayaks, they ferried themselves over to Big Diomede Island, as we call it, and shook off their pursuers.

Big Diomede and its companion Little Diomede, between which runs today the U.S.-U.S.S.R. boundary, are rocky and barren, affording little in the way of food. So our harassed pioneers, unconscious that they were men of destiny, resumed their voyage to a high rocky land that they sighted twenty-five miles to the eastward. This was on the Seward Peninsula of Alaska, and the westernmost point of continental United States. Our Mongoloid pilgrim fathers were the ancestors of the mighty race which Christopher Columbus mistakenly named the Indians.

Alaska to them was a land of promise indeed, for it afforded the first square meals they had had for many a long day. In the rivers and the sea there were salmon, seal, and sea-otter. In the back country there were lots of big, hairy beasts that roared in an amusing manner and rolled over dead when you struck them in a vital spot with your stone-pointed spear; animals whose meat filled the belly and whose pelt kept you warm all winter. And no rival human beings to fight for all this plenty! Our pilgrims so fell in love with this new country that they completely forgot about the old; it never occurred to them to found a Society of Gobi Desert Descendants.

Permit your historians a little flight of imagination before they settle down to hard fact. After all, the consensus of scientific opinion is that the American continent was discovered by man in some such way as we have described. *Homo sapiens* is a relative newcomer on our planet, and in America he seems to have been a post-Pleistocene parvenu. The Indians wrote no histories, and the archæologists and palæontologists cannot answer all our questions; but there is no possibility that the New World developed her own *Pithecanthropus erectus,* because no remains of anthropoid apes or 'low' forms of man have been found here. It seems a little insulting to America that she had to import Man from Asia. But, apparently, big animals like the dinosaur had it all their own way in the pre-glacial age, say fifty thousand years ago and beyond.

This is not to say that all the many million Indians who inhabited North, Central, and South America in 1492 were descended from the passengers on our hypothetical fleet of Mongoloid Mayflowers. Biologically it was perfectly possible, but other migratory bands from Siberia must have followed the same course to safety and a square meal. The migration may have been intermittent, or may have extended over several thousand years. The Eskimo, for instance, belong to the Red Men rather than to the Yellow, but they are very different in physique from their racial brethren, and probably arrived here only ten to fifteen thousand years before the white man. Even today there are Eskimo living under the Hammer and Sickle, as well as under the Stars and Stripes and the Union Jack.

All ancestors of the American Indians came from Asia via Siberia, and America received no addition from any other source, for at least twenty-five thousand years. Africa may have been joined to South America, but that was long before humankind appeared on the earth. The 'lost continent' of Atlantis and Mu are myths. The Polynesians, despite their skill in canoe navigation, never reached America, because in the South Pacific, where the islands are most numerous, the prevailing winds are easterly, whilst in the North Pacific there is a 2000-mile jump from the Hawaiian Islands to California. Easter Island, the furthest east that the southern Polynesians ever reached, is even farther than that from the nearest continental coast in Chile. An occasional Chinese junk or Japanese fishing boat may have drifted across to the coast of Vancouver Island or Oregon; but the human survivors, if any, were undoubtedly killed and probably eaten.

Movements of the Indians after their discovery of America may be traced roughly by remains of their successive cultures that have been excavated; but we need thousands more such finds before we can give them definite timetables and routes. They happened to land in the only part of America north of the present U.S.-Canadian border that was never glaciated. If they arrived earlier than about thirty-five thousand years ago, their movements for many millennia were restricted to northern and central Alaska. As the great ice-cap, which once covered all Canada and a good part of the United States, receded, the Indians passed through the inter-glacial corridor of the Yukon and Mackenzie valleys to the eastward of the Rocky Mountains, and there began to spread out fanwise into the buffalo country and beyond. Before this dispersal took place, they had learned to make watertight baskets in which food could be boiled with hot stones; and after basketry came pottery and weaving. Those who settled down on various parts of the coast learned to fashion dugout canoes holding as many as a hundred people; in such craft the Arawak, whom Columbus first encountered, had reached the islands only a century or so before he did. From Central America to South America the Indians probably passed by land, over the jungle-covered cordillera; and having reached South America some of them became very skilful metal workers and returned to Central America.

Twenty-five thousand years seems little enough for these people to have attained their distribution, as the Europeans found them a mere four and a half centuries ago, or to have developed the differentiation between the primitive savagery of California natives and the highly organized and complex societies of Mexico, Colombia, and Peru.

2. *Some Indian Families*

These differentiations were even wider than those of the peoples of Europe. So, in want of other means of classification, ethnologists have agreed to group the many thousand Indian tribes on a language basis in so-called Stocks or Families, each stock including tribes that have languages with common characteristics. As the ethnologists acquire more knowledge of these languages, they steadily reduce the number through combination. Powell, for instance, recognized fifty-six linguistic stocks in Canada and the United States, but those are now reduced to six. A common or similar language was of little social significance, for some of the deadliest enemies, like the Mohawk and the Huron, understood each other perfectly.

Some of these linguistic stocks, like the so-called Pueblo group, occupied a definite area; others, like the Algonkin, had a continental distribution. The Algonkin, for instance, include the Salish tribes on the Pacific Coast; the Kootenay; the Blackfoot-Cheyenne-Arapaho group; the Cree, Sauk and Fox, Ojibwa, and Shawnee in the Middle West; and all the tribes with which the English settlers made contact in Virginia and New England. It is not known how or when the Algonkin Stock attained so wide a distribution. Over a large portion of their territory they were not the first comers, as the remarkable mounds of the Middle West testify.[1] From the Algonkin the English learned to cultivate corn, tobacco, and the pumpkin, to cook hominy and succotash, to build a wigwam, paddle a birch-bark canoe, and walk on snowshoes. From them our forbears heard about Gitchie Manitu, the ' Great Spirit '; for the Algonkin were religious in a genial Hellenic manner, which made them relatively easy to convert to Christianity. The Algonkin produced many great and even noble characters, such as Pocahontas and Massasoit, Opechancanough and King Philip, Tammany and Pontiac, Tecumseh and Keokuk. Owing to their long contact with the English, both friendly and hostile, the Algonkin characteristics, by and large, are those most familiar to readers of English and North American literature.

Even tougher fighters than the Algonkin were those belonging to the Iroquois Family, who according to their own traditions migrated

---

[1] It was formerly thought that the ' Mound Builders ' were not Indians, but an older American race. Archaeologists have established beyond doubt that they were Indians; but what Indians they were, and what became of them, is still a matter of discussion. See Carl E. Guthe, in *The Maya and Their Neighbors,* pp. 368–74.

from the South along the line of the Appalachians. After the famous Five Nations (Mohawk, Cayuga, Oneida, Onondaga, Seneca) had reached central New York, they were united in a federal league, the most remarkable political organization in North America, by their great leader Hiawatha, who was a contemporary of Columbus. The Tuscarora of the Carolinas, who joined this league as the sixth nation in the early eighteenth century; the Cherokee, who remained in and around central Georgia until removed by President Jackson; the Huron whom the Five Nations almost exterminated; and many other tribes of the Atlantic States were of Iroquoian stock. The Iroquois Confederacy, after protecting the English Colonies from the French and their Algonkin allies for over a century and a half, chose the losing side in the War of Independence, and most of the survivors retreated to Canada. They, too, produced great characters, such as Cornplanter, Brant, Red Jacket, Sequoya, and last but not least, Logan. ' Who is there to mourn for Logan? Not one.'

Belonging to the same language group as the Iroquois is the Muskhogean Family, which dwelt in the Deep South of the United States. These were the first Indians of North America with whom the Spaniards came in contact. The Muskhogean include the Creek, Choctaw, Chickasaw and Natchez, and the Seminole, whose brave and able leader Osceola defeated the armies of the United States in a seven years' war only a century ago, and many of whose survivors still remain in Florida. The others, who had successfully defied the Spaniards for three centuries, were removed to Oklahoma, where they showed an unusual adaptability to American civilization. The Siouan peoples of the Great Plains (including Dakota, Crow, Mandan, Kansas, Iowa, Omaha, Quapaw) are now considered to be of the same language group as the Iroquois and Muskhogean.

Only the Indians of the Great Plains, whose economy was completely tied up to the buffalo, were nomadic. The other tribes which we have mentioned depended largely on hunting and fishing for a livelihood, with agriculture as a secondary source of food; they had definite hunting grounds and moved in a body only when game became scarce. The so-called Pueblo Indians of New Mexico and Arizona, who speak four different languages, have been sedentary husbandmen for almost a thousand years. They were the only Indians north of Mexico who wove cotton cloth. Many of their gigantic communal dwellings of wood, stone, and adobe, which the Spaniards called *pueblos* (towns), were built four and five centuries before

Columbus; and in caves beneath the cliff dwellings, archæologists have found remains of earlier basket-making cultures, the latest being at least eight hundred years old. Partly because of their deep roots in mother earth, partly because of their political cohesion and relatively high development, the Pueblo Indians have more successfully maintained their culture and self-government than any other group of native tribes in the United States.

On the nomenclature of the United States and Canada the Indians have left a permanent impress. The conquering European generally named his settlements after some place in the Old World, or an older part of the New World, or after one of his own saints or heroes; but the second city of the Americas, Chicago, is an Indian name meaning ' place of the skunk.' The names of twenty-five of the forty-eight states and of most of the Canadian provinces are Indian; and native American names were generally preserved by the white man, although often in a garbled or corrupted form, for lakes and rivers.

3. The Maya

Compared with the Maya, the Pueblo Indians were relatively uncivilized. Any North American of today who imagines all Indians to have been an inferior race of low culture, whom his ancestors had a divine right to replace, is invited to contemplate the ruins of the Petén in Guatemala, Copán in Honduras, Chichen Itzá and Uxmal in Yucatán, Teotihuacan in Mexico, or the models and casts of them that are exhibited in North American museums. The glistening white pyramids arising out of tangled jungles; the astronomical observatories and royal palaces carved with plumed serpents, tapirs, exotic birds and strange human figures almost lost in elaborate headdresses; the sculptured glyphs telling stories only part of which modern man has been able to read; the colossal statues representing forgotten gods; the jade carvings, masks, and ceremonial objects, are as impressive to one who sees them for the first time as a Gothic cathedral or the Acropolis of Athens. When these monuments and sculptures were first depicted by the Catherwood drawings in the works of John L. Stephens a century ago, people in the United States and Europe could not believe that such works could have been made by ' Red Indians,' and they devised fantastic theories of Egyptian, Chinese, or East Indian migrations to explain them. Yet one thing is absolutely certain of the three great civilizations of Central and

South America: that they were autocthonous. They arose, after many thousand years' evolution, among primitive savages who originally crossed from Asia to America. The Maya invented complicated designs which they applied to stone, pottery, wood, metal, and textiles, and which too long were regarded by people of European stock as uncouth and repulsive. At length we began to appreciate these native forms as high achievements in the fine arts.

Although the story-glyphs with which an educated priesthood once recorded the history of the Maya have disappeared, a considerable number of the date-glyphs have been deciphered; and it is clear that the Maya were such advanced astronomers as to devise a calendar more accurate than the Julian, which England and her colonies used until 1752. The Maya calendar began to function several centuries before the Christian Era. The first seat of the Maya empire was in the Department of Petén, Guatemala. There a great urban civilization was developed; but about the seventh century A.D. these sites were generally abandoned. Migrating to Yucatán, the Maya built hundreds of stone cities, a few of which, like Chichen Itzá and Uxmal, have been partially excavated and restored; and between A.D. 1000 and 1200 these were united in a league of city states, the League of Mayapan. In the meantime a similar culture was being evolved by the Toltec in Mexico proper. The great Toltec leader Quetzalcoatl, an historic figure who was at once priest-scientist and warrior-king, invaded and conquered Mayapan in 1191; his successors extended their rule over central and southern Mexico, Guatemala, and Honduras. These Toltec both absorbed and added to the Maya civilization, much as the Romans did with that of the Greeks. Under the dynasty of the Cocomes, they remained in control until A.D. 1450, when for unknown causes their culture began to decay and their political organization to collapse.

The Aztec, a hunting tribe from the north, were comparatively late arrivals on the Mexican plateau, reaching in A.D. 1325 the shores of the lake, on an island of which their supposedly impregnable capital was built. They too (like the barbarians who conquered Rome), absorbed much of the Toltec-Maya civilization, and conquered a part of the decaying Toltec empire. When Cortés landed near Vera Cruz in 1519, the Aztec edifice was beginning to show internal weakness, and Montezuma II was somewhat of a Merovingian monarch. In spite of the Spaniards' efforts to stamp out the Toltec-Maya culture, many features of it endure to this day.

In South America the two greatest civilizations were those of the Chibcha in the highlands of Colombia, and of the Inca in Peru. Among these, as in Mayapan, there was a highly complex social organization directed by a ruling class that exploited a voiceless urban and rural proletariat, ' held fast in spiritual and moral slavery to an enormous and baleful priesthood serving a confused throng of fearful gods.' [2] The Inca were inferior to the Maya in certain arts of design, but their equal in textile weaving, and their superior in metallurgy and stone architecture. Population records of their intricate totalitarian commonwealth were recorded by a system of knotted strings that has never been deciphered.

4. *Indian Achievements*

If further evidence is wanted that these high civilizations of the Indians were of purely American origin, we have only to consider the simple things of immemorial use in Europe, which even the most gifted Indians never discovered. Although they learned to mine, smelt and work gold, silver and platinum, tin, lead and copper, their use of iron was limited to chance finds of meteoric deposits. Indians invented the bark and the dugout canoes, cunningly spread the sides of the dugout by filling it with water heated to the boiling point by hot stones; yet only one or two primitive tribes in California learned to build a boat from plank and timber. Although they made pottery that could stand a hot fire, they never discovered the potter's, or any other kind of wheel; the only beasts of burden in all the Americas (apart from the squaw) were the dog and the llama.

The most important discoveries of the Indians, from the point of view of ourselves who profited by them, were in agriculture. One of the greatest agricultural achievements of all time was maize or Indian corn, a hybrid developed by the Indians from certain wild plants that grew in Central America. Second only to that was the evolution of the white potato from a wild tuber-bearing *Solanum* that grew on the west slope of the Andes. We also owe to Indian husbandmen tobacco, the sweet potato, the pineapple, the peanut, maple sugar, various kinds of beans, tomatoes, sisal, squashes and pumpkins, coca, cacao, quinine, vanilla, and even rubber. From caoutchouc they fashioned elastic rubber balls which were used in a game similar to basket-ball that was played from New Mexico to Paraguay, and the

---

[2] Philip A. Means, *The Maya and Their Neighbors*, p. 431.

latex they used for waterproofing bags, shoes, and garments. Even the hunting tribes learned to fertilize their gardens with fish and wood ashes; the Peruvians used guano. Before Columbus arrived, the Arawak already knew how to leach out the hydrocyanic acid from the manioc or cassava plant, using the poison for arrows and the starchy substance for bread. Although they never learned to make distilled liquors, and so were unconditioned to absorb the white man's ' fire-water,' the Indians from Mexico southward made a variety of fermented beverages from maize, palm sap, and several different fruits. They evaporated salt from saline lakes and springs (it was a royal monopoly in Mexico as in France); and in dressing skins and preserving fur they were equal to the best European tanners and furriers. Native herbs were manufactured into such effective drugs and medicine that the ministrations of an ' Indian yarb doctor ' were often preferred by North American pioneers to those of locally trained practitioners.

5. *The Northmen*

Outside Peru, Mexico, Central America, and the Iroquois country, the Indians were completely decentralized; each tribe controlled but a small territory, lived in a state of permanent hostility with its near neighbors, and knew nothing of what went on outside. Hence it was possible for Europeans to impinge here and there on the New World without affecting tribes a few hundred miles away, and without breaking down American isolation. One such impingement, and the only one which is positively known to have occurred, was that of the Norsemen in the eleventh century A.D.

In the ninth century A.D. Scandinavians from Norway occupied Iceland, driving out the Christian Irish colonists who had been living there in isolation for almost two centuries. These Celtic wanderers were bold and skilful navigators in their skin-covered boats, and the sea-voyage from Iceland to Greenland, or from Greenland to the Labrador, is much shorter than that from Ireland to Iceland. Hence, it is possible that Irish from Iceland were the first Europeans to reach the American continent. If so, they were absorbed or exterminated by the Indians, leaving no trace that has been uncovered.

However that may be, it is a matter of historic record that in the late tenth century a tough Norseman from Iceland named Eric the Red discovered Greenland, and founded on the west coast a colony named Brattahlid that flourished for several centuries by raising cattle and exporting walrus ivory and white falcons to Norway. In the year A.D. 1000, Eric's son Leif the Lucky, returning to Greenland from a visit to Norway, was driven out of his course, reached a coast where wild grapes grew, and finally made Brattahild, rather the worse for wear.

A few years later another Icelander named Thorfinn Karlsefni, with a group of Eric the Red's kindred and neighbors, explored the coast of this ' Wineland the Good,' and attempted to found a colony. They spent two winters in an estuary of the North American coast, but the natives, whom they called Skrellings, proved so hostile that the Norsemen gave up and returned to Greenland. Their adventures were related in two sagas which were first written down in the fourteenth century, and which make a most entertaining story.

These Norsemen were not Vikings, and they used a round, one-masted trading ship, not the long Viking ship so often pictured. Ordinary farmers and traders, with weapons little better than those of the Indians, they were unable to cope with the American natives. No certain trace of them has been found along the coast, although fake ' Runic inscriptions ' and planted weapons have been reported from time to time.[3] It is not known how far south they sailed, but the vague and often contradictory descriptions in their sagas fit the Gulf of St. Lawrence better than any other region. After Thorfinn's colony failed, Greenlanders and Icelanders occasionally made voyages to the coasts of the Labrador and Newfoundland to cut wood; and the Greenland colony seems to have lasted until the early sixteenth century, although all communication between it and the outer world was severed before 1450. Greenland appears on a few pre-Columbian maps as a Eurasian peninsula swinging out from Russia over Iceland; but ' Wineland the Good ' is not mentioned later than the chronicles of the eleventh century, and the significance of it as the key to a brave New World never seems to have occurred to the Norsemen, or to anyone else. Leif Ericsson may justly be called the European discoverer of America; but he only lifted a corner of the veil, and his people let it drop. Nothing that he or Thorfinn Karlsefni observed was of any interest to a Europe just emerging from the Dark Ages. And there is no trace of Norse influence in the legends or customs of the northern Indians, or in American fauna and flora.

[3] See Bibliography to this Chapter.

6. *Indian and European*

Thus America enjoyed five centuries more of complete isolation. Nothing was done to prepare for the next European attack, because the existence of Europe and Asia was unsuspected. No Indian tribe or nation knew anything even of his own continent a few hundred miles away. Among them there was nothing even approaching a sentiment of racial or continental solidarity, not even a name for race or country — almost every Indian tribe called itself something equivalent to ' We the People,' and used some insulting title for its near neighbors.[4] Wherever Europeans appeared, for a century or more after 1492, the first thought of the Indians was ' Men from Heaven! ' and the second, ' Not so heavenly after all, but fine allies against our enemies.' European invasions fitted perfectly into the Indian's own pattern of warfare. The white man did not have to divide and conquer, because the Indian continent was already cut up into almost microscopic divisions; he only had to conquer them piecemeal, and he found plenty of native assistance for the task.

Lack of iron and gunpowder, ships and horses, was a handicap to the Indians, but the earliest Europeans who came had few of these, and the Indians in time learned to use them well enough. Certain tribes, like the Cuna Cuna of Panama, have retained their lands and their cultural integrity to this day because they combined the offensive power of poisoned arrows with lack of anything valuable to Europeans. Primarily, the Indian inability to unite was responsible for the European conquest. If, for instance, the Iroquois or a confederacy like theirs had been in possession at the localities where the first Spaniards, English, and Dutch landed, white colonization might have been postponed to the nineteenth century, when European pressures and techniques became irresistible. If the Aztec had had a little more time to consolidate his empire, Mexico might have emerged as a native state like Japan. As it was, the three authoritarian Indian empires were the first to fall. For, as a conquistador put it, when you captured *the* Inca or *the* Montezuma, it was as if a keystone fell from an arch. In Mexico, Peru, and Colombia the Spaniards simply took the place of an Indian aristocracy or theocracy, and exploited the native proletariat for their own behoof.

---

[4] Almost all the tribal names that have come down to us are the native names of the localities (like Iowa, Narragansett), where the white men first found them; others (like Creek, Pueblo) are descriptive of the conditions under which they lived.

Yet there was no consistent pattern of conquest. Certain free but feeble peoples, such as the Arawak of the West Indies, were exterminated by being forced to labor. Others, like the Plains Indians, were humbled and degraded in the nineteenth century because their food supply was destroyed. Still others, like the Carib and a good part of the Algonkin (as in our own day many of the Polynesians), were destroyed by the religion and vices and diseases of white men who wished them well; anthropologists have acertained that if we wish to conserve a people of lower culture, we must respect their religion and folkways, and not attempt to clothe their bodies or dethrone their gods. Some nations managed for many years to live peaceably side-by-side with a European colony. But if the tribe wished to keep its virtue, it had to raid or fight; and the lower sort of white men could always be counted on to provoke hostilities, which at best ended in land cession, removal, and the same thing starting over again. Here and there a successful amalgamation took place: on the St. Lawrence the natives were folded into the French Canadians, as a pastry-cook folds butter into pie-crust dough, and the same process went on in many parts of Central America, between Europeans and Indians, or between Indians and Negroes. Recent social history of Mexico and of several South American republics is essentially the story of the Indian under-dog getting on top again; and hemisphere solidarity is hampered largely by slipping ruling classes, who look wistfully across the Atlantic to a fighting *Volk* who might help them to put the Indians 'in their places.' Even in the United States and Canada, the Indians are so far from being exterminated that their numbers are fast approaching the estimated 800,000 of 1500.

American culture has been greatly enriched by the Indians' contribution. The American character, even among people of unmixed European descent, is very different from what it would have been if this continent had been vacant of mankind when our ancestors arrived. It was a good thing for our forebears that they had to fight their way into the New World; it will be a sorry day for their descendants if they become too civilized to resist nations who covet what they have. The Algonkin warrior of old drank the blood of his fallen enemy in order to absorb his courage; and now that the peoples of America have triumphed in World War II, they may well thank the courageous enemy who made them pay dear for the mastery of a continent.

II

THE ERA OF DISCOVERY

1492–1600

1. *The Decadence of Europe*

AT the end of the year 1492 most men in Western Europe felt exceedingly gloomy about the future. Christian civilization appeared to be shrinking in area and dividing into hostile units as its sphere contracted. For over a century there had been no important advance in natural science, and registration in the universities dwindled as the instruction they offered became increasingly barren and lifeless. Institutions were decaying, well-meaning people were growing cynical or desperate, and many intelligent men, for want of something better to do, were endeavoring to escape the present through studying the pagan past.

Islam was now expanding at the expense of Christendom. Every effort to recover the Holy Sepulchre at Jerusalem, touchstone of Christian prestige, had been a failure. The Ottoman Turks, after snuffing out all that remained of the Byzantine Empire, had overrun most of Greece, Albania, and Serbia; presently they would be hammering at the gates of Vienna. For half a century each successive pope had proclaimed a new crusade, but Europe regarded these appeals to duty as a mere device to raise money. One scandal of Christendom, the great schism, had indeed been overcome, but only at the cost of suppressing reforms within the Church, thus rendering the greater and more permanent Protestant schism all but inevitable; and in 1492 the papacy touched bottom when Rodrigo Borgia, a corrupt ecclesiastical politician, was elected to the throne of Saint Peter as Alexander VI.

If one turned to the Holy Roman Empire, secular counterpart to the Catholic Church, the picture was no brighter. The amiable but listless Emperor Frederick III, driven from his Austrian lands by the king of Hungary, had finally retired to dabble in astrology and alchemy; his son Maximilian was full of promise but short in performance. In England the Wars of the Roses were over, but few expected the House of Tudor to last long. Only in the Iberian peninsula, in Portugal and Castile, were there signs of new life; but these kingdoms were too much on the periphery of Europe to alter the general picture of decay.

With an Empire incurably weak and the Church low in moral prestige, Christians had little to which they might cling. The great principle of unity represented by emperor and pope was a dream of the past that had not come true. Belief in the institutions of their ancestors was wavering. It seemed as if the devil had adopted as his own the principle 'divide and rule.' Throughout Western Europe the general feeling was one of profound disillusion, cynical pessimism, and black despair.

One may catch the prevailing mood by reading the final pages of the *Nuremberg Chronicle*. The colophon of this stately old folio, dated 12 July 1493, declares that it contains 'the events most worthy of notice from the beginning of the world to the calamity of our time.' And that time was painted in the most gloomy colors, suggesting the end of the world; a few blank pages were left to record events between 1493 and the Day of Judgment. Yet, even as the chroniclers of Nuremberg were correcting their proofs from Koberger's press, a Spanish caravel named *Niña* scudded before a winter gale into Lisbon, with news of a discovery that was to give old Europe another chance. In a few years we find the picture completely changed. Strong monarchs are stamping out privy conspiracy and rebellion; the Church, purged and chastened by the Protestant Reformation, puts her house in order; new ideas flare up throughout Italy, France, Germany, and the northern nations; faith in God revives and the human spirit is renewed. The change is complete and astounding. 'A new envisagement of the world has begun, and men are no longer sighing after the imaginary golden age that lay in the distant past, but speculating as to the golden age that might possibly lie in the oncoming future.'[1]

2. *The Discovery of America*

Christopher Columbus discovered America by accident when looking for Japan and China. Few people cared anything about it, when found; and the Atlantic coast of America from Hudson's Bay to the Straits of Magellan was explored by navigators who were seeking a passage to India through or around this unwanted continent. Yet

[1] Sir Charles Oman, *On the Writing of History*, p. 117.

Columbus was the effective discoverer of America for Europe, because he was the first to do anything with it. The ' Enterprise of the Indies,' as he called his plan of sailing west to the Orient, was his very own, suggested by no previous information, produced by no economic forces. He promoted this design for at least eight years before he could persuade any European prince to grant him the modest equipment required; and a less persistent or stout-hearted captain would have been forced to turn back before reaching land. News of his discovery was immediately spread throughout Europe by the recent invention of printing. Columbus personally led the first colony to the New World; he discovered the South American continent as well as the islands; and he obtained the first definite news of the Pacific Ocean. The entire history of the Americas stems from his four voyages.

This great seaman was born at Genoa in 1451, the son of a weaver of woolen cloth. At about the age of twenty he went to sea; and after making voyages in the Mediterranean suffered shipwreck in Portugal, and settled in Lisbon around the year 1477.

Portugal was then the most progressive and western-minded of the European kingdoms. Under the direction of a royal prince, Dom Henrique, the nine islands of the Azores were discovered and colonized between 1439 and 1453; Corvo, farthest west of the Azores, is only 1024 nautical miles from Newfoundland. The Portuguese, supposing that other islands lay to the westward, made many voyages in search of them; but none of these would-be discoverers succeeded. Boisterous westerly winds in the North Atlantic make the westward passage, even in our day, difficult and dangerous for sailing vessels; and the vessels of that day could not sail nearer the wind than 66°; with a heavy sea they could make no progress to windward. Only a lucky break, such as John Cabot evidently had in 1497, plus the certainty of land to the westward, could make that northern route the road to discovery — unless indeed you followed the Iceland-Greenland-Labrador stepping stones; and nobody thought of that, because nobody except the Norsemen had ever known about America, and they had forgotten.

Portugal could use a few more Atlantic islands, but what she really wanted was a sea route to ' the Indies ' (India, China, and the eastern islands), there to obtain at their source the spices, drugs, and gems which reached Europe in small quantities over caravan routes, and the gold and silver about which Marco Polo had told tall tales. The most promising route lay to the southward, along the coast of Africa;

and by the time Columbus settled in Portugal, the mariners of that nation were opening up new stretches of the West African coast every year. As early as 1460 they had passed the site of Dakar, had dispelled the Arabian legends of a ' sea of pitchy darkness,' and disproved what the ancients had said on the uninhabitable nature of tropical countries. Fifteen years later they had completed the exploration of the Gulf of Guinea, and opened up a trade in gold and ivory, slaves and pepper, that made Lisbon the envy of Europe. And for this traffic, which required a round voyage of many thousand miles, the Portuguese developed a type of sailing vessel, the caravel, which was fast, seaworthy, and weatherly. Ships capable of making the voyage to America and back had existed long before Columbus was born; but the caravel, the type he chose, made the voyage far less difficult and dangerous.

Columbus proposed to open a much shorter sea route to ' the Indies ' by sailing west, around the world. A poor mathematician, he had satisfied himself by a series of lucky miscalculations that Japan lay only 2400 to 2500 miles west of the Canaries. In 1484 began his long and arduous efforts to obtain backing for his enterprise. He first offered it to the king of Portugal, and then to the sovereigns of Spain, while his brother Bartholomew hawked it about in the courts of northern Europe. Unfortunately for Columbus, the learned men and mathematicians had much more accurate notions of the size of the globe and the distribution of land and water than he had. Not that he needed to demonstrate that the earth was round. The earth had been known to be spherical for centuries; a spherical earth was taught in all European universities. Everyone agreed that a westward route to ' the Indies ' was theoretically possible, like flying in 1900; but nobody considered it practicable with such means as were then available. In 1488 Bartholomew Dias found his way around the Cape of Good Hope, and was on his way to India when mutinous sailors forced him to turn back; but even Dias was never more than three weeks out of sight of land. Supposing there had been no America, a voyage from Europe to Japan would have required over 100 days, even if the winds favored the entire way.

During his eight years of agitation, the certainty, eloquence, and personality of Columbus made him several enthusiastic friends and backers; but his scheme was rejected by two successive royal committees. Finally the intuition of a woman, Queen Isabella, gave him his chance. After all, the man might be right about the size of the earth.

Nobody really knew — it was simply one theory against another. The equipment he asked for was cheap enough; the honors he demanded were not unreasonable, if he succeeded, and the glory and gain for Spain would be incalculable. If he failed, not much would be lost. Why not try it? So Ferdinand and Isabella, the joint sovereigns of Spain, undertook to pay the bills and to make Columbus viceroy, governor, and admiral over any lands he might discover and acquire. They gave him a Latin letter of introduction to the Emperor of China, and a passport stating that he was on a legitimate voyage ' to regions of India.'

Columbus sailed from Palos on 3 August 1492, as commander of a fleet of three vessels, *Niña, Pinta* and *Santa María,* each about 70 to 80 feet long, all well equipped at the royal expense, and manned by about 90 picked Spaniards. His plan was to sail due west from the Canary Islands, because according to the best available maps these lay on the same latitude as Japan; and a mythical island named Antillia, which he hoped to sight en route, would be a good place of call for food and water. If they were missed, the fleet would be sure to hit China. Their course lay along the northern edge of the belt of northeast tradewinds which blow steadily in the late summer between the Canaries and America. This most important voyage in history was also one of the easiest; during most of the outward passage the Spaniards enjoyed fair wind, soft air, a serene sky, and an ocean smooth as a river. The three vessels dropped the last of the Canaries on 9 September 1492. Mutiny flared up on 10 October but Columbus persuaded the men to go on for three days more; and at 2 a.m. on 12 October the lookout on *Pinta* sighted the sand cliffs of an island in the Bahamas, San Salvador.

Other discoveries have been more spectacular than that of this small low sandy island that rides out ahead of the American continent, breasting the tradewinds. But it was there that the Ocean for the first time ' loosed the chains of things' as Seneca had prophesied, gave up the secret that had baffled Europeans since they began to inquire what lay beyond the western horizon's rim. Stranger people than the gentle Taino, more exotic plants than the green verdure of San Salvador, have been discovered, even by the Portuguese before Columbus; but the discovery of Africa was but an unfolding of a continent already glimpsed, whilst San Salvador, rising from the sea at the end of a thirty-three-day westward sail, was a clean break with past experience. Every tree, every plant, that the Spaniards saw was strange to them, and the natives were not only strange but completely unexpected, speaking an unknown tongue and resembling no race of which even the most educated of the explorers had read in the tales of travellers from Herodotus to Marco Polo. Never again may mortal men hope to recapture the amazement, the wonder, the delight of those October days in 1492 when the New World gracefully yielded her virginity to the conquering Castilians.

With America's virginity went her isolation; neither could ever be restored or re-established, despite all the efforts of soothsayers and statesmen.

The natives of these islands, whom Columbus hopefully called Indians, welcomed the ' men from Heaven ' and several were impressed to act as guides to ' Cipangu ' and ' Cathay.' They piloted Columbus through the Bahamas to northwestern Cuba. There he dispatched his Arabic interpreter inland to meet a cacique whom he took, from the Indians' description, to be the Emperor of China. The village of thatched huts that they found bore little resemblance to the Cambaluk where Marco Polo had hobnobbed with Kubla Khan; but on the way back to the ships the envoys met Indians inhaling cigars through the nostrils, ' to drink the smoke thereof as they are accustomed.' Unknowingly, Columbus had discovered one of the greatest gifts of the New World to the Old.

Eastward along the coast of Cuba sailed the fleet, Columbus eagerly examining every new plant as evidence that this was the southeastern promontory of China. He then crossed the Windward Passage to *La Isla Española,* ' The Spanish Island,' which we still call Hispaniola in English. There he found golden grains in river sands, rumors of a gold mine up-country, and an abundance of gold ornaments on the Indians which they readily swopped for brass rings, glass beads, and bits of cloth. The flagship ran hard and fast on a coral reef, so Columbus built a fort of her timbers and garrisoned it with her crew, and sailed for home aboard *Niña,* accompanied by *Pinta.* Sailing as close to the tradewind as they could, the two caravels worked their way north to the latitude of Bermuda where they caught the winter westerlies and went roaring home, superbly handled through two severe storms. Both dropped anchor the same day, 15 March 1493, in the harbor of Palos whence they had departed.

Columbus and his men were received as heroes, and everyone assumed that they had discovered islands ' in the Indian Sea,' if not the continent of Asia itself. The Pope conferred on Spain the sovereignty of all discoveries already made or to be made, beyond the meridian a hundred leagues (318 nautical miles) west of the Cape Verde Islands. Portugal protested, and by mutual consent in a treaty the next year, the line was moved 270 leagues farther west; and this new line of demarcation gave Portugal her title to Brazil.

After six months in Spain Columbus sailed in command of a gallant fleet of seventeen vessels, discovered all the Caribbee Islands north and west of Martinique, had his first fight with the Carib Indians at St. Croix, called at Puerto Rico, and at Hispaniola, after ascertaining that his garrison had been wiped out, landed men and began building a fortified trading station at Isabela on the north coast.

There his troubles began. The first European colony in America was nothing more than a glorified gold hunt. Columbus expected to obtain the precious metal by trade; but the Indians' demand for jingly trading truck was soon exhausted, and the Spaniards began taking gold by force. As elsewhere in America where Europeans came, the newcomers were first welcomed by the Indians as visitors, then resented as intruders, and finally resisted with fruitless desperation. The Spaniards, who had come for gold and nothing else, resented their governor's orders to build houses, tend crops, and cut logwood; the wine and food supplies from Spain gave out; and before long bands of men in armor were roving about the fertile interior of Hispaniola, living off the country, and torturing the natives to obtain gold. In the summer of 1494, which Columbus spent exploring the southern coasts of Cuba and Hispaniola and discovering Jamaica, the colonists got completely out of hand; and the Admiral's attempts to impose an iron discipline resulted in malcontents seizing vessels and returning to Spain to complain of him and of ' the Indies.' So Columbus, leaving his brother Bartholomew in charge, sailed for home in 1496.

Everybody in Spain had wanted to go to ' the Indies ' in 1493; four years later nobody wanted to go. America seemed a fraud and a delusion; even the gold, it was rumored, was no good; the air was pestilential, the food rotten, and the Columbus brothers were merciless foreign taskmasters. Ferdinand and Isabella would doubtless have dropped the whole thing had not their honor been involved. After a year's lobbying at court, Columbus could only obtain their grudging consent to send out convicts as colonists, and to let him make a new voyage in search of the Asiatic continent.

In the meantime, a second nation had stumbled on America when searching for Asia, and through the efforts of another Genoese. John

Cabot, a compatriot of Columbus but naturalized citizen of Venice, was one of a colony of foreign merchants established at Bristol in England. He had carried spices from the Levant to England, and believed that the Far East could best be reached by sailing westward in the short high latitudes. After making a contract with Henry VII of England similar to that of Columbus with the Spanish sovereigns, he sailed from Bristol on 2 May 1497 in the *Matthew,* a ship so small that she carried a crew of but eighteen men. On 24 June after beating to windward almost eight weeks, he raised an island (probably Scutari off Cape Breton), enjoyed good codfishing, saw some nets ashore but no natives, arrived back in Bristol 6 August, and proceeded to court, where King Henry gave him a pension of £10 a year. That is practically all we know of Cabot's first voyage; and the facts of his second, made in 1498, are impossible to disentangle from later voyages of his more famous son Sebastian. In any event, the English did practically nothing to follow up Cabot's voyages for three-quarters of a century, and their only influence on American history was to give the English Crown a ' legal ' title to North America against the claims of Spain and the Netherlands.

If the Spaniards had heard of Cabot's voyage by 1498, they were not interested in codfish or rocky, spruce-clad shores. Columbus on his third voyage followed a southerly course in search of a continent which, it was suspected, filled the vast unknown spaces of the globe in that direction. On 31 July 1498 he sighted the island of Trinidad, and a few days later entered the Gulf of Paria between it and the mainland, of which he took possession for Spain. He then stretched across the Caribbean to Santo Domingo, the new capital of Hispaniola that had been founded in his absence, and found the island in a turmoil. Most of the Indians had been brought under subjection, but the chief justice, Francisco Roldán — first of a long line of American rebels — was heading a revolt of ex-criminals and robust individualists against the government of Columbus's brother, in the hope of obtaining a larger share of the women and the gold-diggings than regulations allowed. Columbus had so few loyal and healthy followers that he was forced to appease Roldán with a system of land and labor allotments. To each man was granted a tract of land with the Indians who lived on it, whose labors he was entitled to exploit as he saw fit. These *encomiendas* as they were subsequently called, marked the beginning not only of agricultural colonization, but of a system that the Spaniards applied throughout their conquests on the continent, in order to induce settlement and supply the colonists with the cheap labor that they wanted.

In the meantime Vasco da Gama had rounded the Cape of Good Hope, reached Calicut in India, and returned; a triumphant voyage that gave Portugal that sea access to the Orient which Columbus had first sought. Pedro Alvarez Cabral, on his voyage to India in 1500, called at a bay now named after him and took possession of Brazil for Portugal. Several Spaniards who had been officers under Columbus made voyages of their own to the South American continent, and on one of them sailed a Florentine merchant, Amerigo Vespucci. Amerigo's amusingly inflated and pre-dated account of the voyage that he made with Hojeda in 1499 made his name familiar to Northern Europe, and when a German geographer suggested that the new continent be called after him *America,* the name caught on. That was in 1507; three years earlier Columbus, after an unsuccessful fourth voyage, had returned to Spain, where he died in obscurity.

Columbus did not exaggerate when he boasted, ' Over there I have placed under their Highnesses' sovereignty more land than there is in Africa and Europe, and more than seventeen hundred islands, not counting Hispaniola. . . . In seven years I, by the divine will, made that conquest.' And the mystical strain in him, which made him venture unafraid into the unknown, led him to predict, ' Your Highnesses will win these lands, which are an Other World, and where Christianity will have so much enjoyment, and our faith in time so great an increase.' No discoverer in the world's history had such marvellous success as Columbus, even though he never found what he first sought; no navigator save Magellan or Gama may be compared with him for courage, persistence, and skill; no other great benefactor of the human race was so ill rewarded in his lifetime; none other is so justly revered today in the New World of his Discovery.

3. *Exploration of the Carib Sea*

For about twenty years after the first voyage of Columbus, Hispaniola was the only European colony in America; an agricultural and mining colony based on cattle and cotton raising, gold mining, and the culture of the sugar cane, which the Spaniards introduced from the Canaries. In 1512 Hispaniola was exporting annually to Spain not far short of a million dollars in gold. The enslaved Indians died off under forced labor, and were replaced, first by Indians kidnapped from other islands, who suffered the same fate, and — beginning in 1510 — by Negro slaves, bought from the Portuguese, who procured them in Africa.

Santo Domingo was the center from which the rest of America was, to a great extent, explored and colonized. The more adventurous spirits, dissatisfied with the humdrum life of sugar planter, mine overseer, or petty official, obtained royal permission to conquer and colonize other islands, and then the mainland.

Juan Ponce de Leon, the first of these *adelantados* or ' advancers,' explored in 1508 the island of Puerto Rico. It was conquered and colonized, and the native population exploited and exterminated, in much the same manner as Hispaniola.

Jamaica, the second colony to be founded from Hispaniola, was easily conquered in 1509–10. Diego Velásquez, between 1511 and 1515 founded seven towns in Cuba, including Baracoa, Santiago, Trinidad, and the original Havana at Batabanó, which was transferred to the present site in 1518. No gold was found in Cuba, and the redoubtable cacique Hatuey, first protagonist of *Cuba Libre,* made Velásquez pay dear for his conquest.

Next, the Spaniards extended their explorations to the mainland. Ponce de Leon had heard the story of a marvellous spring on Andros in the Bahamas which restored youth and vigor to the old and impotent. This seemed to fit in with a classical myth of the waters of the terrestrial paradise; and Ponce, who at the age of 53 was pretty well used up by fighting and rapine, decided to search for it. In April 1513, after threading his way through the Bahamas and ascertaining (what Columbus might have told him) that there were neither springs nor streams in these coral islands, Ponce landed near the mouth of the St. John's river, and named the land Florida after that fair Easter season (*Pascua Florida*). Hugging the coast to avoid the Gulf Stream, he named and rounded the Florida Keys and sailed up the gulf coast, possibly as far as the site of Pensacola. But he returned without an ounce of gold or a drink of invigorating water; and the tough Seminole Indians thwarted his attempt to found a colony on the peninsula in 1521. St. Augustine was founded by Menéndez de Aviles in 1566 in order to protect the treasure fleets from French and English marauders; within two years he had established a string of posts from Tampa Bay to Port Royal, South Carolina, and was prepared to welcome colonists and convert the natives. Missionaries ranged as far north as Chesapeake Bay, and several missions were later established on the gulf coast, among the Creek Indians; but the few settlers who came soon withdrew, the Indians remained hostile, and Florida during three centuries of Spanish rule was little more than a military outpost of Mexico and Cuba.

The acquisition of Mexico and South America almost ruined the Spanish colonies in the Caribbean. Hispaniola in 1574 contained only a thousand Spaniards, less than Columbus brought over in 1493, and 12,000 Negro slaves. Spanish Hispaniola has never to this day recovered her pristine prosperity; it is as if the tortured Indians had put a curse on the land. Cuba in 1574 had a total Spanish population of 240; Puerto Rico and Jamaica had about the same, and neither the Lesser Antilles nor the Bahamas were ever occupied by the Spaniards. Jamaica, under English rule since 1655, became for a time the wealthiest colony of the British Empire; but it was not until the eighteenth century that Cuba and Puerto Rico became populous and prosperous, through producing the world's best sugar and tobacco.

While these first beginnings of settlement were being made in the Greater Antilles, other Spaniards were making attempts to found trading posts on the continent, in the present republics of Venezuela and Colombia. But the Indians of those regions would stand no nonsense; and many years elapsed before the Spaniards could make nuclei of settlements at Santa Marta and Cartagena. From a third and relatively insignificant Spanish post, Santa María de la Antigua on the Gulf of Darien, the Pacific Ocean was discovered.

4. *On to the Orient*

Vasco Núñez de Balboa, a stowaway from Hispaniola who made himself master of this settlement, obtained information from a local cacique of the great Inca Empire of Peru; and the Indians whom he had helped in their local wars offered to guide him across the isthmus of Darien. Nobody has used that route for at least seventy-five years; the last scientific expedition that tried to, perished in the jungle. As it was, Balboa had several hundred Indians to hack the way across for him and his 189 hidalgos in 1513; the distance was only forty-five miles as the crow flies, but it took them twenty-five days to reach the spot where ' silent, upon a peak in Darien,' he first stared at the Pacific. The discoverer was soon after put to death by his rival Pedrarias, whose energy was so vast that small sailing vessels and their gear were transported across the divide in sections, and set afloat on

El Mar del Sur, the great South Sea. Presently the city of Panama was founded, and Spain had a Pacific base.

Across that ocean — how far across nobody had yet guessed — lay the Spice Islands, whence King Manuel the Fortunate of Portugal was deriving far greater wealth than did his Spanish cousins from the gold-washings of Hispaniola. So the discovery of Balboa only stimulated efforts to get around, through, or by America. For a time it seemed that the Portuguese would discover the western as well as the eastern route to the real Indies, for their exploration of the Brazilian coast took them farther and farther south, to the River Plate and beyond, by 1514. Juan Díaz de Solís, a veteran Spanish pilot, rounded Cape Santa Maria early in 1516, only to be eaten by the Indians at his first Uruguayan port of call.

In Portugal a short, stocky, and dour captain named Ferdinand Magellan was making preparations for a fresh attempt to sail west to the Orient. Magellan had spent seven years with the Portuguese in the Far East and believed that the Spice Islands — the modern Dutch East Indies — could better be reached the other way round; King Manuel was not interested, so Magellan appealed to the Emperor Charles V, who gave him a fleet of five ships. They sailed from Seville in August 1519, and reached the River Plate in January. A careful search proved that this great estuary was no strait, and the voyage continued south along the coast of Patagonia. While the fleet was wintering at Port St. Julian in latitude 49° 15′ S, the captains of four ships mutinied, hoping to return to Spain; Magellan won, hanged and quartered some of the leaders, and marooned others. At the Antarctic summer solstice the voyage was renewed, and on 21 October 1520, at latitude 52° 20′ S, Magellan discovered the entrance to ' that Strait which shall forever be honored with his name.' [2]

The fleet, now reduced by shipwreck and desertion to three, required thirty-eight days to thread the three hundred and twenty-five mile passage that cuts through the tail end of the Andes. Tortuous channels, many of them dead-ends that lead only to destruction; cliff-rimmed waters so deep that a ship will crack before she can anchor; icy squalls that blow right down the mast at a moment's notice; damp, penetrating cold and dangerous fog; the Straits have everything that a seaman dreads, and in modern times the tempestuous passage of Cape Horn with its violent head winds and monstrous seas has been

[2] *Lusiads,* x. 141.

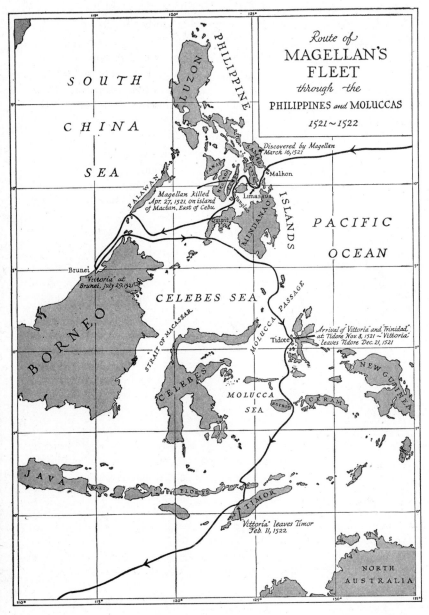

Route of Magellan's Fleet
through the Philippines and Moluccas 1521–1522
Prepared by S. E. Morison for The Growth of the American Republic

preferred as the lesser evil. Yet three of Magellan's ships sailed safely through on 28 November 1520.

Then came the most terrible part of the voyage. This South Sea was calm enough, once they were off-shore — that is why Magellan renamed it the Pacific Ocean — but they were fourteen weeks without sight of land, excepting two small coral atolls where neither anchorage nor food was obtainable. The scurvy-ridden men were reduced to eating sawdust and biscuit which had become mere powder swarming with worms, even to broiling the leather chafing-gear of the yards. Relief was obtained on 6 March 1521, at Guam, in the group that Magellan named the Ladrones; and ten days later they reached the island of Samar in the Philippines. There West met East for the first time. Sailing through the Surigao Straits, the fleet anchored at Limasaua off Leyte, where Magellan's Malay servant, whom he had brought home with him on a previous voyage, was able to make himself understood. At Cebu the Moslem rajah pretended to embrace Christianity in order to obtain Magellan's aid against a local enemy; and in the fight at Mactan, on 27 April 1521, as Magellan was covering the retreat of his men to the boats, he lost his life.

One ship was now abandoned and burned, as there were not enough men left to handle all three. *Vittoria* and *Trinidad* crossed the Sulu Sea to Palawan and Brunei in North Borneo, then doubled back, calling at Zamboanga on Mindanao, to the tiny islands of Ternate and Tidore, which the Portuguese had already discovered to be spice emporia. It was now November 1521. *Trinidad* attempted to recross the Pacific, but could not make it against the easterly trades, and was beaten back and abandoned. *Vittoria* set forth alone, on 21 December 1521, under Captain Juan Sebastian del Cano. She threaded the Molucca Passage, crossed the Banda Sea to Timor, sailed out through the Savu Sea into the Indian Ocean, crossed that ocean to South Africa, rounded the Cape of Good Hope, and on 9 July 1522 called at São Tiago in the Cape Verde Islands for provisions, her first call in two months. Captain Del Cano was grieved to find his sea journal to be a day fast, and could not imagine the cause. There, too, the Portuguese arrested a shore party, and *Vittoria* was forced to slip her cable and make sail with only eighteen Europeans and four Malays. On 9 September 1522, this greatest voyage of all time ended at Seville, with only 18 of the 239 men who set forth three years earlier. But the cargo of spices more than paid expenses, Captain Del Cano was ennobled and granted these arms: Two cinnamon sticks in saltire proper, three nutmegs and twelve cloves, and on a chief gules a castle. Crest: a globe bearing the legend *Primus Circumdedisti Me,* ' Thou first didst circumnavigate me.'

The most substantial fruit of this marvellous voyage for Spain was the Philippine Islands, as they were named after the infante who became King Philip II in 1556. Permanent occupation of this archipelago began with the expedition of Miguel López de Legaspi in 1564. Owing to Legaspi's tact, the friendly attitude of the natives, and (not least) the fact that they had no gold or other precious commodities,[8] the Philippines were conquered, converted, and held by a mere handful of soldiers and friars. So Castile, the nation which had rolled back the westernmost wave of Islam from Europe, met and checked the eastern wave of Mohammedanism in the Philippines.

Manila, founded by Legaspi in 1571, became a wealthy trading post between West and East, such as Columbus had hoped to establish on his first voyage. A yearly galleon traded back and forth between Acapulco in Mexico and Manila, sailing westward by the southern route laden with ingots of Mexican silver, and eastward by the northern route with all manner of China silk and Indian cotton, oriental gems and porcelain, and Malayan spices. The entire Spanish community in Manila had an interest in each cargo, the Church was supported by it, and the rest of the Philippines were left to the natives and the missionary friars.

5. Conquest of a Continent

The entire east coast of South America had been explored, and Magellan was already on his way around the world, before the two most splendid native civilizations in America, those of Mexico and Peru, had yielded their secrets.

In 1519 the governor of Cuba, wishing to establish a trading post on the Mexican coast, sent an expedition of 11 ships, carrying in all only 550 Spaniards, under young Hernando Cortés. Arriving at a time when the natives of Mexico were chafing under the cruel sovereignty of the Aztecs, Cortés was welcomed by many as their fabled hero, Quetzalcoatl, and he had the wit to take advantage of it. For

---

[8] The Philippines in 1939 held fifth place among the gold-producing countries of the world, after South Africa, Canada, the United States, and Australia; but the Spaniards did not discover the gold deposits.

all that, the conquest of Mexico was one of the most amazing military and diplomatic feats in the world's history. The march up from Vera Cruz to the great interior plateau, the audacious capture of Monte-zuma's lake-rimmed capital (1521), and the defeat of a vast army on the plains of Teotihuacan completed the ruin of the Aztec power and firmly established Cortés as master of Mexico.

The results of this conquest in terms of treasure were spectacular, and the prospect of more to come was infinite. Hence America for the first time became popular in Europe. Certain districts of Spain were depopulated by the gold rush to ' the Indies '; the Antilles were de-serted by all but the less vigorous colonists. It might be supposed that liquidation of the Aztec Empire and exploitation of Mexican sources would employ the energies of Spain for a century. Yet this conquest was only a beginning. The whole southern section of the United States from South Carolina across to California was explored by Spanish conquistadors in search of more valuable treasure, new em-pires that might challenge Mexico, and the fabled Strait of Anian which was supposed to cross North America from east to west, and might be the long-sought passage to India.

Pánfilo de Narvaez, who had been badly treated by Cortés, chose Florida for his field of glory, and sailed thither from Spain in 1527. Pánfilo was the most unfortunate of the conquistadors. After losing two ships in a hurricane, he landed somewhere on the gulf coast of Florida, fought his way up to the site of Tallahassee, retreated to the coast, and there built a fleet of boats from native wood fastened with spikes fashioned from spurs and stirrups, rigged with hair cordage and hide sails from the horses which his men had eaten. In these crazy craft he sailed past the mouths of the Mississippi, only to be wrecked on the coast of Texas. The sole survivors, Cabeza de Vaca, two other Spaniards and a Negro, spent six years among the Indians, and eventually reached Mexico with tales of wild ' hunchback cows ' that covered the plains as far as eye could see, and of cities with emerald-studded walls, of which they had heard. These ' Seven Cities of Cibolá ' were more readily believed in than were the buffalo.

In 1539 the viceroy of Mexico sent a Franciscan named Fray Marcos, accompanied by Esteban, the Negro companion of Cabeza de Vaca, up into the future New Mexico in search of the fabled Seven Cities. There they discovered the disappointing foundation of this myth, the Zuñi pueblos, and so reported; but the honest tale of Fray Marcos was so blown up by popular imagination that the viceroy sent north the most splendid exploring expedition of all, that of Francisco Vásquez Coronado, while a co-operating fleet sailed up the Gulf of California. One of Coronado's lieutenants discovered the Grand Canyon in 1540; Coronado himself marched eastward across the panhandle of Texas into eastern Kansas, only to prick another rumor; and returned, disappointed, to Mexico.

Hernando de Soto, who had served under Pizarro in Peru, in the meantime had obtained a grant of Florida from the king. Landing at Tampa Bay, he marched about the interior of the future gulf states for many months, led on by those tales of splendid cities. In 1541 he came upon the Mississippi near Memphis, crossed to the west bank, spent the winter near Fort Smith, Arkansas, returned to the Father of Waters, and there died. His men built boats, descended the Mississippi, crossed the Gulf, and reached Tampico in safety, after an absence of over four years.

Owing to the failure to find treasure or a strait, these Spanish explorations of North America had no immediate result; the tide of conquest turned toward South America. Only at the end of the sixteenth century, when the frontier of settlement and mining in Mexico had been pushed so near to the Rio Grande that conquest of the Pueblo Indians seemed desirable, Juan de Oñate formally took possession ' of all the kingdoms and provinces of New Mexico.' The Pueblos promptly submitted, colonization began, and the next governor founded Santa Fe in 1609. Thus New Mexico, last but one of the forty-eight states to be admitted to the Union, was settled at the same time as the first English colony of Virginia.

By that time Spain had conquered almost the whole of South America down to the River Plate. Francisco Pizarro had overthrown the mighty Inca empire of Peru and founded Lima by 1535. Other conquistadors swarmed southward and eastward, overrunning the whole of the continent. By mid-century the foundations had been laid for every one of the twenty republics of Central and South America, excepting the Argentine.

There has been no other conquest like this in the annals of the human race. In one generation the Spaniards acquired more new territory than Rome conquered in five centuries. Genghis Khan swept over a greater area, but left only destruction in his wake; the Spaniards organized and administered all that they conquered, brought in the arts and letters of Europe, and converted millions to their faith. Our forebears in Virginia and New England, the pathfinders of the Great West, and the French-Canadian pioneers were stout fellows indeed; but their exploits scarcely compared with those of Spanish conquistadors and friars who hacked their way in armor through solid jungle, across endless plains, and over snowy passes of the Andes to fulfil their dreams of gold and glory, and for whom reality was greater even than the dream.

There is another side to the picture: the inordinate greed for gold and the revolting cruelty to which the Indians were often subjected; yet too there was the faith and the chivalrous courtesy that their descendants have inherited, and the arts that followed fast on the trail of conquest. Mexico, and Lima the ' City of Kings,' became seats of urban civilization within fifteen years of the conquest; in each a university was founded in 1551; the first printing press in the New World came to Mexico City in 1539, and the first imprint was a Compendium of Christian Doctrine *en lengua Mexicana y Castellana* composed for the Indians by the Bishop of Teotihuacan. Even today an air of superb magnificence rests on the churches and palaces built by these ' children of the sun ' in their provincial capitals hundreds of miles from the sea.

Thus, the Spanish Empire in America had more than a century's head start on the English and French; and the results of that conquest, materially as well as spiritually, were amazing, stupendous, and the envy of every European power. Spanish prestige reached its height in the year 1580 when Philip II succeeded to the throne of Portugal as well as that of Spain, uniting in his person the two vast empires that stretched their arms around the world. At that moment not another nation had placed a single permanent settler on the shores of the New World; not even a fort or trading post challenged the monopoly of Spain and Portugal in America.

Yet the end of that monopoly was near. The autumn gales of 1580 blew up the English Channel and into Plymouth harbor Francis Drake in the *Golden Hind,* worm-eaten and weed-clogged after her three years' voyage around the world, laden with the spoil of a Peruvian treasure ship. Only eight years more, and Spain suffered her first major defeat on the ocean that she had mastered; twenty years more, and Virginia was founded.

6. *In Northern Waters*

Spanish conquest was too swift and successful for the health of Spain. American treasure ruined her manufactures, financed useless military adventures of her kings, and led to poverty and ineptitude in the next century. Yet the immediate success, which alone was visible, stimulated three other nations, France, England, and the Netherlands, to acquire colonial possessions of their own. As early as 1521 some French corsairs bagged part of the booty that Cortés was sending home; and this process of muscling into the Spanish empire continued until England and France were firmly established in North America, and the Dutch in the Far East.

John Cabot discovered the teeming cod-fisheries of the Grand Bank of Newfoundland, but French and Portuguese fishermen were first to profit by them. Norman fishermen were on the banks by 1504, and the Portuguese were so active about Newfoundland for a generation after Corte-Real's discovery, that even today the principal bays and headlands of Newfoundland have Portuguese names. These fishermen were practical men who were only concerned in catching and curing the firm-fleshed cod of northern waters that found a ready market in Europe. The important explorations in northern waters, as along the Spanish Main, were made by navigators seeking a passage to India.

Francis I of France, who liked to be in the swim, engaged a Florentine navigator to find for him the water route to China. This Giovanni Verazzano in the summer of 1524 made the first voyage (of which we have definite record) along the Atlantic coast of the United States from Cape Fear to Maine, searching for the Strait. He entered the future New York harbor, but decided that the Hudson was not a passage; he tried Narragansett Bay and again drew a blank; he sailed among the spruce-clad islands of Maine, and then home. By that time Francis I had been captured at the Battle of Pavia, and could no longer finance exploration. Verazzano's brother made a map of his voyages that showed a mythical gulf of the Pacific stretching to within a few miles of Chesapeake Bay. Probably the efforts of Indians to tell about the Great Lakes was the origin of this 'Sea of Verazzano,' the search for which lasted almost two centuries. Every Englishman who marched inland from the Atlantic coast, even Governor Spotswood as late as 1716, hoped to play Balboa at the first crest of the Blue Ridge.

Jacques Cartier is the Columbus of French Canada. This hardy seaman of St. Malo made three voyages to the Gulf of St. Lawrence (1534–41) in search of the passage to the Orient. On the second he discovered the rock of Quebec, in a region which the natives called Canada, and then proceeded up-stream, past Mont Real (so named by him), to the lowest rapids of the St. Lawrence, which he humorously called La Chine. He wintered near the mouth of the Saguenay, and collected from the Indians a cycle of tall tales about an inland kingdom of that name, where gold and silver were as plentiful as in Mexico or Peru. King Francis I of France, much excited at this prospect, then equipped Cartier with a fleet so formidable that the Spanish government seriously discussed sending naval vessels to sink it. But the Spanish king wisely concluded that it would be a good thing to keep the French busy chasing northern will o' the wisps. Cartier brought back nothing but a shipload of iron pyrites or fool's gold, and of quartz crystals that he believed to be diamonds.

France then fell into a cycle of religious wars, and although every year Norman and Breton fishermen visited the banks and cured their fish ashore, and traded with the natives for fur, no progress was made toward establishing a French-American empire until the next century. The settled history of Canada began when Samuel de Champlain in 1608 planted the white standard of St. Louis on the rock of Quebec.

7. Enter England

England approached America very gingerly; the Cabot voyages were not her only false starts. For England was a small and poor country, hemmed in by enemies. Independent and hostile Scotland sat on her northern border; the hereditary enemy France lay across one channel; and Ireland, who still refused to admit she had been conquered, across another. English monarchs of the House of Tudor were cautious, impecunious, and anxious to placate the Spanish sovereigns. Henry VII played safe; Henry VIII (1509–1547) built up the royal navy, but wasted money on the continent. The chief overseas effort of his reign was to the northeast; the Muscovy Company, first of a long line of joint-stock corporations that carried the English flag to the far corners of the world, opened a trade with Ivan the Terrible by way of the White Sea and Archangel.

England was growing stronger year by year. No small share of the treasure from Mexico and Peru went to buy English woolens; for woolen garments were still the fashion for both sexes, even in warm climates. In 1500 English foreign trade had been largely in the hands of foreigners; gradually the Italians and Portuguese were squeezed out, and the exclusive privileges of the Hanseatic League for northern trade were revoked. Henry VIII's break with the Roman Catholic Church, whatever his motive, stimulated English nationalism and made a break with Spain sooner or later inevitable. The secularization of the monasteries released capital for foreign trade, and young men for adventure. Many a youth who might have found a safe career in the Church under a Catholic regime now had to seek a living from the sea.

Under Queen Elizabeth, England definitely aligned herself with the Protestant Reformation, which made it a religious as well as a patriotic duty to ' singe the king of Spain's beard.' The obvious place to harry that monarch's whiskers was in the West Indies. Spanish commerce with her overseas possessions was conducted by convoys and staple towns on the coast. The outward-bound fleet from Spain made the West Indies at Guadeloupe and then split, separate squadrons proceeding to Santo Domingo, Cartagena, Porto Bello on the Isthmus of Panama, and Vera Cruz, the port of Mexico. All commerce with Peru and the West Coast was conducted through Panama; the precious metals were transported by mule train across the isthmus to Porto Bello, where at the time of the annual fair, ingots of silver were piled up in the market place like cordwood. On the homeward passage, galleons from Caribbean and Gulf ports sailed through the Yucatán Channel and made rendezvous at the Havana, whence the Gulf Stream bore them up through the Straits of Florida to the zone of westerly winds.

In the 1560's John Hawkins of Plymouth began to make slaving voyages from England to Africa and then to Spanish America, where his courtly manners and attractive prices ensured a good reception, albeit that trade was against the law. Then, on his ' third and troublesome voyage ' he was set upon by the Spanish fleet in Vera Cruz and roughly handled. His captain, Francis Drake, became the most implacable enemy to Spain, raiding the isthmus and the coast towns again and again, and, on his memorable voyage to California and round the world, striking terror along the coasts of Chile and Peru. Thomas Cavendish, a sea captain who in his early twenties commanded the second English voyage around the world, bagged the grandest prize of all, a Manila galleon; his ships entered the Thames rigged with silken sails, and each sailor wore a chain of pure gold around his neck.

The great age of Elizabeth and of Shakespeare, in which English genius burned brightly in almost every aspect of life, was reaching its acme.

> This happy breed of men, this little world,
> This precious stone set in the silver sea,

then awakened from long lethargy to a feeling of exuberant life, such as few people had known since ancient Greece. That was an age when the scholar, the divine, and the man of action were often one and the same person — for the Elizabethans knew what many of us have forgotten, that life is empty without religion, that the tree of knowledge is barren unless rooted in love, and that learning purchased at the expense of living is a sorry bargain. Man in those days was not ashamed to own himself an animal, nor so base as to quench the divine spark that made him something better; but above all, he exulted in the fact that he was a man. Chapman, in *Byron's Conspiracy,* spoke for his age and generation when he cried out, ' Be free, all worthy spirits, and stretch yourselves! '

The age of discovery in England was closely integrated with English literature, promoted by her governing class, and a matter of great moment to the government. Sir Humfrey Gilbert, Oxonian, educational reformer, and courtier, published a *Discourse of a Discovery for a New Passage to Cataia* (i.e. China), and attempted the first English colony. His half-brother Sir Walter Raleigh, courtier, soldier, and historian, founded Virginia and sought El Dorado up the Orinoco. And the Rev. Richard Hakluyt, student of Christ Church in Oxford, compiled his great collection of *Navigations, Voyages and Discoveries of the English Nation,* in order to fire his countrymen to worthy deeds overseas. The English empire down to the American Revolution was but a fulfilment of the plans made by Hakluyt, Gilbert, Raleigh, and a number of other promoters in the reign of Queen Bess.

What these men wanted was an overseas empire that would make England self-sufficient, and employ a great merchant marine. It should be in a climate where Englishmen might live, and where they and the natives would provide a new market for English woolens. The colonies should produce tar and timber for shipbuilding, gold and silver, dyewoods, wine, spices and olives, and everything else that England was then buying from abroad. The Indians must be converted to Protestant Christianity, in order to stay the progress of the Counter-Reformation. A passage through was sought to the real Indies, that would serve as an English Straits of Magellan. Yet, with all this energy, gallantry, and enthusiasm, the chronicle of English colonization in the sixteenth century is one of repeated failure. Martin Frobisher sought gold and the Northwest Passage in the 1570's, discovered Hudson's Strait, and brought back shiploads of worthless fool's gold. Sir Humfrey Gilbert took possession of Newfoundland for the Queen in 1583, but was lost on the voyage home. Sir Walter Raleigh then took over his patent to the whole of North America above Florida, named it Virginia, and planted two successive colonies on Roanoke Island. The first gave up after a year; the second, a well-chosen group of 117 men, women, and children, had completely disappeared by the time a relief expedition arrived in 1590.

Reasons for these and other failures are not far to seek. England had a national policy of overseas expansion, but her efforts were left to individuals, and the experience of Gilbert and Raleigh proved (what they might have learned from the Spaniards) that 'it is a difficult thing to carry over colonies into remote countries upon private men's purses.' The English Crown was too impecunious to finance colonies; and individual enterprise preferred the gay adventure and almost certain profit of raiding Spanish possessions and capturing Spanish ships. These activities increased both the confidence and the sea-knowledge of the English, and so contributed in the end to imperial achievement; but as long as the war with Spain lasted (and it lasted as long as did Elizabeth), it was impossible to obtain enough capital or men for the prosaic business of planting and maintaining a colony. So the sixteenth century closed like the fifteenth, without a single Englishman on American soil — unless survivors of Raleigh's lost colony were still wandering through the forests of Carolina.

All this was most discouraging; but the English were past discouragement. For, underlying all their efforts, the earlier failures as well as later successes, was a powerful drive which thrust them forward no matter what happened; an ideal motive similar to the terrific missionary fervor of the Spaniards. This *daimon* of the English was the burning desire to found a new England, a new society, in which all the best of the past would be conserved, but where life would have a different and better quality from anything then conceivable in Europe.

It was typical of an English discoverer that Sir Humfrey Gilbert when last seen on the quarterdeck of the *Golden Hind,* was reading a book; and from the phrase that he joyfully shouted to his men — ' We are as near Heaven by sea as by land ' — that book must have been Sir Thomas More's *Utopia.*[4] The Utopian ideal for America which was in the mind of every important group of English pioneers from Massachusetts to Georgia, takes off from this *Utopia* of Sir Thomas More, first printed in 1516. The ideal commonwealth to that saintly mind is described as an island set in the Ocean Sea, somewhere in the New World. It is in the north zone, the ' air soft, temperate, and gentle; the ground covered with green grass,' ' full of people, governed by good and wholesome laws ' (but no lawyers), where everyone is honestly employed, and no one exploited or overworked. In the cities, planted not less than a day's journey apart, dwell the handicraftsmen and men of learning; but each city possesses a great rural district studded with co-operative farms. Burghers and farmers change places every two years, so that each has his share of necessary labor, and nobody becomes bored with his occupation. All alike labor six hours a day, leaving ample time for recreation, and eight hours for sleep. Husbandry is made pleasant and easy by having oxen to do all the heavy work, and by inventions such as incubators for raising chickens. In the cities the streets are laid out ' very commodious and handsome,' twenty feet wide, and ' the houses be of fair and gorgeous building,' each of three stories, fireproof, amply windowed, provided with a garden, and drained by a system of canals. None are owned privately; all change hands every decade. Government is carried on by a series of town meetings; they choose an electoral college, which elects a council of philosophers and a prince who holds his office for life. Free and compulsory education is continued for adults by daily lectures, which all attend except such as wish ' to bestow the time well and thriftly upon some other science, as shall please them '; for Utopians like nothing better than ' free liberty of the mind, and the garnishing the same '; and ' often it chanceth that a handicraftsman doth so earnestly bestow his vacant and spare hours in learning, and through diligence so profiteth therein, that he is

---

[4] ' The way to heaven out of all places is of like length and distance.' One of the maxims of Raphael the Portuguese, who discovered Utopia, in Book 1.

taken from his handy occupation, and promoted to the company of the learned.' Greek literature is the favorite study of these workers' educational classes.

Utopia cultivates community life as well as individual achievement. Everyone residing on the same farm or in the same city ward dines and sups in a great hall, and after supper there are debates and community music. The Utopians' time is not taken up with superfluities, for they build solidly, dress simply, care nothing for gambling, cruel sports, or wasteful display, and despise gold, silver, and jewels. All products are considered common; each head of a family helps himself at the storehouse to what he needs, and the aged or infirm are provided with all their wants. Attendance by physicians and free hospitalization are provided for everyone. Whoever wishes to make a pleasure trip is provided by the government with an ox wagon, but he has to work in the farms or cities that he visits, in order to eat. The Utopians hate warfare 'as a thing very beastly,' yet both men and women submit to compulsory military training in case other and less happy people seek to invade them, or attack countries that are their friends. All their wars heretofore have been in defense of friendly countries, the Utopians knowing that if these were conquered by tyrants their turn would come next. Timely offensive they count the best defense, and 'engines for war they devise and invent wonders wittily.'

The Utopians enjoy complete religious liberty; and although they cultivate virtue, which they define as 'life ordered according to nature . . . they judge it extreme madness to follow sharp and painful virtue, and . . . banish the pleasure of life.'

Thus, out of the welter of misery, insecurity, and corruption that were the lot of common man in the England of 1516, came this vision of a new and better society: the American dream. One constant thread of American history has been this quest for peace, liberty, and security; this effort, often frustrated, never realized but in part, yet ever hopeful, ever renewed, to make true the Utopian dream of the blessed Thomas More.

III

THE FIRST FOUNDATIONS

1600–1660

1. *Virginia*

ALL but one of the thirteen English colonies which federated as the United States of America were founded as the result of two great waves of colonizing activity in the seventeenth century. The first, which began in 1606 and lasted until 1637, planted three groups of colonies: 'The Two Fruitful Sisters Virginia and Maryland' on the Chesapeake, with their off-lying sister Bermuda; the Puritan commonwealths of New England; and the British West Indies. The same period saw the establishment of the French in L'Acadie (Nova Scotia), more firmly at Quebec, and side-by-side with the English in the West Indies.

The death of Elizabeth and the accession of James Stuart in 1603 brought about a liquidation of the secular struggles with Spain and Scotland, and released capital and English man power for more fruitful purposes. The lesson that 'private purses are cold comforts to adventurers' had been well learned. Excellent results had already been obtained in foreign trade by joint-stock corporations, which combined the capital of many under the management of a few, chosen by the stockholders. The Muscovy Company and the Levant Company, first of these overseas trading corporations, had done very well trading with Russia and the Near East; spectacular profits were in store for the East India Company. Each company received a monopoly of English trade with specified portions of the world, and full control over whatever trading posts or colonies it might see fit to establish. They may be compared with the great western railroad corporations of the United States before the Interstate Commerce Act; like these, they used capital and labor primarily for profit, and incidentally for the good of the nation and the development of new resources.

In such wise the English colonization of Virginia was effected. Two groups of capitalists were formed, the one centering in Bristol and the other in London. The price of a share was £12 10s, and every stockholder could take part in the quarterly meetings (called General Courts) and had a vote in choosing the board of directors, known as the Treasurer and Council.[1] Between these two Virginia Companies, the English claim to North America was divided. Northern Virginia, renamed New England in 1620, fell to the Bristol group; Southern Virginia, which also included the future Maryland and Carolina, to the Londoners.

The Northern Company's one attempt to plant came to grief because of an 'extreme unseasonable and frosty' Maine winter; the 'Old Dominion' of Virginia was established by the London Company. That corporation was no mere money-making scheme, although the expectation of profit certainly existed; rather was it a national enterprise with hundreds of stockholders great and small. The leading spirits were Sir Thomas Smith, a veteran merchant adventurer; Sir Edwin Sandys, a parliamentary leader; Nicholas Ferrar; and the Earls of Southampton, Pembroke and Montgomery, to whom Shakespeare's First Folio was dedicated.

Three ships under Captain Christopher Newport, *Sarah Constant, Goodspeed,* and *Discovery,* dropped down the Thames at Christmastide 1606, cheered by Michael Drayton's 'Ode to the Virginia Voyage':

> Britans, you stay too long,
> Quickly aboord bestow you,
>   And with a merry gale,
>   Swell your stretch'd sayle,
> With vows as strong
> As the winds that blow you.
>
> And cheerefully at sea,
> Successe you still intice,
>   To get the pearle and gold,
>   *And ours to hold,*
>   VIRGINIA,
>   Earth's only Paradise, . . .

'Virginia's Tryalls,' (as an early tract on the colony was entitled) began at once. The voyage, by the Columbus route, was long and tedious and fatal to 16 of the 120 men aboard — no women were taken. Almost everything was done wrong. The Virginia Company,

---

[1] In the reorganizations of 1609 and 1612; in the original charter, the Council was appointed by the king.

having inherited the ample ambitions of the Hakluyt and Gilbert era, expected to convert Indians, locate gold mines, discover the North-west Passage, produce ' all the commodities of Europe, Africa and Asia, and supplye the wantes of all our decayed trades.' But no gold was found, neither the James nor the Chickahominy rivers led to the Pacific, and the only commodities sent home for several years were of the forest, such as oak clapboard, cedar and walnut panelling. The company proposed to establish a new home for the unemployed who swarmed into English towns, when ousted from the land, but these ' sturdy beggars' did not care to emigrate as landless wage-slaves to a company. So the first colony consisted largely of decayed gentlemen, released prisoners, with a few honest artisans who found nothing to do. The company provided them with an absurd sort of local government; and although Captain Newport was instructed to choose a healthy location, he selected for Jamestown a site so malarial that it was eventually abandoned. As in Columbus's first colony over a century earlier, the men were racked by disease, poisoned or starved by the strange food, drenched through flimsy housing (for the tight, warm log cabin of the American frontier was a later Swedish contri-bution), and pestered by the Indians. By the spring of 1608 only 53 Englishmen were left alive; and they were saved only through the bustling activity of Captain John Smith in placating Indians and planting corn.

The Virginia Company would not hear of failure. Relief was sent in 1608, and again in 1609 — a fleet of nine ships under Sir Thomas Gates. The flagship was wrecked on the Bermudas, pro-viding material for Shakespeare's *Tempest,* and procuring for Eng-land the lovely islands that are now her oldest colony.[2] When the sur-vivors reached Jamestown in a vessel they constructed of Bermudian cedar, the colony was reduced to the last stage of wretchedness. ' Everie man allmost laments himself of being here,' wrote the gov-ernor in 1611. He despaired of making a success with ' sutch disor-dered persons, so prophane, so riotous . . . besides of sutch diseased and crased bodies.' He hoped the king would send to Virginia, out of the common jails, all men condemned to die; they at least might be glad ' to make this their new Countrie.' One is not astonished at the ' murmurs' and ' treasonable Intendments' of these workers

---

[2] Newfoundland puts in the same claim, but although Newfoundland was formally taken possession of in 1583, the permanent English settlement there dates only from the eighteenth century, whilst that of Bermuda has been continuous since 1612.

when one reads of their regime. Twice a day they were marched into the fields by beat of drum or into the forests to cut wood, and twice a day marched back to Jamestown to eat and pray. Obviously that sort of life would not attract Englishmen; nor could it last. The only thing that kept the colony alive was the deep faith and gallant spirit of men like Gates, Dale, De la Warr, and those nameless heroes who refused to admit defeat. These men believed that they had hold of something which must not be allowed to perish. ' Be not dismayed at all,' says the author of *Newes from Virginia* (1610), ' God will not let us fall ':

> Let England knowe our willingnesse,
>   For that our worke is good;
> *Wee hope to plant a nation,*
>   *Where none before hath stood.*

Virginia needed more than faith and a gallant spirit to ensure permanence. She needed a profitable product, a system of landholding that gave immigrants a stake in the country; discipline to be sure, but also liberty. In ten years' time she obtained all these. Between 1615 and 1625 Virginia was transformed from an unsuccessful trading post, ruled by iron discipline and hated by most of her people, into a commonwealth that began to open a new and wonderful life to the common man of England.

Tobacco culture, which never entered into the founders' plans, saved Virginia. Smoking was probably brought to England by Sir John Hawkins in the 1560's. Tobacco is the Arawak Indian word for the cigars which they inhaled through the nostrils; but North American Indians used long-stemmed pipes, with stone bowls from ' the great Red Pipe-stone Quarry,' if they could get them. The variety of tobacco that the Indians cultivated around Roanoke was praised in the official narrative of the Raleigh colony; but English smokers reported that it bit the tongue viciously, and so continued to import West Indian leaf through Spain. John Rolfe, husband to Pocahontas, is said to have been responsible for procuring seed from the West Indies around 1613, and the leaves grown from this seed on Virginian soil smoked well. Some 2500 pounds were exported to England in 1616; 20,000 in 1617; 50,000 in 1618. Here at last was something to attract capital and labor, and make large numbers of Englishmen wish to emigrate. Unfortunately there was a strong anti-tobacco movement in England led by King James, who described smoking as 'a custome lothsome to the eye, hatefull to the Nose, harmefull to the braine, dangerous to the Lungs, and in the blacke stinking fume thereof, neerest resembling the horrible Stigian smoke of the pit that is bottomelesse.' Tobacco planting was almost too successful for the good of the colony, which was still importing foodstuffs from England a decade after her foundation. Yet nothing could stop the colonists from planting or Englishmen from buying and smoking Virginia tobacco.

Another factor was private property in land. As the indentures of the Virginia Company's hired servants expired, they became tenant farmers on a share-cropping basis; by 1619 the tenant farms extended twenty miles along the James, and the population passed a thousand souls. Groups of settlers organized by some man of substance were granted large tracts called 'hundreds,' which formed autonomous communities within the colony; the Pilgrim Fathers would have had a Virginia hundred, if the *Mayflower* had sailed on time. And in 1618 the company devised 'head-rights,' which became the basis of land tenure in all the Southern English Colonies. By this system persons who emigrated at their own expense were granted fifty acres free for each member of their party, or for any subsequent immigrant whose passage money they paid. Thus private gain and individual enterprise were enlisted to build up the colony, and labor supply kept pace with that of arable land.

English law and liberty came as well. In 1618 the company issued instructions to the new governor, Sir George Yeardley, ordering him to introduce English common law and the orderly processes thereof, and summon a representative assembly, with power to make by-laws, subject to the company's consent in England. Democracy made her American debut on 30 July 1619, when twenty-two 'burgesses,' two from each settled district, elected by the vote of all men aged seventeen and upward, met with the governor's council in the church at Jamestown. The session lasted but six days, the few laws passed had to be validated by the company in England, and another assembly was not chosen until 1621. But the Virginia Assembly of 1619 was the earliest representative body in the New World. From that time forth, government of the people, however limited or thwarted, has been a fundamental principle of the English colonies and the United States. No colony of any other nation obtained representative institutions before the nineteenth century.

As long as it lasted, the parent company in England exerted far more power in Virginia than this popular assembly. But the company itself was democratic in spirit; a movement of the small £12 10s stockholders in 1619 unseated Sir Thomas Smith, the experienced London merchant who had been treasurer and executive head during the most difficult years, and elected Sir Edwin Sandys, a leader of the opposition in the House of Commons, tolerant in religion and liberal in outlook. Convinced that the colony's exclusive preoccupation with tobacco was unsound and politically dangerous, Sandys induced the stockholders to adopt a five-year plan for Virginia. French vines, vintners, and olive trees, lumbermen from the Baltic, ironworkers from England, were procured or hired to start new industries, and thousands of poor Englishmen and women were assisted to emigrate. Unfortunately all this required more expense than the company was able to bear, and the colony was ill prepared to receive an influx of four thousand people in four years. Ships were overcrowded, housing facilities inadequate, and the loss of life from typhus, malaria, malnutrition, and overwork continued to be appalling. Moreover, most of the artisans and specialized farmers, whose passages had been paid, dropped what they were supposed to do in order to cultivate the great cash crop. Plantations were laid out too far apart, defense was neglected, and in 1622 a surprise attack by the Indians destroyed the infant ironworks at the falls of the James river, erased almost every settlement outside Jamestown, and in a night wiped out the gains of three years. This gave the enemies of Sandys a handle against him, convinced the king that the colony had been grossly mismanaged, resulted in legal proceedings against the charter, and the dissolution of the Virginia Company of London.

Virginia now became a royal province or crown colony; but she did not lose the large measure of self-government that she had won. The assembly, the courts of justice, and other organs of local government already being evolved were retained. Governor and council, however, were now appointed by the king of England and subject to royal instructions. This change was not unpopular in the colony; Virginia never has liked economic planning. Charles I, not unaffected by the large revenue he was obtaining from the customs on Virginia tobacco, interfered with the colony less than the company had, and development continued along tobacco plantation lines.

When we think of seventeenth-century Virginia we should first banish from our minds the cavalier myth, of gallants and fair ladies living a life of silken ease, that was created by poets and romantic novelists of the nineteenth century. We must picture a series of farms and plantations lining the James, the York, and the Rappahannock rivers up to the fall line, and beginning to extend along the south bank of the Potomac; there are few houses more than five miles from tidewater. The average farm, not above three or four hundred acres, will be cultivated by the owner and his family and a few white indentured servants of both sexes. The house is a story-and-a-half framed cottage, kept warm in winter by great log fires; around it is a vegetable garden and orchard; beyond, corn and tobacco fields, enclosed by zigzag Virginia fences of split rails; and beyond that, woodland, where the cattle and hogs fend for themselves. In course of a few years, when the original tobacco fields are exhausted, the woodland will be cleared and put under tillage, while the 'old fields,' after a few diminishing crops of corn, will revert to brush and woodland. Few horses and still fewer wheeled vehicles will be seen outside Jamestown until after 1650 when New England begins to export horses; but almost every farmer keeps a yoke of oxen for plowing, and a boat on creek or river. If the owner prospers, he will procure more land from someone who has more head rights than he cares to take up.

The few great plantations, established by men who came out with considerable capital, have large houses and more outbuildings, keep a store for selling English goods to their neighbors, and a wharf and warehouse for handling their tobacco. Every so often the big planter orders the London merchant who handles his tobacco crop to send him out another parcel of indented servants, for each of whom he will obtain fifty acres more land; if no ungranted land is available near the homestead he will 'seat' a second plantation elsewhere, and put his son, or a trusty servant whose time is up, in charge.

Most early settlers of Virginia came from the middle class and the better sort of English farmers. They were seeking both freedom and opportunity. Many of the founders of great families, such as John Washington, ancestor of the General, and Captain Thomas Stegg, whose nephew, the first William Byrd, inherited his estate, were shipmasters who came to Virginia to trade, but became so entranced by 'Earth's only Paradise,' that they planted. A handful of families in Virginia had noble or 'genteel' connections; but with these exceptions the First Families of Virginia became first families in Virginia. Nor can it be denied that they worked hard to win and maintain their position. The diary of William Byrd II at the turn of the century is that of an active farmer, trader, and public servant. He enjoyed far less leisure than did the landed gentry in England, and employed much of the leisure that he had in reading the ancient classics and modern theology.

During the first half century, the manners and customs of Virginia were definitely Puritan. The code of laws passed by the first Virginia Assembly 'Against Idleness, Gaming, drunkenes and excesse in apparell,' might as well have been passed by a New England colony; the Virginia laws against Sabbath-breaking and contempt of the Bible or the ministry were almost as severe as in Massachusetts; days of fasting and humiliation were held in the one colony as in the other to placate Jehovah after a pestilence or an Indian victory; witchcraft was prosecuted in both, although no witches were hanged except in New England, and none burned to death anywhere in the English colonies. The typical library of a Virginia gentleman contained about the same proportion of religious literature as that of his fellow in New England, and usually the same books; for the neo-paganism of Elizabeth's reign had by now worn off, and Englishmen like other Christians were eager to understand the mysteries of life and death, and to stand well with their God. The Church of England was early established in Virginia, and Puritan congregations were outlawed in 1643; the Book of Common Prayer had to be read. Such Puritanism as there was in the Virginia church came from absence of Anglican discipline and authority rather than from an aggressive Puritan doctrine and a cohesive Puritan community. And as time flowed on, and great fortunes were built up from tobacco, the Puritan tinge passed from the Old Dominion.

Below the independent landowners in Virginia were the English indented servants. These were the main source of labor in the Chesapeake colonies throughout this pioneer period, and an important one in New England. Indented servants were mostly lads and lasses in their late 'teens or early twenties, members of large families in the English towns and countryside, who were looking for a better chance than the overcrowded trades afforded by the old country. They were attracted by 'come all ye' ballads like 'The Maydens of London's Brave Adventures':

The Reason, as I understand, why you go to that Nation,
Is to inhabit that far Land, and make a new plantation;
Where you shall have good ground enough, for Planting and for Tilling,
Which never shall be taken away, so long as you are willing.

Then come, brave Lasses, come away, conducted by Apollo,
Although that you do go before, your sweet-hearts they will follow.

Nor were they much deterred by counter-propaganda, such as the ballad of 'The Trapann'd Maiden,' [3] of which these stanzas are a sample:

> I have play'd my part both at Plow and Cart,
>   In the Land of Virginny, O;
> Billets from the Wood upon my back they load,
>   *Even that I am weary, weary, weary, weary, O.*

> Instead of drinking Beer, I drink the water clear,
>   In the Land of Virginny, O;
> Which makes me pale and wan, do all that e'er I can,
>   *When that I am weary, weary, weary, weary, O.*

Many of these boys and girls succumbed to the change of climate, although not nearly so many as in the early years of the colony. Men and women alike performed any sort of labor their master required for a space of five years, which might be extended for ill-conduct; and at the end of that time were dismissed with a few tools and clothes; in Maryland each servant was given fifty acres of land by the Lord Proprietor. The more energetic freedmen would then earn money by wage labor, and set up as farmers themselves. Most of the girls married, while the shiftless drifted to the frontier as squatters, or became rural paupers. A hard system it was, according to modern lights; yet it enabled thousands of poor Englishmen and women, and, in the eighteenth century, tens of thousands of Scots, Irish, Germans, and Swiss, to make a fresh start in life and take an active part in the forming of the American nation.

Possession of capital gave any early settler a great advantage in procuring land and labor by the head-right system. For instance, Captain Adam Thoroughgood had built up as early as 1635 an estate of 5350 acres, in several different parcels on Chesapeake Bay. The nucleus was 2050 acres, granted to him for bringing over his wife, son and 41 servants in 1628. The rest were for sundry ' shipments ' in seventeen different vessels, during the next six years. All these were white servants; but we find William Bannister bringing in ' Bas a Negar ' and ' Anthony, William, Mary, John, Jacob, Negars ' in 1638; whilst Rob-

---

[3] ' Trapanned ' was seventeenth-century English for ' kidnapped,' and also included those who were persuaded to sell their services for five years by false promises.

ert Taliafero had 6300 acres confirmed to him in 1666 for the transportation of 126 persons, of whom 16 were Negroes.[4] Great planters
such as these early secured, and their descendants long maintained, political and social control of the colony. They monopolized the seats in
the Council, all offices of honor and profit; the House of Burgesses,
although elected on a democratic franchise, was largely composed of
relatives or social allies of the great planters.

Negro slavery helped the rich to grow richer in colonial Virginia.
A Dutch ship brought slaves from Africa to Jamestown as early as
1619, but slavery did not become a characteristic feature of Virginia
society until nearly the end of the century. It became so then for three
reasons: England restricted the emigration of white bond servants;
the Royal African Company became more efficient; and a catastrophic
fall in the price of tobacco ruined the small farmers, permitting profits
only to men who had the capital to purchase cheap and self-propagat-
ing labor. Virginia in 1700, with an estimated population of 72,000,
was exporting to England about 11,500,000 pounds of tobacco, half
of which was re-exported to the continent.

Virginia was the most English of the English colonies, and more
rural than any part of England. Until Norfolk and Williamsburg
were founded, at the very close of the century, there was no settlement
with more than a few score persons; even Jamestown was almost
deserted when the council or assembly was not in session. It was so
easy to import articles of necessity and luxury from England in exchange for tobacco that local trades did not prosper. Seeds of antagonism were early sown by the exploitation of Virginia at the hands of
English merchants who, if the assembly pegged the price of tobacco,
cynically raised the price of English goods. The Virginians were intensely loyal to their mother country, and proud of being Englishmen; but they were also firmly rooted in their new homes, and conscious of being Virginians. A traveller reported of Jamaica in 1763,
' the generality of its inhabitants look upon themselves as passengers
only.' That could not have been said of the people of any continental
colony twenty years after its foundation. Conditioning for independence began almost immediately on the shores of Chesapeake Bay.

[4] Nell M. Nugent, *Cavaliers and Pioneers*, I. 22, 94, 548.

2. *Maryland and the English West Indies*

Maryland, a colony with the same soil, climate, economic and social system as Virginia, owed her separate existence and her special character to the desire of a great Englishman to create a feudal domain for his family, and a refuge for members of his faith. Gilbert, Raleigh, and half a dozen lesser men had attempted the like and failed; but the proprietary method of colonization continued side by side with the corporate, because land was the safest investment, and many acres meant social security. Land was something you could not lose except by conquest or confiscation; and if it paid no profit in your own time, it would certainly take care of your descendants, the way population was increasing. The main difficulty was this: the expense of carrying a colony along to a point where it was self-supporting was too great for all but a few individuals.

Sir George Calvert, first Lord Baltimore, was a stockholder of the Virginia Company who aspired to found a colony of his own. He failed once, in Newfoundland; when he settled in Virginia, he was ordered out, because he was a Roman Catholic convert. He then asked for and obtained from Charles I a liberal slice of the Old Dominion, with which, now that the Virginia Company was no more, the king had a right to do as he chose. This original Maryland grant extended from the Potomac river north to New England, but was later cut in on by another royal hand-out, Pennsylvania. Lord Baltimore died while the Maryland charter was going through in 1632, but it was confirmed to his son and heir Cecilius. This second Lord Baltimore and first Lord Proprietor of the Province of Maryland dispatched the first group of colonists, who settled at St. Mary's near the mouth of the Potomac, in 1634. They experienced no ' starving time,' for settled Virginia was near, and the local Indians were friendly; but the Susquehanna tribe that lived along upper Chesapeake Bay later gave the colony much trouble.

Cecilius Calvert intended Maryland not only as a source of profit, but as a refuge for English Roman Catholics. One required as much faith and fortitude to be a good Catholic in the England of that era as in the Germany of Hitler; yet, for reasons yet unexplained, comparatively few English Catholics emigrated to Maryland. Almost from the start the colony had a Protestant majority. Calvert coped with this situation in a statesmanlike manner by inducing the Maryland Assembly to pass a law of religious toleration in 1649. He had summoned an assembly, since his charter required that the laws have the consent of the freemen, but allowed it little power, and conferred most of the lucrative offices on his relatives and Catholic friends. The local civil war that broke out in Maryland in 1654 was essentially a class war of Protestant small farmers against the Catholic magnates and lords of manors. The majority won, and the Act of Toleration was repealed; but Lord Baltimore eventually recovered his rights.

In the West Indies also, English and French used the proprietary method of colonization with success. The Caribbean is the American Mediterranean in a strategic as well as a climatic sense. There the Spaniards established their base for the conquest of Mexico; there, in the late sixteenth and early seventeenth centuries, English, French, and Dutch seized vantage points that destroyed the American monopoly of Spain and rendered her communications insecure; there, in the 1780's, the naval supremacy of the War of Independence was decided; there, in Haiti, Napoleon was forced to renounce his American empire and cede Louisiana to the United States; there the United States has erected the outer defenses of the Panama Canal. The superb arc of islands flung out eastward from Yucatán have an amazing fertility; the extension of sugar culture around 1650 made even the smallest of them immensely valuable, and the slaves imported from Africa thrived beyond all expectation. Far more money and men were spent on defending and capturing these islands in the colonial era than on the continental colonies that became the United States, because they were much more profitable to their owners.

As none of the islands east of Puerto Rico were effectively occupied by the Spaniards, these Lesser Antilles attracted small-time English and French adventurers, who were unable to swing a continental venture like Maryland or Canada. Carib Indians broke up the earliest English and French attempts, in St. Lucia and Grenada, and on the ' Wild Coast ' of Guiana. In 1624 permanent footholds on the island of St. Kitts were secured by Sir Thomas Warner, and by Pierre Belain d'Esnambuc. Warner's men spilled over into near-by Montserrat, Nevis, and Antigua; D'Esnambuc, as governor of Cardinal Richelieu's *Compagnie des Îles d'Amérique,* began pushing out the Caribs from Martinique and Guadeloupe in 1635. Captain John Powell took possession of Barbados, which the Caribs had fortunately vacated, in 1625, and English colonization of it began within two years. The Earl of Carlisle obtained a proprietary patent to all the ' Caribbee Islands,' but, unlike Lord Baltimore, did nothing for them; government and

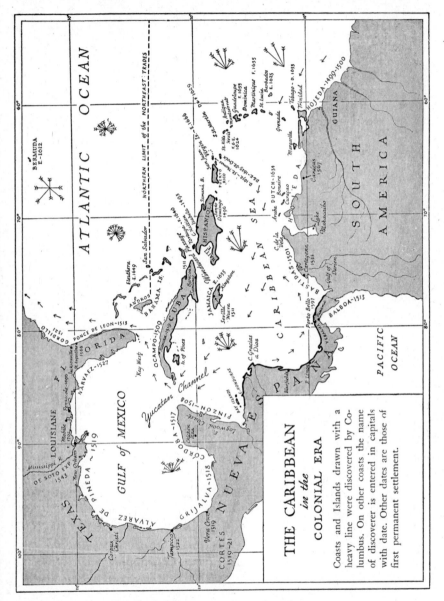

The Caribbean in the Colonial Era

Prepared by S. E. Morison for The Growth of the American Republic

Abbreviations: E–English, F–French, D–Dutch or Danish; all other places settled by Spanish.
The arrows converging on a point indicate by their length the percentage of time that the
wind blows from a given direction over that area in February. This will be a fair average for
the non-hurricane season, 15 November to 25 June. The feathers on the arrows indicate average force of the wind on the Beaufort scale.

profits alike were farmed out. It did not much matter, for the great emigration was under way, and those English who wanted a warm climate and quick profits turned to the islands. Often families split between islands and continent; John Winthrop, governor of Massachusetts, had a son Samuel in Antigua, and another in Barbados, who sent him tobacco that the governor described as 'verye ill conditioned, fowle, full of stalkes and evill coloured.' The John Jefferson who represented Flowerdew Hundred in the first Virginia Assembly, later helped Sir Thomas Warner to found the English colony at St. Kitts, and also became a leading planter in Antigua. Thomas Jefferson is possibly descended from his brother.

Robert Rich, Earl of Warwick, a leading promoter of settlement in New England, Virginia, and Bermuda, attempted a variety of island and mainland colonies all the way from Trinidad to the Bay Islands off Honduras, but none of these lasted long. The Caribbean also became a happy hunting ground for pirates, since its waters were traversed by the valuable supply ships and plate fleets of Spain. Owing to the Spaniards' neglect of Hispaniola, the buccaneers, a rabble of rascals from all countries, established themselves on Tortuga Island near Cape Haitien in the 1620's, hunting the wild hogs and preying on passing vessels. Tortuga, captured by the French in 1640, became the nucleus of their colony of Saint-Domingue, which eventually became the wealthiest European establishment in the West Indies; the buccaneers found other places to operate from. West Indian history is notoriously complicated, and we have had to postpone consideration of the Dutch exploits to a later section of this chapter. Suffice it to say here that the Dutch naval power in the Caribbean was keeping the Spaniards so busy that the French and English colonies were not much troubled, and that the Dutch provided the capital, the appliances and the methods by which the French and English turned from less lucrative crops to sugar cane in the 1650's. Once sugar was in, white labor went out. For instance, Barbados in 1645 had a population of 36,000, of which only 5,680 were slaves. Ten years later there were 23,000 English and 20,000 slaves.

To anyone familiar with the happy-go-lucky poverty of these Lesser Antilles today, their prosperity in the seventeenth century is almost incredible. The French owned only half the 25-mile long island of Saint-Christophe (St. Kitts), but in 1655 they could place in the field 8,000 armed men, and their governor, the Chevalier de Poincy, boasted such an establishment as Virginia did not see for another half-century: a three-and-a-half-story château of brick and stone, maintained by a hundred French lackeys, and with formal gardens, orange groves, a model plantation, and a sugar mill, to which three hundred slaves were attached. Twenty acres in Barbados planted with cotton and sugar cane yielded more profit than a great tobacco plantation in Virginia. Barbados, too, had its representative assembly, which yielded nothing to Massachusetts Bay and Virginia in its solicitude for the liberties of Englishmen.

Thus, within a generation of founding their first continental colonies, at Quebec and Jamestown, France and England had tropical possessions which were small in extent, but worthy competitors to the vast Spanish empire in sugar, dyewoods, cotton, and coffee. In the second half of the century, Spain was despoiled of Jamaica by Cromwell, and of Saint-Domingue by France; while smaller islands such as St. Martin, St. Croix, St. Thomas and Tobago were picked up by Dutch, Norwegians, and Danes. It seemed in 1700 as if the Spanish Empire were on the way out — but it was an unconscionable time a-dying!

These non-Spanish colonies in the West Indies were closely integrated with the next group we have to consider, the English colonies in New England. With slave labor it was more profitable for the planters to concentrate on tropical crops of high profit, and procure elsewhere every other essential to living, such as salt meat and fish, breadstuffs and ground vegetables, lumber and livestock. These were exactly the commodities that New England produced, yet could find no vent for in England; and New England built the ships to carry these products of her farms, forests, and fisheries to the West Indies. The Chesapeake colonies, and later the Middle colonies and the Carolinas, also shared this trade, and like New England imported the molasses and distilled it into the fiery beverage first known as 'rumbustion' or 'kill-devil.' New England, however, would have long remained a string of poor fishing stations and hardscrabble farms, but for commerce with these superb tropical islands set in the sapphire Caribbean.

3. New England

New England was founded without reference to the West Indies, and largely as a result of the religious movement known as Puritanism. Puritanism both as a religion and a social force has been so per-

vasive and permanent an influence in the United States, extending far
beyond New England and the colonial period, that we may well pause
to inquire what it was at the beginning.

The Puritans were that party in the Church of England who wished
to carry through the Protestant Reformation to its logical conclusion,
and establish both a religion and a way of living based on the Bible
— as interpreted by themselves. The Church of England, a typical
English compromise between Rome and the Reformation, did not
satisfy them. With official Anglican doctrine, as expressed in the
Thirty-Nine Articles of Religion, the Puritans had no quarrel; but
they wished to do away with bishops, deans, and all the clergy above
the rank of parish priests, to abolish the Book of Common Prayer and
all set prayers, and to reorganize the Church either by a hierarchy of
councils (Presbyterianism), or on the basis of a free federation of
independent parishes (Congregationalism). They were disgusted
with the frivolity, extravagance, and moral corruption that pervaded
both extremes of English society in the early Stuart era, with
gaming and ' stage-plays,' and with the rough and semi-pagan fes-
tivals that marked rural life, especially on Sundays. In other words,
they wished to establish such patterns of behavior as would make it
possible for people to lead something approaching the New Testament life. English Puritan divines frowned on idleness as a sin,
eschewed mysticism and monasticism, and taught that a good businessman served God quite as well as a good clergyman, provided he
were honest; hence Puritanism appealed largely to the middle class
of tradesmen and rising capitalists whose center was London. It made
a wide appeal also in certain rural regions such as East Anglia and the
West Country, where ' the hungry sheep look up and are not fed '
(to use Milton's phrase) by the common run of English clergyman,
incapable of delivering a proper sermon. And it enlisted the devoted
support of many young intellectuals in the universities, especially in
Cambridge; hence the stress of the Puritans on education. Puritanism
was no class movement, or ground swell of the underdog, but a dynamic religious movement. A burning desire to know and to do the
will of God seemed to pass through the land; in order to know it
neighbors subscribed to establish Puritan ' lectureships ' in parishes
devoid of a sermonizing pastor, and then met in their homes for the
exchange of religious views and experiences.

These desires of the serious-minded were thwarted in an increasing
degree by the first two Stuart kings. James I, remembering the days

when the Scots reformer John Knox had called him 'God's silly vassal,' promised to harry the Puritans out of the land if they would not conform; and he harried one little band to such good purpose that they founded the first New England colony. Things became worse under Charles I. The Anglo-Catholic polity of Bishop Laud, a move toward re-establishing the Eucharist as the central point of Christian worship, appealed to the king, and was enforced; clergymen who refused to follow this 'back to Rome' movement, as they regarded it, were persecuted, and Puritan lecturers were silenced. These Laudian reforms made it increasingly difficult for conscientious Puritans to remain within the Church; yet they looked on separation from the Church with a horror comparable to the feelings of American unionists toward secession in 1860. A large minority of English Puritans fled from these intolerable conditions to found a New England overseas where they might live and worship as they thought right. The majority formed an alliance with other Englishmen who objected to the royal policy on political grounds, won a majority of seats in the Long Parliament, resisted the king in the name of ancient English liberties, and won the great Civil War.

The Pilgrim Fathers owe their fame not only to leading the Puritan vanguard to New England, but to the moving history of their adventures and sufferings by their leader, Governor Bradford. They were a small band of humble folk, left-wing Puritans of East Anglia, whose religious meetings were so interfered with that they removed to Leyden in 1609 and formed an English Congregational Church. After ten years' exile they decided to remove to America. Sir Edwin Sandys, who recognized the quality of these people although he did not share their faith, procured for them a grant from the Virginia Company, and a group of English merchants consented to finance their migration. After interminable delays the *Mayflower* set sail in the worst season of the year for an ocean crossing, and after a rough passage, anchored on 11 November 1620 in the harbor of Cape Cod, outside the Virginia jurisdiction. Accordingly, with that instinct for self-government which Englishmen even then possessed, the Pilgrims signed a compact to be governed by the will of the majority until permanent provision should be made for their colony.

The grim, almost desperate situation of these people, arriving in a harbor enclosed by barren sand dunes at the beginning of a New England winter, and with very limited food supplies aboard, is vividly described by Bradford:

For summer being done, all things stand upon them with a weather-beaten face; and the whole countrie, full of woods and thickets, represented a wild and savage hue. If they looked behind them, there was the mighty ocean which they had passed, and was now as a maine barr and golfe to separate them from all the civill parts of the world . . . What could now sustaine them but the spirite of God and his grace? May not and ought not the children of these fathers rightly say: ' Our fathers were Englishmen which came over this great ocean, and were ready to perish in this willderness; but they cried unto the Lord, and he heard their voyce, and looked on their adversitie. Let them therefore praise the Lord, because he is good, and his mercies endure for ever.'

No group of settlers in America was so ill-fitted by experience and equipment to cope with the wilderness as this little band of peasants, city workers, and petty bourgeoisie; yet none came through so magnificently. For, as Bradford put it, ' they knew they were pilgrimes, and looked not much on those things, but lift up their eyes to the heavens, their dearest cuntrie '; and, as another wrote to Sandys, ' It is not with us as with other men, whom small things can discourage, or small discontentments cause to wish themselves at home again.' About their only good luck was to find deserted fields ready for tillage at the harbor already named Plymouth by Captain John Smith, and to be joined by Squanto, the Indian who acted as their scout-master, teaching them how to catch fish and grow corn. Half the company died the first winter; the first Thanksgiving feast was held in November 1621, to celebrate the arrival of the *Fortune* with provisions, the gathering of a fair harvest, and ' great store of wild Turkies, of which they took many, besides venison.' ' At which time, amongst other recreations, we exercised our arms, many of the Indians coming amongst us, and among the rest their greatest king, Massasoyt, with some ninety men, whom for three days we entertained and feasted.' [5]

This was an expensive entertainment. With more mouths to feed, the Pilgrims were soon again on short allowance, and for several years the colony ran neck-and-neck with famine. But they never lost heart, or considered giving up and going home. These simple folk were

---

[5] In the hope of settling a question about which we are frequently asked, the date of this ' First Thanksgiving ' is unknown. It came somewhere between 11 November, when the *Fortune* arrived, and 4 December, when Winslow wrote a letter describing it. The custom of appointing an annual Thanksgiving Day by law did not begin in the Plymouth Colony until 1668, and the ' last Thursday in November ' date was first set by a proclamation of President Johnson in 1865.

exalted to the stature of statesmen and prophets in their narrow sphere, because they ardently believed, and so greatly dared, and firmly endured. They set forth in acts as in words the stout-hearted idealism in action that Americans admire; that is why Plymouth Rock has become a symbol. For, as Governor Bradford concluded his annals of the lean years,

Thus out of small beginnings greater things have been produced by his hand that made all things of nothing, and gives being to all things that are; and as one small candle may light a thousand; so the light here kindled hath shone unto many, yea, in some sorte, to our whole nation.

Only small beginnings were apparent for ten years; at the end of that time the total population of Plymouth Colony was but three hundred. In the meantime a dozen straggling fishing and trading posts had been founded along the New England coast from Southern Maine to Massachusetts Bay, with or without permission from the Council for New England. One of these developed into the important Bay Colony. A company of indeterminate name, which planted a small settlement at Salem in 1628, was taken over by a group of leading Puritans, including Sir Richard Saltonstall, Thomas Dudley, and John Winthrop, who wished to emigrate. Obtaining from Charles I a royal charter as the Massachusetts Bay Company in 1629, when the Anglo-Catholic pressure on those of their faith began to be severely felt, they voted to transfer charter, government, and members to New England. A fleet of seventeen sail bearing nine hundred to one thousand men and women, the largest colonizing expedition yet sent out from England, crossed in the summer of 1630 to Massachusetts Bay, founded Boston, and six or seven towns near by.

This transfer of the Massachusetts Bay charter had an important bearing on colonial destiny and American institutions. As long as the charter remained in England, their settlement at Salem had the same relation to the company as Jamestown had to the Virginia Company until 1624. With charter and company in America, the colony became practically independent of England. The 'freemen,' as stockholders were then called, became voters; the governor, deputy-governor, and assistants whom the freemen annually elected, and who in England had been president and directors of a colonizing company, were now the executives, upper branch of the legislative assembly, and judicial officers, of a Puritan commonwealth. A representative system was devised, as it was inconvenient for the freemen to attend the 'general court' or assembly in person, and by 1644 the deputies and assistants had separated into two houses. Neither king nor parliament had any say in the Massachusetts government. The franchise was restricted to church members, which prevented non-Puritan participation in the government; but this did not matter in the long run. What mattered was that this organization made for independence, and that the annual election on a definite date of all officers — governor and upper branch as well as deputies — became so popular in the colonies as to be imitated wherever the king could be induced to grant his consent. It was an integral feature of the state constitutions of 1776–82 and even survives in the Federal Government, with the election of presidential electors, senators, and representatives on the same day. This corporate precedent has given the American system of government a very different complexion from the parliamentary system that was slowly developing in England. American institutions began to diverge from English institutions in 1630.

John Winthrop was a superior man of noble character, deeply concerned with his Puritan commonwealth. It is clear enough from his writings what sort of a community he and his fellows of the ruling class intended New England to become. With the greater part of their English heritage they had no quarrel. Their new communities were to preserve the liberties of the ' free-born Englishmen,' foster education and learning, and preserve the distance betwen social classes that Englishmen of all eras seem to value. But they proposed to subordinate everything to the establishment and maintenance of what they deemed to be true religion. This included, besides a particular form of Congregational worship, and strong community spirit, an insistence on sobriety of manners, purity of morals, and an economic set-up that would neither exalt the rich nor degrade the poor.

Church and State in New England were dominated by the covenant idea. ' We are entered into a covenant' with God ' for this worke,' preached Winthrop on the voyage over. ' We have taken out a Commission; the Lord hath given us leave to draw our own Articles,' and He ' will expect a strict performance.' Each Congregational church was formed by a new covenant, and so each new settlement. Thus there was a social and a religious sanction, as well as a civic obligation. Justice however must be tempered by mercy; and the punishments for offenses in New England were no more severe than in Virginia, and less so than in contemporary England.

It soon appeared that Massachusetts Bay was the sort of colony that

English Puritans wanted; for the great Puritan migration promptly set in, and continued until the outbreak of civil war in England, when New England had some twenty thousand people. Most of this emigration, unlike that which was going on at the same time to Virginia, Maryland, and the West Indies, was against the will of the royal government; but nothing could stop it. According to a popular ballad, satirizing the Old Testament names beloved by Puritans,

> Our Company we feare not —
>   There goes my cousin Hannah;
> And Reuben doe persuade to goe
>   His sister, faire Susanna;
> With Abigail and Lydia
>   And Ruth noe doubt comes after,
> And Sarah kinde will not stay behinde
>   My cousin Constance' daughter
>   *Then for the truth's sake come along, come along!*
>   *Leave the place of superstition,*
>   *Were it not for we that brethren be,*
>   *You'd sink into perdition.*

The community character of the New England migration dictated the method of land settlement. Neighborhood groups from the Old Country, often accompanied by an ousted parson, insisted on settling together, obtained a grant of land from the General Court, established a village center, laid out lots, and so formed what was called in New England a town. As soon as one of the older settlements felt itself short on pasturage, a few hardy spirits broke off, and repeated the process a little further west. Around each village green were seated the meeting-house (as the Puritans called a church edifice), the parsonage, and the house of the principal settlers. Each person admitted as an inhabitant received a house lot, a planting lot for his corn, and a strip of river mead or salt meadow for winter forage. The cattle ranged the common woods for most of the year, attended by the town herdsman. By a town meeting, in which everyone took part, each town settled local affairs such as support of the school, laying out highways, regulations for cutting timber, and deciding when cattle could be turned into meadows and cornfields. Here democracy seeped into New England, unwanted and unsuspected by the founding fathers.

This community form of settlement, which extended throughout New England and later had its effect on the federal land system, had an important bearing both on defense and on education. The frontier advanced in an orderly manner, as fast as the Indians could be persuaded to retire. In order to keep them persuaded, universal military training was early adopted. Each male settler eighteen years old and upward had to provide himself with a flintlock musket ' not under three foote nine inches in length,' a pound of gunpowder, 20 bullets and ' 2 fathom of match.' He took part in frequent drills on the village green, and annual regimental musters. Civilian defenders took turns at a nightly ' watch and ward' against prowling wolves and Indians; and boys from ten to sixteen years of age were instructed ' in the exercise of armes, as smale gunnes, halfe pikes, bowes and arrowes.'

Education was a particular concern of the Puritans. Their movement was directed by university-trained divines, and embraced largely by middle-class merchants and landowning farmers, who enjoyed the benefits of education in Elizabethan England. Moreover, it was necessary for godliness that everyone learn to read the Bible. There had come to New England by 1640 about one hundred and thirty university alumni, a very high proportion for so small and poor a population; and these men insisted that their children have the same advantages as themselves, or better. Consequently, in the New England colonies, parents were required to teach their children and servants to read, or to send them to a village school for that purpose. Above these primary schools, about a dozen of the larger New England towns had secondary public grammar schools on the English model, supported by taxation, which boys entered at the age of eight or nine, and where they studied Latin and Greek, and little else, for six years. At the end of that time they were prepared to enter Harvard College, founded by the Massachusetts government in 1636, and named after a young clergyman who bequeathed to it his library and half his estate. There, the more ambitious New England lads (with some from other colonies as far as Bermuda) studied the same seven arts and three philosophies as at Oxford, Cambridge, or Dublin, using the same Latin manuals of logic and metaphysics, Greek texts, Euclids, and ' Hebrew in Twenty-four Hours,' as in European universities. Scholarships were founded by family contributions of corn and wampum, the small change of the Indian trade, and for want of currency students paid their term bills in all manner of agricultural products. About half the graduates entered the Puritan ministry, and became the pastors of frontier communities, where they labored a lifetime to maintain civilized standards; others became magistrates, merchants, physicians, or plain farmers.

Coeval with Harvard College was the first, and for a generation the only, printing press in the English colonies, with a considerable output of almanacs, catechisms, primers, and such locally delivered sermons as London publishers rejected. Nor were the fine arts neglected. Seventeenth-century New Englanders had a natural good taste in house design and village lay-out; artisans like John Hull, John Coney, and Timothy Dwight fashioned beautiful articles of silver for home and communion table; writers such as Anne Bradstreet, Urian Oakes, and Edward Taylor produced religious and occasional poetry of great charm. Thus the classical and humanist tradition of the English went hand in hand with conquering Puritanism into the clearings of the New England wilderness.

Although the founders of Massachusetts Bay hoped to stretch her borders to include all New England, except the Plymouth Colony whose separate existence they somewhat grudgingly respected, there was too much individualism among the Puritans for complete unity. Massachusetts did succeed in annexing New Hampshire for a time, and the population of southern Maine also turned to Boston for protection; but three other colonies, which formed two states of the Union, sprang up before 1640. Under the lead of Master Thomas Hooker, the first westward migration in the English Colonies took place in 1636, to the Connecticut river, where a Bible Commonwealth was organized on the Massachusetts model. New Haven, founded by a London merchant named Theophilus Eaton and his pastor the Rev. John Davenport, maintained a separate existence from Connecticut until 1662, and spread along both shores of Long Island Sound.

Both these colonies were like-minded with the Bay Colony and Plymouth; but Rhode Island, the creation of four separate groups of Puritan heretics, was distinctly otherwise-minded. As everywhere in the field of Protestantism, so in Massachusetts the rulers were unable to maintain religious conformity. Anne Hutchinson of Boston, who set up as a personal prophetess, and Master Roger Williams, who differed with the Bay authorities on many matters, were banished, and formed settlements on Narragansett Bay which federated as Rhode Island and the Providence Plantations in 1644. Roger Williams, the most interesting as well as the most modern of the Puritans, believed in religious liberty. Anywhere else in Christendom toleration of dissenters might or might not be allowed as a political concession, while one ' true ' church was always established. Revolutionary Williams believed in the individual's God-given right to worship as he chose, or not at all; and that right was enforced in Rhode Island. Moreover he coupled democracy with religious liberty; he treated the Indians as men and brothers; and he wrote these principles into the laws and customs of Rhode Island.

One thing these New England colonies had in common until 1680: all were virtually independent commonwealths, acknowledging allegiance to whatever authority had control in England, but making their own laws, trading where they pleased, defending themselves without help from home, and working out their own institutions. Their connection with the mother country was one of sentiment and tradition rather than compulsion; they were every bit as self-reliant and independent as the British dominions of today.

4. New Netherland

Between New England and Virginia the indomitable Dutch, with that uncanny instinct for sources of wealth that has always characterized their commercial ventures, planted a colony that in due time became New York. The Seven United Provinces of the Netherlands (commonly known as the Dutch Republic) accomplished great things overseas before their struggle for independence from the House of Hapsburg was securely won, because the struggle itself forced them to seek empire.

The Dutch merchant marine, largest and most efficient in the world, in the sixteenth century obtained the lion's share of distributing oriental spices from Lisbon throughout Western Europe. As punishment for their rebellion, Philip II of Spain, who acquired the Portuguese crown in 1580, forbade the Dutch access to Lisbon. Consequently they had to procure the spices themselves. As early as 1595 Dutch traders reached Java; in 1602 Dutch capitalists organized the Netherlands East Indies Company, a corporation in comparison with which the Virginia Company was a petty affair. Persistently but inexorably this company pushed the Portuguese out of most of their trading posts in the Far East. In 1611 Batavia was founded in Java, and within thirty years the Dutch Company had established trading stations on the coasts of Sumatra and Formosa, had taken Malacca, conquered Ceylon, discovered Australia and New Zealand, founded the Cape Colony, and created an empire that in 1941 joined the United

States in a struggle for existence. As the Netherlands had a very small population, these far-eastern conquests absorbed the men and money that might otherwise have secured North America for the Dutch race and speech.

Nevertheless, that nation managed to make a permanent and valuable contribution to the future United States. The East Indies Company, interested in finding a shorter way to the Orient than the stormy and dangerous Cape route, made several efforts to find a northeast or a northwest passage to India. That is what Henry Hudson was looking for in 1609 when he sailed the *Half-Moon* up the noble river that shares his name with the mighty bay where he met his death. Yet the Hudson river proved to be a passage indeed, to the heart of the Iroquois Confederacy and the richest fur-bearing country south of the St. Lawrence. Hudson's employers were not interested in the fur trade, but other Dutchmen were; and after skippers Block and May had explored the coast from Maine to the Delaware Capes, fur traders began to frequent the rivers and trade with the natives. A fort was constructed on Castle Island a little below Albany in 1614, but was shortly abandoned.

A turning-point came in 1621. In that year the twelve years' truce between Spain and the Netherlands expired. The grim prospect of that fierce war being renewed impelled the Pilgrim Fathers to leave Holland for America, and inspired the founding of the Dutch West India Company.

Privateering against the Spaniards in the Caribbean, not colonization, was the main purpose of this corporation. But for the enterprise of its fighting traders and of the Dutch navy, Philip IV would certainly have attempted to destroy the English colonies in North America; and as James I had adopted a policy of appeasement, and the Spanish armies in Europe seemed irresistible, it is possible that Philip IV would have gotten away with it. Certainly it was the aggressiveness of Dutch sea power in the Caribbean that enabled the English, French, and Dutch to make establishments in the Lesser Antilles right under the eyes of Spain. In 1628 Admiral Piet Hein pulled off the trick that every seaman had dreamed of for a century past — scooping an entire Spanish treasure fleet. Six years later the company occupied Curaçao, Bonaire, and Aruba off the Venezuelan coast; the first, with a fine harbor, proved to be the ideal base for an interloping trade with the Spanish possessions. A small cluster of islands in the Leeward group was also acquired. In 1624 the company conquered Brazil but within thirty years it was recaptured by the Portuguese. Even in West Africa the company had more of a stake than in North America.

New Netherland began as a trading-post colony in 1624, with the foundation of Fort Orange (Albany) up the Hudson. Fort Amsterdam on the tip of Manhattan Island was permanently established in 1626, Fort Nassau on the Delaware river near Camden, N. J., in 1623 and Fort Good Hope on the Connecticut river, near Hartford, in 1633. As the Dutch looked east rather than west, and even the West India Company was primarily interested in privateering, the future State of New York received very little attention from the company, and still less from their High Mightinesses, the States General of the Netherlands. New Netherland was governed much as Virginia had been before 1619, by a governor and council appointed by the company, without representative institutions. New Amsterdam was the center of the fur trade — it was from Dutch traders that the Pilgrim Fathers learned the use of wampum — and a base for the Dutch merchant ships that entered the Virginia tobacco trade. As early as 1630 it was a typical sailormen's town, with numerous taverns, smugglers, and illicit traders, as well as a Dutch Reformed Church, and a number of substantial houses. Everywhere they went, from New York down to Curaçao and Brazil, or around the world to Ternate and Timor, the Dutch imposed their architecture, their neatness and their good business methods.

When in 1638 the States General threw open the seaborne trade of New Netherland to all Dutch subjects, New Amsterdam became practically a free port. A half-hearted attempt to encourage settlement was made by the company in 1629 by issuing the Charter of Privileges to Patroons. Anyone who brought out fifty families of tenants at his own expense could have an extensive tract of land, with full manorial privileges of holding court, issuing fishing and hunting licenses, and mill monopoly. The directors of the company, such as Kiliaen Van Rensselaer, promptly snapped up all the best sites, like Staten Island and the Hudson valley above Poughkeepsie; and these privileges, which were confirmed under the English regime, meant that the most valuable land in New York was held in vast estates on a feudal basis. Van Rensselaer even levied duties on vessels coming up-river. A certain number of Dutchmen and Walloons acquired 'boueries' (farms) outside the wall on Manhattan, or in the pretty villages of Haerlem, Breucelen on Long Island, or Bergen across the North (as the Dutch called the Hudson) river; a few hundred New England Puritans spilled over into Westchester County and Long Island. Yet New Netherland did not prosper; it was the neglected child of a trading company whose main interests were elsewhere.

'Diedrich Knickerbocker' (Washington Irving) created a myth of New Netherland that will never die; the jolly community of tipplers and topers, of waterfront taverns, broad-beamed *haus-fraus,* and well-stocked farms. The actual New Netherland was rather a frustrated community. The successive governors, Wouter van Twiller, William Kieft, and Peter Stuyvesant, of whom Irving drew such comic pictures, were in reality petty autocrats and grafters, who ruled New Amsterdam with a rod of iron, used torture to extract confessions, and mismanaged almost everything, especially Indian relations. Kieft, assuming that if the Dutch did not exterminate the natives, the reverse would happen, attacked in cold blood a tribe of River Indians who were disposed to be friendly because they dreaded the Iroquois; but these Indians declined to be exterminated, and put up so stout a fight that assistance had to be summoned from New England before the burghers of New Amsterdam dared venture north of Wall Street. In 1644, at a time when Virginia, New England, and the Caribbean colonies were humming with activity, a committee of the Dutch colonists wrote home: [6]

Our fields lie fallow and waste, our dwellings and other buildings are burnt . . . the crops which God permitted to come forth during the past summer remain on the fields standing and rotting . . . There are among us those who, by the sweat and labor of their hands, for many long years have endeavored, at great expense, to improve their lands and villages . . . The whole of these now lie in ashes through a foolish hankering after war. For all right-thinking men here know that these Indians have lived as lambs among us, until a few years ago; injuring no man; affording every assistance to our nation.

Peter Stuyvesant, who had been governor of Curaçao, and lost a leg storming a French fort at St. Martin's, attempted to pull things together by crushing political or religious dissenters and jailing his critics. Some of these obtained the ear of the company and procured a concession of municipal privileges to New Amsterdam; but Stuyvesant insisted on appointing the burgomasters himself. The colony expanded to the westward by seizing the Swedish colony that cen-

[6] John R. Brodhead, *History of the State of New York,* I. 398–99.

tered about Fort Christina (Wilmington) on the Delaware, but Fort Good Hope on the Connecticut was squeezed out by English settlers, who were now pouring in such numbers into eastern Long Island and New Haven colony that it was but a matter of time before New Netherland should be overwhelmed.

English governments, royal, commonwealth, and colonial, had never ceased protesting against the existence of New Netherland as an intrusion on English America; and as the Dutch and English in Europe drew apart from their traditional alliance and engaged in naval and commercial wars, a clash in the New World was inevitable. One Anglo-Dutch war was concluded in 1654 just in time to call off a Cromwellian expeditionary force against New Netherland, and for almost a decade more Peter Stuyvesant retarded development of the superb advantages which Manhattan Island offered for trade and commerce. He ended the free-trade policy which had brought vessels to New Amsterdam. He did nothing to conciliate the varied population of the colony, or to cultivate a local or community pride. The West India Company, bankrupt after its costly venture in Brazil,[7] and unable to secure even the profits of the fur trade from corrupt officials, took less and less interest in its North American colony. And when a small English fleet appeared off New Amsterdam one summer's day in 1664 with orders to surrender, Peter Stuyvesant stomped his wooden leg in vain. Nobody, not even the Dutch, would fight, and New Netherland became New York without a blow or a tear. The population of the city had then reached only fifteen hundred, and that of the colony less than seven thousand; New England outnumbered New Netherland ten to one. But the Dutch stamp was already placed indelibly on New York, and most of the Dutch families, such as the Van Rensselaers, Van Burens, and Roosevelts, kept their property and prospered under English rule. Dutch stubbornness, which helped the Roosevelts to beard Peter Stuyvesant in the 1640's, is a useful trait in the President of the United States three centuries later.

5. Two Decades of Neglect

That 'salutary neglect' by England, which Edmund Burke later asserted to be one of the main reasons for American prosperity, was

---

[7] An interesting result of the Portuguese recapture of Brazil was the emigration of a small number of Portuguese-speaking Jews, to whom the Dutch extended toleration, from Brazil to New Amsterdam.

never more evident than in the twenty years from 1640 to 1660. The civil war and other commotions which lasted from 1641 to 1653, when Oliver Cromwell became Lord Protector of the English Commonwealth, afforded all three groups of colonies a chance to grow in their own way, with a minimum of interference from home; and Oliver decided to let well enough alone. They were thrown on their own resources, sought their own markets, undertook their own defense, and developed their own institutions. When interference was threatened, colonies as wide apart as Massachusetts and Barbados stood stiffly on their privileges. The Barbadian assembly declared in 1651, ' Shall we be bound to the government and lordship of a Parliament in which we have no representatives? . . . This would be a slavery far exceeding all that the English nation hath yet suffered.' Massachusetts declared, ' Our allegiance binds us not to the laws of England any longer than while we live in England, for the laws of the Parliament of England reach no further.' In other words, dominion status was asserted by Barbados implicitly and by Massachusetts explicitly. The Long Parliament, Puritan itself, respected the Puritan colonies overseas, and interfered in New England only to the extent of protecting Rhode Island from being partitioned by her three neighbors. Parliament sent a fleet to blockade Barbados in 1651, but the commander, in return for nominal allegiance, agreed that no taxes be imposed save by act of the assembly, and that free trade with the Dutch continue. The Virginia assembly, which proclaimed Charles II king after hearing of the execution of Charles I, capitulated without a blow to a parliamentary fleet in 1652, and in return was allowed to elect the governor and council. In Maryland, the only colony where English events touched off a civil war, Lord Baltimore triumphed in the end.

Perhaps the most significant colonial development of the period was the formation of the New England Confederacy in 1643, largely for defense against the Dutch, the French, and the Indians. A board of commissioners representing Plymouth, Massachusetts, Connecticut, and New Haven, the ' United Colonies of New-England,' formed a ' firme and perpetuall league of frendship and amitie, for offence and defence, mutuall advice and succore upon all just occasions.' Several boundary controversies between the constituent colonies were ironed out, and one with the Dutch; provision was made for the return of runaway servants, contributions were taken up for Harvard College, and an English fund for the conversion of the Indians was administered. In several respects the New England Confederation anticipated the Confederation of 1777; and although a New England war on the Dutch over the fur trade was prevented in 1653 through the opposition of Massachusetts, the league held together long enough to direct offensive and defensive operations during the Indian war of 1675–76.

During the brief rule of Cromwell as Lord Protector, he entertained a 'Western Designe' to obtain more tropical colonies for England at the expense of Spain. An expedition under Admiral Penn (the father of William) was sent to conquer Hispaniola. That attempt was a miserable fiasco, but the fleet proceeded as second choice to Jamaica, where the Spanish population was thin, and in 1655 easily acquired that beautiful and fertile island for the English empire. Under the new regime, with the aid of slave labor Jamaica became the most valuable of England's tropical colonies. As early as 1670 it had a population of 8,000 souls and was producing sugar, cacao, and indigo; shortly it became a depot for English manufactures on their illegal way into Spanish America, and so a center of English influence in the western Caribbean. The logwood colony of Belize or British Honduras is an offshoot of Jamaica, and even today, owing to the enterprise of the colonial merchants and buccaneers, the Indians and 'maroons' on the coasts of the Spanish Main from Honduras to the Gulf of Darien speak more English than Spanish, while Jamaica-bred Negroes lord it over those of the other islands and of Panama.

Thus, in only a little more than half a century since the founding of Jamestown, the English and Dutch had taken a firm grip on the shores of four American areas — the Chesapeake, the Hudson and Delaware, New England, and the West Indies, and had planted those attitudes, folkways, and free institutions which were destined to spread across the North American continent. In 1660 New England, Virginia, and Maryland were already full-fledged commonwealths possessing most of the apparatus of civilized life as developed up to that time, reproducing or attempting to improve on the institutions of the homeland, yet conscious of their peculiar interests and capable of defending themselves against any foreign enemy who had yet threatened them. Utopia was still far off, but the essential nuclei of the American Republic were already formed.

IV

THE EMPIRE COMES OF AGE

1660–1713

1. *Colonial Policy*

IF the English colonies were already conscious of themselves, England was hardly yet conscious of them. The average Englishman of the governing class still regarded these overseas settlements as 'plantations' of slight worth compared with the Spanish imperial domain; like the average American in respect of the Philippines, he only began properly to value his empire when another nation tried to get it away from him. Every English colony except Virginia had grown up through the unco-ordinated efforts of individuals and small groups of Englishmen. The home authorities as yet had no clear policy about their trade, their development, or their connection with the central government.

With the restoration of the monarchy in 1660 came a perceptible drift into something that may be called a colonial policy. New Netherland was conquered, and the gap between New England and Maryland filled by four new English colonies. The southern frontier was extended by the founding of the Carolinas until it clashed with that of Spain in Florida. Parliament laid down a definite economic policy for the empire in the Acts of Trade and Navigation. An attempted consolidation of the continental settlement was attempted by James II, and thwarted by his exile; William and Mary, in a more tactful manner, brought all American colonies under a considerable measure of political control. And an epic struggle began between the English on the one side and the French and Spanish on the other, for the control of North America.

We may first outline the new economic policy, which outlasted the American Revolution. By 1660 the economic doctrine known as mercantilism, which has been defined as the pursuit of economic power in the sense of national self-sufficiency, was taken for granted by the ruling classes of every western European state except the Netherlands. Mercantilism had been implicit in the founding of Virginia; it now became explicit in the Acts of Trade and Navigation. Everyone, even colonists, admitted that the profits of an empire should center in the mother country. Spain and Portugal had seen to that since the beginning; but England, what with haphazard colonization and civil tumults, had allowed her overseas subjects to trade with foreign countries in almost everything except tobacco, and even tobacco was often carried abroad in foreign ships. Now, through the series of Acts of Trade and Navigation (1660–72), an effort was made to make the English empire a self-sustaining unit, and to confine profits to English subjects.

These acts embodied three principles. All trade between England and her colonies must be conducted by English-built or English-colonial vessels, owned and manned by English subjects. All European imports into the colonies, with the exception of perishable fruit and wine from the Western Islands, must first be ' laid on the shores of England ' — i.e. unloaded, handled, and reloaded — before being sent to the colonies; a large part of the duties were repaid on re-exportation. And, finally, certain colonial products ' enumerated ' in the laws must be exported to England and England only. In the seventeenth century the only ' enumerated ' products were tobacco, sugar, cotton, and other tropical commodities grown only in the West Indies. Rice and molasses, furs, and naval stores (tar, pitch, turpentine, and ships' spars) were added between 1705 and 1722, but nothing more until 1764.

Opinions still differ about how much good, or harm, this system did to the English colonies. It certainly did not stop their amazing growth and prosperity in the century after 1660. But the cutting off of direct tobacco exports to the European continent, which had been common in the Cromwellian period, helped to depress the price of tobacco in Virginia. As time went on, more and more colonial products were added to the enumerated list, until, on the eve of the American Revolution, the only important non-enumerated article was salt fish. As England developed a special technique in handling, grading, and marketing her colonial imports, the ' enumerated ' principle was not too severe. All in all, it has been calculated, the system brought annual profits of something more than a million pounds into English pockets by the seventeen sixties. That was not an excessive tribute in return for the protection afforded to the colonies by the armed forces supported by the English taxpayers, and for the bounties paid by Parliament to the colonial producers of naval stores and indigo. Moreover, the growing of tobacco was prohibited in England, and preferential duties excluded the Cuban and other Spanish-American leaf in favor of the tobacco of the Chesapeake colonies.

American colonists, like other English subjects, were also excluded from trading with Asia by the East India Company's monopoly. All English colonists, continental and insular, were encouraged to trade with each other, and the British West Indies continued after 1660, as before, to furnish the principal market for the Northern Colonies. Nor was there any legal English bar to trade with the French and other foreign West Indies. In fact a large part of the specie circulating in the continental colonies until the Revolution consisted of French and Spanish coins which were procured in the West Indies in exchange for the products of northern farms, forests, and fisheries. Outside lawful trade, New Englanders obtained smuggled European goods from the English fisheries at Newfoundland in exchange for rum, and were responsible for smuggling many foreign West Indian sugar products into England under false invoices. Scotland was a foreign country so far as the Acts of Trade were concerned until the Act of Union in 1707, and Ireland remained so until after the American Revolution, except that Irish 'servants, horses and provisions' could be exported directly to the English colonies.

A curious feature of this system, according to modern notions, was the English customs tariff on colonial products, which yielded so large a revenue to the Crown that its abolition was never even contemplated. There were export duties payable in the colonies on certain products, in order to support the colonial governments, import duties in England on almost everything that came from the English colonies, and import duties in the colonies on European goods that came through England, and on foreign West Indian products. As colonial collectorships were regarded as sinecures, the laws were very inefficiently enforced, and the cost of the establishment generally exceeded the income until just before the American Revolution.

In 1660, also, the English adopted a new policy respecting emigration. The Earl of Shaftesbury wrote, 'I take it for granted that the strength and glory of your Majesty and the wealth of your Kingdom depends . . . on the multitude of your subjects . . . We must stop the drain that carries our natives from us.' Accordingly, skilled artisans were forbidden to leave England for the colonies, and as there was no serious unemployment problem in the last third of the century, English emigration to her colonies dwindled to a mere trickle.

The new colonies established or conquered after 1660 drew for their population largely on the older colonies, on foreign countries, and on Africa. A leading English interest was the supplying of the colonies with Negro slaves, a traffic in which colonial ships and merchants participated to a very limited extent.

It followed from these mercantilist ideas and policy that the most valuable colonies from the English point of view were those from the Chesapeake south, which produced with slave labor tropical or semitropical raw materials that England wanted, and imported almost every luxury and necessity of life from home. And the least valuable colonies were those of New England, which were Old England's competitors rather than her complements. In the year 1698 seven-eighths of England's American trade was with the West Indies, Virginia, Maryland, and the Carolinas; the New England and Middle Colonies, with Newfoundland and Hudson Bay, accounted for only one-eighth. As time went on, and the Northern Colonies acquired wealth through the West Indies trade, this unequal balance was redressed. By 1747 half of England's colonial exports were to the colonies north of Maryland; and by 1767, two-thirds.

2. The Carolinas

After 1660 the impulse toward colonial expansion came mainly from three sources: English merchants and shipowners who wanted new areas for trade and exploitation, courtiers and politicians who planned to recoup their shattered fortunes with great colonial estates, and religious dissenters who sought to establish new refuges for members of their faith. The first two only were concerned in the Carolina venture.

Restoration of the Stuart monarchy set all doubtful English colonial claimants polishing up their old claims and seeking validation from Charles II. Among the minor ones was that of the Mason family to a part of New England, which was bought by the Crown. That territory became the royal province of New Hampshire in 1679. Among the major claims was that of Sir William Heath, which was purchased by the Carolina Proprietors. This group of eight promoters and politicians obtained from Charles II a proprietary patent to all North America between the parallels of 31° and 36° N (and the next year had this enlarged to embrace all the territory between Daytona, Florida, and the Virginia-North Carolina boundary), under the name Carolina. The two leading spirits among the proprietors were Sir John Colleton, a wealthy Barbadian planter who sought new homes for the surplus white population of Barbados, and Anthony Ashley Cooper, better known by his later title of Earl of Shaftesbury, Chancellor of the Exchequer, and founder of the Whig party. Shaftesbury, in collaboration with John Locke, wrote a sort of constitution for the colony, the 'Fundamental Constitutions of Carolina' in 120 articles; an extraordinary document which attempted to provide for the new colony a romanticized feudalism, with five 'estates,' eight supreme courts, a chamberlain and lord high admiral, and native titles of baron, cassique, and landgrave, depending on the amount of land one bought from the proprietors. After several false starts, a small number of colonists from England and several hundred Barbadians founded Charleston in 1670.[1]

Ten years later the proprietors obtained a group of French Huguenots, and in 1683 a band of Scots settled Port Royal at the site of an abandoned Spanish post. The Spaniards broke it up three years later, but the Scots kept coming. Thus South Carolina was racially heterogeneous from the first. By 1700 the population of the colony was about five thousand, about half of them Negro slaves; the principal exports were provisions for the West Indies trade, naval stores, and peltry. These early South Carolinians were as expert fur-traders as the French Canadians, sending agents around the southern spurs of the Appalachians into the future Alabama in search of deerskins; while they followed the example of the Spaniards in enslaving Indians. At the turn of the century the cultivation of rice and indigo began on the low coastal plain and along the rivers; and these gradually replaced the more pioneer pursuits. By 1730 South Carolina was a planting colony like Virginia, with a different staple, and a centralized instead of a dispersed social and political system; there were no county or local units of government. Every planter had a town house near the Battery in Charleston where he spent the summer months, when river plantations were unhealthful. The French Huguenots, the most important element in the ruling class, imparted a high-spirited and aristocratic tone to the colony; unlike other foreigners in the English colonies they quickly adopted the English language and joined the established Church of England.

In the meantime a wholly different form of society was developing

---

[1] The original site was 25 miles up the Ashley river; the present site, on the best harbor between Chesapeake Bay and the Gulf of Mexico, was chosen in 1680.

in the northern or Albemarle section of the province, which became North Carolina. There the original settlers had been runaways or discharged white servants from Virginia; and as these settlements were separated from Charleston by several hundred miles of forest, the proprietors granted them a separate governor and assembly. Apart from the Swiss settlement of New Bern there were few foreigners before 1713, and still fewer colonists of family or means; the principal products were tobacco and naval stores; and lack of harbors suitable for seagoing vessels meant heavy transportation costs. North Carolina was poor, turbulent, and democratic, with relatively few slaves. In 1736 the white population was estimated to be one-third greater than that of the southern colony, but the production was very much less.

On the whole, the proprietors of Carolina did a very good job in planting these two colonies, but they reaped more headaches than profits from them. Hence they were glad to sell out to the Crown in 1729, when the two halves became the royal provinces of North Carolina and South Carolina.

In both colonies the first land system, apart from the few big purchases made by persons who desired a title of nobility, was a modification of the Virginia head-right system, the amount granted for each person varying from twenty to eighty acres at different times. An attempt was made to delimit the frontier by surveying ' squares ' of 12,000 acres which were to be granted out before new land was opened; but this was unpopular, and in both colonies the Virginia system of indiscriminate location prevailed over the New England one of prior survey and compact settlement. Wherever the land could support a profitable staple, which was mostly in South Carolina, men of capital brought in Negro slaves from the West Indies or from Africa, and by combining their head-rights, created large plantations. In North Carolina it was unprofitable to do this; consequently the northern province became a community of small farms. As early as the sixteen nineties the proprietors began to sell land outright, reserving an annual quit-rent the payment of which was a constant bone of contention between them and the settlers; and the assembly in order to check speculation limited individual holdings to 640 acres.

3. *New York and the Jerseys*

The Duke of York's brief and unsuccessful reign as James II
should not blind us to the fact that he was an excellent seaman and
an able administrator. His brother Charles II appointed him Lord
High Admiral at the age of 26; he brought the Royal Navy to a high
state of efficiency and accompanied the fleet into action in the Dutch
War of 1664. As head of the navy he wished to deprive the Dutch of
their base at New Amsterdam, and as an impecunious member of
the House of Stuart he needed a profitable colony. England had consistently protested against the Dutch seizing upon a section of the
coast discovered by John Cabot, and now was in a position to make
that protest good. With parliamentary approval the king conferred
on his brother in 1664 the most extensive English territorial grant of
the century. ' The Duke of York's Grant ' included all the continent
between the Connecticut and Delaware rivers, together with Long
Island, Nantucket, and Martha's Vineyard, and Maine east of the
Kennebec. On 18 August a small English fleet entered the Narrows
of New York Harbor, and obtained the surrender of New Netherland without firing a shot. The Duke of York, aged 30, was now in
possession of a section of America with boundless possibilities, one
destined to be the wealthiest area in the world. As Lord Proprietor,
unhampered even by the Maryland proviso of obtaining consent of
the freemen for his laws, he was absolute master of this domain under the king.

The Duke's rule of New York, as he renamed the old Dutch colony, was fairly enlightened. He summoned no assembly, but ordered
his governor, Richard Nicolls, to treat the Dutch with ' humanity
and gentleness,' and made no effort to impose the English language
or his own religion on them. But he intended to make money out of
the colony, and drew up his own schedule of customs duties, quit-
rents, and taxes. That made trouble. There were already too many
English in the colony for any proprietor to practise taxation without
representation very long. A code of laws, ' The Duke's Laws,' similar to those of New England, was promulgated for Long Island; but
the English there were discontented because they had no hand in
them, and were taxed without ' consent,' so the governor had to keep
the taxes low. And the cost of administering a government that extended from eastern Maine to Maryland was so great that the Duke
was still in the red in 1673 when New York was recaptured by the

Dutch. They restored it to England by treaty in 1674. Again there was trouble about taxation, and finally the Duke's Irish governor, Thomas Dongan, summoned a representative assembly in 1683.

Convinced that he had bitten off a little more than he could chew, the Duke began giving away slices of his grant as early as 1664. To his friends Lord John Berkeley and Sir George Carteret, both proprietors of Carolina, he ceded the lands between the Hudson and Delaware rivers as the 'Province of Nova Caesaria or New Jersey.' A few hundred Dutch and English Puritans from New England were already there, and, in order to attract more, Berkeley and Carteret promulgated the 'Concessions and Agreements of the Proprietors of New Jersey,' granting freedom of conscience, liberal terms for land, and an assembly. In 1674 Berkeley sold out his half share in New Jersey to two Quakers, who took the southwestern half of the province, while Carteret kept the northeastern part. Carteret's widow in 1680 sold out East New Jersey for the modest sum of £3400 to a group of proprietors, and the two Quakers let William Penn in on West New Jersey. The net result of this was a heterogeneous settlement, a minimum of social cohesion, and a bad confusion in land titles which bedevilled New Jersey politics until the Revolution.

4. *The Holy Experiment*

Pennsylvania, more than any other American commonwealth, is the lengthened shadow of one man and of his faith in God and in mankind.

Out of the religious ferment of Puritan England came a great leader named George Fox who founded the Society of Friends, commonly known as Quakers. These were the anarchists of the Protestant Reformation. Puritans substituted the authority of the Bible for the authority of the Church, but the Quakers denied both, and rested on the Word of God as spoken to the human soul. They required no church and no priesthood; every man was his own priest, and so all were equal, addressing one another as 'thee' and 'thou,' and literally observing the divine command 'thou shalt do no murder,' even under the name of war. To persecution they opposed passive resistance; and like the early Christians they gathered strength from oppression and victory from defeat. Over three thousand Quakers were imprisoned in England during the first two years of the Restoration; yet the sect spread like wildfire, and as far as Russia made converts eager to wear the martyr's crown. In 1652 the first Quaker missionaries appeared in the English colonies. Severe laws were passed against them in every colony but Rhode Island, and in Boston three were hanged; but finally by passive resistance they wore down the authorities and won a grudging toleration. The same thing happened in England. Fox and his courageous missionaries converted thousands of Puritans and Anglicans who were tired of the austerities of the one or the indifference of the other, and who sought brotherhood and peace. As Puritanism had been in 1600, and as Methodism would be in 1770, so was Quakerism the dynamic form of English Protestantism from about 1650 to 1700.

Even without William Penn the Quakers would have had a small colony of their own, West New Jersey; with William Penn they obtained one of the greatest. The founder of Pennsylvania, born in 1644, was the son of Admiral Sir William Penn, conqueror of Jamaica. Although he had showed sufficient interest in unfashionable religion to be expelled from Christ Church, Oxford, as a lad, young William was not converted to Quakerism until 1667, when, after a grand tour of the continent, and residence at the gay viceregal court of Dublin, he listened to the sermon of a Friend on the text 'There is a Faith that overcometh the World.' And for the remaining fifty-one years of his life, William Penn was steadfast in that faith.

The Admiral, who swore and threatened when he heard this news, was reconciled before his death and left his Quaker son a considerable fortune. A share of West New Jersey far from satisfied the young man's ambition. What he wanted was a proprietary colony of his own, where he could experiment with political as well as religious liberty. The Friends no longer needed a refuge; but, like the Puritans of half a century before, they wanted a colony where they could live their ideal of the New Testament life, free from the pressure of bad examples and worldly corruptions. In 1677 Penn made a journey to the continent with George Fox. In Germany he met members of several German sects, some akin to the Quakers in doctrine, who were uneasy and eager to leave. That continental tour enlarged his conception of a colony from a libertarian experiment to a refuge for the persecuted of every race and sect.

Fortunately, Penn's conversion had never caused him to break with his father's friends, among whom was counted the Duke of York. A tactful reminder that the Admiral had lent his brother £16,000 that had never been repaid secured to William and his heirs in 1681 a generous slice of the Duke's grant, which at the grantor's insistence was named Pennsylvania. The king implemented this grant by a charter creating the province a proprietary one on the model of Maryland.

Settlement began without delay. In 1681 Penn published in English, French, German, and Dutch *Some Account of the Province of Pennsylvania*, which (in accordance with Quaker business ethics) underestimated rather than exaggerated the natural advantages; urged peasants and artisans to come, and get-rich-quick adventurers to stay away; gave instructions for the journey and the outfit; and promised political and religious liberty. Even more persuasive were the easiest terms for land yet offered in North America: a fifty-acre head-right free; two-hundred-acre tenant farms at a penny an acre rent; estates of five thousand acres for £100, with a city lot thrown in. In three months Penn disposed of warrants for over 300,000 acres, and in 1682 he came over himself.

Neither the banks of Delaware Bay nor the lower reaches of the rivers were a wilderness in 1682. About a thousand Swedes, Finns, and Dutch were already settled there. These were given free land grants, and proved useful in providing the first English colonists with food, housing, and labor. Choosing an admirable site for his capital, Penn laid out Philadelphia between the Delaware and the Schuylkill rivers in checkerboard fashion — which had a permanent and pernicious effect on American city planning — and undertook the government himself.

William Penn liked to allude to his province as ' The Holy Experiment.' It is difficult for us to put ourselves in the place of those seventeenth-century idealists, Winthrop and Calvert, Williams and Penn, who actually tried to found Cities of God in the wilderness. Yet, even though they made idealism pay dividends — at least Calvert and Penn did — there is no reason to doubt their sincerity. Penn, unlike the Puritans, believed in the essential goodness of human nature. ' When the great and wise God had made the world, of all his creatures it pleased him to choose man his deputy to rule it,' reads Penn's *Frame of Government* for Pennsylvania. ' And to fit him for so great a charge and trust, He did not only qualify him with skill and powers but with integrity to use them justly. This native goodness was equally his honor and his happiness.' Herein the note later stressed in American history by Jefferson and Emerson is first boldly struck. And as Quakers regarded it as nobody's business how a man worshipped, if he worshipped at all, Penn made religious liberty and trust in humanity the twin cornerstones of his experiment. Roger Williams had earlier established religious liberty in Rhode Island; but Rhode Island had been concerned only with left-wing Englishmen. And the Maryland Toleration Act had been repealed before Pennsylvania was founded. Penn put the principle to the severest test by inviting people of all sects and nations to participate.

Yet Penn never ceased to be cavalier when he went Quaker, or gentleman when he became democrat. His instincts and tastes were those of the English aristocracy; he appreciated a thoroughbred horse, a well-built ship, good food and drink, and handsome women. It was Penn who brought over Tamerlane, sire of famous American race-horses; and the six-oared rowing barge, in which he was conveyed from his country seat on the Schuylkill to Philadelphia, he loved more than his house.

As a friend and admirer of Algernon Sidney, John Locke, Sir William Petty, and other radical publicists of the day, Penn believed in the traditional liberties of Englishmen, and intended that they should be respected in his province. Indeed, he had earlier figured in Bushell's Case, a test case of the liberty of a jury to have its verdict respected by the judge. He had been made to feel in his own person the value of civil liberties, and the aristocrat in him made him fight back when his rights were infringed, a thing that the average Quaker was too poor or pacifistic to do. Yet Penn was no nineteenth-century democrat. He believed in government for the people, by liberally educated gentlemen like himself. And the first Frame of Government that he issued for Pennsylvania in 1682 reflected this idea. He was the governor. He provided a small council, elected by taxpayers from landowners ' of best repute for wisdom, virtue and ability,' to initiate the laws; and a large elective assembly to accept or reject the bills — but if the assembly ' turn debaters, you overthrow the charter,' said he. Such a system was unpalatable to discussion-loving Englishmen. It worked fairly well in 1682–84 when Penn was in his province, for his generous nature and personal charm would have made any system work; but when he returned to England, his government almost blew up. He was a poor business man, and his too great trust in human nature led him to make unsuitable appointments of land agents who robbed him, and of deputy governors who antagonized or scandalized the people.

When Penn's patron James II was exiled from England, Pennsylvania became for a short time a royal province under the Governor of New York, but in 1694 the proprietary rights were restored, and the assembly secured the initiative in law-making. Penn returned to Philadelphia in 1700 and issued a Charter of Privileges, which remained the constitution of the province until 1776. It provided the usual colonial set-up of a governor and council (appointed by the proprietor but confirmed by the king), and an assembly composed of four representatives for each county, elected by a property franchise.

The three 'Lower Counties,' as the future State of Delaware was then called, were purchased by Penn from the Duke of York, much against the wishes of Lord Baltimore, who regarded that region as part of Maryland. The Lower Counties acquired an assembly of their own in 1702, but the Charter of Privileges was their charter too, and the Governor of Pennsylvania was their governor.

Pennsylvania started with the most generous grant of religious liberty and the most liberal and humane code of laws in the world. Capital punishment, which existed for a dozen different offenses in the other English colonies and for a score or more in England, was inflicted in Pennsylvania only for murder. The grant of religious liberty was never retracted, but a crime wave at the turn of the century caused the criminal code to be stiffened up to such a point that the Privy Council in England rejected half the new laws. Accordingly, by 1717, there was little difference between Pennsylvania and other colonies in the rigor of their laws.

Pennsylvania prospered as no other early settlement did. Founded at a time when business was good in England, and when political proscription in England (the Popish Plot, Rye-house Plot, Monmouth Rebellion) and religious persecution on the continent made thousands of good people eager to seek peace, liberty, and prosperity overseas, the province attracted both labor and capital, and found a ready market in the West Indies for agricultural produce. In two years' time Philadelphia boasted 357 houses; in 1685 the population of the province was little short of 9,000. Germans of the Mennonite sect, mostly linen-weavers from Crefeld, settled Germantown in 1683 under their cultivated minister, Francis Daniel Pastorius; Welsh Quakers founded Radnor and Haverford; a Free Society of Traders, organized by English Quakers, started fisheries and established brick kilns, tanneries, and glass works. Penn could state without boasting in 1684, 'I have led the greatest colony into America that ever any man did upon a private credit, and the most prosperous beginnings that were ever in it are to be found among us.'

In spite of this early invitation to all peoples and races, which was accepted by numerous German societies in the early eighteenth century, the tone of the colony was set by English-speaking Friends. It was fortunate that Pennsylvania was settled not by the first but by the second generation of Quakers, men and women who had sloughed off the frenzy and fanaticism of Fox's first converts, while retaining the serene strength, high ideals, and sturdy pacifism that were the fairest flowers of their sect. They had the same ambition as Virginians and New Englanders to transplant the finer things of English civilization. Since Friends required no educated priesthood, the impact of Ben Franklin was needed to found a college; but they early established good secondary schools; and Quaker compassion provided Philadelphia with the best hospitals and charitable institutions in the English colonies. James Logan, classical scholar and scientist, imported the first copy of Sir Isaac Newton's *Principia* that reached America; his fine collection of books became the nucleus of the Library Company of Philadelphia.

> Philadelphia, that great Corporation,
> Was then, is now, our choicest Habitation.

reads the rhymed *Description of Pennsylvania,* which was the first imprint (1692) of William Bradford's press, the first printing press in the English colonies outside New England. By 1715 Philadelphia was a more cultivated city than New York, and was running Boston hard for first place in culture and in population.

William Penn himself fell on evil days at the turn of the century. After his second visit to the Province, he hastened home to England to forestall another attack on his charter; and although he managed to remain on good terms with Queen Anne, his business affairs went from bad to worse. He had a continuous boundary controversy with Lord Baltimore and Maryland — eventually settled in 1767 by Mason and Dixon's Line. William's eldest son, the second proprietor, turned out a spendthrift and a rake. Living in great style at Holland House in London, with a country estate as well, William Penn ran deeply into debt, and was even confined in debtors' prison for some months. The quarrels among council and governor and assembly distressed him; 'For the love of God, me, and the poor country,' he once wrote to Thomas Lloyd, leader of the opposition, 'Do not be so litigious and brutish! ' But he never lost faith in the Holy Experiment, or in human nature.

Pennsylvania was a portent of America to be; the first large community in modern history where different races and religions lived under the same government on terms of equality. The experiment was not so successful as Penn had hoped, since there was much quarrelling and contention between the races; yet, for all that, they did not fly at one another's throats. For these reasons Pennsylvania interested liberal philosophers of eighteenth-century Europe as a successful experiment in the life of reason; Voltaire never tired of holding it up as proof that man could lead the good life without absolute monarchy, feudalism, or religious and racial uniformity. The liberalism of William Penn, one may say, not only forged the small vessel which grew to the great American melting-pot; it also prepared the way for the Revolution. And if the American experiment has so far withstood the assaults made upon it by totalitarian powers, William Penn and his ' Holy Experiment ' are more directly responsible than any other colonial founder, or any other colonial commonwealth.

5. *The Older Colonies*

Virginia, most loyal of the colonies to the house of Stuart, suffered most from their restoration. In 1672 Charles II even proposed to grant the whole of Virginia to two courtiers, Lords Arlington and Culpeper. That was prevented, but Culpeper got the Northern Neck, between the Potomac and the Rappahannock rivers. Sir William Berkeley was reappointed Governor of Virginia, and in a wave of loyalty the people elected a house of burgesses in 1661 which proved so pliant that Berkeley kept this ' Long Assembly ' going for fifteen years by successive adjournments, and managed to get the whole machinery of government, central and local, in the hands of his particular clique of great planters.

More serious for the Old Dominion was the overproduction and low price of tobacco. Virginia's population had doubled in the sixteen fifties, from 15,000 to 30,000. Then came the Acts of Trade and the Dutch wars, curtailing the foreign market and raising the cost of transportation. In 1662 Governor Berkeley reported tobacco so low that it would not pay the cost of freight. ' Forty thousand people are impoverished,' he wrote, ' in order to enrich little more than forty merchants in England.' In 1668 tobacco prices in Virginia reached an all-time low of a farthing a pound, far less than the customs tariff on it in England. The assembly for ten years made attempts to curtail production and peg prices; these were thwarted partly by Maryland refusing to come in, partly by difficulty of enforcement, and partly because the English merchants raised prices of goods sent in exchange when they could not make their usual profit. Fifteen years after the Restoration, Virginia, the land of opportunity for poor and industrious Englishmen, had become a place of poverty and discontent. There the first farmers' revolt in American history broke out.

The immediate cause of Bacon's Rebellion was the Indian question. At this time the Iroquois were putting pressure on tribes nearer the coast, all the way from New England to the Virginian frontier. Governor Berkeley, who was interested in the fur trade, was anxious to stand in well with the Indians, and took no proper measures to protect the frontier. The people could get no relief from their poverty or protection against the Indians from Berkeley's oligarchy and the Long Assembly. A scalping affair in 1675 so alarmed and infuriated the poorer settlers that, placing at their head a gentleman planter named Nathaniel Bacon, described by his enemies as 'a man of ominous pensive melancholy and of a pestilence and prevalent logical discourse tending to atheism,' they marched against and defeated the wrong Indians, and then advanced on Jamestown. Bacon is said to have exclaimed, 'Damn my blood, I'll kill Governor, Council, Assembly and all.' As this improvised rebel army approached Jamestown, Berkeley decided to dissolve the Long Assembly and issued writs for a new one, which met shortly and passed some important bills for relief, reform, and defense. The rebels retired; Berkeley plucked up courage, called out the loyal militia of the Eastern Shore, appealed to England for troops, and civil war began. Exactly how far Bacon intended to go is not clear: there is some reason to believe that he had ideas of a general colonial revolt against royal and proprietary government; but in October 1676, while carrying everything before him, he died and his death took the heart out of the rebellion. Berkeley rounded up the leaders and had thirty-seven of them executed for treason. 'That old fool has hanged more men in that naked country than I have done for the murder of my father,' exclaimed Charles II.

Many years elapsed before the economic structure improved by reason of increased demand for tobacco and higher prices. No longer could a yeoman farmer 'make a crop' with the aid of his family; indented servants could not earn their keep. The rich, who could afford to import slaves, grew richer; and the poor grew poorer.

New England fared much better, as the increase of sugar pro- duction in the West Indies created a greater demand for her ships and products. It might be supposed that self-government of these Puritan colonies would now be overthrown; on the contrary. Mas- sachusetts Bay was allowed to continue for a quarter-century more under her corporate charter, and Connecticut and Rhode Island obtained similar charters from the Crown in 1662 and 1663, through the efforts of the scientist-governor John Winthrop, Jr., and of Dr. John Clarke of Newport. The Connecticut charter included the old New Haven Colony in its boundaries, which impelled some die-hard Puritans of New Haven to found Newark, N. J. Both charters not only granted complete self-government, as had existed in Plymouth and Massachusetts from the beginning, but protected them against various court claimants who were seeking to carve up their terri- tory. Charles II, to be sure, cheerfully granted to his brother every- thing east to the Connecticut river two years after that colony had been defined as extending west to the South Sea; but the Duke of York was reasonable, as the present boundaries attest.

New England experienced in 1675–77 the most devastating war in her entire history. King Philip's War, as it was called after the Wampanoag chief who began hostilities, was a result of pressure from both sides, from the Mohawk nation of the Iroquois confed- eracy, and from the English, who were now beginning to found settlements in the interior, far from tidewater. As the Indians had interior lines, with the powerful Narragansett tribe at the tip of a wedge that touched the ocean, and as they now were skilled in the use of firearms, they were able at first to attack frontier townships at will, destroy crops, cattle, and settlements, and endanger the very existence of four Puritan colonies. But the Puritans had the New England Confederacy, while the Indians were not united; some four thousand Indians converted by Puritan missionaries remained loyal to England; and gradually the tough, well-disciplined New England militia, accompanied by loyal Indian scouts and fighting chaplains, broke up Indian concentrations, destroyed their food supply, and hunted down their bands one by one. The power of the natives in southern New England was broken forever; but the

Abnaki of Maine and New Hampshire turned to Canada for aid, and kept the English at bay in northern New England for another seventy-five years.

Not until 1720 did New England recover the frontier thrown back by this fierce war. The losses in men and property were relatively severe. And the royal government chose this time to bring the Bay Colony to book for her recalcitrance. Massachusetts offended Charles II by coining the pine-tree shilling, and by purchasing from the Gorges proprietors the Province of Maine, which the king intended to grant to one of his bastards. She refused to obey the Navigation Acts on the ground ' that the lawes of England are bounded within the fower seas, and do not reach America. The subjects of his majestie here being not represented in Parliament, so wee have not looked at ourselves to be impeded in our trade by them.' She declined to allow appeals to English courts, or to grant freedom of worship and the franchise to Anglicans. Consequently, in 1684, the High Court of Chancery declared the old Massachusetts Bay charter to be ' vacated, cancelled and annihilated.' The government was now in the king's hands to do as he saw fit; and the death of Charles II threw the problem into King James's lap.

James II, like most members of his family, was an enemy to representative institutions; and as a professional sailor he thought it an easy matter to throw them overboard. The colonial situation was disquieting. Even with the Massachusetts government gone, there were three separate colonies in New England and four in the middle region, each with its own assembly; and all flouted the Acts of Trade and Navigation as far as they dared. French Canada, with which the English had lived on fairly good terms hitherto, was beginning to loom as a menace; for it was now a united crown colony under a great administrator, Count Frontenac, who sent explorers to the Far West and down the Mississippi, and attempted to seduce the Iroquois from their English alliance. Obviously there must be unity in administration to meet this danger.

The royal solution to these colonial problems was consolidation. Between 1685 and 1688 the New England colonies, New York, and the Jerseys were combined into one viceroyalty called the Dominion of New England, governed by an appointed governor (Sir Edmund Andros) and council, but with no representative institutions. This reform, as it was intended to be, appealed to the non-

Puritan minority and to some of the wealthier merchants of New England who were weary of the ' rule of the Saints '; but to nobody else; and the merchants soon wished they were back under the Saints, who accounted it no sin to smuggle. Andros and his council respected the Puritan churches, schools, and colleges; they were moderate according to standards of the day, but they did question the validity of land titles, which alarmed every farmer in New England, and they tried to tax without a legislative grant, which no Englishman would allow. One curious result of the autocratic government was a currency shortage, brought on by the suppression of piracy; for pirates, as good spenders who ' put money in circulation ' had been treated tenderly by the former governments at Boston, Newport, and New York.

If James II had succeeded in suppressing English liberties at home, he would probably have combined the other continental colonies in a second dominion, and the English empire would have been governed like the Spanish viceroyalties of Mexico and Peru. But he was expelled from England in the ' Glorious Revolution ' of 1688, which brought in William III and Mary II as joint sovereigns of the British Isles. As soon as news of this event reached the colonies, a succession of popular revolutions overthrew dominion authorities, and put the several colonies back where they had been before 1685. The only conspicuous leader in these revolts was Jacob Leisler, a New Yorker of German birth. Leisler, by flouting important groups in his colony, managed to let them place him in a position where he could be accused of treason; he was judicially murdered, and his property confiscated in 1691. Otherwise the Dominion of New England fell apart with scarcely a blow.

6. *Colonial Reorganization*

Colonial reorganization was now up to William and Mary. It was done gradually, extending over into the next reign, and by a series of typical English compromises. Rhode Island and Connecticut were allowed to keep the corporate charters which they had reassumed. New York, and later the Jerseys and Carolinas, became royal provinces. Pennsylvania for two years and Maryland for twenty-three years were governed as royal provinces, but finally restored to their proprietors, in deference to the growing theory of vested rights among the Whigs who had brought in the new regime. A part of the Dominion of New England was salvaged by creating a new royal province of Massachusetts Bay that included the old Plymouth Colony and the future State of Maine. In all these units, representative institutions were confirmed or granted, and, by an act of Parliament of 1696, a new system of admiralty courts was instituted to enforce the Acts of Trade and Navigation. Submission of all acts of colonial assemblies to the privy council for possible disallowance was insisted on, and appeals from colonial courts to the privy council were encouraged.

This reorganization was manifestly incomplete. After the admiralty courts, which required no jury trial, began to function, it became possible with the aid of revenue cutters to suppress the grosser forms of piracy and smuggling. A certain amount of European goods leaked into the Thirteen Colonies by way of Newfoundland and Jamaica, but direct importation from continental Europe was definitely stopped. Acts of Parliament, such as those organizing the postal service, or granting bounties on colonial products, were enforced. The Crown had means of preventing colonial legislation that it considered undesirable, both by the royal governor's veto, which could not be overridden, and by the royal disallowance. About two and a half per cent of all acts passed by colonial assemblies were disallowed by the privy council; and most of those so disallowed, such as laws discriminating against religious minorities, laws for emitting unbacked paper currency, and laws discriminating against ships, products, or subjects of neighboring English colonies, should never have been passed.

These colonial laws were disallowed after an investigation and report by the Board of Trade and Plantations. That body, appointed by the king under a parliamentary act of 1696, was the nearest thing to a colonial office in the English government; but it had other duties as well, such as administering the poor laws and negotiating commercial treaties, and its powers were only advisory. Most colonial matters were routed through the Board, which meant a certain uniformity in administration, but the decisions were made either by the Secretary of State, the King in Council, the Lords of the Admiralty, or the war department. In other words, the imperial system, as it existed from 1689 to 1776, was a mere outgrowth of the government of the realm; it would have been cumbrous and ineffi-

cient even if competently and honestly administered, as it was
not.

The principal officials in the colonies who were expected to enforce imperial laws and regulations were the royal and proprietary
governors. The former were appointed by the king during his good
pleasure; the proprietary governors had to be acceptable to the Crown.
All observed considerable pomp and circumstance, but fell into that
most unfortunate political category of officials who enjoyed responsibility without power. All except the governors of Virginia and
of certain West Indian islands were dependent on the assemblies
for their salaries. Executive patronage, which might have been an
important lever, was taken away from them both by the Secretary
of State, who needed it for his own henchmen, and by the assemblies, which generally elected the colonial treasurer and other minor
officials themselves. The royal governors on the whole were honest
and able men; no small number of them were colonists; but they
had rather an unhappy time of it, expected as they were to enforce
the regulations of an overseas government without the power to do
so. In the proprietary as in the royal governments, the assemblies,
as representing local interests, demanded greater control of their
local affairs than the governors' instructions permitted; the governors upheld more royal and proprietary prerogation than the people
were disposed to admit; and distance, as well as the power of the
purse, tended to keep the governor's power at a low ebb.

Even in time of war, each colonial assembly had the privilege of
honoring or dishonoring the requisitions made upon it by the home
government for men, money, and supplies. War grants generally
had a number of strings attached which prevented the governor
from employing colonial troops to best advantage, and often the
grants were forthcoming only after concessions had been made on
some issue over which governor and assembly had long been quarrelling.

7. Imperial Wars

King William brought the English colonies into the orbit of world
politics. As stadholder of the Netherlands he had organized a league
of European states to resist the pretensions of Louis XIV to the
hegemony of Europe. With the English crown on his head, he made
that league into the Grand Alliance, which automatically brought

the English and French colonies to blows. There then began the first of the international colonial wars,[2] which took up a large part of colonial effort and energy, and which ended with the complete overthrow of French power in North America.

Although the English colonists at the time of the Revolution were able to make out a good case for 'foreign entanglements' being the cause of these wars, informal hostilities between England and Spain on the southern border had been going on since 1655, and a clash between English and French on the northern border was inevitable from the centrifugal nature of Canadian society, and the central position of the Iroquois Confederacy. Although Louis XIV wished Canada to be a loyal and religious peasant society like that of Normandy and Brittany — which eventually it became under English rule — the Canadians of 1650-1750 had different views. Every young man of spirit became an explorer or a *coureur de bois,* and the more adventurous of these travelling salesmen of the fur business had reached the Dakotas before any Englishmen had attained the crest of the Appalachians. On the other hand, the Iroquois Confederacy, whose sphere of influence covered up-state New York, most of Pennsylvania, and the old Northwest, remained faithful to their alliance with the Dutch and the English, who could provide them with cheaper blankets and liquor than did the French; [3] and the Iroquois not only remained impervious to French missionary efforts, but occasionally indulged in raids on the French-allied Indian nations of the St. Lawrence basin. Consequently French fur traders had to travel north of and around the Iroquois country in order to reach the upper Mississippi valley, which by 1715 had become a more valuable source of fur than the basin of the Great Lakes.

In the summer of 1682 the Sieur de la Salle, greatest of French ex-

[2]   SUMMARY OF THE COLONIAL WARS

Colonial Name	European Name	Dates	Peace Treaty at
I King William's War	War of League of Augsburg	1689-97	Ryswick
II Queen Anne's War	War of Spanish Succession	1702-13	Utrecht
III King George's War	War of Austrian Succession	1745-48	Aachen
IV Old French and Indian War	Seven Years' War	1754-63	Paris

King George's War began in the Southern Colonies and Caribbean in 1739 as the 'War of Jenkins's Ear' between England and Spain.

[3] Rum was an effective agent of English imperialism, because it was so cheap. The French Government discouraged the manufacture of rum in its West Indian colonies in order to protect French cognac.

plorers, after thirteen years' effort to establish a new peltry empire, sailed and rowed down the Mississippi, planted the white banner of St. Louis on its banks below New Orleans, and named the region Louisiana. This was so far from fitting in with the royal policy respecting Canada that the king declared La Salle's expedition to be 'altogether useless,' and ordered the Governor of Canada to prevent further enterprises of that nature. La Salle, back in France, managed to 'sell' Louisiana to his sovereign on the ground that a post on the Gulf would annoy the king of Spain, with whom France was then at war; he was then allowed to recruit a few score Frenchmen, mostly convicts, to make a settlement near the mouth of the great river. Unfortunately on his next voyage La Salle missed the Passes and pitched his colony on the gulf coast of Texas, where he was killed by his own men, who were then finished off by the Comanche Indians. The only effect was to force Spain's hand. The Viceroy of Mexico promptly founded the first Spanish post in Texas on the Neches river; the Comanches squeezed it out in 1693, and the place was not reoccupied until 1716. Also as a protection against a possible French colony on the Gulf, Pensacola was founded by Spain in 1696. La Salle's expedition was not aimed at the English, nor did they take much notice of it; and this exploration, one of the glories of French enterprise, so little affected French policy that in 1696 Louis XIV actually issued an edict ordering the Canadian *coureurs de bois* to take wives, settle down, and cease exploring the wilderness in search of fur. For Louis was entering his pious old age, and the Church objected to these adventurers spoiling the pitch for the missionaries. Nevertheless Count Frontenac, who was hand in glove with the fur-trading interests, largely ignored his sovereign's orders.

Louis XIV, however, had no objection to Count Frontenac using *coureurs de bois* and friendly Indians to raid the frontiers of New England and New York. So King William's War and the next one took on the character of a series of winter attacks on English frontier settlements. Schenectady, New York, was the first place to be destroyed. Other raids followed against the Maine and New Hampshire frontiers, while Canadian privateers from Acadia (Nova Scotia) preyed on Yankee fishermen and traders. New England's reply was a successful capture of Port Royal on the Bay of Fundy (1690), and an unsuccessful expedition against Quebec, led by Sir William Phips, the Maine-born buccaneer who had been knighted for recovering Spanish treasure from the ocean north of Hispaniola.

Despite his failure before Quebec, Phips was rewarded by being commissioned the first royal governor of Massachusetts; he took office at the time when the uneasy and harassed New Englanders were in the throes of the famous Salem Village witchcraft panic, and did not intervene in the process of judicial murder until nineteen men and women had paid the penalty of popular hysteria by being hanged for alleged naughty practices in league with the devil.[4]

King William's War ended in Europe with the Treaty of Ryswick (1697), which did not change a single colonial boundary but restored Port Royal to the French; it dragged along in New England until 1699, when Governor Bellomont made peace with the Abnaki Indians. By that time there was hardly a white settler left in the province of Maine.

During the interval between King William's and Queen Anne's Wars, Spain strengthened her position on the northern and eastern borders of Mexico, and as Spain was England's enemy in the next three colonial wars, that was important. Father Kino founded the mission of San Xavier near Tucson, Arizona, in 1696, which became the center of a border province called Pimería Alta. New Mexico, whence the Pueblo Indians drove out the Spaniards in the sixteen eighties, had been reoccupied by 1700; and Pensacola in West Florida was founded by the Spaniards in 1696. The next year Count Frontenac sent Le Moyne d'Iberville to take effective possession of Louisiana. Owing to the difficulty of sailing vessels up the Mississippi, he pitched his first settlement at Biloxi, and shifted it to Mobile in 1702. About the same time the Canadians founded three posts — Kaskaskia, Cahokia, and Vincennes — in the Illinois country, partly as a check to Iroquois influence, and partly as connecting links between Canada and Louisiana.

In 1700 came a shifting of European alliances. The king of Spain died without issue; Louis XIV claimed the throne for his grandson; the Grand Alliance supported a rival claimant, the Elector of Bavaria; and the War of the Spanish Succession, Queen Anne's War as the colonists called it after their new sovereign, began. This was the war in which Eugene of Savoy and the Duke of Marlborough

---

[4] Although it was formerly alleged that the Salem Village witchcraft panic was whipped up by the New England clergy, especially Increase and Cotton Mather, as a device to bolster their waning power, a more judicious consideration of the affair shows that Increase Mather was responsible for persuading Phips to dismiss the indictments, while Cotton was instrumental in preventing a similar outbreak in Boston.

distinguished themselves, in which the battles of Blenheim and Ramillies were fought, and in which England captured Gibraltar. France and Spain now became allies, and the feeble little colonies of Louisiana and Florida were friends; they found a common enemy in the vigorous young English colony of South Carolina.

Owing to the lack of an Appalachian barrier to the west, the South Carolinians developed very much the same sort of fur-trading frontier as the Canadians had in the North. In this region deer and buffalo skins, which European carriers valued as a raw material for fine leather, were the most important peltry. By 1700 the Carolinian traders had penetrated the entire region back of the eastern Gulf of Mexico, and were even obtaining skins from the Quapaw across the Mississippi. The Yamassee Indians, who had revolted against the Spaniards in Florida, established themselves in South Carolina, and made slaving raids on the Creek and the Cherokee, selling their captives to the English of Charleston, who in turn sold them to good advantage in the West Indies and even in New England. Le Moyne d'Iberville in turn allied with the Choctaw, and Queen Anne's War on this southern border took on the character of a preliminary skirmish in the contest for mastery of the Mississippi; a contest that ended only with Jefferson's Louisiana purchase and Jackson's victory before New Orleans. And, just as Massachusetts was begging the English Crown for help to conquer Canada, so the South Carolina assembly urged on the Board of Trade in London the advantage of extending Carolina to the ' Mischisipi ' river, since ' half the Canada fur trade and skins must of necessity come this way, besides a vast internal trade of furs and skins.' Throughout the last three colonial wars the flank English colonies of Massachusetts and South Carolina were more imperialist than the home government, ever urging action on the part of England; while the Middle and Chesapeake colonies, protected as they were by the Iroquois, hung back until they were directly menaced.

A little help from England would have enabled Carolina to satisfy her ambition, and to snuff out the infant colonies of Louisiana and West Florida. But she did not get it. The Spaniards attacked Charleston in 1706 but failed; the Carolinians burnt Pensacola town in 1707, but failed to take the fort. In the meantime d'Iberville's Choctaw allies protected Mobile, and that nucleus of Louisiana endured. A small French naval expedition, procured by d'Iberville to carry the war against Carolina, turned its attention to the British West

Indies. Here, again, was another constant factor of these colonial wars. The West Indian sugar islands were so much more valuable to Europe than the continental colonies, and those waters were so rich in possible prizes that French or British naval forces almost always concentrated on the Caribbean, where their success did not help the mainland settlements or secure the great West for either side.

On the northern frontier, Queen Anne's War began with border raids by the French and Indians, of which the most famous, rendered classic by Parson Williams's account of his captivity and by Francis Parkman, was the attack on Deerfield. Massachusetts countered with companies of frontier scouts equipped with snowshoes, since the Indians usually attacked in winter when the going was good. An importation of ski technique from Norway might have turned the scales! New York remained neutral almost to the end of the war, largely because of the desire of the Albany merchants to continue supplying those of Montreal with rum and woolens for the Indian trade. Massachusetts, after two failures, and a bitter disappointment when a promised English expeditionary force was diverted to Portugal, captured Port Royal, this time permanently; it became Annapolis Royal. In 1711 the English Government sent a fleet with 12,000 men under incompetent leaders, to co-operate with the New Englanders in an attack on Quebec, while a land force moved up the Hudson valley toward Montreal. As in the previous war the land force stalled at Lake Champlain, and the naval-military expedition turned back after some of the ships had run aground in the Gulf of St. Lawrence.

The Treaty of Utrecht (1713), which ended this war, was a landmark in the territorial history of North America. Great Britain obtained French recognition of her imperium over Hudson's Bay, where the great fur-trading corporation of that name had been operating since 1670, and of Nova Scotia; but the value of this latter cession to New England was largely nullified by allowing France to retain Cape Breton Island, where Louis XV constructed Louisbourg, the 'Gibraltar of the New World.' The negotiators at Utrecht paid no attention to the southern frontier. There the Tuscarora Indians in the piedmont of North Carolina rose against the English in 1711, Virginia and South Carolina had to come to the aid of their neighbor, and after a defeat the Tuscarora tribe was removed to the Iroquois country and became the sixth nation of that confederacy. The Yamassee in South Carolina also revolted, and were driven into Spanish Florida in 1715.

Although the Treaty of Utrecht did not resolve any of the power politics that were constantly bringing the American colonies to blows, it did mark the beginning of a generation of peace, broken only by the short King George's War, an era in which the English colonies expanded westward, drew on new sources for their population, diversified their economic life, and began to enjoy the 'century of enlightenment.'

V

A HALF–CENTURY OF EXPANSION

1713–1763

1. *New Lands, New People*

THE Treaty of Utrecht begins the last half-century of the old British empire, a period which is marked by change and expansion in almost every department of colonial life. Only two new continental colonies, Nova Scotia and Georgia, were founded; but immigrants poured into the other twelve, and the frontier of settlement marched westward, creating a new section, the 'Old West,' that ran along the back country from New Hampshire to South Carolina. The empire was integrated by war, and by the governmental processes inaugurated under earlier reigns, but disintegrated by the creation of this 'Old West,' and by the growing consciousness of the colonists that they were Americans rather than Englishmen. Population and trade increased many-fold, and began to strain at the bonds of the Acts of Trade and Navigation. Religion took a new turn with the Great Awakening; many new schools and colleges were founded; and in the eastern section an upper class, growing in wealth and in self-confidence, acquired the refinements and the sophistication of the eighteenth century. In 1713 nobody predicted or suspected that the English colonies would ever seek union, unless in an imperial war, much less free themselves from English rule; in 1763 the Declaration of Independence was only thirteen years away.

In 1713 the population of the twelve continental colonies was not far from 360,000. In 1760 it was roughly 1,600,000, a fourfold increase; and the area of settlement had about tripled since 1713.

Whence came this vast increase, proportionally greater than that of any subsequent half-century of our history? In part from the large families, for whom there was always plenty of employment; in part from immigration. The outstanding feature of this immigration was its non-English character. The two most important contributions were German and Scots-Irish. William Penn had made contact with elements in Germany who were discontented with their homeland on economic and religious grounds: 'Palatines' ruined by French invasions of the Rhenish Palatinate; sects such as the Mennonites, Moravian Brothers, and Dunkards, who were not accorded freedom of worship in the German states; and Pietists whose relation to the Lutherans was somewhat similar to that of the early Puritans to the Church of England. Many of the vanguard were assisted by the English Government to come to England, whence they embarked for America and were given grants of land; many thousand others came over directly as 'redemptioners' given free passage by the shipowners, who recouped themselves by selling the passengers as indented servants. The great majority of Germans entered the colonies at Philadelphia, whence they spread out fanwise into the back country; but small groups were also to be found in all the colonies from Dresden, Maine, to Ebenezer, Georgia. In Pennsylvania thrifty Germans took up the best land, in the triassic belt that runs diagonally across that state, and became the most prosperous and successful agriculturalists in North America. They brought their own language and culture, established printing presses and newspapers, and, at Bethlehem, a musical tradition that eventually flowered into the annual festival devoted to the works of Johann Sebastian Bach.

Equal in importance to the German-speaking immigrants were the English- (and sometimes Gaelic-) speaking Scots-Irish from Ulster. These were largely descendants of the Scots who had colonized Northern Ireland when the English were first settling Virginia. After 1713 the pressure of the native Catholic Irish and the restrictive legislation of the British Parliament forced them to emigrate in droves. As land was dear in the East, these fighting Celts drifted to the frontier. By 1763 they formed the outer belt of defense against the Indians all the way from Londonderry, New Hampshire, to the upper country of South Carolina. A considerable number of southern Irish, mostly Protestants but including Catholic families like the Kavanaghs of Maine and the Carrolls of Maryland, came at the same time; but these were mostly men of property who invested in land and remained in the older-settled regions.

A third non-English strain was the Huguenots of France. The revocation of the Edict of Nantes by Louis XIV in 1685 destroyed their religious liberty, and sent tens of thousands of the most solid and enterprising French subjects to enrich Germany, the Netherlands, England, and the English colonies. Comparatively few Huguenots came to America; but those that did were of such high quality that they soon rose to positions of prominence, and acquired an influence out of proportion to their numbers. They were particularly prominent in South Carolina (Legaré, Petigru), Virginia (Maury), Massachusetts (Revere), and New York (Jay, DeLancey).

After 1713 new and speculative methods of land allotment were evolved from older systems in which the profit motive did not enter. In the seventeenth century it was possible for any immigrant to obtain free allotments in a New England township, or free farms by the head-right system in the Middle and Southern Colonies. The Crown, or the proprietor, looked for profit from an annual quit-rent rather than from original sale. But by 1713 the older settlers and their descendants saw no reason why they should not profit by this new flood of immigration by buying land cheap and selling dear. In New England the colonial legislatures began the practice of laying out belts of six-mile-square townships beyond the settled frontier, which were granted to groups of veterans of earlier colonial wars. Most of the veterans then cashed in on their shares, which were bought up by a small group of proprietors, who organized, granted home lots to a selected number of pioneers, and sold the remaining land, or part of it. In the Middle and Southern Colonies land was sold outright in small lots by the proprietors or the assemblies, and immense free grants were made (such as Lord Fairfax's six million acres of the Northern Neck of Virginia, Lord Granville's of the northern strip of North Carolina) to English or colonial land speculators who promised to obtain settlers. In Maryland, for instance, the fourth and fifth Lords Baltimore allowed their friends and supporters to take out land warrants to extensive territories in the western part of the state, and to postpone paying the legal fees or complying with the legal requirements of building a house and cultivating, until they had obtained a sufficient number of paying settlers to make a good profit. Even by 1720 so much land had been taken up by these methods that the only recourse for a poor man who had not the wherewithal to satisfy a land speculator, was to 'squat' without leave on Crown or proprietary land; and if he did not move on to repeat the process, selling out his improvements to a later comer who had the means to pay, his descendants had to wait until the Revolution to secure a good title.

Governor Spotswood's gay cavalcade of the 'Knights of the Golden Horseshoe' explored the Shenandoah valley in 1716, and opened up large sections of it and the piedmont to settlement. About

1726 Germans and Scots-Irish who had entered America at Philadelphia began to pour into this valley at Harper's Ferry. Their motive was cheap land; for William Penn's heirs, reversing his policy, charged £10 for a hundred acres, as against £2 in Maryland, or 10*s* by some of the Virginia speculators. The 'Old Wagon Road' up the valley became a veritable funnel of the frontier. Some pioneers settled along it and sprinkled the Shenandoah valley with log cabins and German names; others turned south, through one of the many 'gaps' in the Blue Ridge, into the piedmont of Virginia and the Carolinas. For a long time there was an unsettled strip of piedmont; for Richmond, on its eastern edge, was founded only in 1729, but during the eighteenth century small farmers and indented servants from the Tidewater pushed into the piedmont and to the great valley beyond.

In North Carolina the defeat of the Tuscarora opened up not only the piedmont but part of the coastal plain, and that colony increased sixteenfold in population between 1713 and 1760. At the latter date it contained more people than New York, where the Iroquois mastery of the Mohawk valley and the feudal institutions of the Hudson river patroons retarded settlement.

The important social fact of this settlement of the 'Old West' was the building up of a new internal tension in many of the colonies. South of New England and New York, the older-settled region was English in race and Anglican or Quaker in religion; the 'Old West' was a mixture of German, Scots-Irish, and English in race, and either Presbyterian, Baptist, or German sectarian in religion. The eastern belt of settlement, controlling the assemblies, managed to keep the frontier under-represented; and by levying most of the taxation on polls rather than property, by forcing the frontiersmen to travel long distances to get justice, by denying to their ministers the right to make legal marriages, and by buying frontier products cheap and selling imported goods dear, the Easterners built up a sectional antagonism that broke out, later, in movements like the Paxton Boys, the Regulators and Shays's Rebellion. So fast were western grievances against eastern ruling classes accumulating in 1760, that a civil war within the colonies seemed more likely than a war for independence from Britain.

2. *Georgia and Nova Scotia*

Georgia and Nova Scotia, the two new continental colonies founded in this period, were designed by the Crown as bastions against the Spaniards and the French in preparation for the next imperial war; but the first was promoted by private initiative, and the dynamic motive was a desire to give a new start in life to the poor and unfortunate in England. Georgia, therefore, was no mere incident in power politics; it belongs in the cycle of ' holy experiments ' portended by More's *Utopia*.

The eighteenth century is full of contradictions and paradoxes, as was natural for an age when new modes of thought and action, new forms of society and industrial experiments were struggling to be born from the womb of the past. On the one hand, it was an era of formalism, indifference, and decay in the established churches; on the other, it saw the birth of new religious and philosophical movements, such as Methodism in England, Jansenism in France, the ' natural religion ' that stems from Newton, the idealism associated with Berkeley, and the rational philosophy that prepared the way for the French Revolution. Or, confining ourselves to the British Isles, it is equally true that the age was one of social smugness and complacency toward poverty and other social evils, and of the brutality recorded so graphically in the paintings of Hogarth; yet it was also an age of benevolence and humanitarianism, when the first effective protests were made against evils such as the slave trade, high infant mortality, and imprisonment for debt. While the colonies as a whole were exploited for the benefit of ruling classes in England, a steady back-flow of charitable funds reached the colonies from England for the foundation of libraries, schools, and colleges, for the conversion and education of Indians and Negroes. Georgia was the result of the combination of several charitable individuals and forces for a single well-defined object.

Thomas Bray ' the great little man,' a small but energetic Anglican clergyman, was the initiator of several of these schemes. Sent out to Maryland in 1699 to organize the Church of England there, he was impressed with the dearth of good books in the colonies, and the want of means for colonial clergymen to keep abreast of good literature. Accordingly he founded parochial libraries for each of the thirty Anglican parishes of Maryland, many more for the Anglican churches from Boston to Charleston, South Carolina, and a number of laymen's libraries as well. These were the first semi-public libraries in the colonies after those of Harvard and William and Mary Colleges; for Dr. Bray insisted that 'any inhabitant' should have the right to 'borrow any Book out of the Library, . . . promising to return it' within one to four months, depending on the format. Returning to England, Dr. Bray was instrumental around 1700 in founding two great missionary societies which still exist: the Society for the Propagation of the Gospel, and the Society for the Promotion of Christian Knowledge. In 1723 he organized his particular friends as 'The Associates of Dr. Bray,' for carrying out other benevolent schemes.

One of the four Associates, a London parishioner of Dr. Bray, was a very different type of man from the busy little parson. Captain Thomas Coram, a big, tough, two-fisted shipmaster with a tender heart, made a fortune trading with the colonies after he retired from the sea, and devoted it to various charitable enterprises. Moved by compassion for abandoned infants, bastards of sailors' drabs who were left by the roadside in the hope that some passer-by might take pity on them, he founded the great Foundling Hospital of London in 1735; yet yearned to do still more for suffering humanity. Already, in 1717, Coram had planned to have Maine east of the Kennebec detached from the Province of Massachusetts Bay, and erected into a colony called Georgia, with the object of providing new homes for discharged soldiers and other unemployed, and of exploiting the forest resources of northern New England for the benefit of the British navy and merchant marine. Unfortunately the Bay Province and various claimants to Maine under seventeenth-century grants frustrated his scheme. All that came of it was a settlement of Scots-Irish and New England frontiersmen at Pemaquid, around 1730.

A second Associate of Dr. Bray was Lord Percival (later the Earl of Egmont), a disciple of the Irish philosopher George Berkeley, Dean of Derry. Dean Berkeley had planned a college for Negroes in Bermuda, to be the beginning of a system of Negro schools on the American continent; he had spent the years 1729–31 at Newport, Rhode Island, waiting for a parliamentary appropriation that never came. Percival was the connecting link between the Associates of Dr. Bray and Oglethorpe.

James Edward Oglethorpe was a young gentleman of rank and fortune who left Oxford to fight under Eugene of Savoy in the

War of Germany against Turkey. After the war he entered Parliament, where, ' driven by strong benevolence of soul ' (as Pope wrote of him), he served with Percival on a committee to inquire into the state of jails. That state was bad indeed; so horrible that a released prisoner was apt to be a broken man for life. The worst part of the system was imprisonment for debt; a debtor once committed to jail could not be released until his debt was paid, and in jail he had no means of discharging it; if released by charity after many years, he was usually incapable of supporting himself. It occurred to Gen. Oglethorpe that the way to meet this social evil was to assist poor debtors to emigrate to America under conditions that would enable them to start afresh and lead happy and useful lives. At his instance the Associates of Dr. Bray petitioned the Crown for a grant of land in Carolina, and then founded a new corporation, which obtained a proprietary grant of the land between the Savannah and the Altamaha rivers, under the name of Georgia.

The Trustees of Georgia were men prominent in English society, politics, and business. They financed the biggest publicity campaign that any English colony ever enjoyed. Inspired accounts of the healthy climate and fertile soil of Georgia were liberally paid for in the now flourishing newspaper press of London; pamphlets were printed and circulated. As several of the trustees were members of Parliament, they were able to obtain grants of public money, in order to transport and settle deserving poor. So Georgia began as a colony de luxe, the pet project of wealthy and powerful philanthropists. The royal charter created it a proprietary colony with limited tenure; after twenty-one years the jurisdiction should revert to the Crown, which appointed the customs officials from the first. English officials welcomed the colony as a cheap buffer for the Carolina frontier.

General Oglethorpe was appointed by the trustees the first governor, came out himself with the first consignment of poor debtors in 1733, and founded Savannah. During the first year 618 persons, over 500 of them objects of charity, emigrated. A fifty-acre farm was granted to each charity colonist; and five hundred acres were given to any self-supporting settler who brought out a family of six. The trustees also sought recruits, in competition with Pennsylvania, among the Protestants of Germany; a colony of Scots settled Frederica; and several groups of New Englanders were induced to try their luck in Georgia. Slavery was absolutely forbidden, and an effort was made to exclude rum and other hard liquor. Friendly relations were cultivated with the near-by Lower Creek Indians, and an effort was made to keep irresponsible traders away from them.

Georgia did not prosper under this benevolent despotism of her trustees. The settlers found it impossible to live off fifty acres, or without slave labor; one of them wrote home, 'Its hard living here without a servant, one man being incapable to remove trees, etc., and fence before he can plant.' Lacking a supply of quinine or other febrifuge, rum was a necessity of life in the malarial lowlands. Jealous peltry traders of South Carolina had the Indian monopoly disallowed in England. The contrast with South Carolina, where people were growing rich through applying slave labor to rice and indigo plantations, made the fifty-acre freeholders envious and discontented, and the more ambitious drifted away to the older colony, even though in so doing they forfeited their land in Georgia. The trustees gradually liberalized the conditions of land-owning and removed the slavery and liquor prohibitions in 1750; an assembly was granted in 1751; but the colony had made such slow progress, and caused the trustees so many headaches, that in 1752, when their twenty years' proprietorship lapsed, they were glad to turn Georgia over to the Crown. It was still so poor and thinly populated that the Crown paid almost all government expenses in the province until the Revolution. Gradually the economy of Georgia was assimilated to the rice-plantation system of South Carolina, and eventually it received an up-country population by way of the intermountain trough. But at the outbreak of the Revolution Georgia was still the weakest and least populous of the Thirteen Colonies. Yet the enterprise cannot be considered a failure in organized philanthropy, for it did assist several thousand men, whose lives would have been wasted in England, to a new life in the New World.

Captain Coram, although he had consented to serve as a trustee of Georgia, never approved of planting a charity settlement so far south; and after 'that wretched colony,' as he called Georgia, had been started, he began agitating for a northern counterpart in Nova Scotia. Horace Walpole the elder recommended Coram to his brother Sir Robert the Prime Minister, as 'the honestest, the most disinterested, and the most knowing person about the plantations I ever talked with'; and Coram was almost at the point of having Nova Scotia made a colony of unemployed artisans in 1745 when King George's War broke out and the scheme was postponed. At the end of that war, in 1749, Halifax was founded by the British Government on the magnificent Chebucto Bay with some four thousand veterans and other well-chosen colonists, and the settled history of the fourteenth British continental colony began. Most of the pioneers of Nova Scotia during the next quarter-century came from New England; but the British Government did so much for the people of that colony, and so far avoided the mistakes it had made in the others, that in 1765 Nova Scotia obeyed the Stamp Act, and in 1775 remained loyal to the empire.

3. Industry and Commerce

Despite the increasing controls of the imperial system — perhaps to some extent because of them — industry and commerce prospered as never before and seldom since, during the half-century following the Treaty of Utrecht.

The key to this prosperity was a rise in prices for colonial produce in the British Isles and continental Europe. This rise kept so far ahead of production that the fourfold increase of population in the continental colonies did not dilute prosperity.

In the West Indies the increased European demand for colonial produce was first felt; and West Indian prosperity almost automatically affected those continental colonies which were dependent on the West Indian market. The British West Indian planters, annoyed by the competition of the French colonies of Saint-Domingue and the Windward Islands, induced Parliament in 1733 to pass the Sugar or Molasses Act, charging a prohibitory duty on foreign molasses and sugar entering English colonies. By that time, the rum industry had been so developed in the seaports from Portsmouth to Philadelphia that the French Antilles, where molasses was cheapest and most abundant, were necessary to them as a source of supply; and the act was simply ignored. Yankee shipmasters found no difficulty in obtaining false invoices at Jamaica to cover their shipments from French islands, which proved satisfactory to the underpaid and complacent British customs officials on the continent.

Baltimore was founded in 1729, largely because the local river bearing the humble name of Jones Falls afforded water power for mills which ground the wheat of German-settled Pennsylvania and up-country Maryland into flour, for which there was a brisk demand in the West Indies. Before many years the export of grain and flour from Chesapeake Bay was pushing that of tobacco for first place. Philadelphia remained the principal place of export for grain and provisions. And, as in the previous century, the West Indies trade was vital for southern New England. The islands appeared to have an indefinite capacity to absorb salt fish, wood for boxes, barrels, and house construction, live horses, salt meat, and vegetables.

In northern New England and North Carolina, the export to England of ship timber and naval stores, such as pitch and tar, was of great importance. Virginia recovered her ancient prosperity with a rise in the price of tobacco, and shared in the flour trade as well. In South Carolina fortunes were built up out of rice and indigo a few years after the Treaty of Utrecht. In the year 1731, over 200 vessels cleared from Charleston, carrying 42,000 barrels (or about 21 million pounds) of rice, 14,000 barrels of pitch, tar, and turpentine, about 250,000 deer skins, and a large quantity of provisions. Rice was an enumerated product in the Acts of Trade; but as the market was almost exclusively continental, making a detour through England costly and increasing the risk of damage, Parliament in 1729 allowed rice to be sent directly to all European ports south of Cape Finisterre. By 1771, South Carolina was sending over 9,000,-000 pounds of rice to the Western Islands (Madeira and the Azores), over 13,000,000 pounds to the West Indies, and almost 40,000,-000 pounds to Great Britain (which re-exported most of what she received) and Southern Europe. This great increase of rice production accounted for South Carolina's becoming the principal slave-importing continental colony. Indigo, stimulated by a production bounty from the British Parliament, was introduced into South Carolina from the foreign West Indies about 1740, and quickly produced a crop of ' indigo millionaires.' Both rice and indigo required a substantial capital and a large labor force for profitable cultivation, and thus accelerated the development of the slave system and the division of classes among the whites.

New York was still the principal port of export for furs. The merchants of Albany had a monopoly of trade with the Six Nations, who by this time were acting as middlemen, and obtaining their peltry from an extensive watershed in the Far West. Governor Burnet founded the trading post at Oswego and attempted to break up a secondary activity of Albany merchants, supplying rum and woolens to England's rivals in Canada; but Albany had sufficient influence at Whitehall to have Governor Burnet removed to Massa-

chusetts, and the prohibition repealed. As a result, there was a gradual infiltration of French influence among the Iroquois, which
broke down what contemporaries called the 'impenetrable fence'
around the Middle Colonies, and lessened its usefulness to the British Empire in subsequent colonial wars.

Although the English ruling classes did not object to the colonists
indulging in crude manufacturing processes, such as milling grain,
distilling molasses into rum, making candles from spermaceti, and
preparing tobacco, timber products, and naval stores for export,
they always endeavored to clamp down on colonial competition
with any leading English industry, which by the mercantilist
conception of the nature of things should have a monopoly of the
colonial market. Emigration of skilled artisans to the colonies with
the tools or implements of their trade was always forbidden, but,
fortunately, the prohibitions were generally ignored. Three acts of
Parliament in particular were aimed at protecting English staples.
The Woolens Act of 1699 forbade colonial woolen cloth to be sold
outside the place or plantation where it was woven; but as most
rural families carded, spun, and wove their own wool, this caused
no hardship in America. On complaint of London's Worshipful
Company of Hatters that the colonists were beginning to make up
their own furs into the wide-brimmed beaver hats of the era, instead of importing all their headgear from England, a law was passed
in 1732 limiting the number of hatter apprentices. And in 1750 the
British iron interests induced Parliament to remove British duties
from colonial pig and bar iron, in the hope of encouraging Americans to supplant the importations from Sweden to England; and
to forbid the establishment of new slitting mills (which slit bar
iron into nail rods) or plating forges using a trip hammer, or steel
tool furnaces, in order to protect the export of English ironmongery
and steel. But this law had little effect. The export of colonial iron
to England increased only from 3,000 to 7,500 tons between 1750 and
1771 — not enough to rob Sweden of her English market; and the
prohibition of new mills and forges was so flagrantly disregarded
that Pennsylvania, New Jersey, and Massachusetts even granted
bounties for new plants after the Iron Act was on the statute books!
By 1760 there was a thriving colonial iron industry wherever the
combination of surface deposits of iron ore, wood for smelting, and
water power, was found. There were actually more 'furnaces'
(where pig iron was produced) and 'forges' (where pig was re-

smelted into bar or wrought iron) in the Thirteen Colonies than in England and Wales, in 1775. Most of them were very small, employing but a few dozen hands at the most; but the average annual production — 300 tons of pig iron for each furnace, and 150 tons of bar iron for each forge — was about the same as in England. So, even though the acts restraining manufactures were restrictive in motive, they were hardly so in practice; and before indulging in virtuous indignation over them, we should remember that it has long been the policy of Congress to levy tariffs or set quotas on Philippine products, such as sugar, which compete with those of the United States.

Far more serious than all the Acts of Trade and Navigation as brakes on colonial enterprise were the English restrictions on the colonial use of money, and the attempts of colonial assemblies to get around them. Currency problems, like those of war and peace, seem destined never to be solved; but the treatment of the colonial money problem by Parliament was both selfish and irritating. No precious metals were produced in any of the English colonies, and the balance of trade with the mother country was against them; so their want of metallic currency was constant. Yet Parliament refused to allow the export of English coin to English colonies, or to allow them to mint coinage of their own [1] from the foreign bullion that they obtained through trade with the West Indies. In part this prohibition was a survival of the 'bullionist' doctrine that the wealth of a country is measured by its store of precious metals; in part it was due to a fear that if the American towns acquired a stock of specie they would acquire a money economy and invest in manufacturing or other enterprises that would render them less dependent on England.

Colonial assemblies endeavored to meet this situation in a variety of ways. Each colony or group of colonies established a currency of account, 'lawful money' as it was called, in pounds, shillings, and pence that were worth less than sterling in England. The common standard for this 'lawful money' was the Spanish-milled dollar or 'piece of eight' weighing 17½ pennyweight, which was the commonest foreign coin that came into the continent from the Caribbean, and so eventually chosen as standard for the United States silver dollar. The Spanish dollar was worth 4s 6d in terms of

[1] The Massachusetts 'pine-tree' coinage, begun in 1652 without authorization, was stopped in 1684 when the Bay Colony lost its charter.

English sterling, but in South Carolina and Georgia it was valued at
4s 8d, in New England and Virginia at 6s, in New York at 8s, and
in the other colonies at 7s 6d. This meant that a New York pound of
account was worth only half an English pound sterling, and a 'York
shilling' only sixpence sterling or 12½ cents; in New England and
Virginia one pound 'lawful' was worth about two-thirds of a pound
sterling, and a shilling, 16⅔ cents. The colonial assemblies fondly
imagined that by this overvaluation of foreign coins in terms of
sterling, these coins would stay in the colonies and not be re-exported;
and that the colony which overvalued them most would acquire
the whole stock; but the only result was a corresponding mark-up
of all prices of English goods in the local £ s d of account, and frequent consignments of foreign bullion to England in order to pay
for goods ordered there.

Since overvaluing the Spanish dollar and undervaluing sterling
did not help the colonists, they resorted to paper money. Personal
promissory notes, tobacco-warehouse receipts, and bills of exchange
had long been used as money in the colonies, even for very small
sums. In Virginia, for instance, a man might pay his reckoning at
a tavern with an order for the amount on the London merchant
who handled his tobacco. From this it was a short step for the Massachusetts Assembly in 1690 to issue official promissory notes to pay
for Sir William Phips's expedition against Quebec, in anticipation
of loot and of tax collections. The loot did not materialize and the
taxes were not sufficient to 'sink' the notes, so they stayed in circulation a couple of years. These Massachusetts notes of 1690 are
said to have been the first official paper money in the modern world,
except for a slightly earlier emission in Sweden. Before the close of
Queen Anne's War eight or nine colonies had followed suit. This
earlier colonial paper currency was generally not legal tender except
for taxes, and though not redeemable in silver it did not depreciate
greatly, because the colonial governments bought it back from the
holders fairly promptly.

These 'bills of credit' (whence we derive our phrase, a dollar
'bill') so well relieved the currency shortage in time of war that a
demand grew up for issuing them in time of peace. The American
farmer believed then (as in the main he still believes) that currency
inflation, raising prices of farm produce, would benefit him and ease
his burden of debt. Massachusetts and South Carolina, which had

borne a disproportionate share of the war burden, continued issuing bills after the Treaty of Utrecht, and in the southern colony the
two houses of assembly, the council representing the creditor-
mercantile, and the commons the debtor-farmer interest, became
completely deadlocked on the subject. In some colonies, notably
Pennsylvania, where Benjamin Franklin urged the value of the
system in a growing country, issues of paper currency were promptly
redeemed, and depreciated very little. They were, in effect, a lien
on future prosperity, like government debts today. In a small colony like Rhode Island, whose possibilities of future growth were
limited, one issue succeeded another, until prices in terms of paper
money rose about thirtyfold.

South Carolina thought up another scheme that the farmers
liked even better — the so-called Land Bank. Under this system
the colony, instead of issuing bills in the first instance to merchants
who furnished the government supplies, lent them to farmers on
landed security. It was a wonderful game for the land-poor farmer
— practically a gift of money: for if he could not redeem the paper
debt, he and his fellows could generally induce the assembly to
' stay ' collection, or to let him discharge it in produce at an inflated
value. In order to make the bills effective, the assemblies had
to declare them legal tender for all payments. But nothing that
a colonial assembly did in the way of fiat money could legally discharge debts due to English merchants; hence it was the country
storekeeper or seaport merchant who suffered from this sort of legislation, and sought redress in England. Royal governors were always
instructed to veto paper-money laws unless they provided for prompt
redemption out of taxes; and when the governor was forced by political pressure to disobey his instructions, the law was disallowed
by the Privy Council.

Massachusetts was almost torn apart by a land bank controversy
in 1741. The farmers even planned a march on Boston to intimidate
the merchants, but the latter appealed to England, and induced Parliament to declare an act of 1720, aimed at the South Sea Bubble and
other wild-cat English schemes of that speculative era, to be applica-
ble to the colonies and to have outlawed the Massachusetts land
bank. This tactless act of power left much embittered radicalism
in New England (the father of Sam Adams was ruined by it), and
was responsible in part for that clause in the Federal Constitution

against *ex post facto* laws. Parliament passed an act in 1751 prohibiting the New England colonies from erecting new land banks or making paper currency legal tender.

Although few of the colonial assemblies showed sufficient wisdom and restraint to be entrusted with so dangerous a sovereign power as the issuance of paper money, it must be said that the British Government did nothing to provide a substitute. By forbidding the colonies to import English coin, or to mint the bullion they acquired from the Spanish West Indies into coin, they made some other form of currency necessary and inevitable. The social effect was to create a tension between debtors and creditors in each colony rather than to arouse antagonism against Great Britain; the debtors had things pretty much their own way during the Revolution, but sound money advocates won in the Federal Convention.

4. Society and Religion

While the Thirteen Colonies were increasing their trade, population, and wealth, diversifying their racial content, and becoming conscious of sectional interests, their social and intellectual ties with England were becoming closer. Every royal governor's mansion was a little court where the latest London fashions were displayed and London coffee-house gossip was repeated. Transatlantic travel, except during three or four winter months, was relatively safe in the small packet ships and ' constant traders' of the day. British naval superiority meant that travel went on even in time of war. Merchants in the seaport towns made a point of visiting London every few years, and sent their sons on long voyages as supercargos; the sons of rich Southern planters often went to school or university in England; or, if they studied at a colonial college, took a medical course at the University of Edinburgh or read law in the Inns of Court. Even so middle-class an American as Benjamin Franklin managed to spend many years in England, and was no worse an American for that. English books and periodicals reached the colonies only a few months late. Thirteen colonists were accorded the highest scientific honor in the English-speaking world, a fellowship in the Royal Society of London, between 1713 and 1773,[2] and

[2] These colonial F.R.S.'s, exclusive of those from the West Indies, were Cotton Mather, William Brattle, John Leverett, Paul Dudley, Thomas Robie, Zabdiel Boylston and John Winthrop the astronomer, all of Massachusetts; John Winthrop III of Connecticut, John Mitchell and John Tennent of Virginia, Benjamin Franklin and John

several others contributed to the famous *Philosophical Trans-actions*.

Commerce and land speculation were the principal ways to wealth in all the colonies, Virginia included; although some large fortunes were made in the Chesapeake colonies and South Carolina by planting combined with land speculation and official position. New families were rising through wealth into the class of gentry every year. Professional architects were very few; Peter Harrison of Newport, Rhode Island, who catered to the slave-trading aristocracy of that flourishing city, appears to have been the earliest in the colonies; when Harvard College wanted a new building in 1764, Governor Bernard obligingly drew the plans. Local builders, with the aid of books of design from England, erected mansions in the balanced, well-proportioned Georgian style, and churches modelled on those of Sir Christopher Wren. Even the middling sort of town and farm houses reflected the 'century of enlightenment.' When young Ben Franklin, around 1720, cracked his head on a low smoke-blackened beam in the Rev. Cotton Mather's antique house in Boston, that sententious cleric gave him a maxim that stood him well through life — 'When you come to a low place, stoop!' Had it been a new house, there would have been one saying of 'Poor Richard' the less; for the beam would have cleared Ben's head, and probably have been concealed under plaster. After 1720 paint was used freely to preserve the exterior and adorn the interior of wooden dwelling houses; square-paned sash windows replaced the leaded casements of the seventeenth century, and white panelled doors surmounted by graceful fanlights replaced the massive nail-studded oak portals that were designed to resist Indian tomahawks. Fireplaces were built much smaller, now that wood was less plentiful, and Franklin made them more economical with his stove; the chimneys were placed at the ends instead of the center, allowing a vista from front door to garden. Gambrel roofs with dormer windows afforded good space in the attic story; the greater mansions were built in three stories, surmounted by a low roof and a classic balustrade. In the South we have the first colonnaded porches, as at Mount Vernon, a balanced layout with detached offices and kitchen (for the eighteenth century was becoming susceptible to smells), and landscaped grounds. In

---

Morgan of Pennsylvania, and Alexander Garden of South Carolina. In addition, John Winthrop, Jr., of Connecticut and William Byrd II of Virginia were elected before 1713.

the back-country and new settlements from Maine to Georgia the log cabin, made either of round logs or of squared timbers well mortised together, and chinked with chips and clay, became universal.[3]

The recent reconstruction of Williamsburg, Virginia, most of whose buildings are subsequent to 1720, affords a living picture of a colonial court town. Broad streets, well laid out, a Governor's Palace with formal garden, a Capitol or State House with large chambers for the two houses of assembly, and offices for other colonial officials; a tavern with a large room for banquets, concerts, stage plays, and dances; a Georgian church with high-backed square pews; fair brick dwelling houses with extensive gardens; and a jail which was the most sanitary building in town. Even colonial towns of two or three thousand inhabitants afforded more social amenities in the eighteenth century than American cities of many times their population today. There would always be a market house and merchants' exchange, a tavern where the latest English gazettes were taken in and where clubs of gentlemen or tradesmen met for talk, smoke, wine, and singing; a dancing assembly for the social élite; a circulating library; and, in five or six places, a musical society. Philadelphia had a theatre as early as 1724, and in 1749 an excellent English company of players began trouping through the colonies south of New England, for in the Puritan colonies only private theatricals were permitted. College commencements, horse-races, and fairs gave entertainment to everyone. Williamsburg, for instance, established two annual fairs for livestock, goods, and merchandise in 1739; the *Virginia Gazette* advertised:

And for the Entertainment and Diversion of all Gentlemen and others, that shall resort thereto, the following PRIZES are given to be contended for, at the Fair, viz.

A good Hat to be Cudgell'd for; and to be given to the Person that fairly wins it, by the common Rules of Play.

A Saddle of 40s value, to be run for, once round the Mile Course, adjacent to this City, by any Horse, Mare or Gelding, carrying Horseman's Weight, and allowing Weight for Inches. A handsome Bridle to be given to the Horse that comes in Second, And a good Whip to the Horse that comes in Third.

A Pair of Silver Buckles, value 20s, to be run for by Men, from the Col-

---

[3] Although there are good examples throughout the old Thirteen States, Annapolis is the best town for the study of Georgian domestic architecture. The much-admired dwellings of Salem, Providence, and Charleston are mostly of the Federal period, or later.

lege to the Capitol. A Pair of Shoes to be given to him that comes in Second. And a Pair of gloves to the Third.

A Pair of Pumps to be danc'd for by Men.

A handsome Firelock to be exercis'd for; and given to the Person that performs the Manual Exercise best.

A Pig, with his tail soap'd to be run after; and to be given to the Person that catches him, and lift him off the Ground fairly by the Tail.

The fifteen years from 1740 to the French and Indian War were the golden age of the Old Dominion. The old roughness and crudeness were passing away. Peace reigned over the land, high prices for tobacco ruled, immigrants were pouring into the back country; the traditional Virginia of Thackeray and Vachel Lindsay — 'Land of the gauntlet and the glove ' — came into being. Living in Virginia at that time was like riding on the sparkling crest of a great wave just before it breaks and spreads into dull, shallow pools. In that wholesome rural society with lavish hospitality, a need for constant vigilance and organization, and a sense of civic pride and public spirit, was bred the ' Virginia dynasty ' that (with some help from elsewhere, one must admit!) guided the destinies of the young republic yet unborn.

In religious history this period was marked by increasing missionary effort on the part of the Anglican church, both among the English colonists and the Indians, and conducted largely by missionaries sent out by the Society for the Propagation of the Gospel. These efforts seldom reached the Old West, which was served mainly by Baptists, Presbyterians, or parsons of the German sects; and the Church of England's organization in the colonies always remained decentralized and haphazard because of the lack of any higher official than a commissary. All English colonies belonged in the diocese of London. It was necessary for any candidate for Anglican orders to visit the mother country for training and ordination; consequently a large number of colonial priests were men who for one reason or another could obtain no parish at home. Bishop Sherlock proposed in 1749 that the English Government provide for the consecration of a number of colonial bishops; but this notion provoked a violent controversy from colonists, both Anglican and dissenters, who feared increased control, taxes, and tithes; so nothing was done.

In Rhode Island and in the second group of colonies founded after 1660, where toleration prevailed, dissenting sects enjoyed a large measure of religious liberty, but in the rest of New England, Baptists,

Quakers, and Anglicans were constantly struggling against being forced to contribute to the Congregational churches; in Maryland the Catholics were severely discriminated against by the established Church of England, now that the lords proprietors were Protestant; and in Virginia the dissenters (in the English sense) were taxed for the Anglican church, which had a monopoly of performing marriages. By mid-century, however, the dissenters in every colony had made tremendous gains, especially among the common people, through the religious revival known as the Great Awakening. Arising out of their deep desire to know and do the will of God, this was the first important and spontaneous movement of the American people — far more pervasive than the wars and political squabbles of the period. Altogether outside the sphere or influence of government, it crossed colonial boundaries, emphasized class lines, and stimulated democracy.

As proof that a revival of religion was due in the colonies, and that existing churches were not providing what the people wanted, the Great Awakening began almost simultaneously in three different colonies. Theodore Frelinghuysen, a German immigrant parson of the Dutch Reformed Church, started a revival in the Raritan valley, New Jersey, in 1719. William Tennent, a University of Edinburgh graduate who emigrated to Philadelphia about 1717, began soon after to train young men privately for service on the frontier, and in 1736 established the so-called Log College for revivalists at Neshaminy, Pennsylvania. In 1734 Jonathan Edwards, graduate of Yale and minister of Northampton, Massachusetts, began his famous imprecatory sermons in order to recall his people to a sense of sin and bring them to the sense of communion with God which the evangelicals call conversion. His description of this revival, *A Faithful Narration of the Surprising Work of God in the Conversion of Many Hundred Souls in Northampton* (Boston, 1737), was promptly reprinted in London and Edinburgh, translated into German and Dutch, and became, as it still is, a classic. John Wesley read it afoot between London and Oxford — 'Surely this is the Lord's doing,' he wrote in his journal; presently he began to obtain the same effects with his own preaching, and in a little while the Methodist Church was born. George Whitefield, an eloquent young minister sent out to Georgia by the trustees, read *A Faithful Narration* in Savannah, and his amazing career as a revivalist dates from that hour.

Whitefield began the second phase of the Great Awakening by

preaching at Philadelphia in 1739, and touring New England in 1740. In 73 days he rode 800 miles and preached 130 sermons. His voice could be heard by 20,000 people in the open air. He made violent gestures, danced about the pulpit, roared and ranted, greatly to the delight of the common people who were tired of gentlemanly, unemotional sermons from college-bred ministers. He introduced the second stage of revivalism with which many parts of America are still familiar — sinners becoming vocally and violently ' saved.' Gilbert Tennent, son of the proprietor of the Log College, and several score of lay exhorters and itinerant preachers followed Whitefield; and the ' New Light,' as their followers called themselves, proved to be the first blossom of that amazing tree that was to bear the Shakers and the Mormons, Holy Rollers and the Millerites, and a score of other sects. Not a colony was free from the Great Awakening. Intermittently, but over the entire decade of the seventeen forties, it raged through New England, the Middle Colonies and the South.

The net result of the Awakening in terms of pure religion is impossible to estimate; in terms of sociology it is more palpable. It brought more people into the Protestant churches, but split them up, setting congregations against their ministers, and reviving intolerance. Connecticut, for instance, repealed its toleration act in 1743. Once ignorant and emotional people had tasted the strong drink of revivalism they cared no more for traditional worship; new congregations were formed, some of which died out after a few years, while others became Baptist, Methodist, or ' New Light ' Presbyterian. Calmer souls sought refuge in the Anglican churches or Quaker meetings, which were the least affected by the Awakening.

Jonathan Edwards stayed with the movement, although he deplored its excesses; but the backwash of reaction drove him from the pleasant Connecticut valley of his ministry. He became a missionary to the Indians in Stockbridge, and there, in the solitude of the wilderness, wrote three of his greatest works — *The Nature of True Virtue, Original Sin,* and *Freedom of the Will.* His collected works, in ten volumes, which poor college students used to save their pennies to buy, are now gathering dust on library shelves. Even in Scotland, whither he was invited to remove after Northampton and where he had the greatest and the longest reputation, Jonathan Edwards is read no more. Yet he faced, as few modern men have dared or cared to face, the problem of evil and the problem of free will. The system of theology that he and his disciple Hopkins worked out, neo-Calvinist in general character, gave the New England churches a new lease of life. And certain passages in his works express more effectively the beauty of holiness, and the supreme importance to man of his relation with God, than any in American literature.

Indirectly the Great Awakening gave to the colonies three new colleges; for the 'New Lights' soon perceived that without seminaries to educate an evangelical ministry, their movement would be killed by ignorant hot-gospellers. The College of New Jersey at Princeton (1746), the first colonial school of higher learning to be founded since Yale (1701), was the Presbyterian seminary, founded in order to replace the Tennents' Log College; Dartmouth (1769) was founded by Eleazar Wheelock, a disciple of Edwards and Whitefield, ostensibly for the training of Indian preachers; and the Baptists, who hitherto had been without an educated ministry, were driven by competition to found the College of Rhode Island (later Brown University) at Providence in 1764. King's College (Columbia University), founded in New York City in 1754, was Anglican; Queen's College (Rutgers University), founded at New Brunswick, New Jersey, in 1766, was Dutch Reformed. The Philadelphia Academy (University of Pennsylvania), founded as a secondary school in 1740, was the only colonial college whose impetus and control was non-sectarian.

All these colleges were very small, according to modern standards; the largest student body was 200, and the record colonial graduating class 63 in number. Several, including the older William and Mary (1693), had to maintain preparatory schools in order to secure freshmen fit to follow college studies. William and Mary had the finest buildings and maintained a professor of law; all gave graduate training in theology; Philadelphia and King's established medical schools in 1765 and 1767. But the great majority of undergraduates followed a prescribed course in rhetoric, philosophy, mathematics, and the ancient classics (including a good deal of political theory), which proved to be an excellent preparation for public life. Out of 56 signers of the Declaration of Independence, 29 were alumni of colonial or British schools of higher learning; and most of the important framers of state and federal constitutions were college-trained men.

Nevertheless, only one of the three greatest Americans of the age, Jonathan Edwards, was a college graduate. George Washington (b. 1732) attained his superb poise and self-discipline and his character that met every test, through manly sports, roughing it in the wilderness, and contact with his gentle neighbors, the Fairfaxes of Belvoir, who employed him as a surveyor in his young manhood. They introduced him to the Stoic philosophy that breathes through Plutarch's *Lives,* Seneca's *Dialogue's,* and Addison's *Cato:*

> Turn up thy eyes to Cato!
> There may'st thou see to what a godlike height
> The Roman virtues lift up mortal man,
> While good, and just, and anxious for his friends,
> He's still severely bent against himself;
> Renouncing sleep, and rest, and food, and ease,
> He strives with thirst and hunger, toil and heat . . .

Benjamin Franklin, born in 1706, and only three years Edwards's junior, was the very antithesis of New England's saint in character and career. Essentially worldly and careerist, adopting just enough morality and religion to make a good impression, he found little time for deep philosophic thought, and none for manly sports. Yet his indefatigable industry enabled him to accumulate a competence early, after which the application of his inquiring mind to sundry problems made him one of the first scientists of his day. His pioneer work on electricity was of the highest significance, and led eventually, after countless experiments by others, to the dynamo, the telephone, and radio communication. Franklin suggested or initiated theories that required a century to verify and realize. His passion for improvement made him the first inventor of his time. Finding that most of the heat from open fireplaces went up the chimney, he designed the Franklin stove. Worried by the fires set by lightning, he invented the lightning rod. In an age when night air was popularly supposed to breed distempers, he advised people to sleep with open windows, in order to avoid colds. And during the long ocean passages in sail, of which he made many, he thought up improvements in seafaring technique, many of which have since been adopted. He was over a century ahead of naval architects in pointing out that wind resistance should be taken into account when designing the hulls and rigging of vessels, and that the same amount of canvas, if divided into a number of jib-headed sails, will give more speed than a few big square sails.

Franklin perhaps knew the art of living better than any other American or European of his day. He was on good terms with the world that he was eager to improve. He urged reform with a joke and a smile; he was never angry with stupid people who preferred the ways of their ancestors. He was a lover of music, played four different instruments, and invented a fifth, the glass harmonica, for which Mozart and Beethoven composed music. The most eminent statesmen, scientists, and men of letters in England and France consorted with Franklin, and valued his conversation; yet he never ceased to be a good democrat. Unlike many clever and successful men who have risen from lowly origins, he believed in the common people; and so they believed in him. He certainly knew more people, and more types of people, than anyone in his day, for colonial Philadelphia, as we have seen, was a microcosm of the America of the future. In that future, Franklin firmly believed. Of all Americans of his day, he was the greatest optimist; yet his vision fell short of the reality.

Franklin's college was a newspaper office, which many even today regard as the effective seat of education; certainly the ' fourth estate ' has done more, in recent years, to awaken Americans to the coming assault on them, than the colleges, churches, and politicians all together. Colonial journalism began with the colorless *Boston News-Letter* in 1704; seventeen years later Ben's elder brother James, with Ben (in his teens) as printer's devil and anonymous contributor, brought out *The New-England Courant.* ' Mr. Coranto,' as this paper called itself, was a sprightly sheet that attacked Harvard College and the Mather dynasty, even when those clerical autocrats (whose efforts to popularize scientific knowledge have never received their just due) were leading public opinion by advocating inoculation for smallpox. So far, so good; but when Mr. Coranto attacked the assembly, he got in trouble; and Ben left Boston for Philadelphia. There and in London Franklin continued his trade of printer; and he was one of the first to sense the use of almanacs to enlighten farm folk who could not afford a newspaper. In 1725 there were only five newspapers in the continental colonies; by 1765 there were twenty-five, two of them in German, and every colony but Delaware and New Jersey had at least one. All were four-page weekly journals, filled largely with foreign news clipped from London papers, but carrying a certain amount of local items, entrances and clearances of vessels, death notices, laws and debates of the assembly, advertisements of runaway slaves and ' fine assortments ' of English and West Indian goods for sale, notices of proprietors' meetings and public vendues, and texts of new laws and proclamations.

Libel laws in all the colonies were severe, and governments had to be criticized by innuendo rather than directly; yet one of the landmarks in the long struggle for the freedom of the press was the Zenger case in New York. John Peter Zenger, publisher of *The New-York Weekly Journal,* lent his columns to Lewis Morris's criticism of Governor Cosby, who haled him into court for false and scandalous libel. Andrew Hamilton, the most aged and reputable lawyer of Philadelphia, was imported to defend Zenger, and offered the defense that the articles complained of told the truth. Chief Justice De Lancey laid down the English principle that ' it is nevertheless a libel that is true,' defining a libel as anything understood to be ' scandalous and ironical.' Hamilton made a ringing appeal to the jury, declaring that the cause of English liberty, not merely the liberty of a poor printer was at stake, and won a verdict of ' not guilty.' This outcome was of the greatest importance for freedom of discussion in the future, when liberty was indeed the issue; Gouverneur Morris called the Zenger case ' the morning star of that liberty which subsequently revolutionized America.'

In another realm it was significant, too: the rise of a lawyer class. In the seventeenth century there was no legal profession in the colonies except in New York and Maryland; practitioners were regarded with contempt, and usually deserved it. With the increase of commerce after 1713 came an increase of litigation, and the need for skilled lawyers; and in one colony after another the men of best repute who had defended clients in the courts formed a bar and adopted rules of entry and of conduct that had the force of law. Prominent lawyers naturally were elected to the assemblies, where they were very clever in tying up the royal governors in legal knots, and making every local dispute a matter of the ' liberties of Englishmen.' So, when weightier matters were at issue in the seventeen sixties, the legal profession as well as the press were prepared.

5. Politics

Imperial organization from 1713 to 1760 continued along the lines already laid down under William and Mary. Several times the Board of Trade recommended that the charters of the two incorporated colonies (Connecticut and Rhode Island) and the two remaining proprietary provinces (Pennsylvania and Maryland) be vacated, and royal governors appointed; but the Whig ministries of Walpole, Pel-

ham and Newcastle, which governed England from 1721 to 1757, respected vested rights and did not wish to increase the power of the
Crown. Apart from these four jurisdictions (and Georgia until
1752), the Thirteen Colonies were royal provinces, governed theoretically by the king's instructions to his governors, and subject to a
double control over their laws, to appeals from their justice, and to
parliamentary legislation in all matters of trade, manufacture, and
navigation.

Actually the lower houses of the assemblies prevented the English
Government from reaping full results from this relative uniformity
in colonial administration, because they controlled both the purse
and the patronage; and colonial politics are largely the story of struggles between the assemblies and the royal or proprietary governors.
In such a conflict between colonists with a lively sense of their rights
and interests, and the representatives of a central government with
not so keen a sense of imperial needs or English interests, and which
did not wish to be bothered, the colonists generally won. The system
worked well enough, for the British Government by veto or disallowance was able to prevent things, such as abuse of paper money,
that it did not like; but it was unable to get positive things done,
such as full co-operation in time of war.

Colonial assemblies were not completely representative bodies, according to modern principles. In every colony there was a property
qualification for the franchise. Apportionment of members was everywhere unequal, unduly favoring the seaboard as against the interior. In New Hampshire, Pennsylvania, Virginia, and the Carolinas there was not half so much discontent with the English
Government as with the local governing clique that controlled the
assembly. In New Hampshire, for instance, Governor Wentworth
wished to allow new frontier towns to send representatives, but the
house refused, because the Eastern members feared heavy taxation
for frontier defense if they admitted Westerners. Yet with all these
defects, the assemblies were more representative than the unreformed
House of Commons. Their proceedings were open to public scrutiny and discussion. In some colonies journals of the lower house
were printed and distributed; in others the proceedings were reported
in the press.

Colonial assemblies tended to arrogate to themselves executive as
well as legislative power, because the executive represented an outside interest not responsible to their constituents. This they obtained

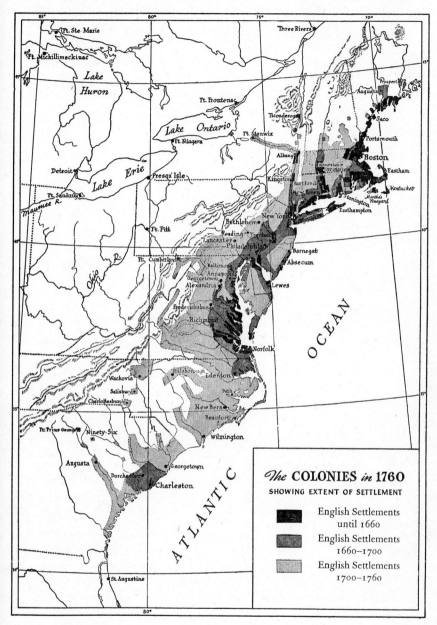

The Colonies in 1760

Adapted from a map prepared under the direction of Marion F. Lansing, from Channing's History of the United States, *courtesy of The Macmillan Company*

by a steady policy of attrition on the royal governors, who were dependent on them for salaries. The Board of Trade reported in 1754, with truth, that the New York Assembly ' have wrested from Your Majesty's governor, the nomination of all offices of government, the custody and direction of the public military stores, the mustering and direction of troops raised for Your Majesty's service, and in short almost every other part of executive government.' South Carolina even pushed encroachment to such an extent that the Anglican churches of the colony were instructed to pray for the assembly instead of the governor!

Royal governors, as the personal representatives of the king, were always treated with viceregal deference and respect by colonists who boasted of their loyalty; but the assemblies were so rich in procrastination and obstruction as frequently to provoke their excellencies to something very like common scolding. For instance, Governor Spotswood of Virginia on one occasion thus addressed his assembly:

> But to be plain with you, the true Interests of your Country, is not what you have troubled your heads about; all your proceedings have been calculated to Answer the Notions of the ignorant Populace; And if you can Excuse your Selves to them, you matter not how you Stand before God, your Prince, and all Judicious men, or before any others to whom, you think, you owe not your Elections.

To do the royal governors justice, most of them were able and honest men, who at best obtained so small a salary, according to eighteenth-century standards, that it is a mystery why the position was so sought after. One governor of North Carolina died with his salary eleven years overdue. They enjoyed no patronage beyond appointing members of the council and commissioning justices of the peace. Many were native Americans — Massachusetts, for instance, had native-born governors for sixty years and Englishmen for only twenty-two — and generally the Englishmen were the more popular. If the English Government had paid the salaries and perquisites of royal governors, its control would have been far more effective, yet never complete; for the governors of Virginia and Maryland, whose income came largely from fixed fees, had no soft time of it. Only occasionally the Crown appointed as governor a man who by taste and personality had the assembly ' eating out of his hand.'

Such a man was William Shirley, governor of Massachusetts from 1741–57. Appointed at a time of financial depression, when the Great

Awakening and a land bank scheme were boiling, and following an acrimonious salary conflict with the last governor, he nevertheless managed to please almost everyone. Far-sighted as regards the danger to New England from Canada, he obtained generous appropriations for defense, and, by the time King George's War broke out in 1744, had Massachusetts well prepared. The people regarded him as their champion, and the assembly allowed him to direct the armed forces during the war, voting him regularly a salary of £1000, without log-rolling. He conceived and carried out the famous siege and capture of Louisbourg by New England troops, with the co-operation of the Royal Navy. Shirley, as one of the small group of Englishmen who were preparing for one grand effort to overthrow French power in America, was able to overcome provincial jealousy and suspicion of the home government, and make Massachusetts a fighting spearhead of the conquering empire.

There were a few others, like Dinwiddie of Virginia and the two Wentworths of New Hampshire, who demonstrated how well the old empire could work with proper human instruments and an English policy at once consistent, firm, and just. Of course the empire could not have gone on in the same relatively haphazard way forever. The system of regulating colonial trade, currency, and manufacturing from London was acquiesced in until 1763, partly because there were many compensating benefits, like bounties and the encouragement of colonial shipbuilding, to balance the restrictions on commerce and manufacturing, partly because the more oppressive acts of trade, notably the Molasses and Iron Acts, were never completely enforced. Given patience in the colonies and wisdom at Whitehall, there might conceivably have been a gradual broadening of colonial autonomy, as has occurred in the latest fifty years of British imperial history, until the Thirteen Colonies had dominion home rule, after which they might peaceably have seceded and set up an independent republic, with consent of the mother country. But such an ideal prolongation and final ending of the colonial period in American history was too much to expect of human nature. Americans are not patient; and the overwhelming victory of 1763 raised new problems which the English ruling class of the reign of George III had not the wisdom to solve.

6. Wars

At the time of the Treaty of Utrecht, Louisiana consisted of the two posts at Biloxi and Mobile. New life was infused into the colony in 1717 when Louis XV conferred a monopoly of its trade for fourteen years on the Mississippi Company, one of the speculative enterprises launched by the Scots financier John Law. New Orleans was founded in 1718; but the French were so slow in sensing the possibilities of Louisiana for trade and settlement, and their sugar islands were so productive, that in 1745 Louisiana had a population of only thirty-two hundred Europeans, and two thousand Negro slaves. Within ten years it had received an important addition in the ' Cajans,' the Acadians forcibly transferred by the British from Nova Scotia. Yet, throughout this period, Louisiana was but a thin line of settlement along the lower Mississippi and the Gulf, up to Spanish Florida where, again, European sovereignty was maintained only by a string of presidios and missions.

Owing to the enterprise of the Carolina peltry and slave traders, English influence was paramount among the Indians of the future Gulf states east of the Mississippi, and among the Cherokee. When war with Spain seemed impending, General Oglethorpe was sent back to Georgia with a regiment of British soldiers; and as there was something about the gallant general that appealed to Indians, he was able to preserve their fidelity during the War of Jenkins' Ear.

That inconclusive conflict between England and Spain arose out of the English traders abusing their *asiento,* the privilege acquired at the Treaty of Utrecht of sending one African slave ship annually to Porto Bello on the Isthmus of Panama. Instead of one ship, the English traders usually sent a fleet, laden with much merchandise besides ' black ivory.' All this was welcome to the people on the Spanish Main, who hated the home monopoly of their trade; but the Spanish Government retorted by commissioning a fleet of *guarda costas* (revenue cutters) manned largely by ex-pirates, which committed abominable excesses on peaceful British traders throughout the Caribbean; that was how Jenkins lost his ears. Another Spanish grievance was the continual cutting of logwood by English, largely from Jamaica, on that section of the Spanish Main which by their persistence eventually became the colony of British Honduras. England declared war on Spain in 1739, and Walpole's government planned to take possession of Central America by attacks on both sides. Both were unsuccessful. Admiral Vernon, with thousands of volunteers from the Thirteen Colonies, nine-tenths of whom never returned (but including George Washington's elder brother who returned to build Mount Vernon), attacked Cartagena fruitlessly in 1741, made a demonstration before Porto Bello, but neglected to co-operate with Oglethorpe in a siege of St. Augustine, Florida that failed (1740). Two years later a Spanish fleet of thirty-six vessels attempted to conquer Georgia; but Oglethorpe, commanding kilted Highlanders from the Scots settlement at Frederica, was too much for them. After that, there were no important hostilities during this war on the southern frontier.

The Pacific end of the English attack was even more unfortunate. Commodore George Anson was given command of a small squadron manned in part by 'the most crazy and infirm' old pensioned soldiers, and sent around Cape Horn to capture Spanish treasure ships, and Peru and Panama, before the Spaniards were warned. The Spaniards were warned, Anson's fleet took a terrible beating off the Horn, scurvy decimated his feeble crews, and except for the temporary occupation of Paita, Peru, and the capture of an immensely rich Manila galleon, the expedition accomplished nothing. Only one of the six vessels reached home, in 1744.

Far more important for the future of America was a voyage in the Pacific that went completely unnoticed by colonials who had high hopes of Anson and Vernon. Vitus Bering, a Danish navigator in the service of Russia, discovered the straits that bear his name in 1728; in 1741 he built two ships at Petropavlovsk in Kamchatka, touched the southern coast of Alaska, discovered the Aleutian Islands, and, driven ashore on Bering Island, there died. Although Russia took no effective possession of Alaska before 1784, her title to that territory which passed to the United States in 1867, was based on Bering's voyage.

In the meantime the most effective exploration of the Far West was being made by French explorers searching out an overland route to the Pacific; for even yet, with no accurate method to ascertain longitude, the great breadth of North America was not suspected. The Chevalier de Varennes de la Vérendrye, in command of a French post on Lake Nipigon, heard tales from the Indians of a great river — possibly the Columbia — that emptied into a salt ocean. In 1731 with his three sons he began a series of expeditions in search of it that covered twelve years, in the course of which he built forts on Rainy

Lake, the Lake of the Woods, Lakes Winnipeg and Manitoba, at the mouth of the Saskatchewan river, and on the site of the city of Winnipeg; he crossed the Black Hills of South Dakota, and reached the foothills of the Bighorn range of the Rocky Mountains before turning eastward again. La Vérendrye was the first explorer to reach the High Plains, and to mingle with the buffalo Indians. Lewis and Clark, sixty-two years later, fulfilled the quest of the gallant Chevalier.

In 1744 the Anglo-Spanish conflict merged into the War of the Austrian Succession, and France again came to grips with England in America. Again there was *la petite guerre* along the New York-New England border; and *la grande guerre* also, but not according to Vauban. The New Englanders' attack on the strong French fortress of Louisbourg, planned by the lawyer-governor Shirley and led by the Maine merchant Pepperell, was one of the maddest schemes in the history of modern warfare, a sort of large-scale ' commando '; but it worked, through amazing bumptiousness and aggressiveness. The Yankee yokels who pitched camp before the ' impregnable ' fortress refused to obey any of the rules of eighteenth-century warfare, and the French governor was so baffled and alarmed by these odd antics that he surrendered (1745). Next year Louis XV sent a large fleet under Admiral the Duke d'Anville to retake Louisbourg and punish Boston; but the fleet was dispersed by a storm and pestilence, and the admiral died. A second formidable squadron, sent out the next year, was intercepted and defeated by an English fleet under Anson the circumnavigator. By the Treaty of Aachen, which ended this war in 1748, the English restored Louisbourg to France in return for Madras; the disappointment of New England was assuaged by the Crown's paying the entire expenses of the expedition.

This treaty was only a truce in the final conflict for mastery in North America. In Virginia, where Spotswood's expedition had called attention to the trans-Appalachian region, Thomas Lee, president of the council, organized in 1747 the Ohio Company, with the object of opening a route from the Potomac to the Ohio for Indian trade, and making a profit from western land by cashing in on Virginia's ancient claim to the Northwest. Shortly after, the Loyal Company and the Greenbrier Company were organized by other prominent Virginians, such as Peter Jefferson the father of Thomas, Dr. Thomas Walker, and Thomas Nelson; while George Fairfax and George Washington's elder brothers were taken into the Ohio Com-

pany. The story of their rivalries and grants, and their efforts to mo-
nopolize the Indian trade of the upper Ohio by employing expert
Pennsylvania fur traders like George Croghan and Thomas Cresap,
is too complicated to relate here; the important point is that they constituted a threat to communications between Canada, the Illinois
Country, and Louisiana, which the French could not afford to
ignore.

In 1749 the governor of Canada sent Céleron de Bienville with
several hundred Canadians and Indians in a fleet of batteaux and
canoes to take possession of the Ohio valley. They carried over from
Lake Erie to Lake Chautauqua, paddled down the Allegheny river
past the site of Pittsburgh into the Ohio, down the Ohio and up the
Miami, and returned to Canada by the Maumee river and Lake Erie.
This expedition was followed up in 1753 by the Marquis Duquesne,
who established a chain of log forts on the Allegheny and upper
Ohio. Now, in 1750 French Canada had a population of only fifty or
sixty thousand farmers and fur-traders, while the English colonies
had one and one-quarter million people. The pretension of the
French to reserve for themselves the unsettled parts of North America was one that the English could hardly be expected to admit. Governor Dinwiddie of Virginia, who was one with the Virginia land
speculators, sent young George Washington up to the Allegheny to
protest, in 1753. Protest being unavailing, the governor commissioned
George (aged 22) a lieutenant-colonel of Virginia militia, and the
next year sent him with one hundred and fifty men to forestall the
French at the forks of the Ohio. But the French had arrived first, and
built Fort Duquesne on the site of Pittsburgh. At Great Meadows in
western Pennsylvania, our young lieutenant-colonel, unmindful that
one must always let the enemy make the first aggression, fired a shot
on a French force under Jumonville that began the last and greatest
of the colonial wars. The enemy rallied and Washington's force was
forced to capitulate and go home; for this was one of these wars that
was not yet a war — it was not declared for two years.

Both Virginia and New England were eager to call it a war and
get going. Virginia wished to preserve her ancient charter rights to
all the territory west and northwest of her settled area; Massachusetts was eager as she had been for the past sixty years to clear the
French out of Canada. But the Duke of Newcastle, First Secretary
of State in England, a timid and vacillating politician, was by no
means eager for war; nor was the government of Louis XV in

France. Pressure from Parliament and from nationalist desire to maintain England's rights to the American West forced Newcastle to do something; but he imagined that he could simply seize the disputed territory in America, and localize the hostilities. So in the fall of 1754 he sent General Braddock to America with only two regiments, and powers of Commander-in-Chief.

Considering that officially there was still peace between George II and Louis XV, things were pretty lively in the colonies in the year 1755. Braddock's expedition marched north and west from Virginia against Fort Duquesne. His defeat when only a few miles from the fort is one of the things one always remembers; it would be better to recall what young Washington, who was with him, wrote: ' General Braddock was unfortunate, and his character was much too severely treated. He was one of the honestest and best men of the British officers with whom I was acquainted; even in manner of fighting he was not more to blame than others.' The public wanted a scapegoat, and Braddock was dead. He took the proper precautions, and he was not ambushed; but all the ' breaks ' went against him; and the ' breaks ' are as important in war as in football.

Braddock's defeat brought the Indians of the Northwest over to the French side, threw back the English frontier, and exposed the western settlements of Pennsylvania, Maryland, and Virginia to a series of devastating attacks.

The other operations of the English in 1755 were inept, though not disastrous. Governor Shirley failed to take Fort Niagara, on which the whole English effort should have been concentrated; for Niagara was the French gateway to the West. William Johnson, a clever Irishman of the Mohawk valley who kept the Six Nations quiet, defeated the French on Lake George and was rewarded with a knighthood, because his was the only English victory that year; but he was unable to capture Crown Point on Lake Champlain, and the French built Fort Ticonderoga to back up Crown Point.

This ' Old French and Indian War,' as our forebears called it, might have been localized but for a shift in alliances in Europe; Austria came over to the side of France, and Frederick the Great anticipated matters by invading Saxony. Russia, Sweden, most of the German states, and (in 1761) Spain allied with France and Austria against England, Portugal, and Prussia. Before the war was over it had extended to all parts of the world. There was naval warfare between England, France, and Spain in the Atlantic, the Mediterranean, the West Indies, and the Indian Ocean; battles on the Asiatic continent between Dupleix and Clive and their East Indian allies. Hostilities even reached the Philippines, where the English captured Manila after the war was over in Europe.

The years 1756–57 were disastrous for England, in America and elsewhere. The Earl of Loudoun, who became Commander-in-Chief in America, was justly described by Governor Shirley as ' a pen and ink man whose greatest energies were put forth in getting ready to begin.' Washington's Virginia militia with great difficulty held the line of the Shenandoah valley against the Indians. Oswego, the English fort on Lake Ontario, was captured by the French General Montcalm, who then advanced down Lake Champlain to Lake George, captured Fort William Henry, and isolated the English garrison there. Three thousand French troops reached Canada, despite all efforts of the British navy, for Newcastle did not dare attack them in narrow seas before war was declared, and Admiral Boscawen failed to catch them off the St. Lawrence. Admiral Byng lost Minorca in the Mediterranean to the French, and was courtmartialled and shot for cowardice, ' pour encourager les autres.' In India, the British lost Calcutta. On the Continent, Frederick the Great was defeated by the French and Austrians, and King George's son, the Duke of Cumberland, surrendered his English and Hanoverian army to the French. At the end of 1757 the military experts confidently predicted that France would win, hands down; and that England and Prussia would soon be compelled to sign a peace, which would give France all North America west of the Alleghenies, and reduce Prussia to a second-rate power.

Yet the whole complexion of the war was changed in 1758 when William Pitt, the future Earl of Chatham, became Secretary of State, head of the ministry, and virtual dictator of the Empire. Pitt was an Englishman with a genius for organization, a knack for grand strategy, and a knowledge of men. While most Englishmen regarded the American scene as a secondary theatre of war, Pitt saw that the principal object for England should be the conquest of Canada and the American West, thus carving out a new field for Anglo-American expansion. Pitt's policy was simple and direct: subsidize Frederick the Great to carry on warfare on the European theatre of war; use the navy to command the high seas and contain the French fleet in French ports; and, finally, concentrate the military might of England in America, under young and energetic generals.

James Wolfe, son of a country squire, was a tall, lanky, narrow-shouldered young man with vivid red hair. Ambition, audacity, genius, and a fierce concentration on becoming master of his profession made Wolfe the most Napoleonic soldier in English history; and if his victory on the Plains of Abraham paved the way for American independence, it was a lucky break for America that he lost his life that day, and did not live to command British armies against the United States. Wolfe was only 31 years old in 1758, when Pitt made him first brigadier general under General Jeffry Amherst, who was just ten years older, and whom Pitt had selected as commander-in-chief by passing over whole columns of senior officers. These two formed a perfect team with Admiral Boscawen in recapturing Louisbourg; and Louisbourg, though infinitely better fortified than in 1745 and more skilfully defended, was captured in July 1758.

The same year Colonel Dudley Bradstreet of Massachusetts, with a force of New Englanders, captured Fort Frontenac, where the St. Lawrence flows out of Lake Ontario; and General Forbes, with George Washington as his right-hand man, marched across Pennsylvania and captured Fort Duquesne, renaming it Pittsburgh after the great war minister. Clive won the upper hand in India, and Frederick the Great broke out from his encirclement of French, Russian, and Austrian enemies, and in swift succession won the battles of Rossbach, Leuthen, and Crefeld.

Then came 1759, England's *annus mirabilis* — the acme of the old empire, when England reached a pinnacle of glory that she had never reached before, and, as Horace Walpole wrote, the very bells of London were worn threadbare pealing out victories. It was then that David Garrick wrote the words for that stirring old song, ' Heart of Oak: '

> Come, cheer up, my lads! 'tis to glory we steer,
> To add something more to this wonderful year;
> To honor we call you as free men, not slaves,
> For who are so free as the sons of the waves?
>> Heart of oak are our ships, heart of oak are our men;
>> We always are ready, steady! boys, steady!
>> We'll fight and we'll conquer again and again.

In Europe, Frederick won the Battle of Minden; on the coast of France, the British navy won the Battle of Quiberon Bay, which rendered the French incapable of sending reinforcements to Canada; in the West Indies, a combined naval and military expedition conquered Guadeloupe; in North America, Sir William Johnson captured Fort Niagara, key to the West.

Yet the greatest campaign that year was the march on Quebec. Wolfe advanced in transports, with a convoy under Admiral Saunders, up the St. Lawrence river to Quebec, where General Amherst with a land force was supposed to co-operate with him. Amherst captured Crown Point and Ticonderoga, but never got within striking distance of Quebec. Thrice in previous wars this failure in co-ordination had meant that Quebec remained French; again, in 1775–76, a similar failure on the part of the Americans meant that it remained British. But Wolfe's forces carried on. He had only four thousand men, with Robert Monckton (aged 33) his second in command, and George Townshend (aged 35) his third brigadier.

Wolfe, for all his youthfulness, was well prepared for his task. So earnest a student of military strategy that some of his brother officers considered him a little queer, he could size up a situation at a glance and tell instinctively what risks to take. Before Rochefort, in 1757, he had learned the absolute necessity of co-operation between army and navy. He anticipated Frederick the Great in recognizing the value of a concentrated musketry. And he was the first English or European officer to train his troops in precision and accuracy of fire. After abortive attacks on Quebec from two sides, and failing also to draw the defenders away, Wolfe worked out his plan of placing a force on the Plains of Abraham above the city by a ruse. And with a single concentrated volley on the Plains of Abraham, a volley withheld until his men could see the white of their enemies' eyes, Wolfe won Canada on 13 September 1759 — as he learned before his death on the battlefield.

After the surrender of Quebec, it remained only to mop up. Montreal surrendered in 1760, and French power ceased on the North American continent. Only in the West war continued with the Indians, who could not believe that their old friends the French were beaten; but after a last flare-up, the conspiracy of Pontiac, that died too.

In Europe the war dragged on, and Spain was dragged in, which gave the British an opportunity to capture Havana and Manila in 1762. In the meantime the new king George III wearied of Mr. Pitt, who was becoming altogether too powerful for royalty, dismissed him, opened negotiations with the enemy, and purchased peace by renouncing a number of the conquests. By this Peace of Paris (1763), all French Canada and the Spanish Floridas were ceded to Great Britain; while France, in order to compensate Spain for her losses, ceded Louisiana and all French claims to the west of the Mississippi to Spain. There was some talk of returning Canada to France in exchange for the sugar island of Guadeloupe; this scheme was defeated not so much by prescience for the future, as from the fear of the British planters that their market would be flooded with sugar.

Even with the return of these islands to France, and of Havana and the Philippines to Spain, the war ended in a mighty victory for the English. The British Empire bestrode the world like a colossus: India gained, all North America to the Mississippi won, and the best of the West Indies; supremacy of the seas confirmed. As the historian Seeley wrote, ' through all that remained of the eighteenth century the nation looked back upon these splendid years as upon a happiness that could never return; . . . long it continued to be the unique boast of the Englishman,

> That Chatham's language was his mother tongue
> And Wolfe's great name compatriot with his own.'

English, Scots, Irish and colonists spilled over with expressions of loyalty; and at a meeting in Boston to celebrate the peace, James Otis declared that the true interests of Britain and her colonies were identical, and warned, ' What God in his providence has united, let no man dare attempt to pull asunder! '

Yet the war was not paid for, and the price of glory comes high. The French menace was ended forever; but a flock of new domestic problems within the empire came home to roost on post-war statesmen, and to clamor for solution.

VI

LIBERTY AND EMPIRE
1754–1763

1. *The Imperial Problem and the Peace of Paris*

THE generation that came to maturity between the Peace of Paris and the inauguration of President Washington had to solve more serious and original political problems than any later generation cf Americans. It was then that the great beacons of American principles, such as the Declaration of Independence, the Virginia Bill of Rights, and the Federal Constitution, were lighted; it was then that institutions of permanent and profound import in the history of America and of liberty were crystallized. The period was not only revolutionary and destructive, but creative and constructive; moreover the British connection was not the most important thing that was destroyed, nor was national independence the most important thing that was created. A new federal empire was erected on the ruins of the old empire, American ideas proclaimed, and the American character defined.

This period from 1763 to 1789 has a singular unity, from which the rush of events and the din of arms can easily distract our attention. We must not let the high-strung debates that preceded the American Revolution, or the vivid events of the War for Independence, hide from us the real meaning of these years. Just as the Greek tragedies of the Periclean Age are concerned not merely with the conflicts of gods and heroes, but with the depths of human nature; just as the stories of the Old Testament explore the mysterious relation between God and man, so we may discern, behind the noisy conflict of words and arms in the American Revolution, the stirring of a political problem older than recorded history: the balancing of liberty with order. That underlay all the tumult and the shouting. And this ancient question between liberty and order resolves itself into two: the horizontal or federal problem of distributing power between one central and many regional governments; and the vertical or democratic one of how far the masses of mankind shall be entrusted with control. These two problems are the warp and woof of American history through the Civil War; and the circumstances of our own time have simply restated these ancient problems in terms of liberty *vs*. security. To what extent shall the federal and state governments regulate the affairs of men, in order to save, and possibly to improve, society? How far shall the masses, having won the right to control, abdicate the exercise of a right that they cannot possibly exercise themselves, to elected and appointed officials? Can there be any liberty worth having, under the complexities of modern society, without security?

In excluding the French from continental North America, the British government took over more responsibility than it could handle. At one stroke the British possessions in North America were more than doubled in extent, and a race alien in language and religion was brought into the empire. Baffling questions of Indian relations, fur trade, land policy, and military and political administration were created. In short, Great Britain faced more urgently than ever before the great riddle of imperial organization; and the history of her relations with her older American colonies during the next twenty-five years can be related largely as an attempt to find a solution. Yet American independence was only a half-solution, for the independent States found themselves confronted with the same difficulties, and did not find a way out until they adopted the Federal Constitution of 1787.

From 1763 to 1775 Americans naturally asserted their rights, while Englishmen reminded them of their duties; yet the thinking men on both sides of the Atlantic were grappling with the same task: how to organize this vast empire so that the military, political, and economic interests of the whole would be furthered, the various parts nicely adjusted to each other, and a certain degree of local autonomy preserved. Men who were at best bewildered by the difficulties and at worst indifferent and ignorant, had to face or to evade these practical issues. Americans argued and until 4 July 1776, fought, not for independence, but for a guaranteed free status within the empire. Englishmen until 1775 agreed, and until 1782 fought, not to reduce Americans to political 'slavery,' but to their 'proper place' in the empire: to a political status similar to that which Puerto Rico enjoys in the American empire of today.

Let us analyze the major elements of this problem of imperial order. For two centuries the British Empire had been a commercial one, dominated largely by merchants in profitable alliance with the landed gentry, and developing in accordance with the philosophy of mercantilism. The interests of this ruling class were primarily commercial, and it regarded the empire, quite properly, as a commercial empire, various parts of which were valuable only in so far as they contributed to the wealth of Great Britain. But the immense acquisitions of the Seven Years' War produced a subtle transition from commercial to territorial imperialism, from the idea of governing colonies with a view to their trade, to governing colonies with a view to their revenue and man power. This meant, as Governor Hutchinson of Massachusetts wrote, that 'there must be an abridgment of so-called English Liberties in America.' The new idea did not replace the old, but reinforced the mercantile idea, so that the Acts of Trade were tightened up and strengthened to an extent that began to work real hardships on important colonial interests. Just as today we find that we need a bigger navy because we have a wider territory and commerce to defend, and also need a larger merchant marine to support the bigger navy; so in the years after 1763 British statesmen felt that a bigger empire required more men and ships. These would cost money, and unless the British taxpayer supplied it all, the colonies must contribute; and revenue could be extracted from the colonies only through a stronger central administration, at the expense of colonial self-government. The Thirteen Colonies tried to escape this vicious circle by squaring it, and finally broke through with independence. Then they found much the same problem of adjustment between parts and whole confronting their new nation. Federalism — a form of government which seemed just as absurd to eighteenth-century Englishmen as squaring the circle does to twentieth-century mathematicians — federalism provided America with a solution.

We have seen how there grew up in the American colonies a large body of English accustomed to managing their own political, economic, and religious affairs. Alongside these, men and women of different races and backgrounds ranged themselves. Scots, Irish, Germans, Swiss, French, and others had come to the New World; people alien to the English tradition, but falling easily into the American temper. Indeed the numerous Scots-Irish and Germans who established themselves on the frontiers took very unkindly to control of any sort.

These then were the elements with which the imperial statesmen of eighteenth-century England had to contend: colonists trained to self-government and impatient of interference; self-reliant and enterprising merchants, politically conscious mechanics, planters proudly refractory to imperial discipline, yeomen of the uplands who knew little and cared less for laws and regulations of the empire; Scots-Irish who remembered Londonderry, Catholic Irish who had had not forgotten Cromwell; Germans who loved their new homes but knew not Britain; colonial assemblies sensitive to any infringement on what they regarded as their constituents' rights. And it was ominous for the future that very few Americans were capable of thinking imperially; that all but a small minority were aggressively determined to go their own ways and live their own lives here in the America they had converted from a wilderness to a home.

2. *The Albany Plan*

Before the Seven Years' War an attempt was made to bring the imperial machinery up to date. On the instance of the Board of Trade, a congress of delegates elected by the assemblies of seven colonies met at Albany in June 1754. After declaring a colonial union ' absolutely necessary for their preservation,' the Congress adopted a plan drafted by Benjamin Franklin. This Albany Plan of Union, though never adopted, was prophetic. With remarkable foresight it allotted matters of general concern to a central body and left those of a local nature to the individual colonies: much as the Constitution of 1787 divided power among the Federal Government and the states. There would have been a President-General appointed and supported by the Crown, and a Grand Council chosen triennially by the colonial assemblies; the number of representatives from each colony to be determined by the amount paid by that colony into the general treasury — a typical bit of Franklin foxiness. This government would have had power to make war and peace with the Indians, to regulate their trade, to purchase Indian lands, found and regulate new settlements, to raise military and naval forces, to levy taxes and customs duties ' such as may be collected with the least inconvenience to the people,' and to appoint a general treasurer and a particular treasurer in each colony to collect these moneys. Franklin always believed that the adoption of this system might have averted the Revolution. It was certainly a practical solution to the problem of imperial order, and served as a basis for the later attempts to

solve the same problem within the United States. There is a definite continuity between the Albany Plan, the Articles of Confederation, and the Federal Constitution; and Franklin was the author of
the one, principal architect of the second, and an important member of the body which adopted the third.

The Albany Plan failed, however, of adoption. ' The Assemblies
. . . thought there was too much *prerogative* in it,' wrote Franklin,
' and in England it was judged to have too much of the *democratic.*'
The colonial assemblies objected to granting to any ' foreign ' body
any taxing power; and it was not until they had experienced two
great wars that in 1788 they finally made up their minds to do that.
Hence the colonies weathered the war without any further union
than came from the old imperial organization. Although that war
was waged for American objectives of trade, land, and security;
and although the colonies asked for and obtained sufficient aid from
England to attain these objectives, their own part in it was secondary.
Massachusetts, Connecticut, New York, and New Jersey alone contributed their full quota of soldiers to the common cause. Elsewhere there was a woeful lack of co-operation. Requisitions of men
and money were flouted. Commercial regulations were evaded.
Trade with the enemy flourished. This was not due to disloyalty,
for the colonies were eager to win; but to lack of sufficient imperial
control to override the petty bickerings and jealousies within each
colony. Pennsylvania would not levy taxes unless her proprietor
conceded what he considered his right of tax-emption. Virginia,
whose most unmilitary spirit was deplored by young Lieutenant-
Colonel Washington, would have her levies controlled by a board of
directors, until the Governor gave up his ' fee of a pistole.' The most
pressing exigencies of defense were used by colonial assemblies, proprietors, and royal governors, to score points on one another, or to
force some concession on internal matters. It was left to the regular
army and navy, directed by the matchless strategy of Pitt, to gain the
victories that won the war.

Naturally experience such as this taught all thoughtful men that
the imperial fabric was defective, and that a thorough reformation
was necessary before the next war came. And the fruits of victory
placed a fresh strain on the fabric, which broke asunder.

3. *The West*

The West was the third and most immediate element in the problem of imperial reorganization. There had been difficulties of adjustment between the old-settled, the newly-settled and the un-settled regions for at least a century before 1763, and there were such difficulties for more than a century after. This Western problem may be likened to a rope of many strands, now twisted in a regular pattern, but more often tangled with each other, and with strands from other ropes, or tortured into Gordian knots which only war could sever. Of these strands we can distinguish as the most important, the international and military problem, the Indian problem, the fur trade, the problem of territorial administration and land policy, and the political problem, particularly with reference to the French Canadians.

The international aspect of it: whether the American West would be won by France, Spain, or Great Britain, or partitioned among them, was only partially solved by the Seven Years' War. To the south and west of the new British possessions lay the Spanish empire, wealthy and well organized, if sparsely populated. Spain was still a power to be reckoned with, still the largest and the most powerful empire in the New World, covering all South and Central America and Mexico, together with the coast of California, Texas, and the west bank of the Mississippi. Under Charles III, the ablest monarch since Philip IV, Spain became aggressive and expansive for a brief space. Jealously she guarded Mexico; and in spite of her acquisition of a new bulwark in the shape of Louisiana, she was eager to recover the two Floridas which had gone to England, and the east bank of the Mississippi as well.

Although the Peace of 1763 finally disposed of the French danger to the English colonies, they were by no means sure of it; and events both in America and in Europe have proved that France does not lightly renounce territory which she has relinquished by force. Indeed Napoleon's recovery of Louisiana in 1800 vindicated English fears in 1770. The French government continued mischievous intrigues with its former Indian allies, and kept its finger on the pulse of colonial discontent.

While the danger from French and Spanish ambition always loomed on the horizon, the Indian danger was very real and present. Pontiac's conspiracy of 1763 was the most formidable Indian outbreak of the century. Goaded to desperation by the tactics of the English traders and trappers, affronted by the refusal of the English to continue the French practice of annual gifts, and foreseeing the occupation of their hunting grounds by English settlers, the Indians of the Ohio valley formed a grand confederacy under the leadership of Pontiac, chief of the Ottawa. Every western fort except Detroit and Pittsburgh was captured by the savages, the frontier was ravaged from Niagara to Virginia, and hundreds of pioneer families were wiped out. Virginia and Maryland struck back at the foe; but Pennsylvania, the worst sufferer, failed to provide adequate defense for her frontiersmen. The uprising was finally crushed not by Americans, but by British red-coats. If the colonies could not even co-operate for their own defense against the Indians, could there be any doubt that stronger imperial control was needed?

Nor was the Indian question merely one of military offense; it was much more complicated than that. How were the Indians to be treated after they had been brought to terms? Should their hunting grounds be reserved for them in the interests of humanity and the fur trade, or, if not, by what means were they to be secured against speculators and land-hungry frontiersmen? In short it was imperative to work out some broad Indian policy; to provide not only for present emergency but for future developments. Such a task was pre-eminently one that required centralized control.

Closely connected with the Indian problem was the fur trade. Peltry still dominated the economic life of Canada and West Florida, and was a leading interest of New York, Carolina, and Louisiana. This fur trade was always a major stake in the winning of the West; it was a main factor in American foreign relations through the War of 1812, and again in the struggle for Oregon and the upper Missouri. It was not merely an international rivalry, but a ruthless competition among people of the same country, in a business which knew no ethics; and this competition became more intense when the Peace of Paris opened up a new field for colonial and English greed. Lord Shelburne declared in 1775, 'The peltry or skin trade, my lords, is a matter which I presume to affirm is of the last importance to the trade and commerce of the colonies and this country. The regulation of this business has cost his Majesty's ministers more time and trouble than any one matter that I know of.' As fast as the peltry of one region was exhausted, the trappers and traders moved farther west, where they competed with the Spaniards for an Indian clientele; or by too eager salesmanship they stirred up the nearer Indians, who retaliated on the nearest white family. So here was another ungrateful task for the harassed officials at Whitehall: regulation of a group of unprincipled traders who could not be brought to see that contented Indians produced the most fur. And this aspect too of the Western problem was inherited by the United States government.

More perplexing and more permanent than any of these questions was the problem of territorial administration and land policy. This problem, again, was as old as the first English settlement in America and has remained to vex American politics almost until the present day. Should the extensive domain acquired from the French, Spaniards, and Indians be conserved as an Indian and hunting reserve or opened in whole or part to white settlement? If the latter, should land be regarded as a source of revenue, and assessed with quit-rents, or should quick settling be encouraged? And if so, how? By ceding it to land companies in large tracts, or in small farms to individual settlers? And for what price? Although the home government did not go very deeply into this question, it sincerely desired so to regulate settlement as to protect the settler and profit the empire.

All these questions of policy, baffling enough in themselves, were complicated by politics and by land speculation. The prize of millions of acres was a very alluring one, and excited cupidity and rapaciousness both in America and in England. Land companies, as we have seen, had been formed, even before the war, with a view to securing large tracts in the contested region. As soon as the war was over, the Board of Trade was bombarded with petitions for more grants of land in the newly acquired West. Yet whose was the West to grant?

Almost every colony had claims. The rights of some, such as Virginia, were long-established and well-founded; the claims of others, such as New York, were doubtful and tenuous. Almost any policy Great Britain adopted would step on someone's corns. But everyone will now admit that the land question was essentially imperial, and that a land policy ought to be administered by a central authority. At least the United States afterwards acted upon that assumption.

Finally, there was the political problem. If new settlements were to be established in the West, what degree of self-government should be permitted them, and what should be their relation to the older colonies and to the mother country? Moreover, the Treaty of 1763 had given England jurisdiction over some sixty thousand French Canadians, men alien in race and tongue and faith, and unaccustomed to English traditions of law and administration. Some general scheme of government had to be provided for these new additions to the empire and some method discovered to gain the friendship and support of the powerful Catholic Church which largely controlled the *habitans* of Canada.

The Western problem proved to be permanent. Before 1775 the diverse strands of defense, Indian relations, furs, land policy, and politics were English and colonial problems; after that time they entered into the web of American development, and all of them continued to occupy a prominent position in American politics far into the nineteenth century.

4. *British Politics and George III*

Since Parliament initiated the new colonial policy to which the colonists objected, and passsed the laws which finally precipitated the War of Independence, British politics were a factor in the American Revolution. In general, the British political system of that era has been too much simplified by historians. There was no clean-cut division between Pitt, Burke, and liberty-loving whigs on the one side, and a tyrannical king and sinister tories on the other. The old tory party no longer existed; the new tory party of Canning and Castlereagh had not yet arisen. In fact the English political situation in 1760–70 was not unlike that of the United States in the ' era of good feeling.' The whigs had successfully eliminated the tories by fastening on them the stigma 'pro-French' and of supporting the Jacobite uprising in 1745, just as the Jeffersonian Republicans later eliminated the Federalists by the stigma of disloyalty and the Hartford Convention; in both instances, the dominant party broke up into factions. Even King George called himself a whig, and all the ministries with which the colonists had to deal were whig ministries. And to carry the parallel further, George III played the rôle of Andrew Jackson in reviving the two-party system, although, like our ' Old Hickory,' he thought party opposition highly unnecessary and even slightly treasonable.

For twenty years from 1760, British ministries were formed much as they were formerly in France: by making a *bloc*. The king asked someone to be premier, and he made a combination of leaders who controlled enough votes in the House of Commons to carry on the king's government, without much or any regard to political principles. Ministries fell because the *bloc* was weakened by some important person not getting the job he wanted for a relative or supporter, and so voting his gang against the government; or because the premier did not satisfy the king. The American question did not cause a single ministerial crisis until 1782. In fact American questions were of secondary importance in British politics until 1774. Almost every year there were rumors of war with France or Spain or both; there were many absorbing domestic questions such as what should be done about Jack Wilkes; and the game of politics took about all the time that ministers could spare from their sports, their gaming, and their dinners.

Of the different whig factions, the one which showed most sympathy for the Americans was the 'old whig,' so-called because it claimed to inherit the whig traditions of 1688. The 'old whigs' included the Duke of Richmond, General Conway, the Marquess of Rockingham and his sometime private secretary Edmund Burke; Charles James Fox joined them in 1774. Usually allied with them was William Pitt and his large personal following. Pitt and the 'old whigs' were the most liberal groups in British politics, and the most conservative; indeed they opposed the taxation of the colonies as much because it was new as because it was unfair. Although willing to make many concessions in practice to colonial demands, they firmly believed in the legislative supremacy of Parliament over the entire empire. Pitt, in his speech against the Stamp Act, declared, 'It is my opinion that this kingdom has no right to lay a tax upon the colonies. At the same time I assert the authority of this kingdom over the colonies to be sovereign and supreme.' If, however, the Americans ventured to attack the Acts of Trade, they would have no support from him. 'I would not permit them to manufacture a lock of wool or a horseshoe or a hobnail.' So it is not surprising that few colonists ever did attack the Acts of Trade before 1776; that would have lost them their chief support in British politics. Actually, the continental colonies were manufacturing not only their horseshoes and hobnails, but most of the ironmongery and tools that they needed, and exporting a surplus to the West Indies.

Pitt's following included the Duke of Grafton, who succeeded him as prime minister in 1767, and Lord Shelburne, who had a broader comprehension of colonial problems than any English statesman of his time, especially of the Western question. Shelburne was sent to France for his education, and returned with a polish and politeness that made him an object of suspicion to the English — for this was the ' Goddamme Sir! ' age in English manners. Highly intelligent, he tried to get what he wanted by indirect methods rather than go to the trouble to explain to ignorant colleagues, and so earned his nickname ' The Jesuit of Berkeley Square ' — the place of his stately town mansion.

Unfortunately the ' old whigs,' though rich in talents, were poor in leadership. Rockingham, a young man better known on the turf than in politics, was well-meaning but weak, and a halting speaker in the House. Pitt, a peerless leader in time of war, was inept in time of peace; and some strange malady thrust him out of the picture almost as soon as he became premier, in 1767.

Next, there were a number of factions following such political free-lances as George Grenville and the Duke of Bedford, whose ' Bloomsbury gang ' was notorious for being on hand when the plum-tree was shaken; and finally there was the king and his friends.

George III, only twenty-two years old at his accession in 1760, was brought up under the tutelage of his mother, a strong-minded German princess. His private life was as impeccable as that of George V. His simple tastes ran to farming and country sports. A strong sense of duty made him precise and methodical, and a glutton for work. ' George, be a *king!* ' was his mother's frequent injunction, which he appears to have interpreted as ' George, be a politician! ' The young man knew what he wanted, and got it, even though it cost him an empire. He wished to beat the whigs at their own game, and restore the power of the Crown, so diminished under his predecessors, by creating and eventually governing through a political party of his own. By this means he hoped to rescue England from the baneful effects of party politics, and govern the realm with an eye single to the public weal. His first ministry, under his personal friend Lord Bute, was a failure. He then induced George Grenville to construct a ministry, but inserted enough personal friends into it so that nothing could be done against his will. Grenville fell, not because the colonists made a row about the Stamp Act, but because he endeavored to turn out Stuart Mackenzie, one of the king's numerous ' North Briton ' friends; and the next ministry, Rockingham's, resigned rather than admit some of Mackenzie's henchmen to office. Finally, after the heterogeneous Pitt-Grafton ministry had crumbled, George III obtained exactly the government he wanted under his subservient friend and successful borough-monger, Lord North; and it was this ministry that drove the colonists into revolt, and lost the war.

For the first ten years of his reign, George III was conciliatory toward the colonists. He ordered his friends in Parliament to vote for the repeal of the Stamp Act. When Lord Hillsborough in 1769 proposed to punish Massachusetts for her Circular Letter of 1768 by altering the Massachusetts charter, the king refused to adopt what he called an 'odious measure' which would 'increase the unhappy feudes that subsist rather than to asswage them.' But the Boston tea-party, the first challenge to his personal rule, aroused his liveliest resentment. For the Coercive Acts of 1774, and for the inefficient conduct of the war, he was in great measure responsible, through his choice of ministers. If George III, for all his private virtues and well-meaning patriotism, is a pitiable figure in history, it is largely for the opportunities he lost. He might have been a patriot king indeed, by reaching out over the heads of the politicians to his people in the colonies, who were devotedly loyal, and attracted by his youth and personality. He did his best for the empire according to his lights; but his best was not good, and his lights were few and dim.

The British electoral system, with its rotten boroughs and family controls, was a strange mixture of medieval survival and eighteenth-century cynicism; but there is no reason to suppose that a more uniform or democratic system would have produced any different result, so far as the colonies were concerned. It was corrupt, in the opinion of Americans like Benjamin Franklin who viewed it from close quarters; elections to Parliament were purchased, and many members were kept faithful by pensions and positions, though very rarely with money. However, that sort of thing goes on in practically every representative government. The worst feature of the system, from the colonial point of view, was the lack of continuity, and the necessary preoccupation of ministers with local politics. No sooner did a really capable man like Halifax or Shelburne come to know the colonial ropes, than out he went. And a man like Burke, whose intelligent imagination enabled him to grasp exactly how to deal with the colonists, never received a responsible position. It is true that every ministry, even North's, meant well toward the Americans and wished to keep them quiet and happy, since their grievances made a talking-point for the opposition; but none save Grenville's made a real study of the colonial and imperial problem, or adopted anything but temporary expedients. And in 1774 the North ministry acted on emotion rather than knowledge. Seventy years later, when Canada rebelled, Parliament sent over a royal commission under a real statesman to find out what was the trouble and recommend a policy; and the report of that Durham commission was the beginning of the modern system of dominion home rule. But this statesmanlike way of meeting a situation occurred to nobody when the Thirteen Colonies were making trouble.

George III's ministers were no gang of unprincipled villains, subservient to a royal tyrant. Lord Dartmouth, for instance, who sponsored the Coercive Acts, was a kind and pious gentleman, patron of an American college and protector of the poet Cowper. But all save a few were incompetent. The situation of 1760–76 called for statesmanship of the highest order; and the political system which George III manipulated to his personal advantage put statesmanship at a discount, political following at a premium. In the end it was this unresponsiveness to crying needs and issues, rather than corruption or deliberate ill will, which convinced the Americans that their liberties were no longer safe within the British Empire.

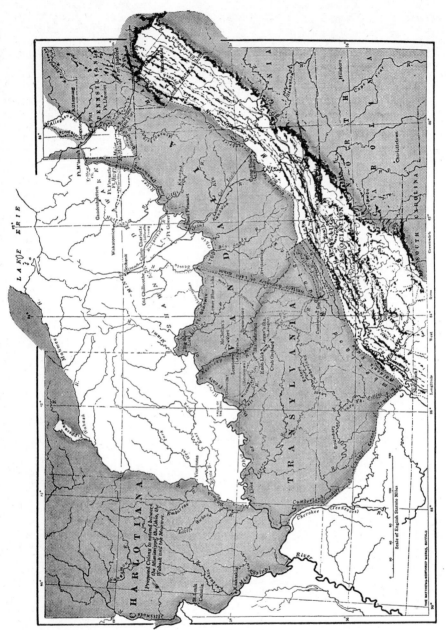

The West, 1763–1776

From F. M. Avery History of the United States, Vol. V.

VII

IMPERIAL REORGANIZATION
1764–1774

1. *The Organization of the West*

THE most pressing task that confronted the Crown on the close
of hostilities was the organization, administration, and defense
of the new acquisitions. To this problem the ministry of George
Grenville, which succeeded Bute's in 1763, addressed itself. Various
policies had been under consideration for some years, but the Western problems were at once so complex, so remote, and so unfamiliar
as to be evaded rather than faced, an attitude which the vicissitudes
of English politics made almost inevitable. The series of measures
adopted in 1763 and 1764 and inspired largely by Lords Shelburne
and Halifax, must be looked upon, then, as largely provisional, as
emergency measures to meet what was thought to be a temporary
situation.

The ministry decided that settlers must be excluded from the
trans-Alleghany country until the Indians were pacified, and a definite land policy worked out. This decision, dictated by sound reason, had been anticipated in 1761 when the colonial governors were
instructed to prohibit future land purchases in the West. It was
now given formal expression in the famous Royal Proclamation
of 7 October 1763. By the terms of this Proclamation 'the extensive
and valuable acquisitions secured to our Crown by the late Treaty'
were erected into four new governments: Grenada (embracing
several West Indian Islands), East Florida, West Florida, and Quebec. The Proclamation reserved all the western territory between the
Alleghanies, the Floridas, the Mississippi, and Quebec, for the use of
the Indians. ' We do strictly forbid, on pain of our displeasure, all our
loving subjects from making any purchases or settlements whatever
in that region.' Thus at one stroke the Crown swept away each and
every western land claim of the Thirteen Colonies. Shelburne had
originally planned to have the new boundary observe all vested
rights, and weave in and out of western settlements; but in the
critical condition of Indian affairs, he made haste to draw a simple
'Proclamation line' on the map, along the crest of the Alleghanies.

In the following year, 1764, an elaborate plan for the regulation of Indian affairs was advanced. As early as 1755 General Braddock had laid the foundations of an imperial Indian policy by appointing two highly capable colonists, Sir William Johnson and John Stuart, superintendents respectively of the Northern and Southern Indians. The 'Plan of 1764' recommended a well-organized Indian service under the control of these superintendents, licenses, regulations, and fixed tariffs for traders, and the repeal of all conflicting colonial laws — a program too ambitious for immediate fulfilment but looking in the right direction.

Before opening the country west of the Proclamation line to progressive settlement, it was necessary to purchase territory and establish an Indian boundary line west of the Alleghanies. Superintendents Stuart and Johnson, though seriously embarrassed by lack of funds, gave the problem immediate attention. In 1763 Stuart negotiated with the Cherokee nation the Treaty of Augusta, establishing the Indian boundary line west of Georgia and the Carolinas. The Treaty of Hard Labour of 24 October 1768 extended this boundary north to the Ohio at the confluence of that river with the Great Kanawha. This line called forth a storm of protest from Virginian land speculators and was subsequently adjusted to meet their views. In the same year, 1768, William Johnson established the line north of the Ohio by the Treaty of Fort Stanwix. By the terms of this Treaty the Iroquois ceded for some £10,000 their rights to a large part of central New York and Pennsylvania and their rather dubious claims to all the territory south of the Ohio river.

Intimately associated with Indian affairs was the pressing question of defense. 'What military establishment will be sufficient? What new forts to be erected?' inquired the Secretary of State of the Board of Trade. Pontiac's rebellion made the issue acute, and the estimate of military needs was somewhat exaggerated. The Board of Trade proposed establishing a chain of garrisons from the St. Lawrence to Florida and from Niagara to Michilimackinac. They estimated that ten thousand soldiers would be required to garrison these forts and maintain the military establishment in America. This estimate was excessive, if protection of the frontier were the only object — double the number that Lord Amherst, the Commander-in-Chief in America, asked for. It is so seldom in history that a government proposes to provide more soldiers than the generals want, that one naturally inquires whether some other motive than frontier defense was not involved in this generous estimate, especially since almost all the troops retained in the colonies were withdrawn to New York, Halifax and Quebec, where they were more likely to be useful for suppressing popular movements in the middle colonies, Boston and Canada, than for protecting the frontier. Obviously if the colonies could be persuaded to pay for ten thousand men, a number of deserving veterans of the Seven Years' War would be taken care of without expense to the people of Great Britain; and the Stamp Act of 1765 was an effort to force the colonies to pay for this military establishment. With the failure of the Stamp Act, the cost of maintaining ten thousand soldiers soon proved to be prohibitive. But for the time being adequate defense had been provided, the frontiers sufficiently garrisoned, the Indians pacified, the malpractices of Indian traders stopped, and an Indian demarcation line drawn. Large areas west of the Proclamation line were therefore available for settlement under propitious conditions.

Nevertheless the prohibition of settlement in the Proclamation of 1763 was never withdrawn. Shelburne, who alone of the British Ministers had some understanding of the Western problem and had caught a vision of America's future, was forced out of office, and his place taken by Lord Hillsborough. Confused by the claims of land speculators, the schemes of fur traders, and the perplexities of American politics, the new ministry abandoned the generous plans of Shelburne and Halifax for the development of the West and endeavored to make the region an Indian reservation for the use of the fur traders. 'Let the savages enjoy their deserts in quiet . . . were they drove from their forests, the peltry trade would decrease,' wrote General Gage to the Board of Trade, and the ministry snapped up this bright thought as a reason for doing nothing further about the West. At the same time the Indian service suffered for want of funds, and the problem of defense was transferred to the colonial governments. Thus the Royal Proclamation of 1763, intended as a provisional measure antecedent to opening the West to colonization, became a permanent policy of exclusion. But American backwoodsmen were not to be stopped in their westward march by imperial proclamations, and the inevitable result was a knock-down, drag-out fight between Indians and frontiersmen. Lord Dunmore, the Scots peer who became Governor of Virginia in 1772, wrote thus to the Colonial Secretary:

I have learnt from experience that the established Authority of any government in America, and the policy of Government at home, are both insufficient to restrain the Americans; and that they do and will remove as their avidity and restlessness incite them. They acquire no attachment to Place: But wandering about Seems engrafted in their Nature; and it is a weakness incident to it, that they Should for ever immagine the Lands further off, are Still better than those upon which they are already Settled But to be more particular . . . In this Colony Proclamations have been published from time to time to restrain them: But impressed from their earliest infancy with Sentiments and habits, very different from those acquired by persons of a Similar condition in England, they do not conceive that Government has any right to forbid their taking possession of a Vast tract of Country, either uninhabited, or which Serves only as a Shelter to a few Scattered Tribes of Indians. Nor can they be easily brought to entertain any belief of the permanent obligation of Treaties made with those People, whom they consider, as but little removed from the brute Creation.

Governor Dunmore, accordingly, followed the line of least resistance, and sought to gain popularity in Virginia by supporting the pioneer in border conflict which they had provoked with the Shawnee, whose hunting grounds they were beginning to occupy. He led in person a force of frontiersmen, advancing down the Ohio from Pittsburgh:

Our Royal Governor Dunnmore, he being of high renown
With fifteen hundred jovial men, he marched towards their town
With a full resolution, to slay both old and young
For all the barbarous actions, the savages had done.

Another column under Colonel Lewis gathered in the Valley of Virginia and defeated the Shawnee at Point Pleasant, at the mouth of the Great Kanawha, on 10 October 1774:

The Army of Indians, in Battle array,
Under Cornstalk and Elnipsicow,
Was met by the forces of Lewis that day,
On the Banks of the Ohio.

They brought on the battle at breaking of day,
Like heroes they slaughtered the foe,
Till two hundred Indians or more, as they say,
Were slain by the Ohio.

As a result of this battle, and of Dunmore's diplomacy, the Delaware, Shawnee, and Mingo tribes renounced all their hunting rights south of the Ohio. Yet, a little more than a year later, Lord Dunmore was driven from Virgina by the very men he had led against the Indians!

Dunmore did not even have the consolation of pleasing his king, for while he was marching through the wilderness with his jovial band, the British government sought to put a stop to all such doings by ordering all royal governors to grant no land, and permit no new settlements, except after prior survey, allotment, and sale by auction. Although not put into effect outside Canada, this order of 1774 called forth Thomas Jefferson's bold *Summary View of the Rights of British America,* denying the Crown's right to dispose of Western land at all. It furnished one more grievance for the Declaration of Independence, and in many details anticipated the American land ordinance of 1785.

At the same time Parliament passed the last and most important act dealing with the West — the Quebec Act of 22 June 1774. This law, dictated by an enlightened liberalism rare in that or any other age, was intended to correct certain mistakes in the Proclamation of 1763, and to secure the loyalty of the French Canadians. To these it granted complete religious liberty and the restitution of their peculiar legal and political institutions. But at the same time it annexed to the Province of Quebec all the territory north of the Ohio river, thus nullifying the Western claims of four colonies and thwarting the plans of the American land companies. With this the far-sighted plans of Shelburne and Halifax for the development of the American West came to an inglorious and ineffectual climax. The solution of the Western problem was left to Americans, and it was one of the most perplexing of all the issues that faced the new nation after 1776.

2. *Financing Colonial Reform*

This organization of the West and erection of an extensive military establishment meant a heavy financial burden which the British government was ill prepared to assume. The attempt to assess a part of that burden upon the American colonies led in turn to a series of financial and constitutional controversies which ended only with the break-up of the empire. The national debt of Great Britain on the conclusion of the Seven Years' War had mounted to some £130,-000,000, an increase of over £70,000,000 since 1756, while the extensive acquisitions in two hemispheres greatly increased administrative expenses. The annual cost of maintaining the civil and military establishments in America alone had risen from some £70,000 in 1748 to well over £350,000 in 1764. In the light of this situation, George Grenville, Chancellor of the Exchequer, felt that it was both necessary and just to increase the revenue from the American colonies. Parliament greeted this proposition with enthusiastic approval, and even the level-headed Franklin anticipated no trouble from America.

As early as 1763 Lord Egremont had inquired of the Board of Trade, 'In what mode least burthensome and most palatable to the colonies can they contribute towards the support of the additional expense which must attend their civil and military establishments?' Lord Shelburne wisely refrained from committing himself, but Grenville, who felt himself peculiarly qualified to solve just such problems, was not so cautious. A man of great and generally recognized abilities, of tireless devotion to duty as he understood it, George Grenville was an administrator rather than a statesman, a man more interested in the machinery of government than in its ends. His vision was circumscribed, his spirit uninspired and his pedantic mind bound by the traditions and precedents of the law; but he was neither unintelligent nor ungenerous. Contemporaries considered him the ablest man of business in British politics and supported most of his well-meant measures. It was in April 1763, that he succeeded Bute in office, and at once he set about to reduce the American administrative and financial chaos to order. Early in the following year he introduced into the House of Commons a series of resolutions for securing a revenue from America, and upon these the Sugar Act and the Stamp Act were based.

The exact extent of colonial contributions to the upkeep of the empire is not easy to determine. English landowners, paying an income tax of twenty per cent, felt that the colonists could well afford to shoulder some of their burden. But the Americans insisted that they were already carrying their full share, and contributing, directly and indirectly, to the maintenance of the imperial government up to the limit of their capacities. The colonies had incurred a debt of over £2,500,000 for the prosecution of the war, and, notwithstanding the generosity of Parliament in assuming a part of that debt, a large portion of it remained. Massachusetts, for example, with a population of approximately 300,000, was raising no less than £37,500 annually for the payment of her war debt. Propertied members of that colony asserted, with considerable justice, that they were taxed as heavily as propertied Englishmen; but few inhabitants of other colonies could make the same claim. If little direct revenue was derived from the American customs or the royal lands, it must be remembered that the mercantilist system was not designed to levy tribute on colonies. The indirect contributions in the form of English port duties and the monopoly of colonial trade were considerable, and William Pitt estimated that the colonial commerce brought an annual profit of not less than £2,000,000 to British merchants. All of these factors must be taken into consideration in weighing the justice of the new revenue measures. Events proved their inexpediency quickly enough, whatever the right may have been.

The Revenue Act of 1764 — often known as the Sugar Act — was the first of these measures. This law had a double purpose: to provide revenue, and to tighten the mercantilist system by strengthening the Acts of Trade and Navigation. The American customs service was notoriously inefficient; it was maintained at a cost of some £8000 annually but brought in less than one-fourth of that sum. Of course this deficit might have been made good by economies in the civil service and by the elimination of unnecessary pensions at home, but it was no more to be expected that politics would be free of extravagance in eighteenth-century England than in twentieth-century America. The Act reduced from six to three pence the duty on foreign molasses, but levied additional duties on sugar and numerous luxuries such as wines, coffee, silks, and linens, while drawbacks (duty refunds) on European goods re-exported from England to the colonies were to cease. At the same time customs officers were ordered to repair to their posts in America, writs of assistance were authorized, and jurisdiction over revenue cases given to the admiralty courts.

It was not so much the duty of three pence per gallon on molasses as the prospect of its actual collection that caused consternation among New England merchants. For over a generation these had been accustomed to disregarding the provisions of the Molasses Act of 1733 and importing the larger part of their molasses from the French and Spanish West Indies. The Rhode Island distillers, for example, imported less than one-sixth of their molasses from the British Islands, a situation which gave profound concern to the British sugar planters, well represented in Parliament. This universal smuggling was made possible, of course, only by the connivance of the underpaid customs officers. 'The real cause of the illicit trade in the provinces,' wrote Governor Hutchinson of Massachusetts, 'has been the indulgence of the officers of the customs.'

The threat to American distillers and business men was ominous. 'It is no secret,' asserted John Adams later, 'that rum was an essential ingredient in the American Revolution.' But the most serious aspect of a stringent enforcement of the new customs regulations was that it threatened to deprive the colonial merchant of the one customer with whom he had a favorable balance of trade, and cut off the one reasonably secure source of money at a time when increased duties and rising prices made the continuance of this income imperative. The Southern colonies had staple products that they sold in England, but the colonies north of the Mason and Dixon line depended on their markets in the French and Spanish West Indies.

So far as imperial reconstruction was concerned the most unfortunate part of the Revenue Act of 1764 was the preamble, for it gave the colonials an opportunity to rationalize their discontent on constitutional grounds. As yet few persons had cared to look into the constitutional relationship between colonies and mother country. It would have been better for imperial unity had none but humorists done so! The preamble to the Act states 'Whereas it is expedient that new provisions and regulations should be established *for improving the revenue of this Kingdom* . . . and whereas it is just and necessary that a revenue should be raised . . . for defraying the expenses of defending, protecting and securing the same . . .' The power of Parliament to tax colonial commodities for the regulation of imperial trade was universally acknowledged; the power of Parliament to tax colonial commodities for revenue was debatable. This early constitutional issue became an entering wedge that finally split asunder the empire. 'One single act of Parliament,' wrote James Otis, 'has set people a-thinking in six months, more than they had done in their whole lives before.' Merchants, legislatures, town meetings protested against the expediency of the law, but colonial lawyers such as Samuel Adams found in the preamble the first intimation of 'taxation without representation.' The opposition was as yet, however, unorganized, localized, and sporadic. Grenville's next revenue measure was to crystallize and mobilize that opposition, to give it general support and driving force. This was the fateful Stamp Act of 22 March 1765.

3. *The Stamp Act*

The idea of a stamp tax was not original with Grenville. This means of indirect taxation had been long prevalent in England, and its extension to the American colonies had frequently been proposed by colonial governors with more zeal than perception. Easy-going Robert Walpole had earlier rejected such a proposition, and the far-sighted Pitt had 'refused to burn his fingers with an American Stamp Tax.' But Grenville was energetic and short-sighted. 'No tax,' he announced, 'appears so easy and equitable as a stamp duty,' and he decided to impose one. With well-intentioned but unfortunate fairness he announced his purpose a full year in advance, thus, as Burke sarcastically remarked, 'allowing time for all the discontents of that country to fester and come to a head, and for all the arrangements which factious men could make toward an opposition to the law.'

This opposition was not so apparent in 1764 as later. The colonial agents did, indeed, protest against the proposed law, but even they were unable to suggest any alternative method of raising a revenue except the customary one of requisitions which had so often been found wanting. Under these circumstances Grenville advanced confidently with his plan and early in 1765 introduced his bill to Parliament. It provided for revenue stamps costing (in specie) from a halfpenny to upward of twenty shillings sterling, to be affixed to all newspapers, broadsides, pamphlets, licenses, commercial bills, notes and bonds, advertisements, almanacs, leases, legal documents, and a number of similar papers. All the revenue was to be expended in the colonies under the direction of Parliament solely for the purpose of 'defending, protecting and securing the colonies.' Offenses against the law were to be tried in the Admiralty Courts. As a sugar-coating to the pill only Americans were to be appointed as agents, and a number of unsuspecting colonials such as Richard Henry Lee and Jared Ingersoll applied for such positions. The measure, if extended to the West Indies, was calculated to secure an annual revenue of over £60,000; the costs of collection, it was hoped, would be relatively small, and the burden of the tax so evenly and lightly distributed as to arouse little opposition.

The measure, indeed, appeared reasonable to the majority of Englishmen, and passed Parliament without any difficulty. The debate in the Commons which Burke described as 'languid' was enlivened only by a memorable passage at arms between Charles Townshend and the fiery young Colonel Isaac Barré, in which the latter endeared himself to Americans by referring to them as Sons of Liberty. Despite the Colonel's eloquence, the bill passed the Commons by a vote of 204 to 49.

The reception of the Stamp Act in the Thirteen Colonies was so violent that it astonished moderate men everywhere, and has puzzled not a few historians. It was the peculiar misfortune of the Act that it aroused the hostility of the most powerful and the most articulate groups in the colonies: merchants and business men, lawyers, journalists, and clergymen, and that it bore equally on all sections of the country, North, South, and West. Soon the merchants of New York, Philadelphia, and Boston, whose every bill of lading would be taxed, and who faced the prospect of a ruinous drain of specie money, organized for resistance and formed non-importation associations. Lawyers, bankers, land-dealers, and newspaper men were aroused to opposition and even the clergy joined in the din. Business came to a temporary standstill, the trade with the mother country fell off £600,000 in the summer of 1765; respectable men organized as 'Sons of Liberty' and political opposition soon descended into violence. A mob, inflamed by the harangues of Samuel Adams or the sermons of Jonathan Mayhew, paraded the crooked streets of Boston, gutted the fine mansion of Lieutenant-Governor Hutchinson and threw his splendid library to the winds. 'Our presses have groaned, our pulpits have thundered, our legislatures have resolved, our towns have voted; the crown officers have everywhere trembled, and all their little tools and creatures been afraid to speak and ashamed to be seen,' wrote the exultant John Adams. From Massachusetts to South Carolina the Act was nullified, mobs forced luckless agents to resign their offices, and destroyed the hated stamps.

The great significance of the Stamp Act, however, was not the mobbing and violence that it aroused. It crystallized the constitutional opposition to the program of imperial reorganization; and forced Americans to formulate a theory of empire that would accommodate itself to American conditions.

The first step in this direction was taken by the Virginia Assembly, dominated by proud planters of the Tidewater such as George Mason and Richard Bland, and impetuous leaders of the Piedmont such as Patrick Henry. 'Virginians,' the English traveler Burnaby observed, ' are haughty and jealous of their liberties, impatient of restraint, and can scarcely bear the thought of being controlled by any superior power. Many of them consider the colonies as independent states, not connected with Great Britain otherwise than by having a common king and being bound to her with natural affection.'

On the 30th of May Patrick Henry, who had already achieved notoriety as an orator and popular leader in the famous Parsons' Cause, introduced a set of seven resolutions on the Stamp Act, and supported them with ' sublime torrents of eloquence' that later became grossly distorted by historians. Only the first five of the seven resolutions were actually passed by the closely divided legislature, but all seven of them were published in newspapers throughout the colonies. The gist of the matter was to denounce taxation without representation as a dangerous and unprecedented innovation and a threat to colonial liberties. These Virginia resolutions were an ' alarum bell to the disaffected' in Boston (said Governor Bernard), and pointed the way to common colonial action.

A few days after Henry had stirred up the Virginia Assembly, the Massachusetts House adopted a circular letter inviting all the colonies to appoint delegates to a Congress in New York to consider the Stamp Act menace. This Congress, which met in October 1765, was the first intercolonial meeting summoned by colonial initiative, and may be regarded as the opening move in the Revolution. Delegates from nine colonies were present, among them James Otis of Massachusetts, John Dickinson of Pennsylvania, and Christopher Gadsden of South Carolina — bold and able men ready to seize on this opportunity to mobilize colonial opinion against Parliamentary interference in American affairs. The note was sounded by Gadsden: ' We should stand upon the broad common ground of natural rights. . . . There ought to be no New England man, no New-Yorker, known on the continent, but all of us Americans.' After considerable debate the Congress adopted a set of resolutions more moderate than those of Virginia, but asserting once more that ' no taxes ever have been, or can be constitutionally imposed on them, except by their respective legislatures,' and that the Stamp Act had a 'manifest tendency to subvert the rights and liberties of the colonists.'

The constitutional issue was thus drawn, and it centered on the question of representation. In the American colonies there had developed the custom that a representative must reside in the district which he represented. From the colonial point of view, therefore, it was impossible for the colonies to consider themselves represented in Parliament, unless they actually elected members of the House of Commons. And they knew very well that it would do them no good to elect members to a Parliament where they would be in a hopeless minority, at least for many years. The orthodox English principle was that of 'virtual representation' — representation of classes and interests rather than by locality, and English parliamentarians insisted that the American colonies were represented in the same way as the cities of Liverpool, Sheffield, or Birmingham.

There were flaws in both the colonial and the English arguments, and these were fully revealed in the great debate in Parliament over the repeal of the Stamp Act. From the strictly legal point of view, the English contention was probably correct: virtual representation was the accepted practice of the British Constitution, and the power of Parliament to legislate for the colonies could scarcely be controverted on the grounds of law or precedent, unless you skipped the eighteenth century and went back to Stuart England for your arguments. Even the great Pitt, friend of America, insisted on the right of Parliament to exercise every power whatsoever. Yet 'virtual representation' was one of those glib phrases that cover a multitude of flaws. As Hutchinson carefully pointed out, every English *interest* was represented in Parliament, even if most English individuals were not: ' But the colonies have an interest distinct from the interest of the nation; and shall the Parliament be at once party and judge?' Daniel Dulany of Maryland, one of the ablest pamphleteers of the period, exposed the fallacy of the theory of virtual representation, and Pitt denounced it as 'the most contemptible' idea 'that ever entered into the head of man.' ' I rejoice,' he declared, ' that America has resisted. Three thousand people so dead to all feelings of liberty as voluntarily to submit to be slaves would be fit instruments to make slaves of the rest.' James Otis swept away the distinctions of lawyers with his impatient cry: ' To what purpose to ring everlasting changes to the colonists on the cases of Manchester, Birmingham and

Sheffield? If these now so considerable places are not represented, they ought to be.'

It is doubtful whether the eloquence of Pitt, the logic of Dulany, or the indignation of Otis, would have induced Parliament to repeal the Stamp Act had it not been for the pressure brought to bear by business men throughout the kingdom who were suffering from the American boycott on British goods and refusal to pay debts. These had no special tenderness for the American colonies, but they could not remain passive before the prospect of bankruptcy; and while merchants bombarded Parliament with memorials and petitions, the unemployed rioted outside the doors of the House. Under these circumstances the king and the new Rockingham ministry had the Stamp Act repealed by Parliament in March 1766.

At the same time Parliament passed, without division, a Declaratory Act asserting in sweeping terms the power of King and Parliament to 'make laws and statutes of sufficient force and validity to bind the colonies in all cases whatsoever.' This flat assertion of Parliamentary sovereignty was couched in the very phraseology of the odious Irish Declaratory Act of 1719, and so indicated the British government's intention to assimilate the American colonies to the same subordinate position in the empire as Ireland long occupied. Few Americans, however, stopped to inquire into the implications of this Act. They were too busy celebrating the repeal of the Stamp Act, and raising statues to the king and Pitt. Nor did certain changes in the trade laws imposing a uniform duty on British and foreign molasses and thus transforming a law for the regulation of trade into one for raising revenue, receive any notice. On the contrary, a wave of loyalty and gratitude swept through the colonies. It would have been well for imperial relations had the English government capitalized that loyalty and refrained from further acts which might weaken it, or raise delicate constitutional questions. Instead, the accident of politics placed Charles Townshend in temporary leadership of the government, and that ill-starred politician ripped open the whole controversy over colonial liberty and imperial order.

4. The Townshend Acts

The history of the decade from the repeal of the Stamp Act to the Declaration of Independence is one of drifting and muddling. Had a wise and statesmanlike comprehension of the problem of imperial order obtained at Whitehall, the War of Independence might have been avoided and the break-up of the empire postponed to a future generation. But larger issues of imperial organization were lost sight of, and when any American issue arose petty questions of right and prestige came to the fore; and as the king obtained more control over his government, the quality of ministers notably declined. Shelburne, for instance, was frozen out in 1768. Actual unity was sacrificed to theoretical unity. Few periods in history illustrate more convincingly the disastrous effects of applying doctrinaire principles to the larger problems of politics.

At least, that is how the broad issues appear to us. But a different view is reasonable, and has been held by many historians to this day. Admitted that the whole colonial system needed overhauling, which would cost money, and that the Thirteen Colonies had gained enormously in power and security from the conquest of Canada and the West, was it not fair that they should either pay some part of the cost, as Parliament directed, or propose some constructive alternative? Did not the experience of earlier wars prove that voluntary requisitions — the only alternative they proposed — were not constructive? And did not Parliament twice back down before colonial insistence, in 1766 and 1770, only to find the colonists preferring new claims and discovering new rights? Perhaps, say those who ask these awkward questions, if Parliament had been a little more unyielding in 1765 they would have prevented trouble in 1775. Or, putting it another way, if old whig politicians in England had not encouraged rebels in the colonies, these rebels would soon have acquiesced in Parliamentary regulation. To which one can only reply, with Sir Philip Francis, that the fates of empires are not to be judged by forms, and the principles of police administration cannot be extended to imperial administration; or, one may point to the complete failure of a 'hard boiled' British policy toward Ireland, over a period of centuries. England has maintained her empire, or rather transformed it into a league of free Commonwealths under George VI, by following a policy diametrically opposed to that of George III, one strikingly similar to what Jefferson and John Adams demanded in 1774 as the price of colonial loyalty.

The Rockingham ministry repealed the Stamp Act; but for reasons of internal politics and royal pleasure the Rockingham ministry fell in 1766. King George then turned to the great Pitt as the one man of outstanding ability who commanded the confidence of

Parliament and was not unalterably opposed to the royal pretensions. The great Commoner — now created Earl of Chatham — formed a ministry of talents, including three known friends to the American colonies, Shelburne, Conway, and Camden, and others like the Duke of Grafton and Charles Townshend, who were not so friendly. 'Indeed, a very curious show, but utterly unsafe to touch and unsafe to stand on,' as Burke remarked. Then at the critical juncture Chatham was laid low by a mysterious malady, and the government drifted. It was under these distressing circumstances, 'while the western horizon was still in a blaze with his descending glory, on the opposite quarter of the heavens arose another luminary, and, for his hour, became lord of the ascendant.' This was Charles Townshend, brilliant, ambitious, and unprincipled, 'Champagne Charley' of melancholy eminence in imperial history, whose startling career was cut short by death before the empire had reaped the results of his sowing.

Townshend, who was Chancellor of the Exchequer, saw in the temporary incapacity of his chief an opportunity for bridging the gap between the king's friends and the old whigs. With breathtaking audacity he proposed in the Commons to reduce the land tax from twenty to fifteen per cent, and meet the resulting deficit of some £400,000 partly by reducing the military establishment in the American colonies, and partly by increasing the revenue from the colonies. This revenue was to be realized by import duties in the colonies on English paint, lead, paper, and tea. It was expected to yield not less than £40,000 annually. The colonial distinction between internal and external taxes Townshend held to be 'perfect nonsense,' but since the point seemed of such importance to Americans he affected to observe it by providing for these 'external' taxes only. For the more efficient collection of the duties the customs service was strengthened and reorganized, and a Board of Commissioners of Customs was established at Boston: an important administrative reform. New vice-admiralty courts were created, and writs of assistance, whose legality had been challenged by Otis, were specifically authorized. Most important of all, the moneys thus raised in the colonies, instead of going to support the garrisons, were to be used to create a colonial civil list and thus render the royal governors and judges independent of the colonial assemblies.

To meet this new threat a new formulation of the colonial argument was necessary. Townshend, with admirable cleverness, had but adopted the colonial distinction between internal and external duties, but this only made the pill more bitter for American merchants and politicians. John Dickinson, a Pennsylvania country gentleman who had read law in London and practised it in Philadelphia, now wrote his *Letters of a Pennsylvania Farmer* (1768), where he discovered an essential difference between duties for the regulation of trade and duties for revenue. The latter were, according to the Farmer, clearly taxes, and as such beyond the power of Parliament to levy. Duties for the regulation of trade were, on the other hand, a necessary part of the administrative power of an imperial government. The distinction was a nice one, but led the more forthright Franklin to assert:

The more I have thought and read on the subject the more I find myself confirmed in the opinion that no middle ground can well be maintained. I mean not clearly with intelligible arguments. Something might be made of either of the extremes: that Parliament has a power to make *all laws* for us, or that it has a power to make *no laws* for us; and I think the arguments for the latter more numerous and weighty than those for the former.

Aside from the question of duties, the declared purpose of the English government to create a civil list, and its high-handed dictation to several of the colonial assemblies at this time, brought to the fore the question of legislative independence. It had long been for Americans a matter of peculiar pride that through the control of the purse they were able to check the pretensions of royal officials in the colonies. Furthermore the English ministry had dissolved the New York Assembly in 1767 for its refusal to comply with all the provisions of the Quartering Act. In 1768 the General Court of Massachusetts was dissolved for refusing to rescind its circular letter to sister colonies protesting against the Townshend Acts, and the Virginia Assembly was dissolved for receiving it. Thus the question of legislative prestige and power was raised, as well as that of taxation.

The agitation that followed the Townshend duties was marked by less violence than that of the period of the Stamp Act, except in Boston. Merchants once again resorted to non-importation agreements, and although little enforced in some places, importations fell off by one-half in Boston, by two-thirds in Philadelphia, and by four-fifths in New York. Men dressed in homespun, women found substitutes for tea, students used colonial-made paper, and houses went unpainted. New colonial industries sprang up, and an agreement among planters to purchase no more slaves is estimated to have cost English slave traders £250,000. Yet, owing to the opening up of new markets for English goods in Europe and the East, the colonial opposition of 1768–69 was less effective in British trading circles than the earlier non-importation agreements.

In New England alone, where the mercantile interests were most sensitive to any interference, were the new customs regulations attended with violence. When customs officials sought to collect duties from John Hancock's sloop *Liberty* they were set upon by the Boston populace and roughly handled. This led Governor Bernard to demand two regiments to protect the Commissioners, and these were duly sent from Halifax and quartered upon the town of Boston. The presence of the red-coats in the old Puritan town was a standing invitation for disorder, and the natural antagonism between citizens and soldiery flared up after eighteen months of resentment, in the so-called Boston Massacre of 5 March 1770. A harmless snowballing of the red-coats degenerated into something like a mob attack. Someone gave the order to fire, and four Bostonians lay dead in the snow. It is wrong to dignify this brawl with the name 'massacre,' but radicals such as Adams and Warren seized upon it for purposes of propaganda. It is well to remember that Captain Preston and the British soldiers were defended by young John Adams and Josiah Quincy, and acquitted of the charge of murder brought against them. Governor Hutchinson was forced to remove the offending soldiery from the town to Castle William, however, and all the strategic advantage lay with the radicals.

On the day of the Boston Massacre, the North Ministry, concluding that colonial duties on English manufactures were preposterous, repealed all the Townshend duties except that on tea. A tax of three pence per pound was kept on this article primarily as an assertion of Parliamentary authority. 'A pepper-corn in acknowledgment of the right is of more value than millions without it,' George Grenville had said; and Lord North, well-disposed as he was, acquiesced in this glib fallacy.

Despite such untoward incidents as the Boston Massacre, the *Liberty* affair, the riot on Golden Hill in New York, and the burning of the British revenue-cutter *Gaspee,* two years later, the decade of the seventies opened auspiciously for imperial relations. Constitutional calm succeeded the agitation of the sixties. Yet Parliamentary taxation was an established fact, and the unrepealed duties, including the tax on tea, were being efficiently collected by the new American customs service. The income from customs duties rose to over £30,000 annually, while the cost of collection averaged only £13,000 —a sum which did not include, to be sure, the expense of maintaining the two regiments in Boston. In the ten years beginning with 1767, out of £257,000 taken in at colonial customs houses, £83,000 was remitted to England, and £32,000 expended on colonial civil lists. This allocation had an important effect on the colonial governments, especially in Massachusetts, where the native-born Governor Hutchinson began to use a high hand with his Assembly. At the same time the penalties for violation of the customs laws rose from £473 in 1769 to £2395 in 1774, and smuggling well-nigh ceased.

Yet prosperity was increasing, and most colonial leaders were willing to let the future take care of itself. 'The people,' wrote Connecticut's agent in England, 'appear to be weary of their altercations with the mother country. A little discreet conduct on both sides would perfectly re-establish that warm affection and respect towards Great Britain for which this country was once remarkable.' And for three years the relations between colonies and mother country were unmarred by any serious crises. Inertia and neglect seemed to succeed where bolder policies had failed. The moderate element, everywhere predominant in the colonies, welcomed this peaceful interlude; and the amiable Franklin, still a friend of peace, composed a ditty he was later to repudiate:

> Know too, ye bad neighbours, who aim to divide
> The sons from the mother, that still she's our pride,
> And if ye attack her, we're all on her side,
> Which nobody can deny, deny,
> Which nobody can deny.

5. Organizing for Revolution

Only the left-wing radicals such as Sam Adams and Warren in Boston, Isaac Sears and John Lamb in New York, Henry in Virginia, and Gadsden in South Carolina, were disgruntled. In order to arouse his fellow country-men from their lethargy Adams organized committees of correspondence. Soon a network of these committees covered New England, and the system was quickly extended to the middle and southern colonies. Together with Warren, Adams drafted a statement of the 'Rights of the Colonies' with a list of infringements which was circulated in pamphlet form throughout the colonies. 'It told them a hundred rights, of which they had never heard before,' growled Solicitor-general Wedder-burn, 'and a hundred grievances which they had never before felt.'

It was the famous Boston tea party of 16 December 1773 that broke the long calm. The powerful East India Company, finding itself in critical financial straits, had appealed to the government for aid, and had been granted a monopoly on all tea exported to the colonies. The Company decided to sell its tea through its own agents, thus eliminating the independent merchants, and disposing of the tea at a price considerably under the customary one either in America or in England. It was this ill-considered step that aroused the colonial merchants and threw them into alliance with the radicals. It was not so much the loss of the tea trade alone, valuable as that was, but the principle of monopoly, that stung the merchant class to action. 'America,' wrote one of them, 'would be prostrate before a monster that may be able to destroy every branch of our commerce, drain us of all our property, and wantonly leave us to perish by the thousands.' These fears were probably groundless, but none the less powerful. Burke gauged well the American temper, in his speech on Conciliation. 'In other countries, the people, more simple and of a less mercurial cast, judge of an ill principle in government only by an actual grievance; here they anticipate the evil, and judge of the pressure of the grievance by the badness of the principle. They augur misgovernment at a distance, and snuff the approach of tyranny in every tainted breeze.'

The colonial reaction to the monopoly on tea took various forms. In Charleston the tea was landed, but was not offered for sale; at Philadelphia and New York the consignments were rejected and returned to England. It was in Boston alone that violence occurred. Here, on the night of 16 December, a band of men disguised in the paint of Mohawk Indians boarded the three tea ships and dumped the offending leaves into the water. 'Many persons,' wrote the exultant John Adams, 'wish that as many dead carcasses were floating in the harbor as there are chests of tea.' The radicals had called the Ministerial bluff. They had refused even the pepper-corn in acknowledgment of right, and by confusing the legal and economic issues, had succeeded in committing a large part of the merchant class to opposition.

The results of this momentous jettison were six-fold: it brought to a head the long-smouldering conflict over home rule; it committed the 'patriots' to violent measures; it forced the more moderate merchant element into the hands of the radicals; it inflamed public opinion in England; it strengthened the 'die-hard' element in Cabinet and Parliament; and it produced an unwise attempt at punishment and cure. This took the shape of a series of laws closing the port of Boston to commerce until the tea were paid for, radically changing the form of government in Massachusetts, and providing for the transportation of certain offenders to England for trial. These 'Intolerable Acts' threatened the very life of Boston, for the attempt to exclude her from the sea, the element that made her great, was a punishment comparable to the destruction of Carthage.

Instead of isolating Massachusetts, as they had been planned to do, these measures demonstrated a parliamentary power more dangerous to colonial liberty than mere taxing, and thus rallied twelve continental colonies to Massachusetts. On 27 May 1774 a rump assembly, meeting in the historic Raleigh Tavern at Williamsburg, Virginia, sent out a call for a congress of all the American colonies. One by one the other colonies fell into line, and on 5 September the delegates of twelve of them assembled in Carpenter's Hall, Philadelphia, 'to consult upon the present unhappy State of the Colonies.' This was the famous Continental Congress.

'Clouds, indeed, and darkness,' said the great Burke, 'rest upon the future.'

6. Federalism Emerging

Thus after a decade of muddling with the imperial organization the English government indicated that it had no solution to the problem but coercion. No one of the events of these troubled years was of sufficient seriousness to account for the final split, but the cumulative force of dissension and bickering over a period of years was such that it drove men unwillingly, and often unwittingly, to extremes. Moderates everywhere, in England and in the colonies, were forced to take sides, and issues were raised which might well have been avoided had common sense rather than legalism obtained. The larger question of imperial order was transformed by the British Government into one of sovereignty; the welfare of the empire sacrificed on the altar of authority.

Constitutionally the importance of this decade of controversy is in the evolution of two ideas central to the American political system: the idea of a fixed constitution, and the idea of a federal system. In the course of their quarrel with Parliament Americans appealed from their charter rights to their rights as Englishmen under the British Constitution. Refusing to recognize the flexible and evolutionary nature of that Constitution, they insisted that it was 'fixed'; that it was, in the words of John Locke, 'a standing law to live by.' Not only was the Constitution unalterable, but it contained in it the immutable laws of Nature. Just what these laws were was nowhere made clear, but that they included 'life, liberty, and property' was universally acknowledged. Finally, Parliament itself was bound by the Constitution, and by the laws of Nature. 'As the supreme legislative derives its authority from the constitution,' asserted the Massachusetts Circular Letter, 'it can not overleap the bounds of it without destroying its own foundations.' And if Parliament should, nevertheless, pass its constitutional limits, its acts would be null and void and of no force. Thus ran the American argument; the British held, of course, to the contrary theory that 'what Parliament does no power on earth can undo.'

It is bootless to debate the legal correctness or incorrectness of the American argument. Historically its importance is that Americans were setting up ideals of a fixed constitution, a constitution which embodied natural law, and a government that was limited in its powers, and insisting that acts contrary to this constitution were void. All of these concepts were later embodied in American institutions.

When Americans came to set up their own governments they resorted to written constitutions, with precise limitations of powers, and they established courts with the power of passing on the constitutionality of laws. There had been written constitutions in America since the first Virginia charter, but it was the experience of Americans in the revolutionary period that made them inevitable in the future. Having had unhappy experience with a constitution that was not 'fixed' they determined that their own should be definite and rigid. The doctrine of judicial review, too, though its roots may be traced deep into the historic past, was a normal product of the colonial insistence that all authority is limited, that certain human rights are not subject to the vagaries of executive or legislative bodies. In other words, the constitutional controversy of the revolu-tionary period was essentially constructive in nature, and not merely destructive of the British connection.

Of equal importance was the emergence of the idea of federalism. Benjamin Franklin had outlined a federal empire as early as 1754, in the Albany Plan of Union, and he had not ceased to advocate it since that time. Forced to defend their contention that Parliament, although sovereign in the empire, did not have control over the in-ternal affairs of the colonies, Americans such as Franklin, Jefferson, James Wilson, and John Adams had discovered in the empire the essentials of a federal system — a distribution of powers between governments. When, in 1773, Governor Hutchinson asserted that ' no line can be drawn between the supreme authority of Parliament and the total independence of the colonies' and, 'it is impossible that there should be more than two independent legislatures in one and the same state,' John Adams, on behalf of the lower House of Massachusetts, cut through this dialectic with the reply that the Brit-ish Empire was not a centralized but a federal one. There actually were, Adams insisted, a number of independent legislatures in the empire; and furthermore 'if they interfere not with one another, what hinders but that, being united in one head and common sov-ereign, they may live happily in that connection and mutually sup-port and protect each other?' Adams's argument may not have fitted the legal theory of the British Constitution in the eighteenth cen-tury, but it was remarkably close to the historical reality. Actually the British Empire of the eighteenth century was a federal em-pire with powers and authority distributed between governments; and prior to the imperial reorganization of 1763 there had been no attempt to interfere with this arrangement. Had the structure of the empire of 1763 been petrified, it would have been obvious to everyone in a later generation that it was a federal structure. The unwillingness of British statesmen to abandon the legal fiction of centralization and sovereignty for the historical fact of federalism spelled the failure of imperial organization. But the federalism of the old empire became the basis for the American federal system, and, with a much greater emphasis on states' (i.e., dominions') rights, the basis of the British Empire under the last two Georges.

VIII

SECTIONAL AND CLASS DIVISIONS
1760–1775

1. *Classes, Interests, and Sections*

FULLY as important as the question of home rule in the empire was the question of who should rule in the colonies. The
first was more the subject of talk than of thought before 1765; the
second lay under the surface and was more thought about than discussed. Some colonies, such as North Carolina, were relatively democratic; and others, like New York, fully aristocratic in their social
structure. In some, such as Massachusetts and New Hampshire, the
franchise was fairly broad; in others, such as South Carolina, it was
very narrowly restricted. But no one of the thirteen was really democratic in political or social structure, much less 'dedicated to the
proposition that all men are created equal.' Class distinctions had
been brought from England by the colonists, and since maintained;
and class distinctions, in the seventeenth and eighteenth centuries,
implied political privilege.

In all the colonies in 1760 the franchise was limited by property
qualifications, which were much higher for office-holding; and the
newly settled regions were under-represented in colonial legislatures,
and in many other ways treated unfairly by colonial politicians and
men of wealth. There was nothing new in this, but the majority
were beginning to resent it, and the political controversy with the
mother country enabled them to make this resentment felt. An internal quarrel, partly class and partly sectional, cut athwart the larger
contest between colonies and mother country. There were really
two American revolutions at the same time: the sectional revolt of
thirteen colonies against imperial centralization; and a class upheaval against vested interests and local governing classes.

The upper colonial class consisted of merchants, landed gentry,
clergy of the established churches, lawyers and officials. These
groups had rival economic interests, and were often inspired by
opposite political views and religious affiliations; but they were
agreed in general that the direction of local and colonial affairs
should lie in their accustomed hands. They controlled the colonial

assemblies, in certain colonies owned most of the land, sat on the county courts, directed the important economic activities, controlled credit by individual loans (for there were as yet no banks) and set the social and cultural standards. Graduates of the nine colonial colleges filled the ranks of the learned professions, and, whatever their social origin, became gentlemen by virtue of their classical education. Members of this upper class, even in the few instances when they were not of English race, were English conscious and intensely proud of their English heritage. They provided most of the principal leaders of the Revolution in the years that followed: men such as the Otises, Adamses, and Trumbulls of New England; the Jays, Schuylers, Livingstons, Dickinsons, and Stocktons of the Middle Colonies; the Howards and Carrolls of Maryland; the Lees, Masons, and Washingtons of Virginia; Willie Jones of North Carolina and the Pinckneys, Rutledges, and Izards of South Carolina.

Next in the social scale came the middle class, which often shared political power with the gentry, but could not measure up to them on the economic and social scale. This class was the backbone of the colonies. It included the average farmer, city shopkeeper and master workman of New England and the Middle Colonies; the lesser planters and county-seat merchants of the South; the lawyers in the larger towns. There were more of them in regions settled at least fifty years, and less as you approached the frontier. This middle class was educated at least to the point of reading newspapers and following politics, and it produced not a few of the important leaders of the American Revolution, such as Ben Franklin and Patrick Henry. In New England and Virginia the middle class had broken into local politics; in Pennsylvania and the Carolinas it had only a foot in the door. Less intelligent than the upper class, it was more quickly responsive to emotional movements. The gentry drank the tea, but the middle class dumped it, at Annapolis and Boston.

Below the middle class came what for want of a better word we must call the lower class of freemen: people who were often referred to as ' the peasants ' or ' the meaner sort,' in eighteenth-century writings. The line between these and the middle class is hard to draw, and perhaps easier to describe historically. The lower class included, first, the many thousands of German, Scotch, and Irish immigrants who had come to America in the course of the eighteenth century, mostly since 1730. A few halted in seaports where they entered the 'ower ranks of labor; but the great majority pushed toward the fron-

tier, where land was cheap. Very many had come as indentured servants from the humbler ranks of society, accustomed to class distinctions in the Old World but hoping to rise in the New. Second, this
class included many small farmers of English stock, who had been
squeezed out of eastern sections by the growing dearness and scarcity
of land, and the large families of the period. Frontier New England,
for instance, was composed of such people. A third element in the
lower class was the urban mechanics and laborers, the tenantry of
New York, the coast fishermen and sailors, and the ' poor white ' of
the older-settled South. The lower class were little concerned with
political theory or imperial organization, but tremendously interested
in anything that affected their economic welfare, religious privileges,
and political rights. They were better off than people of their class
anywhere else in the world. But in no colony were they fairly represented in the legislature, and in few colonies did their interests and
grievances receive much consideration. Many, probably most, of
them had no vote; few even reached the lower house of a colonial
assembly; and in most colonies representation was so apportioned
as to favor the older-settled regions. They were a simple people,
unschooled and often unlettered. Those who were artisans worked
long hours at their lasts or their looms, and looked forward to
being independent farmers; the majority were on the way to become
just that, by clearing the wilderness and tilling the soil with rude
wooden implements. They were religious, but not ritualistic; intense
and emotional Protestants to whom the Great Awakening appealed.
Free land and voluntary religion were their two great objects; and
while neither of these were real driving forces of the American Revolution, they were the ' boosters ' which got the patriot locomotive
over many a stiff grade on its journey to independence.

Finally, there was a servile class of indentured white laborers and
Negro slaves, which we may ignore in 1760, as it does not come into
the political picture for fifty years. When Jefferson or Madison mentioned 'the people,' they did not intend to include this class at all.
There were Negro slaves in every one of the Thirteen Colonies, but
in New England and Pennsylvania they were few in number and
had little economic significance, being used chiefly for domestic service. It is a good indication of how far democratic ideas and economic
opportunity had already gone, that white domestic servants were
difficult to obtain in 1760, except by indenture.

These class divisions were not rigid, not even as clear and distinct as we have to state them in so brief a space; nor were conditions the same from one generation to another. American society of the eighteenth century was dynamic, not static. In New England the community was generous in helping poor scholars into college, whence they could become ministers or lawyers: John Adams was just such a man; and shrewd Yankee boys were constantly working up from the ranks to become merchants and shipowners. In New York many an alliance of ambitious lawyers or rising merchants with proud patroon was consummated by marriage. The Quaker society of eastern Pennsylvania was sufficiently democratic to enable men like Benjamin Franklin to get ahead — but no aristocracy, however rigid, could have kept Ben Franklin down! Even in the more aristocratic South, alliances of 'first families' and middle-class families were not unusual: as with the parents of Thomas Jefferson and John Marshall.

The division in the colonies, however, was not so much one of classes as of sections. Sectionalism — the political, economic, and social response of people to their geographic environment — has played an important rôle in American history from the seventeenth century to the present time. In 1760 there were two main sections in the American colonies: the coastal region or Tidewater, as it was called in the South, and the interior or up-country, as it was then called — the 'Old West,' as we have named it.

The coastal section has already been described in terms of its dominant class, the merchants and planters. The southern part of it, generally known as the Tidewater, extended in an uneven belt from Maryland to Georgia, and west to the 'fall line' — an imaginary line connecting the falls which mark the head of navigation of the rivers. Accessible to ocean-going ships by countless indentations of the sea, it was in close touch with the mother country. In Maryland, Virginia, and South Carolina, the Tidewater was a section of large plantations, devoted to the cultivation of staple crops under the slave system.

The Old West included most of the sparsely settled regions of northern New England, the Mohawk valley and Ulster County, New York, central and western Pennsylvania, the Shenandoah valley and western Virginia, and in the Carolinas most of the Piedmont, between the fall line and the mountains. This great up-country section contained, on the eve of the Revolution, not far from a million inhabitants. It was a sturdy, self-sufficient, democratic community, the home of a primitive radicalism in politics, of emotional revivalism in religion. This was an expansionist, imperialist section, regarding the Indians as having no more right than wild beasts to the land, which belonged to white folks by natural right; a fierce, land-hungry people, the vanguard of those pioneers who followed the setting sun across the continent to the Pacific.

The Old West suffered under grievances and discriminations as we have seen: under-representation in colonial assemblies, poor transportation and marketing facilities, taxation for the benefit of established churches, indebtedness to seaboard merchants. The Old West seized upon and adopted as passionate convictions the more democratic ideas which were set floating in the American Revolution. Ethan Allen was a perfect representative of this region — except for his impiety; Patrick Henry well represented its windy and thoughtless eloquence; Jefferson, who had a bit of the Old West in him, succeeded in making a complete fusion of frontier prejudice and democratic dogma; but adaptable Ben Franklin the typical bourgeois was also the favorite statesman of the frontier.

2. *The South*

The Southern Colonies present the keenest edge in the sectional cleavage. In Virginia, most populous of the American colonies, the conflict between Tidewater and back-country was particularly sharp, and was even recognized by local nicknames for the people of the two sections: ' Tuckahoes ' and ' Cohees.' At the same time, there were certain factors which made it possible to present a united front against the mother country.

The large plantations of eighteenth-century Virginia were acquired in various legitimate ways, and also by fraud and corruption. The second William Byrd increased his holdings from twenty-six thousand acres to seven times that area. Governor Alexander Spotswood deeded himself sixty thousand acres of the best Virginia land. The great estates were seldom concentrated in one locality, but scattered in largish parcels throughout Tidewater and Piedmont. They furnished the foundation for the wealth and social consequence of the ' First Families of Virginia,' such as the Lees, Randolphs, Carters, Beverleys, Ludlows, Blairs, Masons, and Pages, whose estates were kept intact through the feudal institutions of primogeniture and entail. A relatively small group of inter-related planter families controlled Virginia. They sat in the Governor's Council, composed the majority of the Burgesses, and filled the county bench which controlled most local matters. By virtue of their power to lay out new counties and apportion representation, they were heavily over-represented in the legislature: thus Elizabeth City County in the Tidewater, with a white population of 1574, had the same representation as Berkeley County, in the Shenandoah valley, with a white population of 16,781.

Here, as elsewhere in the South, the Anglican Church was established, and all inhabitants were required to pay taxes to its support. Tidewater gentry might acknowledge that there were many roads to Heaven, but they were convinced that a gentleman could take only the Anglican way. Dissenting churches existed only by sufferance, and not infrequently a Baptist preacher or Presbyterian clergyman was refused a license to preach. The English Act of Toleration of 1689 was not definitely extended to Virginia until 1755. Yet by the middle of the century the communicants of the Established Church composed a decided minority of the population.

The Virginia back-country — Piedmont and valley — contained over two-thirds of the white population of some 300,000, on the eve of the Revolution. While the Piedmont was settled by farmers and former servants from the coast, the Shenandoah valley was almost entirely peopled by Germans and Scots-Irish who followed the natural route from Pennsylvania, attracted by the excellent limestone soil, the climate, and the relative cheapness of land. The 'Cohees' or back-countrymen were socially democratic — 'simple' was the word then — and although one of them later wrote, ' We were accustomed to look upon what were called gentle folks, as beings of a superior order,' they nursed many grievances against the gentry. Negro slavery they hated, not because they regarded the black man as a brother, but because possession of him was a badge of privilege and the road to wealth. Their first spokesman was the eloquent Presbyterian preacher, Samuel Davies, leader of the Great Awakening, who had been instrumental in securing an extension of the Toleration Act to the colony. Davies, in turn, inspired one of the greatest and the most popular of frontier leaders, Patrick Henry.

Patrick Henry, tall, red-headed, and raw-boned, was a true child of the frontier. To low-country gentlemen he was a dangerous demagogue: to up-country democratics an inspired spokesman, a flaming genius around whom they might rally in their struggle against injustice. He had won widespread fame in the Parsons' Cause, where he skilfully turned a bad legal case into a stirring appeal for religious liberty and independence from royal control. Early in 1765 he was sent down to Williamsburg as burgess from Louisa County, and there struck an alliance with a young and discontented aristocrat named Richard Henry Lee. Together they uncovered a record of misuse of public moneys by Speaker Robinson and his Tidewater friends, shook the confidence of the colony in the ruling class, and became heroes of the democracy.

Yet despite this cleavage between Tidewater and back-country, the two sections were able to unite against the mother country. And despite the aristocratic nature of Tidewater society and the intimate connections of planters with the mother country, there were proportionately fewer tories in Virginia than in any other colony. This may be accounted for on several grounds, of which economic determinists would choose western lands and debts.

The tradition of colonial autonomy was very strong in the ' Old Dominion.' That very name, and the motto on the colony arms, *En dat Virginia quintam* under the leopards of England, the lilies of France, the lion rampant of Scotland, and the harp of Ireland, suggested that Virginia was a separate dominion of the Crown, not a part of the English realm. The governing class valued this implication, without any conscious sacrifice of loyalty. During generations of governing the colony with no serious interference from Crown representatives, the planters had developed a proud spirit which would suffer no challenge to their rights and traditions. Nurtured in the tradition of Hampden and Milton, familiar with the doctrines of Harrington and Sidney, they were political liberals without being democrats; royalists and republicans too.

The most socially reputable way to grow wealthy in Virginia was by speculation in land. We have seen how even before the Seven Years' War, land companies had been organized by Virginians and others to obtain and exploit the Ohio valley, and how the policy of the British government defeated them. Yet there is no evidence that land hunger gave any appreciable boost to the independence movement. The organizers of land companies always worked through politically prominent Englishmen, and through colonial agents in England like Franklin; and they had not yet given up hope when independence was declared.

Then, indebtedness tended to alienate the planter class from the mother country. Like the present-day farmer who sells in a world market and buys in a protected one, the tobacco planters sold their crop at a price fixed in England, and made all their purchases at prices fixed by their agents. These debts, Jefferson wrote, ' had become hereditary from father to son for many generations, so that the planters were a species of property annexed to certain mercantile houses in London,' and he estimated that at the opening of the Revolution at least £2,000,000 were due from Virginians to British merchants. Planters of Maryland and the Carolinas were in a similar position, but the problem was most acute in Virginia. Tom Moore gibed in verse:

> Those vaunted demagogues, who nobly rose
> From England's debtors to be England's foes
> Who could their monarch in their purse forget
> And break allegiance but to cancel debt —

but considering that only independence could bring about repudiation, Virginia's reluctance to consider independence for a year after the war began disproves this mercenary motive.

If we turn to the Carolinas we find conditions differing in detail only from those we have noted in Virginia. In North Carolina, indeed, the antagonism between plain and Piedmont was present in exaggerated form, and the colony was the scene of the first serious violent sectional conflict. A small group of seaboard gentry, in close alliance with the royal governor and his hand-picked council, composed an inner ring that ruled the colony. Though a small minority of the population they controlled four-fifths of the representation: the coastal counties sending five members each to the legislature, while the inland counties had two apiece. The system of taxation also was unfair, and quit-rents were everywhere assessed, though not successfully collected. Although the great majority of the population belonged to the dissenting churches, as late as 1769 no marriage was legal unless celebrated by an Anglican clergyman, of whom there were only six in a colony of 230,000 souls. The administration and the judiciary were shot through and through with corruption, and a report of 1770 revealed at least one defaulting sheriff in every county.

Up-country North Carolina, beyond the unsettled pine barrens, was more democratic than any other section of the American colonies, excepting possibly Vermont. This region had long been a refuge for the discontented of Virginia, and during the latter part of the eighteenth century it filled up rapidly with the Scots-Irish and Germans streaming down through the great valley.

In the decade of the seventeen-sixties the grievances of the up-country became intolerable; and repeated petitions to the government for redress proved futile. One from Anson County enumerated particular causes for discontent, including disproportionate taxes, venal lawyers and judges, lack of paper money, quit-rents, abuse of land laws, and religious intolerance, and, adopting the language of Tidewater politicians, asserted that, 'notwithstanding our sacred privileges, we have too long yielded ourselves slaves to remorseless oppression.' The discontent culminated in the organization of so-called Regulator associations in 1768. Two years later violence broke out all along the frontier, and Governor Tryon called out the militia and marched into the back-country to suppress this radical threat to the established order. The result was the total defeat of the Regulators at the battle of Alamance in May 1771. Some of the leaders were hanged for rebellion; hundreds of the rank and file took an oath of allegiance to the government, and thousands fled across the mountains to the fertile lands along the Watauga and Holston rivers. The battle of Alamance was not the first battle of the Revolution, as it has often been called, but a chapter in the story of the internal sectional conflict: the civil war of East against West which has so often threatened to break out in America, but never materialized. For the alignment has always been broken up by a new arrangement of forces: in this instance, the War of Independence.

South Carolina, smaller than any of the Southern colonies except Georgia, was dominated by the planter-merchant aristocracy of Charleston. Here the Rutledges and Ravenels, Bees and Hugers, Pringles and Petigrus formed the most exclusive and delightful society in the American colonies. A Charleston gentleman declared that he would rather be buried in St. Michael's or St. Philip's churchyard than live anywhere else. Wealthy rice and indigo planters such as the Pinckneys and Draytons allied with prosperous merchants such as the Manigaults and Izards to form a landed-commercial interest not unlike that which prevailed in New York. Like the planters of Virginia they were liberal and independent in imperial politics, but ultra-conservative in questions of domestic government.

Qualifications for office-holding were the highest in America — five hundred acres of land and ten slaves or property to the value of £1,000, for membership in the lower House, which was called the House of Commons. The Charleston gentry controlled the government, the administration, and the judiciary. They owned most of the desirable land along the coast and on the Santee, Pedee, Ashley and Cooper, Edisto and Savannah rivers, and engrossed large tracts in the up-country. The Anglican Church was firmly established. And here, alone in the colonies, the slaves outnumbered the white population.

The South Carolina up-country was a cosmopolitan as well as a democratic society: a melting pot of Germans, Swiss, Scots-Irish, English and Welsh, staunchly dissenting in religion, levelling in political principles. Their rôle in the government was purely passive. As in North Carolina, and for the same reasons, Regulator associations were organized in 1764. Hostilities were barely averted in 1769 when armed Regulators and militia met on the Saluda river. Peace was patched up, and some of the Western grievances were remedied. Sectionalism cropped up again during the War of Independence, and the Federalist era; but it never came to blows as in North Carolina.

Thus, for the Southern people the question of who was to rule at home was more immediate than the problem of home rule in the empire. We shall see how the War of Independence interrupted the growing sectional conflict, retarding it in some colonies, accelerating it in others, but everywhere giving it larger scope and new objectives.

3. The Middle Colonies

The sectional division in Pennsylvania and New York was, in a general way, similar to that in the South, but complicated by a larger urban population, and distinguished by the absence of religious issues. Pennsylvania was a proprietary colony, with all ungranted land owned by the Penn family, who also drew annual quit-rents from much of the land already granted. It was a Quaker province, still dominated by the merchant aristocracy of the Delaware valley; but it contained the largest proportion of non-English stock of any American colony, and Philadelphia was the largest and wealthiest town on the Atlantic seaboard. Pennsylvania and New Jersey were largely agricultural, but these two colonies also had the

most important iron industries in the colonies; it was by accident
that the Valley Forge, one of several hundred Pennsylvania furnaces and forges, became famous. Despite the Iron Act, the Potts
family, among others, were building new slitting mills and steel
furnaces in the Schuylkill valley, and 535 workmen were imported
in 1765 in order to build and operate the four blast furnaces
and seven forges of the American Iron Company in New Jersey.
It was not yet time for 'big business,' and this company soon
folded up.

Scarcely a century old, the colony of William Penn had developed
more rapidly and prosperously than any other in America, and contained, on the eve of the Revolution, a population well over 250,000.
The natural advantages of soil and climate, the religious toleration
that obtained, and the once enlightened form of government made
Pennsylvania the Mecca of the poor and discontented in Europe.
In the course of the eighteenth century tens of thousands of Germans from the Palatine, the upper Rhine, and Switzerland, and of
Scots-Irish from Ulster, poured into the back-country, squatting on
the proprietors' lands, and disquieting the older Quaker group.

The Germans were a stolid, God-fearing people. They tilled the
rich limestone soil of the Delaware, the Schuylkill and the Lehigh
valleys, clung tenaciously to their language and folkways, and formed
a solid German community in the heart of the English colonies.
Many had come over as indentured servants (redemptioners, the
Germans called them), and most were poor; but with thrift and
industry they wrung wealth from the soil, became a powerful middle-
class group and commanded the respect of their neighbors. Benjamin
Rush, the eminent Philadelphia physician, thus described these
'Pennsylvania Dutch':

A German farm may be distinguished from the farms of other citizens
by the superior size of their barns, the plain but compact form of their
houses, the height of their enclosures, the extent of their orchards, the
fertility of their fields, the luxuriance of their meadows, and a general
appearance of plenty and neatness in everything that belongs to them.

By the time of the Revolution these numbered not far from 90,000
— over one-third of the population of the province.

Another story was the Scots-Irish immigration into Pennsylvania.
Harried out of Scotland into northern Ireland in the seventeenth
century, they were forced, in the eighteenth, to abandon oppressed

Ulster for America, and throughout the century Pennsylvania attracted a larger proportion of them than any other colony. As early as 1729 Penn's secretary, James Logan, wrote:

It looks as if Ireland is to send all its inhabitants hither, for last week not less than six ships arrived, and every day, two or three arrive also. The common fear is that if they continue to come, they will make themselves proprietors of the province. It is strange that they thus crowd in where they are not wanted.

Finding the best lands in the east already occupied, the Scots-Irish poured out along the frontier and squatted on the proprietors' lands without leave or license. The very year after Logan wrote, they seized 15,000 acres on Conestogoe manor, declaring that 'It was against the laws of God and of Nature that so much land should remain idle while so many Christians wanted it to labor on.' Of the 670,000 acres occupied between 1732 and 1740, no less than 400,000 were taken by squatters, principally of this energetic, fighting people. Presbyterian to a man, land-hungry, individualistic, and living on the farthest frontier, the Scots-Irish bore the full brunt of Indian warfare, and were partly responsible for the peculiar savagery of the border wars. By 1775, although many had re-emigrated across Maryland to the Shenandoah valley, they and the Southern Irish who were beginning to arrive in appreciable numbers, constituted one-third of the Pennsylvania population.

Between these two back-country groups and the Quakers of Philadelphia, Chester, and Bucks counties along the Delaware, there was a natural hostility, complicated by the proprietary form of government and by the presence in Philadelphia of a large body of unfranchised mechanics, tradespeople, and laborers.

Although William Penn himself had lived in the colony for some time, and took an enlightened interest in the welfare and development of his vast estate, his descendants came to look upon Pennsylvania as a private domain destined by God to support them in the upper circles of English society. Between the reigning proprietor and his personally selected governor on the one hand, and the Quaker-controlled Assembly on the other, there was constant friction, sharpened by the unwillingness of the Penns to pay taxes on their wild lands. They claimed all the emoluments of government and ownership, without any of the expenses or responsibilities. Their attempts to collect quit-rents, the high price that they charged for land, and the inadequacy of defense against the Indians aroused against the proprietors the hostility of the westerners.

The city of Philadelphia was dominated by a wealthy Quaker aristocracy, many of whom had intermarried with the more progressive German families. They controlled the business, the trade and shipping, the finances, and the politics of the province, and lived in a luxury that excited the envy of the less fortunate. The division between the classes was a deep one. 'A poor man,' wrote one Philadelphia democrat, 'has rarely the honor of speaking to a gentleman on any terms, and never with any familiarity but for a few weeks before the election.' Even the genius of Benjamin Franklin, first citizen of America, could not bridge the social gap; he was always looked down upon by the 'best people' of the City of Brotherly Love. The political situation mirrored the social one: the franchise was limited to those who possessed £50, which successfully disqualified nine out of ten men; and the city of Philadelphia had only two representatives in the Assembly, while the rest of Philadelphia County, with less population, had eight. The discontent of the disfranchised element in the city threw them into alliance with the disgruntled westerners, and created a fighting combination that proved irresistible when the critical struggle came.

The causes of discontent in back-country Pennsylvania were similar to those in the Southern colonies. It was grossly underrepresented in the Assembly. The three Delaware river counties of Philadelphia, Chester, and Bucks returned eight representatives each; the five western counties had only eleven representatives altogether. If representation had been based either on population or on the number of taxables, the figures would have been reversed. Further, the western counties of York, Lancaster, Berks, and Northumberland were so large that it was difficult for many of the residents to get to the county seat, and until 1770 the Quaker oligarchy resisted subdivision. At the same time, representation was increased. But at no time prior to 1776 was it possible for any combination to outvote the Quaker aristocracy of the east.

Of more importance, probably, were the economic grievances of the western counties. These involved land, roads, and markets, taxation and paper money. The men of Ulster, who had left Ireland to get rid of rent, insisted that the land belonged to those who cultivated it, and resisted the collection of quit-rents. The natural market of the Delaware watershed was Philadelphia; that of the Susquehanna,

Baltimore. The best roads led to Baltimore, where the inhabitants of central and frontier Pennsylvania sold their crops and purchased their supplies. Naturally Philadelphia merchants resented this. The westerners also felt that they paid a disproportionate share of the taxes, because the Assembly, instead of raising revenue from real estate and business, supported the expense of government by poll taxes, the interest on paper money lent to landowners, and an excise on alcoholic spirits. The frontiersmen fiercely resented the excise tax of 1771 on whiskey; and yet the Assembly consistently refused to vote necessary taxes for the defense of the frontier.

Border warfare was the most serious western grievance. On the frontier fell the full burden of Indian depredations, and the chronicle of the border wars of eighteenth-century Pennsylvania is a dark and bloody one. The proprietors refused to provide for adequate defense, and the Assembly, taking refuge behind the anti-war doctrines of the Quaker church, refused to vote any military support or supplies. In fact both Governor and Assembly were inclined to lay the responsibility for the Indian wars at the door of the Scots-Irish themselves — and they were probably right. As a result the west bore not only the danger, but the full military and fiscal burden of the defense of the whole province. It was this situation that led to the famous raid of the 'Paxton Boys' in 1764. Infuriated by Indian attacks — which they had provoked — a band of frontiersmen fell on a little settlement of peaceable Christian Indians, massacred them, and then marched on Philadelphia to demand the wherewithal to continue the campaign. Only Benjamin Franklin's diplomacy averted an open conflict between the Paxton Boys and the authorities, but the episode revealed a bitter sectional hatred. If the Crown had exploited this feeling, it might have won the western vote here, as in North Carolina; for the westerners contrasted the aid given them by British regulars in the Pontiac rebellion with the utter neglect of them by their own Assembly.[1] It is true that the Scots-Irish of the eighteenth century were even more bitterly anti-English than the Catholic Irish — for the strident loyalty of Ulster is a very recent phenomenon — but the Philadelphia Quakers were a little more English than the English themselves, and socially superior in a very offensive way. As Charles Biddle observed on the legislators from the two sections: 'Those from the westward look upon the people in any of the commercial towns as little better

[1] See, however, Lord Dunmore's war, above, pp. 144–145.

than swindlers, while those of the east consider the western members a pack of savages.' William Smith, Provost of the Philadelphia Academy, described the Germans as ' a body of ignorant, proud, stubborn clowns,' and advocated their disfranchisement.

From 1763 on there was a continuous struggle in the colony between the conservative Quakers of the east and the Scots-Irish of the west in alliance with most of the Germans and disfranchised inhabitants of Philadelphia. The discontented groups were skilfully led, not to say exploited, by intelligent men such as Benjamin Franklin, Joseph Reed, Thomas McKean, and Judge George Bryan. Here, as elsewhere in the colonies, the liberal doctrines that were being hurled against England proved boomerangs in the domestic scene. ' By liberty,' sniffed the aristocratic Alexander Graydon, ' the people meant anarchy, since hallowed by the phrases of Equality, and the Rights of Man.'

Just as two series of tides, combining in a narrowing estuary, form a wave of destructive violence; so in Pennsylvania the rising tide of democracy met and coincided with the rising tide of home rule; and the result was independence. The War of Independence furnished an opportunity for the democratic and western element to get what they wanted — guaranteed, as they fondly hoped, by the most radical of revolutionary constitutions. Although quit-rents were high, the Pennsylvania land system was well managed, so that land titles were secure. In New Jersey, the contrary was true. That province, in 1765, was just settling down to peace and prosperity after a decade of land riots, lawlessness, and anarchy in the northern half, owing to laxity and unbusinesslike methods in granting land. It had been a conflict over land titles and quit-rents between squatters from New York and Scotch and New England settlers on the one side, and descendants of the English proprietors on the other. In the end the populace won most of what they wanted, obtaining good titles for small sums, and ' the Jersies ' were brought into the revolutionary movement more by the attraction of their powerful neighbors than from any political or social grievances of their own.

In the royal province of New York can be found the same elements as in Pennsylvania, but the antagonism was neither so deep nor so clean-cut. New York was one of the smaller colonies, both in settled area and in population. Only on the islands at the mouth of the Hudson and in the comparatively narrow valleys of the

Hudson and Mohawk rivers was there any considerable settlement; and the population in 1770 was less than that of Connecticut, or Maryland, or North Carolina. This was due partly to the powerful Iroquois confederacy which held all central New York, and partly to the illiberal land system inherited from New Netherlands.

The colony was dominated by a great land-owning aristocracy, whose princely estates surpassed those of Virginia planters in extent and value: the Van Rensselaers, Philipses, Livingstons, Van Cortlandts, De Lanceys, Morrisses, Schuylers, and others — descendants of the Dutch patroons or of the Duke of York's favorites. Six manorial estates in Westchester embraced over half the area of the county; Rensselaerwyck in Albany County covered nearly 700,000 acres; and the estate of Sir William Johnson along the Mohawk was even larger, while speculators like Cruger and Duane held title to almost unlimited lands in the back-country. Governor Bellomont declared the 'whole province' already 'given away to thirty persons,' and Governor Colden wrote, in 1764, that three estates contained

above a million acres each, several others above 200,000. . . . Although these grants contain a great part of the province, they are made in trifling acknowledgments. The far greater part of them still remain uncultivated, without any benefit to the community, and are likewise a discouragement to the settling and improving the lands in the neighborhood of them for from the uncertainty of their boundaries the patentees of these great tracts are daily enlarging their pretensions, and by tedious and most expensive law suits, distress and ruin poor families who have taken out grants near them.

This, indeed, had been the fate of the German Palatines who had come over in 1710, and their unfortunate experience had deterred others from settling land in this province.

The great proprietors not only engrossed the land, but through their control of the Assembly evaded taxation, and even a careful scrutiny of their titles. And here, as in South Carolina, the landed gentry strengthened their position by marriages with the wealthy merchant and professional families of New York City, such as the Alsops, Beekmans, Roosevelts, and Jays.

After a protracted struggle the New York Assembly, controlled by this upper-class combination, had gained ascendancy over the royal governor. The political differences that agitated the colony were largely of a factional nature, led by the De Lancey and the Livingston interests. The so-called Popular party was popular only in so far as it opposed royal control, but not at all in its constituency. The high suffrage qualifications successfully excluded the great majority of the adult males from politics, and the landlords could usually control the politics of those tenants who were able to meet the suffrage requirements. In only four counties was the Anglican Church established — New York, Westchester, Queens, and Richmond — but these counties contained one-half the population in 1700 and one-third of it in 1770. Land, trade, politics, law, the church, society, all were controlled by the landlord-merchant aristocracy. The life of this privileged class on great manorial estates along the Hudson, as described in the charming memoirs of Anne Grant, was probably more delightful than any that could be found north of the Potomac; but it contained no promise of the American life that was to be.

At the other end of the scale were the tenant farmers, small freehold farmers, and the mechanics and laborers of New York City and Albany. These, the large majority of the population, were out of the political picture altogether. Very few could qualify for the suffrage with a £40 freehold. They were an inarticulate and unorganized group, looking to the landlord for guidance and support — and often very happy in that relationship. A more democratic community was to be found in the Mohawk and Schoharie valleys, where numbers of Germans and Scots-Irish had settled, and where frontier conditions made for equality and self-sufficiency.

In between the aristocracy and the unenfranchised was a middle class of £40 freeholders, small merchants, tradespeople, lawyers, and professional men. These constituted less than ten per cent of the population, and had little cohesion, but counted heavily politically, by holding the balance of power between the upper-class factions. Isaac Sears, John Lamb, and the brilliant young lawyer, John Morin Scott, led this middle-class group. Their names were as prominent as those of Patrick Henry and Sam Adams among the radical whigs of the continent.

Dissatisfaction with the feudal structure of New York politics and society was general by 1760, but unorganized and inarticulate. Here, as elsewhere, the controversy with the mother country brought it out into the open. Organized opposition to the Stamp Act afforded the opportunity for the discontented to strike out at authority, and in the winter and spring of 1766 New York was troubled everywhere by mobs and rioters. The tenants of Westchester and Dutchess counties refused to pay their rents and 'prescribed law to their land-lords,' while five hundred men marched on New York City ripe for rioting and lawlessness. And the turmoil and rebellion of the Green Mountain Boys in the New Hampshire grants that went on during the ensuing decade was directed rather against the New York government and landlords than against England. New York was experiencing serious domestic difficulties when the controversy with the mother country substituted a common enemy for the sectional and class antagonisms, and obscured for a generation the domestic issues.

4. New England

The sectional and class cleavages in New England were less distinct, less organized and less concentrated than elsewhere in the American colonies. They do not appear to have had much to do with bringing the section into the American Revolution. In New England, the War of Independence was not accompanied by any internal revolution in the structure of society or of government. Merchants, lawyers, and clergy led the revolutionary movement, and remained in control after the war, their position materially strengthened by the prestige of victory. The situation in New England was analogous to that of Virginia, where the Tidewater planters stayed in power by espousing a popular and successful cause.

The history of New England during the eighteenth century exhibits three notable processes: a general secularization of life, the growth of industry and commerce, and the expansion of population. The ablest graduates of the New England colleges were showing a tendency to go into the law instead of the Church; but the clergy was still powerful enough in forming local opinion, and, on the issues with England, saw eye-to-eye with the lawyers and the merchant aristocracy. Nature was niggard to the Yankees in soil, climate, crops, and natural resources, but it gave a magnificent stand of timber, excellent harbors, and tempting off-shore fishing banks, which drew the people to shipbuilding, fishing, and carrying goods for more prosperous neighbors. New Englanders were the most inveterate fishermen in North America, and the most expert whalers in the world: it was the island of Nantucket that created that deep-sea whaling whose peculiar blend of enterprise, dare-deviltry, and ruthlessness forms one of the most lively memories of America's past. Shipbuilding by native craftsmen (partly for English order, as the cost was much less), and the operating of locally owned vessels with native thrift and shrewdness, surpassed fishing in economic importance: distribution, not production, brought the large profits. From every harbor of the New England coast — from Falmouth (Portland, Maine), Portsmouth, N. H., and Newburyport; from Salem, Marblehead, and Boston; from Plymouth, New Bedford, Providence, Newport, New London, New Haven, and Bridgeport, hundreds of little schooners, sloops, and ketches put forth each year for coastwise traffic, and scores of brigs and ships for England, the Mediterranean, the Gold Coast, and the West Indies. During the War of Independence the West India Islands were often near starvation for want of the Yankee provision ships; and the loss of this principal market for New England farms, forests, and fisheries produced agrarian unrest at home. In 1660 New England traded for a living; in 1760 New England lived for trade. The old clerical and magisterial families were supplanted by those whose wealth was drained from the sea: Langdon, Dalton, Cabot, Derby, Gerry, Hancock, Quincy, Delano, D'Wolf, Hillhouse — to take only one from each principal port. These formed a substantial upper-class society, as in New York, Philadelphia, and Charleston. With the aid of country storekeepers, who were often in debt to them, they controlled politics; without any competition from landed gentry they established the social standards, patronized painters such as Copley, silversmiths such as Paul Revere, and parsons too numerous to mention; and ran their communities like their ships, from the quarter-deck. Hence their interests and their pride were affected by the acts of the British government regulating West India and other trade, in 1764–67, just as the interests of the Virginia planters were affected by the new Western policy. This economic solidarity of the seaboard explains why four New England colonies came into the revolutionary movement as a unit, although two of them, Rhode Island and Connecticut, did not have the usual irritant of a royal governor and other crown-appointed officials. Rhode Island, in fact, was the center in North America for the evasion of the Acts of Trade and the rum distillery, both of which interests would have been ruined if the new parliamentary policy had taken effect. This stout little colony in 1764 was annually importing 14,000 hogsheads of molasses, from which some 1,750,000 gallons of rum were distilled; and a large part of this went for purchasing slaves in Africa to sell in the Carolinas and the West Indies. Massachusetts Bay found vent for over half her rum production (which was even greater than Rhode Island's) in Newfoundland, where it was exchanged for fish, fur, and European goods that the English fishermen brought over for trade.

If there was little democracy in these seaboard communities, there was on the other hand little discontent. By and large the mechanics, ship-carpenters, and seamen were bound by ties of common interest to the merchants and shipowners. The lot of the fisher-folk of Gloucester and Marblehead was less happy: John Adams thought their condition ' as abject as that of slavery.' These submerged groups, eager like all Yankees to rise in the world, found their leader in Samuel Adams, and their medium in the town meeting. They suffered most sharply from the regulative or coercive measures of imperial reorganization, for their margin of living was very narrow; hence they furnished a rich field for the agitator, and were ready for mob violence when leaders who spoke their language gave the word.

Expansion is the third note in New England history during the eighteenth century. Land hunger was as strong among the hard-scrabble Yankee farmers as among the placid Dutch of Pennsylvania or the frontiersmen of Virginia and the Carolinas. By 1760 practically all southern New England had been taken up. On the conclusion of the Seven Years' War, the teeming population swarmed into northern New England. In fifteen years prior to the Revolution one hundred towns were planted in New Hampshire, seventy-four in Vermont, and over twenty in Maine. The frontier was being pushed forward with unprecedented rapidity.

In the Maine district of Massachusetts there was ill feeling between settlers and groups of merchant proprietors in Boston, who had bought for a song ancient crown grants; but that caused no serious trouble until after the war. New Hampshire was rather a special case in New England, with some points of resemblance to Pennsylvania and North Carolina. For one thing it had a valuable natural product in white pine. The small assembly, in order to avoid taxes for frontier defense, or sharing the land-grant graft with uncouth democrats of the frontier, denied representation to interior towns. As late as 1773, of 147 communities only 46 were represented, and by 34 members. And this does not count all the 138 townships which the Wentworths laid out beyond the Connecticut river, in a region claimed by New York, whose claims they did nothing to quiet. So the New Hampshire frontiersmen welcomed the Revolution as a chance to be quits with the Portsmouth gang, which conveniently went tory. The Green Mountain Boys organized their section as the State of Vermont; the rest of the population got a new constitution, and soon transferred the state capital from Portsmouth to Concord.

So, generally speaking, New England had a nascent or suspended, rather than an actual, frontier grievance. It broke out after the war in disturbances like Shays's Rebellion, and finally turned into Jeffersonian Republicanism.

More palpable were the causes of New England's early primacy, with Virginia, in the patriot cause. Parliamentary prohibition of the Land Bank of 1740 'raised a greater ferment in this province than the Stamp Act did,' said John Adams, and aroused a fierce antagonism against some of the Boston families like the Olivers and Hutchinsons, who welcomed British aid to the cause of sound money. In Connecticut, a 'New London Society United for Trade and Commerce,' a wild-cat scheme, somewhat similar to the Massachusetts Land Bank, had an even shorter and more disastrous career. In that eastern section of Connecticut the religious radicalism engendered by the Great Awakening bit deeper than elsewhere, creating several religious societies with a grievance outside the established church. And a contemporary remarked that both the economic and the religious grievance combined to make that section the most radical part of Connecticut when the Stamp Act was announced.

Especially irritating to the backwoods enemies of 'conservation' was the attempt of royal officials to keep settlers out of certain well-timbered lands, on the theory that the tall pines were reserved for masts in the royal navy. Apprehension lest the mother country establish American bishops in the colonies was widespread throughout New England. That such a project was ever seriously considered by Parliament is doubtful; but the fear of it acted on politics like the fear of 'popery' in a recent presidential campaign. When Parliament in 1774 granted liberal privileges to the Catholic Church in Canada, some of the patriot leaders in New England began to insinuate that George III, like James II, had gone 'papist.'

In New England there was no acute class conflict; but the existence of a multitude of puritan, frontier, and maritime bristles, which were rubbed the wrong way by almost everything Parliament did, good or bad, on the American problem, explains why that section bore the first brunt of attempted coercion, and went in whole-heartedly for independence.

*　　*　　*　　*

Now, as we have been chronicling divisions and grievances to the neglect of unities and contentments, we have perhaps unwittingly given the impression that the people of the Thirteen Colonies were all ready to spring at one another's throats, or at England's, on the slightest provocation. That is not correct. Rare indeed is the community and golden the age where complaints and clashes cannot be found; but they are not always significant. It is only when some new element is added, or an unusual issue arises, and when able and energetic men are willing to risk their necks to head the cause that latent grievances become patent, and passive causes, dynamic. So it was in France, when the monarchical régime proved unable to make both ends meet. So it was in Russia, when a determined group of Communists played on the war weariness of the people. So it was in Germany, when a new leader promised relief from poverty and humilitation. So it was in the American Revolution. The taxation controversy, and the naked issue of power that arose with the Coercive Acts of 1774, set all the colonial bees a-buzzing and a-stinging; and it was many years before they settled down to making honey again, in a new federal hive.

IX

THE REVOLUTION PRECIPITATED

1774-1776

1. *Gathering Clouds*

THE Congress which assembled in Philadelphia in September 1774, had been summoned by popular demand — not for independence but for liberty, as Americans understood that word. They expected Congress to take steps to ward off parliamentary wrath, vigorously to assert colonial rights, and, so far as Americans could, to restore imperial relations to their former happy status. This Continental Congress was an extra-legal body chosen by provincial congresses, or popular conventions, and instructed by them. This meant that the patriot party, which did not fear extra-legal action, was in control of the situation, and that extreme conservatives who would have nothing to do with resistance to the laws were not represented. Otherwise the membership of Congress was a fair cross-section of American opinion. Here were extremists like John and Samuel Adams from Massachusetts, Stephen Hopkins from Rhode Island, Thomas Mifflin of Pennsylvania, Richard Henry Lee and Patrick Henry of Virginia, and Christopher Gadsden of South Carolina; moderates like Peyton Randolph and George Washington of Virginia, John Dickinson of Pennsylvania, and the Rutledges of South Carolina; conservatives like James Duane and John Jay of New York and Joseph Galloway of Pennsylvania. The varied interests of the colonies were well represented. Every colony save Georgia sent at least one delegate, and the total number was fifty-five — large enough for diversity of opinion, small enough for genuine debate and effective action.

Able as this Congress was, it faced a distressing dilemma: it must give an appearance of such firm unanimity as would persuade or frighten the British government into concessions; and at the same time avoid any show of radicalism or 'spirit of independency' that might alarm conservative Americans. To brandish the sword and proffer the olive branch simultaneously was a feat that required no little skill. At the same time Congress did not wish to encourage the spirit of lawlessness and levelling that was already abroad in the country.

Peyton Randolph, chosen president of the Congress, struck a key-note of caution; but the presentation of the Suffolk Resolves precipitated Congress into the hands of the radicals. These famous resolves from a convention of Suffolk County, Massachusetts, declared that no obedience was due to the Coercive Acts, which should be resisted ' as the attempts of a wicked administration to enslave America.' They were presented in such a way that unless Congress endorsed them it would appear to have abandoned Massachusetts to her fate. It endorsed them, and by that endorsement the bolder and more reckless spirits won a victory that they exploited to the full. Hard upon this came the rejection of Joseph Galloway's Plan of Union. The essence of his plan was to unite the colonies and elect a continental legislature which would have co-equal control with the British Parliament over all colonial affairs. No Act of Parliament would apply to America unless accepted by the continental legislature, which would have control over Indians, Western land grants, and raising men and money in war time, subject to veto of the British government. Although not so well worked out as Franklin's federal plan of 1754,[1] Galloway's was so plausible that it was lost only by a majority of one. The division of opinion, as stated by Galloway himself, is probably not exact but illuminating. Those who favored his plan ' were men of loyal principles, and possessed the greatest fortunes in America; the others were congregational and presbyterian republicans, or men of bankrupt fortunes, overwhelmed in debt to the British merchants.' If the Galloway plan had been presented before the Suffolk Resolves, it would certainly have been adopted, and the next move would have been up to Great Britain.

Congress then proceeded to a series of retaliatory measures against the Coercive Acts. Mindful of the success of commercial boycott in 1765–70, it adopted new and stringent non-importation, non-exportation, and non-consumption agreements. John Adams, unsatisfied, confided to his *Diary,* ' When Demosthenes (God forgive the vanity of recollecting his example) went as ambassador from Athens to the other States of Greece . . . he did not go to propose a non-Importation or non-Consumption Agreement.' But Lee of Virginia was certain that this ' Association ' would wring immediate

[1] See above, p. 131.

concessions from Parliament, while Chase of Maryland believed that
they would reduce England to bankruptcy.

Having agreed upon this counter-offensive, Congress passed a
Declaration of Rights and Grievances addressed to the people of
Great Britain and the colonies, and, as a sop to the moderates, a
petition to the king. These papers, taken together, led the great
Chatham to admit that 'for solidity of reason, force of sagacity and
wisdom of conclusion under a complication of difficult circumstances, no nation or body of men can stand in preference to
the general Congress at Philadelphia.' The Declaration of Rights
summed up anew the traditional arguments of American protest
and anticipated in many particulars the grievances of the Declaration of Independence. It did, however, concede parliamentary
regulation of external commerce and strictly imperial affairs: for
Chatham had given America due warning that otherwise Americans
could expect no sympathy from his party.

This concession, it must be admitted, was not pleasing to the radicals. Quite independently of one another, James Wilson, a close-
reasoning Scot of Pennsylvania, Thomas Jefferson, and John Adams
had reached the conclusion that Parliament had absolutely no jurisdiction over the colonies. 'All the different members of the British
Empire are distinct States,' said Wilson, 'independent of each other,
but connected together under the same sovereign in right of the
same Crown.' Wilson's *Considerations on the Authority of Parliament,* Jefferson's *Summary View,* and Adams's *Novanglus* papers
published this startling theory between August 1774 and February
1775. Historically they found no ground for Parliament's authority,
although they admitted that the colonies had weakly accepted it;
logically there was no need for it, since the colonial legislatures were
competent. The colonists should love and honor the king, follow
his lead in war, observe the treaties he concluded with other princes;
but otherwise govern themselves. So these three Americans in 1774-75
demanded for their colonies the exact dominion status which
Canada, South Africa, Australia, New Zealand, and the Irish Free
State now enjoy in the British Empire, and which is now the official
basis of the British Commonwealth of Nations. Here was the complete theory of federalism, already worked out before the War of
Independence. But these doctrines had no remote chance of acceptance in England. Very few Englishmen except Lord Camden
— who pointed out the analogy of the Channel Islands — could

understand how a community could be in the empire, unless parliamentary authority over it were sovereign and complete. It is one of the ironies of history that the British Empire should finally have officially adopted the federal theory of these three American thinkers, which had been dismissed as insincere and fanatical ravings in 1775.

The most important work of the Congress was 'The Association.' This provided for a system of committees of inspection in every town or county, in order to supervise the non-importation, non-exportation, and non-consumption agreements. The Association was charged to inspect customs entries, to publish the names of merchants who violated the agreements and to confiscate their importations, and even to 'encourage frugality, economy, and industry . . . and discountenance every species of extravagance and dissipation, especially all horse-racing, and all kinds of gaming, cock-fighting, exhibitions of shews, plays, and other expensive diversions and entertainments.' This play for the religious vote was a master-stroke.

Thus a Congress called to protest against parliamentary usurpation of rights ended by creating a powerful and extra-legal machinery for supervising the daily life of Americans. The Association introduced an element of illegality and rebellion that caused moderates to draw back in alarm. For many the issue now became: submission to parliamentary authority, or to the petty tyranny of a self-constituted vigilance committee. 'If we must be enslaved,' wrote the loyalist Samuel Seabury, 'let it be by a King at least, and not by a parcel of upstart, lawless committeemen.'

The Association favored the spirit of lawlessness that was already abroad in the colonies. By placing power squarely in the hands of the radicals, and making nonconformity synonymous with toryism, it forced large numbers of moderates to go along with the current, and widened hopelessly the breach between patriots and loyalists.

Even now the Crown might have effected an alliance with the large body of conservative opinion in the colonies, and by timely concession have averted hostilities. For not willingly would the propertied men in the colonies ally themselves with levellers and democrats, mob leaders and snooping committees. But the king had no intention of making concessions; and what the king said went, in the North administration. In September 1774, George III, scoring a petition of Philadelphia Quakers asking concessions, wrote, 'the dye is now cast, the Colonies must either submit or triumph;

I do not wish to come to severer measures but we must not retreat . . . there must always be one tax to keep up the right, and
as such I approve of the Tea Duty.' And in November: 'the New
England Governments are now in a State of Rebellion, blows must
decide whether they are subject to this Country or independant.'
In February 1775, Lord North pushed through Parliament a resolution providing that if any colony would raise of its own authority
the cost of its own government, with a proper quota (determined in
England) for defense, Parliament would forbear to tax that colony,
and would pay the customs duties collected within its borders into
the colony treasury. The king liked this because it would, so he
fondly thought, 'put an end to Congresses,' and North defended
it because it gave up no British right, which was certainly true; but
from the American point of view the North Conciliatory Resolve
conceded nothing on taxation, and failed to meet the latest issue
of closing a port and altering a government. And news of it arrived
in America at a moment fatal to any reconciliation — just as the
news of Lexington and Concord was being shouted through the
length and breadth of the land.

2. *Hostilities Begin*

General Thomas Gage, an amiable gentleman with an American
wife, was in command of the garrison at Boston. Dr. Joseph Warren,
one of the leading radicals of that town, where political activity
had wholly replaced trade, wrote to an English friend on 20 February 1775:

It is not yet too late to accommodate the dispute amicably. But I am
of the opinion that if once General Gage should lead his troops into the
country with the design to enforce the late Acts of Parliament, Great
Britain may take her leave, at least of the New England colonies, and,
if I mistake not, of all America. If there is any wisdom in the nation,
God grant it may be speedily called forth! Every day, every hour widens
the breach. A Richmond, a Chatham, a Shelburne, a Camden, with their
noble associates, may yet repair it; it is a work which none but the
greatest of men can conduct.

Unfortunately these gentlemen and their noble associates were
in opposition, without a dog's chance of ousting the king's well-
nursed majority; and General Gage's duty was to enforce the Coercive Acts. News that the Massachusetts patriots were collecting
powder and military stores at Concord came to his ears. On the

night of 18 April he sent a strong detail of his garrison to confiscate these munitions. But the signal was given: Paul Revere and Will Dawes aroused the whole countryside. When Major Pitcairn, after a night of marching, led his column of light infantry into the village of Lexington, he saw through the mists of the early morning a grim band of minute-men lined up across the common. There was a moment of hesitation, cries and orders from both sides, and in the midst of the noise somebody fired. Then firing broke out along both lines and the Americans dispersed, leaving eight of their number dead on the green. The first blood of the War for American Independence had been shed. Who first fired, American or Englishman, is one of the unsolved riddles of history; but the patriots managed to circulate their own view of it as a brutal and wanton attack on peaceful villagers.

The British continued their march to Concord, where the 'embattled farmers' at the bridge 'fired the shot heard round the world.' Their purpose partially accomplished, the British regiments began their return march. All along the road, behind stone walls, hillocks, and houses, the militia arriving from 'every Middlesex village and farm' made targets of the bright red coats. When the weary column finally stumbled into Boston it had lost 247 in killed and wounded. And inside of a week Boston was a beleaguered city.

It was while the country was still resounding with the alarms and 'atrocities' of Lexington and Concord, that the Second Continental Congress assembled in Philadelphia (10 May 1775). The prophetic words of Patrick Henry were still ringing in the ears of the delegates: 'It is vain, sir, to extenuate the matter. Gentlemen may cry "peace, peace" but there is no peace. The war is actually begun! The next gale that sweeps from the north will bring to our ears the clash of resounding arms! Our brethren are already in the field! Why stand we here idle?' Why, indeed? Congress was in no conciliatory mood. War had already begun. Would it be accompanied by independence? Even as delegates were asking these questions, timidly or boldly, Ethan Allen and his Green Mountain Boys were crashing through the defenses of Fort Ticonderoga and raising the standard of revolt in the North. Control of affairs was rapidly drifting out of the hands of hesitant and law-abiding men, and Congress had little to do but register, in one form or another, the accomplished facts.

This second Congress was as distinguished a group as ever assembled in America, and they have achieved historical immortality as 'the signers.' John Hancock, a wealthy Boston merchant, was chosen President. Young Thomas Jefferson was there, fresh from composing his *Summary View,* and the venerable Dr. Franklin, so discouraged by his vain search for conciliation in London as to be an exponent of independence. Yet the radicals did not push through their program of accepting war and declaring independence without a severe struggle. John Dickinson again raised his voice in favor of conciliation, and persuaded his reluctant colleagues to adopt another petition to the king.

The real temper of Congress was revealed by a stirring Declaration of the Causes and Necessity of Taking up Arms, the joint product of Dickinson and Jefferson.

Our cause is just. Our union is perfect. Our internal resources are great, and, if necessary, foreign assistance is undoubtedly attainable. . . . The arms we have been compelled by our enemies to assume, we will . . . employ for the preservation of our liberties, being with one mind resolved to die free men rather than live slaves.

And then came the ominous if oblique threat,

We mean not to dissolve that union which has so long and so happily subsisted between us. Necessity has not yet driven us into that desperate measure, or induced us to excite any other nation to war against them. We have not raised armies with ambitious designs of separating from Great Britain, and establishing independent States. . . .

The inference was unmistakable, and even as the Declaration was being debated Congress took the militia besieging Boston into Continental service, and appointed Colonel George Washington commander-in-chief of the American forces. And on 23 June Washington rode off from Philadelphia to take charge of the army, only to be met by breathless couriers with the stirring story of Bunker Hill. And shortly after Congress authorized a project which the British could only consider as wantonly aggressive: an overland expedition to Quebec under Benedict Arnold,[2] to bring Canada into the Union as the fourteenth colony.

3. *Independence*

Still, the idea of independence was repugnant to many members of Congress and to a large part of the American people. The osten-

[2] See next chapter.

sible purpose of the two Continental Congresses had been to get the Coercive Acts repealed, restore imperial relations as before 1763, and thus avert both war and independence. As late as the autumn of 1775 the legislatures of North Carolina, Pennsylvania, New Jersey, New York, and Maryland went on record against independence. Public opinion was not yet ready for any drastic action. Yet the colonies could not forever remain half in, half out of the empire, professing allegiance while refusing obedience. Moderates persuaded themselves that they were not fighting the king or the mother country, but the 'unprincipled hirelings of a venal ministry.' They referred to the enemy as the 'ministerial,' not the British army; they hoped for a political crisis in England that would place their friends in power; as late as January 1776 the king's health was toasted nightly in the officers' mess presided over by General Washington. Radicals acquiesced in this policy because they expected that it would have the contrary effect, and make Britain more uncompromising; as it did.

As the months wore on, the difficulties of prosecuting a war while still a part of the empire became more and more patent. Independence was desirable for military success; without it the colonies could scarcely expect that assistance from France upon which they based great hopes. Furthermore, it became clearer every day that the first Congress's policy of non-importation and non-exportation was a complete failure. Commercial pressure was not effective after fighting had aroused passion. It simply prevented the Americans from getting needed supplies, and hurt them more than it did the British. And after so many lives had been lost, at Bunker Hill and in the vain assault on Quebec (December 1775), there came a feeling that something of permanent value ought to be achieved.

No compromise came from England. King George, naturally regarding as insincere an 'olive-branch' petition from a body that was carrying on armed rebellion, refused to receive it, and instead issued a proclamation declaring the colonies to be in a state of rebellion (23 August 1775). And on 22 December 1775, all trade and intercourse with the Thirteen Colonies was interdicted by Parliament. The triumphant comment of John Adams reveals how this Act helped the American radicals:

I know not whether you have seen the Act of Parliament called the Restraining Act or Prohibitory Act, or Piratical Act or Act of Independency — for by all these titles it is called. I think that the most apposite is the Act of Independency; the King, Lords and Commons have united in sundering this country from that, I think forever. It is a complete dismemberment of the British Empire. It throws thirteen colonies out of the royal protection, and makes us independent in spite of supplications and entreaties.

In January 1776 Thomas Paine's pamphlet *Common Sense* was published. This book was to the American Revolution what *Uncle Tom's Cabin* was to the Civil War. Sweeping aside dialectic and sentiment, Paine stated the case for independence in a crisp, vigorous language, that appealed to the ordinary American. It presented in popular form the natural rights philosophy that was to be embodied in the Declaration of Independence. 'Society in every state is a blessing, but Government, even in its best state, is but a necessary evil; in its worst, an intolerable one. Government, like dress, is the badge of lost innocence; the palaces of kings are built upon the ruins of the bowers of Paradise.' With ruthless disregard for tradition and sentiment Paine attacked the monarchy, the British Constitution, and the empire. Monarchy itself, he argued, is an absurd form of government; one honest man worth 'all the crowned ruffians that ever lived'; and George III, 'the Royal Brute of Great Britain,' the worst of monarchs. Such words were sweet music to democratic ears. How absurd, too, that a continent should be governed by an island! Such an unnatural connection merely subjected the colonies to exploitation, and involved them in every European war. Separation would not only avert these evils, but bring positive benefits — such as a world market for American trade. Anticipating the idea of isolation, Paine announced it to be 'the true interest of America to steer clear of European contentions, which she can never do while, by her dependence on Great Britain, she is made the make-weight in the scale of British politics.'

Thus with persuasive simplicity Paine presented the alternatives: continued submission to a tyrannous king, an outworn government, and a vicious economic system; or liberty and happiness as a self-sufficient independent republic. The loyalists he lumped together and denounced as 'interested men who are not to be trusted, weak men who *cannot* see, prejudiced men who will not see, and a certain set of moderate men who think better of the European world than it deserves.' And he closed with the eloquent peroration:

O! ye that love mankind! Ye that dare oppose not only the tyranny but the tyrant, stand forth! Every spot of the old world is overrun with oppression. Freedom hath been hunted round the Globe. Asia and Africa have long expelled her. Europe regards her as a stranger and England hath given her warning to depart. O! receive the fugitive and prepare in time an asylum for mankind.

The influence of this amazing pamphlet cannot well be exaggerated. Within a few months it had been read by or to almost every American. It rallied the undecided and the wavering, and proved a trumpet call to the radicals. 'Every Post and every Day rolls in upon us Independence like a Torrent,' observed John Adams exultantly. Among the makers of the new nation few played a more dynamic part than Thomas Paine, sometime staymaker of Norfolk in old England.

In each colony now a keen struggle was going on between conservatives and radicals for control of the delegations in Congress. As yet only a few delegations were definitely instructed for independence: it was the task of the radicals to force everyone into line. The struggle coincided with the class and sectional divisions which we have already described as present in most of the colonies. Everywhere the radicals were using the powerful lever of independence to oust the conservatives and put themselves in control, and, under cover of a popular war, push through their programs of democratic reform. The alternative that faced the conservatives in such colonies as New York, Pennsylvania, Maryland, and South Carolina was not pleasant. If they tried to stem the popular tide, they would see themselves denounced as tories, hurled out of office, and old institutions exposed to the mercies of the radical democrats. They could maintain their accustomed position and influence, and save their property, only by acquiescing in a policy of war and separation. In Pennsylvania the struggle was particularly bitter, coinciding as it did with the ancient feud of Scotch-Irish frontiersmen and the city artisans against the Quaker oligarchy and the wealthier Germans. The success of the radicals here was achieved only by overthrowing the old government, establishing a new one with full representation of the frontier counties, and drawing up a new constitution. This new revolutionary government promptly instructed the Pennsylvania delegates for independence. The effect of this radical victory upon the Congress, sitting in Philadelphia, was tremendous.

Events now moved rapidly toward independence. In January 1776 came the burning of Norfolk by the patriots to prevent it falling into the power of Lord Dunmore, and Virginia loyalists had to seek the protection of the British fleet. The next month the embattled farmers of the South repulsed royal troops and native loyalists at Moore's Creek Bridge. In March the legislature of North Carolina instructed its delegates to declare independence and form foreign alliances. Congress then threw the ports of America open to the commerce of the world, and sent an agent to France to obtain assistance. On 10 May Congress advised the states to establish independent governments, as several had done already. On 7 June Richard Henry Lee, pursuant to instructions from his native state, rose in Congress and moved ' That these United Colonies are, and of right ought to be, Free and Independent States.' After a terrific debate in which sturdy John Adams pled the cause of independence, Lee's motion was carried on 2 July. Meantime Congress had appointed a committee consisting of Thomas Jefferson, John Adams, Benjamin Franklin, Roger Sherman, and Robert Livingston to prepare a formal declaration ' setting forth the causes which impelled us to this mighty resolution.' This Declaration of Independence, written by Thomas Jefferson, was adopted 4 July 1776.

4. The Great Declaration

The Declaration of Independence not only announced the birth of a new nation; the philosophy which it set forth has been a dynamic force in the entire Western world throughout the nineteenth century. 'Out of a decent respect to the opinions of mankind,' Jefferson summed up, not only the reasons which impelled Americans to independence, but the political and social principles upon which the Revolution itself rested. The particular ' abuses and usurpations' which are charged against the king, and which fill a large part of the Declaration, are not advanced as the basis for revolution, but merely as proof that George III had ' in direct object the establishment of an absolute tyranny over these states.' The Declaration rests, therefore, not upon particular grievances, but upon a broad basis which commanded general support not only in America but in Europe as well. The grievances are scarcely those which appeal to the student of that period as fundamental; examined in the candid light of history many seem distorted, others inconsequential, some unfair. One of the strongest, an indictment of the slave trade, was struck out at the insistence of Southern and New England delegates. But the historical accuracy of the grievances is not the yardstick by which they are to be measured. Jefferson was making history, not writing it.

Jefferson's indictment is drawn against George III, despite the fact that for twelve years the dispute between the colonies and Britain had centered on the question of parliamentary authority. The only reference to Parliament is in the clause, 'He has combined with others to subject us to a jurisdiction foreign to our constitution and unacknowledged by our laws, giving his assent to their acts of pretended legislation.' Entire odium of parliamentary misdeeds is transferred to the hapless George III. The reason for this shift was not that the king's influence over politics was understood, but that Congress had finally accepted the position of Adams, Jefferson, and Wilson regarding Parliament as merely the legislative body of Great Britain, each colonial legislature being a co-equal and co-ordinate body, having exclusive power (with the king or his representative) over that particular colony.

The political philosophy of the Declaration is set forth clearly and succinctly in the second paragraph:

We hold these truths to be self-evident, that all men are created equal, that they are endowed by their creator with certain unalienable rights, that among these are life, liberty, and the pursuit of happiness. That to secure these rights governments are instituted among men, deriving their just powers from the consent of the governed. That whenever any form of government becomes destructive to these ends, it is the right of the people to alter or abolish it, and to institute new government, laying its foundation on such principles and organizing its powers in such form, as to them shall seem most likely to effect their safety and happiness.

'These truths' were not the creatures of Jefferson's mind; they formed a political theory 'self-evident' to his generation. The obvious sources for this philosophy were Harrington and Sidney, John Locke's *Second Treatise on Government,* and the actual experience of Americans. It is unnecessary to seek further.

And what was the nature of this ideal government? It was one created by social compact. Originally, so Locke and Jefferson held, men lived equal in a state of nature. When necessity required some form of control, they got together and set up a government by popular consent. It is the function and purpose of government to protect men in their life, liberty, and property. Jefferson substituted for the term 'property' the phrase 'pursuit of happiness': a characteristic and illuminating stroke on the part of this social philosopher who throughout his life placed human rights first. If government fails to perform these functions, 'it is the right of the people to alter or abolish it altogether, and to institute new government' — as the Americans were doing. To the troublesome charge that such popular power would lead to anarchy, Jefferson replied, 'all experience hath shown that mankind are more disposed to suffer while evils are sufferable, than to right them by abolishing the forms to which they are accustomed.'

It is futile and irrelevant to argue that this theory of the origin of government does not square with nineteenth-century experience and twentieth-century anthropological knowledge. Whatever the origin of government may have been in prehistoric times, in America it often arose just as Jefferson described. As in the Mayflower Compact of 1620, so in countless frontier settlements from the Watauga to the Willamette, men came together spontaneously and organized a government. Jefferson's political philosophy seemed to them merely the common sense of the matter. And the ideas of the Declaration were vital throughout in the nineteenth century. Historical facts derive their significance not as they are judged correct or incorrect by some abstract criterion, but by the place they come to hold in the minds and imaginations of men. By a curious transfer of ideas Jefferson's doctrine that all men are *created* equal has gradually come to mean that all men *are* equal, or that if not they ought to be. And although Jefferson did not mean to include slaves as men, public opinion finally came to regard slavery as inconsistent with the Declaration. Most of the great liberal reform movements of the nineteenth century — abolition, universal suffrage, labor laws, popular education; most of the nationalist movements — in Ireland, Finland, Italy, Germany in '48, Czecho-Slovakia — based their philosophy on the Declaration of Independence; and the American Union could not have been saved in 1861–65 without it. The timelessness of its doctrines and the haunting beauty of its phrasing insure immortality to the Great Declaration.

5. *The Loyalists*

The Declaration of Independence divided those who hoped to solve the problem of imperial order by evolution from those who preferred to solve it by revolution. By calling into existence a new nation it made loyalty to King George treason; and in most colonies patriot committees went about forcing everyone, on pain of imprisonment of person and confiscation of property, to take an oath of allegiance to the United States. Thus it strengthened the hands of the patriots or whigs, and gave to the loyalists or tories the unpleasant alternative of submission or flight.

This party was important in quantity and impressive in quality. There were loyalists in every colony and in every walk of life. In New York, New Jersey, and Georgia they probably composed a majority of the population, and they were very strong in Pennsylvania and the Carolinas, the regions where British arms were most successful. The loyalists were weakest in Virginia, Maryland, and Massachusetts: the oldest settled colonies with the proudest traditions. Although it is impossible to ascertain their number, the fact that over seventy thousand loyalists left the country during the Revolution, and that everyone admitted those to be a minority of the party, gives some index of their strength. The greater part of the loyalists took the required oaths and paid taxes, while praying for the defeat of the American cause, simply because they had no place to go. As late as 1830 there were old ladies in New York and Portsmouth, N. H., who celebrated the king's birthday, but drew all their curtains and closed their shutters on the Fourth of July!

Loyalism was strongest in the upper classes. The royal officials went tory as a matter of course; so, too, most of the Anglican clergy, whose Book of Common Prayer prescribed loyalty to one's lawful sovereign as a Christian virtue. Outside Virginia and Maryland, most of the greatest landowners were loyal, although many remained passive during the war to save their property. The merchants in the North, except in Boston and the smaller New England seaports, were pretty evenly divided; and many lawyers remained faithful to the king. In general the older, conservative, established, well-to-do people — always excepting the Virginia planters and New England merchants — were inclined to oppose revolution, actively or passively; but many families such as the Randolphs of Virginia, Morrises of New York, and Otises of Massachusetts were divided;

and most of the earliest and most prominent leaders of the Revolution were gentlemen. It is easy to understand that they could not carry their entire class into a revolution which involved not merely separation from the mother country, but the stability of American society. The question of home rule in the empire could not be divorced from the question of who was to rule in America. The country was much less united in 1775 than in 1765. When the conservatives realized that liberty could be won only by opening the floodgates to 'dirty democrats,' many drew back in alarm; others, like John Jay, held their noses and carried on, to be rewarded by capturing the government in 1789 — and being let down once more in 1801. Of these perhaps the most distinguished was John Dickinson, who opposed independence to the last but when it finally came acquiesced and fought under Washington. Even some of the radical patriots had their bad moments. John Adams, riding home from the Continental Congress, was accosted by a countryman who exclaimed, so he tells us:

'Oh, Mr. Adams, what great things have you and your colleagues done for us. We can never be grateful enough to you. There are no courts of justice now in this province, and I hope there never will be another.' Is this the object for which I have been contending? said I to myself, for I rode along without any answer to this wretch. Are these the sentiments of such people, and how many of them are there in the country? . . . If the power of the country should get into such hands, and there is a great danger that it will, to what purpose have we sacrificed our time, health and everything else?

To what purpose indeed! This question forced itself upon the consideration of every thoughtful man, until finally, when independence was achieved, it became the dominant question of American society.

It is hardly necessary to tell the present generation that the old popular view of the tories as perfidious traitors is false. Intellectually and morally the loyalists were good men, and their principles were respectable. The attitude of those Americans who fought to hold the empire together in 1776 was no different from that of Southern Unionists like General Thomas and Admiral Farragut in 1861; and the difference between success and failure, more than that of right and wrong, explains the different 'verdict of history' toward these two great civil wars.

X

THE WAR OF INDEPENDENCE
1775-1783

1. *A Civil War*

IF Americans had really been so united and determined as the ringing phrases of the Declaration of Independence suggest, they could have achieved independence within a year. For they already controlled ninety-nine per cent of the country; the English people were half-hearted in the war; and the difficulties of conquering a determined people three thousand miles overseas were enormous. But there was so much loyalist feeling and sheer apathy that Congress found it very difficult to keep an army together and to feed those who fought. And there were so many American sympathizers in Great Britain that German mercenaries had to be hired. In other words, the War of Independence was a civil war, one in which, like the recent civil war between loyalists and fascists in Spain, assistance from outside was a very important factor. American loyalists were incapable of carrying on the struggle a week without British assistance, and but for French aid the American patriots would have had to give up complete independence in 1775, or take a bad beating around 1780.

Indeed the surprising thing about the War of Independence when you compare it with other wars of liberation is not that the Americans won, but that they did not win more easily. The continent was theirs, in 1775, from Quebec to the borders of Florida, and from the sea to the mountains — except for the acreage occupied by a few thousand British troops at Boston; and all the Americans had to do to win independence was to hold what they had. The British, on the contrary, had to reconquer a vast territory in order to win. It was the military problem of 1861, on a vaster scale, and with the dice loaded in favor of the 'rebels.' For the British government, in order to get troops in action against the 'rebels' of 1775-81, had to send them by bulky, slow-moving sailing vessels which never took less than five weeks and often twelve to cross the Atlantic against the prevailing winds. Many men succumbed to ship fever, and the rest had to be conditioned after they landed, weak and groggy, in a strange land with a perplexing climate. Moreover, those who 'came three thousand miles and died, to keep a king upon his throne,' had to be armed, clothed, and even partly fed from England, which meant more shipping, more delays, more losses from American privateers and hazards of the sea, and such expense as had never been known in English history.

Several English military experts thought the reconquest of America hopeless from the start. The Adjutant-General of the army called it 'as wild an idea as ever controverted common sense,' and Lord Barrington, the veteran war secretary, agreed. He proposed to bring the rebels back to their bounden duty and service by withdrawing all land forces, and smothering the rebellion by a strict blockade. Not being a sailor, Barrington did not appreciate that you cannot maintain a blockade without bases; but if the British had concentrated on holding three or four seaports as fortified naval bases, and sent not a single company inland, they would have had a fair chance of saving something besides honor.

However, that was not to be. The Secretary of War was not in the cabinet, and the conduct of the war came under the Colonial Secretary of the North ministry, Lord George Germain, who is always represented in the savage political cartoons of the day as wearing a white feather. He had been dismissed from the army after the Battle of Minden for something that looked like cowardice, yet had risen in politics through a combination of personal effrontery, family influence, and royal favor. The feelings of British officers and generals at having to take orders in war time from a man who had been declared by a court martial unfit to serve in any military capacity may well be imagined. Lord George did not see eye to eye with Lord Barrington. He saw no essential difference between this war and any other. A British army was already in the country; honor and prestige demanded its reinforcement; then let it defeat or disperse the rebels, and ravage or occupy the country. It was all so simple, as you looked on a neatly colored map of North America, and ignored the ocean and the wilderness.

Congress could not afford to let a British army parade about the country unopposed. Many members of Congress inherited the traditional English aversion to standing armies, and believed the war could be fought by militia alone; but the wiser saw that a regular army was absolutely necessary if only as a stiffener to the rest; that it took time to train a soldier. They had to reckon, however, with

American individualism, hostile to the necessary discipline of a regular army, and with a very slight spirit of sacrifice among the people at large. The Revolutionary War was fought under the peculiar condition of want of enthusiasm on each side — nothing comparable to that of 1917, or even 1861. The king was obliged to hire German mercenaries, his own subjects were so reluctant to enlist; though no doubt this was as much due to the hard conditions of British army life, with severe discipline and low pay, as to indifference. Soldiers were not supposed to be patriots in those days, or even to know what the war was about; soldiering was simply a trade like any other. There were, however, very many instances of British officers who resigned their commissions rather than fight their overseas brethren; and the late Sir G. O. Trevelyan in his brilliant history of the American Revolution, which so well represents the 'old whig' point of view, gives instance after instance of the most open sympathy by prominent Englishmen with the American 'rebels,' whom they regarded as fighting for English freedom from arbitrary monarchy as much as for American independence. Sir John Fortescue, the historian of the British army, regards the 'treason' of those liberty-loving Englishmen as a principal factor in the American victory. One of them, the irrepressible John Wilkes, M.P., declared in October 1775 that the war was 'unjust, felonious and murderous,' that the greater part of America was already lost, and could never be reconquered, since the Americans propagated children much faster than the British could kill their patriot soldiers. 'The Americans, sir, are a pious and religious people. With much ardour and success they follow the first great command of Heaven, *Be fruitful and multiply*. While they are fervent in these devout exercises, while the men continue enterprising and healthy, the women kind and prolific, all your attempts to subdue them by force will be ridiculous and unavailing.'

On the other side, the greatest disadvantage of the Americans was the small number who were willing to fight or to make any sacrifice for independence. Washington himself wrote, when trying to get the New England troops to re-enlist in the fall of 1775, 'Such a dearth of public spirit, and want of virtue, and stock-jobbing, a fertility in all the low arts to obtain advantages of one kind or another, I never saw before and pray God I may never be witness to again. . . . Could I have foreseen what I have, and am likely to experience, no consideration upon Earth should have induced me to accept this command.' He was to experience less virtue and more politics as the war went on; but his own steadfast patriotism never wavered for a moment, and he endured a degree of neglect, disobedience, and even disloyalty, which would have induced almost any other general in history to resign his sword and give up the cause.

Washington was more than a general: he was the embodiment of all that was noblest and best in the American people. With no illusions about his own grandeur, no thought of the future except an intense longing to return to his beloved Mount Vernon, he assumed every responsibility thrust upon him, and fulfilled it. He not only had to lead an army, but to write constant letters to Congress, state leaders, and state governments, begging them for the wherewithal to create and maintain an army. He had to compose quarrels among his officers, many of them volunteers from Europe, and placate cold, hungry, unshod troops. Intrigues against himself he always ignored, and always the intriguers came to grief. After France sent aid, he had quasi-diplomatic functions to fulfil. Although asking and receiving no salary, he sometimes from his own pocket bought clothing for his men, and sent aid to the destitute families of his companions in battle. Thus Washington brought something more to the cause than his military ability and statesmanship; he contributed the priceless gift of character.

The Declaration of Independence gave a brief fillip to patriotism, but for only a short period; and it was the comparative indifference of the vast majority that made the task of Washington and the handful of devoted and self-sacrificing men and women who sustained him so difficult. For the Americans were not then — nor are they now — a military people. They were eager for a fight perhaps; but sustained warfare demands other qualities than those needed to fight Indians and wild-cats. The sort of warfare they enjoyed was militia warfare: turning out under some popular local leader like John Stark or Francis Marion to repel an invasion or do a little bushwhacking, and then home to plant the corn or get in the hay. Steady service in an army so ill-fed, paid, clothed as Washington's was distasteful; and the average American, though he wished his side to win, saw no need of continuous fighting. When New England was cleared of the enemy, it was difficult to get Yankees to go to the aid of the Middle States or the South; after the first enthusiasm of 1775 it was equally difficult to get Southerners to serve in the

North; and the people of the Middle States, where most of the fight-ing occurred, hung back even there. The total enlistments in the war, regulars and militia — i.e., the total number of men who counted as veterans and as ancestors for members of 'patriotic societies' — was several hundred thousand. But Washington's army reached its peak of strength with eighteen thousand in the summer of 1776. It fell to five thousand by the end of the year, and seldom if ever went higher. It is true that no provision was made for the fam-ilies of men in service, and no pensions were paid to the dependents of those who fell, so enlistments were practically restricted to the very young, the adventurous, the floating population, and the super-patriotic. But with all these allowances the fact remains that a disgracefully small number of Americans were willing to do any sustained fighting for their country's cause.

The existence of a loyalist minority was an important factor in prolonging the war. Those who fled to England whipped up British public opinion by their stories of persecution (unfortunately for the most part true); and they were forever telling anyone who would listen that if Lord George would only dispatch a few regiments to my section of the country, Sir, the countryside would rise as one man, Sir, and flock to the colors! This policy was occasionally tried, but the loyal rustics learned very early in the war that if they rallied to a British force, it presently marched away and left them at the mercy of patriot committees. There were never enough loyalists any-where to control the country; even in the South, every county snapped back into patriot hands as soon as Cornwallis had passed by. There were enough, however, to do some very effective fighting for the king. Somewhat late in the war, the British discovered that Americans were the best people to fight Americans. Several tory regiments were then organized. New York furnished more soldiers to George III than to George Washington. Loyalist forces which were quartered in New York City frequently harried the shores of Long Island by marauding expeditions, and did other dirty work with which the regulars would not soil their hands. It was Butler's Tory Rangers and St. Leger's Loyal Greens who with Mohawk Indians perpetrated the Wyoming massacre in northern Pennsyl-vania, the surpassing horror of the war. In the South, the large num-ber of fighting loyalists made the warfare in that section more bitter and inhumane than elsewhere, for neighborhood feuds and personal grudges gave a sharper edge to the conflict. The Battle of Camden

was really an American loyalist victory, won by Tarleton's Legion
and Rawdon's Volunteers of Ireland. King's Mountain was the
rebel revenge. Gallant Patrick Ferguson with a handful of British
regulars and over a thousand tories took his stand on the summit and
challenged ' all the rebels outside of hell ' to dislodge him; and he
must have thought that most of them were there when the firing began from every rock and bush on the mountain side. Half the loyalists were killed, and all the rest but 21 surrendered.

How far was race a factor in the American Revolution? In a
general way, it is probable that the racial heterogeneity of the
colonies in comparison with England weakened the bond between
the two; but George III was a German prince as well as an English
king. Thomas Jefferson in his original draft of the Declaration of
Independence spoke as one Englishman to another. His indignant
reference to the king's sending over ' Scotch and foreign mercenaries
to invade and destroy us ' had to be deleted because James Wilson
and John Witherspoon resented the 'Scotch'! Members of every
non-English race then in America can be found on American army
rolls; but so can they also be found on British army rolls and lists
of loyalists. One of the best tory regiments was Rawdon's Volunteers
of Ireland. The Pennsylvania Germans were notoriously slow to
take fire in this cause, as in most things; although the Mühlenbergs
were leaders both in war and politics. Mrs. Ravenel, the historian
of South Carolina, declares that the Huguenot element of that
colony, grateful to England for many benefits, failed to turn out in
large numbers until their hero Marion called them. The Scotch
Highlanders of North Carolina, who had been fighting the local
whig gang in the ' War of the Regulation,' generally remained loyal
to the Crown. And thousands of backwoodsmen from Pennsylvania
to Georgia emigrated beyond the mountains rather than pay war
taxes and perform war service. Conversely, many officers who were
English or Irish born and bred, such as Gates, Charles Lee, St.
Clair, Montgomery, and Conway, joined the American army; and
Tom Paine wrote for it rather more effectively than they fought
for it. So one might go on claiming and counter-claiming, and all
to no purpose; for the truth is that Americans were not race-conscious
in the eighteenth century, and race played no part in the choice of
sides. All peoples then represented in America played an honorable
part on the patriot side; and an equally honorable part on the loyalist
side.

2. *Supply and Finance*

The government of the country contributed to this slackness in the fight. All the state and local governments of the Thirteen Colonies, except the few places under British occupation, were in patriot hands; but the central government, which alone can successfully wage war, was very weak. Until the Articles of Confederation were ratified the Continental Congress had no legal authority. It was little more than an inter-allied conference. It passed resolutions, not laws; it issued requisitions, not orders, for men, money, and supplies. Although Congress had the good sense to give Washington supreme control of military operations, and to resist all intrigues to deprive him of it, it did not support him adequately — indeed it could not, dependent as it was on the good will of the states and the people for the wherewithal to carry on the war. Washington organized his army in line regiments, each one coming from a specific state; and the states were supposed to keep these filled. Congress made requisitions on states for so many recruits, for so many months' or years' service. The states generally passed on the responsibility to the counties or towns, and these local units advertised for recruits, paying bounties in money or kind, which steadily increased as the war continued. Near the end of the war Virginia was offering recruits a choice between £60 specie and 300 acres of land with 'a healthy, sound negro'; while Beverly, Mass., to fill her local quota, paid each man an amount of sugar, coffee, beef, corn, and cotton, to the value of £1600 in continental currency.

In the matter of arms and munitions, Congress, aided by generous supplies from France, captures by privateers, and local enterprise, did rather well; and no battle was lost for want of arms or powder. But in the matter of feeding and clothing the army it did very ill.

The story of the sufferings of the Revolutionary army has usually been regarded as a glorious proof of endurance and patriotism, and this it is; but it is also proof of weakness and folly on the part of Congress and the Country. Undoubtedly, liberal allowance should be made in judging a young, ill-organized people, who were inexperienced in great affairs, and whose circumstances were peculiarly unfavorable to executive efficiency. Yet the fact remains that the army starved, not because the country could not furnish food, but because the people were unwilling to endure taxation, and because Congress themselves did not understand the importance of administrative centralization. Some of the hardships that the army endured were, indeed, unavoidable; but the greater part of them were caused by incompetent or negligent officials, bad management, and an excess of paper money.[1]

The war was financed by national bills of credit (the famous continental currency), state bills of credit, requisitions on the states in money and in kind (which were met by state loans or taxes), domestic loans and foreign loans. Of these the most important was the continental currency, the first of which was issued shortly after the Battle of Bunker Hill. It was expected that each state would make these bills of credit legal tender, and make provisions for 'sinking' (redeeming) its share of them, according to congressional apportionment; but while the states were ready enough to legalize the bills for all payments, they failed to provide for their redemption at the times fixed, and instead issued bills of credit of their own. Consequently both continental and state bills depreciated rapidly from 1778 on, and acted as a forced loan on the people, each holder losing part of the value as prices rose and the currency was inflated. In all, continental bills to the par value of about $241,500,000, and state bills to the par value of $210,000,000 were issued. Congress recognized in 1780 that continental currency was worth only one-fortieth of its specie value, and began receiving it for state requisitions at that rate, and issuing 'new tenor' bills at five per cent interest, redeemable in specie; and they soon depreciated. The old continental currency within a year ceased to pass as currency, and became a by-word and a jest — 'not worth a continental' was a rustic phrase for complete worthlessness well into the nineteenth century.

Requisitions of money on the states began in 1777. These, like the old parliamentary requisitions on the colonies during the French and Indian Wars, were honored or not as the states saw fit. Three specie requisitions to the amount of over ten millions in the desperate year 1780 yielded only a million and a half. Consequently Congress resorted to requisitions in kind: so much beef, pork, flour, and rum; so many blankets, coats, and stockings. The states were apt to re-assess these requisitions on counties or communities, with corresponding ineffectiveness.

Domestic loans were floated from 1776, at first at four and then

[1] L. C. Hatch, *The Administration of the American Revolutionary Army*, pp. 121–22.

at six per cent; but with the lack of liquid capital in the states, or of banks to make what there was of it available, only some $67,000,000 in paper (about $10,000,000 specie) was subscribed to 1780, when the loan offices were closed. The French subsidies (gifts) amounted to $1,800,000.[2] The loans from France, which began in 1777, yielded $6,352,000 in specie value; and, while most of this was spent on supplies in Europe, enough specie came to America to pay the interest on the domestic debt until 1782. Spain also lent about $150,000 in 1781–82; and John Adams borrowed $1,304,000 from private bankers in the Netherlands during the peace negotiations.

American Revolutionary finance used to be held up to ridicule as an example of everything vicious in public finance; but since the inflation of the World War and the years that followed, we have become more tolerant. All in all, considering the primitive economic organization and means of transport in the United States, the large proportion of the population disaffected to the American cause, the lack of authority in Congress, the ineffective committees that managed finance, and the popular prejudice against taxation (with or without representation), it is surprising that the war did not collapse for want of financial support. There was a great improvement after 1781, when Congress appointed Robert Morris, a wealthy Philadelphia merchant, Superintendent of Finance. Morris stopped waste and corruption in spending, introduced proper administrative methods, placed government finance on a specie basis, organized the first American bank of deposit and issue (the Bank of North America), fed the army by contract, and procured decent uniforms, so that during the last year of the war, after Yorktown, the army was better paid, clothed, and fed than during the 'times that tried men's souls.' But he did not and could not improve revenues; and it was mainly the increased financial help from France at this time, the slackening of war efforts, and the specie circulated by the French and British armies, that enabled Morris to do as well as he did. Practically the whole country was on a specie basis by 1782, and European bankers were so favorably impressed by the results of Morris's efforts, that the new loan in Holland was obtained at the low interest of five per cent. But a financial collapse was just around the corner.

[2] Excluding the supplies bought through Beaumarchais.

3. Military Operations, 1775–1777

Even before the Declaration of Independence there were military operations which had an important influence on the outcome of the war. The crushing of the North Carolina loyalists by patriot militia at Moore's Creek Bridge near Wilmington, N. C., on 27 February 1776, made it impossible for the British to erect a military base in that region. That was the object of a new expeditionary force from Ireland commanded by Lord Cornwallis, with a detachment of British regulars from Boston under Sir Henry Clinton. They were forced to try Charleston, S. C., instead. Charleston is a remarkably hard nut to crack, as Spaniards, British, and Yankees have discovered to their cost. Washington detached Charles Lee to take charge; but before he arrived, the local patriots had erected Fort Moultrie, which drove the attacking ships off when they endeavored to force a passage (28 June 1776). Clinton and Cornwallis, baffled, retired to join Howe in his attack on New York. So the British acquired no southern base in 1776, and the large number of Carolina loyalists had to fend for themselves.

About the time of the Moore's Creek fight, Washington, who had been besieging Boston for eight months with an army composed of New England militia and Southern riflemen, decided to finish up. Seizing and fortifying Dorchester Heights, which the British had neglected after their dearly bought capture of Bunker Hill, Washington placed his artillery in a position to bombard the enemy out of Boston. General Sir William Howe decided it was time to leave, and, happily for modern Boston, chose St. Patrick's Day, 1776, to evacuate his army.

After Ethan Allen had taken Ticonderoga and Crown Point on Lake Champlain early in 1775, Benedict Arnold, an enterprising Connecticut militia officer, persuaded Congress to authorize a march on Canada in two divisions. The French Canadians were expected to revolt on the appearance of an American force, and bring in Canada as the fourteenth member of the half-formed American Confederation. But England had gone far toward conciliating the French Canadians by the Quebec Act of 1774, which, in turn, had provoked such outbursts of anti-Catholic bigotry in the northern colonies that few French *habitans* cared to change masters. Seldom has religious intolerance been so promptly chastised by the ' frowns of Providence.'

Richard Montgomery, with a little over a thousand men, taking the classic route of the Hudson and Lake Champlain, captured Montreal on 12 November 1775. About six hundred of Benedict Arnold's equal force got through the wilderness of Maine to Quebec, after incredible hardships. They poled, pushed, and dragged their way in flat-bottomed boats up the Kennebec river, across a twelve-mile carry, through a complicated chain of ponds and small streams, across a snow-covered mountain pass, and — those who had boats left — down the rapids of the Chaudière river, while the rest, cold and starving, stumbled along deer trails, until they met with assistance from the French Canadians. Rendezvous was made with Montgomery near Quebec. As many of the troops' terms of enlistments expired on New Year's Day 1776, Montgomery and Arnold delivered a premature assault on Quebec, the strongest fortress in America, in a blinding snowstorm on the last night of 1775. Montgomery was killed, Arnold wounded; and although Congress sent reinforcements, the position of this expeditionary force so far from its base proved untenable. Arnold was forced to retreat by Lake Champlain in the spring, and Canada remained British. Yet, taking a long view of it, the Arnold-Montgomery campaign had an important bearing on the war. It alarmed the British Government for the safety of Canada, induced Germain to divide the largest force of regulars yet despatched across the Atlantic, and send almost half to Quebec. The attempt of this section under Burgoyne to push through to New York in 1777 resulted in the most decisive American victory of the entire war.

Before that took place, the Americans had lost in succession New York and Philadelphia. Washington, rightly foretelling that New York would be the next British objective, marched thither from Boston in April 1776, with as much of his army as could be induced to stay under the colors. Had it not been for the presence of Washington's force in New York City that colony would certainly have stayed loyalist: as it was, the Provincial Congress did not vote for independence until 9 July 1776, and the patriot committees had the greatest difficulty in keeping the tories quiet by strong-arm methods. If the British expeditionary force had arrived in April or May, there would have been a different story to write. But Sir William Howe, after retreating from Boston on 17 March, had to wait at Halifax, N. S., until 7 June for reinforcements to arrive from England; and his transports and convoying fleet, commanded by his

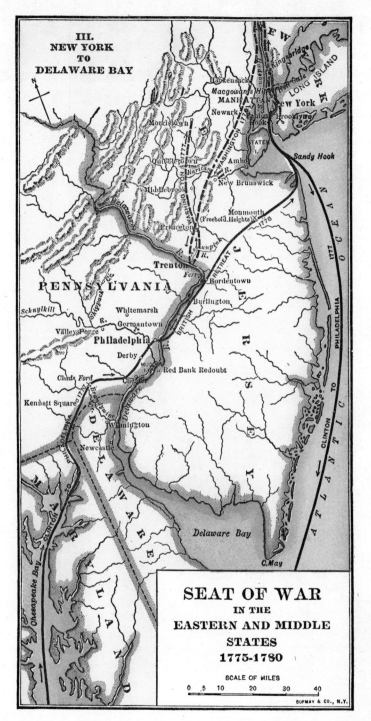

III.
NEW YORK
TO
DELAWARE BAY

SEAT OF WAR
IN THE
EASTERN AND MIDDLE
STATES
1775-1780

SCALE OF MILES
0   5   10   20   30   40

BORMAY & CO., N.Y.

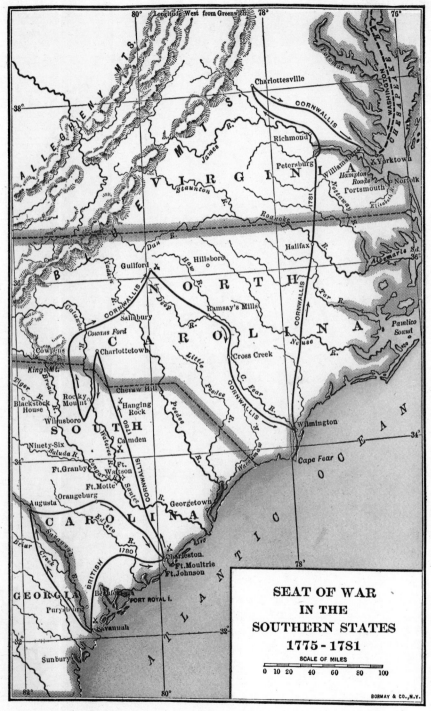

SEAT OF WAR
IN THE
SOUTHERN STATES
1775-1781

SCALE OF MILES
0 10 20   40   60   80   100

BORMAY & CO., N.Y.

The War of Independence

The Seat of War in the United States

The Seat of War in the Southern States

From Harper's Atlas of American History

brother, Admiral Lord Howe, did not sail through the Narrows of New York harbor until 2 July 1776.

The Howe brothers, whig in politics and friendly to America, brought an olive branch as well as a sword. All they had to offer (so Ben Franklin drew from them at a conference on Staten Island) was the king's clemency to the rebels if they would stop fighting, but no guarantee of future liberty within the empire. Franklin, as instructed, refused to negotiate save on the basis of independence. It would have been well for both countries if the British had accepted this condition then, instead of six years later; but national honor forbade them to relinquish the Thirteen Colonies without a fight. And with thirty thousand men and a navy to oppose Washington's land force of eighteen thousand, it seemed as if the fight would soon be over.

Washington, on his side, felt that he could not honorably abandon New York City without a struggle. Commanded both by Brooklyn Heights and by ships already in the harbor, the metropolis was difficult to defend. Washington promptly fortified the Heights, and prepared to defend them; but Howe landed his army safely in the rear. In the ensuing Battle of Long Island (27 August 1776) Washington's plan was faulty, his generals did not execute their assignments, all the breaks went against him, and the British numbers were overwhelming. Brooklyn Heights became untenable, and Washington on 29 August executed a masterly retreat in small boats to the Manhattan shore. Providentially the wind held north, so the British warships could not come up the East River, and Sir William Howe apparently never knew what was going on. He lost his greatest chance to end the war by a single stroke: for if Washington's army had then been captured, it would have been impossible for the Congress to have raised another. Indeed the War of Independence was remarkably punctuated by 'ifs.'

After a delay for the futile conference on Staten Island, Howe easily seized New York City, forcing Washington to retire to Harlem Heights; and during the remainder of the war that city remained a British base and a tory refuge. Arnold, in the meantime, was stubbornly contesting every mile of the American retreat from Canada; and to such good purpose that Sir Guy Carleton, after fighting his way to Ticonderoga with heavy loss, withdrew to Montreal, and gave up for that year an attempt to form a junction with Howe. Thus Benedict Arnold a second time helped to save the cause he later betrayed.

Washington, his army weakened in morale as in men by the militia contingents going home, was unable to hold his position to the north of Manhattan Island. He retreated into New Jersey. General Charles Lee, the showy, loud-mouthed type of military man which impresses simple folk, was given by Congress what amounted to an independent command, and refused to co-operate with Washington, hoping to be made commander-in-chief. Congress retreated from Philadelphia to Baltimore on the appoach of Howe, and General Washington retreated, since there was nothing else to do in face of a vastly superior force; he must save his army to save the cause. By the end of the year his army was hardly five thousand strong. The rest had simply dwindled away: deserted, gone absent without leave, or left when terms of enlistment were up. These were 'the times that tried men's souls,' wrote Tom Paine. And how few souls survived the ordeal!

Howe, in that dreary autumn, lost several chances to capture Washington's army; for Howe waged war in the dilatory manner of European campaigns. There seemed to be no hurry. Every month the American army grew weaker; Jersey loyalists were hospitable; gentlemen did not fight in winter. And so Washington led his entire army to the further bank of the Delaware before Howe's outposts reached it. Five days later Charles Lee, still in the Jersies, was captured. It was well for the American cause that he was, for his army was now placed under Washington; unfortunate that he was later exchanged.

Desperately, as an animal at bay, Washington lashed back at the enemy, and after recrossing the Delaware on a snowy Christmas eve, captured a thousand Hessians at Trenton. The cause at once looked up; men whose enlistments would expire New Year's Day re-enlisted — for six weeks. And in a rapid and brilliant manœuvre Washington evaded Cornwallis, who had been sent by Howe with eight thousand men to 'bag the old fox,' defeated a portion of his force within sight of the college at Princeton, and retired to a strong position in the highlands of New Jersey, about Morristown. The British returned to New York City, leaving the Jersey loyalists to their fate. Congress now invested Washington with power to appoint and replace all officers except the generals, who had to be apportioned more or less among the states for political reasons. And Congress recruited vigorously. But in March 1777, when the roads began to thaw, Washington had only four thousand men.

For the year 1777 Lord George Germain, in consultation with General Burgoyne and the king, worked out a plan of campaign which was perfectly sound from the point of view of persons sitting in London and playing military chess on maps of America. The idea was to reunite at New York the forces which had been divided in 1776, by reason of the American threat to Canada. Burgoyne was to bring eight thousand men south by the line of Lake Champlain and the Hudson to Albany, where they would be placed under Howe's command, while Howe, detaching a force to meet Burgoyne up-river, would himself capture Philadelphia, and perhaps proceed farther south. The danger to the American cause lay in concentrating at New York a force so overwhelming that it could conquer other American seaports piecemeal. The weakness of the plan lay partly in the difficulty of obtaining co-ordination at such a distance. Germain was in such a hurry to get away from London for a week-end that he forgot to send an important dispatch, and Howe did not learn that he was expected to help Burgoyne until 16 August, when the bulk of his force was in Chesapeake Bay. But the fatal mistake was ignoring the physical and human conditions of warfare in America. The several transfers between Lake Champlain, Lake George, and the Hudson meant an enormous apparatus of baggage and portable boats, many delays, and plenty of warning to the enemy. Lexington and Concord had showed on a small scale what would happen to a British force advancing into a hostile country. And European tactics were helpless against a countryside in arms: for the countryside in Europe never rose; warfare over there was a professional game.

In the early summer of 1777, while Washington waited at Morristown, not knowing what to expect, General Howe embarked the bulk of his army on transports, in order to attack Philadelphia from the sea. He chose the longest way, by Chesapeake Bay instead of the Delaware, which was so well fortified that the seamen had no stomach for covering the landing. Howe did not reach Elkton, Maryland, at the head of the Chesapeake, until 25 August; so Washington had plenty of time to bar the road thence to Philadelphia. All he could do against greatly superior forces was to retard Howe's advance, at the Brandywine Creek. Howe occupied Philadelphia on 27 September 1777, and Washington's gallant attack on his forces at Germantown (4 October) was a complete failure. The British settled down to a comfortable winter in the former seat of Congress, while Washington went into most uncomfortable winter quarters at Valley Forge, only a few miles away.

In the meantime, the greatest American victory of the war had been won, on the line of the Hudson. The army of Canada, some seven thousand strong, began its southward advance in good season and with bright prospects. On 6 July, Burgoyne took Fort Ticonderoga. By 29 July he had reached Fort Edward on the upper Hudson, and was forced to wait for more supplies from Canada. 'Gentleman Jack' Burgoyne would make no concessions to wilderness conditions; he must have his service of plate, his champagne, and thirty wagons for his personal baggage. Baron Riedesel, the commander of the Brunswick mercenaries, was accompanied by the Baroness, who has left us a most vivid account of the series of splendid picnics that marked her hero's advance. Burgoyne's ideas of American geography were not as hazy as those of Bernard Shaw, who in his delightful play, *The Devil's Disciple,* places New Hampshire south of Boston; but he did seem to imagine that it would be an easy matter for a raiding force to march in two weeks across Vermont to Bellows Falls, down the Connecticut river to Brattleborough, and back 'by the great road to Albany,' collecting at least thirteen hundred cavalry horses, together with beef and draught cattle and wagons for the use of his army! For this exploit he chose three hundred and seventy-five dismounted German dragoons, the slowest marchers in his army, and about three hundred tories, Canadians, and Indians. They did not even reach the Vermont line. John Stark and his Green Mountain Boys marched out from Bennington, Vermont, to meet them; and very few of the Germans ever returned. In the meantime General Herkimer and the German-American settlers of the Mohawk valley held up the British general St. Leger, who was trying to join Burgoyne by that route; and on the approach of reinforcements under Benedict Arnold, St. Leger retreated to Canada.

In militia fighting, nothing succeeds like success. The Battle of Bennington brought a general turnout of the fighting population of northern New England, and Burgoyne's delay at Fort Edward enabled Washington to despatch regulars from the lower Hudson. In early September Burgoyne finally got his unwieldy force in mo-

tion, and marched into a hornets' nest of Yankee militia, flushed
with the success of their fellows, stiffened by regulars, and well commanded by an adequate general of the regular army, Horatio Gates.
As the early frosts were turning the foliage of the upper Hudson
to colors bright as the British soldiers' coats, the fighting began.
At the battle of Stillwater, on Freeman's farm (19 September) Burgoyne reached his farthest south. Only a quick retreat could have
saved him then; but he had little notion of what stout fellows were
mustering behind the screen of woods; and Sir Henry Clinton
appeared to be coming up the Hudson to his rescue. On 7 October
Burgoyne lost another fight on Freeman's farm; and retreated to
Saratoga. The autumn rains began, the Germans deserted in shoals.
Americans were in front, rear and flank in overwhelming numbers:
and on 17 October 1777 Burgoyne surrendered his entire army, still
over five thousand strong, to General Gates. This was the decisive
blow of the war, for it brought England's hereditary enemy to the
American side.

4. Enter France

France had been watching and waiting for her *revanche* since
1763; and America was ready to gratify her. As early as November
1775, Congress appointed a committee of foreign relations and the
next spring sent Silas Deane to France to purchase clothing, munitions, and supplies, which he was successful in obtaining from the
government through the medium of a bogus company, organized
by Beaumarchais, the playwright. After Independence had been declared, Franklin and Arthur Lee were sent to join Deane, with instructions to obtain secret or open assistance, and to offer a treaty
of amity and commerce. John Adams then, and always, was against
an 'entangling alliance.' But the American military situation became
so desperate toward the close of 1776 that Congress authorized
Franklin to conclude an offensive-defensive alliance if necessary to
get France into the war.

Enthusiasm in France for the American cause ran high. The
intellectual world, though far as yet from republicanism, was in
revolt against feudalism and privilege. Voltaire had taught the
French to admire the society of Pennsylvania, where men had
showed it possible to live the good life on the basis of religious
liberty, and thus had paved the way for a warm reception to Frank-

lin. Condorcet was so charmed with what he read of simple, rustic
Connecticut that he signed one of his tracts *Un Bourgeois de New-
Haven;* Rousseau imagined the Indians to be genuine children of
nature. The Declaration of Independence was greeted ecstatically;
Washington seemed a new Cincinnatus; and ardent young men, of
whom Lafayette was easily the first, hastened to place themselves
under his command.[3] The Virginia Bill of Rights and the state
constitutions of 1776 were hailed as harbingers of a new era, sub-
jecting the civil authorities to the popular will, bringing into practical statecraft those principles of liberty which had hitherto been
mere speculations of philosophers.

If intellectual France was ready to fling up her cap for independence, the rulers of France had more solid and practical reasons
for helping the United States. A shrewd, practical statesman, the
Comte de Vergennes, directed the foreign affairs of the rather
stupid young monarch, Louis XVI. England must be humbled and
the balance of power redressed in favor of France, whose lowered
prestige had lately been signalized by a partition of Poland without
her consent or participation. 'Providence has marked this era,'
Vergennes wrote to the Spanish government in 1778, 'for the
humiliation of a proud and greedy power . . . glory and inestimable advantages will result for the two crowns.' And the French
manufacturers were eager for a new market in America, closed
to them by the British Acts of Trade. 'Always keep in mind,' wrote
Vergennes to the Minister of Finance after the war was over, ' that
in separating the United States from Great Britain it was above all
their commerce which we wanted.' And so for practical reasons of
state, the French government from the first gave the United States
unneutral aid in the shape of munitions and supplies, and welcomed
Yankee privateers to French seaports. But Vergennes shrank from
the expense of direct intervention and open war with England.

This policy lasted until after the news of Burgoyne's surrender
at Saratoga; and then changed, because Vergennes feared lest this
disaster induce the English government to make such liberal concessions as would reunite the empire. He was not far wrong. Lord

[3] Other foreign officers who greatly helped the American cause were Baron Steuben, who introduced a modified Prussian drill and discipline in the Continental
Army; Thaddeus Kosciuszko of Poland, an admirable artillery officer; Count Casimir
Pulaski of Poland, mortally wounded at Savannah; the Baron de Kalb, who died
of his eleven wounds at the Battle of Camden; and the Chevalier du Portail, an
accomplished officer of engineers.

North was eager to recognize American independence as soon as he heard of the defeat at Saratoga; but the king forbade it. North repeatedly offered to resign; Rockingham and his party were ready to take office and bear the ignominy of treating with rebels; but the king declared he would rather lose his crown than submit to the old whigs and abandon his own party. Nevertheless, the king was ready to concede everything short of independence in order to keep the American states nominally under his sovereignty. A bill which North introduced in November 1777, but which owing to the long Christmas holidays of Parliament did not pass until February 1778, appointed a peace commission with authority to make the following offer: parliamentary taxation of the colonies to be renounced; no military forces to be kept in the colonies without their consent; the Coercive Acts of 1774 and all other Acts of Parliament to which Congress objected — even the Acts of Trade — to be repealed, if America would but acknowledge the sovereignty of the king; and these concessions to be guaranteed by treaty. In other words, England was ready to place the Thirteen Colonies on the same dominion status as Canada today. If the peace commission had reached America in advance of the French alliance, its terms would in all probability have been accepted; for the British still held New York, Newport, and Philadelphia; and Washington was at Valley Forge. But, as usual, the British offer of conciliation came too late.

On 6 February 1778, eleven days before the conciliatory bills passed Parliament, Franklin signed with Vergennes treaties of commerce and of alliance. Each nation promised to make common cause with the other until American independence was recognized. It was a generous treaty, in which America obtained everything and promised nothing except to defend French possessions in the West Indies. Vergennes had been brought to this point by Franklin's cleverly playing on his fears that otherwise the British offer would be accepted. Great Britain promptly declared war on France, and the War of Independence became world wide. Spain entered it as an ally of France in 1779, and proved very useful to the American cause by making New Orleans a base for privateers, and by taking the British posts in West Florida. The Netherlands, which had been reaping a fortune as the principal neutral sea power, was forced into the war by England in 1780; and Catherine II of Russia formed a League of Armed Neutrality which considerably cramped the operations of the British navy against neutral traders. United, the enemies of England would have been irresistible; but of them only France and America acted in concert, and that not until 1780.

So, by 1780, the shot at Concord bridge had literally been heard around the world. There were naval operations on the Atlantic Ocean, the Mediterranean, the Caribbean, the North Sea, the English Channel, even the Indian Ocean. And in far off Hindustan Warren Hastings was fighting native troops and princes to create a new empire for England in the Far East.

5. Naval and Military Operations 1778–1781

Sea-power was a decisive factor in the War of Independence, as Washington appreciated from the first; but it was not until 1780 that the allies were able to challenge British sea supremacy. An American navy was improvised by Washington from some Marblehead fishing schooners during the siege of Boston, and before 1776 the New England states began to fit out privateers with letters of marque and reprisal authorizing them to capture British merchantmen wherever found; there were also a few state navies. These three American naval forces, Continental, state, and private, engaged almost exclusively in commerce-destroying, for there was no money to provide capital ships, and naval warfare had to pay for itself.

The state navies accomplished very little. The story of the Continental navy is one of successful prize-taking and gallant naval combats by single ships or small squadrons, commanded by men such as Esek Hopkins (a Rhode Islander), Joshua Barney (a Marylander), John Barry (an Irishman), and John Paul Jones (a Scot). Captain Jones was sent across the Atlantic in the *Ranger* in 1777 to announce the capture of Burgoyne. Using Brest as a base, he raided English shipping in the narrow seas, and spiked the guns at Whitehaven near his old home in Scotland. In command of an old French Indiaman, the *Bonhomme Richard,* he won a desperate fight against the *Serapis* off Flamborough Head on 23 September 1779. Paul Jones's exploits had slight military value, but he became the hero of countless ballads, chapbooks, and fireside tales. After the French entered the war, Congress gradually dismantled the Continental navy. There were thirty-four vessels in commission in 1777; only seven in 1782.

At least two thousand American privateers were commissioned during the war, about three-quarters of them from New England.

Privateering was primarily a business: each man got a certain percentage of the prize money, according to his rank. Some privateers were built for speed, able to run down trading vessels and flee from the large, slow-sailing men-of-war; others were armed merchantmen which made it their main business to trade with France, Spain, and the West Indies, and only took prizes as a side line. Yet in helping themselves the privateersmen served the cause, for they intercepted military supplies, made the British trade routes unsafe, forced up insurance to unheard-of figures, and obtained valuable goods for the army and the people. Enormous sums were made out of privateering during the war — especially by the merchants who handled the prize cargoes — but most of the gains were lost before the war ended.

The year 1778 was one of incompetence and failure on all sides, redeemed only by the indomitable patriotism of Washington. While Washington's troops went barefoot and hungry in the snow at Valley Forge, Sir William Howe was revelling on the fat of the land in Philadelphia. But Howe was recalled in the spring of 1778, and his successor, Sir Henry Clinton, was ordered to evacuate the city and concentrate on New York in preparation for a new campaign. Washington attacked Clinton's retiring army at Monmouth Court House, in New Jersey: a confused battle in which an American disaster was barely averted by Washington sending incompetent Charles Lee off the field, and saving the day himself. Clinton reached New York safely; and all that Washington could do was to encamp at White Plains, fortify West Point, and look on. The only successful American campaign of 1778 was that of George Rogers Clark in the West, acting under the State of Virginia. Floating down the Ohio from above Pittsburgh to the mouth of the Cumberland, he marched his little force across the wilderness to take the British post of Kaskaskia in Illinois, and, instead of settling down for the winter, made an overland march in February 1779 to Vincennes, and took that by surprise. By several historians Clark is credited with saving the West for his country; but if the peace negotiators were aware of his exploits in 1782, they did not allude to them in a single one of their numerous notes and dispatches.

Fortunately for America, the French navy had been reorganized since 1763, and was at a high point of morale and efficiency; while the British navy, under Lord Sandwich, the most corrupt and inefficient First Lord of the Admiralty in history, was full of dry rot and mismanagement. The loss of the *Royal George* 'with twice four hundred men,' mourned by William Cowper, was due to dockyard graft. And England at this time had in high command only one sea-dog worthy of her tradition, Admiral Rodney.

On 11 July 1778, the first direct French aid arrived off Sandy Hook, in the shape of a gallant fleet under a too cautious commander, the Admiral Comte d'Estaing. The British had prepared for him by fortifying the Narrows, and D'Estaing did not have the nerve to force a passage with his great men-of-war. He left New York to attack the other British base at Newport; but, after landing a force to co-operate with the New England militia, hurriedly recalled them when the wind turned northeast. His fleet was blown out to sea by a gale, and put in at Boston to refit. Despite John Hancock's hospitality the feeling between the allies at Boston was very bad. There were duels between officers and murderous riots between men; the French alliance seemed a broken reed. In 1779 D'Estaing's squadron sailed away for the West Indies to pick up sugar islands for King Louis.

After France entered the war it was more difficult than ever to get Americans to enlist. Washington's army remained so small in 1779-80 that he could do nothing more than defend the Hudson from Clinton. In the meantime the British embarked on a new plan of campaign: to establish bases in the lower South, conquer the Carolinas, and roll up the tide of rebellion northward. A beginning was made by the capture of Savannah on 29 December 1778, but no more was accomplished for another year. In December 1779, as soon as D'Estaing's fleet was out of the way, Clinton sent from New York seven thousand men who besieged Charleston and captured the city together with an American force in May 1780. Then began a fierce bushwhacking war between Southern whigs and tories, aided by regulars of both sides, with an occasional pitched battle such as Camden, King's Mountain, the Cowpens, and Guilford Courthouse (15 March 1781). By that time the Carolinas were practically out of the war, and the British began to prepare a new military and naval base at Yorktown on the Chesapeake. There would have been a limit to American endurance if every seaport had become a British base, and if British sea-power enabled her to strike where and when she pleased.

6. The Yorktown Campaign

The early months of 1781 were the darkest for the American cause. It seemed as if nothing could induce the country to give Washington a proper army. Continental currency became almost worthless

The states would not even honor requisitions in kind. The Pennsylvania line regiment mutinied, exasperated at broken promises for pay and clothing. But it was the darkness before the dawn.

Lafayette visited Versailles in the winter of 1779–80 and persuaded his government to make a real effort to bring the war to an end. Hitherto Louis XVI had kept his army at home, in case Frederick the Great made trouble. Now, with the European horizon clear, he sent over a splendid expeditionary force of six thousand men under General Rochambeau, which occupied Newport in the summer of 1780. For a year it did nothing except enrich the Rhode Island farmers and fascinate their daughters. Nothing could be done against the British as long as they held the naval superiority off the American coast. Washington, far ahead of his time, grasped the implications of sea-power. In a note to Rochambeau he declared, ' In any operation, and under all circumstances, a decisive naval superiority is to be considered as a fundamental principle, and the basis upon which every hope of success must ultimately depend.' Rochambeau's army was of no use without a French high-seas fleet, and in January 1781 Washington sent a special envoy to France to ask for naval aid.

Louis XVI promptly sent to the West Indies a powerful fleet under the command of a first-rate seaman, the Admiral Comte de Grasse. He arrived at Haiti in May, with orders to clean up in the West Indies and then repair to that part of the coast of the United States where he could do the most good. Clinton with the main British army, and Admiral Graves with a large British fleet, were still in New York. Lord Cornwallis, after several victories in North Carolina, was then marching north into Virginia, where he made junction with another British detachment under the traitor Benedict Arnold. In August 1781 Cornwallis settled down to fortify Yorktown. But already measures had been started to close a net about him. The military-naval campaign of Yorktown was one of the most brilliantly conceived and smoothly executed operations in the history of warfare, considering that it involved co-ordinated movements between two French fleets, an American army and a French army, all widely separated, and with no better means of transport or communication than sailing ships and horses.

In May a small French fleet under the Comte de Barras slipped into Newport with dispatches for Rochambeau, stating that De Grasse would sail north that summer with 3,000 soldiers. Rochambeau promptly called a conference with Washington at Wethersfield,

Conn. They agreed to move jointly against New York City *or* York-town, according as De Grasse decided to attack the one or the other. Washington naturally would have preferred to dislodge the British from New York; but he wisely decided that the French navy ' must have the casting vote.' And thus De Grasse was informed, by the frigate *La Concorde,* which was detained some time by contrary winds, but sailed from Boston 20 June, and arrived at Cape Haitien on 26 July. In the meantime Rochambeau pulled up stakes at New-port, leaving his siege artillery to be loaded on De Barras' fleet, and marched his army across Connecticut to White Plains, N. Y., where he made junction with the American army under Washington on 6 July, and awaited news of Admiral de Grasse's decision.

De Grasse, who in the meantime had won sea supremacy in the West Indies and returned to Cape Haitien, took only two days to decide that he would strike Cornwallis's army at the Chesapeake, rather than Clinton's at New York, a harbor difficult for a hostile fleet to enter. He despatched *La Concorde* north with this news on 28 July, and himself sailed on 5 August with his grand fleet, 4,000 men of the Haiti garrison, and an ample supply of money, borrowed from the Spanish authorities at Havana.

In the meantime, by a lucky break for the Americans, Admiral Rodney sailed for England on leave of absence on 1 August, taking with him four battleships. He ordered the rest of his fleet, under Sir Samuel Hood, to sail to New York, reinforce Graves, and warn the British there to look out for De Grasse. The frigates sent ahead to warn the British in New York either ran aground or were cap-tured, so that when Hood's fleet anchored off Sandy Hook, on 28 August, Graves and Clinton supposed the grand French fleet to be at Havana, and attached no great significance to the movements of Rochambeau. It took them about three days to grasp the situation, and on 1 September the combined fleets of Graves and Hood sailed for the Chesapeake.

On 12 August the despatch frigate *La Concorde* entered New-port, only two weeks out from Haiti, with news from De Grasse that he was on his way to the Chesapeake. A swift courier brought the despatch to Washington, who now knew that he had the naval superiority for which he had pleaded so earnestly. He and Rocham-beau were now ready to undertake the vigorous offensive operations for which their armies had so long been held in readiness.

Between 21 and 25 August they ferried their 6,000 men (two-thirds

of them French) across the Hudson at King's Ferry. Four thousand
Americans were left behind to guard the northern approaches to
New York, and to mislead Clinton. On 25 August the fleet of Ad-
miral de Barras sailed from Newport for the Chesapeake, conveying
Rochambeau's siege artillery.

De Grasse with his fleet anchored within the Capes of the Chesapeake on 30 August. On 2 September the allied armies were still
marching across New Jersey. Washington wrote Lafayette, who with
a small American force was endeavoring to hold Cornwallis at Yorktown until everything was set, ' I am distressed beyond expression
to know what has become of the Count de Grasse, and for fear that
the English fleet, by occupying the Chesapeake, . . . may frustrate
all our flattering prospects in that quarter.' On 5 September, at
Chester, Delaware, Washington heard of De Grasse's arrival. In
view of what we have been told about Washington's unbending
dignity, it is interesting to note that the French officers who brought
the news reported that he had never seen a man shed so much
joy. The General ' acted like a child whose every wish had been
gratified.'

Washington would have been still more pleased had he known
what was happening that afternoon. The Battle of the Capes of
the Chesapeake was on. As Graves's fleet with nineteen battleships
approached from the north, De Grasse's fleet, with twenty-four battleships, got under way from its anchorage off Lynnhaven Bay, and
tacked to weather Cape Henry. Graves missed a chance to attack
the French before they had formed line of battle. The two fleets
gradually converged on the same tack, sailing seaward, but owing
to the inadequacy of his signalling system, Graves's orders were mis-
understood, and the small portion of his fleet that was engaged took
a bad beating. During the next five days De Grasse kept an eye on
the British fleet without attacking again, in order to let De Barras
slip into the Chesapeake. By 11 September, when he returned, De
Barras was there.

The French were now masters of the Chesapeake and the coastal
waters. Washington's and Rochambeau's armies were ferried in
naval boats down the bay, and took regular siege positions about
Yorktown, the siege of which began on 30 September, under the
direction of French engineers. The combined allied armies under
Washington, Rochambeau, Lafayette, Saint-Simon, together with
Virginia militia totalled fifteen thousand men; Cornwallis had about

half that number, but his position was well fortified. After two of his redoubts had been carried — by American and French assaulting parties, the former led by Colonel Alexander Hamilton — and after an unsuccessful attempt to escape across the York River, Cornwallis surrendered his entire force on 17 October. General O'Hara delivered his commander's sword to General Benjamin Lincoln, and as the British passed through the allied lines to stack arms, their bands played 'The World Turned Upside Down.'

Lafayette joyfully wrote the news to Vergennes, at Paris, concluding, 'The play is over, Monsieur le Comte; the fifth act has just come to an end.'

7. *The Peace of Paris*

If the soldiers had spoken all their parts, the sailors still had something to say; and the diplomats were just warming up. Before Cornwallis's surrender, it rather looked as if the United States could only obtain peace and independence on the basis of a *uti possidetis* truce — 'keep what you have' — which would have meant Great Britain retaining the principal seaports from New York to Savannah, and Spain holding both banks of the Mississippi and the shores of the Gulf of Mexico. Vergennes, in a memorandum written in February 1781 for his sovereign, expressed his readiness to accept such peace terms for America, but his unwillingness that France propose anything so 'lacking in delicacy.' The game was to let the Emperor of Austria and the Empress of Russia, who were eager to pose as pacificators, propose the *uti possidetis* basis. This they did, in May. John Adams, who had already been sent to Paris to entertain peace proposals, was outraged when he heard of these. The game was not spoiled, however, by his virtuous indignation, but by George III, who regarded imperial mediation as an unwarranted interference in a domestic British brawl. So no progress had been made toward peace when news of the happy victory at Yorktown reached Europe. The king, after he heard the news, declared he would never sanction 'getting a peace at the expense of a separation from America'; and when Lord North, who had been threatening to resign almost every month since Burgoyne's surrender (even thrice in one week), finally threw up the sponge, George III went so far as to draft a message of abdication. But he thought better of it, and called Rockingham — the same minister who had repealed the Stamp Act — to form a party government again, together with

Shelburne, Charles James Fox, and others who were traditional friends of America. This was in March 1782. Shelburne at once sent Richard Oswald to Paris to sound Dr. Franklin, and Fox sent an emissary of his own. Both proved remarkably complacent when Franklin suggested not only independence and peace, but the cession of Canada to the United States to prevent future quarrels. It was perhaps lucky for British Canada that the negotiations were not pushed through at once, for at that time Shelburne was willing to concede almost anything to get home the thirty thousand troops who were doing nothing in America at enormous expense. But there were endless complications and delays.

Franklin, however, was not to be the sole negotiator, but one of a commission of five appointed by Congress four months before Yorktown, and given a complete discretion as to the peace terms they should accept, provided France consented. These instructions, practically dictated by the French minister at Philadelphia, were intended to place the United States, in the forthcoming negotiations, completely under the guidance of Vergennes. Franklin seems to have been willing to play the rôle; but fortunately John Jay, a member of the peace commission who arrived in time to take part in the negotiations, was congenitally suspicious. As a member of Congress he had witnessed the intrigues of the French minister at Philadelphia to detach the West from the United States, in favor of Spain. Jay was suspicious too of Shelburne, the 'Jesuit of Berkeley Square,' who became premier on the death of Rockingham, 1 July 1782. So that when Oswald presented credentials that were rather unhappily phrased, and it looked as if the United States must negotiate as 'dependent states,' Jay insisted he must return to London and get a new commission. It was a mistake to have made so much of a phrase, for every month the British position improved, the American spirit became more apathetic, and the French treasury more empty. Admiral Rodney beat De Grasse badly at the Battle of the Saints in the West Indies on 12 April 1782, and Gibraltar held out against the joint siege by a French fleet and a Spanish army. Oswald did not return to Paris with credentials satisfactory to Jay until 28 September, almost a year after Yorktown.

In the meantime, Jay believed that he had discovered evidence of Vergennes's attempting to double-cross America, by a scheme to partition the West between England and Spain. It is true that Spain's territorial pretentions in North America were absurdly high. The

Spanish ambassador at Paris proposed to Jay that the boundary between his royal master's empire and the United States be a line dropped from the west end of Lake Ontario to the St. Mary's in Florida! When Jay rejected this, Vergennes took a hand, and through his secretary proposed a compromise by which Great Britain would keep everything north of the Ohio, and the Spanish-American boundary follow the Cumberland from its mouth to its source, and thence straggle down across Tennessee and Alabama to the northwest corner of the Florida peninsula. Having delivered to Jay this proposal, which, as Franklin said, evinced a desire 'to coop us up within the Alleghany Mountains,' the same secretary departed on a secret mission to London, where he gave Shelburne to understand that France rather preferred the Ohio to be the boundary between the United States and Canada.

Before condemning the French government for this attitude, we must remember that Vergennes was the minister of the French king, and not of the United States, to which Louis XVI had promised independence, but no specific boundaries. France was indeed in a bad dilemma. She needed peace as much as anyone; but she had promised Gibraltar to Spain, and her best efforts failed to extract that English thorn from the Spaniard's leg. Hence Vergennes hoped the United States might relinquish a share of the West in order to buy Spain's consent to peace without Gibraltar, or that England might cede Gibraltar in return for the Ohio boundary.

As a counter-move, John Jay sent a secret messenger of his own to London to persuade Shelburne that it was the interest of Britain 'immediately to cut the cords which tied us to France,' and to start negotiations at once. As a result of this suggestion, a new commission was made out to Richard Oswald enabling him 'to treat with the Commissioners appointed by the Colonys, under the title of Thirteen United States.' This change in the wording was taken by the American plenipotentiaries to mean a recognition of independence, and formal negotiations began at Paris toward the end of September. John Adams arrived from The Hague late in October, and took the same point of view as Jay; Franklin, too, was converted to this separate negotiation with England. Jay, however, is the one who deserves the greatest credit, for it was he who smoked out Vergennes and who, in spite of the instructions from Congress to be guided in all things by France, insisted on a direct negotiation and honorable terms. The preliminary treaty was signed 30 November 1782, with the proviso that it was not to take effect until France concluded peace with Great Britain. There was not even an Anglo-American armistice until 20 January 1783, the day that England and France ceased hostilities; and the definitive peace was not concluded until 3 September 1783.

The preliminary treaty contained one very unwise provision, proposed by Jay — a separate and secret clause to the effect that if Britain recovered West Florida from Spain before the final peace, the United States would accept as her southwestern boundary the parallel through the mouth of the Yazoo instead of 31°. Jay was so obsessed with the notion of Spain as a dangerous neighbor that he would even have released the British army from New York before the close of hostilities, in order to facilitate the reconquest of West Florida. Fortunately the British were not much interested in the Floridas, which they ceded at the general peace to Spain; and Spain sold them to the United States in 1819.

Apart from this, there were only trifling differences between the preliminary and the definitive treaties of Paris. This Peace of Paris certainly gives the lie to the epigram that 'America never lost a war, or won a peace conference.' Considering that the British still held New York, Charleston, Savannah, and seven posts in the Northwest, that Washington's army was almost incapable of further effort, and the British navy commanded the sea, it is surprising what wide boundaries and favorable terms the United States obtained. Almost every article except the one acknowledging the independence of the United States was subject to double construction, and occasioned long diplomatic controversy. The northeast boundary was laid down in a very sketchy manner, and not settled until 1842. The northern boundary along the line of the St. Lawrence and the Great Lakes was fairly definite, except where it went among the islands, until it reached the Grand Portage on Lake Superior; it was left completely in the air between the 'northwest corner of the Lake of the Woods' and the source of the Mississippi. Franklin had hoped to get the whole of Canada, and the Quebec fur interests expected that the Ohio river boundary of 1774 would be retained. Shelburne, always a friend to westward expansion, probably accepted the compromise [4] in the hope that it would leave

[4] The Americans gave the British the choice of two. The rejected alternative, 45°, would have given the Ontario peninsula to the United States, but cost four degrees of latitude in the West.

both countries free to expand along parallel lines; but, as we shall see, the Canadian fur interests did not give up hope of recovering the Ohio river, and it was long before Spain admitted the Mississippi as the western boundary of the United States.

As for the other articles, the Americans retained fishing privileges in the territorial waters of British North America, which they had enjoyed as British subjects. That was Yankee John's contribution to the treaty. Article IV provided that 'creditors on either side shall meet with no lawful impediment' to the recovery of pre-war debts. As unpaid bills for goods furnished America before the war to the amount of several million pounds were still in the strong-boxes of English merchants, this proved a strong plea for ratification; but it was an article which the United States found itself powerless to enforce for many years. The problem of the loyalists caused the greatest difficulty. Shelburne dared not face Parliament without some provision that would take those unfortunate exiles off the books of the treasury, by giving them restitution or compensation. Franklin, contrary to his usual benevolence, cherished most ferocious sentiments against the loyalists (perhaps because his son had gone tory), and even circulated false atrocity stories to prejudice European opinion against them. He refused to go beyond an innocuous agreement that Congress should 'earnestly recommend' to the several states to restore tory property, and a positive stipulation that no future confiscations should be made. Both parties knew that the earnest recommendation would amount to nothing, but Shelburne accepted it to save the ministry's face before Parliament.

In the other treaties signed the same day between England and France and Spain, a clause of great interest to the United States provided for the retrocession of West and East Florida to Spain, as compensation for England's keeping Gibraltar. So North America was divided between Spain, the British Empire, and the United States, Spain retaining the lion's share: everything west of the Mississippi and south of the thirty-first parallel of latitude. This marked an important step in the history of the Western question, but the expansion of the United States in another generation wiped out the Florida and the Mississippi boundaries, and by 1848 flung back the Spanish-American frontier to the Rio Grande. France got nothing out of the war but a few West India islands, a bankrupt treasury, and the prospect of a new market and an ally in America: a prospect which failed to materialize.

The comment of George III, in a letter to Shelburne, was characteristic:

I cannot conclude without mentioning how sensibly I feel the dismemberment of America from this Empire, and that I should be miserable indeed if I did not feel that no blame on that Account can be laid
at my door, and did I not also know that knavery seems to be so much
the striking feature of its Inhabitants that it may not in the end be an
evil that they become Aliens to this Kingdom.

A very different reception was accorded to the new republic by the
enlightened and generous souls of Europe. In England itself, Washington remained a hero to the liberals; and many old whigs, though
smarting with the sting of defeat, consoled themselves with the
thought that the king's personal rule had been forever discredited.
On the Continent the general feeling about America may be gathered
from a vivid account by Henrich Steffens, a Norwegian who later
made a brilliant career in Germany, of his boyhood impressions at
Elsinore in Denmark:

I was well enough instructed on the significance of the North American War to be vitally interested in a people that fought so boldly for
freedom. Among the great men of that time Washington and Franklin
stood forth, and the verse of Juvenal with which the latter was greeted

Eripuit coelo fulmen sceptrumque tyrannis [5]

made a great impression on me. The hero aroused my wonder, but more
enviable appeared to me the career of Franklin, who from a simple
bourgeois family (the son of a printer) rose to be a famous writer and
distinguished scientist, as well as representative of his struggling people,
admired by the most intelligent men of his time. There were very few
lively young fellows in the countries then at peace who did not follow
North American affairs . . .

When we ponder the significance of this war by which the gleaming
spark that later burst forth into the mighty flame of Revolution was first
thrown into France, it is interesting to remember how near that spark
came to our quiet family circle in a far-off, peaceful land. I still remember
vividly the day when the conclusion of peace, the victory of struggling
liberty, was celebrated at Elsinore and in the harbor. It was a fair day,
the harbor was full of merchant ships of all nations, men-of-war too. All
the vessels were dressed, their mastheads adorned with long pennants; the
most splendid flags were hoisted on the main flagstaffs, and there were
others on the jackstaffs and strung between the masts. There was just

[5] 'He snatched the thunderbolt from Heaven, and the sceptre from tyrants.'

wind enough to make flags and pennants fly free. This unusual decoration, the joyful people who swarmed over the decks, and the gun salutes from warships and from every merchantman that possessed a pair of cannon made the day festive for us all. Father had invited home a few guests, and, contrary to the prevailing custom, we boys were bidden to table; father explained the significance of this festival, our glasses too were filled with punch, and as toasts were drunk to the success of the new republic, a Danish and a North American flag were hoisted in our garden. The victory of the North Americans and the liberty of other peoples were discussed in lively fashion; and a certain anticipation of the great events to be derived from this victory was in the minds of those rejoicing. It was the friendly morning light of a bloody day in history.[6]

[6] Translated from Henrich Steffens, *Was Ich Erlebte* (Breslau, 1840), i. 78–80.

XI

FROM COLONY TO COMMONWEALTH
1775–1792

1. *The Formation of New Governments*

HAVING followed the external history of the American Revolution to the winning of independence, we must now turn back to take up the internal history: the transformation of colonies into commonwealths, the creation of new political institutions, the class and sectional conflict, and the readjustment of American society and business to the new conditions. The Revolution furnished Americans the opportunity to give legal form and expression to their political ideals as indicated in the Declaration of Independence; and to remedy some of their sectional and class grievances through the state constitutions, through legislation, and to some extent by a shift in the balance of political power. As James Madison wrote, ' Nothing has excited more admiration in the world than the manner in which free governments have been established in America; for it was the first instance, from the creation of the world . . . that free inhabitants have been seen deliberating on a form of government, and selecting such of their citizens as possessed their confidence, to determine upon and give effect to it.'

Americans are so accustomed to living under written constitutions that they take them for granted; yet the written constitution was developed in America, and these were among the earliest in history.[1] ' In all free states the constitution is final,' as John Adams wrote; Americans everywhere demanded ' a standing law to live by.' The written constitution was the natural, the inevitable result.

As early as 10 May 1776 Congress passed a resolution advising the colonies to form new governments ' such as shall best conduce to the happiness and safety of their constituents.' Some of them, such as New Hampshire and South Carolina, had already done so, and Massachusetts, to meet the Coercive Acts, had established a pro-

---

[1] In one sense, the Connecticut, Rhode Island, Virginia, and Massachusetts charters, and the frames of government promulgated by William Penn were constitutions; two of these served as such; but none were so fully developed or had so broad a popular basis as the later state constitutions.

visional government as early as the fall of 1774. Within a year after the Declaration of Independence every state except Massachusetts, Connecticut, and Rhode Island had drawn up a new constitution.[2] Massachusetts labored under her provisional government until 1780, while the two others retained their colonial charters, with a slight change in the preamble, until well into the nineteenth century.

The Pennsylvania constitution quaintly thanked God for ' permitting the people of this State, by common consent, and without violence, deliberately to form for themselves such just rules as they shall think best for governing their future society.' Here indeed was the Americans' opportunity to put into practice their favorite theories that government is of the people, rests upon the consent of the governed, and should be given form in a fixed constitution. Yet a method of giving effect to this 'compact' theory was not easily found. War, political disturbances, and the need of haste caused the states to adopt new constitutions in a variety of ways. The South Carolina, Virginia, and New Jersey constitutions of 1776 were framed by legislative bodies without any specific authorization, and were promulgated by them without express popular consent. In New Hampshire, Georgia, Delaware, New York, and Vermont the legislative bodies or provincial congresses which framed the constitutions did so by express authority, but failed to submit the finished products to popular approval. In Maryland, Pennsylvania, and North Carolina constitutions framed by authorized legislatures were in some manner ratified by the people. Only Massachusetts (1780) and New Hampshire (1784) had constitutional conventions specifically elected for that purpose alone, with a popular referendum on the result, and this has become the standard method of constitution making.

Massachusetts illustrates the most deliberate and effective transition from colony to commonwealth, as well as the first successful use of the constitutional convention with popular referendum. The process took five years, and the delay was fortunate, for in Massa-

[2] The dates of the adoptions of new state constitutions are as follows:

New Hampshire (1)	6 Jan. 1776	North Carolina	18 Dec. 1776
South Carolina (1)	26 Mar. 1776	Georgia	5 Feb. 1777
Virginia	29 June 1776	New York	20 April 1777
New Jersey	2 July 1776	Vermont	8 July 1777
Delaware	22 Aug. 1776	South Carolina (2)	19 Mar. 1778
Pennsylvania	28 Sept. 1776	Massachusetts	15 June 1780
Maryland	11 Nov. 1776	New Hampshire (2)	13 June 1784

chusetts the sort of people who made John Adams wince by shouting 'no courts, no taxation,' were very numerous. The hired men, tinkers, and village drunkards who had enjoyed tarring and feathering tories, ransacking the premises of suspected profiteers, and turning out with the militia for a few days or weeks, were a force to be reckoned with, and almost every rural township had a village demagogue and a crack-brained scheme of government. But in addition there was much shrewd common sense in the New England population, which sustained the leaders in establishing a sound state constitution.

The last General Court (legislature) of Massachusetts under the Crown was dissolved by the last royal governor in September 1774. The lower house met alone, and resolved itself into a Provincial Congress. On 5 May 1775 the Provincial Congress deposed Governor Gage and ordered the election of a regular General Court, as though the royal charter were in force and the governor absent. This made such an awkward government that the General Court, in September 1776, requested the people to empower it to draw up a constitution. Permission was eventually given, but Concord town meeting seized the opportunity to lay down the principle that a specially elected convention was the only proper body to draft a constitution, and that the people should have a whack at it before it went in force. A legislature, they declared, was no fit body to form and establish fundamental law, since one of the objects of a constitution was to secure the people against legislative tryanny. Further, if a legislature established a constitution, it could by the same power amend it, which would be no security to the citizen. This Concord idea became so rapidly popular, that when the Massachusetts legislature drafted a poor sort of state constitution, and submitted it to the people, they rejected it by a five-sixths majority. The chastened legislature then put into effect the new method. Early in 1779 it requested the people to decide in their town meetings whether or not they wanted a constitutional convention. They so voted. The legislature then ordered the towns to elect as many delegates to the convention as they were entitled to send representatives, and expressly provided that every resident freeman twenty-one years of age or over should vote. The convention duly met and chose a committee to draft a constitution, and on that committee John Adams did all the work. His amended draft was adopted 2 March 1780, when the convention asked the freemen to discuss the constitution in their town meetings, to point out objections and suggest improvements, to vote on it article by article, and to empower the convention to ratify and declare it in force if two-thirds of the men aged twenty-one and upward were in favor; or, if not, to alter it in accordance with the popular will as expressed in the returns, and ratify it as thus amended. This complicated procedure was followed. The town meetings that spring had a beautiful time discussing the constitution clause by clause, and drafting criticisms that in the main were sensible. When the convention tabulated the returns, it found a two-thirds majority for every article,[3] and declared the entire constitution ratified and in force on 15 June 1780.

It would be difficult to devise a more deliberate method of securing a government by popular consent. In fact the process of ratification was over-elaborate. At every step the rights of the people were safeguarded, and their views consulted. By the constitutional convention, the written constitution, and popular ratification, Americans had discovered a way to legalize the revolutionary doctrine.

2. The New State Constitutions

The writing of the state constitutions was a splendid opportunity for the democratic elements to remedy their grievances and for the better educated patriots to realize their ambitions for sound government. Most of the new constitutions showed the impact of democratic ideas, but none made any drastic break with the past, and all but two were designed to prevent a momentary popular will from overriding settled practices and vested interests. They were built by Americans on the solid foundation of colonial experience, with the timber of English practice, using Montesquieu as consulting architect. And there was a remarkable uniformity in the new governments. The reason was that the main work of drafting a constitution must always be done by a few men, and those few selected saw eye to eye on the fundamentals of popular government. 'Government is a very simple, easy thing,' declared a local convention in Maine. ' Mysteries in politics are mere absurdities.' But when simple men tried to draft a constitution they found it not so easy. Except in Pennsylvania

[3] Actually there was only a bare majority for the article on religion and the article on amendments, but the convention juggled the returns so that these appeared to be accepted as well. Although the constitution was voted on by manhood suffrage, there was a two-thirds majority for the clause adopting the colonial property qualification for voting.

and Vermont, the actual drafting was entrusted to college-educated men. That of New York, for instance, one of the best, was written by three young graduates of King's: John Jay, Robert Livingston, and Gouverneur Morris, of whom the first two were just over 30, and the other, 24 years old.

The same political philosophy that dictated the Declaration of Independence was fundamental to the state constitutions. Naturally the first object of the framers was to secure those ' inalienable rights,' the violation of which by George III had caused them to repudiate the British connection. Consequently, each constitution began with a declaration or bill of rights. That of Virginia, framed by George Mason of Gunston Hall (a gentleman so liberal that he could not swallow the Federal Constitution, yet so aristocratic that he regarded Washington as an upstart), served as a model for other states. It included a declaration of principles such as popular sovereignty, rotation in office, freedom of elections, separation of powers; and then enumerated the fundamental liberties for which Englishmen had been struggling since Magna Carta: — moderate bail and humane punishments, militia instead of standing army, speedy trials by the law of the land, and judgment by one's peers — together with others, based on recent experience, which Englishmen had not yet completely secured: — freedom of the press, of conscience, of the right of a majority to reform or alter the government, prohibition of general warrants. Other states considerably enlarged this list by drawing upon their own experience, or upon English constitutional documents such as the Bill of Rights of 1689: — freedom of speech, of assemblage, of petition, of bearing arms, the right to a writ of habeas corpus, inviolability of domicile, equal operation of the laws. State governments were generally forbidden to pass *ex post facto* laws, to define treason in such a way as to ' get ' undesirables, to take property without compensation, to imprison without warrant, or to apply martial law in time of peace.

Truly no governments on earth have ever been instituted with so little authority to do ill, as those of the American states. Yet, not content with that, the framers of constitutions even limited their governments' power to do good, lest it be perverted to their hurt. American colonists had long English memories. The English people in the seventeenth century had tasted absolutism under Charles I, the Long Parliament, Cromwell, and James II; and the unhappy experience of these four totalitarian régimes impressed the English

mind with the need for separation between those who make laws
(the legislative), those who execute the laws (king, governor, or
executive council), and those who interpret the laws (the judiciary);
and with the need for checks even within these departments. By 1700
the English had obtained a government in which the legislative and
executive functions were separated,[4] and the judges had obtained
tenure during good behavior. George III upset this balance by acquiring an undue influence over Parliament, which was all the more
reason for the Americans harking back to what they conceived to be
the 'true principles' of the British Constitution, as brilliantly ex-
pounded by their Bible of political wisdom, Montesquieu's *Spirit of
Laws*. Moreover, their colonial experience of royal governors, popularly elected assemblies, and judges appointed during the king's
pleasure, made them the more sensible of the value of a separation of
powers.

Accordingly, all the state constitutions paid allegiance to the theory
of separation of powers, and attempted to carry it out in fact. John
Adams's constitution of Massachusetts, for example, provided that
'In the government of this commonwealth, the legislative department shall never exercise the executive and judicial powers or
either of them; the executive shall never exercise the legislative and
judicial powers or either of them; the judicial shall never exercise
the legislative and executive powers or either of them; to the end
it may be a government of laws and not of men.' By the same token,
internal checks were provided in the executive and legislative departments — a council on the governor, a senate on the house.

This principle was much less consistently carried out in the constitutions of 1776. The Virginia framers seem to have been impressed
by Locke's dictum, 'The legislative is the supreme power of the commonwealth'; for they allowed the legislature to elect governor, council, and all judges except justices of the peace. The Pennsylvania
constitution was consciously drafted by radicals to give the popular
will immediate effect. No one could be a member of the Pennsylvania
legislature more than four years in every seven, or of the executive
council (out of which a president was chosen), more than three years
in seven. This rotation was prescribed, the constitution explained, in
order to preclude 'the danger of establishing an inconvenient aris-

---

[4] Their subsequent blending in the modern parliamentary system, took place
almost entirely after the American Revolution, and so was outside the experience of
Americans at that time.

tocracy.' The classical education of leaders of American opinion, memories of what Julius Caesar did to the Roman Republic, were reflected in antipathy to the executive power; and in every state but New York and Massachusetts that branch was conspicuously weak. Massachusetts alone granted him the veto power. The judiciary in most states was appointed by the legislature, and in three for a limited term; but every state endeavored to make the judiciary independent by protecting the judges from arbitrary removal or pressure through reduction of salaries.

Although the people were everywhere recognized as sovereign, every constitution but that of Vermont placed control of the government in the hands of persons possessing more or less property. The accepted idea was that the body politic consisted of those who had a ' stake in society.' Even the democratic Franklin declared that ' as to those who have no landed property . . . the allowing them to vote for legislators is an impropriety.' There were property qualifications for voting, and proportionately higher ones for office-holding. Pennsylvania, New Hampshire, and Georgia gave the suffrage to all who paid at least a poll tax; Virginia, Delaware, and Rhode Island to landholders; other states had various property qualifications. In most states, too, there were religious qualifications for office-holding, or offensive oaths of office that were designed to keep Roman Catholics out.

Few of the early constitutions provided any special method of amendment; yet when necessity arose, amendment could be effected by a new convention. Despite the haste with which many of the constitutions were drafted, five lasted over half a century, and the deliberately formed constitution of Massachusetts is still in effect, although much amended. A number of mistakes and crudities were to be expected; but these amateur constitution-makers fully proved themselves worthy of their trust, and their states ripe for self government.

3. Political Reform

In almost every state the writing of the new constitutions precipitated a struggle between democratic and conservative elements. In most states the former were at a considerable disadvantage, because talents, education and leadership were on the other side. In states such as New York, Massachusetts, South Carolina, Maryland, and Virginia, where the conservative classes had taken the lead before

1775, they were in a position to direct the course of events and stem the democratic tide. 'However unexceptionable a democratic government may appear at first view,' said Governor Rutledge of South Carolina, 'its effects have been found arbitrary, severe, and destructive.' In Pennsylvania, North Carolina and Georgia, where the initial decision in favor of independence had been a radical victory, the democratic elements had things much their own way.

The constitutional history of three typical states, Pennsylvania, Virginia, and South Carolina, illustrates the clash of classes and the essential continuity of this period with the pre-war years.

In the Quaker commonwealth the struggle between east and west culminated early in 1776 in a complete reapportionment of representation, a smashing victory for the western counties. Triumph tasted sweet, and the radicals wanted more. They called a convention to adopt a new constitution and take over the government of the state. Delegates were chosen by popular vote, without property qualifications. The constitution that they produced was drastically democratic; the principal authors were George Bryan, an intense and idealistic Irishman, James Cannon, a Scotch professor of mathematics, and Benjamin Franklin. It did away with governor and upper chamber, and provided for a council of censors to examine the operation of the government every seven years. As one conservative bitterly lamented:

We might at least have prevented ourselves from being ridiculous in the eyes of the world were it not for a few enthusiastic members who are totally unacquainted with the principles of government. It is not only that their notions are original, but they would go to the devil for popularity, and in order to acquire it, they have embraced leveling principles, which you know is a fine method of succeeding.

There were no qualifications for voting or office-holding, except the payment of a state tax and the touching proviso that membership in the House should consist of 'persons most noted for wisdom and virtue.' Representation, proportioned to the number of taxables in each county, gave the more numerous Scotch-Irish and Germans of the interior the majority; and their natural allies, the working people of Philadelphia, obtained a larger share of power than they had ever known. These groups promptly swept away many of the unpopular features of proprietary and Quaker control, and much good with the bad: the Philadelphia College, for instance.

Just as in Pennsylvania the radicals, middle classes and frontiersmen who took the lead in the Revolution drafted a radical constitution, so in Virginia the gentry who led the patriot party wanted a conservative constitution, and got it promptly, even before the Declaration of Independence was adopted. Archibald Cary, Robert Carter Nicholas, James Madison, George Mason, and Patrick Henry were on the drafting committee; Jefferson and even John Adams exerted some influence from Philadelphia, where they were busy on more important matters. The constitution was a compromise, weighted on the conservative side. On the one hand, a conservative plan of Carter Braxton for a high-toned government with a Senate elected for life obtained no consideration. On the other hand, colonial property qualifications for voting and office-holding remained unchanged, and the eastern counties retained their control of the legislature through the device of giving each county exactly two members. As the western counties were large, populous, and growing fast, this disproportion became greater every year. In 1790 the five Valley counties with an average white population of 12,089 had two representatives each, and five Tidewater counties with an average white population of 1,471 had two representatives each. Also, the Valley Presbyterians were disappointed in not obtaining separation of church and state. Yet the Virginia constitution, as we have seen, was also distinguished for its noble Declaration or Bill of Rights, which served as a model for other states, and even for France.

Although the Virginia gentry were unyielding in matters such as sectional representation which threatened their political supremacy, they went further in reform legislation than the governing class of any other state, not excepting Pennsylvania. Their constitution, brief and flexible, allowed this; and within a few years, under the driving leadership of Jefferson, Madison, and Mason, quit-rents, primogeniture, and entails were abolished, church and state separated, the legal code revised, and the slave trade abolished.

This Virginia constitution of 1776 was radical in comparison with the South Carolina constitution of 1778, which perpetuated those class and sectional inequalities that made trouble in the colonial period. Suffrage was limited to men with a fifty-acre freehold, and property qualifications for office-holding were almost prohibitory. A Senator had to hold an estate worth £2000, while the Governor, Lieutenant Governor, and councillors must own property to the value of £10,000. There were special provisions for absentee voting and representation, making it possible for wealthy planters who resided in Charleston to be elected from communities where they owned land. The coastal region continued to be grossly over-represented in the House, with 144 members, and the up-country under-represented with 58. The Anglican Church was disestablished, but only Protestants were guaranteed civil rights. Quit-rents and entails had already been done away with; primogeniture lingered on until 1791. This triumph of the conservatives left that state under the control of low-country planters, and made it the stronghold of Southern conservatism for three-quarters of a century.

4. Social Progress

These typical states of Pennsylvania, Virginia, and South Carolina give some indication of the general trend of political reorganization, but we must look elsewhere as well to appreciate what progressive forces were released by the Revolution. The war did not give the ' people ' control of their governments, but it did help the poor to acquire a stake in society. With land selling at a few cents an acre, as it did in many states when confiscated tory property was thrown on the market, it was a sorry fellow indeed who could not acquire fifty acres, or a forty-shilling freehold, which would entitle him to the vote. If property qualifications for office remained, they were seldom prohibitory, and thousands of poor men had a taste of power during these years. In the Northern states representation was generally reapportioned according to population, allowing the back-country for the first time its full weight. Relics of feudalism such as titles of nobility, quit-rents, entails, primogeniture, and tithes were swept away. The crown lands, the extensive domains of proprietors such as the Penns and Calverts, and the princely estates of loyalists such as Lord Fairfax of Virginia, Sir William Johnson of New York, James Wright of Georgia, Henry Harford of Maryland, Governor Wentworth of New Hampshire, and others, were confiscated by the states and in part redistributed to small farmers and war veterans. The estate of Roger Morris of New York, for example, went to two hundred and fifty persons, that of the De Lanceys to even more. Considerable progress was made in achieving complete religious freedom and separation of church and state, and a concerted attack upon slavery or the slave trade was made in every state. The democratic philosophy of the Revolution percolated through politics into the structure of American society, and the force of it was not spent for a century.

When the War of Independence broke out, the Anglican Church was established in every colony from Maryland to Georgia and in part of New York; and the Congregational churches enjoyed a privileged position in Massachusetts, Connecticut, and New Hampshire. Only in otherwise-minded Rhode Island, and in Pennsylvania, New Jersey, and Delaware, was there a separation of church and state. The dissenting groups were discriminated against in various ways, and their discontent was part of the internal upheaval that accompanied the War of Independence. An important leader in the movement was the Presbyterian minister John Witherspoon, who came to America after fighting the established church in Scotland, became President of the College of New Jersey at Princeton, and a signer of the Declaration of Independence. He was forever preaching that mere toleration was not enough, for that implied superiority and condescension; the only proper principle for a republic was complete liberty to worship how one chose or not at all, and every church should be supported by its own members or funds without help from the taxing power of the state. Witherspoon's pupils, among whom James Madison was conspicuous, were apt to be found on the side of religious liberty.

The issue was early raised in Virginia; but the struggle by Madison, Jefferson, and R. H. Lee to have that principle expressed in concrete terms, was long and arduous. Dissenters were still forced to pay tithes, and none but the Episcopal clergy could perform the marriage ceremony. It took ten years of what Jefferson called the severest contest in which he was ever engaged to do away with these privileges. Patrick Henry supported a counter-scheme to establish all the churches of whatever denomination, and support them all by taxation, as in New England; but complete religious liberty prevailed. 'There had been a time,' one dissenting clergyman observed of his brethren, 'when they would have been satisfied to have paid their tithes, if they could have had liberty of conscience; but now the crisis was such that nothing less than a total overthrow of all ecclesiastical distinctions would satisfy their sanguine hopes. Having started the decaying edifice, every dissenter put his shoulder to push it into a irretrievable ruin.' In January 1786, after a state-wide campaign of education, the legislature passed the noble Statute of Religious Liberty which Jefferson had introduced seven years earlier, and which he accounted one of his three great contributions to his country.[5] It was a re-enactment, with an eloquent preamble, of Article II of the Pennsylvania Declaration of Rights, to the effect that no man be compelled to attend or support any ministry or place of worship; with this difference, that Pennsylvania allowed by implication an atheist to be deprived of civil rights, whilst Virginia declared that no religious profession whatsoever might ' diminish, enlarge or effect' a person's ' civil capacity.'

In Maryland, where the Anglican Church was unpopular both with the Catholics of the coast and the Presbyterians of the interior, it was separated from the state in 1776. In North Carolina the feeble establishment completely disappeared, and the constitution of 1776 stated simply that ' there shall be no establishment of any one religious church or denomination in this State in preference to any other.' There was a struggle in South Carolina, where the church was firmly intrenched in the affections of the ruling class; but the constitution of 1778 provided that all Protestant churches should enjoy equal civil and religious liberties.

In the Middle Colonies where religious liberty already existed, the principle was embodied in the new constitutions as a matter of form; and it was incorporated into the Northwest Ordinance of 1787 and the First Amendment to the Federal Constitution. Only in New England did it fail of recognition. Here the Congregational clergy had been early and eloquent on the winning side; the Rev. Thomas Allen of Pittsfield even led his parishioners into action at Bennington. It was argued that the town church like the town meeting and town school had made New England, and should be equally respected. Rhode Island had always had religious liberty; Vermont adopted it at once; but the other three states adopted a sort of quasi-establishment, according to which everyone had to pay a religious tax to the Congregational church of the parish within which he lived, unless he belonged to a recognized dissenting church. In that case the dissenting pastor received the tax. The Episcopalians in Connecticut and the Baptists elsewhere attacked this system intermittently, but it lasted in New Hampshire until 1817, in Connecticut until 1818, and in Massachusetts until 1833.

The Congregational churches, therefore, were left in exactly the same position after the war as before; they had no central organiza-

---

[5] The other two were the Declaration of Independence and the establishment of the University of Virginia.

tion to be troubled by political changes. The Methodists, on the contrary, seized this opportunity to form a separate church, and the Anglicans were forced to separate from a church that acknowledged the king of England as supreme head. The Methodists had been a religious society within the Church of England that operated through conferences; and in a time when (as Francis Asbury said) the minds of men were 'full of sin and politics,' they did not prosper. Asbury, who had been John Wesley's superintendent before the war, became an American citizen, and at the Baltimore Conference of 1784 organized the Methodist Episcopal Church of America with himself as first bishop and premier circuit rider — his horseback mileage averaged five thousand annually for the next five years. The Anglican communion, although decimated by loyalism and the withdrawal of English support, had sufficient strength and spirit to organize as the Protestant Episcopal Church of America at a series of conventions between 1784 and 1789. The present constitution of the Church, giving far more power to the laity than in England, was then adopted, references to English royalty were deleted from the Book of Common Prayer, and apostolic succession was secured through the election of three bishops and their consecration in England and Scotland. In 1785, when Bishop Seabury (the former tory pamphleteer) returned to his new diocese in lawn sleeves, the Massachusetts legislature laid a stamp tax; which caused the Boston *Gazette* to exclaim, 'Two wonders of the world — a Stamp Act in Boston and a Bishop in Connecticut!'

No religious body was so well prepared for independence as the Presbyterians. They had numbers, wealth, Scotch respect for learning, Irish *gaudium certaminis,* and a great leader in President Witherspoon. At a series of synods between 1785 and 1788 a form of government and discipline, a confession of faith, a directory of worship and two catechisms were adopted for the Presbyterian Church in the United States.

The various German and Dutch sects also broke loose from their old-world organizations; only the Quakers and the Catholics made no constitutional change. The one had so loose and informal an organization that independence did not matter; whilst revolutions were an old story to Rome. Nevertheless, there was a sharp struggle between English, French, and Irish Catholics for control of the Church in the United States, which in 1785 counted but 24 priests and as many thousand souls, almost all in Maryland and around

Philadelphia. The London vicar apostolic made no effort to exercise jurisdiction after 1776; but in France there was an active movement, led by that Bishop of Autun who is better known in history as M. de Talleyrand, to place American Catholics under a French vicar apostolic, and provide a seminary at Bordeaux for training their priests. Pope Pius VI appointed the Rev. John Carroll of Maryland his prefect apostolic in 1784, but that office did not carry enough authority to keep the French and Irish Catholics in order; and in 1786 a chapter of the Maryland clergy petitioned the Holy See to grant the Church in the United States episcopal government. Two years later the Pope gave his American clergy permission to choose their bishop; and John Carroll was duly elected, confirmed, and consecrated Bishop of Baltimore, a diocese that covered the entire United States until 1804.

The next issue was personal liberty. When the War of Independence broke out there were about half a million slaves in the American colonies.[6] The inconsistency of demanding life, liberty, and happiness for themselves while denying those 'natural rights' to the Negroes was apparent to Americans even before unfriendly English criticism called it to their attention, and they proceeded to do what they could about it. Historians are fond of pointing out the yawning chasms between the theory that 'all men are created equal' and the fact that thousands were born into slavery. Be it said to

---

[6] It is impossible to ascertain the exact number of slaves in the American colonies in 1776. The table below gives the approximate number in 1776 and the number according to the census of 1790.

	1776	1790
New Hampshire	700	157
Rhode Island	4,000	958
Connecticut	6,000	2,648
Massachusetts	5,249*	0
New York	20,000	21,193
New Jersey	10,000	11,423
Pennsylvania	6,000	3,707
Delaware	?	8,837
Maryland	70,000	103,036
Virginia	200,000	292,627
North Carolina	70,000	100,783
South Carolina	100,000	107,094
Georgia	10,000	29,264
Kentucky	?	12,440
Southwest Territory	?	3,417
	501,949	699,374

* Including free Negroes.

the credit of the theorizers that they did everything in their power to bridge the gulf.

The first point of attack was the slave trade. Time and again the American colonies had protested against the traffic, maintained chiefly for the benefit of the Royal African Company, but their protests had been in vain and their prohibitory laws had been disallowed by the Privy Council. As late as 1776 the pious Lord Dartmouth denounced the colonies for their attempts 'to check or discourage a traffic so beneficial to the nation.' One of the first acts of the Continental Congress was to conclude a non-importation agreement prohibiting the slave trade. Soon the states took separate action. Delaware prohibited the trade in 1776, Virginia under Jefferson's leadership in 1778, Pennsylvania in 1780, and Maryland in 1783, where Luther Martin argued pointedly that the traffic was 'inconsistent to the principles of the Revolution and dishonorable to the American character.' Even in South Carolina the trade was temporarily prohibited, while North Carolina placed a heavy tax on all slaves imported into that state. Within ten years after independence every state except Georgia had prohibited or severely restrained the traffic, and Georgia followed tardily in 1798 with an absolute prohibition. But a good many ships from New York and New England continued to bring slaves illegally from Africa, and sell them in the West Indies and the lower South.

The struggle for emancipation was more difficult, and marked by a more distinct sectional character. It was relatively easy for the Northern states, where slavery was unprofitable, except as a means of providing cooks and butlers for the wealthy; and in the North the progress of emancipation was rapid. As early as 1774 Rhode Island provided that all slaves thereafter brought into that commonwealth were to be free, and the reason given is illuminating:

Whereas . . . the inhabitants of America are generally engaged in the preservation of their own rights and liberties, among which that of personal freedom must be considered as the greatest, and as those who are desirous of enjoying all the advantages of liberty themselves should be willing to extend personal liberty to others.

The constitution of Vermont abolished slavery outright. In Massachusetts, Quock Walker sued his master for freedom on the ground that the state constitution declared: 'All men are born free and equal.' He won his suit (1781), and slavery ended in that state. The

New Hampshire courts, under a similar clause, freed only the *post nati*. Pennsylvania, stronghold of anti-slavery Quakers, provided for gradual emancipation in 1780; Connecticut and Rhode Island followed four years later. New York and New Jersey made similar provisions in 1799 and 1804. So the Revolution put slavery well on the way to extinction, north of the Mason and Dixon line.

In the South slaves were so numerous that to free them would not only shake the economic and social system to its foundation, but substitute a Negro problem for a slavery problem. The dilemma of liberal Southerners is well presented in a letter that Patrick Henry addressed to his friend Robert Pleasants:

I take this Oppertunity to acknowledge the receit of Anthony Benezets Book against the Slave Trade. I thank you for it. . . . Is it not amazing, that at a time when the rights of Humanity are defined and understood with precision in a Country above all others fond of Liberty: that in such an Age and such a Country, we find Men, professing a Religion the most humane, mild, meek, gentle and generous, adopting a Principle as repugnant to humanity, as it is inconsistent with the Bible and destructive to Liberty — . . . Would any one believe that I am Master of Slaves of my own purchase! I am drawn along by the general Inconvenience of living without them; I will not, I cannot justify it. However culpable my Conduct, I will so far pay my devoir to Virtue, as to own the excellence and rectitude of her Precepts and to lament my want of conformity to them. I believe a time will come when an oppertunity will be offered to abolish this lamentable Evil. — Everything we can do, is to improve it if it happens in our day, if not let us transmit to our descendants together with our Slaves a pity for their unhappy Lot, and an abhorrence for Slavery.

'I tremble for my country,' Jefferson wrote, 'when I reflect that God is just; that his justice cannot sleep forever.' Yet proposals for gradual emancipation were defeated in every Southern state, although several states encouraged manumission by the masters, and thousands of Negroes obtained their freedom by this means. Except in South Carolina and Georgia, almost every Southerner looked upon slavery as an evil, but a necessary one; in time it became so necessary that it ceased to appear evil. The anti-slavery forces, however, scored a signal victory in the provision of the Northwest Ordinance dedicating the territory north of the Ohio to liberty.

Important as all these reforms were, it would be an exaggeration to describe the American Revolution as a social revolution, like

those of France and Russia. No class as such was expropriated,
slavery was not abolished, the structure of society was not altered.
Our Revolution was primarily political, like the English Revolution
of 1640–60. Even the confiscation of loyalist property affected the
relations of persons rather than of classes: one set of proprietors
was impoverished, and another enriched; and it was not long before
the patriots who obtained tory farms and mansions were just as
conservative as the former owners. Yet the Revolution was a powerful catalytic agent in American society. It released pent-up energies
and gave them form and direction. It crystallized the American
character and institutions. The established order of things was questioned if not replaced. Ideals heretofore nebulous were given concrete formulation; hopes and aspirations heretofore formless were
realized. Jeffersonian democracy would have been impossible but
for the fillip that war and independence gave to the democratic
elements in American society.

5. Arts, Letters, and Education

Revolutionary liberalism also found expression in efforts of an
intellectual and humanitarian nature. Remarkable were the efforts
to enlarge opportunities for higher education, especially in the South,
where before the war there had been but one college. Governor
Jefferson, as chairman of the board of regents, partly secularized the
College of William and Mary in 1779 by turning the chairs of divinity and Hebrew into professorships of law and modern languages,
and by allowing students considerable latitude of choice in their
studies. It was also during the war that William and Mary students
founded the Phi Beta Kappa Society, and initiated a young Harvard
graduate who established chapters at his alma mater and at Yale.
Although much disturbed by the Virginia campaigns of 1780–81,
the College of William and Mary just after the war, under Bishop
Madison as president, probably had the best liberal arts course in the
country. But the charter gave so much control to the Episcopal
Church as to prevent the College from becoming a state university;
Presbyterians and Baptists objected. The Presbyterians founded at
least four new colleges in the seventeen eighties: Hampden-Sydney,
Virginia (1782); Liberty Hall, which became the nucleus of Wash-
ington and Lee University; Dickinson College (1783) at Carlisle,
Pa.; and Transylvania Seminary (1785), the first institution of

secondary education beyond the mountains, one which a decade later became a college. The Lutherans and Dutch Reformed Church, with the aid of a contribution from Benjamin Franklin, established the German-speaking Franklin College at Lancaster, Pa., in 1787; and the Protestant Episcopal Church between 1782 and 1785 founded Washington College at Chesterton, Md., St. John's at Annapolis, and the College of Charleston in South Carolina. Bishop Carroll founded the Roman Catholic Georgetown College in 1789. Within the same period the legislatures of Maryland, Georgia, and North Carolina took the initiative in providing state universities.

All the older colleges were injured by the war, but most of them picked up rapidly thereafter, Yale graduating a record-breaking class of 70 in 1785.[7] The Harvard boys had a little revolution of their own in 1780 and chased President Langdon out; the governing boards then chose as his successor the Rev. Joseph Willard, a good amateur scientist, employed young Albert Gallatin to teach French, and opened a medical school before the war was over. No new colleges were founded in New England until the nineties, but the Phillips Academies at Andover, Mass. and Exeter, N. H., opened respectively in 1778 and 1783, were soon attracting students from various parts of the country. King's College was closed during the British occupation of New York, but reopened as Columbia College in 1784, under a distinguished president, William Samuel Johnson. Franklin's beloved Philadelphia College was abolished when his back was turned, in 1779, by the democratic legislature of Pennsylvania, because most of the trustees were tories or conservatives. The property was vested in a new state university, which existed largely on paper; and although the trustees of the College recovered their rights ten years later and merged with the University of Pennsylvania, higher education in Philadelphia suffered a blow from which it did not recover for many years. Yet the distinguished Benjamin Rush made the Pennsylvania Medical School the best in the country, and Quaker influence made Philadelphia easily the leading city in humanitarian enterprises — a college of physicians, a free medical dispensary for the poor, an abolition society, and a society for the relief of prisoners were founded there under the Confederation.

In other branches of arts, letters, and learning this era of war and

---

[7] The numbers of other graduating classes that year, so far as is recorded, are: Harvard, 32; Princeton, 10; Dartmouth, 20; Brown, none (15 in 1786); Columbia, none (9 in 1786); Pennsylvania, 4.

upheaval was equally productive. Judge Francis Hopkinson, signer of the Declaration of Independence, was better known to contemporaries as poet, painter, pamphleteer, musician, organist of Christ Church, Philadelphia, and designer of the American flag, which Betsy Ross may have cut out and sewed together. Hopkinson's *Battle of the Kegs* (1778) was a roaring satire on an incident of the Revolution; his oratorio *The Temple of Minerva* was performed in 1781 'in Presence of His Excellency General Washington and his Lady.' David Rittenhouse, the Philadelphia mathematician and astronomer, was the first man of science in America at this time; but everywhere ingenious people were making inventions and seeking out the secrets of nature. In Essex County, Mass., for instance, the Rev. Manasseh Cutler during the war prepared the first systematic account of New England flora, measured (very inaccurately) the height of Mt. Washington, observed eclipses, and in 1787 promoted the Ohio Company; the Rev. John Prince invented a new air pump in 1783; and the Rev. Joseph Willard recorded all manner of phenomena. In the Philosophical Library that this group formed at Salem, largely from an Irish scientist's library brought in by a local privateer, young Nathaniel Bowditch, the future navigator, first fed his appetite for mathematical science. Philadelphia even before the war had her literary-scientific academy, the American Philosophical Society, of which Franklin was the founder and Rittenhouse the president; in 1780 the Boston and Salem virtuosi founded the American Academy of Arts and Sciences.

It was in 1783 that a twenty-five year old schoolmaster named Noah Webster declared, 'America must be as independent in *literature* as she is in *politics*, as famous for *arts* as for *arms*.' And he did more than his share to make her so. His famous blue-backed speller, the first edition of which appeared in 1783, became one of the best sellers of all time: over fifteen million copies sold in the author's lifetime; sixty million in a century. It was followed in 1787 by his *American Selection*, the first school reader, including rules for elocution, a brief American history, and a geography of the United States. Webster became an ardent Federalist, and published one of the best arguments for a more perfect union, when he discovered that the Confederation could do nothing to protect literary property; a book had to be copyrighted in all thirteen states. Joel Barlow, Webster's classmate at Yale, wrote his epic *Vision of Columbus* in the intervals of preaching, fighting, and teaching, and had it sumptuously printed at Hartford in 1787; by that time he and other ' Hartford Wits' were contributing squibs on democracy and Dan Shays to *The Anarchaiad*. When poor Dan fled to New York he once more unwittingly contributed to American Literature, for Royal Tyler, sent thither to demand Shays's extradition, saw Sheridan's *School for Scandal* and was inspired to write *The Contrast*. This delightful comedy was professionally produced in 1787.[8] John Trumbull, son of the Governor of Connecticut but educated at Harvard, served in the war, studied painting at London under the expatriated Pennsylvanian Benjamin West, and there in 1786 completed his two famous paintings, *The Battle at Bunker's Hill near Boston,* and *The Death of General Montgomery*. St. John de Crèvecoeur's *Letters of an American Farmer* were published in 1782; and four years later appeared the first collected edition of the poems of Philip Freneau. The concluding stanzas of one of them, ' On the Emigration to America and Peopling the Western Country,' well express the spirit of this age:

> O come the time, and haste the day,
> When man shall man no longer crush,
> When Reason shall enforce her sway,
> Nor these fair regions raise our blush,
> Where still the *African* complains,
> And mourns his yet unbroken chains.
>
> Far brighter scenes a future age,
> The muse predicts, these States will hail,
> Whose genius may the world engage,
> Whose deeds may over death prevail,
> And happier systems bring to view,
> Than all the eastern sages knew.

6. *Western State Making*

While the thirteen seaboard colonies were being metamorphosed into states and adjusting themselves to the conditions of independence, new commonwealths were being created in Vermont and in the trans-Appalachian country. Here, under primitive conditions, the processes of commonwealth building and state making were go-

---

[8] *The Prince of Parthia* by Thomas Godfrey of Philadelphia, there produced in 1767, was the first play by an Anglo-American to be put on professionally; *The Contrast* was the second.

ing on simultaneously throughout the revolutionary period, and here the democratic theories of that era were given a rude and effective application. Nothing more eloquently bespeaks the vitality and creative energy of Americans of this generation than the rapidity and vigor with which, during the years of war and reconstruction, they hewed new empires out of the wilderness and peopled them with sturdy and independent citizens.

The history of Vermont from 1770 to 1790 illustrates in a most illuminating fashion the complexities and cross-currents of the Revolution. This land between the Connecticut and the Hudson rivers, long in dispute between New Hampshire and New York, began to be settled about 1763. By the time of the war the population was thirty thousand or more — enough to furnish the Green Mountain boys who harassed Burgoyne's army. Yet, stout fighters as they were, the Vermonters and their leaders, Ethan, Ira, and Levi Allen, cared less for the independence of the United States than for the autonomy of Vermont, which was refused admission to the Confederation because New York and New Hampshire each claimed it as a part of their territory.

Ethan Allen was the first leader of the Vermonters. A combination of patriot and speculator, adventurer and capitalist, he was typical of those frontier leaders who directed the expansive forces of the American people. Defying a pre-war decision of the Privy Council allotting the Green Mountain country to New York, defying also Congress and Governor Clinton and General Washington, who regarded this decision as valid, the Allens and their party created and defended an independent commonwealth. In June 1777, a revolutionary convention adopted the name Vermont and drafted a state constitution modelled upon that of Pennsylvania, and even more democratic. It provided for a unicameral legislature, a plural executive, and septennial 'council of censors,' 'whose duty it shall be to inquire whether the Constitution has been preserved inviolate in every part.' No property qualifications were established for voting or office-holding, religious liberty was upheld, and slavery prohibited.

Although the Allen brothers used the vocabulary of patriotism, and spoke glibly of oppression, tyranny, and sacred liberties, they and their numerous followers were primarily interested in land. The Allen family controlled a land company which claimed title to over three hundred thousand acres in central Vermont, and Ethan him-

self thus stated their position: 'He and his family have large fortunes which they do not intend to lose, if there is a possibility of
saving them. At all risks, he is determined that Congress shall not
have the parcelling of his Lands to their avaricious Minions.' That
this event should not come to pass they carried on intrigues with
Governor Haldimand of Canada, looking to a guarantee of independence in return for neutrality during the war, or even a return
to the British Empire after the war. Like true Vermonters they acted
with such silent shrewdness that only recently have the archives revealed their doings. In 1789 Levi Allen went to London to obtain
a commercial treaty, and offered, 'to raise a regiment of Green
Mountain boys for His Majesty's service.'

Meantime the body of people, who knew naught of these intrigues,
had been loyal and active supporters of the American cause. Yet
Congress was estopped from recognizing their claims to statehood
by fear of antagonizing New York. After a checkered history the
Green Mountain State succeeded in vindicating her independence
and escaping foreign entanglements. In 1790 New York finally relinquished her claims, a convention at Bennington ratified the Federal Constitution, and on 18 February 1791 Congress admitted Vermont as the fourteenth state.

The creation of new commonwealths west of the Appalachians
was attended with even greater difficulties than in Vermont. Lured
by the finest hunting their race had found in a thousand years and
the richest land yet spied out in America, the pioneers poured into
the 'dark and bloody ground' of Kentucky and Tennessee. As early
as 1769 settlers from western Virginia, defying the royal proclamation, established a small community on the upper waters of the
Watauga, one of the tributaries to the Holston. In the following
years James Robertson and John Sevier, the two great figures in
the early history of Tennessee, led a body of eighty men from North
Carolina to the Watauga settlements; and Jacob Brown established a
small community on the Nollichucky. These far-flung outposts of
settlement were shortly reinforced by the arrival of large numbers
of Regulator refugees from the civil war in North Carolina, and by
1775 there were several thousand settlers scattered along the banks
of the Watauga, Holston, and other tributaries of the Tennessee river
in the northeast corner of the present state of Tennessee. These
settlements were separated by mountain ranges and by hundreds of
miles from the centers of political authority in the East. Uncertainty

whether they were within the jurisdiction of Virginia or of North Carolina, the rapid increase in population, together with the want of law, justice, and common defense against Indians, made some form of political organization imperative. As early as 1772 the Watauga inhabitants drew up a written compact of government — the first of its kind in the region west of the Appalachians. They governed themselves for four years, until North Carolina organized the region as a county, in 1776. When in 1784 North Carolina ceded this region to the Confederation, she stopped payments promised to the Cherokee Indians, who promptly attacked the settlements. In this critical situation, with no prospect of the impecunious Confederation doing anything for them, the Watauga leaders called a convention at Jonesboro, decided to organize a separate state, and elected John Sevier governor. This Virginia-born aristocrat, the outstanding military and civil figure in the West, had long been associated with the Tennessee settlements. In December a new convention met and drafted a constitution modelled closely on that of North Carolina, and named their new state Franklin. But the state of Franklin was short-lived. Factional quarrels divided it into hostile camps, and North Carolina hastened to reassert her jurisdiction over the region. As soon as North Carolina completed the cession of her western lands to the Federal Government, the demand for separate statehood arose again. Franklin was finally included in Tennessee, which was admitted to the Union in 1796.

Central Kentucky, the blue-grass country, began to be settled shortly after the Watauga. This region was the scene of a colossal land speculation that assumed the full panoply of sovereignty — the Transylvania Company, of which the leading spirit was Judge Richard Henderson of North Carolina. On 17 March 1775 this company purchased from the Cherokee Indians for a few thousand pounds all lands lying between the Kentucky, the Ohio and the Cumberland rivers. They had no authority from king or colony to make the purchase, and the Cherokee had no exclusive right to make the sale; but the company always referred to this transaction as the 'treaty of Sycamore Shoals.' A few bold pioneers, encouraged by the defeat of the Shawnee in Lord Dunmore's War, had already found their way into the blue-grass, and founded Harrodsborough. Boone and Henderson now conducted a few dozen more to a place on the Kentucky river that they named Boonesborough; and there on 23 May 1775, under a great elm in the clover-carpeted meadow, Henderson called a meeting of delegates from all settlements in the domain claimed by the Transylvania Company. The convention drafted articles of government, passed laws, organized the 'Transylvania Colony,' and petitioned the Continental Congress for recognition as such, in order to validate the company's dubious title to the land. It is possible that if Patrick Henry had been taken into the Transylvania Company, the Congress would have complied; but this was not done. Virginia was not ready to surrender title and jurisdiction over seventeen million acres of her western territory, Henderson alienated settlers by attempting to collect quit-rents, and the upshot was that most of the settlers sought protection from Virginia, which, in spite of protracted lobbying by the company, organized the region as Kentucky County in 1776. The Transylvania Company obtained two hundred thousand acres by way of compensation, for it had done much to open up Kentucky; it was Henderson who employed the celebrated scout Daniel Boone to hew out what later was known as the Wilderness Road.[9] After fourteen years' agitation Virginia relinquished her jurisdiction over this region, and on 1 June 1792 Kentucky was admitted to the Union as the fifteenth state.

The third nucleus of settlement in the West was in central Tennessee. In 1779 James Robertson led a small band of pioneers two hundred miles into the heart of the wilderness to the bend of the Cumberland and established the town of Nashborough. The following year the tiny community received accessions from the Watauga and Holston settlements, one intrepid group going down the Tennessee river to the Ohio and back up the Cumberland river to Nashborough. On 13 May 1780 a body of men signed the Cumberland compact, providing a government on the basis of a Virginia county court. The community was to be administered by a court of twelve judges, chosen by vote of all men over twenty-one years of age, and subject to recall. It is eloquent of the dangers of pioneer life in this era that of the 256 signers to the Cumberland compact,

---

[9] The Wilderness Road, which remained a mere trail until about 1796, began at the Holston and Watauga settlements, swung north at Knoxville, passed through the Cumberland Gap where it joined the Indian 'Warrior's Path' that led to the junction of the Scioto and Ohio rivers, branched off by a buffalo trace northwesterly across the Rockcastle, crossed the Kentucky river at Boonesborough, and continued to Lexington. Just before the crossing of the Rockcastle the Wilderness Road forked, and the west branch, which led to Crab Orchard, Danville, and Louisville, soon became the most heavily travelled.

scarcely a dozen were alive a decade later; yet but one died a natural death!

A fourth region that seemed marked out by nature for independence was that of the Vandalia Company's claim along the headwaters of the Ohio. The inhabitants of this region petitioned in 1776 to be organized into the state of Westsylvania, claiming a flourishing population of 25,000 souls — an obvious exaggeration. Although this petition was rejected, it may be regarded as the beginning of the movement which bore fruit almost a century later in the state of West Virginia.

Despite their isolation from the main theatres of conflict, the Kentucky and Tennessee settlements suffered severely during the war. They were exposed to merciless Indian warfare, the attacks of tories, and the ravages of the desperadoes and cattle-thieves who always flock to the frontier. Yet these communities throve lustily, and the end of the war attracted a flood of emigration from the older states. Settlers from North Carolina and Virginia pressed through the Cumberland Gap into the fertile river bottoms of Kentucky, the hardwood forests between the Cumberland and the Tennessee, or the rolling blue-grass prairies; while another stream of settlers from Maryland and Pennsylvania followed the Potomac or the Juniata to their headwaters, then crossed the Alleghanies to Wheeling or Pittsburgh, and floated down the Ohio into the promised land. The trans-Appalachian population, but a few thousand on the outbreak of the war, numbered well over 120,000 by 1790.[10] In the year ending November 1788, 967 boats containing 18,370 men, women and children floated down the Ohio, while almost equal numbers were spilling over the mountain barriers to the South.

The most striking features of this migration were its spontaneity and the intense individualism of its members. California was taken possession of by Spain, with methods derived no less from pagan than from Christian Rome; not so the 'dark and bloody ground' by the American pioneer. No government provided his means of transport, or protected him at his destination. No church or benevolent society provided him with priest or minister, school or poor relief. But — and this exception is as American as the rule — he gen-

---

[10] The census of 1790 gave the population of Kentucky as 73,677, that of Tennessee as 35,691. The Tennessee census was very incomplete, with five districts missing. It is estimated that there were between four and five thousand inhabitants north of the Ohio.

erally had to secure a land title from speculators. His ideal and his practice were individual liberty, restrained only by spontaneous organization to secure defense, and to protect property from his more lawless fellows. His earlier settlements were in stockades, or 'stations' as he called them. Perhaps twenty or thirty families lived within a wooden palisade, with blockhouses at the corners, encircled by a swath cleared from the surrounding forest as a precaution against surprise. Thus, ten centuries before in England, countless 'stokes' looked out on unbroken fen and forest. But the American stockades were fortuitous and temporary. Some vague instinctive fear, perhaps, that village life would mean serfdom to him as to his Saxon ancestor broke up the stations before it was safe to do so, and each pioneer made haste to satisfy his ambition for a wilderness farm with clearing and log cabin in the center. And the instinct for self-government, the yearning for improvement, were only submerged, never lost by privation and danger. It was typical of West as well as East when the Watauga leaders of 1784 declared: 'If we should be so happy as to have a separate government, vast numbers from different quarters with a little encouragement from the public, would fill up our frontier, which would strengthen us, improve agriculture, perfect manufactures, encourage literature and everything laudable.'

XII

THE CONFEDERATION
1777–1789

1. *Articles of Confederation*

A S early as 7 June 1776, Richard Henry Lee moved that Congress appoint a committee to draw up articles of confederation
among the several states. A committee of one member from each
state was chosen, and on 12 July presented a plan of Articles of Confederation and Perpetual Union drafted by John Dickinson. This
plan was severely altered in Congress, and not finally adopted until
November 1777. Since ratification by all the states was necessary,
the Articles did not go into effect until 1781. The delay was principally caused by Maryland's refusing to accede to any formal union
until the Western lands had been disposed of to her satisfaction.

The Articles of Confederation represent the first American experiment in reconciling unity with localism — the old problem of
imperial order. Independence had merely transferred the solution
from London to Philadelphia and complicated it by the peculiar
circumstances of war, unfavorable for the cool consideration of
political problems. The states, having just won full powers over
taxation and commerce from Parliament, were not ready to grant
them out again; and Tom Paine's theory that all government at
best was a necessary evil, something to be feared, limited, and circumscribed, had bitten deep into the American brain. And although
the problem was restricted in scope, its major elements were still
the same: taxation, regulation of commerce, Western lands, Indian
affairs, paper money, military co-operation in time of war.

What was the Confederation, a government or a treaty? In the
preamble it is described as a 'perpetual Union'; in Article II 'Each
state retains its sovereignty, freedom and independence'; and in
Article III the states 'enter into a firm league of friendship.' Each
state had one vote in Congress, no matter how many delegates it
sent. Unanimous consent was necessary for any amendment. The
states retained complete control over taxation and regulation of
commerce. The relations between the members were essentially in-

ternational: each state gave full faith and credit to the records, acts, and judicial proceedings of all other states; citizens of one state were entitled to all the privileges and immunities of those of other states, and must extradite criminals.

On the other hand, the powers of the central government were so broad as to cast doubt on the reality of state sovereignty. Congress was granted authority to make war and peace, send and receive ambassadors, make treaties and alliances, regulate coinage, weights, and measures, establish a post-office, manage Indian affairs, borrow money on the credit of the United States, raise an army and equip a navy, make requisitions upon the states for men and money, and decide disputes between states. The essence of federalism is the distribution of powers between governments, and the success of a federal system depends upon the accuracy with which powers of a general nature are allotted to the central government and those of a local nature reserved to the local governments. This distribution was not well done in the Articles of Confederation; but they did outline a federal system, and represent a great improvement upon the constitution of any previous league in modern history.

The main defects in the Articles — failure to give Congress control over taxation and trade, want of a federal executive or judiciary, and lack of any sanction for federal powers — were results of the general situation. The Thirteen States were not yet ready to grant a federal legislature what they had refused to an imperial Parliament, or to surrender the substance of sovereignty for the shadow of union. Even when the inadequacies of the Articles became glaringly apparent, unanimous consent for amendments was impossible to obtain. Rhode Island defeated one proposal to provide Congress with a five per cent customs duty; and when Rhode Island was later induced to part with this 'most precious jewel of sovereignty' the proposal was rejected by the legislature of New York.

Yet it was not so much *powers* that the Confederation wanted as *power*. Requisitions might have served in lieu of taxes had Congress possessed the authority to enforce them. As James Madison observed in a paper written in 1787:

A sanction is essential to the idea of law, as coercion is to that of government. The federal system being destitute of both, wants the great vital principles of a political constitution. Under form of such a constitution, it is in fact nothing more than a treaty of amity of commerce and of alliance, between independent and Sovereign States.

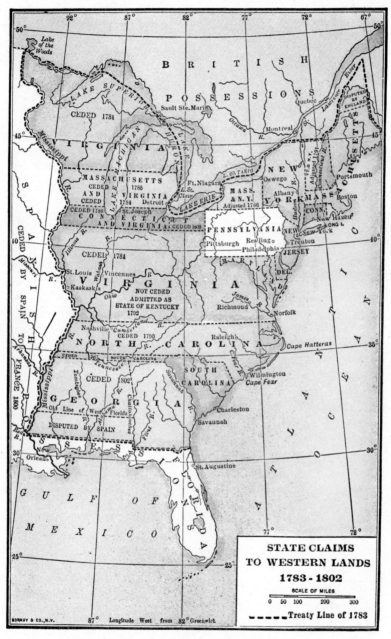

State Claims to Western Lands, 1783–1802
From Harper's Atlas of American History

Noah Webster pointed out the same defect, and indicated the remedy that was eventually adopted:

> The general concerns of the continent may be reduced to a few heads; but in all the affairs that respect the whole, Congress must have the same power to enact laws and compel obedience throughout the continent, as the legislatures of the States have in their respective jurisdictions.

But all this was apparent only to a few. It took time and bitter experience to convince men of the folly of particularism. Furthermore, the Confederation was launched under distressing economic circumstances. The years after Yorktown were years of profound economic depression and decline in property and security values. The ultimate breakdown of the Confederation, then, was due not so much to the defects of the Articles as to the psychological unreadiness of Americans to submit to any outside control, and to the 'hard times' which made any government an adventure.

2. A New Colonial System

And now the old Western question comes home to roost. All those pesky problems of land, Indians, fur trade, settlement, and government of dependencies, which had troubled Grenville and Shelburne and Chatham and North from the Peace of Paris to the Quebec Act, were now up to Congress to settle. In these Western matters it did well, formulating policies and inaugurating practices during the troubled years of the Confederation, which made a permanent mark on American history.

During the colonial period Virginia, the Carolinas, Georgia, New York, Massachusetts, and Connecticut had extensive and often overlapping claims to land beyond the Appalachians. The Quebec Act abrogated most of these titles by attaching the land north of the Ohio to the Province of Quebec. Upon the outbreak of the war the states revived their claims, and Virginia sent a military expedition to recover her Western territory.

The prospect of a few more fortunate states winning this rich territorial prize was unpleasant to states without Western claims. Maryland made herself the spokesman for this group, and her representatives early introduced into Congress a resolution that the Western lands,

If wrested from the common enemy by the blood and treasure of the thirteen States, should be considered as common property, subject to be parcelled out by Congress into free and independent governments. . . .

The states which hoped to use their Western lands to finance the war and reward their soldiers did not appreciate the idea of pooling them; and the resolution did not pass. Until they should feel more generous Maryland refused to ratify the Articles of Confederation, and thereby rendered a great service to the nation.

In 1780 New York led the way by ceding her claims to the United States. Congress immediately passed a resolution which contained in it the germ of American future colonial policy.

The unappropriated lands that may be ceded or relinquished to the United States . . . shall be disposed of for the common benefit of the United States, and be settled and formed into distinct republican States, which shall become members of the Federal Union, and have the same rights of sovereignty, freedom and independence as the other States.

Inspired by this guarantee, and by New York's example, Connecticut and Massachusetts followed suit.[1] Virginia, whose claims were the largest and the soundest, surrendered her lands north of the Ohio in 1781, Governor Jefferson writing:

The lands . . . will remain to be occupied by Americans, and whether these be counted in the members of this or that of the United States will be thought a matter of little moment.

By 1783, with the successful termination of the war, it was apparent that Congress would come into possession of all the lands north of the Ohio, and probably of all west of the Alleghanies. This common possession of millions of acres of land was the most tangible evidence of nationality and unity that existed during these troubled years, and gave a certain substance to the idea of national sovereignty. Yet possession itself was fraught with difficulties. Ancient problems of land, Indians, and administrative policy pressed for a solution.

Congress feebly attempted to regulate the fur trade. It obtained land cessions from the Iroquois and the Northwest Indians, who in alliance with Britain had waged a terrible and relentless war

---

[1] Wrathful over an adverse decision in the Susquehanna dispute, Connecticut withheld a strip of land extending westward from Pennsylvania 120 miles along the shore of Lake Erie — the Western Reserve. This was finally ceded in 1800.

against the backwoods settlements; but most of these treaties it was unable to enforce. New forts were built on the Ohio, and in 1787 a detachment of the United States army moved down the right bank, burning the cabins of frontiersmen who had staked out claims there by 'tomahawk right'; but it was not strong enough to prevent repeated Indian forays into Kentucky and Virginia. In the transmontane region south of the Ohio, where *de facto* state governments had been set up by the pioneers, and where no land claims had been made over to the Confederation, the period 1785–88 was one of bitter race warfare. The westward movement had obtained such a start that even the stronger Federal Government of 1789 could do little more than give the Indians a breathing-space, pending their final removal or extinction.

With land disposal and the questions of government, Congress adopted the right principles, without advancing very far toward solving the problems. It appointed a committee to take each subject under consideration, and Jefferson was made chairman of both. In 1784 he brought in the draft of an ordinance for the political organization of the entire trans-Appalachian territory. This plan provided for a temporary government and ultimate self-government of the West, which was to be divided into sixteen states,[2] eventually to be admitted on a basis of absolute equality with the original Thirteen. Jefferson's original draft excluded slavery, but the Southern states got that deleted. This Ordinance of 1784 was adopted by Congress, but never put into effect.

The report of the committee on land was incorporated into the Land Ordinance of 1785. This Ordinance provided for a rectangular survey of lands and a division into townships of six miles square. Each township was to consist of thirty-six sections of 640 acres each, and the sections could be subdivided as necessity arose. Land offices were to be established at convenient points in the West and lands sold in orderly progress at a price of not less than one dollar an acre. Four sections of every township were to be set aside for the United States Government, and one section reserved for the maintenance of public schools. This land system was modelled in a general way on that of New England, with some features derived from the projected imperial land survey of 1774. It adopted the principle of using the national domain as a source of revenue rather than

---

[2] Some of the names that Jefferson suggested for these states are: Sylvania, Polypotamia, Pelisipia, Cherronesus, and Michigania.

granting it free, or on easy terms, to settlers. And as not less than one section could be sold, and $640 was too much for a pioneer farmer to pay, the states and private land companies did most of the land-office business for many years. Although there were numerous changes in detail during the next fifty years, the Ordinance of 1785 remained as the basis of American land policy until the Homestead Act of 1862.

It was the activities of private land companies that forced Congress to make some provision for the political administration of its Western territory. The most important of these land companies were the Ohio and the Scioto, promoted in New England largely by officers of the Revolutionary army. In the summer of 1787 General Rufus Putnam and the Reverend Manasseh Cutler appeared before Congress requesting the sale of millions of acres of land north of the Ohio river on favorable terms. The prospect of an immediate revenue proved irresistible, especially when coupled with the promise of offices and perquisites, and the purchase was finally agreed upon at bargain prices. The Ohio Company of Associates obtained 1,500,000 acres of land along the banks of the Ohio and Muskingum rivers at an average price of less than nine cents an acre.[3] The Scioto Company negotiated for an even larger tract of land along the Scioto river, but it later became involved in financial difficulties and the sale was never consummated.

With this immediate prospect of settlement in the Ohio country, Congress had to make some immediate provision for government, and on 13 July 1787 adopted the Northwest Ordinance, largely the work of Nathan Dane, Rufus King, and Manasseh Cutler. This famous Ordinance bridged the gap between wilderness and statehood by providing a system of limited self-government, the essence of which has been repeated for all the continental and most of the insular possessions of the United States. The Northwest Territory was organized as a single district and ruled by a governor and judges appointed by Congress. When this territory should contain five thousand free male inhabitants of voting age it could elect a territorial legislature, with the status of a subordinate colonial assembly, and send a non-voting delegate to Congress. No more than five nor less than three states were to be formed out of this territory, and whenever any one had sixty thousand free inhabitants it was to be

[3] One section in each township was reserved for educational and one for religious purposes. Two entire townships were set aside for a university.

admitted to the Union ' on an equal footing with the original States in all respects whatever.' Six ' articles of compact between the original States and the people and States in the said Territory ' guaranteed the customary civil rights and liberties, and declared ' Religion, morality, and knowledge, being necessary to good government and the happiness of mankind, schools and the means of education shall forever be encouraged.' Further, ' There shall be neither slavery nor involuntary servitude in the said territory.' . . .

Thus a new colonial policy based upon the principle of equality, was inaugurated. The time-honored doctrine that colonies existed for the benefit of the mother country and were politically subordinate to her and socially inferior, was definitely repudiated. In its stead was established the principle that colonies were but the extensions of the nation, and entitled, not as a privilege, but as a right, to all the benefits of equality. The Ordinance of 1787 is one of the great creative contributions of America, for it showed how to get rid of that friction which had always been a canker in the relations of colony to metropolis. The enlightened provisions of the Land Ordinance of 1785 and the Northwest Ordinance of 1787 laid the permanent foundations for the American territorial system and colonial policy, and enabled the United States to expand westward to the Pacific, and from thirteen to forty-eight states, with relatively little difficulty.

3. Liquidating the Treaty of Paris

The Treaty of Paris was satisfactory neither to England nor to the United States, and its terms were fruitful of future quarrels. Boundary disputes, arising from the loose wording of the treaty, were fortunately postponed to a later generation, but there were immediate controversies over matters in which one or the other party failed to fulfil its obligations, such as debts, the treatment of loyalists, and the presence of British garrisons on United States soil. Congress on 14 January 1783 duly made the required ' earnest recommendation ' to the states to restore confiscated loyalist estates and a few actually complied to some extent: Pennsylvania, for instance, paid the Penn family $650,000 in compensation for their proprietary rights — but most of them, being under no obligation, failed to act. The treaty requirement that loyalists should be free to reside twelve months in any part of the United States, in order to endeavor to recover their property, was not always respected

Many loyalists managed to recover their property, by assigning it to some patriot friend or kinsman, whose exertions and whose honor seldom failed them in this period of blasted hope; but tory rangers or partisans who returned to the districts they had ravaged were fortunate to get off with a term in jail. More often they were given a coat of tar and feathers and escorted out by a mob. A second requirement, 'that there shall be no future confiscations made,' nor fresh prosecutions commenced against loyalists, was generally obeyed. New York passed a Trespass Act, encouraging owners of property formerly within the British lines to recover damages against loyalist occupants through actions of trespass. But Alexander Hamilton successfully defended the first loyalist so prosecuted, in the case of Rutgers v. Waddington, and obtained a judgment from the Mayor's Court of New York, nullifying the statute on the ground of its conflict with the treaty. South Carolina authorized fresh confiscations in 1783, but rescinded them in 1786. Other states passed laws having reference to the disposition of property already confiscated during the war, taking the ground that the treaty had no retroactive effect, a construction vigorously maintained by the British Government in respect of a different article which forbade British commanders to deport negro slaves.

America often had law on her side in her treatment of loyalists; but few will contend that she had justice. In extenuation one may observe that American tories were less harshly treated than royalists in the French Revolution, or than bourgeois and Catholic in more recent upheavals. It was too much to expect of human nature that the Americans should forgive a class of people who, with all their acknowledged merits, had contributed greatly both to the ferocity of the war and to its prolongation. And, after all, the sixty to eighty thousand loyalists who were driven from the United States during the war, and left it voluntarily afterwards, were but a minority of the loyalist party. After 1776, tories who paid their taxes refrained from hostile action, and kept their mouths closed were in most states permitted to continue the enjoyment of their property; and practically all of this class remained in the country. John Adams admitted that the tory vote helped to obtain the ratification of the Federal Constitution. Even in New York most of the tories remained, and many of the exiles drifted back — men such as Cadwallader Colden, who became mayor of the city, and commanded a regiment in the War of 1812; and Henry Cruger, elected to the

New York senate while still a member of Parliament. If, then, the bulk of the loyalists became good American citizens, the country might well have repatriated all who were willing. A young republic could ill spare such men as the scientist Benjamin Thompson (Count Rumford), John Singleton Copley the artist, and Justice Howe of Nova Scotia, though American schoolboys were saved some future pain through the departure of that loyal grammarian Lindley Murray. America's loss was Britain's gain; without the United Empire Loyalists of Canada, and the equally loyal refugee families in the West Indies, it is unlikely that those dominions would still belong to the British Empire.

A second clear obligation placed on the Thirteen States by the peace treaty was to open their courts freely to British subjects seeking to recover their pre-war debts. There is no doubt that this article was violated both in letter and in spirit. Virginia, where the debts were heaviest, and the general attitude toward financial obligations was aristocratic and feudal, led the way in passing laws hampering the recovery of British debts. Both French and British armies left plenty of gold and silver in the country, but the Americans — like others in similar circumstances — spent it on luxuries instead of paying off their pre-war debts. Hard times followed, and domestic creditors suffered equally with the foreign. John Jay induced Congress to send a circular letter to the states, adverting strongly on their breach of public faith, and requesting the repeal of their illegal acts. Most of them had complied by 1789, when the Constitution superseded all state laws contrary to treaty obligations, and opened the new federal judiciary to British litigants. Thereafter, the recovery of British debts was a matter of judicial process, and no impediment was imposed save the law's delay. This, however, was so prolonged that the matter was finally adjudicated by Jay's Treaty, where the determination of uncollected debts was left to a mixed commission which failed to agree. Finally, by a convention of 1802 the United States paid a lump sum of £600,000 in complete satisfaction of the bona fide debts and interest.

Article VII of the treaty of peace required all British garrisons on American soil to be withdrawn 'with all convenient speed.' New York was completely evacuated by December 1783. Seven military and fur-trading posts[4] on the American side of the new Cana-

---

[4] From east to west these posts were Dutchman's Point and Pointe-au-Fer at the head of Lake Champlain, guarding the military and trading route between Montreal

dian boundary remained in British possession. The general in command refused, in August 1783, to discuss arrangements for turning over these posts with an emissary of Washington. On 8 April 1784, the day before George III ratified the treaty of peace, his Home Minister wrote the Governor of Canada that the posts would not be evacuated, 'at least until we are enabled to secure the fur traders in the Interior Country,' because the United States had not complied with even one article of the treaty. They were not evacuated until 1796, after a convenient delay of twelve years. Now that the archives have yielded up their secrets, it is clear that prior violations by the United States were a mere excuse. Unwillingness to abandon the fur trade and the Indians of the Northwest was responsible for retention of the posts.

It was partly in order to conserve the fur trade and control the redskins that the Province of Quebec had been extended from the Ottawa to the Ohio river in 1774. Scotch-Canadian fur merchants, Grants and McGills and Mackenzies and McTavishes, brought new capital and business acumen, which made an irresistible combination with French-Canadian personnel, technique, and Indian connections. During the next ten years they so developed this trade that peltry to the annual value of £200,000 passed through Montreal on its way to London. Then, in the peace treaty, Shelburne made a free gift to the United States of this immense imperial asset, the land between the Lakes and the Ohio river. At least, so the cession appeared on the Canadian side of the boundary. But we must remember that the Thirteen Colonies had prior claims to this region as against Canada. A glance at the map, and a forward reference to the annexation of Texas, suggest that sooner or later the American settler would have rushed across the Ohio, with another Anglo-American war as a result. Lord Shelburne's statesmanship is indicated by the unarmed Canadian-American boundary, which enabled the two countries to expand along parallel lines.

As soon as the news of the treaty terms reached Canada, petitions and remonstrances from the Montreal fur merchants began to pour in upon the Governor General. American possession of the Northwest posts, they complained, would divert the fur trade to New

---

and Albany: Oswegatchie on the St. Lawrence river, near Ogdensburg, N. Y.; Oswego, N. Y., on Lake Ontario, guarding the portage route to the Mohawk; Niagara, on the American side of the falls; Detroit, on the river between Lakes Erie and Huron; and Michilimackinac, on an island in the strait between Lakes Huron and Michigan.

York and Philadelphia, and alienate the loyal Western Indians who had been guaranteed the Ohio boundary in 1768. The Canadians only requested a reasonable delay to reorganize the trade before evacuating the posts. It was in answer to these petitions that the Home Office gave orders to retain the Northwest posts until further notice.

By this deliberate breach of treaty obligations the United States were excluded from territory, trade, and Indian control that were rightly theirs. Yet there were even more serious implications in the act, though the actors may have been unconscious of them. Detroit and Michilimackinac were sally-ports of empire, looking towards New Orleans. Twice the Thirteen Colonies had fought to keep French Canada from their back doors. Must the Thirteen States fight again to keep British Canada within her legal boundaries? Would the United States ever be secure until British power, like French power, was expelled from the North American continent?

4. *Foreign Affairs during the Confederation*

Isolation, free trade, and westward expansion were American aspirations as old as the Thirteen Colonies, but frustrated by the colonial status. Unless independence could achieve them, independence was a delusion. American foreign policy from the seventeenth century onward has been the median of vertical and horizontal forces: repulsion from European politics, attraction for European principles. Geography accentuates the one; cultural unity keeps the other alive. It was idle for European philosophers to warn the Americans that they could attain political isolation only by commercial isolation; that, like China, they must renounce foreign trade in order to preserve their virtue. What would become of the Southern states, without a market for their tobacco, naval stores, and rice; or of the Northern states, without a market for their grain, fish, and timber, or employment for their shipping? The Western settlements, if they could not secure an outlet for their peltry by the Mississippi or the St. Lawrence through the efforts of the Federal Government, were certain to turn to some other power. The United States might be independent politically of the British Empire; but for a generation to come they would encounter the ships and soldiers of that empire on the high seas, in the mouths of their harbors and at the gateways to the Great West.

America emerged from the War of Independence entangled by an alliance with France — the only treaty of alliance the United States has ever ratified. Isolation was not likely to be achieved until that alliance ended; and until the two gates that closed westward advance — Britain's in the Ohio country, and Spain's along the Mississippi — swung open on their hinges at Montreal and New Orleans. Not until then could America pretend 'to dictate the terms of the connexion between the old and the new world,' as Hamilton predicted in *The Federalist*. Until then the United States must balance France against Britain in the old world, and Spain against Britain in the new.

Lord Shelburne, who alone of English statesmen of his generation had the wisdom to base British policy on what America might be rather than on what she was, proposed to heal the wounds of war and to consolidate Anglo-American friendship. The liberal terms of the Treaty of Paris had been a step in this direction. Now, at his suggestion, on 3 March 1783 young William Pitt introduced a bill restoring to the ships and products of the United States practically the same privileges they had formerly enjoyed within the British Empire. British shipowners vigorously attacked the bill, and the Commons amended it out of all recognition. Within a month Shelburne's ministry was succeeded by the coalition that united Fox and North.

In the meantime Lord Sheffield had brought out his *Observations on the Commerce of the American States*. Sheffield argued that England could now absorb the commerce of America without the expense of governing her, and without concessions to the American interests.

Our great national object is to raise as many sailors and as much shipping as possible. Parliament should endeavour to divert the whole Anglo-American trade to British bottoms. America cannot retaliate. It will not be an easy matter to bring the American States to act as a nation. They are not to be feared as such by us . . . We might as reasonably dread the effects of a combination among the German as among the American States.

And he concluded with the tempting suggestion that the United States were breaking up; that New England, if made to feel the rod of British maritime power, might return to her old allegiance.

Sheffield's policy prevailed. Pitt's bill was lost; the commercial negotiation with the American diplomatists at Paris dragged along for a year, until the Foreign Office cut it short. By a series of Orders in Council of 1783 American vessels were excluded absolutely from Canada and the West Indies. In British ports they were placed on the same footing as the ships of any European country, in carrying the produce of other European countries. American tobacco, timber, and other raw materials, however, were admitted to British ports in American or British bottoms, practically on a colonial footing; provided they came directly from America.

This privilege was a great concession: no European country enjoyed as much from Great Britain. It was not, however, secured by a commercial treaty, but revocable at pleasure. And, for all its apparent liberality, the Order in Council of 1783 was carefully designed for ' strangling in the birth ' American shipping, as the loyalist author of it boasted. It might well have done so, if the American states had not formed an effective combination somewhat more promptly than those of Germany.

The immediate success of this policy established Sheffield's reputation, and discredited the free traders; although it was the free-trade element in it — the free admission of American materials — that made it successful. By 1789 the Board of Trade could boast that British exports to the United States had recovered pre-war dimensions; and that their excess over imports from America was even greater than in 1772. Anglo-American trade was so largely triangular that the exclusion of American vessels from the West Indies, and from all but a direct trade in American products with England, threw the traffic into British bottoms. The Confederation of 1781–89 had no jurisdiction over commerce, and all efforts of the states to retaliate separately were completely futile. If Massachusetts closed her ports to British ships, British goods came overland from New Hampshire and Rhode Island; Connecticut and New Jersey similarly poached trade from New York City.

America had no right to expect colonial privileges after she had repudiated the colonial status; but the fact that other nations granted them made the British refusal seem invidious. France opened up her West Indian ports to American shipping and to most American products, and admitted American-built vessels to French registry. Havana and Santiago de Cuba were opened by the Spanish about the same time; and the Dutch were completely hospitable. Four Continental powers concluded commercial treaties with the American Confederation. If American friendship were worth winning and possible to win, it would be the part of wisdom for Great Britain to make some concessions of a similar nature.

American relations with Spain were scarcely more satisfactory than those with Great Britain. Between the two nations there was a natural conflict of interests, inherited from the ancient feud between Great Britain and Spain, and not ultimately resolved until 1898. During the War of Independence Spain had offered an alliance to the United States in return for the region south of the Ohio, between the Mississippi and the Appalachians, which she was pleased to call 'Eastern Louisiana.' Her object was not so much to acquire territory as to dam the flood of western migration at the mountains, lest it overrun the Mississippi to the plains of Texas and the valley of Mexico. Florida Blanca, the able premier of Charles III, foretold the expansive tendencies of the United States, and the danger of republican institutions to the Spanish Empire.

Congress refused to cede the West, but Spain joined the war as an ally of France, though not of the United States, and obtained from Britain, as the price of peace, East and West Florida. It was too late to stop the gaps in the Appalachians; but not too late to make them an international boundary, with 'Eastern Louisiana' a Spanish protectorate. To accomplish this policy, Spain not only used Indians, and retained posts on United States territory, but choked the southern outlet of the West, and corrupted some of its leading men.

In 1784 the Creek, Choctaw, and Chickasaw Indians, who inhabited the territory of the United States south of the Tennessee river and west of Georgia, were persuaded to conclude treaties with His Catholic Majesty, who became virtually their protector. A loyalist refugee from Georgia organized the firm of Panton, Leslie & Company, which, with Spanish approval, established trading posts in Florida and sent its factors, with ammunition and other Indian truck, up the rivers towards the Tennessee frontier. Creek and Cherokee, now well furnished with weapons, began to harry American settlements on the Cumberland and upper Tennessee rivers, and in Georgia. The frontiersmen were not slow to retaliate on Indian villages, and they found the southern tribes better organized and less elusive than those along the Canadian frontier. During 1787–88 the border from Nashville to southern Georgia was the scene of hideous barbarities.

Natchez, on the left bank of the Mississippi well within the boundary of the United States as recognized by Great Britain, had been captured from British loyalists in 1779 by the Spaniards, who refused to surrender it to the United States, as not England's to grant. Natchez and New Orleans gave Spain the control of the lower Mississippi — a powerful means of pressure on the West. The people of Kentucky, Tennessee, western Virginia, and even western Pennsylvania, discovered that the long river journey south was their only practical way to market. Their cheap and bulky products could not stand the cost of being sweated over the Appalachian passes. But the Mississippi river led to natural markets in lower Louisiana, where the Creole planters preferred to concentrate on sugar cane, and purchase their livestock, horses, corn, and bacon. New Orleans was the natural post of transshipment for the New York and European markets.

As General James Wilkinson of Kentucky wrote in 1789, 'Spain ought to consider the navigation of the Mississippi as one of the most precious jewels of her crown. For, whatever power shall command that navigation, will control all the country which is watered by that river, and by those streams which fall into it.' Conversely, permission to navigate the lower Mississippi, and to enjoy a 'right of deposit' or free transshipment at New Orleans, was for the American West a question of life and growth, or strangulation.

Although formally denied to the United States as a right, both navigation and deposit were frequently accorded as a privilege, by the dispensing power of Governor Miró, in favor of such Westerners as would promise to serve Spanish policy — to detach their communities from the United States. Wilkinson, who accepted not only favors but bribes to make his state a 'bastion of Mexico,' was the most notorious of these Western conspirators. When John Jay, secretary of the Confederation for foreign affairs, proposed in 1786 to waive the right of deposit temporarily in return for privileges to American shipping in Spanish ports, Spain's Western following increased. A surprising number of backwoods politicians accepted Spanish gold, and intrigued for secession, because they had lost hope of obtaining their outlet from the United States. What made matters worse was that many leading Easterners, disliking frontiersmen as political bedfellows, wished the West well out of the Union.

It was a strange diplomatic combination, that of polished don and rough-necked pioneer. One may well wonder that the latter showed less resentment against the nation who egged on the Cherokee and Creek, than against the power who supported the Shawnee and Miami. It was not merely that the Spaniard had more to offer. However fiercely your backwoodsman might hate the Canadian loyalist, he respected British power, whilst for Spaniards and their diplomacy he had a fundamental contempt. To the northward, moreover, he wanted nothing but his rights; to the southward his ambition knew no limit but Panama and the Pacific. As the Germans in the dark Teutowald yearned for the sunny, fertile plains of Italy, so the backwoodsman of Tennessee, as he tilled his patch of corn in the shade of girdled trees, while kinsmen watched with loaded rifle, dreamed of the day when he would go whooping down the great river of the West to loot the Spaniard of his undeveloped land. And his dream, like the other, came true.

5. *The Day of the Debtor*

Most of the difficulties under which the United States labored during the first five years of peace were the necessary effects of a war that loosened the bonds of society, and cut the connection with a trading empire. But they were aggravated by the weakness of government, and the failure of co-operation on the part of the states. The radical weakness of the Confederation, as we have seen, was its complete dependence — like the old German Diet and the recent League of Nations — upon the good will of the sovereign states. Congress wanted power to fill the treasury, to enforce the laws of the Union, to regulate trade and commerce with foreign nations. The government languished upon the meagre results of requisitions which the state legislatures sometimes could not, but more often would not, honor. Only half a million dollars on the average was annually paid into the federal treasury by the states between 1781 and 1786: a sum hardly sufficient to meet the running expenses of government, let alone war costs and the interest on foreign loans.[5] Robert Morris, the able finance minister of the Confederation, was fortunate to prevent repudiation, and, by the grace of loans from Dutch bankers, to stave off bankruptcy. So hopeless had the financial situation become by 1783 that Morris resigned, in despair, confessing ' it can no longer be a doubt . . . that our public credit is gone.'

[5] In 1783 the foreign debt of the United States stood at $7,885,085. By 1789 the principal of foreign debts had increased to $10,098,706, and the arrears of interest to $1,760,277. Approximately $350,000 of interest had been remitted by the French government.

Overdue interest on the debt accumulated, Continental securities fell below 15, and demobilized army officers had to sell at a heavy discount the scrip they had received in lieu of pay. In the four years after the war the finances of state and central governments alike fell into hopeless confusion, and after emitting hundreds of millions of dollars of paper money, repudiation, partial or complete, was the order of the day.

The device of legal-tender paper currency had often been used in colonial days, when Parliament was not looking. The financial necessities of the war forced state and confederate governments to resort to this panacea, as we have seen; and some $451,500,000 in paper money was emitted during the war years. The greater part of this depreciated to utter worthlessness, but, ethical considerations aside, this was perhaps as satisfactory a way to finance the war as any other that could have been found. It served as a substitute for taxation, and distributed the losses over a long period and among the entire population. ' This Currency as we manage it,' observed Franklin cynically, ' is a wonderful Machine. It performs its Office when we issue it; it pays and clothes Troops, and provides Victuals and Ammunition; and when we are obliged to issue a Quantity excessive, it pays itself off by Depreciation.' At the close of the war most of the states stopped issuing paper money, and tried to pay off their war debts and collect taxes long overdue. And just when the loss of markets injured their capacity to pay, various factors tended to increase the normal indebtedness of rural and frontier districts to merchant-bankers and storekeepers. There were war damages to repair, especially in the South; discharged soldiers took up new land on credit; and after seven years of war, people generally purchased more European luxuries than they could afford. A currency famine made matters worse. Debtors began to press state legislatures for relief in the form of ' tender acts ' making land or produce at fixed prices a legal discharge, ' stay laws ' postponing the collection of debts, and laws providing cheap money. It was this radical movement within the states, threatening the property interests, which, according to James Madison, ' contributed more to that uneasiness which produced the Constitution, and prepared the public mind for a general reform ' than any political inadequacies of the Articles of Confederation. Seven states issued paper money in 1786, when the economic depression was at its worst. This virtual confiscation seemed intolerable to many when the necessity of war was removed. ' They are determined,' wrote General Knox to Washington, 'to annihilate all debts, public and private, and have agrarian laws, which are easily effected by the means of unfunded paper money.' North Carolina purchased tobacco from the farmers at double the specie value. In Charleston young radicals formed the Hint Club, which made a practice of sending sections of rope to planters who would not receive state paper for their rice. Rhode Island, where the debtors put through their whole program, furnished an example of what the gentlemen might expect elsewhere. The state lent large sums of paper money to landowners, and forced it on others by heavy penalties.[6] If a creditor refused to accept state paper to the face value of his due, the debtor could discharge his obligation by depositing the currency with the nearest judge. Of course the merchants shut up shop and fled the state to escape purchasers, as did hundreds of harassed creditors, pursued by implacable debtors seeking to make the legal proffer of paper money! But before the New England farmers had time to learn this economic lesson, civil war broke out in Massachusetts.

In that state the case of the farmers was really deplorable, and they lacked the political power to obtain relief. Farm produce was a glut on the market, owing to the stoppage of West India trade, and taxes were heavier than elsewhere. The commercial interests, having rigged the state constitution, had succeeded in shifting the weight of taxation onto land and polls — the latter accounting for no less than forty per cent of the entire taxes. Courts were clogged with suits for debt, the cost of justice was exorbitant, and lawyers were more grasping than usual. All through the summer of 1786 popular conventions and town meetings demanded reform in the state administration, the removal of the capital from Boston, and an issue of fiat money as in Rhode Island. One petition read:

We beg leave to informe your Honours that unless something takes place more favourable to the people, in a little time att least, one half of our inhabitants in our oppinion will become banckerupt . . . Sutes att law are very numerous and the atturneys in our oppinion very extravigent and oppressive in their demands. And when we compute the taxes laid upon us the five preceding years: the state and county, town and class taxes, the amount is equil to what our farms will rent for. Sirs, in this

---

[6] The attempt of the state to enforce its paper money laws by substituting summary trial by judges for a jury trial led to the famous case of Trevett v. Weeden, 1786. In this case the Court boldly declared the state law unconstitutional, null and void.

situation what have we to live on — no money to be had; our estates dayly posted and sold, as above described. . . . Suerly your honours are not strangers to the distresses of the people but doe know that many of our good inhabitants are now confined in gole for det and for taxes; many have fled, others wishing to flee to the State of New York or some other State.

No relief, however, was to be had from the legislature, where the state senate wished deflation to take its natural course. Even Sam Adams, grown cautious with age, denounced the unhappy farmers as 'wicked and unprincipled men.' The process of distraining upon cattle and land for the debts and accumulated taxes of five lean years went rigorously on. That many yeomen, facing a debtor's prison and loss of ancestral farms, resorted to violence is not so surprising as the sense of law and order that prevented the majority of sufferers from following them.

In the autumn of 1786 mobs of farmers, under the somewhat un-willing lead of a former army captain, Daniel Shays, began forcibly to prevent the county courts from sitting. The object of the leaders appears to have been to prevent further judgments for debt, pend-ing the next state election. They met with stout resistance from the state government. John Hancock, scenting trouble, had retired from the governorship; his successor, James Bowdoin, was a tough-minded merchant who kept the legislature firm. The mobs were or-dered to disperse, the leaders declared outlaw, and a price placed upon their heads. Shays and his comrades then resolved to become rebels indeed. For a few days there was danger that the state gov-ernment might be besieged in Boston by an infuriated yeomanry, as had happened to the last royal government in 1775. But the rebels lacked firearms, and their attempt to capture the federal arsenal at Springfield was repulsed with grape-shot. Loyal militia, financed by forced contributions of merchants, was set in motion from the eastern counties, and college boys formed a cavalry regiment to terrify the country folk. The rebel bands, armed for the most part with staves and pitchforks, were scattered into the barren hills of central Massachusetts, where they were hunted in the heavy snow like game. Many fled to the western wilderness; cold and hunger forced the remnant to surrender. There was a threat of inflicting the death penalty on the leaders, but wiser counsels prevailed, and a general amnesty was finally granted to all those concerned in the rebellion. Only after the uprising had been crushed did the legislature consider the justice of the grievances which had caused it, and take steps to remedy them.

So ended Shays's rebellion. Its effects went deeper than any event since the Boston tea-party. Unlawful force was discredited, and a government based on rebellion showed that it could deal with rebellion. But how narrow had been the escape from civil war, if indeed it were an escape. 'There are combustibles in every State which a spark might set fire to,' wrote Washington. 'I feel infinitely more than I can express for the disorders which have arisen. Good God! Who besides a Tory could have foreseen, or a Briton have predicted them?'

Some conservatives turned in despair to monarchy. The President of Congress even sounded Prince Henry of Prussia whether he would accept an American throne. Others learned their lesson from the powerlessness of the Confederation even to protect its own property, much less to help a state in distress. Out of it all came an emotional surge — without which nothing great can be accomplished in America — towards a new Federal Constitution.

XIII

THE FEDERAL CONSTITUTION
1787–1789

1. *Thermidor*

THERE comes a time in every revolutionary movement when the people become tired of agitation and long for peace and security. They then eliminate the radicals, trouble-makers and warmongers, and take measures to consolidate their government, hoping to secure what has already been gained through turmoil and suffering. *Thermidor* this time is called in leftist language, from the counter-revolution in France that overthrew Robespierre and ended the reign of terror. Thus, the establishment of Cromwell as Lord Protector was the Thermidor of the English Revolution in the seventeenth century; and the Stalin dictatorship and exile of Trotsky marks the Thermidor of the Russian Revolution. Every taking of the Bastille, it may be said, is inevitably followed by Thermidor, since human nature craves security, and the progress of a revolution must be stopped somewhere short of anarchy.

In America the thermidorean reaction began in different states at different times; in South Carolina as early as 1778, in Massachusetts with the adoption of the constitution of 1780, in Pennsylvania not until 1791, when the constitution of 1776 was replaced by a new one that safeguarded property. The movement that led to the Federal Constitution was essentially thermidorean in its nature. Shays's rebellion conjured up a horrid vision of disorder, disintegration, and foreign intervention, that would have made the last state of America infinitely worse than submitting to George III in 1775. Naturally it was the men of property and education whose interests were primarily affected by the menace of disunion, and who assumed leadership in the constitutional movement. But we are not to assume that it was for any exclusively selfish or class interest that they were acting. The plain people had the most to lose by disunion — their liberty, and opportunity for future economic betterment — and the most (as the event proved) to gain by a more perfect union. Seldom has a class acted more wisely for the good of the whole, than the Federalists, the self-constituted party of property owners, publicists, and professional men that framed the Federal Constitution, procured its ratification, and built a new federal state within its frame. The American Thermidor, moreover, was effected quietly and peaceably, without purges, exiles, executions, or assassinations. ' Jacobins ' like Patrick Henry and Sam Adams retained all their rights, and lived to be governors and senators. For Americans were already mature in their political habits, and civilized in their political processes.

While Shays's rebellion was at its height, the advocates of a stronger central government managed to turn another movement in that direction. Owing to disputes over the navigation of the Potomac, Madison induced the Virginia legislature to propose an interstate convention, to adopt a uniform system of commercial regulation. This convention met at Annapolis, Maryland, in September 1786. Delegates from only five states were present, but among them were Madison and Hamilton. The last-named induced his colleagues to report that commerce was too much bound up with other questions, and the situation too serious, to be dealt with by so unrepresentative a body as themselves. They recommended a general convention of all the states 'to take into consideration the situation of the United States, to devise such further provisions as shall appear to them necessary to render the constitution of the federal government adequate to the exigencies of the Union, and to report such an act as . . . will effectually provide for the same.' Thus prompted, the Congress of the Confederation, on 21 February 1787, invited the several states to send delegates to a convention at Philadelphia on 14 May, ' for the sole and express purpose of revising the Articles of Confederation.' So the Annapolis Convention, under the clever guidance of Hamilton and Madison, became a stalking horse for a Federal constitutional convention.

2. The Federal Convention

The story of the Federal Convention is fundamentally the search for a new balance between liberty and order, and for a new distribution of powers between states and nation. A confederacy of coequal, sovereign states had been tried and found wanting. Since 1777 the gruelling experience of the war and the years after had persuaded many more people to consider the problem candidly and without prejudice. It was not, however, a mere technical question of political science. As Andrew C. McLaughlin has written:

Supposing that the cleverest adjustment of powers, the most accurate assignment of authority, was at last discovered, what security could there be that the states would regard the system, play their parts, and abide by their obligations? Could any method be found for making certain the observance of the Articles of Union, for making certain the power of the central authority to perform the duties bestowed upon it? Could this be done without destroying the states as political entities or reducing them to mere districts? That was a question that might well have confused the clearest brain of the time; no more delicate and intricate problem in practical politics and statecraft ever confronted a thinking people. If a system could be found which did not involve the destruction of the states, which preserved an equitable distribution of authority between the centre and the parts, the great problem of imperial organization had found a solution. If this could be done, America would make one of the greatest contributions ever made by a nation to the theory and practice of government.[1]

It was an assembly of notables that met in the State House at Philadelphia in May 1787 as the Federal Convention. The legislatures sent the best men of their respective states: leaders with ample experience in colonial and state governments, in Congress, on the bench, and in the field. The delegation from Virginia was particularly brilliant. George Washington, although doubtful of changing the prevailing popular temper, consented to serve and was unanimously chosen president of the Convention. James Madison, who at the age of thirty-six had a ripe knowledge of political theory and practice, came prepared with a study of ancient and modern confederacies—a study fruitful in lessons of what to avoid. George Wythe, the law tutor of Jefferson and Marshall at William and Mary College and one of the greatest lawyers of his generation; George Mason, author of the Virginia Bill of Rights; and Governor Edmund Randolph were also of the delegation from the Old Dominion.

North Carolina sent ' respectable characters ' rather than ' brilliant luminaries; ' but South Carolina shone with General Charles Cotesworth Pinckney, his young cousin Charles Pinckney, John Rutledge, and Pierce Butler, the one of ancient Irish family, the other Irish born. Massachusetts sent Rufus King and Elbridge Gerry, young

[1] *Confederation and Constitution* (Harpers, 1905) pp. 176–77.

men of ability and of experience, destined for high office. Yankee shrewdness was represented by Roger Sherman of Connecticut, shoe-maker turned judge; Oliver Ellsworth, a future Chief Justice of the United States; and W. S. Johnson, president of Columbia College and a former loyalist. From New York came Alexander Hamilton, just turned thirty, and already famous. The Pennsylvania delegation, led by the aged but still lively Franklin, vied in distinction with that of Virginia. James Wilson, born and educated in Scotland, was the most useful member of the convention after Madison. Gouverneur Morris, the brilliant debater and keen observer of human weaknesses, and Robert Morris, the English-born financier of the Revolution, represented the same state. John Dickinson, the 'Pennsylvania Farmer' of 1768 and reluctant revolutionist of 1776, was sent by Delaware. From New Jersey came William Paterson and from Maryland Luther Martin, two eminent lawyers who distinguished themselves as representatives of the interests of small states. Every state but Rhode Island was represented. The total number of delegates who attended was 55, of whom three-quarters had served in Congress, and nine were foreign-born. Their average age was 42, the youngest, Jonathan Dayton, being 27, and the oldest, Franklin, 81.

The Federal Convention, it may be said, was the first American 'brain trust.' Of the 55 members, at least 31 had been educated at colonial colleges or the equivalent abroad, and many others, like Mason and Franklin, had had more than the equivalent from private tutors or their own reading. Two university presidents (Baldwin and Johnson), three university professors (Wythe, Wilson, and William C. Houston), and several who at one time or other had been schoolmasters, were included. Indeed, the only 'brains' absent from the convention that might have helped it were those of John Jay, who was then Secretary of Foreign Affairs, and of John Adams and Thomas Jefferson, who were on foreign missions.

It is always a temptation to read present interests into past events. Richard Hildreth, when writing about the Federal Convention in 1849, featured slavery. George Ticknor Curtis and George Bancroft, writing in 1854 and 1882, stressed state rights against nationalism. Charles A. Beard's *Economic Interpretation of the Constitution* (1913) sounded the note of economic determinism, and several writers of that school, with less reverence for fact than Mr. Beard, have pictured the Convention as preoccupied with the protection of property interests and the exploitation of the common people. Another school of thought, building upon Jefferson's qualification of the framers as ' demi-gods ' (a phrase that he lived to regret), regards them as inspired to draft a document of almost divine sanction. And in the year 1937, when the sesquicentennial of the Federal Convention was celebrated, the public was assured that the framers foresaw all future evils, and did their best to protect the United States against communism, radical labor, and the New Deal.

A careful reading of Madison's and Yates's notes on the debates — a luxury in which popular writers on the convention seldom indulge — reveals that slavery interested the members only as an aspect of sectional balance, that there was substantial agreement on the extent to which the states should yield powers to the Federal Government, that the members were looking to remedying the ' defects, the deformities, the diseases ' of the Confederation (as Madison said) rather than endeavoring to legislate for all future time, and that they were much more interested in political technique — in the organization of the government, and the distribution of powers — than in safeguarding particular interests. That members were conscious of those interests is true; and some examples of that consciousness will be quoted shortly. But the main, central and determining consideration that appears throughout the debates, is to erect a government that would be neither too strong nor too shocking to popular prejudices for adoption, and yet be sufficiently strong and well-contrived to work. Moreover, there was no disagreement over some of the most important claims of the Constitution such as federal control of defense and of interstate and foreign commerce.

The temper of the Convention, in marked contrast to that of the French Constituent Assembly of 1789, was realistic and objective, rather than idealistic and theoretical. ' Experience must be our only guide. Reason may mislead us,' was the keynote struck by Dickinson. Collectively, the members well represented the political intellect, statesmanship, and great property interests of the country. Luther Martin of Maryland was the only champion of the debtors and small farmers. Most of the members were public creditors, who stood to lose personally by a dissolution of the Union, and to gain by a restoration of public credit; but it would be unjust to attribute their views to property alone, as it is absurd to pronounce them superior to forces that move the best of men. All the members hoped to remedy the proved defects of the Articles of Confederation. A few of them saw that something more was at stake. As Madison said from the

floor, ' They were now to decide the fate of republican government.'
No fair-minded person can read their debates without wonder that
a country of four million people could produce men of such intellect,
common sense, and enlightened vision.

3. *The Convention at Work*

The Convention had been authorized merely to draft amendments
to the Articles of Confederation. But events at the beginning gave
nationalists like Madison and Wilson, who wished to scrap the Articles, a start over those who thought that tinkering would suffice.
The nationalists, or large-state party as they came to be called, had
quietly organized their forces even before the convention opened
and at a series of private meetings decided to bring in a plan for a
new national government. The convention opened on 25 May 1787,
and on the 29th Randolph presented the result of these preliminary
efforts — the Virginia or large-state plan. This plan, foreshadowing
the stronger government that was subsequently adopted, became the
first basis of discussion. It provided a ' National Executive,' a ' National Judiciary,' and a ' National Legislature ' of two branches, with
members apportioned according to population, empowered ' to legislate in all cases to which the separate States are incompetent.' As
for the basic question of how the states could be persuaded to abide
by these Articles of Union, the Virginia plan offered three solutions:
an oath of office, a negative on all state laws contravening the constitution, and power to call forth the forces of the Union to coerce
recalcitrant states. All this was not essentially different from the
methods that prevailed under the British connection. A negative on
state laws was no better than the practice of disallowance by the
Privy Council, and the power to coerce a state was little improvement on the Coercive Acts of 1774. The Virginia plan did not begin
to get at the root of the problem of maintaining a federal state. This
is all the more remarkable, since both Madison and Wilson had
shown a real grasp of the federal idea. It would seem that the terror
inspired by Shays's rebellion, or over-enthusiasm for strong government, had deflected them from the course that they later followed to
a brilliant conclusion.

For two weeks the convention developed the Virginia plan in
committee of the whole, when William Paterson presented a counter-
project, the New Jersey or small-state plan, containing almost every

feature of the Articles of Confederation that made for weakness and uncertainty. A single legislative body in which each state was equally represented, and whose acts were to be enforced by armed coercion of the states, was the central feature of this plan. Yet it did contain one clause of far-reaching importance, which in a modified form became the key clause of the Federal Constitution. ' All Acts of the United States in Congress made in pursuance of the powers hereby and by the articles of confederation vested in them, and all Treaties made and ratified under the authority of the United States shall be the supreme law of the respective States . . . and the Judiciary of the several States shall be bound thereby in their decisions, anything in the respective laws of the individual States to the contrary notwithstanding.' Here we see the germ of the doctrine that the Constitution is supreme law, that acts contrary to it are void, and that the courts are the proper agents to enforce it.

To this New Jersey plan the smaller states rallied. Some of their delegates preferred the Virginia plan, but thought it too 'highmounted' for popular acceptance; others were influenced by the fact that their states enjoyed equality with the larger ones in the Congress of the Confederation, and did not propose to give up that privilege. This division between large and small states, which threatened time and again to wreck the work of the convention, was most unfortunate because it rested upon prejudice rather than logic. There was no natural antagonism between the interests of large and of small states as such — between Pennsylvania and New Jersey, or Virginia and Maryland. The real divisions of interest in the country were sectional and economic in character: divisions between North and South or East and West, between the commercial and the agrarian interests, the creditor and the debtor. But as Hamilton remarked in the acrimonious debate that followed the introduction of the smallstate plan, ' It is a contest for power, not for liberty.'

By using their superior voting power the large states were able to shelve the New Jersey plan, and make that of Virginia again the order of the day. But the small states' delegates were unappeased. July brought hot weather, bad temper, and deadlock. Even Franklin the sceptic could only suggest that the sessions be opened henceforth with prayer. Fortunately the large states met the small half way. After all it was not the best possible constitution that must be drafted, but the best that the people would be likely to accept. The same practical consideration ruled out Hamilton's plan for a centralized unitary constitution that would leave the states mere subordinate corporations — a plan that revealed how completely Hamilton failed to grasp the value of federalism.

The deadlock was finally broken by the appointment of a grand committee of one member from each state to deal with the vexatious problem of representation. This committee finally brought in a report distinctly favorable to the small states — known as the Connecticut or Great Compromise. By the terms of this compromise every state was conceded an equal vote in the Senate irrespective of size, but representation in the House was to be on the basis of the 'federal ratio' — an enumeration of the free population plus three-fifths of the slaves. At the same time it was provided that all money bills should originate in the popularly elected House of Representatives.

The alignment of large against small states then dissolved; but almost every question raised new parties and was resolved only by a new compromise. State delegations were not even united within themselves. Certain members wished no branch of the Federal Government to be popularly elected, whilst others, like Wilson, thought that the 'federal pyramid' must be given as broad a basis as possible in order that it might be 'raised to a considerable altitude.' In the end the qualifications for voting for the House of Representatives had to be left to each state to decide for itself. Gouverneur Morris struggled by means not wholly fair to exclude the growing West from statehood, arguing that 'The busy haunts of men, not the remote wilderness, was the proper school of political talents. If the Western people get the power into their hands they will ruin the Atlantic interests.' Fortunately, others like Wilson and Mason had a vision of future expansion, and eventually Congress was given full discretion in the matter. There was no serious difference of opinion on such national economic questions as paper money, tender laws, and laws impairing the obligation of contracts. These were forbidden to the states with little or no debate. But there was a distinct balancing of sectional economic interests. Charles Pinckney remarked in debate

that there were five distinct commercial interests. (1) The fisheries and West India trade, which belonged to the New England States. (2) The interest of New York lay in a free trade. (3) Wheat and flour the staples of the two middle States (N. J. and Penn.). (4) Tobacco the staple of Maryland and Virginia, and partly of North Carolina. (5) Rice and indigo, the staples of South Carolina and Georgia. These different interests would be a source of oppressive regulations if no check to a bare majority should be provided.

The Southern states long contended for a two-thirds majority of both houses for laws such as a navigation act, regulating interstate or foreign commerce. They were induced to abandon this demand by the Northern states agreeing to a prohibition of export taxes (which would obviously have fallen largely on the South), and to prevent the Federal Government from meddling with the slave trade for twenty years. The fear of the Southern States lest they be kept permanently in a minority, as they were by the estimated population in 1787, brought the requirement of a decennial census as a basis for reapportionment of the House.

During sixteen weeks the convention held sessions every weekday, except when it adjourned for committees to catch up; it was practically continuously at work. Finally the Constitution was entrusted to a committee on style, where the brilliant Gouverneur Morris polished up the language, and in so doing rubbed out a few little things he did not like. At length, on 17 September 1787, the finished Constitution was engrossed and signed 'By unanimous consent of the States present.' As Washington arose from his armchair inscribed with a gilded half-sun the venerable Franklin observed:

I have often and often in the course of this session, and the vicissitudes of my hopes and fears as to its issue, looked at that . . . without being able to tell whether it was rising or setting; but now at length I have the happiness to know that it is a rising and not a setting sun.

The Federal Convention was over. The members 'adjourned to the City Tavern, dined together, and took a cordial leave of each other.'

Yet the crucial part of the struggle for a more perfect union had not begun. For the document upon which the Federal Convention had expended so much thought and labor required the consent of popularly elected conventions in at least nine states to become a constitution.

4. *The Federal Constitution*

The Federal Constitution it has always been called, and the organism that it created is still known as the Federal Government. This term was used advisedly, in order to spare current susceptibilities against a consolidated national government; but according to the accepted meaning of a *federal* government in 1787, a league resting upon the good faith of the parties, it was somewhat mis-leading. For the essence of the Constitution, and a secret of its suc-cess, was the complete and compulsive operation of the central gov-ernment upon the individual citizen, within (of course) the scope of its limited powers. It was carefully discussed whether the new gov-ernment, like the old, should depend upon the sanction of state governments, and, in the last resort, upon the coercion of sovereign states by force of arms; or whether the Federal Government should create its own sanctions, enforce them by its own courts and officials, and, in the last resort, by the coercion of individuals. The latter system, which Ellsworth called the coercion of law, was finally adopted.

Congress shall have power . . . to make all laws which shall be neces-sary and proper for carrying into execution the . . . powers vested by this Constitution in the Government of the United States. (Art. I Sec. VIII § 18.)

This Constitution, and the laws of the United States, which shall be made in pursuance thereof, and all treaties made, or which shall be made, under the authority of the United States, shall be the Supreme Law of the land; and the judges in every State shall be bound thereby, anything in the Constitution or laws of any State to the contrary notwithstanding. (Art. VI. § 2.)

Further, state legislators and executive and judicial officers are 'bound by oath or affirmation to support this Constitution' (Article VI), in order to emphasize the fact that the police power of every state is required to enforce the laws of the Union as well. State authorities, in these national aspects, are under the oversight of the federal courts, which have jurisdiction over 'all cases . . . arising under this Constitution, the laws of the United States, and treaties made . . . under their authority.' As a last resort, Congress has power 'to provide for calling forth the militia' under the President's command 'to execute the laws of the Union.'

These are the central clauses of the Constitution. They went far to solve the more perplexing problems of the period since the war. They grew out of the cumulative experience of these years, and emerged in their present form from the debates in the convention over the New Jersey plan. They provide the Federal Government with means for a peaceful enforcement of its laws in normal times, and for coercion of organized law-breaking in abnormal times. The

Congress of the Confederation, in contrast, had been powerless to enforce its law on the people of a recalcitrant state. That a great Civil War occurred in spite of these provisions is true; but it is no less certain that without them the Federal Government would have been successfully defied by several states before the Constitution had been in effect a generation.

Yet the Constitution is not a unitary one, for the government it creates lacks complete sovereign power. It is a government supreme within its sphere, but that sphere is defined and limited. As the Tenth Amendment made clear in 1791, ' the powers not delegated to the United States by the Constitution, nor prohibited by it to the States, are reserved to the States respectively or to the people; ' and the supremacy of federal laws is limited to such as ' shall be made in pursuance of the Constitution.' The states are co-equally supreme within their sphere; in no legal sense are they subordinate corporations. Both governments rest on the same broad bottom of popular sovereignty. And although the scope of federal power has been widely extended by amendment, by implication, by judicial interpretation, and by the necessities of national crises, so has that of the states. Even in the twentieth century, the American citizen comes more frequently in contact with his state than with the national government. To the states belong, not by virtue of the Federal Constitution but of their own sovereign power, the control of municipal and local government, factory and labor legislation, the chartering of corporations, the statutory development and judicial administration of civil and criminal law, the supervision of religious bodies, the control of education, and the general ' police power ' over the health, safety, and welfare of the people. And the Federal Constitution cannot be amended without the consent of three-fourths of the states.

Article IV of the Constitution, copied almost word for word from the Articles of Confederation, has an international flavor. Each state shall give ' full faith and credit ' to the public acts, records, and judicial proceedings of its sister states, shall extend to their citizens every privilege of their own, shall extradite criminals and return fugitive slaves. The United States guarantees to every state its territorial integrity, a republican form of government, and protection against invasion or domestic violence — another reflection of Shays's Rebellion. The Supreme Court is open to suits by states and has appellate jurisdiction over disputes between citizens of different states.

As the Supreme Court later held, 'For all national purposes embraced by the Federal Constitution, the States and the citizens thereof are one, united under the same sovereign authority, and governed by the same laws. In all other respects the States are necessarily foreign to and independent of each other.'

In conferring powers on the new government, the convention included all those of the Confederation, such as the conduct of war and foreign and Indian relations, posts, coinage, fixing the standards of weights and measures, and administering the western territories. To these were added the taxing power within certain limits; a general supervision over state militia; copyright, patent, naturalization, and bankruptcy laws; and the regulation of foreign and interstate commerce. The power to pass all necessary and proper laws for executing these defined powers rendered the Federal Government sufficiently elastic to meet the needs of later generations, and of a greatly expanded body politic. Between the powers expressly or implicitly granted to the Federal Government, and those reserved to the states, is a sphere of possible governmental action in which the lines between federal power, state power, and concurrent power have as yet been merely pricked out by decisions of the Supreme Court.

Madison thus concludes his analysis of the nature of the new Constitution:

The proposed Constitution . . . is, in strictness, neither a national nor a federal Constitution, but a composition of both. In its foundation it is federal, not national; in the sources from which the ordinary powers of the government are drawn, it is partly federal and partly national; in the operation of these powers, it is national, not federal; in the extent of them, again, it is federal not national; and finally, in the authoritative mode of introducing amendments, it is neither wholly federal nor wholly national.

Thus almost without knowing it, the framers of the Constitution had realized the principle that they believed to be implicit in the Constitution of the British Empire, and that they had maintained so boldly in face of the counter-theory of parliamentary sovereignty and centralization. They proved that federalism and nationalism were not mutually exclusive terms; they gave a new meaning and value to the federal principle; they made the most successful reconciliation in modern history between liberty and empire.

5. *The Frame of Government*

'Let the government be as the materials be.' This wise advice of a pilgrim father was followed by the Convention, in erecting its frame of government. Colonial or state forms to which the people were habituated were used wherever possible. Instead of the parliamentary system, which the British Dominions have preferred, the Convention of 1787 adopted a system immediately derived from state constitutions, and ultimately from the colonial charters and joint-stock trading corporations of the sixteenth century: a legislature and executive elected at stated intervals, and responsible to the same authority, the freemen. Practically every feature of the Federal Constitution was ultimately of English origin, in the same sense that the British Constitution is of Norman and Germanic origin; but there is hardly a clause in it which cannot be traced to state constitutions or to colonial practice. Yet in its grand outlines, in the distribution of powers between central and local governments that is the essential characteristic of a federal system, the Constitution follows the unwritten constitution of the British Empire as it was prior to 1763. The same general powers that were exercised by King and Parliament in the empire were now granted to the central government; the same local jurisdiction that was allocated to the colonies was now reserved to the states.

The principle of separation of powers, familiar in most of the colonial governments, had already been given a fair trial in most of the state constitutions and discovered to be sound.[2] In distributing functions and determining relations between the legislative, the executive and the judiciary, the Federal Constitution followed closely on the constitution of Massachusetts, of which John Adams was the political architect.

The two-year term of the House of Representatives was a compromise between the current American practice of annual elections and the four-year presidential term; the six-year term of the Senators, expiring biennially by thirds, was meant to be a brake on the will of the people. Compared with other second chambers, the Senate has a very small membership: 22 in 1789, gradually increasing to 96 in 1913. Until that date, when the Seventeenth Amendment was ratified, Senators were chosen by their state legislatures. The Senate

[2] See above, p. 121.

was intended both to defend the somewhat imaginary interests of the small states — that was the talking point for it outside the convention — and to protect the very concrete interest of property against numbers. In one of the most realistic and at the same time prophetic speeches delivered in the convention, Madison said (according to the notes of Judge Yates),

We are now forming a body on whose wisdom we mean to rely, and their permanency in office secures a proper field in which they may exert their firmness and knowledge. Democratic communities may be unsteady, and be led to action by the impulses of the moment. Like individuals they may be sensible of their own weakness, and may desire the counsels and checks of friends to guard them against the turbulency and weakness of unruly passions. Such are the various pursuits of this life, that in all civilized countries, the interest of a community will be divided. There will be debtors and creditors, and an unequal possession of property, and hence arises different views and different objects in government. This indeed is the ground-work of aristocracy; and we find it blended in every government, both ancient and modern. Even where titles have survived property, we discover the noble beggar haughty and assuming.

The man who is possessed of wealth, who lolls on his sofa or rolls in his carriage, cannot judge of the wants or feelings of the day laborer. The government we mean to erect is intended to last for ages. The landed interest, at present, is prevalent; but in process of time, when we approximate to the states and kingdoms of Europe; when the number of landholders shall be comparatively small, through the various means of trade and manufactures, will not the landed interest be overbalanced in future elections, and unless wisely provided against, what will become of your government? . . . If these observations be just, our government ought to secure the permanent interests of the country against innovation. Landholders ought to have a share in the government, to support these invaluable interests and to balance and check the other. They ought to be so constituted as to protect the minority of the opulent against the majority. The Senate, therefore, ought to be this body; and to answer these purposes, they ought to have permanency and stability. Various have been the propositions; but my opinion is, the longer they continue in office, the better will these views be answered.

John Dickinson hoped that the United States Senate would bear ' as strong a likeness to the British House of Lords as possible.' But the Senate has become a much more powerful chamber than the Lords, by virtue of its co-equal legislative power with the House, and its share in the President's powers of appointment and treaty making. The two-thirds requirement for ratifying treaties, without which the United States would have joined the League of Nations, was a relic of the Articles of Confederation, retained for fear lest the interests of one section of the country be sacrificed to those of another, as John Jay had been accused of doing in his negotiation with Spain. Madison attempted to procure an exception in favor of treaties of peace, but was overruled.

The executive department gave the Federal Convention more trouble than any other part of the Constitution. Questions of powers, qualifications, term of office, mode of election, relations with the other departments and the like, inspired prolonged debates, and were settled in most instances by compromise. The method of electing the President was particularly perplexing. It was finally provided that each state legislature should choose or cause to be chosen, quadrennially, a number of presidential electors equal to its whole representation in House and Senate. The presidential electors of every state form the electoral college, though each state group meets separately and a majority of electoral votes is necessary for choice. It was expected that the presidential electors would nominate a number of 'favorite sons,' no one of whom would obtain a majority; in that case the final choice among the top three candidates was to rest with the House. Madison thought this could happen 'nineteen times out of twenty'; but the two-party system has allowed it to happen but twice, in 1801 and 1825. Political parties have made the nominations since 1792, and the presidential electors merely register the will of the state pluralities. That they should do so is now an unwritten convention quite as strong as any provision of the written Constitution; and although some state legislatures appointed presidential electors as late as 1860, a popular vote has become the accepted and universal method. It is interesting to note that in this one department where the Federal Convention was largely without experience, it created a clumsy system which had to be supplemented by the Twelfth Amendment and by the intervention of political parties.

If the method of electing the President was clumsy, the office of President was clean-cut. This was the boldest feature of the new constitution, for most of the states had a mere figurehead of a governor, chosen by the legislature; but the example of Massachusetts, where a strong and popularly elected chief magistrate had put down rebellion, encouraged the convention to clothe the President with ample powers. He is not only the responsible head of the executive and administrative branches, but supreme war chief and, by virtue of his suspensive veto over acts of Congress, a part of the legislative branch as well. He is not hampered by a council, although the Senate shares his appointing and treaty-making powers. He is responsible only to the people. It has often been said that the President of the United States is a republican monarch and a monarchical premier rolled into one; but the comparison is inexact. He is more independent of the legislative power than either, but Congress is independent of him. He cannot dissolve Congress and can adjourn it only in case of disagreement between House and Senate as to the time, which has never occurred. The state authorities issue writs of election for the House of Representatives every two years, and the Constitution requires Congress to assemble every December.[3]

6. Judicial Review

The Federal Constitution is a very brief document, as constitutions go; the framers had the good sense not to endeavor to anticipate every need or provide for every eventuality. They were content to provide means of electing or appointing the great departments of government, to give certain powers like commerce regulation to the federal legislature, to provide for the immediate operation of federal law on individual citizens, and to forbid the states to exercise certain powers that had been grossly abused. They left it to Congress, the President, and the courts to supplement and implement much that was left optional or inchoate in the constitution itself. For instance, the convention once adopted the clause, ' The Legislature shall discharge the debts . . . of the United States,' but reconsidered it after Mason and Johnson — both men of wealth and creditors of the nation — had objected to the mandatory character. The Constitution, after enumerating the payment of debts as a legitimate object of the taxing power, simply declares that all debts against the United States shall be ' as valid . . . under this Constitution, as under the Confederation.'

In no department is this preference of ' may ' over ' must ' more evident than in Article III on the judiciary, which required an organic act of Congress to become operative. The framework and jurisdiction of the federal courts and the judges' tenure are covered

---

[3] According to the Twentieth Amendment (1933) ' at least once in every year,' and normally on January 3.

in two sections of some four hundred words. Owing to this brevity, the power of the Supreme Court to declare acts of Congress unconstitutional has frequently been challenged when an unpopular decision was handed down. Hence we must inquire at this point where if anywhere the federal courts obtained the power of judicial review.[4]

In the first place, from the Constitution:

The Judicial power shall extend to all cases, in law and equity, arising under this Constitution, the laws of the United States, and treaties made, or which shall be made, under their authority; . . . (Art. III, Sec. II)

This Constitution, and the laws of the United States, which shall be made in pursuance thereof; and all treaties made, or which shall be made, under the authority of the United States, shall be the Supreme Law of the land; . . . (Art. VI. § 2)

These words, it may be argued, are not very explicit. But the debates in the Convention prove that they were explicit enough for the framers. As former English colonists they were familiar with judicial review by the Privy Council of acts of colonial assemblies that were deemed 'contrary to the laws of England.' State courts had already in several instances declared acts of state legislatures void, as contrary to the state constitution or to 'natural right.' In the North Carolina case of Bayard v. Singleton (1787) the Court said:

It was clear, that no act they [the legislature] could pass, could by any means repeal or alter the constitution, because if they could do this, they would at the same instant of time, destroy their own existence as a Legislature, and dissolve the government thereby established. Consequently the constitution (which the judicial was bound to take notice of as much as of any other law whatever) standing in full force as the fundamental law of the land, notwithstanding the act on which the present motion was grounded, the same act must of course, in that instance, stand as abrogated and without any effect.[5]

---

[4] 'Judicial review' as commonly used, includes review in the course of judicial proceedings both of acts of subordinate legislatures (in this case the states) and of the co-ordinate legislature (in this case Congress). The right of the federal courts to review acts of the state legislatures, and declare such as contravene the Federal Constitution to be invalid, has seldom been challenged since the Civil War. We are here concerned with the review of acts of Congress.

[5] North Carolina Reports, I Martin, 42. Many other alleged state precedents, however, notably Commonwealth v. Caton, have been proved either apocryphal or irrelevant. See L. Boudin, *Government by Judiciary*, vol. i, appendices B and C.

The Federal Convention was much concerned with the problem of keeping the powers of Congress within constitutional bounds. The Virginia Plan provided a 'council of revision' consisting of the executive and a number of federal judges, with power to veto any act of Congress, not only those that were deemed unconstitutional, but those considered by the council to be unnecessary or 'improper.' In the debate on this clause, Elbridge Gerry doubted whether the judiciary ought to form part of such a council,

as they will have a sufficient check against encroachments on their own department by their exposition of the laws, which involved a power of deciding on their Constitutionality. In some States the Judges had actually set aside laws as being against the Constitution. This was done too with general approbation. It was quite foreign from the nature of the office to make them judges of the policy of public measures.

This argument appears to have prevailed, for the convention first struck the judges out of the council of revision, and then by amendments turned it into the presidential veto, which might be overridden by a two-thirds vote of both houses. When, later in the convention, Wilson attempted to revive the council of revision, Luther Martin said:

As to the Constitutionality of laws, that point will come before the Judges in their proper official character. In this character they have a negative on the laws. Join them with the executive in the Revision, and they will have a double negative. It is necessary that the Supreme Judiciary should have the confidence of the people. This will soon be lost, if they are employed in the task of remonstrating against popular measures of the Legislature.

And the council of revision was again defeated.

Madison said, when arguing in favor of submitting the Constitution for ratification to state conventions, 'A law violating a constitution established by the people themselves, would be considered by the Judges as null and void.' Hamilton discussed the question of judicial review in No. 78 of *The Federalist* — one of the best expositions of the theory that we have. Oliver Ellsworth in the Connecticut ratifying convention declared the Supreme Court to be 'a constitutional check' if Congress 'should at any time overleap their limits.' Similar statements can be found in the debates of ratifying conventions in Virginia, Maryland, and Pennsylvania. It was Ellsworth who drafted, and President Washington who signed the Judiciary

Act of 1789, which set up the machinery for testing the constitutionality both of state and of national laws by the Supreme Court.[6] In the
case of Hylton *v.* United States that came before the Supreme Court
in 1796, Justices Paterson and Wilson, both prominent members of
the Federal Convention, exercised the right to pass upon the constitutionality of an act of Congress. But in the same case Justice
Chase said:

it is unnecessary at this time for me to determine whether this court constitutionally possesses the power to declare an Act of Congress void, on
the ground of its being made contrary to, and in violation of the Constitution; but if the court have such power, I am free to declare, that I will
never exercise it but in a very clear case.[7]

And in 1811 William Tilghman, a former federal judge who was then
Chief Justice of Pennsylvania, stated the rule so far followed by the
Supreme Court of the United States: ' that an Act of the legislature
is not to be declared void unless the violation of the Constitution is
so manifest as to leave no room for reasonable doubt.'

Whether the Supreme Court has, on the whole, exercised this
power of the judicial review wisely, with a decent respect for other
departments of the government, or in accordance with Judge Tilghman's rule, are questions that we need not here consider. But there
is no doubt that the power of judicial review, already familiar to the
framers of the Constitution, was conferred on the judiciary in the
Constitution with full intention that it should be exercised.

7. Ratification

The Federal Convention decided to submit its work for ratification
to popularly elected state conventions, rather than to state legislatures, in order to give the Constitution a broad bottom of popular
consent. Further, the convention made a clean-cut, revolutionary
breach with the Confederation by declaring that the Constitution
would be in force when ratified by nine of the thirteen states.

In September 1787, when the convention adjourned, the prospect
of ratification seemed dark indeed. Mason, Randolph, and Gerry
refused to sign the finished Constitution, while Lansing and Yates

[6] See Chapter xv § 3, below.
[7] James B. Thayer, *Cases on Constitutional Law,* ii. 1315–20.

of New York and Martin and Mercer of Maryland had already left the convention and were urging their states to reject its handiwork. Popular politicians like George Clinton, Patrick Henry, and Willie Jones were certain to whip up local patriotism against the loss of state power. Debtors and paper-money advocates were furious with the convention. The Constitution flouted such catchwords as rotation in office, annual elections, and legislative supremacy, while the absence of a bill of rights caused profound misgivings among democrats everywhere. For many, it was enough to condemn the Constitution that it granted more power to President and Congress than King and Parliament had ever exercised over the Thirteen Colonies. It was a generation that had been taught to view all government, and especially a centralized, distant, and powerful government, with fear and suspicion. The idea of state sovereignty was generally accepted and particularism was rampant. William Pierce of Georgia predicted, 'Some will oppose it from pride, some from self interest, some from ignorance, but the greater number will be of that class who will oppose it from a dread of its swallowing up the individuality of the States.'

The Federalists, as the protagonists of the Constitution tactfully called themselves, could count on the support of merchants and the seaport towns, public creditors, speculators in western lands, officers of the late army, the pulpit, and most of the press. It was an inestimable advantage that Washington consented to stand for the Presidency. The *Federalist* papers written by Hamilton, Madison, and Jay were first in permanent value of thousands of editorials, pamphlets, and handbills that were issued to persuade the doubtful and enlighten the ignorant. The Federalists, too, could appeal to popular prejudice: the instinct for law and order so recently aroused against Shays's Rebellion, the fear of anarchy, and the latent spirit of American nationalism. Their most powerful argument was to contrast the impotence of the Confederation against British seapower and Spanish intrigue with the means for a vigorous foreign policy that the Constitution afforded. It is significant that both the French minister and the British consuls at New York and Philadelphia were unfriendly to the new Constitution, fearing lest it enable the United States to become the leading American power.

Unless the Federalists had been shrewd in manipulation as they were sound in theory, their arguments could not have prevailed. In Pennsylvania they rushed through the election of a state con-

vention before the Anti-federalists had time to stir up their natural
supporters, the German farmers and Scotch-Irish frontiersmen. Pennsylvania, accordingly, ratified on 18 December 1787. Several of the
smaller states, grateful for an equal vote in the Senate, adhered
shortly after. Massachusetts suffered the first sharp contest. There
was an Anti-federalist majority in the state convention when it met
at Boston. Agrarian discontent was still rife in that state, and ' Many
of the insurgents are in the Convention, even some of Shays's officers,'
wrote General Lincoln to Washington. The note of opposition was
struck by a rustic delegate, Amos Singletary:

> These lawyers, and men of learning and moneyed men, that talk
> so finely, and gloss over matters so smoothly, to make us poor illiterate
> people swallow down the pill, expect to get into Congress themselves;
> they expect to be managers of this Constitution, and get all the power
> and all the money into their own hands, and then they will swallow up
> all us little folks like the great *Leviathan;* yes, just as the whale swallowed
> up *Jonah!*

In order to meet the popular objection to the lack of a bill of rights,
the Massachusetts Federalists drafted amendments which their commonwealth, in ratifying the Constitution, might propose to her
sister states subsequent adoption. This clever device won many
of the waverers there and helped the Federalist cause elsewhere.
Governor Hancock, who was waiting to see which way the band-
wagon went, had the Vice-Presidency dangled before his expectant
gaze. Doubtful members from the rural districts were plied with
flattering hospitality and converted by persuasive eloquence. Finally
the Massachusetts convention ratified the Constitution by a margin
of 19 votes in 355. Maryland followed, despite the efforts of Samuel
Chase and Luther Martin, and South Carolina fell into line. By the
end of May 1788, eight states had ratified; but the key states of Virginia and New York were still to be heard from.

In no state was the event so doubtful, or the discussion so able
as in Virginia. Here, alone in all the states, the Constitution received a thorough and searching analysis; here alone its merits were
fully revealed, its defects candidly exposed. And here, too, the opposition met the Federalists on equal terms: Patrick Henry, George
Mason, James Monroe, and Richard Henry Lee were fully able to
hold their own against James Madison, John Marshall, Edmund
Pendleton, and George Wythe. Mason presented the state convention
with a reasoned Anti-federalist view; Henry, the greatest American

orator of the day, thundered against the Constitution as undemo-
cratic, tuned its every clause with local or popular prejudice, and conjured up a horrid spectacle of the President sallying forth at the head
of his army to 'make one bold push for the American throne.' Madison, Marshall, and 'Lighthorse Harry' Lee replied; but it is doubtful
whether their arguments would have been convincing had they not
previously made sure of Governor Randolph. That weak and vacillating member of an ancient family was the most popular Virginian after
Henry. In the Federal Convention he split with Madison, and refused
to sign the Constitution on the ground that it would lead to monarchy or aristocracy. Washington and Madison, however, won him
back to Federalism before the state convention met; and his skillful
advocacy of the Constitution in that body carried weight. The sectional divisions of Virginia also counted heavily in the decision.
The Piedmont, where Patrick Henry's influence was strong and the
planters were heavily in debt, mustered very few votes for the Constitution; but the Tidewater on general conservative principles was
for it, and the Shenandoah valley Presbyterians, though still in a
frontier stage of culture, were so eager for free interstate trade, for
more equable taxation, and for a prompt execution of the treaty of
peace, that they cast a unanimous vote for ratification. Virginia,
therefore, was an exception to the generalization that the Constitution was carried by upper class and seaboard against interior and
West. In the Old Dominion it was an alliance of the two ends,
'Tuckahoe' and 'Cohee,' against the middle; and the Federalists
had only ten votes to spare out of 168 when the Constitution was
adopted, on 25 June 1788.

New Hampshire had come in a few days previously; Virginia
made the tenth state, and the Constitution could now go into effect.
Yet with New York out of the Union the new nation would be
divided in the middle and hopelessly incomplete. In New York,
wrote Washington, there was 'more wickedness than ignorance'
in Anti-federalism. A determined opposition of the landed interest
prolonged the contest another month. Hamilton led the Federalist
forces with consummate skill, but it was only after a threat to detach New York City from the rest of the state that the convention
finally ratified by a majority of 3 in a total vote of 57. North Carolina
and Rhode Island alone remained outside the new Union, which
could now well afford to await their pleasure.

The Congress of the Confederation arranged for the first presidential election, declared the new government would begin operations on 4 March 1789, and quietly expired.

On 10 July 1788 the New York *Public Advertiser*, under the heading ' Ship News — Extra,' noted the entrance of the good ship *Federal Constitution*, Perpetual Union master, from Elysium. Her cargo included thirteen large parcels of Union, Peace, and Friendship; on her passenger list were Messrs. Flourishing Commerce, Public Faith, and National Energy. Below is noted the clearance of *Old Confederacy*, Imbecility master, with a cargo of paper money, legal-tender acts, local prejudices, and seeds of discord; and the total loss with all hands of the sloop *Anarchy*, wrecked on the Rock of Union.

8. *The End of an Era*

The Federal Constitution was the outcome of a twenty-five year contest with the problem of imperial organization: parliamentary sovereignty, rejected by the colonists; dominion status, rejected by the North ministry only to be offered too late in 1778; Articles of Confederation, imperfect and too rigid. Over the dead bones of all these solutions rejected or attempted, the Federal Convention worked out a new federal system, a successful distribution of powers between central and local governments, all resting upon popular sovereignty. The creation of this federal system is undoubtedly the greatest original contribution of the United States to the art and science of government. Republics there had been before, and democracies; but nothing to reconcile liberty and empire over vast areas and disparate interests.

Yet federalism was not the only political contribution of this generation. Vital for the extension of this federal system over wider areas and for adapting it to an expansive people was the discovery of a new colonial system, in the Northwest Ordinance. Herein was first adopted the policy of treating colonies as equals of the mother country, a policy which enabled the United States to expand from thirteen to forty-eight commonwealths under the same government. And other Western problems were put in the way of solution by the land Ordinance of 1785. The compact theory of government, formulated in the Declaration of Independence, was given concrete shape by the device of a constitutional convention, which made it possible to abolish, alter, or create government by peaceful process.

These — federalism, a new colonial system, and the constitutional convention — were the positive contributions of the Revolutionary era, and mark that period as creative and constructive. Less palpable but no less significant was the growth of democracy. That would have come without revolution, as in the British dominions and in England itself; but the war and the transfer of power from London to thirteen states greatly accelerated the process. In 1789, however, the democratic movement was in abeyance, and a 'thermidorian reaction' in full swing. The democratic discontents of 1760–75 had only partially been placated, and, largely for want of effective leadership, had broken out into demands that threatened property values. Hence the Federal Constitution put a stopper on those levelling and confiscatory demands of democracy by making contracts sacred, by prohibiting paper money (just as Parliament had done), and by the system of checks and balances which made the satisfaction of an immediate popular will highly improbable.

If democracy found itself checked and hampered by the new government, every liberty compatible with good order was secured. America was very fortunate to achieve political independence without loss of liberty, even without loss of cultural values. There is something cramping to the human spirit in a dependent relation, and it is doubtful whether America could have produced such statesmen as Jefferson, Hamilton, and Madison, or such creative artists as Irving, Poe, Whitman, and Emerson, had it remained a series of colonies. Certain humanitarian reforms, such as the abolition of the slave trade, could now be realized; although independence was the means of giving slavery itself a longer life than in the British Empire. Full scope, too, was given by the Revolution to that business enterprise which has become the leading factor of the United States; the Acts of Trade and Navigation no longer existed for America, her ships were no longer confined to the Atlantic Ocean, and her workmen could never again be told that they might not 'manufacture a lock of wool or a horseshoe or a hobnail.' On the political thought of the western world, the Revolution exerted a tremendous influence. In the words of Lord Acton, 'It was from America that the plain ideas that men ought to mind their own business, and that the nation is responsible to Heaven for the acts of the State — ideas long locked in the breast of solitary thinkers, and hidden among Latin folios — burst like a conqueror upon the world they were destined to transform, under the title of the Rights of Man.'

XIV

THE UNITED STATES IN 1790 [1]

1. *Generalities*

ONLY twenty-five years since the Stamp Act; only fourteen years since the Thirteen Colonies declared 'to a candid world' that they were 'and of right ought to be, free and independent States.' It is already time to take stock, and see what sort of country it was when the Federal Constitution was newly established, and Washington had been President for less than a year.

Much had been said in the debates over the Constitution about the enhanced prestige that it would give to the United States. Official Europe was not impressed. Not that they perceived danger in American republicanism. With Washington's army disbanded, and the navy dismantled, the United States was hardly a feather in the balance of power. Merchants and traders, however, were not so indifferent to the new nation, if it could be called a nation. As a source of raw materials for Europe, the United States was not yet in a class with the West Indies; but for a country of such vast empty spaces, it was an important market. Even with the Mississippi as its western boundary, the United States was equal in area to the British Isles, France, Germany, Spain, and Italy. Less than half this territory had yet come under the effective jurisdiction of the United States or of any state; and the population of four millions, including seven hundred thousand negro slaves, was dispersed over an expanse of coastal plain and upland slightly more extensive than France. But if the trans-Appalachian country were ever settled, it would surely break off from the Thirteen States. So at least believed the few Europeans who gave the matter a thought.

Whatever the future might promise the United States in wealth and power seemed to be denied by political vagaries. America was attempting simultaneously three political experiments, which the accumulated wisdom of Europe deemed likely to fail: independence, republicanism, and federal union. While the British and the Spanish

---

[1] We have taken the year 1790, rather than 1789, as the central point of this description, because it was the year of the first federal census, which supplies the first statistics, incomplete to be sure and not very accurate, for the United States.

empires touched the states on three sides, their independence could hardly be maintained without more of that European aid by which it had been won; and an independence so maintained would be only nominal. Republicanism promised instability; and federalism, dissolution. Since the Renaissance, the uniform tendency in Europe had been towards centralized monarchy; federal republics had maintained themselves only in small areas, such as the Netherlands and Switzerland. Most European observers believed that the history of the American Union would be short and stormy.

It was still too early to aver that the Americans had conquered the forest. Volney wrote that during his journey in 1796 through the length and breadth of the United States, he scarcely travelled for more than three miles together on open and cleared land. 'Compared with France, the entire country is one vast wood.' Only in southern New England, and the eastern portion of the Middle States, did the cultivated area exceed the woodland; and the clearings became less frequent as one approached the Appalachians.

The larger part of the American people then lived under isolated conditions, but in a land of such plenty that exertion had no attraction for the unambitious. The ocean and its shores yielded plenty of fish; the tidal rivers teemed with salmon, sturgeon, herring, and shad in due season, and the upland streams with trout; every kind of game was plentiful, from quail and raccoon to wild turkey and deer; and at times the flights of wild pigeon darkened the air. Cattle and swine throve on the woodland herbage and mast; Indian corn ripened quickly in the hot summer nights; even sugar could be obtained from the maple, or honey from wild bees. The American of the interior, glutted with nature's bounty and remote from a market, had no immediate incentive to produce much beyond his own actual needs; yet the knowledge that easier life could be had often pressed him westward to more fertile lands, or to a higher scale of living. Hence the note of personal independence that was, and in the main still is, dominant in American life. 'The means of subsistence being so easy in the country,' wrote an English observer in 1796, 'and their dependence on each other consequently so trifling, that spirit of servility to those above them so prevalent in European manners, is wholly unknown to them; and they pass their lives without any regard to the smiles or the frowns of men in power.'

However independent of those above him the average American

might be, he was dependent on those about him for help in harvest, in raising his house-frame, and in illness. In a new country you turn to your neighbors for many offices and functions that, in a riper community, are performed by government or by specialists. Hence the dual nature of the American: individualism and herd instinct, indifference and kindliness. Isolation in American foreign policy is an authentic outcome of community isolation, as are the recent American relief organizations of primitive interdependence.

In 1790 there were only six cities (Philadelphia, New York, Boston, Charleston, Baltimore, and Salem) in the United States with a population of eight thousand or over; and their combined numbers included only three per cent of the total population.[2] Their aspect was not unlike that of provincial towns in Great Britain, for a native American architectural style had not yet been invented. Brick houses in the Georgian style, often detached and surrounded with gardens and shrubbery; inns with capacious yards and stables; shops and stores with overhanging signs; places of worship with graceful spires after Sir Christopher Wren; market houses or city halls of the same style, often placed in the middle of a broad street or square, with arcades to serve as stalls or merchants' exchange; somewhat ramshackle unpainted wooden houses where the poorer people lived, but hardly one without a bit of garden or yard. Wealth was not a conspicuous feature of the United States in 1790. Almost a century had to elapse before a European could find here anything impressive in the way of shops, mansions, architecture, or high living. Nor was there anything to match the poverty of a European city; and even the slave population of the Carolina rice-fields was less wretched than the contemporary Irish peasant.

Except for iron, the vast mineral resources of the country were practically untouched, and iron smelting remained primitive, owing to the abundance of wood, long after the British had made technical improvements. Agriculture was the main occupation of nine-tenths of the people. Except along the Hudson, practically every farmer was a freeholder. Except among the Pennsylvania Germans and the more enlightened country gentry of the South, the methods of agriculture were incredibly wasteful and primitive, with little sign of the improved culture and implements that were then transforming rural England. Wheat bread was largely an upper-class

[2] The proportion of urban to rural population did not pass ten per cent until after 1840.

luxury. Indian corn was the principal food crop, with rye a poor second. Brown 'rye and Injun' bread, corn-pone or hoe-cake, and hasty-pudding or hominy, with salt pork or codfish, washed down by rum, cider, or whisky, according to locality, formed the farmer's staple diet from Maine to Georgia. As early as 1780 the Marquis de Chastellux noted the prevalence of hot biscuits, the bountiful breakfasts of the South, and 'the American custom of drinking coffee with meat, vegetables, or other food.' Frontier conditions still prevailed over the larger part of the 'Old West' which had been settled within the last fifty years. The houses were commonly log cabins of one or two rooms and a cock-loft; the fields were full of stumps, and acres of dead trees strangled by girdling were a depressing sight to travellers.

Bad roads were one of the penalties that Americans paid for their dispersed settlement and aversion from taxation. In 1790 the difficulties of communication were so great that a detour of several hundred miles by river and ocean was often preferable to an overland journey of fifty miles. It was almost as difficult to assemble the first Congress of the United States as to convene church councils in the Middle Ages. There was a main post-road from Wiscasset in Maine to Savannah in Georgia, over which passengers and mails were transported by light open stage-wagons, in approximately so many days as the railway now requires hours. It took twenty-nine days for the news of the Declaration of Independence to reach Charleston from Philadelphia. Bridges were few, even over the rivers and streams that were unfordable; the wooden pile structure across the Charles at Boston was considered an immense feat of engineering. Washington managed to visit almost every state in the Union in his own coach without serious mishap; but he had to choose a season when the roads were passable, and to undergo discomfort and even danger. Most of the roads were merely wide tracks through the forest, full of rocks and stumps and enormous holes. Many that are marked on the early maps were mere bridle-paths or Indian trails, that would admit no wheeled vehicle. Northern farmers reserved their heavy hauling for winter, when snow made even the worst trace practicable for sledges; whilst upland Southerners got their tobacco to tidewater by pivoting a pair of shafts to a hogshead, and rolling it down on the bilge. Inns were to be found at frequent intervals along the main roads; but they commonly fulfilled the function of neighborhood pot-house better than resting-place for the weary wayfarer. The food was cheap and plentiful, but meals could be had only at stated hours — as in the largest American hotels within recent memory. A traveller was fortunate to secure a bed to himself, or to arrive on the first evening after the sheets were changed. Lieutenant Anburey, late of Burgoyne's army, regretted that he could not safely horsewhip the landlord who overcharged him. He might have fought the landlord, however, with bare fists, and been thought a better man for it.

Now that America has become famous for its sanitation, and for hotels with as many thousand baths as bedrooms, it is worth noting that in the eighteenth and early nineteenth centuries America impressed European tourists as an uncommonly dirty country. From persons at that time accustomed to London or Paris, this meant a good deal. Even in the larger towns streets were seldom paved and never cleaned, offal was deposited in the docks, and, without wire screens, houses were defenseless against the swarms of flies and other winged pests that summer brought. As no one had yet heard of disease germs, there were intermittent outbreaks of typhoid and yellow fever in the seaports as far north as New Hampshire; and the frontiersmen were racked every summer by malarial fevers and agues, transmitted by mosquitoes. Flower gardens were rare; and the pioneer, regarding trees as enemies, neither spared them nor planted them for purposes of shade. Country farmhouses in the older-settled region were almost invariably of wood, usually unpainted, resembling dingy boxes surrounded by unseemly household litter. Stoutly and honestly built as they were, the colonial houses that have survived long enough to acquire white paint, green blinds, lawns, shrubs, and century-old shade trees, are seen to have both distinction and beauty. In the eighteenth century, however, no one found much to admire in America in the works of man; and few Americans had the taste or leisure to appreciate the rugged grandeur of their mountains and forests, and their majestic rivers, swift rapids, and mighty waterfalls.

The United States of 1790 was not a nation, by any modern standard. Materials of a nation were present, but cohesive force was wanting. An English origin for the bulk of the people made a certain cultural homogeneity; the Maine fisherman could understand the Georgian planter much more readily than a Kentishman could understand a Yorkshireman, or an Alsatian a Breton. Political institutions, though decentralized, were fairly constant in form through the length and breadth of the land. But there was no tradition of union behind the War of Independence, and it was difficult to discover a common interest upon which union could be built. Most citizens of the United States in 1790, if asked their country or nation, would not have answered American, but Carolinian, Virginian, Pennsylvanian, Jerseyman, New Yorker, or New Englander. A political nexus had been found, but unless a national tradition were soon established, the United States would develop a particularism similar to the states of Germany and Italy. Already the problem was becoming complicated by the formation of settlements on the western waters, beyond the Appalachians. In the meantime, it would require the highest statesmanship to keep the thirteen commonwealths together, so widely did they differ in origin, tradition, religion, and economic interests. The Federal Constitution made it possible; but few observers in 1790 thought it probable.

2. New England

In New England, climate, soil, and religion had produced in a century and a half a strongly individualized type, the Yankee, perhaps the most persistent ingredient of the American mixture.

The Yankee was the American Scot; and New England was an eighteenth-century Scotland without the lairds. A severe climate, a grudging soil that had to be cleared of boulders as well as trees, and a stern puritan faith, dictated the four gospels of education, thrift, ingenuity, and righteousness. By necessity rather than choice, the New Englanders had acquired an aptitude for maritime enterprise and trading. They hailed with joy the new and wider opportunities for seafaring opened by freedom from the Acts of Trade. The seamen of Salem had already ventured to the East Indies with much success when Boston, in 1790, celebrated the return of her ship *Columbia,* laden with tea, silk, and porcelain, from a voyage around the world. On her next voyage the *Columbia* sailed up a great river that Vancouver had passed by, gave it her name, and to its banks her flag.

The five New England States were divided, politically, into townships, about thirty square miles on an average, containing from a hundred to several thousand people. Each was a unit for purposes of local government, conducting its own affairs by town meeting and selectmen, supporting common schools by local taxes, and electing annually to the state legislature a representative, whose votes and doings were keenly scrutinized by his constituents. The nucleus of every township was the meeting-house, part town hall, part place of worship, bordering on the village green. Outlying farms, by 1790, in most places outnumbered those with a village house-plot; and the common fields had been divided in severalty, and enclosed by un-cemented stone walls. There was plenty of wood to supply the large open fireplaces. Families were large, but estates were seldom divided below a hundred acres; a Yankee farmer hoped to make a scholar or minister out of one son, to provide for a second with a tract of wilderness, and let the rest earn their living by working for hire, going to sea, or learning a trade. Until 1830 or thereabouts the Ameri-can merchant marine was manned largely by New England lads who were seeking the wherewithal to purchase land and set up housekeeping.

Puritanism had become less grim than in the seventeenth, less petty than in the nineteenth century. 'Holy days' were still pro-scribed, and the puritan Sabbath was still observed; but there was plenty of frisking at rural barn-raisings and corn-huskings; and much drinking on public occasions such as ship-launchings, ordinations, college commencements, and Thanksgiving Day — the puritan sub-stitute for Christmas, which in course of time became an additional day of merry-making. On the whole, living was plain in New Eng-land; and the ample, generous tone of new countries was little in evidence. Even in the family of President Adams, we are told, the children were urged to a double portion of hasty-pudding, in order to spare the meat that was to follow. Idleness was the cardinal sin. If a Yankee had nothing else to do, he whittled barrel-bungs from a pine stick, or carved a model of his latest ship; and he usually had much else to do. New England housewives spun, wove, and tailored their woolen garments, and made cloth for sale. Small fulling mills and paper mills were established at the numerous waterfalls, and distilleries in the seaports turned West India molasses into that grateful if dangerous beverage, New England rum. Wooden ware was made by snow-bound farmers for export to the West Indies, nails were cut and headed from wrought iron rods at fireside forges, and in some parts there was a domestic industry of shoe-making. Connecticut, in particular, had attained a nice balance be-tween farming, seafaring, and handicraft, which made the people of that state renowned for steady habits and mechanical ingenuity.

Before the century was out, Eli Whitney of New Haven devised the cotton gin and interchangeable parts for firearms: inventions which, for weal or woe, have deeply affected the human race. New England was ripe for an abrupt transition from handicraft to the factory system; but the success of her seafarers, and the facility of emigration, postponed industrial revolution for another generation. The intellectual flowering was all in the future.

For a good inside view of New England by an outsider, we are indebted to the South American patriot Francisco de Miranda, who travelled through that region in the summer of 1784. An intelligent member of an old Spanish family, brought up in Carácas and familiar with Spain, Miranda found much in New England that was kindly, pleasant, and in good taste. At New Haven he is taken over Yale College by President Stiles, converses with a classically educated miller who had been a cavalry captain in the late war, and views the famous Blue Laws in the town archives. Proceeding to Wethersfield, he attends Sabbath meeting, and admires the manner in which the psalms and responses are sung by the congregation, trained by a music master. At Windsor, the men are ill-dressed and the women ill-favored, but he enjoys a lively literary conversation with John Trumbull, as well as with the innkeeper. This worthy is discovered reading Rollin's *Ancient History,* and discusses with Miranda the comparative merits of the ancients and the moderns, stoutly maintaining Ben Franklin to be a better man than Aristides. Thence to Middletown, and a boat excursion on the river with General Parsons and other good fellows, drinking copiously of punch 'in pure republican style,' which was probably not so different from the present style. Newport he thought justly called the paradise of New England, containing, besides hospitable natives, a large company of ladies and gentlemen from Charleston, S. C., who were already using the place as a summer resort. The leading lights of Providence, on the other hand, were provincial and vulgar, Commodore Esek Hopkins even insisting that there was no such place as the City of Mexico.

Miranda entered Boston armed with letters of introduction to the 'best people,' whose ladies he found vain, luxurious, and too much given to the use of cosmetics. Boston society was so fast, in that year of post-war extravagance, that he predicted bankruptcy within twenty years. Samuel Adams, however, was still faithful to republican simplicity. After carefully inspecting Harvard College, Miranda reports it better suited to turn out Protestant clergymen than intelligent and liberal citizens. He visits the studio of the self-taught painter, Edward Savage, and predicts that with a European education his talent will take him far. (Savage never visited Europe, but his portrait of Washington is the best likeness we have of that great man.) From Boston, Miranda takes the eastward road to Portsmouth, N. H., and is much impressed by the thrift and prosperity of the North Shore of Massachusetts. 'Liberty inspires such intelligence and industry in these towns . . . that the people out of their slender resources maintain their large families, pay heavy taxes, and live with comfort and taste, a thousand times happier than the proprietors of the rich mines and fertile lands of Mexico, Peru, Buenos Aires, Carácas, and the whole Spanish-American continent.'

The New Englanders were very well satisfied with themselves in 1790, and had reason to be; for they had struck root in a region where nature was not lavish, and produced a homogeneous, cohesive, and happy society. Disorderly as colonists when royal governors attempted to thwart their will, the Yankees quickly passed through the cruder phases of democracy. For another generation the leadership of their clergy, well-to-do merchants, and conservative lawyers would not be successfully challenged. Outside New England, where they were familiar as traders and pedlars, the Yankees were regarded much as Scotchmen then were by the English: often envied, sometimes respected, but generally disliked.

3. The Middle States

New York State was heterogeneous in 1790, and was never destined to attain homogeneity. The Dutch 'Knickerbocker' families shared a social ascendancy with the descendants of English and Huguenot merchants. There were many villages where Dutch was still spoken, and Albany was still thoroughly Dutch, ruled by mynheers who lived in substantial brick houses with stepped gables. But the Netherlandish element comprised only one-sixth of the three hundred thousand inhabitants of New York State. For the rest, there were Germans in the Mohawk valley and Ulster county; a few families of Sephardic Jews at New York City; an appreciable element of Scotch and Irishmen, and a strong majority of English, among whom the Yankee element was fast increasing.

New York was only the fifth state in population in 1790: a four-fold increase in thirty years made it first in 1820. It was the settlement of the interior that made the difference. In 1790 the inhabited area of New York followed the Hudson river from New York City to Albany, whence one branch of settlement continued up the Mohawk towards Lake Erie, and a thin line of clearings pushed up by Lake George and Lake Champlain, which Burgoyne had found a wilderness. There were also a few islands of settlement such as Cooperstown, where James Fenimore Cooper was cradled in the midst of the former hunting grounds of the Six Nations. Socially, New York was still the most aristocratic of the states, in spite of the extensive confiscation and subdividing of loyalists' estates; for most of the patroons managed to retain their vast properties. One out of every six New York families held slaves in 1790, and nine more years elapsed before gradual emancipation began. The qualifications for voting and for office were high. For a generation the story of New York politics was to be, in the main, a struggle for the prestige and profit of office between the great whig families, struggles waged by the means familiar to English politics of the time. These landlords were wont to improve their fortunes through alliances with mercantile families, with lawyer-statesmen like Hamilton and Rufus King, and by speculation in Western land.

New York City owed its prosperity, and its thirty-three thousand inhabitants, to a unique position at the mouth of the Hudson river, the greatest tidal inlet between the St. Lawrence and the Plata. It was the natural gateway to the Iroquois country, which was settled between 1790 and 1820; and in 1825 the Erie Canal, following the lowest watershed between the Atlantic States and the Lakes, made New York City the principal gateway to the West, and the financial center of the Union. The merchants did not need to be so venturesome as those of New England and Baltimore, and they spent more on good living than on churches and schools. They too had a family college — Columbia (late King's); but while Boston was forming learned institutions, and Philadelphia supporting a literary journal and a Philosophical Society, New York was founding the Columbian Order, better known as Tammany Hall. Yet it was in the midst of this wealthy, gay, and somewhat cynical society that Alexander Hamilton reached manhood, and Washington Irving was born.

New Jersey, a farming state of less than two hundred thousand people, has been compared with a barrel tapped at both ends by

New York and Philadelphia. Travellers along the road between these two cities admired the Jersey apple orchards, the well-cultivated farms, and, at the pleasant village of Princeton, the College of New Jersey whose Nassau Hall, 180 feet long and four stories high, was reputed to be the largest building in the Thirteen States. At the falls of the Passaic river, near Newark, an incorporated company had just founded Paterson, the first factory village in America. South of this main road was a region of pine barrens and malarial marshes.

Pennsylvania, the second largest state in the Union, with a population of 435,000, had acquired a certain uniformity in diversity. Her racial heterogeneity, democratic polity, and social structure, ranging from wealthy and sophisticated merchants to the wildest frontiersmen, made Pennsylvania a microcosm of the America to be. Philadelphia, with its evenly spaced and numbered streets crossing at right angles, had been the principal port of immigration for a century previous to 1825; and the boat-shaped Conestoga wagons of the Pennsylvania Dutch needed but slight improvement to become the 'prairie schooner' of westward advance.

Pennsylvania was still in the throes of democratic experiments. Her radical state constitution, with a unicameral legislature and a plural executive, had become notoriously factious and incompetent. In 1790 a new constitution with a bicameral legislature was adopted, but manhood suffrage was retained; and this laid a firm foundation for subsequent democratization of Pennsylvania.

Philadelphia, admirably situated at the junction of the Delaware and Schuylkill rivers, and with a population of forty-five thousand in 1790, was easily the first city in the United States for commerce, architecture, and culture. During the next ten years it was the seat of the Federal Government and of a more brilliant republican court than the city of Washington was to show for a century to come. Owing largely to Quaker influence, Philadelphia was well provided with penal and charitable institutions, amateur scientists and budding literati. It was 'by Delaware's green banks' that Tom Moore in 1804 found Dennie and Ingersoll and Brockden Brown, but for whom

> Columbia's days were done,
> Rank without ripeness, quickened without sun.

These 'sacred few' were producing pallid imitations of the *Spectator,* dreary tragedies of medieval Europe, novels of mystery and horror; ignoring the rich color and wilderness flavor of youthful Pennsylvania.

A few miles from Philadelphia one reached the garden spot of eighteenth-century America, a belt of rich limestone soil that crossed the Susquehanna river, and extended into Maryland and the Valley of Virginia. The fortunate inhabitants of this region were reaping huge profits in 1790 by reason of the European crop failures of 1789; and were to prosper still more through the wars that flowed from the French Revolution. 'The whole country is well cultivated,' wrote a Dutch financier who passed through this region in 1794, 'and what forests the farmers keep are stocked with trees of the right kind — chestnut, locust, walnut, maple, white oak. It is a succession of hills, not too high, and the aspect of the country is very beautiful.' Lancaster, with four thousand inhabitants, was the largest inland town in the United States. Here and in the limestone belt, the bulk of the farmers and townspeople were German. They were by far the best husbandmen in America, using a proper rotation, with clover and root crops. Their houses were commonly of stone, and heated by stoves; their fences of stout posts and rails; but what most impressed strangers were the great barns, with huge gable-end doors, through which a loaded wagon could drive onto a wide threshing-floor, flanked by spacious hay-lofts, cattle and sheep pens, and horse stables. The Germans were divided into a number of sects, some of which, like the Amish Mennonites, have retained their quaint costumes and puritanism into the twentieth century. They supported six weekly newspapers in their own language, and were as keen household manufacturers as the Yankees; but Chastellux found them lacking in public spirit, compared with the English-speaking Americans, 'content . . . with being only the spectators of their own wealth,' and with the standards of a German peasant.

Lancaster was the parting point for two streams of westward emigration. One wagon road took a southwesterly direction, crossed the Potomac at Harper's Ferry, and entered the Shenandoah valley of Virginia, between the Blue Ridge and the Unakas. The Pittsburgh wagon road struck out northwesterly, crossed the Susquehanna by ford or ferry at Harrisburg (the future capital of Pennsylvania), and followed the beautiful wooded valley of the Juniata to its headwaters. This region was inhabited mainly by Ulstermen, although in the easternmost section they were rapidly being bought out by the more thrifty and land-hungry Germans. North of it, and west of the upper Susquehanna, Pennsylvania was still a mountain-ous virgin forest. After a long, painful pull up the rocky, rutty wagon road, to an elevation of some 2,500 feet, you attained the Alleghany front, an escarpment from which, by a rolling, densely wooded plateau, you descended westward to where the Alleghany and Monongahela rivers come together to form the Ohio. At this point you reached Pittsburgh, a thriving village in the midst of virgin coal and iron deposits, the most important of three inner gateways to the far West. Already fleets of covered wagons were bringing in settlers destined for Kentucky, and goods to be dis-tributed down the mighty valley of the Ohio and Mississippi.

4. *The South*

Twenty-five miles south of Philadelphia the post-road crossed the Mason and Dixon line,[3] an internal boundary that bulks large in American history. Originally drawn to divide Pennsylvania from Delaware and Maryland, in 1790 it was already recognized as the boundary between the farming, or commercial, and the plantation states. From 1804 to 1865 it divided the free and the slave states; and even yet it is the boundary of sentiment between North and South.

Delaware, formerly an autonomous portion of the Penn proprie-tary, was the least populous state of the Union; and apart from the flour-milling regions about Wilmington, a farming community, steadfastly conservative in politics. Maryland, with 320,000 souls, one-third of them slaves, was the northernmost state where slavery was an essential part of the economic system. The old English Catholic families still retained some of the better plantations on both shores of Chesapeake Bay; the Irish Carrolls of Carrollton provided a 'signer,' a United States Senator, and the first Roman Catholic bishop in the United States. Maryland produced the best wheat flour in America, and a variety of tobacco chiefly appreciated by the French. The lowland planters were famous for hospitality, and for the various and delicious methods devised by their black

---

[3] The Mason and Dixon line is the parallel latitude of 39° 43' 26.3" between the southwestern corner of Pennsylvania and the arc of a circle of twelve miles' radius drawn from Newcastle (Delaware) as a center; and along that arc to the Delaware river. It was run in 1763–1767 by two English surveyors named Mason and Dixon, in consequence of Lord Hardwicke's decision, in 1750, of a long-standing controversy between the proprietors of Maryland and Pennsylvania. But there have been interstate controversies about parts of it even in the present century.

cooks for preparing the oysters, soft-shell crabs, terrapin, shad, canvas-back ducks, and other delicacies afforded by Chesapeake Bay. Annapolis, the pleasant and hospitable state capital, had just been made the seat of St. John's College. Later, the town was to be saved from decay by the United States Naval Academy.

Baltimore, a mere village before the War of Independence, was approaching Boston in population. A deep harbor on Chesapeake Bay, water-driven flour mills, and proximity to wheat-growing regions made it the metropolis for an important section of Pennsylvania, in preference to Philadelphia. Baltimore was already famous for belles, one of whom married Napoleon Bonaparte's brother Jerome, and for swift schooners, the Baltimore clippers that made excellent privateers and successful pirates. The Maryland Piedmont was much like the limestone belt of Pennsylvania: a rich rolling grain country tilled by English and German farmers, with the aid of a few slaves. This region, in combination with Baltimore, neutralized the Tidewater aristocracy, and gradually drew Maryland into the social and economic orbit of the Northern states.

From Baltimore a road that long remained the despair of travellers traversed Maryland to Georgetown, just below the Great Falls of the Potomac. Here, at the head of navigation, the City of Washington was being planned. Crossing the river, one entered the Old Dominion, with a population of 748,000, of which forty per cent were slaves.[4]

Virginia is today but a fragment of the imperial domain that was granted to the Virginia Company in 1606; and less than half the size of the state in 1790. Kentucky was lopped off as a separate state of the Union in 1792, and West Virginia in 1863. But even without Kentucky, Virginia was the most populous, proud, and wealthy American commonwealth.

The Tidewater or coastal plain of Virginia, east of the fall line which passes through Washington, Richmond, and Petersburg, consists of a series of long narrow peninsulas separated by the navigable estuaries of the Potomac, Rappahannock, York, and James rivers. There were no towns excepting Portsmouth and Norfolk, and scarcely even a village. County seats were merely a court house, church, and tavern at some convenient cross-roads. Tobacco warehouse-receipts, and bills of exchange on your London merchant, who did your shopping in the metropolis, served as currency. 'Even now,'

---

[4] Not including the 74,000 in Kentucky (17 per cent slaves).

wrote John Randolph in 1813, 'the old folks talk of "going home to England."' But by 1790 the Tidewater had seen its best days. The state capital had been transferred to Richmond, at the falls of the James; only William and Mary College kept Williamsburg alive. Norfolk, not yet recovered from the fire of 1776, was a poor-looking seaport of less than thirty-five hundred people. The forest was reconquering exhausted tobacco fields, the wiser planters were laying down their lands to wheat and grass, and the wisest were emigrating to Kentucky. One of the best plantations of the Virginia Tidewater, Davies Randolph's 'Presqu'ile' at Bermuda Hundred on the James, was described by the Duc de la Rochefoucauld-Liancourt, in 1795. It contained 750 acres, of which 400 were wood and marsh, and 350 were cultivated by eight negroes, two horses, and four oxen. This area was divided into forty-acre fields by the usual Virginia or worm fence, made of split rails, notched near the ends, and intersected in a zigzag pattern in order to dispense with posts. 'No sort of fencing is more expensive or wasteful of timber,' wrote Washington; but those improving farmers who attempted hedges were thwarted by the enterprise of American hogs and cattle. Mr. Randolph used manure on but one of his fields. His system of rotation was corn, oats, wheat, rye, fallow: an improvement over the customary one of corn, wheat, and pasturage, which John Taylor called a scheme of tillage founded in contempt of the earth and terminating in its murder. With a modest average yield of ten to twelve bushels per acre, Presqu'ile brought its owner from $1,800 to $3,500 annually; and he valued the plantation at $20,000. The proportion of labor to acreage was so small that the condition of the land compared 'very indifferently with the most ordinary husbandry of Europe.' Apart from the mansion houses, the appearance of Virginia plantations, with their ill-cultivated fields, straggling fences, and dilapidated negroes' cabins, was slovenly in the extreme. A traveller going south from Pennsylvania looked in vain for tidy agriculture until he reached the rice plantations of South Carolina.

By 1790 the Virginia Piedmont between the fall line and the Blue Ridge, for the most part a fruitful, rolling country, had become the seat of all that was healthy and vigorous in the plantation system; and Richmond, as the principal outlet of the James river valley, was flourishing. Most of the great Virginia statesmen of the revolutionary and early republican eras were either born in this region or grew to manhood in its wilder margins. The 'First Families of Virginia,' a rural aristocracy of native origin, reproduced the high sense of honor and public spirit of the English aristocracy, as well as the amenities of English country life. They frequently combined planting with the practice of law, but left trade to their inferiors, commerce to the agents of British mercantile firms, and navigation to the Yankees. Prepared by private tutors or at schools kept by Scotch clergymen for Princeton or William and Mary, trained to administration by managing their large estates, and to politics by representing their counties in the Virginia Assembly, the planters stepped naturally and gracefully into the leadership of the nation. It was no accident that Jefferson of Virginia drafted the Declaration of Independence, that Washington of Virginia led the army and became the first President, that Madison of Virginia fathered the Federal Constitution, that Marshall of Virginia became the greatest American jurist, and that he and Taylor of Virginia led the two opposing schools of American political thought.

If the proper object of society be to produce and maintain an aristocracy, Virginia had achieved it. If it be to maintain a high general level of comfort and intelligence, she had not. Below the 'first families,' but continually pushing into their level by marriage, was a class of lesser planters, to which Patrick Henry belonged: a class generous and hospitable, but uneducated, provincial, and rude. Below them was an unstable and uneasy class of yeomen, outnumbering the planters in the Piedmont. Descended largely from indentured servants and deported convicts, these peasants, as the gentry called them, were illiterate, ferocious, and quarrelsome. Self-contained plantations, with slave artisans and mechanics, left small demand for skilled white labor, and made small farms unprofitable. Hence the Virginia yeoman had but the alternative of migrating westward, or of becoming 'poor white trash' despised even by the slaves. It was already doubtful in 1790 that any community could endure half slave and half free; presently it would be doubtful if the nation could thus endure.

In the lowlands the slaves outnumbered the whites; in the Piedmont they comprised about one-third of the total population. They supported the economic system, and contributed much to the quality of Virginia leadership. Jefferson's oft-quoted passage, that 'the whole commerce between master and slave is a perpetual exercise of the most boisterous passions,' can only have applied to new and inexperienced members of the planter class; for the successful management of Negroes required tact, patience, forbearance, an even temper, and a sense of humor. Few denied that slavery was a moral evil and a menace to the country. Almost every educated Virginian hoped to make real the opening words of his Bill of Rights ' that all men are by nature free and independent.' But a state whose population was forty per cent black naturally quailed before such a social revolution. Jefferson counted on the young abolitionists that Chancellor Wythe was making in William and Mary College. But in a few years' time the cotton gin gave chattel slavery a new lease of life; and, shortly after Jefferson died, a young professor of William and Mary began to preach the doctrine that Negro slavery was justified by history and ordained by God.

As one rode westward across the Virginia Piedmont, with the crest-line of the Blue Ridge looming in the distance, the forest became more dense, the large plantations less numerous, the farms of independent yeomen more frequent, and the cultivation of tobacco gave place to corn and grazing. Between the Blue Ridge and the higher folds of the Appalachians lies the Shenandoah valley peopled as we have seen by Scotch and Germans, and feeling itself a province apart from lowland and Piedmont until 1861. It was here, in Rockingham county, that Abraham Lincoln, grandfather of the President, lived until 1784; and at Staunton in Augusta county, Woodrow Wilson was born in 1856. Still less did the trans-Appalachian part of Virginia, a densely wooded plateau sloping to the upper Ohio, resemble the Virginia of the planters. In 1790 it was a frontier more primitive even than Kentucky. In 1861 it refused to follow the Old Dominion out of the Union, and became the State of West Virginia.

South from Petersburg in Virginia, through a level, sandy country of pine forest, a two days' journey took you to Halifax, one of several petty seaports of North Carolina. This ' tar-heel state ' possessed a very different character from her neighbors on either side. Her population was the result of two distinct streams of secondary and fairly recent colonization: Virginia yeomen who settled in the coastal plain, outpouring from the Shenandoah valley into the Piedmont and the Great Smoky mountains. Along the Roanoke river there was an overflow of plantations from Virginia; but the greater part of the coastal plain, a hundred miles or more wide, consisted of pine barrens with soil too sandy for wheat or tobacco, and extensive marshes like the Dismal Swamp. The river mouths were landlocked against vessels drawing above ten feet by the barrier beaches that enclosed Pamlico and Albemarle Sounds. This region, therefore, was sparsely settled, and its chief exports were naval stores: tar, turpentine, and pine timber. President Washington, travelling through it in 1791, found it 'the most barren country he ever beheld,' without 'a single house of an elegant appearance.'

The Piedmont of North Carolina was a thriving region of upland farms, supporting a large population of Germans, Ulstermen, English, and Highland Scotch. There was little communication between coast and Piedmont through the pine barrens, and less sympathy. Petersburg, Va., and Charleston, S. C., were nearer or more convenient markets for the upland farmers than the petty ports of their own state. Local particularism was so strong that the legislature abandoned Governor Tryon's 'palace' at Newbern, and became peripatetic. Only by creating a new state capital, at Raleigh on the falls of the Neuse river, could it manage to settle down.

The plantation system never obtained a strong foothold in North Carolina; the state remained a farming democracy, aided by rather than based upon chattel slavery. Among its white population of three hundred thousand in 1790, less than one-third owned slaves; and the proportion was even smaller in 1860.[5] For such a community a democratic policy was natural and inevitable; but without the leaven of popular education, a landlocked region was not apt to make much progress. Honest mediocrity was typical of North Carolina statesmanship from the eighteenth century to the twentieth, when the industrial revolution brought wealth, material progress, enthusiasm for learning, and accomplishment in the arts.

There was no such dearth of great figures, as we have seen, in South Carolina. The coastal plain of that state has a sub-tropical climate. In Charleston, its only city, the ravages of war were quickly repaired and the gay old life was resumed; in 1790, with a population of sixteen thousand, it was the fourth city in America, and metropolis of the lower South.[6] The Rev. Jedidiah Morse in his *American Geography* (1789) wrote, 'In no part of America are the

[5] With a total population of 400,000 in 1790 (one-quarter slave), North Carolina was the fourth state in the Union, just ahead of New York. But North Carolina's interior had already been settled, and New York's had not. New York reached the million mark in 1810; North Carolina only in 1870; in 1920 North Carolina had three million to New York's twelve and a half; and its largest city fell short of a hundred thousand.

[6] In 1930 Charleston had only 62,265 inhabitants, but more distinction and flavor than any one of the hundred American cities that exceeded it in size.

social blessings enjoyed more rationally and liberally than in Charleston. Unaffected hospitality, affability, ease in manners and address, and a disposition to make their guests welcome, easy and pleased with themselves, are characteristics of the respectable people of Charleston.' One can well imagine that stiff New England Calvinist succumbing to the graceful attentions of a Charleston family, while he sipped their Madeira wine on a spacious verandah overlooking a tropical garden.

The South Carolina planters went to their country houses in November, when the first frosts removed the danger of fever; and took their families back to Charleston for the gay season from January to March. Early spring, a most anxious period in rice culture, was passed in the plantation mansion — shaded by a classic portico, and surrounded by groves of live oaks, hung with Spanish moss. The hot months would be spent at a summer house in the pine hills, or at Newport. Popular education was little attended to, but the College of Charleston was established in 1785, and the more opulent families continued to send their sons to Old England or New England for higher education.

Rice, the economic basis of the lower country, required intensive cultivation, along such parts of the tidal rivers as permitted artificial flooding with fresh water. These regions were so unhealthy for white people that black labor, immune from malaria, was a necessity; and in no part of the United States were slaves so numerous. Out of sixteen hundred heads of families in the rural part of the Charleston district, in 1790, thirteen hundred held slaves to the number of forty-three thousand. South Carolina not only blocked abolition of the African slave trade in the Federal Constitution, but reopened traffic by state law in 1803.

Indigo culture had been abandoned with the loss of the Parliamentary bounty; but the South Carolina planters, in 1790, were experimenting with the long staple sea-island cotton; and the next year Robert Owen spun into yarn the first two bags of it that were sent to England. The short staple upland cotton, which could be grown inland, was so difficult to separate from its seed as to be unmarketable until after the cotton gin was invented in 1793. One effect of this momentous discovery was to extend the plantation system into the Piedmont, the more populous section. In 1790 the upland people had just won their first victory by transferring the state capital up-country, to Columbia; but the Piedmont was still under-represented in the legislature, and poor men were denied office by high property qualifications. John C. Calhoun, who was destined to weld the South and divide the Union, was a boy of eight in the upper country, in 1790.

Across the Savannah river from South Carolina lay Georgia, which retained few traces of General Oglethorpe's pious experiment. The objects of his benevolence, poor debtors and Scotch highlanders, wedged between hostile Indians on one side and a plantation colony on the other, had led a miserable existence. As soon as the prohibition of rum, slaves, and large holdings was removed, Georgia developed, as had South Carolina, a slave-holding rice coast, a belt of infertile pine barrens, and a rolling, wooded Piedmont of hunters and frontier farmers, who racially belonged to the usual Southern mixed upland stock. These Georgia 'crackers' were vigorous and lawless, hard drinkers and dirty fighters. Desperately eager to despoil the Creek Indians of their fertile cornfields across the Oconee river, the up-country Georgians gave constant trouble to the Federal Government.

5. 'America the Hope of the World'

Such, in their broader outlines, were the Thirteen States, and the people thereof, seven years after the war. They were singularly fortunate and happy. Of such a people, so circumstanced, the friends of liberty in Europe had high expectations. The French statesman Turgot wrote in his famous letter of 1778 to Dr. Price:

This people is the hope of the human race. It may become the model. It ought to show the world by facts, that men can be free and yet peaceful, and may dispense with the chains in which tyrants and knaves of every colour have presumed to bind them, under pretext of the public good. The Americans should be an example of political, religious, commercial and industrial liberty. The asylum they offer to the oppressed of every nation, the avenue of escape they open, will compel governments to be just and enlightened; and the rest of the world in due time will see through the empty illusions in which policy is conceived. But to obtain these ends for us, America must secure them to herself; and must not become, as so many of your ministerial writers have predicted, a mass of divided powers, contending for territory and trade, cementing the slavery of peoples by their own blood.

Dr. Price printed Turgot's letter in 1785, together with some hundred pages of his own advice to the young republic. Slavery must

be abolished. America must adopt a system of education that will
' teach *how* to think, rather than *what* to think, or to lead into the
best way of searching for truth, rather than to instruct in truth itself.'
The American States should foster an equal distribution of property;
and to this end they must renounce foreign trade, as well as foreign
alliances.

The Atlantic must be crossed before they can be attacked. . . . Thus
singularly happy, why should they seek connexions with Europe, and
expose themselves to the danger of being involved in its quarrels? —
What have they to do with its politics? — Is there anything very important to them which they can draw from thence — except *infection?*
— indeed, I tremble when I think of that rage for trade which is likely
to prevail among them.

Here is the policy of isolation, laid down in terms that America
found too Spartan; and something more than a suggestion of the
political system later known as Jeffersonian democracy. But there
was one dominant force in United States history that no one foresaw
in 1785: the expansive force. With such a prize as the West at their
back doors, the people of the United States would have been more
than human had they been content with a ' state of nature ' between
the Atlantic and the Appalachians. For a century to come, the sub-
duing of the temperate regions of North America to the purposes
of civilized life was to be the main business of the United States. In
1790 the boundaries of the republic included eight hundred thousand,
in 1860 three million square miles. In 1790 the population was four
million; in 1930 one hundred and twenty-two million. This folk
movement, comparable only with the barbaric invasions of Europe,
gives the history of the United States a different quality from that of
modern Europe; different even from that of Canada and Australia,
by reason of the absence of exterior control. The advancing frontier,
with growing industrialism, set the rhythm of American society,
colored its politics, and rendered more difficult the problem of union.
Yet, as Turgot warned us, only union could secure the gain and
fulfil the promise of the American Revolution.

Thomas Bland Hollis, another English radical who looked to the
rising star in the West, wrote to the President of Harvard College
in 1788: 'Our papers mention that there is an intention of having
the Olympic games revived in America. All her friends wish it and
say she is capable of it: having acted upon Greek principles you

should have Greek exercises.' Her friends saw no reason why literature and the arts should not spring into new life in a new world, fostered by liberty. One of them, ten years later, recorded with his disappointment the popular excuse: 'We are but a young people — let us grow.' How often has that excuse been repeated, and how constantly has it been true! Grow they did; but not as Rome, neither as Greece. Their astounding expansion was a continuous adventure in pioneering, a constant renewal of the nation's youth through fresh contact with a receding frontier. The American of today, with all his wealth, pride, and power, is still unmistakably young and inexperienced in the ways of the world that he is now called upon to set right for the second time in one generation.

The frontier has vanished with the wild Indian, and America's youth is waning fast. Some thought, during the great depression, that it had altogether gone, and that a premature old age was settling over American society. They were wrong. It is the story of a youthful people that you are to read; of a people constantly in movement, expanding and upheaving, blithely accepting new forces that were to strain their body politic, seeking to assimilate them to the democratic principle and to recover equilibrium between liberty and order, or security. And, as we write, America, with all the confidence and idealism of youth, is organizing her power as never before in a mighty offensive against the gangster nations who would strike her down. Possibly that effort will destroy her youthfulness forever. We believe not; and that, on the contrary, the faith and energy of the United States are still, in an even deeper sense than in 1778, 'the hope of the human race.'

XV

ORGANIZING A GOVERNMENT
1789–1792

1. *The Prospect*

W ITH their new constitution the Americans challenged their own future. It remained to be seen whether a federal and republican government was workable on such a scale, whether local interests would not choke national sentiment, whether the political fabric had the strength to withstand war, or the elasticity for social and territorial growth.

The prospect seemed fair enough, outwardly, on that bright morning of 30 April 1789, when Washington, a picture of splendid manhood, stepped out onto the balcony overlooking Wall Street, New York, and took the oath: 'I do solemnly swear that I will faithfully execute the office of President of the United States and will, to the best of my ability, preserve, protect, and defend the Constitution of the United States.' A clean, new ship of state, under the old, tried master: what more could the patriot desire? Yet many of the commissioned officers were filled with anxious forbodings, and the master himself, on setting out from Mount Vernon to take command, wrote to his future Secretary of War:

My movements to the chair of government will be accompanied by feelings not unlike those of a culprit, who is going to the place of his execution; so unwilling am I, in the evening of a life nearly consumed in public cares, to quit a peaceful abode for an ocean of difficulties, without that competency of political skill, abilities, and inclination, which are necessary to manage the helm. I am sensible that I am embarking the voice of the people, and a good name of my own, on this voyage; but what returns will be made for them, Heaven alone can foretell. Integrity and firmness are all I can promise. These, be the voyage long or short, shall never forsake me, although I may be deserted by all men.

Let us consider the state of the country in 1789, and the nature of Washington's task. The new Constitution possessed neither tradition nor the backing of organized public opinion. The new government had to create its own machinery. Every revolutionary government of Europe has taken over a corps of functionaries, an administrative system, and a treasury: the American Confederation left nothing but a dozen clerks with their pay in arrears, an empty treasury, and a burden of debt. There were no taxes or requisitions coming in, and no machinery for collecting taxes existed. The new Congress quickly imposed a customs tariff; but months elapsed before an administration could be created to collect it, in a loose-jointed country two thousand miles long. Until a federal judiciary could be established, there was no means of enforcing any law. The country itself was just beginning to experience the return of prosperity; but free capital was exceedingly scarce, and Washington, reputed the wealthiest of Americans, had to borrow £600 from a friend in order to meet the expense of his removal to New York. England and Spain, as we have seen, controlled spheres of influence on United States territory. A secession movement in the West threatened to split the Union along the crest of the Appalachians. The American army consisted of 672 officers and men; the navy had ceased to exist.

Yet, there were saving elements in the situation. In 1789 economic conditions were vastly improved over the panic year of 1786; and by 1790 a time of easy money had returned. Virginia and the Carolinas had recovered their pre-war volume of exports in tobacco, naval stores, and rice. Poor crops in France gave a better market for the grain of the Middle States. The West India trade, mainstay of New England, was doing service once more by 1789. Jamaicans and Barbadians, hampered by the British regulations that lessened their supply of provisions from the Northern states, were helping Yankee shipmasters to smuggle. New markets had been discovered. Northern shipowners, with specie borrowed from English merchant-bankers, were driving a roaring trade in Calcutta and Canton, where the number of American entries, in 1789, was second only to those flying the British flag. All this had been effected by good fortune, enterprise, and individual energy, before the new government came into operation; but the Federalists were quick to claim credit for the tide on which their ship was launched.

The Federal Government could count on a good press, and a favorably expectant public opinion. Not that there was any enthusiasm for the Constitution, even among its advocates. Washington, indeed, considered it a hopeful experiment, and Madison was pleased with what was chiefly his handiwork; but Hamilton, in his more cheerful moments, regarded it as a makeshift; and, in bad humor, as a 'frail and worthless fabric.' John Adams believed it would not outlast himself. Every Federalist, however, was determined to do his best for the Constitution, as the sole alternative to anarchy; and the same attitude, to their lasting credit, was taken by the Anti-federalists. Patrick Henry declared, when he recognized his defeat in the Virginia ratifying convention: 'I will be a peaceable citizen. My head, my hand, and my heart, shall be at liberty to retrieve the loss of liberty, and remove the defects of that system in a constitutional way.' His party throughout the union showed the same fine spirit of fair play. Consequently there was no organized, irreconcilable party, or even important man, committed to overthrowing the Constitution, however people and parties might differ as to its interpretation. The United States had no Bourbon pretenders or Trotskyites, no would-be Hitlers or Mussolinis. English-speaking people had long ago worked that sort of thing out of their systems.

A federal bill of rights, promptly passed by Congress and ratified by the states, quieted some honest fears of tyranny; but the Anti-federalist type of mind persisted. The habit of considering a government dangerous in direct ratio to its effectiveness was too ingrained to disappear in a decade, or even in a century. Less than three years elapsed before many of the Anti-federalists were again found in opposition; but it was a constitutional opposition.

Washington accepted the Presidency with great reluctance. It had been his hope and wish to spend the remainder of his days at Mount Vernon as a scientific farmer, improving American husbandry by experiment and example. Washington studied the best works on the subject, corresponded with English experts such as Arthur Young, imported improved implements, and applied new methods. Tobacco culture, which had exhausted the soil of Tidewater Virginia, was relinquished at Mount Vernon as early as 1765. Wheat, flax, and root crops were substituted for corn, pasturage was increased, a five-year rotation of crops adopted, and sheep folded on turnips or clover.

Mount Vernon, unlike the modern ' gentleman's country estate ' that is supported by income from other sources, supported its proprietor; and Washington's relation to it was more like that of an industrial manager to his plant. Washington inherited an estate of 2500 acres and added about 5500 more, until Mount Vernon stretched ten miles along the broad Potomac. The 3500 acres under cultivation around 1790 were divided by tracts of woodland into separate farms, each with its own force of slaves and an overseer, who must report weekly how he had employed every hand. There were great wooden barns, with cow stables and spacious threshing-floors. The pastures, enclosed by worm fences, produced a thin, poor turf in that land of hot, dry summers. Brood-mares and blooded stallions occupied the best watered of them. Royal Gift, a fifteen-hand jackass presented by the King of Spain, had a special paddock and groom, as befitted the ancestor of the American army mule. The cattle were undersized and of low breed; the hogs ran at large through the woodlands, affording illicit sport for a pack of French boar-hounds, an unwelcome gift from Lafayette.

Mount Vernon was an industrial as well as an agricultural unit. There were slave blacksmiths, carpenters, and even bricklayers; a cider press and a still-house, where excellent rye and Bourbon whisky were made, and sold in barrels made by plantation Negroes from home-grown oak. Herring and shad fisheries in the Potomac provided food for the slaves; a grist-mill turned Washington's improved strain of wheat into the finest grade of flour, which was taken to market in his own schooner. There was a weaving-shed, where a dozen different textiles were produced from local wool and flax, and West India cotton. Picture Washington rising at sunrise, break-fasting at seven, and superintending from the saddle the work on his several farms, frequently dismounting and stripping his coat to demonstrate with his strong back and large, capable hands how things should be done. His good lady, in the meantime, would be directing the work of a large force of household slaves, and helping to cut and piece home-woven cloth for the Negroes. Dinner at three ended the day's work in the field; but there were usually accounts and problems enough to occupy the master until supper.

For recreation there was fox-hunting with his own and his neigh-bors' packs; taking toll of the great flights of wild duck, goose, and pigeon; dancing assemblies at Alexandria. A constant stream of rela-tions and friends flowed through the mansion house, few distin-guished travelers came South unprovided with a letter to the great man, and no gentleman could be turned away from his door. The guests, in fact, ate up most of the increase not consumed by the slaves, whose children Washington was too humane to sell away from their parents.

This was the life that Washington loved, and in which he hoped to spend his declining years. No detail was too small for his atten-tion, no slave too humble to attract his interest, no blight too devas-tating to command his patience. Even on his campaigns, and in the

Presidency, he would write sixteen-page letters of instruction to his overseers; and one suspects that, like Sir Robert Walpole, he read their reports before he turned to the affairs of state. 'The more I am acquainted with agricultural affairs, the better I am pleased with them,' he wrote to Arthur Young in 1788. 'How much more delightful . . . is the task of making improvements in the earth than all the vain glory which can be acquired from ravaging it by the most uninterrupted career of conquests.'

The qualities that made Washington the first farmer and the first soldier in America also made him the first statesman. As landed proprietor no less than as commander-in-chief, he had shown executive ability, the power of planning for a distant end, and a capacity for taking infinite pains. Neither drought nor defeat, nor, as it proved, political abuse, could turn him from a course that he discerned to be proper and right. In describing himself as one who inherited 'inferior endowments from nature,' Washington was too modest; but we shall underestimate the difficulties of his task if we forget that his superiority lay in character, not in talents. He had the power of inspiring respect and trust, but not the gift of popularity; directness but not adroitness; fortitude rather than flexibility; the power to think things through, not quick perception; a natural presence and dignity, but none of that brisk assertiveness that has often given inferior men greater political influence. The mask of dignity and reserve that concealed his inner life came from shyness, humility, and stoical self-control. A warm heart was revealed in numerous kindly acts to his dependents and subordinates. And beneath the cool surface of him there glowed a fire that under provocation would burst forth in immoderate laughter, astounding oaths, or Olympian anger.

2. *The First Presidential Administration*

The Federal Government was not only limited in scope, but hampered within its proper sphere by 'checks and balances.' Yet, however anxious the 'Fathers' might be to prevent bad legislation, their chief point in establishing a new constitution was to enable the nation to get things done. For this, not only ample federal powers, but leadership was necessary; and leadership in policy was expected to be one of the functions of the President. It was impossible to write this desire into the Constitution itself. An attempt to define the Presidency as either Roosevelt administered it would have been considered plain tyranny in 1788. The Presidency was left purposely vague in its relation to Congress, and with such executive departments as Congress might establish. Hence the personality of the first President would go far to determine the scope of his office.

It was here that Washington's character and prestige counted heavily. The heads of departments had to be appointed by the President with the consent of the Senate. But Congress, according to colonial usage, might have made them responsible to itself, and removable by the Senate. Instead, it made the Secretaries of State and of War responsible to the President alone, and subject to his direction within their legal competence. Moreover, when the first question of dismissal from office came up, the Senate admitted that the President could remove officials without its consent. The effect of this precedent was to make the entire administrative force and diplomatic service responsible to the chief magistrate.

For heads of the State, War, and Treasury departments, there was not a large field of choice, as the Confederation had given small scope for civil administration. As Secretary of State someone with diplomatic experience was needed. The only available candidate was Thomas Jefferson, then minister to France. Robert Morris suggested Alexander Hamilton for the Treasury, which fell in perfectly with Washington's inclinations. Henry Knox, Washington's chief of artillery, was given the War Department, and Edmund Randolph, whose term as governor of Virginia had expired, was appointed Attorney-General.

The making of minor appointments turned out to be, as Washington feared, the 'most difficult and delicate part' of his duty. He deemed it necessary to reward war service, to conciliate factions, and to avoid any suspicion of personal or sectional partiality. Washington scrutinized applications most conscientiously, asking the advice of senators and representatives from the applicant's state, and sought out able men where none applied. The federal civil service began with principles of efficiency and honesty that were in sharp contrast to the jobbery and corruption in contemporary European governments, and in several of the state governments.

A Vice-President was created by the Federal Constitution in order to provide an acting chief magistrate in the event of the death or disability of the President, without the need of a special election. In order to give him some regular occupation, he was made President of the Senate, with a casting vote in case of tie. John Adams, the first Vice-President, regarded his office as 'the most insignificant . . . that ever invention of man contrived, or his imagination conceived.' Adams suffered all his life from the notion that he was not properly appreciated. A sound political scientist, and a useful drafter of state constitutions, he had a foible for titles and ceremonies. But his efforts to introduce the elaborate ceremonial of the British Parliament met with no success. Senator Maclay of Pennsylvania was shocked at Adams's reference to the President's inaugural address as 'His Most Gracious Speech,' and reminded the Senate that the removal of royal trappings was an object of the Revolution. The Vice-President was offended. Rising from his chair he declared 'that he was for a dignified and respectable government,' and that if he had suspected we should ever come to this, 'he never would have drawn his sword.' Outbursts of this sort prevented more than one summons to a cabinet meeting being issued to John Adams.

Although most of the first senators were friends to the administration, their chamber early developed that *esprit de corps* which has been the bane of wilful presidents. 'Senatorial courtesy,' the practice of rejecting any nomination not approved by the senators from the nominee's own state, soon began. In the matter of treaties, however, the Senate's sense of its own dignity defeated its ambition. The Constitution grants the President power, 'by and with the advice and consent of the Senate, to make treaties, provided two-thirds of the senators present concur.' On one memorable occasion Washington appeared before the Senate, like the Secretary for Foreign Affairs in the House of Commons, to explain an Indian treaty and see it through. Hampered in freedom of debate by the august presence, the senators voted to refer the papers in question to a select committee. The President 'started up in a violent fret.' 'This defeats every purpose of my coming here,' he said. After that he dispensed with advice until a treaty was ready for ratification. This practice has generally been followed by his successors.

'Impressed with a conviction that the due administration of justice is the firmest pillar of good government,' wrote Washington in 1789, 'I have considered the first arrangement of the judicial department as essential to the happiness of our country and the stability of its political system.' The Constitution left this branch of government as inchoate as the others. The scope of federal judicial power was defined, the mode of appointing judges was determined, and their tenure fixed during good behavior. But it remained for Congress to create and organize the inferior federal courts, to determine their procedure, and to provide a bridge between state and federal jurisdiction. All this was done by the Judiciary Act of 24 September 1789, the essential part of which is still in force. It provided for a Supreme Court consisting of a chief justice and five associate justices, for thirteen district courts consisting of a single federal judge, and three intermediate circuit courts consisting of the district judges included in that circuit, together with two Supreme Court justices. Procedure, powers, and respective jurisdictions are worked out in great detail. The procedure for judicial review, and the problem of getting cases that involve jurisdictional disputes out of state courts and into federal courts, in order that the Constitution, laws, and treaties of the United States might indeed be 'the supreme law of the land,' was solved in the twenty-fifth section of this law. A final judgment in the highest court of a state

where is drawn in question the validity of a treaty or statute of, or an authority exercised under the United States, and the decision is against their validity; or where is drawn in question the validity of a statute of, or an authority exercised under any state, on the ground of their being repugnant to the Constitution, treaties or laws of the United States, and the decision is in favour of such their validity, . . . may be re-examined and reversed or affirmed in the Supreme Court of the United States upon a writ of error, . . .

This section is quite as essential to the smooth working of the federal system as the Constitution itself. Without it, every state judiciary could put its own construction on the Constitution, laws, and treaties of the Union. With it, a case involving any of these three factors may originate either in the state or the lower federal courts; but its final determination belongs to the Supreme Court of the United States.

John Jay was appointed Chief Justice by Washington; and on 2 February 1790 the Supreme Court began its first session, at New York. The judges assumed gowns of black and scarlet, but honored Jefferson's appeal to 'discard the monstrous wig which makes the English judges look like rats peeping through bunches of oakum.' Under Chief Justice Jay the federal judiciary assumed its place as the keystone to the federal arch. As early as 1791, in a case involving British debts, one of the circuit courts declared invalid a law of Connecticut which infringed Article VI of the treaty of peace. In 1792 a state law of Rhode Island was held unconstitutional, as impairing the obligation of contracts. The same year another circuit court, in the first Hayburn case, refused to execute an act of Congress requiring the federal courts to pass on pension claims, on the ground that this was a non-judicial function, beyond the constitutional power of Congress to impose, or of the courts to assert. Thus the power of judicial review over both state and federal legislation was asserted during Washington's first administration. Later, when party and sectional interests perceived the implications of it, judicial review was vehemently attacked behind the cover of state rights and democracy; but in the early years of the republic it went almost unchallenged.

Washington was unwilling to come to any vital decision without taking the advice of people in whom he had confidence. Thence came the American cabinet, a body different in origin and in functions from the British cabinet. There had been much talk in the Federal Convention of providing the President with a privy council, but the project was not developed. The Senate was given a check on the appointing and treaty-making powers, but it was expected that the President would call upon such heads of departments as Congress might create, for informal consultation. That is exactly what he did. In 1793 we find some forty-six meetings of the three secretaries and the Attorney-General at the President's house. These officials were already known collectively as the President's cabinet; but not until 1907 was the cabinet officially recognized as such by law.

This lack of co-ordination between executive and legislature is one of the distinctive and less useful features of American government. Colonial in its origin, the practice received the sanction of theory from Montesquieu, and of experience as a reaction from George III's close relations with an unreformed House of Commons. The Federal Constitution guarded against executive control through 'placemen' by disqualifying civil or military officials for membership in either house; and by forbidding the appointment of members during the term of their election to an office created, or given increased salary, during that term. There was nothing, however, to prevent a cabinet official appearing in person before either house. The clause requiring the President to recommend measures to Congress reflected a desire that the executive should take the lead in legislation.

Washington had not the temperament to do this alone. He wanted some young and energetic man to give the impulse, and attend to his relations with the legislature. Fortunately the right man, Alexander Hamilton, was in the right office, the Treasury. For the primary problems of Washington's first administration were fiscal.

3. Alexander Hamilton

If the character of Washington fortified the new government, the genius of Hamilton enabled it to function successfully. As Henry Adams wrote, he ' had at once the breadth of mind to grapple with the machine of government as a whole,' the practical knowledge to find ways and means, and ' the good fortune to enjoy power when government was still plastic and capable of receiving a new impulse.'

Alexander Hamilton was thirty-two years old in 1789 when Washington appointed him Secretary of the Treasury. No American equalled him in administrative genius; few surpassed him in maturity of judgment. As an undergraduate of seventeen at King's (Columbia) College he had brilliantly defended the rights of the colonists. At twenty he had earned a place on Washington's staff. In his twenty-fifth year he indicated the fatal defects of the Confederation, wrote a remarkable treatise on public finance, and commanded the storming party at Yorktown. Admitted to the New York bar at the conclusion of peace, he quickly rose to eminence in the law. With Madison he dominated the convention at Annapolis; in the Federal Convention he played a spectacular though hardly a useful part. His contributions to *The Federalist* helped to obtain the ratification of a constitution in which he did not strongly believe. One of the greatest of Americans, he was the least American of his contemporaries: a statesman rather of the type of Colbert, whose innate love of order and system was strengthened by the lack of those qualities among his slack, turbulent, and suspicious fellow citizens. Intellectually disciplined himself, Hamilton was eager to play political schoolmaster. He had bold plans and definite policies where others had cautious notions and vague principles. When Congress was thinking of what the people would say, Hamilton told them and the people what they ought to do.

The Treasury Department was the creation of Congress, not of the Constitution; and the organic Act of 1789, still in force, was framed with the intent of making the Secretary responsible to the House. Fortunately the same members who feared executive power also disliked select committees. Hence all financial questions, even routine matters such as petitions, were referred to the Secretary of the Treasury. Hamilton, quick to perceive the opening, acquired a quasi-ministerial lead in legislation, which might have developed into a parliamentary system had he possessed more tact and patience. On his retirement in 1795, the House seized the opportunity to create a ways and means committee, which gradually assumed the initiative in questions of supply. It is only in the twentieth century that a director of the budget has to some extent bridged the gap.

Hamilton's financial policy was determined by his conception of the governmental problem in 1789; and that, in turn, by his political philosophy. The key may be found in his speeches in the Federal Convention:

Take mankind as they are, and what are they governed by? Their passions. . . . One great error is that we suppose mankind more honest than they are. Our prevailing passions are ambition and interest; and it will ever be the duty of a wise government to avail itself of those passions in order to make them subservient to the public good. . . . All communities divide themselves into the few and the many. The first are the rich and well-born; the other the mass of the people . . . turbulent and changing, they seldom judge or determine right. Give therefore to the first class a distinct, permanent share in the Government.

The Federal Constitution, he believed, could only be made an instrument for good and a guarantee of order by ' increasing the number of ligaments between the government and interests of individuals.' The old families, merchant-shipowners, public creditors, and financiers — in other words the Federalists who had procured the Constitution — must be welded into a loyal governing class, by a straightforward policy favoring their interests. That was the object of Hamilton's domestic and foreign policy. He proposed to use the Federal Government to enrich a class, in order that this class might strengthen the Federal Government. Instead of his political policy having an economic object, his economic policy had a political object. As Thomas Cromwell fortified the Tudor monarchy by distributing confiscated land, and as Bonaparte promoted his own fortune by the Concordat, so Hamilton would clothe the Constitution with the sword of sovereignty and the armor of loyalty, by giving definite individuals a distinct interest in its permanence.

In September 1789, ten days after he took office, the House of Representatives called upon Hamilton to prepare and report a plan for the ' adequate support of public credit.' The report was laid before the House at its next session, on 14 January 1790. Based on the tried expedients of English finance, it was worthy of an experienced minister of a long-established government.

Hamilton first laid down principles of public economy, and then adduced arguments in support of them. America must have credit for industrial development, and commercial activity, and the operations of government. Her future credit would depend on how she met her present obligations. The United States debt, foreign and domestic,

was the price of liberty. The faith of America has been repeatedly pledged for it. . . . Among ourselves, the most enlightened friends of good government are those whose expectations [of prompt payment] are the highest. To justify and preserve their confidence; to promote the increasing respectability of the American name; to answer the calls of justice; to restore landed property to its due value; to furnish new resources, both to agriculture and commerce; to cement more closely the Union of the States; to add to their security against foreign attack; to establish public order on the basis of an upright and liberal policy; these are the great and invaluable ends to be secured by a proper and adequate provision, at the present period, for the support of public credit.

Precise recommendations of ways and means ensued. The foreign debt and floating domestic debt, with arrears of interest, should be funded at par, and due provision should be made by import duties and excise taxes to provide interest and amortization. The war debts of the states should be assumed by the Federal Government in order to bind their creditors to the national interest. A sinking fund should be created in order to stabilize the price of government securities and prepare for repayment of the principal. The want of banking facilities should be filled by a Bank of the United States, on the model of the Bank of England, but with the right to establish branches in different parts of the country.

This daring policy could not have been carried out by Hamilton alone. Every proposal was matured by the cool judgment of the President; and in House and Senate he found eager co-operation. Congress passed a customs tariff, with tonnage duties discriminating in favor of American shipping — both essential parts of Hamilton's system — before Hamilton took office; and his other projects were altered and in some respects improved in the process of legislation. The foreign and domestic debt was funded at par, largely through loans from the same Dutch bankers who had tided us over the last years of the war. Most of the debts of the states were assumed by

Congress, after a bitter struggle not unmixed with intrigue. The Bank of the United States was chartered, and its capital subscribed in four hours after the books were open. By August 1791 United States six per cents were selling above par in London and Amsterdam; and a wave of development and speculation had begun.

All Hamilton's immediate plans were adopted. He turned dead paper into marketable securities, and provided for their redemption by taxes that the nation was well able to bear. He set standards of honesty and punctuality that were invaluable for a people of crude financial conceptions. His youthful country, so lately on the verge of bankruptcy, acquired a credit such as few of the nations of Europe enjoyed. Yet Hamilton failed to achieve his ultimate end of consolidating the Union. If he created an interested government party, his measures encountered a dangerous opposition. Instead of attaching new interests to the Federal Government, he endowed with new privileges those who were already attached to it. His measure of financial corn tempted only those horses in the paddock that had tasted corn; when Jefferson turned them out to grass, they threatened to jump the fence into John Bull's cornfield.

4. The Sectional Test

To understand where and why Hamilton failed, we have only to glance at the effect of his measures on two commonwealths: Massachusetts and Virginia. From the earliest colonial times to 1865, these two illustrate the contrast of North and South. Massachusetts was the second state of the Union in population. Her premier interests were maritime; her upper class, composed of shipowning merchants, voted for the new Constitution in the hope of substantial benefits, which Hamilton and Congress accorded. Her fishing villages benefited by the new bounties on dried codfish; her foreign trade benefited by the low tariff, and her shipyards by the tonnage duties favoring American-built vessels. Good business men themselves, the merchants knew the value of sound credit and honest finance. Their war-time gains from privateering and profiteering were largely invested in government paper that gained enormously in value by the funding system. Massachusetts, with the largest war debt of any state, profited most from the assumption of state debts by the Federal Government. Maritime prosperity, percolating from the market towns to the interior, raised the price of country produce, and healed the wounds of Shays's Rebellion. Washington's foreign policy completed the process; and Boston, once the home of radical mobs and loud-mouthed demagogues, became a pocket borough of the new Federalist party. The 'Essex junto' of Massachusetts: Cabots, Higginsons, Lowells, and Jacksons, who had been to sea in their youth and viewed politics as from a quarter-deck, hailed Hamilton as their master, and kept his flag flying in the Bay State long after his death. With them, in general, were the solid men of Rhode Island and Connecticut, of New York City, and the seaports south of it. But the great mass of the American people was untouched, either in imagination or in pocket, by Hamilton's policy. It would have been otherwise had the public debt remained in the hands of its original possessors; but the phenomena incident to falling prices had appeared. Farmers, discharged soldiers, petty shopkeepers, and the like who held government securities representing service rendered, goods supplied, or money advanced during the war, had been forced to part with them at a ruinous discount during the hard times that followed. By 1789 the bulk of the public debt was in the hands of the 'right people' at Philadelphia, New York, Boston; and the nation was taxed to pay them at par, for what they had purchased at a tremendous discount.

By the same economic test, a system that appeared sound and statesmanlike in Massachusetts seemed unwarranted and unconstitutional in Virginia. Although well provided with a long sea frontage where small, fast vessels were built, not many of them were owned in Virginia. The Virginia planter knew little of business, and less of finance. A gentleman inherited his debts with his plantation, why then should debt trouble the United States? Why not pay it off at market value, as a gentleman compounds with his creditors? Virginians had sold their government paper as low as 15; why should they be taxed to assume the debts of other states? For men such as these, in love with 'republican virtue' of the pristine Roman model and ignorant of not only public finance, but of the simplest principles of accounting, Hamilton's system was incomprehensible, therefore suspect. It must portend colossal taxation as in England, jobbery and corruption as in England — perhaps monarchy as in England.

Patrick Henry, who a quarter-century before wrote the Virginia resolves, drafted a remonstrance against the federal assumption of state debts which the Virginia Assembly adopted. Therein, on

23 December 1790, were expressed the misgivings of plain folk throughout the country, as well as those of the Virginia gentry.

They discern a striking resemblance between this system and that which was introduced into England, at the Revolution [of 1688], a system which has perpetuated upon that nation an enormous debt, and has moreover insinuated into the hands of the executive an unbounded influence, which pervading every branch of the government, bears down all opposition, and daily threatens the destruction of everything that appertains to English liberty. The same causes produce the same effects! In an agricultural country like this, therefore to erect, and concentrate, and perpetuate a large monied interest, is a measure which your memorialists apprehend must in the course of human events produce one or other of two evils, the prostration of agriculture at the feet of commerce, or a change in the present form of federal government, fatal to the existence of American liberty. . . . Your memorialists can find no clause in the constitution authorizing Congress to assume the debts of the States!

A vision of the Civil War flashed across Hamilton's brain as he read this remonstrance. 'This is the first symptom,' he wrote, 'of a spirit which must either be killed, or will kill the Constitution of the United States.'

Hamilton was making new enemies to the administration. But Virginia could hardly form an opposition party without aid from some of her citizens who were highly placed in the Federal Government. Washington, national in his outlook, and convinced that Hamilton's policy was honest and right, signed every bill based on his recommendations. Richard Henry Lee, in 1788 elected to the Senate as an Anti-federalist, became a convert to Hamilton's views. Thomas Jefferson, Secretary of State, and James Madison, leader of the House, wavered — but found the Virginia candle stronger than the Hamiltonian star.

The breach between Jefferson and Hamilton, which we are about to describe, was not personal. The Republican and Federalist parties were in no sense the projections of rival personalities; and only in a limited sense were they a division between democracy and aristocracy, or between radicalism and conservatism. They were the political expressions of a deep-lying antagonism between two great American interests — the planting-slaveholding interest, typified by Virginia; and the mercantile-shipping-financial interest, typified by Massachusetts. These interests preceded Hamilton and Jefferson by a century. In the Federal Government they found a stake worth fighting for; and in Hamilton and Jefferson they found natural leaders. American political history until 1865 is largely the story of these rival interests, capitalist and agrarian, Northern and Southern, contending for the control of the government — undermining each other's vote, interfering with each other's labor, bidding for Western support, gambling with petty wars, and finally staking everything on civil war. Principle also divided the parties, particularly in their infancy; but principles were both changed and exchanged, while Massachusetts and Virginia remained the intellectual foci after they ceased to be the economic nuclei of the two systems.

5. *Thomas Jefferson*

When Thomas Jefferson returned to Virginia in November 1789, on leave of absence from his diplomatic post at Paris, he was surprised to learn of his nomination to the Department of State. Only Washington's urgent request persuaded him to accept. Ambition to found a political party was remote from Jefferson's mind. 'If I could not go to heaven but with a party, I would not go there at all,' he wrote that year. Yet his name and reputation are indissolubly bound up with the party that he was the first to lead.

Jefferson was fourteen years older than Hamilton, and much more experienced in administration. As the author of the Declaration of Independence and the *Notes on Virginia* he was famous in both continents. As representative of the United States in France, he became a sort of consulting attorney on revolution. While the National Assembly was in session at Versailles, the leaders met at his dinner-table, and were surprised at his moderate advice; for Jefferson, despite his later reputation as an ideologue, had an inductive rather than a deductive mind. A democrat in a country with a democratic social basis, he was not even republican in France. Science, literature, and the fine arts attracted Jefferson as much as they had Franklin; and he was easily the first American architect of his generation. In England the Adam country houses and formal gardens interested him more than the British Constitution. His Virginia mansion, Monticello, designed by him and superbly situated on a hill-top facing the Blue Ridge, was as admirable for its architecture and landscape gardening as Mount Vernon for efficient husbandry. Bremo in Fluvanna County, the mansion that Jefferson designed for his friend John Hartwell Cocke, is perhaps the most beautiful country house in America today. The only perfect college quadrangle in America is his design. Jefferson wrote upon Neo-Platonism, the pronunciation of Greek, the Anglo-Saxon language, the future of steam-engines, American archaeology, and controversial theology. But there was one subject of which he was ignorant in practice yet self-confident in theory: and that was Hamilton's specialty, finance.

Hamilton's political theories had more validity for the future America than for the simple society with whose common mind and condition Jefferson's theories agreed. Yet if America outgrew Jefferson's principles, she is still indebted to them for whatever liberalism and idealism she has preserved in an industrial society. Hamilton wished to concentrate power; Jefferson, to diffuse power. Hamilton feared anarchy and thought in terms of order; Jefferson feared tyranny and thought in terms of liberty. Hamilton believed republican government could only succeed if directed by a governing class; Jefferson, that republicanism was hardly worth trying if not fused with democracy. Hamilton took a gloomy view of human nature; Jefferson, the hopeful view of Jean-Jacques Rousseau. The people, according to him, were the safest and most virtuous, though not always the most wise, depository of power; and education would protect their civic virtue and perfect their wisdom. (He would have been sorely puzzled to account for the failure of the American educational system to produce a more intelligent and public-spirited electorate.) Hamilton would diversify American economic life, encouraging shipping and creating manufactures by legislative enactment; Jefferson would have America remain a nation of farmers. All those differences in temper, theory, and policy were bracketed by two opposed conceptions of what America was and might be. Jefferson shared the idealistic conception of the new world to which Price and Turgot paid homage — an agrarian republic of mild laws and equal opportunity, asylum to the oppressed and beacon-light of freedom, renouncing wealth and commerce to preserve simplicity and equality. To Hamilton all this was sentimental and mischievous nonsense. Having assimilated the traditions of the New York gentry into which he had married, Hamilton believed that the only choice for America lay between a stratified society on the English model and a squalid ' mobocracy.' Jefferson, who knew Europe, wished America to be as unlike it as possible; Hamilton, who had never left America, wished to make his country a new Europe.

Their appearance was as much of a contrast as their habits of mind. Hamilton's neat, lithe, dapper little figure, and general air of brisk energy, went with his tight, compact, disciplined brain, that could conceive a system, and carry it out relentlessly. Yet Hamilton's written style was heavy and often lifeless. Unlike Jefferson, he could not have composed a classic state paper such as the Declaration of Independence; yet Jefferson's mind in comparison was somewhat untidy, constantly gathering new facts and making fresh syntheses. 'His whole figure has a loose, shackling air,' wrote Senator Maclay in 1790. 'I looked for gravity, but a laxity of manner seemed shed about him.' His discourse 'was loose and rambling and yet he scattered information wherever he went, and some even brilliant sentiments sparkled from him.' His sandy complexion, hazel eyes, and ill-fitting, much-worn clothes, gave him the look of an indolent Scotch laird; while Hamilton had the fair complexion, light hair, and personal charm of his French mother.

Jefferson assumed his duties as Secretary of State in March 1790, when Hamilton's financial policy was well under way, and government circles were ringing with his praises. Jefferson approved the payment of the domestic and foreign debt at par. He did not approve in principle the assumption of the state debts. But he saw 'the necessity of yielding to the cries of the creditors in certain parts of the Union for the sake of union; and to save us from the greatest of all calamities, the total extinction of our credit in Europe.' A few days after, according to Jefferson's own account, he arranged with Hamilton the famous bargain by which the federal capital was transferred from New York to Philadelphia for ten years, pending removal to the new federal city of Washington on the Potomac. Jefferson induced two Virginian congressmen to vote for assumption, and Hamilton rounded up Yankee votes for the Potomac.[1] But from the date of Hamilton's report recommending a national bank (13 December 1790), Jefferson's attitude toward him and his policy began to change. To George Mason of Virginia he mentioned a ' sect ' high in office who believed the British Constitution to be the goal of perfection; and intimated that Congress was under the control of ' stock-jobbers.' The President called for opinions on the constitutionality of the bank bill from his cabinet. Jefferson, in a rather incoherent report that foreshadows the ' strict construction ' school of interpreta-

---

[1] Congress adjourned at New York on 12 August, and met in Congress Hall, Philadelphia, on 6 December 1790, when Philadelphia officially became the capital.

tion, declared flatly that the bill was unconstitutional. According to him the congressional power 'to make all laws necessary and proper for carrying into execution' its delegated powers of taxation and the like did not include laws merely convenient for such purposes. A national bank was not strictly necessary — the existing state bank at Philadelphia could be used for government funds.

Hamilton replied with a nationalistic, 'loose-construction,' interpretation of the Constitution:

> Every power vested in a government is in its nature sovereign, and includes by force of the term, a right to employ all the means requisite . . . to the attainment of the ends of such power. . . . If the end be clearly comprehended within any of the specified powers, and if the measure have an obvious relation to that end, and is not forbidden by any particular provision of the Constitution, it may safely be deemed to come within the compass of the national authority.

Congress, he pointed out, had already acted upon that theory in providing lighthouses and buoys, necessary and proper to the regulation of commerce. A bank has a similar relation to the specified powers of collecting taxes, regulating trade, and paying the debt. This opinion satisfied Washington, and he signed the bank bill; it only needed the clarifying process of Chief Justice Marshall's brain to become the great opinion of 1819, which read the doctrine of implied powers into the Constitution.

Jefferson was neither silenced nor convinced. The Federal Constitution, from his point of view and Madison's, was being perverted into a consolidated, national government. To what end? Before many months elapsed, the two Virginians thought they knew. Hamilton was simply juggling money out of the pockets of the poor into those of the rich, building up through financial favors a corrupt control of House and Senate; and 'the ultimate object of all this was to prepare the way for a change from the present republican form of government to that of monarchy, of which the English constitution is to be the model.' That belief remained a fixed tenet of Jefferson for the rest of his life.

Virginian suspicions were deepened by the brisk speculation in lands, bank stock, and government funds that began in the year 1790. No sooner did Hamilton's financial reports come out, than Northern speculators began to comb the Southern countryside for depreciated paper. Several of Hamilton's friends and subordinates were implicated in larger transactions of a shady character. William Duer, his first assistant secretary, and Henry Knox, the Secretary of War, floated a colossal speculation in wild lands. Duer and Macomb, an associate of Hamilton's father-in-law, formed a blind pool to speculate in government bonds: an operation which landed Duer in jail and produced a financial flurry in New York. Hamilton sincerely deprecated all this, and his own hands were clean — but the speculators were very close to him.

Jefferson's opposition, then, was based on agrarian theory and Virginian prejudices reinforced by financial ignorance and sharpened by misapprehension of Hamilton's aims. He did not, however, create an opposition; he joined and organized the elements of opposition. The antagonism of the Northern mercantile and creditor elements to Southern agrarian and debtor elements can be found in congressional debates before either Hamilton or Jefferson took office; a full year before the Virginia remonstrance we have quoted. Hamilton had six months to organize his natural supporters before Jefferson appeared on the scene. If Hamilton was taking the country to the dogs, must not Jefferson lead it back? If the Treasury had its party, why not the Department of State?

6. The Virginia-New York Alliance

Political parties were in bad odor at the end of the eighteenth century. No provision for party government had been made in the Constitution, although parties or factions existed in all the states as in all the colonies. Ought Jefferson to resign from the cabinet, leaving Hamilton in undisputed control? Was it proper for him openly to support opposition to a policy that Washington had accepted? The President, believing that every month and year the Constitution endured was so much gained in future stability, endeavored to keep the smouldering fire from bursting forth. To Jefferson he preached charity and to Hamilton forbearance. Both were entreated to remain in office, and both consented. But Jefferson, believing Hamilton's policy to be dangerous, used every means short of open opposition to check it; while Hamilton spared no effort to thwart Jefferson, when his management of foreign affairs appeared to be mischievous. The conduct of neither man, in view of the unprecedented circumstances and the uncertain position of the cabinet, can be called dishonorable.

A most important step toward forming an opposition party was an understanding between Virginian malcontents and those of New York. The politics of that state were divided into two factions, of which the one that interested Jefferson was led by Governor George Clinton (the son of an Irish immigrant), the Livingston clan, and attorney-general Aaron Burr, who had discovered the political value of a city benevolent society called the Sons of St. Tammany. Opposed were the 'aristocratic' party of De Lanceys and Van Rensselaers and General Schuyler, whose daughter Alexander Hamilton had married. George Clinton had won the governorship, but having bet on the wrong horse in opposing the Federal Constitution, he obtained no federal patronage in New York, which was most exasperating for a highly practical politician. Clinton wanted Jefferson's support, and Jefferson needed his. On a 'botanizing excursion' that led Jefferson and Madison up the Hudson in the summer of 1791, they undoubtedly found occasion to study *Clintonia borealis* and other hardy perennials in Ulster County and the neighborhood of Albany. They also arranged to bring Madison's classmate Philip Freneau, the poet-journalist, from New York to Philadelphia to publish an opposition newspaper, the *National Gazette,* and ' unmask ' the monarchical schemes of Hamilton. Freneau, partially supported by a clerkship in the Department of State, abused the 'monarchists' to such good purpose that in the presidential election of 1792, Virginia, North Carolina, and New York gave their second electoral votes to George Clinton for vice-president, as against John Adams. From this 'botanizing excursion,' then, we may date the Virginia planters' first political alliance, a combination that set the pattern of the Jeffersonian Republican party, and of all its successors. For 150 years the ' Solid South ' and Tammany Hall have been the two constant faithful factors in the Democratic party. After a brief estrangement in 1928, the year 1942 finds them united under a gentleman democrat like Jefferson.

Washington, dismayed by the growing opposition to his administration, was eager to retire in 1793. Hamilton and Jefferson both urged him to accept another four-year term; the one for obvious reasons, the other because he trusted Washington to suppress any further ' monarchical tendencies,' and believed the opposition needed further nursing to become an effective party. The President was unanimously re-elected. He began his new term in March 1793, in the shadow of a European war which was soon destined to precipitate all floating elements of political dissension into two national parties, around the nuclei of Massachusetts shipping and Virginia planting — the Federalists, led by Hamilton and inclining towards England; and the Republicans, led by Jefferson and favoring the French Revolution. These parties held the national stage for the next generation; and the Republican and Democratic parties of to-day are respectively their descendants.

XVI

PARTY POLITICS AND THE FRENCH REVOLUTION
1789–1797

1. *The Two Poles*

WASHINGTON'S foreign policy may be summed up in three words: peace, union, and justice. Peace, to give the country time to recover from the material and moral wounds of the Revolutionary War, and to permit the slow work of national integration to continue. The less diplomacy, the more likelihood of peace; but justice could not be done, nor the Federal Union maintained, without a vigorous foreign policy.

It was certain that the Westerners would not long remain in the Union unless Washington could secure to them the navigation of the Mississippi; that the support of the trading classes would be lost if their commerce were not protected; and that there would be irresistible demand for war with Britain if the Northwest posts were not shortly surrendered. The Federal Government would become as contemptible as the Confederation unless it could satisfy all parts of the country that their essential interests were being protected.

Jefferson and Hamilton agreed with Washington's objects, although by different processes of reasoning; and they also agreed that the first step towards securing them must be a good understanding with England. But they disagreed absolutely as to the means of obtaining that understanding. Jefferson had been minister to the court of Versailles before taking the Department of State. 'You will perceive,' he wrote from France in 1788, 'that my object is to strengthen the connection between this country and my own in all useful points. . . . This friendship we ought to cultivate closely, considering the present dispositions of England towards us.' Those dispositions Jefferson had tested two years previously, as joint commissioner with John Adams at London. He concluded: 'That nation hates us, their ministers hate us, and their King more than all other men.' Jefferson returned this hatred with interest, and for reasons more profound than foreign policy. English society, government, and manners were the sort of things that he wished his country to avoid. With Hamilton and his friends daily avowing their admiration for the British Constitution, British finance, and English society, Jefferson believed it to be their object to make the United States a mere transatlantic copy of the mother country. It was repulsion from them and their ideas, rather than attraction for France as such, that led Jefferson to regard the French alliance as his polar star. The French Revolution made him all the more eager to cling to that course, regardless of the rocks that Hamilton pointed out ahead.

Hamilton believed that the essential interests of Great Britain and the United States were complementary, not competitive. 'I cannot foresee any solid grounds of difference between us,' he told an Englishman in 1790. Jefferson would probably have agreed, with the reservation that Britain must undergo a revolution at least in commercial policy, before the point of view of her governing class could be friendly to the sort of country that he wished America to remain. When he saw signs of the desired transformation taking place, in 1823, he was willing to contemplate 'fighting side by side with her in the same cause.' Until then, he feared America would have to fight her way up to a place in the sun.

Although Hamilton never attempted to graft the British Constitution on the Federal one, he did believe that Americans had many political lessons to learn of their mother country. 'We think in English.' England, for him, had found the just balance between liberty and order. The influence of her friendship could only be wholesome for a young nation, sprung from her loins, and which needed above all things integration and stability. Hamilton really liked Frenchmen, who in turn found his personality more sympathetic than that of Jefferson. For, after all, Hamilton was one-quarter French in blood. But on the French Revolution Hamilton saw eye-to-eye with Burke. It was most disconcerting, just when there seemed some hope of America settling down, to have her favorite nation blow up and invite everyone else to follow suit!

2. Pressing for the Posts

Before matters had progressed further with Great Britain, the Nootka Sound affair gave Washington's administration a serious question of high diplomacy. A dispute between Spanish cruisers and

British traders in that estuary in far off Vancouver Island suddenly flashed into European diplomacy, shook the balance of power, and reverberated on American politics.

Spain's renewed colonial activity under Charles III — one aspect of which, as we have seen, was the distribution of gold in the Kentucky backwoods — led to the effective occupation of the California coast. In 1769 a naval expedition was despatched from Mexico, and two parties were sent overland to occupy Alta California. One of the ships took one hundred and ten days to reach San Diego and another was never heard from; but the overland party, under Gaspar de Portolá, pushed north along the coast as far as the site of Drake's landing; and then, turning south, came upon the magnificent Bay of San Francisco, which had strangely eluded earlier explorers. A chain of Indian missions, whose mellowed buildings still reflect the California sunshine, were founded by the Franciscan father Junípero Serra; and in 1775 General Anza conducted a band of colonists northwestward from Arizona, and founded the *presidio* of San Francisco. Little they dreamed that within a man's lifetime California would become a state of the American Union.

In order to keep interlopers from this new colony, the Spanish *guarda costas* patrolled the Pacific coast as far north as Alaska. There, Russian fur traders had founded another colony that eventually fell to Uncle Sam. New rivals soon appeared. As a result of Captain Cook's voyage, both American and English shipowners learned that fat profits could be made through buying furs from the Pacific coast Indians and selling them in China. Nootka Sound was the center of this traffic. In 1789 both the Spanish and the British governments planned to take effective and exclusive occupation. The more powerful Spanish ship seized the Englishmen and sent them prisoners to Mexico. Reparation and apology were demanded. A European war was threatened, and Jefferson had an opportunity to play international politics.

At least so he hoped; but before any concession to the United States could be fished from the troubled waters of Nootka Sound the storm subsided. The one important result for the United States was Jefferson's conviction that, in order to protect America neutrality in a future war between England and Spain, and to secure an outlet for the West, the whole west bank of the Mississippi must become American territory — a conviction upon which he acted when he became President.

Spain consented to negotiate with the United States over the navigation of the Mississippi and the Southwest posts. But in the meantime she established two new posts on the American bank of the Mississippi. The negotiations dragged on at Madrid for two years, when the American commissioners concluded 'that a few ships of the line would have more weight in securing peaceably the territorial rights of the United States, and those with respect to the Mississippi than all the most unanswerable arguments or incontestable proofs that could be adduced in support thereof.'

It was not until his second term of office that Washington could gather the fruits of his patient diplomacy and forbearance. In the meantime the Union was strengthened by fresh accessions. North Carolina ratified the Constitution before the end of 1789; Rhode Island joined in 1790, after Congress had threatened to exclude her from commercial intercourse. The admission of Vermont in 1791, as the fourteenth state, put an end to the separatist movement in that quarter. Kentucky was admitted in 1792; Tennessee in 1796; but the separatist movement continued in the West until the Mississippi outlet was secure.

The longer Britain retained the Northwest posts, and refused to conclude a treaty of commerce, the more difficult Hamilton found it to restrain Congress from retaliatory measures.

3. Neutrality and the French Revolution

In the meantime events in Europe were making a peaceful solution of these difficulties highly improbable. Americans followed the French Revolution with the keenest interest and sympathy; few perceived the difficulties ahead. Lafayette, Tom Paine, and the Declaration of Rights seemed to make that revolution a continuation of theirs. News from Paris, arriving in huge stale batches by infrequent vessels, was printed at large in the newspapers, discussed eagerly in mansions, taverns, and the log cabins of the frontier. In December 1792 arrived the news of the previous summer — the storming of the Tuileries, the declaration of the French Republic, and the Battle of Valmy. Hard on its heels came the decree of 19 November, the 'war of all peoples against all kings.' Enthusiasm then became hysterical, as is apt to be the case when American emotions are stirred. In puritanic Boston, where dramatic instincts found an outlet in political form, there was a civic feast in French style. A procession of 'citizens eight deep' escorted a roasted ox, labelled 'a Peace Offering to Liberty and Equality,' together with sixteen hundred loaves of bread and two hogsheads of punch, to a spot rechristened Liberty Square. As the punch fell lower in the hogsheads the spirits of the citizens rose, and what was said and sung was not complimentary to John Bull.

A series of westerly gales prevented any vessel arriving from Europe for three months. Then, in April 1793, came news that brought war to the edge of the three-mile limit, and made the French Revolution an issue in American politics. France had declared war on Great Britain and Spain; the king had been guillotined; the Girondin party was in power; and Citizen Genet was coming over as minister plenipotentiary of the French Republic.

America was still, formally, an ally of France. In the treaty of 1778 the United States had guaranteed French possession of her West India islands. As the British navy was certain to attack them, it was difficult to see how America could honorably refuse to enter the war, if France demanded it. Most Americans wished to help France; and war would enable them to discharge both their debt of gratitude to her and their feeling of resentment against Britain.

On 18 April 1793 a cabinet meeting was held at Philadelphia. Washington, though dismayed at the turn of events, still wished the French well, but thought of his own country first. Hamilton, loathing the French Revolution, wished to declare the treaty of 1778 in suspense now that the king was dead, declare American neutrality, and reject the French minister. Jefferson considered the cause of France 'the most sacred cause that ever man was engaged in,' but was equally anxious to keep America out of the war. To an immediate declaration of neutrality he was opposed; partly on constitutional grounds, but mainly because he regarded American neutrality, without some equivalent, as a free gift to England that she would receive only with contempt. To Washington such bargaining seemed unworthy of a self-respecting nation. Neutrality must be declared on its merits, not as part of a bargain. Accordingly, on 22 April 1793, the President issued his famous neutrality proclamation. It declared the 'disposition of the United States' to 'pursue a conduct friendly and impartial toward the belligerent powers,' and warned citizens that 'aiding or abetting hostilities,' or unneutral acts committed within the country, would render them liable to prosecution in the federal courts.

In the meantime Citizen Genet, quaintest of the many curious diplomatists sent by European governments to the United States, had landed at Charleston. Genet's instructions called upon him to use the United States as a base for privateering; and before presenting his credentials to Jefferson he undertook to fit out privateers against British commerce. He was instructed to recruit forces for the conquest of Florida and Louisiana, ' and perhaps add to the American constellation the fair star of Canada.' Several fighting land speculators like George Rogers Clark, who had some dubious claims to Western land still held by Spain, showed great enthusiasm for war with that country. To them Genet distributed French military commissions, forming the *cadres* of an *Armée du Mississippi* and an *Armée des Florides*. In other words, France expected the same sort of aid from her sister republic that she herself had given in 1776; aid which was as certain to embroil the giver with Britain. But Hamilton refused to provide Genet with funds, in the shape of advance instalments of the debt to France. So for want of pay and subsistence, the volunteers had to return empty-handed to their log cabins. Jefferson welcomed the arrival of Genet as a sort of refresher for the opposition party, yet he enforced Washington's neutrality policy with loyal and even-handed justice. He insisted on a strict construction of the French treaty privileges, and lectured Genet on the law of nations.

When Genet found he could do nothing with the government, he conceived the brilliant notion of turning it out. His official notes became inconceivably truculent. In Charleston he had presided at the birth of a local Jacobin club, whose legitimacy was recognized by the parent organization at Paris; and his progress through the states was marked by similar progeny of ill portent. After a few weeks of him, Jefferson concluded that Genet was likely to become the Jonah of the Jeffersonian party: ' He will sink the Republican interest, if they do not abandon him.' In August 1793 the cabinet unanimously voted to request his recall. Robespierre gladly consented, and in return asked for the recall of Gouverneur Morris, whose intrigues at Paris had been quite as mischievous as Genet's in Philadelphia. Early in 1794 a new French minister arrived in the United States, with an order for his predecessor's arrest. Instead of returning to feed the guillotine, Genet married the daughter of Governor Clinton, and settled down to the life of a country gentleman on the Hudson.

The year of the passing of Citizen Genet, 1794, saw the definite crystallization of all those unstable political elements that had been oscillating between the Massachusetts and Virginian poles, into two national parties.

Edges were blurred, issues confused, but the political cauldron was seething. Men were asking whether the American experiment in self-government had passed its zenith. Could the Republic be saved only by old-world expedients: national debt and accumulation of capital, army and navy and governing classes, perhaps even church and king? Must the Federal Constitution be merely the British Constitution writ large? Or, on the contrary, was the American Revolution just begun? Were the people of the United States destined to shake off every fetter that enslaves men's bodies and minds, and face the world, united indeed, but enlightened, free, and equal? In the tumultuous year 1793 Americans gazed on the French Revolution as into a crystal ball, for an answer to their hopes and fears. Presently they looked up, satisfied, with a hearty ' Yes! ' or a thumping ' No! '

European issues reach America without shadings, all black and white. Thus the French Revolution seemed to some a clean-cut contest between monarchy and republicanism, oppression and liberty, autocracy and democracy; to others, simply a new breaking-out of the eternal strife between anarchy and order, atheism and religion, poverty and property. The former joined the Republican party; the latter, the Federalist. Sectional and economic groups were polar to the completed parties; but in the reverse order to general expectation. Democratic New England and the seaports, rivals as they were to Liverpool and Bristol, became the headquarters of the pro-British Federalists; while the landed interests, particularly in slaveholding communities, was swept by gallomania.

The explanation is both social and economic. In New England the clergy had been worrying over the younger generation: undergraduates who preferred reading Voltaire and Gibbon to studying Jonathan Edwards and Rollin. Tom Paine's *Age of Reason* appeared in 1794. That scurrilous arraignment of the Bible sent liberal Christians hot-foot to the standard of reaction, eager for anything to exclude ' French infidelity.' Paine himself, by a fierce attack on Washington the next year, completely identified Jeffersonianism with Jacobinism, in the mind of the average New Englander and Middle-State Presbyterian.

The basis of Virginia's opposition to Northern capital we have already examined. Her opposition to British capital and sea-power was of the same nature. But to the merchant shipowners of New England, New York, Philadelphia, Baltimore, and Charleston, British capital was an indispensable instrument of credit; and commerce with Britain the first condition of American prosperity. Their overseas trade was largely financed by London merchant-bankers; and after the French armies had sucked Amsterdam dry, public loans could be obtained nowhere else than in London. Like Hamilton, they did not care to risk a quarrel with the power that could give or withhold. British spoliations on neutral trade might annoy American shipowners; but they soon discovered that British sea-power gave compensation, while French sea-power did not. Although the Acts of Trade and Navigation were technically in force in the West Indies, they were not strictly enforced after 1792. During the entire period of the French war, as in 1914–17, American shipowners could make immense profits by submitting to British sea-power when they could not evade it; whilst French attacks on neutral commerce, like those of the German submarines, tended to destroy the only traffic that the British navy permitted.

Thus it came about that great Virginia planters of English race and tradition — men like John Randolph of Roanoke who would wear no boots unless made in London, and read no Bible printed outside Oxford: men whose throats would have been the first cut and whose lands the first divided if Jacobinism infected America — screamed for the Rights of Man and railed at Britain. Thus it came about that Boston Unitarians like William Ellery Channing and Harrison Gray Otis, whose creed was more subtly subversive of traditional Christianity than the crude outbursts of the Paris commune, beat the tomtom against French impiety and anarchy.

Around these two poles American opinion crystallized in 1793–95. You were either for the Republicans and France, or for the Federalists and Britain — there could be no compromise. Emotion for a principle, and for the kind of country you wanted America to be, joined interest and policy. It was not Britain and France corrupting American opinion, but American merchants and farmers stretching out to Europe for support. As a French observer wrote, 'Each party will use foreign influence as it needs, to dominate.'

4. *The Party Structure*

Both American parties, the Republicans (ancestors of the Democrats of today) and the Federalists (of whom the present Republicans are residuary legatees), accepted the Federal Constitution as their common basis, although each accused the other of wishing to subvert it. Both believed in free trade, though for different reasons. Their respective principles were agrarianism and the Revolution, against capitalism and Britain. If the one in 1794 stood for states' rights, and the other for a strong Federal Government, it was only because the one was out and the other in. The distinction was accidental, and was exchanged after the Republicans came in and the Federalists went out.

Each party attempted to undercut the other on its home field, by appealing to some local interest or feeling contrary to the dominant one. Thus in Virginia, Federalists were found in the wheat-growing Shenandoah valley, which hated the planter aristocracy. Similarly the Republicans reached out to the under-dog in New England. Maine, the frontier district of Massachusetts, was largely Republican; and the Baptists, Methodists, and other dissenters, who disliked the privileges of the Congregational churches, were faithful Jeffersonians. All of which is an early illustration of another factor in American politics that makes them so puzzling to outsiders — the fact that both in motive and in purpose national politics are partly local. Thousands of votes in every presidential election are dictated by state politics, local hatreds, and neighborhood feuds.

Outside New York, where the Clintons and Burr proved more than a match for Hamilton and Jay, the most important group of Northern Republicans was in Pennsylvania. Here were the genuine radicals and the professional politicians of the party. Pennsylvania politics had long been a matter of class and race, as we have seen. The back-country refused to pay Hamilton's excise; the mechanics were becoming class-conscious. Philadelphia carpenters struck for a twelve-hour day in 1791. Journeymen shoemakers organized in 1792 the first American labor union, which by strikes and boycotts managed to force up their wages almost one hundred per cent, in the prosperous years of neutral trade. In 1805 one of these strikes occasioned the first labor conspiracy case in American judicial annals. The defendants were fined $8 and costs each, for 'entering into a combination to raise their wages.' These, and their compeers in New

York, were the men who welcomed Genet and formed Jacobin clubs, and who stoned Hamilton when he spoke for Jay's treaty. The New York and Pennsylvania democracy became a firm ally to the Virginia aristocracy. But the Boston shipcaulkers and shoemakers, stout fellows who had done the mobbing for Sam Adams and Jim Otis in the 1770's, were won over by a younger Otis to the party that fostered shipping. The most lively hope of the Republicans was the West. Here was the most favorable soil for the growth of a party that opposed strong government, financiers, and Britain. The gallomania of 1792 lasted for some years beyond the Appalachians. Republicanism increased as backwoods population increased; and the Federalists, realizing that they were doomed to a minority position, adopted after 1800 an anti-Western policy that could end only in the division of the Union, or the submergence of Federalism.

Jefferson and Hamilton typified Goethe's two eternal spirits that contend for the government of all that men do or say: the spirit that creates and the spirit that denies, the hope that man can raise himself through the ages a little nearer God, and the mocking doubt that human nature can ever change its ways. There was not the same difference between the two parties that they organized. The Republicans may have had the greater share of optimism, and the Federalists of pessimism; but both had something to give their country, and both were guilty of appealing to men's fears and appetites. Jefferson's 'botanical excursion' of 1791 began the infiltration of practical politics, bringing into his party elements moved only by a desire to win; while the character of Washington, the genius of Hamilton, and the intellect of Marshall sublimated from a material and cynical policy the ideals of national integrity and international justice.

5. *Neutral Rights and Jay's Treaty*

The follies of Genet, and his disgrace, cooled American ardor for France. Yet no sooner had he been disposed of than fresh dry timber was thrown on the hot embers of Anglo-American relations. By March 1794 the frontier and commercial controversies had become roaring furnaces; and it was doubtful whether the cool, calm temper of Washington was adequate to quench them.

Lord Grenville informed the American minister in London, near the end of 1793, that the British government proposed to hold the

Northwest posts indefinitely, frankly abandoning all pretence that they would be evacuated when the United States gave full satisfaction for the debts. Washington's patience, Jefferson's forbearance, and Hamilton's long, uphill pull towards good understanding had apparently come to naught. What was left but war, for America to secure her own? The other burning issue of Atlantic commerce was flaring a like signal.

When England is at war, and the royal navy is measuring the extent of neutral rights, neutral commerce with her enemy is apt to thin out. The weaker naval powers had long endeavored to build up a positive law of neutral rights, with the doctrines of effective blockade, limited contraband, and 'free ships make free goods': doctrines which publicists long labored to write into law, only to see them go smash in 1914. The United States had subscribed to these principles in her treaties with Holland, France, and Prussia. As a neutral in the war of the French Revolution, she hoped to benefit by them. But a British Order in Council of unprecedented severity was issued on 6 November. Among other things, it directed the detention and adjudication of all ships laden with French colonial produce, whether French or neutral property; and all vessels carrying provisions to the French colonies.

The Caribbean was swarming with Yankee schooners and brigs when the order reached naval officers on that station. It was executed in a manner that reflected the navy's sharp hunger for prize-money, and the low salaries of admiralty judges in the West Indies. Everything was fish that came to their net. If a Maine schooner, laden with plank and salt cod, ventured into the harbor of St. George's, Bermuda, she was boarded by a gang of ruffians, stripped of her rudder and sails, spoiled of her stores, her seamen consigned to a calaboose if not impressed, and the vessel libelled in His Majesty's court of vice-admiralty. The burden of proof that the cargo was not somehow tainted by French association was placed upon the Yankee skipper. Of course he could appeal to a British court from the almost certain condemnation: an illusory privilege for the masters of small craft.

News of these captures brought consternation to the American trading community, which was the backbone of Hamilton's party. Hamilton himself was exasperated. Congress began war preparations, and clapped an embargo on the seaports. In the midst of the crisis, news leaked into the American papers of a truculent speech by Governor Lord Dorchester of Canada to an Indian delegation, encouraging them to look for the king's aid shortly in driving the ' long knives ' across the Ohio for good and all.

A new British invasion of American territory had occurred, but fortunately was not yet known. As a ' defensive measure ' the Lieutenant-Governor of Upper Canada built and garrisoned a new fort, on American soil at the Maumee rapids, a hundred miles southwest of Detroit.

In Congress the Republican party was not eager for war, but for Jefferson's and Madison's favorite plan of commercial retaliation, which would surely have led to war, as it did when Jefferson and Madison later tried it. The Federalists, scorning such measures as mischievous and futile, were beginning to think that war was inevitable, when Lord Grenville revoked the Order in Council under color of which the commerce spoliations had been perpetrated. This information was communicated to Congress on 4 April 1794; and on the 16th Washington nominated Chief Justice Jay as envoy extraordinary to Great Britain.

' My objects are, to prevent a war,' Washington wrote the Secretary of State, ' if justice can be obtained by fair and strong representations . . . of the injuries which this country has sustained from Great Britain in various ways,' injuries which ' leave very unfavorable impressions of their friendship, and little to expect from their justice.' Jay's nomination was confirmed by the Senate, and he left immediately for London. Through the influence of the new French minister with the Republicans, the embargo was allowed to lapse. A large fleet of provision ships then sailed from the Chesapeake and slipped safely into Brest, in time to relieve the famine that accompanied the reign of terror.

The appointment of Chief Justice Jay as envoy extraordinary to the Court of St. James's was not a happy one for the United States. John Jay was a model of abstract propriety and unblemished character, but his leaning toward Britain was too pronounced, and his self-esteem opened the way to judicious flattery. ' He can bear any opposition to what he advances, provided that regard is shown to his abilities,' Grenville was advised. ' Mr. Jay's weak side is Mr. Jay.'

The treaty of London, 19 November 1794, has always been known as Jay's treaty. Jay did secure the main object of his mission, the evacuation of the Northwest posts. In return, he had to admit British fur-trading over the northern border. No renunciation of the pretended right to meddle with the Indians on the American side of the border could be obtained. Jay did, however, prevent a rectification of frontier in the Northwest, which would have given Canada a corridor to the site of St. Paul, Minnesota; and eventually would have made the international boundary the forty-fifth instead of the forty-ninth parallel of latitude. Questions of British spoliations on American commerce, of uncollected debts, and of the Maine-New Brunswick boundary, were wisely referred to mixed commissions — a precedent of great value for subsequent diplomacy.

In the commercial articles of the treaty, which were limited to ten years' duration, the principle of most-favored nation was established. Jay acquiesced in the British doctrine of contraband and neutral rights, contrary to the previous policy of the United States, and obtained no stipulation on impressment, which was already beginning to disturb Anglo-American relations. Article XII, which was struck out before ratification, was the most exceptionable. In return for a limited entry to the British West Indies of American vessels not over seventy tons burden, Jay agreed to the prohibition of export from the United States, in American vessels, of sugar, coffee, cocoa, and cotton; all of which articles, as he should have known, were of increasing importance in American foreign trade. The concession, however, was immaterial, for ports in the British West Indies were almost continuously kept open by local proclamations and orders in council to American ships and products from 1793 to 1813, so dependent were they upon America for provisions.

Jay's treaty was a victory for British diplomacy. The United States was forced to ransom its own property, the Northwest posts, by humiliating concessions as to commerce, shipping, and maritime rights. It embroiled the United States with France, and thus threw American weight into the allied scale, until the Peace of Amiens. In driving so sharp a bargain, Lord Grenville really served his country ill. More generous concessions might have lost British merchants and shippers a few hundred thousand pounds; but would have had the same political result, and left no bitterness behind. Jay's treaty is largely responsible for the American popular tradition that British diplomatists are more to be feared than British battleships.

Washington read the treaty with dismay. In his usual deliberate

manner he gathered the opinions of his advisers; and decided to
accept it, as the only honorable alternative to war. He wrote Morris:

Peace has been the order of the day with me since the disturbances
in Europe, first commenced. My policy has been, and will continue to
be, while I have the honor to remain in the administration of the government, to be upon friendly terms with, but independent of, all the
nations of the earth; to share in the broils of none; to fulfil our own
engagements; to supply the wants and be carrier for them all; being
thoroughly convinced that it is our policy and interest so to do. Nothing
short of self-respect, and that justice which is essential to a national
character, ought to involve us in war; for sure I am, if this country is
preserved in tranquillity twenty years longer, it may bid defiance in a
just cause to any power whatever; such in that time will be its population, wealth and resources.

While the treaty was still before the Senate in secret executive
session, the terms of it leaked out; and a howl of execration went up
from one end of the country to the other. Any British treaty would
have been opposed by some; and it took a long view like Washington's to see the value of Jay's. Randolph, the Secretary of State, was
against ratification, the French Minister actively intrigued against
it, but a bare two-thirds' majority was obtained, and the President
ratified the treaty on 25 June 1795. It was one of his wisest and bravest
acts in a life filled with wisdom and courage.

6. *The Frontier Gates Swing Open*

While Jay was absent on his mission, in October 1793 General
Wayne moved the 'Legion of the United States,' a regular army of
two thousand men, into winter quarters at the site of Greenville,
in the heart of the Ohio wilderness. 'Mad Anthony,' as Wayne had
been called after his gallant storming of Stony Point in 1779, had a
cool head. An admirable disciplinarian, he trained his troops in the
technique of forest warfare, and the Indians gave them plenty of
practice. Several hundred Kentucky mounted riflemen, as hard-
bitten a lot of troopers as ever swung steel, joined him in the spring
of 1794. The lieutenant-governor of Upper Canada bent all his energy
to mobilizing the Indians, despite cautious counsels from the home
government. Wampum belts, 'speeches,' even Yankee scalps obtained
in early skirmishes, were sent out by forest trails, in order to induce
all the braves to join. Provisions, blankets, muskets, powder and

ball, and vermilion warpaint were dispensed from government de-
pots and arsenals to the enemies of a country with which His Bri-
tannic Majesty was at peace.

When the oak leaves were fully out and nature's ambush was
complete, the Indians attacked Wayne's fort. After beating them off,
Wayne took the offensive. Advancing cautiously through the primeval hardwood, protected by a screen of picked scouts, he de-
bouched into the Erie plain, and found himself in the granary of
the Indians. The margins of the Maumee and the Auglaize were one
continuous village, with log cabins, fruit trees, and fields of rustling
corn extending to the forest edge. In the midst of these savage
gardens Wayne built Fort Defiance, a stockade with block-house
bastions. There he offered peace once more, and once more it was
rejected. The Indians retreated to the vicinity of the new British
fort, and took cover behind a natural stockade of fallen trees. There
were fifteen hundred to two thousand of them: Miamis under
Little Turtle who had ambushed St. Clair in 1791, Black Wolf with
his Shawnee, the 'three fires' of the Ottawa, Chippewa, and Pottawatomi under Blue Jacket, Sauk and Fox from Lake Superior, a few
Iroquois die-hards, and seventy white Canadian rangers under an
old loyalist captain. On 20 August Wayne marched forth to meet
them. A squadron of dragoons charged on the Indians' left flank.
Both the American captains were picked off, but a lieutenant took
command, and the troopers, jumping their game little horses over
the fallen timber as in a steeplechase, burst in on the redskins and
gave them cold steel. On their front the infantry and riflemen poured
in a volley of hot stuff, and charged with fixed bayonets before the
Indians had time to reload. In forty minutes it was all over.

This 'Battle of the Fallen Timbers' scattered the distant tribes-
men, and enabled Wayne to destroy the Indian villages and lay
waste their cornfields. Fort Wayne was built at the forks of the
Maumee, and the legion returned to Greenville, to await envoys of
peace.

On 16 June 1795 there were enough sachems and warriors assembled for Wayne to open the peace conference. Imagine a broad
clearing in the forest; the great bark-roofed council house, open at
the sides and with a council fire in the middle; on one side of the
fire a semicircle of war-chiefs, warriors, and sachems, splendid in
their gaudy match-coats, quills, and feathers; on the other General
Wayne and his lean officers; a ring of lounging soldiers beyond;

and a background of hickory, oak, and buckeye trees in the green of early summer. The calumet of peace is passed around, and Wayne opens the conference in the name of the 'Fifteen Fires of America.'

I take you all by the hand as brothers, assembled for the good work of peace. . . . The Great Spirit has favored us with a clear sky and refreshing breeze. . . .

The heavens are bright, the roads are open; we will rest in peace and love; and wait the arrival of our brothers. In the interim, we will have a little drink, and wash the dust out of our throats. We will, on this happy occasion, be merry, without however passing the bounds of temperance and sobriety.

A little drink it had to be, for Greenville was seventy miles from the nearest frontier distillery, and fresh delegations of thirsty redskins came pouring in until warriors and sachems, representing all the tribes between the Great Lakes, the Mississippi, and the Ohio, were assembled to the number of eleven hundred and thirty. The tedious conferences went on through interpreters.

On 20 July the articles were read, and the assembled warriors gave the 'Yo-ha!' of assent. Three days passed in eating and drinking while the treaty was engrossed; and on 3 August 1795 the General signed his name, and the chieftains their marks, to the Treaty of Greenville. By this treaty the Indians ceded the southeastern corner of the Northwest territory,[1] together with sixteen enclaves such as Vincennes, Detroit, and the site of Chicago, in return for annuities to the value of some ten thousand dollars. So ended almost twenty years of fighting: the last phase of the War of Independence. Peace came to the border from the Genesee country to the Mississippi. Pioneers began to swarm up the valleys of the Scioto and the Muskingum, and in ten years' time their insatiable greed for land made the Treaty of Greenville a mere scrap of paper.

Spanish-American relations were badly befogged in 1795, when Jay's treaty came as a clearing breeze. The Baron de Carondelet, governor of Louisiana, continued Miró's policy of cutting out a buffer state from trans-Appalachia, by his method of angling in western waters with golden bait. Not to be outdone by Simcoe, Carondelet established a new fort on American territory, at Chickasaw Bluffs (Memphis), which helped him to control the Mississippi.

[1] See map page 301.

The Creek and Cherokee nations were persuaded to denounce their treaties of 1790–91 with the United States.

When Jay's treaty was published, Spain had made her peace with France, and was preparing to enter the French system of alliances. Her statesman, Godoy, observing that the Western intrigues had failed, deemed it prudent for Spain to meet the United States half-way, rather than risk losing all Louisiana to American filibusters. In the Treaty of San Lorenzo (27 October 1795) His Catholic Majesty accordingly granted the right to navigate the lower Mississippi, as well as the 'right of deposit' at New Orleans so ardently desired by the West; and recognized the thirty-first parallel to the Chatta-hoochee as the southern boundary of the United States. It was not, however, until 1798, after exhausting all its rich resources in pro-crastination, that the Spanish government evacuated the posts it held north of that line. So that, in all, fifteen years elapsed before the United States obtained control of their own territories from Eu-ropean powers.

7. The Whisky Rebellion

In the very week that Wayne crushed the Indians, President Washington was calling out fifteen thousand militia to put down pale-faced rebels in western Pennsylvania. This Whisky Rebellion, as it was humorously named, tested the ability of the Federal Government to enforce federal law. Hamilton's Excise Act of 1791 appeared as unjust and tyrannical to the Westerners as had the Stamp Act to the Colonists. Beyond the mountains distillation was the only practical method to dispose of surplus corn, unless you had gold to grease the palms of Spanish officials down-river. Whisky also did duty as currency — one-gallon jugs of 'moonshine' passing for a quarter in every store on the western slope of the Alleghanies. Modifications of the excise law, which Hamilton wished to enforce more as a measure of social discipline than as a source of revenue, obtained some measure of compliance in the Southern mountains. Western Pennsylvania, however, was peopled by men of the Ulster breed, who had a moral sanction for their interests and appetites. Covenants were formed never to pay the hated tax; there were masked night-riders, and whippings and other methods of terrorism, familiar even yet in parts of the United States. In 1794, when a fed-eral marshal appeared at Pittsburgh with a bundle of writs against delinquent distillers, he and the nearest excise-man were roughly handled. Led by two backwoods demagogues named Bradford and Husband, the people held mass meetings, appointed a committee of public safety, and called out the militia of the four western counties to protect the spirituous liberties of the people. But for the moderating influence of Albert Gallatin, an embryo statesman of the frontier, there would probably have been a declaration of independence. Governor Mifflin of Pennsylvania minimized the affair, and at first refused to lend the aid of state forces.

It was the essence of the Federal Constitution that the Federal Government should have a compulsive operation on individuals. Coercion by law was preferred to coercion by arms; but to deal with forcible obstruction of judicial process, Congress was given power ' to provide for calling forth the militia to execute the laws of the Union.' By law, Congress had authorized the President to call out state militia in such contingency. It remained to be seen whether he would dare exercise the authority, and whether the militia would obey. Washington, on Hamilton's urgent plea, decided to make a test case of the Pennsylvania defiance of federal law.

Everything worked smoothly. The militia of four states, including Pennsylvania, turned out upon the President's proclamation. They were given a good, stiff hike across the Alleghanies in the glorious Indian summer. The more violent leaders of the rebels fled, and the covenanters promptly caved in. Two ringleaders, who were apprehended and convicted of treason, were pardoned by the President. Henceforth, persons and interests who had a grievance against the law, had to carry their state, and evolve the doctrine of states' rights as a shelter against federal authority. That form of resistance was not completely dealt with until 1865.

Hamilton, unable to support an expensive family on his salary, resigned his office after the Whisky Rebellion was suppressed, and resumed his law practice in New York. His intelligence and judgment had so impressed Washington and the cabinet that they continued to consult him by letter on all important questions of foreign and domestic policy. On the determination of both, Hamilton's pen was the most powerful single influence until he broke with John Adams in 1799.

8. Public Land Policy

Now that Jay's treaty and Wayne's victory had caused the gates of the frontier to swing open, it was time to decide how the land ceded by the Indians should be disposed of. An American colonial policy had been determined once and for all by the Northwest Ordinance of 1787, but the land policy blocked out in the Ordinance of 1785 was not binding on the Federal Government. Owing to the attitude of the Northwest Indians, there had been little settlement north of the Ohio before 1796; but now that a good part of the territory was really open to settlement, it was time to decide matters of land disposal.

Every feature of American society that men of Hamilton's stamp disliked — political democracy, rude plenty, undiversified economic system — depended on an ample supply of cheap land for settlers. In the Federal Convention of 1787 Charles Pinckney predicted that the

vast extent of unpeopled territory, which opens to the frugal and industrious a sure road to competency and independence, will effectually prevent for a considerable time the increase of the poor and discontented, and be the means of preserving that equality of condition that so eminently distinguishes us.

Albert Gallatin, in the debate on the Land Bill of 1796, said that

if the cause of the happiness of this country was examined into, it would be found to arise as much from the great plenty of land in proportion to the inhabitants . . . as from the wisdom of their political institutions.

Forty-three years later Lord Durham in his report on Canada asserted ' that the amazing prosperity of the United States is less owing to their form of government, than to the unlimited supply of fertile land, which maintains succeeding generations in an undiminishing affluence of fertile soil.'

Yet the converse is also true. Self-government and democracy were necessary conditions of opening the public domain to the American people. We have already followed the attempts of the British Government to restrict western settlement in 1763-64. The public land system of Canada is a fair example of what the American pioneer would have had imposed upon him if the War of Independence had turned out differently. In order to foster loyalty on the basis of privilege, Lord Dorchester produced a bureaucratic travesty of the New England township system, with extensive crown and clergy reserves, and enormous free grants to loyalists and officials. During the administration of one Canadian governor, almost a million and a half acres were granted to sixty individuals; yet would-be settlers found it almost impossible to obtain land at a reasonable price.

Some such device for keeping the poor from the land would have been adopted in the United States if men like Hamilton, Jay, and Morris had determined the public land policy. Many influential Easterners had land of their own, purchased from the states or from the Confederation, which they wished to dispose of before throwing open the West. Others regarded pioneers as a public nuisance. Hamilton's ideas on the subject were determined by his zeal for a division of American labor. He wished to populate more thickly and exploit more fully the Eastern states, and to retard migration of any sort. With labor running off to the backwoods, how could you build up manufactures? Washington, however, owned western land and was Western-minded. In 1784 he proposed that the public domain be sold at a sufficient price to deter speculators, but to accommodate the more solid sort of settler.

If any member of Congress in 1796 shared Hamilton's views he did not dare avow it. William Smith of South Carolina, who reported the land bill, said that the committee had two objects in view: 'to raise revenue, and to sell land in such lots as would be most convenient for settlers.' Madison, who thought the main thing was 'to fill the treasury as soon as possible,' was for throwing the whole public domain on the market at once, in lots six miles square, in order to pay off the national debt. Gallatin, a backwoods philosopher of noble birth, pointed out that this wholesale disposal would place the public domain in the hands of speculators. He proposed to encourage a gradual alienation to actual settlers, at a fixed price, in lots of one hundred to six hundred acres.

The point of view of this Congress, as of its successors, was quantitative rather than qualitative; yet there were a few members who believed the vital question was not how fast the West could be settled, but the sort of West we would have when it was settled. American colonial experience proved that land tenure and distribution largely determined the nature of society. New England, as we have seen, had been settled by compact groups, detaching themselves successively from the older settlements, and presenting an unbroken frontier line to the wilderness. The proprietary colonies treated their wild land mainly as a source of revenue for the proprietor, who sold it in convenient lots to individual settlers, retaining a quit-rent for himself. In Virginia, and the South generally, the practice of 'indiscriminate location' prevailed. An individual obtained a land warrant entitling him to so many acres; 'located' them wherever he pleased in the public domain, and received a title from the Crown after performing some rite of cultivation or settlement. From this method arose the dispersed settlement, large plantations, loose government, and individualism characteristic of the South, as compact village communities were characteristic of New England. The New England way preserved the rudiments of civilization — the church, the common school, an instinct for orderly government. Kentucky pioneers had as good stuff in them as the Yankees; but circumstances led them to slough off the slight cultural equipment they brought from an individualistic society. Only fifty years ago one could find in log cabins of the Kentucky mountains calf-bound volumes of Pope and Johnson that 'great-grandpaw toted over from old Virginny'; but that great-grandson could not read. The Southern pioneer often had to descend to the redskin's level before he could rise again; and the leaven that made him rise was not infrequently furnished by a New England neighbor or by a Southern aristocrat bringing his library and his traditions together with his slaves.

In the debates of 1796 a few members expressed this qualitative point of view; and, curiously enough, they were not New England members. Robert Goodloe Harper, from the Carolina Piedmont, insisted that the first object of a national land policy should be 'to secure order and good government' in the newly settled regions. William Findlay, a Pennsylvania democrat of Irish birth, pointed out that dispersion had caused much unhappiness on the frontier; whilst compact settlement enabled pioneers to obtain good schools and social intercourse. He did not think it practicable to reproduce the New England system absolutely, 'but he would have it approached to.' A model was ready at hand, the Ordinance of 1785, which adopted the New England unit and method of survey, as opposed to the Southern system of indiscriminate location, which had covered much of Kentucky and Tennessee with a triple layer of irregular and conflicting grants. So by the Congress of 1796, as by the Congress of the Confederation, the township six miles square, surveyed in compact ranges or columns, starting on the western boundary of Pennsylvania, was made the unit of public land. Each township was divided into thirty-six sections of one square mile (640 acres) each. No land was to be placed on sale until surveyed, or surveyed until the Indian title of occupancy was extinguished.

This method of survey made for simplicity, cheapness, and a clear title. It set the pattern of the American West. Ranges, townships, and sections marched across the continent with the pioneer, imposing their rigid rectangles on forest, plain, and mountain.

The question of large plots or small was determined by a compromise, which one member called a wholesale and retail method. The Act of 1796 required alternate townships to be sold in blocks of eight sections; intervening townships in single sections of 640 acres. Government land offices were established at Philadelphia for the sale of the large lots, which it was expected would appeal to moneyed men and speculators, and at Pittsburgh and Cincinnati for the sale of the sections, in order to serve the actual settlers. For both large and small lots the method of sale was public auction, at the upset price of two dollars an acre, to be paid within one year. Salt springs were reserved in order to prevent the monopolizing of that frontier necessity, but the educational reserves of the Ordinance of 1785 were not adopted. Two dollars an acre was fixed upon as a sufficient price to prevent large areas being engrossed by speculators; and it proved to be adequate for a time; but the smallest unit was too large and the price too high for the ordinary sort of pioneer, who at that time could obtain land in Maine, New York, and the Western Reserve, for as little as fifty cents an acre.

The Act of 1796 applied only to the land ceded by the Treaty of Greenville; and, owing to high prices and the delay of Congress in making appropriations for surveys, only fifty thousand acres were sold by 1800. In that year Congress lowered the unit of sale in certain areas to 320 acres (in 1804 to 160 acres), and gave four years' credit. As thus amended the Act was copied for every new acquisition from the Indians in the Northwest Territory until 1820.[2] By that time eighteen federal land offices were open for sales to settlers. When Ohio, the first ' public land state,' was admitted in 1802 the Federal Government adopted the precedent of retaining title to all ungranted land within the state boundaries, excepting a donation of one section in each township to a state fund for education. Thus the Act of 1796, drafted by ordinary members of an average Congress, set the rhythm of American social development for a century to come.

---

[2] In 1803 it was extended to the remainder of the Mississippi Territory that was not covered by state grants; and two years later the system of survey was extended to the Louisiana purchase, although the complicated French and Spanish grants prevented the sale of government land west of the Mississippi until twelve years more had elapsed.

Until 1825 the frontier in the northwest was advanced mainly by pioneers and settlers of the Kentucky type. Adventurous youths of New England and New York contributed their quota to the army of professional pioneers, who acted as a shock battalion for the permanent settlers. These men, inured to hardship and danger, seldom acquired a title to land, and remained in one spot only long enough to deplete the game, or exhaust their clearings by crude cropping with rude implements. When large plantations cultivated by slave labor became established in Kentucky, the hardened pioneer moved southwest or northwest as a stage in his journey to Texas and the Pacific. 'No people are so adapted to encounter the fatigues and privations of the wilderness; none form such efficient pioneers of civilization,' said an English observer. They lightened the labors of the settlers that followed, and provided the trained scouts and sharpshooters for Indian wars. Their wild, free life gave America much of its old-time gusto and savor; and if they left a taint of lawlessness and violence, they also carried forward the robust tradition of individual prowess that has given America its present place in the world.

9. *The Farewell Address*

Organization of a government, establishment of national credit, a wise fostering of maritime commerce, recovery of territory withheld under the Confederation, the crushing of red rebels and white, the establishment of a land policy which set the rhythm of American society, and the preservation of peace: these were the notable achievements of the two administrations of President Washington. By refusing to run for a third term he established the two-term tradition in national politics, and on 17 September 1796, he summed up his political experience in a farewell address to his countrymen.

For a paper addressed to a people in a peculiar stage of their development, its permanent truth and value are surprisingly great. An eloquent plea for union is followed by a pointed exposition of disruptive tendencies: the politician's device of misrepresenting 'the opinions and aims of other districts' in order to acquire influence within his own; the forming of combinations to override or control the constituted authorities; the 'baneful effects of the Spirit of Party,' a spirit 'having its root in the strongest passions of the human mind.' As to foreign policy:

Observe good faith and justice towards all nations; cultivate peace and harmony with all. . . . In the execution of such a plan nothing is more essential than that permanent, inveterate antipathies against particular nations and passionate attachments for others should be excluded; and that in place of them just and amicable feelings towards all should be cultivated. The Nation which indulges towards another an habitual hatred or an habitual fondness is in some degree a slave.

Washington's famous doctrine of isolation is contained in the following sentences:

Europe has a set of primary interests, which to us have none, or a very remote relation. — Hence she must be engaged in frequent controversies, the causes of which are essentially foreign to our concerns. Hence therefore it must be unwise in us to implicate ourselves, by artificial ties in the ordinary vicissitudes of her politics, or the ordinary combinations and collisions of her friendships or enmities. Our detached and distant situation invites us to pursue a different course. . . . 'Tis our true policy to steer clear of permanent alliances, with any portion of the foreign world. . . . Taking care always to keep ourselves, by suitable establishments, on a respectable defensive posture, we may safely trust to temporary alliances for extraordinary emergencies.

The Farewell Address fell on deaf ears in a Europe that was ringing with the exploits of a new hero, Bonaparte. But there it was written, for whosoever cared to read, that a new power considered herself outside the European system. It was little heeded in America, where the leading politicians believed that the dearest interests of their respective parties were bound up with England or with France.

The presidential election of 1796 was the first to be contested by party candidates, but there were no formal nominations; everything was arranged through private consultation and correspondence among the national and state leaders. By the implied terms of the Virginia-New York alliance, the Republicans decided to support Jefferson and Burr for President and Vice-President; the Federalists, to make a balanced ticket, nominated John Adams and Thomas Pinckney. Jay's treaty was the central issue of the campaign. The result was a narrow Federalist victory. Adams obtained the Presidency with 71 votes in the electoral college. Jefferson's 68 votes made him Vice-President by the curious method of choice that then prevailed.

'I now compare myself,' wrote Washington on 2 March 1797, ' to the wearied traveller who seeks a resting place, and is bending his body to lean thereon. But to be suffered to do *this* in peace is too much to be endured by *some*.' During his last year in office the President was assailed with a virulence such as few of his successors have suffered. Jefferson, in a private letter which found its way into print, referred to a certain ' Samson in the field and Solomon in the Council ' whose head had been ' shorn by the harlot England ' — obviously the President! The Philadelphia *Aurora,* on the morrow of Washington's retirement, proclaimed that ' this day ought to be a Jubilee in the United States . . . for the man who is the source of all the misfortunes of our country, is this day reduced to a level with his fellow citizens.'

A generation passed before Washington's services in time of peace were adequately appreciated in his own country; and as his personality has faded into legend, it has been clothed in army uniform. Washington's unique place in history rests not only on his leadership in war, and his influence in organizing the Federal Government; not merely on his integrity, good judgment, and magnanimity, but also on his courageous stand for peace when his countrymen were clamoring to embark on an unnecessary war. This quiet, plainspeaking gentleman of Virginia glimpsed a truth hidden from his more talented contemporaries: that the means by which a nation advances, especially in its adolescence, are more important than the ends which it pursues.

XVII

JOHN ADAMS'S ADMINISTRATION
1797–1801

1. *French Policy and Federalist Apprehensions*

WHEN John Adams became President, on 4 March 1797, he found the situation more difficult than Washington had in 1794. Jay's treaty had embroiled the United States with a more powerful and aggressive France than the country that sent Genet to America. Danton and Robespierre, uniformly friendly to the United States, had been guillotined. France was under the five-headed executive known as the Directory, which had completely abandoned the republican idealism of 1792 for the traditional policy of French hegemony in Europe. With some justice, the Directory regarded Jay's treaty as evidence of an Anglo-American entente, for by accepting the British view of neutral rights, the United States was forced to order French privateers out of her harbors and to permit the capture of provision ships destined for France. James Monroe, who had been received as American minister under an earlier régime with enthusiastic speeches and fraternal embraces, lost his balance and his usefulness under these new circumstances, and was recalled by Washington in 1796. Party feeling was so bitter in the United States that several followers of Jefferson even urged the French minister at Philadelphia to advise his government to retaliate against American shipping — largely owned by Federalists. The Directory, accordingly, loosed its corsairs against the American merchant fleet. The ensuing French spoliations on commerce made those of Britain in 1793 seem mild in comparison. Even provision ships sent to the French islands by French consuls were taken and condemned. In June 1797 the Secretary of State reported that over three hundred American vessels had been captured under color of French authority.

The Directory refused to receive Monroe's successor at Paris, and its official language towards the United States became insolent and provocative. President Adams declared that he would not submit to further indignities, but hoped to maintain Washington's policy of neutrality. Hamilton wished to avoid a rupture with France, until it were known how her negotiations with Britain were coming out. Following the Jay precedent, another effort was made to obtain justice through diplomacy. In order to satisfy the Republicans that he was not seeking a quarrel, Adams appointed Elbridge Gerry, *persona grata* to them and to France; and in order to keep Gerry out of mischief, John Marshall and C. C. Pinckney were joined with him in the mission.

The first year of Adams's administration passed before news arrived from the three ambassadors. In the meantime, the party cleavage became deeper. The Republicans, refusing to believe that the French Government had changed its character since 1792, stoutly defended the spoliations as a proper answer to Jay's treaty. To the Federalists, on the other hand, France had become just such an object of fear and loathing as, in 1920, the Soviet Union became to the American conservatives of our time. Even Hamilton, in reviewing ' the disgusting spectacle of the French Revolution,' bewailed free love and worship of reason, which, he insisted, were still officially supported in Paris. A New England clergyman, reading Robison's *Proofs of a Conspiracy,* spread the news that the French Revolution was simply a conspiracy engineered by the ' Illuminati ' of Bavaria against government, religion, and morality; and that Jefferson was their head agent to subvert American society.[1] This simple explanation of hateful but bewildering phenomena was no less satisfying in 1797 than in the 1920's when professional patriots in England and the United States revived the hoary hoax.

European events gave reason to those who asserted that France was a world menace. The Directory, in its endeavors to conquer the ' natural frontiers ' of France, erected vassal republics abroad by exporting the Jacobinism that it proscribed at home. The civilized world was fast dividing into those who had made terms with France, and those who had not; and at the end of 1797 Britain and the United States were the only two countries who had not. 'If England will persevere,' wrote Senator Cabot, ' she will save Europe and save us; but if she yields, all will be lost.' 'She is now the only barrier between us and the deathly embraces of our dear Allies —

---

[1] President Dwight of Yale predicted in his Fourth of July Sermon of 1798 that Jeffersonian Republicanism meant nothing less than ' our wives and daughters the victims of legal prostitution; soberly dishonored; speciously polluted . . . our sons become the disciples of Voltaire, and the dragoons of Marat.' Similar arguments. based on the Robison *Proofs,* have often been used against liberal and anti-militarist organizations since the World War.

between universal irreligion, immorality and plunder, and what order, probity, virtue and religion is left.' Surely, as in 1917, the alternative was to fight on England's side, or fight alone later.

So reasoned the Federalists. We now know that their fears were exaggerated, for the rulers in Paris were too well informed to try in America their favorite formula of revolution pushed home by invasion. Yet the French designs on Canada, Louisiana, and Florida were more definite and dangerous than even the Federalists supposed. Reviving a policy that brought on the Seven Years' War, the Directory sought to cover both flanks of the United States with French territory, and push back their boundaries to the Appalachians. The *habitants* of Quebec were being plied with propaganda for a Canadian republic under French protection. Pressure was brought to bear on the Spanish court to cede the Floridas and Louisiana to France. Victor Collot, who went on a secret mission for the Directory to the Western country, stated the argument neatly:

France must acquire Louisiana and the Floridas by negotiation, and Canada by force, as the only means to contain the United States within peaceful bounds, to break their exclusive relations with England, to preserve our colonies exclusively to ourselves by feeding them with the products of our own soil, and, finally, to recover in both hemispheres that preponderance to which nature entitles us.

With the Spanish possessions, the Directory proposed to take over Spain's American policy. In 1796 relations were renewed with Genet's unpaid warriors, a fresh lot of agents was sent into the western country, and Milfort, the half-breed 'tastenagy' or war chief of the Creek nation, was commissioned brigadier-general in the armies of the French Republic.

The American peace commission arrived in Paris at an unpropitious moment in October 1797, just after the Directors had pulled off a *coup d'état* against the peace party, and concluded a successful treaty with Austria. The Directors, at least one of whom had a pecuniary interest in privateering, felt they could with impunity continue clandestine war against the United States. A comic, if one-sided, bit of bargaining ensued. Talleyrand, the Directory's minister of foreign affairs, sent some hangers-on (referred to in the dispatches as X, Y, and Z) to play on the fears of the American envoys, and sound their pockets. A bribe for the minister, and a loan

as compensation for the President's message, were the prerequisites
to negotiation. Pressed for an alternative, Monsieur Y hinted at the
power of the French party in America, and recalled the fate of
recalcitrant republics. The American envoys, understanding that
bribery was necessary in dealing with the Directory, were prepared
to come down handsomely for some definite concession; but a loan
of ten million dollars on doubtful security together with a gift of
$250,000 to Talleyrand, seemed excessive for mere recognition. ' Our
case is different from that of the minor nations of Europe,' Marshall
informed Monsieur Y. ' They were unable to maintain their independence, and did not expect to do so. America is a great, and,
so far as concerns her self-defense, a powerful nation.' After several
months of this sort of thing, Marshall and Pinckney took their leave.
Gerry, fondly believing his presence necessary to avert war, remained
in Paris.

The envoys' dispatches, recording in detail their strange experiences, were submitted by President Adams early in 1798 to Congress, and published in April 1798. The public was deeply moved
by this first-hand view of French diplomacy. On the Republicans
their effect was stupefying. ' Trimmers dropt off from the party
like windfalls from an apple tree in September,' wrote Fisher Ames.
Jefferson ' thought it his duty to be silent.' Loyal addresses poured
in on President and Congress, indignation meetings were held,
reams of patriotic poetry were produced, and ' millions for defence,
but not one cent for tribute ' became the toast of the day.

2. Hostilities but not War

Alexander Hamilton, underestimating his old acquaintance Talleyrand, expected the French Government to be so angered by the
publication of the dispatches as to lose all sense of its proper interest,
and declare war. At his advice the Federalists adopted a policy of
armed neutrality, counting on a declaration of war by France to
unite all honest men to their standard. Congress created the Navy
Department, revived the marine corps, fitted for sea the *Constitution,
Constellation,* and *United States* frigates, and purchased several
smaller vessels that were promptly built by maritime communities.
National ships and armed merchantmen were authorized to capture
French armed vessels wherever found. The French treaties of 1778
were formally abrogated. By the end of 1798 there were fourteen

American men-of-war at sea, and some two hundred merchant vessels had taken out letters of marque and reprisal. The picaroons were fairly swept out of West Indian waters, and on 9 February 1799 the *Constellation,* Commodore Truxton, captured off Nevis the crack French frigate *L'Insurgente.*

In the congressional elections of 1798–99 the Federalists won a strong majority, which was destined to be their last. Jefferson and his party appeared to be utterly discredited by their pro-French leanings, but time was preparing their revenge. A rift appeared in the Federalist party between the President and Hamilton, and into this rift Talleyrand insinuated a wedge.

It was a difference in objective and in temperament that caused the trouble. President Adams's object was to teach the Directory good manners, and force it to respect the American flag. He was willing to accept war if declared by France, but hoped to avoid it. The bulk of his party agreed. Hamilton and the New England Federalists, on the contrary, regarded the French imbroglio not as an affair to be wound up, but as an occasion to be improved. It was to be a starting-point for spirited measures that would strengthen the Federal Government, discipline the American people, discredit the Republicans and all that they stood for. Hamilton expected some of the Jeffersonians to help the enemy in case of war, and for this reason, no less than to meet a French invasion, the regular army was increased, the *cadres* for a provisional army created, Washington appointed Lieutenant-General, and Hamilton his second in command. Adams growled over these excessive military preparations, but complied.

The only thing wanting, it seemed, was an open and declared war with France, which France was not so obliging as to offer. Talleyrand, although annoyed at the exposure of his venality to the amused laughter of all Europe, saw the real point: that war with America would mean a new ally for England. Jefferson advised him, and he advised the Directory, to keep cool, and not fall into the trap. No use trying to start a revolution, he said. ' In no country is anarchy so much feared as in the United States.' Hence the French government used every available channel to communicate pacific intentions to America. In evidence of sincerity, West Indian letters of marque were annulled, and the French agents were ordered to respect American ships. An official explanation of the X Y Z episode was issued, in a tone of injured dignity. The American ministers, it appeared, had been imposed upon by charlatans. The Directory had intended to treat with them, but they shut themselves up in their hotel, and went off in a huff before they could be received! For just such a cue the discomfited opposition in America had been waiting. Every Republican paper took up the cry that the X Y Z affair was a Federalist hoax.

These evidences of an accommodating spirit took the war Federalists aback — but only for a moment. 'I hope we shall remember,' declared Secretary of State Pickering in January 1799, 'that the tyger crouches before he leaps upon his prey.' It was decided to treat the French overtures as insincere, to continue war preparations, and to declare war on France as soon as Congress convened.

3. *The Alien and Sedition Acts*

While organizing defense and drumming up war enthusiasm, the Federalists did not neglect their real enemies at home. The Naturalization, Alien, and Sedition Acts of 1798 were aimed at domestic disaffection rather than foreign danger. These laws provoked the first organized state rights movement under the Constitution, and promoted the election of Jefferson to the presidency. They afford an instance of political intolerance which is unfortunately a part of the American character, as of human nature.

Gouverneur Morris had remarked in the Federal Convention that he wanted none of 'those philosophical gentlemen, those citizens of the world as they call themselves, in our public councils.' The French Revolution, however, sent a good many of them to America; and one who came earlier, Albert Gallatin of Geneva, was leading the congressional minority in 1798. Dr. Priestley, accused of trying 'to decompose both Church and State' with his chemical formulae, had found refuge in Pennsylvania after being mobbed as pro-French in England. Thomas Cooper, who followed him, founded a Republican newspaper. The French minister, Adet, who interfered in the election of 1796, was also a chemist by profession; the French botanist Michaux did espionage for his government. Victor du Pont, son of the economist, was one of the French consuls who had to leave the United States hastily in 1798. At the height of excitement that year, the Directory requested passports for a delegation from the Institute of France, under Victor's father, Du Pont de Nemours, to visit the United States 'with the view of improving and extending the sciences.' John Adams replied, 'We have too many French philosophers already, and I really begin to think, or rather to suspect, that learned academies . . . have disorganized the world, and are incompatible with social order.' As these were the persons whom super-patriots wished to expel in 1798, it is interesting to note that Gallatin became one of our greatest statesmen, Priestley a notable figure in the history of science, Cooper a college president; whilst the Du Ponts settled in Delaware and engaged in a highly respectable mode of disorganizing the world — the manufacture of high explosives.

Immigrants who were neither philosophers nor gentlemen gave even more trouble to the Federal Government. Noisy Jacobins began to come over. French agents were stirring up sedition in the West. Equally unwelcome from the Federalist point of view were the Irish refugees, who lost no time in becoming naturalized and in joining the anti-British party. A Federalist senator reported that in a journey through Pennsylvania he had seen many Irishmen, who with few exceptions were 'United Irishmen, freemasons, and the most God-provoking democrats this side of hell! '

As of late, the notion that political refugees were engaged in treasonable activities against the United States produced legislation against them. The Naturalization Act of 1798 extended the required period of residence for citizenship from five to fourteen years; the Alien Act gave the President power to expel foreigners by executive decree. Adams never availed himself of the privilege; but two shiploads of Frenchmen left the country in anticipation.

For the Sedition Act of 1798 there was a legitimate need. There being no common law of the United States, the federal courts required statutory authority before taking cognizance of conspiracies against the government, or libels on high officials. One section of the act, however, declared any speech or writing against President or Congress 'with the intent to defame' or to bring them 'into contempt or disrepute' a misdemeanor punishable by fine or imprisonment; and it was this section only that was enforced. Federalists never recognized the value of party opposition, and from their quarter-deck point of view the Republicans were little better than mutineers. About twenty-five persons were arrested and ten convicted, most of them Republican editors who were conveniently got out of the way by heavy fines or jail sentences.

Another act of the 1798 crop is still on the statute books. Dr. Logan, a Philadelphia Quaker, went to Paris in the hope of pre serving peace. Congress, fearing lest he succeed, passed the Logan Act, declaring it a misdemeanor for an American citizen to correspond with a foreign government on the subject of a dispute between it and the United States. It is still perfectly legal, however, for any American citizen to do his utmost to stir up war with a foreign government.

4. *State Protests and Presidential Action*

Out of this unwholesome atmosphere of persecution came two startling protests from state legislatures: the resolves of Virginia drafted by Madison, and those of Kentucky drafted by Jefferson. Both declared the Alien and Sedition Acts unconstitutional. As to the Alien Act, there is no getting round the doctrine, later adopted by the Supreme Court, that the power of expelling aliens belongs to the Federal Government and not to the states. The Sedition Act stands in a different light, for the Constitution (Amendment I) forbids Congress to pass any law abridging the freedom of speech, or of the press. Federalist lawyers, like many American lawyers today, attempted to extract all meaning from this clause by assuming Blackstone's definition that freedom of the press is merely freedom from censorship, or by asserting that it was not meant to apply in time of war, or by confounding criticism with libel. The First Amendment, however, was written by men who intended to protect critics of the government. A much more drastic sedition law (the Espionage Act) was passed in 1917, and enforced by sentences far more severe than those of the Federalists. But in 1798 the American Revolution was too close for government to punish opinion with impunity.

It is the theory rather than the arguments of the Virginia and Kentucky Resolves that is significant. They develop the ' compact ' or ' state rights ' theory of the Constitution that Jefferson adumbrated in his opinion on the bank bill in 1792. Kentucky declares that whenever Congress palpably transcends its powers. as in the Sedition Act, each state ' has an equal right to judge for itself, as well of infractions as of the mode and measure of redress.' She calls upon her ' co-states ' to ' concur . . . in declaring these acts ' void, and to unite ' in requesting their repeal'; while Virginia hints at ' interposing' state authority between the persecuted citizen and his government.

These principles are not logically expressed, nor is it likely that their implications were yet thought out. Both state legislatures had their eyes on the coming presidential election, and were really engaged in lighting a fiery cross to rally the Republican clans. Yet the principles of the Kentucky and Virginia Resolves of 1798 became a platform to all later movements in state rights. Within ten years the New England Federalists were flinging them back at Jefferson and Madison; and to the Southern particularists of a later generation they became an indispensable gloss on the Constitution.

In any federal government there is a possible conflict between powers of the nation and powers of the states. A minority party, interest, or sectional combination, if ridden too hard or too proud to be ridden at all, will try to escape the consequences of its position by raising the banner of state rights. In American history the ' doctrine' of state rights has not been a cause, but an effect of this condition. Almost every man in public life between 1798 and 1860 spurned it when his section was in the saddle, and embraced it when his constituents deemed themselves oppressed. Almost every state in turn declared its own absolute sovereignty, only to denounce as treasonable similar declarations by other states.

There is no doubt that the ' Federalist reign of terror' alarmed a people who had rather strong notions of liberty. Virginia talked of secession. Congress kept the new army on foot ' to suppress or prevent rebellion'; Thomas Jefferson alone remained hopeful and serene. Strong in his faith that the people would ' recover their true sight,' Jefferson presided impeccably over the Senate, writing letters far and wide to his political lieutenants, and enjoying the spectacle of Federalists hanging themselves on their own rope. ' Hold on then, like a good and faithful seaman,' he wrote a discouraged congressman, ' till our brother sailors can rouse from their intoxication and right the vessel.' It was John Adams, however, who drove the drunken sailors from the quarter-deck — only to bring the ship into port for Thomas Jefferson.

Hamilton, who up to the spring of 1799 had been the power behind the Adams administration, owing to the deference of numerous senators, representatives, and three members of the President's cabinet to his views, did not propose to stop with armed neutrality.

He regarded the imbroglio with France as an occasion to be improved for glory and power. Hints dropped here and there in letters suggest that a grandiose plan was forming in his brain. He would lead the new American army overland against New Orleans, and the British would co-operate in blockading the mouth of the Mississippi. Louisiana and the Floridas having fallen, Hamilton might march into Mexico, while the British navy, in concert with the South American patriot Miranda, liberated the Spanish main. The American West would be reconciled to a Federal Government clothed in all the panoply of sovereignty. Anglo-American friendship would be cemented by dividing the spoils of Spanish America. Hamilton would return laurel-crowned, at the head of his victorious legion, to become the First Citizen of America, as Bonaparte was already the First Citizen of France. And the Jeffersonian party, with all it stood for, would be completely discredited.

But the Hamiltonians reckoned without the President. John Adams was one of the first political philosophers in America, and a very human one, too. In no sense a democrat, he regarded Jefferson's belief in the common man's innate virtue as sentimental nonsense; but he was equally hostile to the development of anything like plutocracy or militarism. For some unaccountable reason he had so far allowed himself to be guided by Hamilton's friends in the cabinet. In March 1799, he suddenly awoke to the dangers into which the ship of state was drifting; and without telling a single person (except the prudent Abigail) about his intentions, President Adams threw a bombshell into the Senate in the shape of the nomination of a minister plenipotentiary to France. Of course that halted the whole war program. Hamilton and his friends were furious, but they dared not reject the nomination and thus give color to the charge that they were seeking war when the President saw the possibility of peace.

Adams compromised to the extent of appointing a commission instead of a single envoy; but Secretary Pickering managed by subterfuge to hold up their sailing, so that the commission did not reach Paris until the year 1800. Napoleon Bonaparte, now First Consul, received them cordially and appointed his brother Joseph as negotiator. For seven months the negotiations dragged, while Napoleon crossed the Alps to thrash the Austrians again, at Marengo. Bonaparte would admit no liability for the French spoliations, unless the United States recognized the treaties of 1778, which Congress had denounced at the height of anti-gallican feeling. No alliance, no money! The Americans, fearing to bring home a renewed entangling alliance, signed a mere commercial convention, each party reserving its rights as to treaties and spoliations. It was high time to come to terms with France, for even England was on the point of making peace.

On the very next day, 1 October 1800, France secretly obtained the retrocession of Louisiana from Spain. But Jefferson later secured by purchase what Hamilton proposed to conquer at incalculable cost.

5. *The Election of 1800–01*

If the French had only been so accommodating as to land even a corporal's guard on American soil, or some ' seditious alien ' had started something, the presidential election of 1800 might have gone very differently; but as time went on, and no enemy appeared, and the new direct tax was assessed, the patriotic fervor of 1798 faded out. In the meantime there were fresh difficulties with England over impressment, the sedition prosecutions were having their effect, and the Republican editors were throwing out a wide net for political martyrs.

Presidential candidates for the election of 1800–01 were selected by party caucuses in Congress. The Republicans, as in 1796, decided to support Jefferson and Burr. The Federalists reluctantly renominated John Adams, with C. C. Pinckney of the X Y Z mission for Vice-President. No sooner was the decision made than the Hamiltonian faction, who vowed vengeance on Adams for making peace, planned to bring in Pinckney over the President's head, by persuading some presidential elector to throw away a vote that should normally have gone to him. Most of the pamphlets published during the campaign were by Federalists attacking one another. A majority of Republican electors was chosen; but as no one of them dared throw away his second vote, Jefferson and Burr tied for first place with 73 votes each, as against 65 for Adams and one less for Pinckney.

The Twelfth Amendment to the Constitution (1804) removed the possibility of a tie between two candidates on the same ticket. But in 1801 the House of Representatives, voting by states, had to choose between Jefferson and Burr, a majority of one state being necessary for election. The Federalists saw an opportunity to thwart their enemies by supporting Burr, thus electing a cynical and pliant corrupt politician over a 'dangerous radical.' Party division was so close that during thirty-five ballots, and until 17 February 1801, the House was deadlocked. There was talk of preventing an election, and of civil war. Finally Hamilton brought his influence to bear, three Federalists cast blank ballots, and Jefferson was elected President by a majority of two states. At the congressional elections in 1800 the Republicans obtained emphatic majorities in House and Senate; and in 1801 the Federalists went out of power in every branch of government except the judiciary. The exception proved important!

So passed into minority the party which contained more talent and virtue, with less political common sense, than any of their successors. The Federalists went down with colors flying; but their usefulness as leaders of the nation had gone. It had been their task to tame the wild forces set loose by the American Revolution, to integrate discordant elements, to lead an inchoate nation to enduring union. The character of Washington, the genius of Hamilton, and the disciplined, intelligent patriotism of their colleagues and lieutenants saved the American union from disintegration before its colors were set; but the events of 1798–1800 proved that the Federalists had nothing more to contribute, outside the judiciary. Their chosen basis, an oligarchy of wealth and talent, was the very thing to tide over a crisis, but insufficiently broad or deep for permanent polity. Their patience and vision were not great enough for their task. Their old-world precepts of vigor, energy, and suppression had become fixed ideas, enclosing them in a network of delusion that set them in antagonism to deep-rooted popular prejudices; and the expanding forces of American life enveloped and overwhelmed them. Yet those forces had been so schooled and molded by twelve years of Federalist rule that, with John Marshall presiding at the supreme bench, even Jefferson and his 'wild men' (as the Federalists called them) were unable to do much more than throw the furniture about when the next session opened.

XVIII

JEFFERSONIAN DEMOCRACY
1801–1805

1. *Jefferson's Ambition*

THOMAS JEFFERSON, ruminating years later on the events of a crowded lifetime, thought that his election to the Presidency marked as real a revolution as that of 1776. He had saved the country from monarchy and militarism, and brought it back to its true principles of republican simplicity. But there never had been any danger of monarchy; it was John Adams who saved the country from militarism; and a little simplicity more or less cannot be deemed a revolution. The Federalists feared that America, with a 'Jacobin' President, was in for a reign of terror. Yet the four years that followed were one of the most tranquil of Republican olympiads, marked not by radical reforms or popular tumults, but by the peaceful acquisition of territory as large again as the United States. The election of 1800–01 brought a change of men more than of measures, and a transfer of federal power from the latitude of Massachusetts to that of Virginia, rather than a weakening of the Federal Government in favor of the states. Jefferson ruled eight years and was succeeded by his Secretary of State, Madison of Virginia. Madison, after eight years, gave way to his Secretary of State, Monroe of Virginia. Monroe ruled eight years, and was succeeded by his Secretary of State, J. Q. Adams. The year 1829, when this second Adams was defeated by a militant democracy, may more properly be termed revolutionary than 1801.

Jefferson was not in any social sense a democrat, and only in a political sense by contrast with his contemporaries. A gentleman philosopher like many of the French *noblesse,* with a classical education, an exquisite taste, a lively curiosity, and a belief in the perfectibility of man, he was of the eighteenth rather than the nineteenth century. Deeply religious without being a churchman, he had the serenity of one to whom now and then the Spirit has not disdained to speak. The extraordinary ascendancy that he enjoyed in the hearts of the masses was attained without speech-making, military service, or catering to vulgar prejudices. The secret of Jefferson's power lay in the fact that he appealed to and expressed America's better self: her idealism, simplicity, youthful mind, and hopeful outlook, rather than those material, practical, and selfish qualities on which Hamilton based his policy. Jefferson's political object was to prove that people circumstanced like the Americans were ripe for 'a government founded not on the fears and follies of man, but on his reason, on the predominance of his social over his dissocial passions.'

It is easy to be cynical about Jefferson. In order to win support, he was forced to give men offices; and Hamilton's financial schemes were mere pleached alleys to the golden vista opened by Louisiana. Yet it was a bold experiment even to attempt to base a government on man's better nature, at a time when France had almost come full circle; and it was something to have kept the country straight to Washington's course in the midst of Napoleonic wars. Jefferson realized that 'an important means of giving free course to this experiment is to keep Europe and its quarrels at a distance,' and his foreign policy was aimed at an isolation that would be cultural and economic as well as political.

Jefferson was sensitive but not sentimental. He loved birds and flowers, lacked a sense of humor, and hated the sight of blood. Unlike most Virginians he did not engage in field sports, and regarded dogs as a useless race, deserving extirpation. But he despised Rousseau's romanticism; and, if he thought mankind perfectible, it was because Americans had advanced so rapidly in his own time. The dead hand of the past had been lifted from their government; why not from their religion and society? And this fastidious gentleman was a finished politician. His inaugural address of 4 March 1801 was eighteenth-century idealism rubbed through the sieve of practical politics. Instead of denouncing the Federalists as monarchists, he invited them to rejoin the true republican church: 'We are all republicans — we are all federalists. If there be any among us who wish to dissolve this Union, or to change its republican form, let them stand undisturbed as monuments of the safety with which error of opinion may be tolerated where reason is left free to combat it.' This government, 'the world's best hope,' must not be abandoned 'on the theoretic and visionary fear' that it is not strong enough. 'Sometimes it is said that Man cannot be trusted with the government of himself. Can he then be trusted with the government of others?'

'Separated by nature and a wide ocean from the exterminating havoc of one quarter of the globe,' 'possessing a chosen country, with room enough for our descendants to the hundredth and thousandth generation' practicing the social virtues, the only thing 'necessary to close the circle of our felicities' is 'a wise and frugal government, which shall restrain men from injuring one another, shall leave them otherwise free to regulate their own pursuits of industry and improvement, and shall not take from the mouth of labor the bread it has earned.'

If a government of that nature ever was attainable, it was so in the simple rural America that the physiocrats admired. In his inaugural address Jefferson dropped a plain hint that shipowners and manufacturers might expect no favors from him. And if the net result of his administration was to bring Hamilton's dream of a warlike and industrial nation nearer fulfilment, it was because of world forces beyond anyone's control.

2. Simplicity and Frugality

Jefferson was fortunate in the circumstances and surroundings of his first administration. His party had a majority in both houses of Congress, and no rival leader was hankering for the succession. The truce of Amiens made a breathing-space in the European war, which left him free to concentrate on domestic problems. The civil service had not yet acquired that *esprit de corps* and resourceful obstruction which have thwarted so many reforming statesmen; and the President had a right to remove any member of it without cause. There was no mess to clear up; John Adams turned over the administration and the Treasury in superb order. And the Federal Government had been transferred from aristocratic Philadelphia to an appropriate setting for Republican simplicity, the new capital city of Washington.

Congress decided in 1790 to fix the federal District of Columbia on the Potomac. President Washington chose the exact site, in a sparsely populated region a few miles up-stream from Mount Vernon, just below the Great Falls. Maryland and Virginia[1] ceded their

---

[1] In 1846 that part of the District on the right bank of the Potomac, including the town of Alexandria, was retroceded to Virginia.

jurisdiction, local landowners were indemnified by federal commissioners, and the capital city of Washington was planned on a generous scale by a French engineer, Major L'Enfant.[2] Ten years had elapsed, but Washington was little more than a cleared space with scattered buildings, between primeval forest and the river. One wing of the Capitol, a graceful Palladian structure on a noble site, was ready for occupancy, and the other wing nearly completed; but the rotunda was open to the heavens. Near by were a few brick houses, wooden cabins of workmen and negroes, and a few poor stores. Pennsylvania Avenue, a broad clearing studded with stumps and alder bushes, led northwestward from the Capitol through a morass to the simple and dignified executive mansion, or White House, designed by James Hoban of Dublin. Around that, on higher ground, were a few hundred houses, mostly of wood, the nucleus of the future residential city. Two miles farther to the westward was Georgetown, a comfortable little college town that afforded the officials an agreeable change from each other's and their landladies' society. The red clay soil of Washington became fine dust in dry weather and liquid cement in rain; swarms of mosquitoes spread malaria among the new-comers, and inoculated the remainder with a parasitic attitude toward life. Several fine groves of tulip-trees were the only features of natural beauty within the city site. Jefferson's one recorded wish for despotic power was to save these trees from the inhabitants, who proceeded to fell them regardless of property rights, and to sell the logs to shivering new-comers. Except for scornful Federalists, and a complaining diplomatic corps, everyone made light of the difficulties, and looked forward to some magic transmutation of their backwoods capital into a seat of commerce and the muses;

> Though nought but woods and Jefferson they see,
> Where streets should run and sages ought to be,

as Tom Moore wrote after his visit in 1804. Eventually the 'city of magnificent distances' grew up to its magnificent plan; but until after the Civil War it was squalid and slovenly compared with Baltimore, Charleston, or the Northern cities.

Washington, then, was a fit setting for experiments in *laissez-faire*. Members of Congress, forced to leave their wives at home and live

[2] Jefferson suggested the spacing of the Capitol and the White House. William Thornton, an American, and B. H. Latrobe, an Englishman with a Pennsylvania mother, designed the Capitol. The two interior wings. still standing, are their work.

in crowded boarding houses, finished the public business in annual sessions of three to five months' duration. Written presidential messages were substituted for the annual 'speech from the throne,' and the answers from both houses were omitted. As a widower, Jefferson was free to establish a new code of republican etiquette. The White House was open to all comers every morning. Anthony Merry, in full uniform of a British minister plenipotentiary, was received by the President in morning undress of faded threadbare coat, red waistcoat, corduroy breeches, and slippers. White House dinners were well cooked by a French chef, and Jefferson's wine bill for one year was $2800. But the rule of first come first served, which he adopted to do away with precedence, was not understood by the diplomatic corps or relished by the secretaries' wives; and Washington has since become the most precedence-ridden capital in the western world.

Jefferson's inaugural pledge of the honest payment of the public debt, and promise to preserve 'the general government in its whole constitutional vigor,' created joy in the Federalist camp. Hamilton, who had prophesied that his rival would pursue a temporizing rather than a violent system, viewed the inaugural message 'as virtually a candid retraction of past misapprehensions, and a pledge to the community that the new President will not lend himself to dangerous innovations, but in essential points will tread in the steps of his predecessors.' That, in the main, was what Jefferson did. He took over Washington's administrative machine 'in the full tide of successful experiment,' but fed a slightly different material into it.

Madison became his Secretary of State. For Secretary of the Treasury he chose Albert Gallatin, an off-shoot of aristocratic Geneva who had arrived young in the land of promise, made his living in the backwoods of Pennsylvania, and risen by character and ability to the opposition leadership in the House. He and Jefferson regarded the national debt as a mortgage, to be paid off without delay. Gallatin would even have retained the excise on distilled liquors, which his former constituents had resisted; but Jefferson insisted on removing this detested relic of Federalism, and made his name immortal in the mountains. This made the government even more dependent than formerly on customs revenues, so that the stoppage of foreign trade seriously embarrassed federal finances on the eve of the War of 1812.

Gallatin, who had been an unsparing critic of Hamiltonian financial methods, now gave Washington's minister the compliment of continuing them with little change. An act passed late in the Adams administration required the Secretary of the Treasury to prepare and submit an annual report. This led to an improvement in accounting methods. In Washington's administration, it had been customary for Congress to appropriate lump sums to the different departments, to spend with considerable discretion. The opposition naturally disliked this, and President Adams's Secretary of the Treasury complained: 'The Legislature will not pass laws in gross: their appropriations are minute. Gallatin, to whom they yield, is evidently intending to break down this department by charging it with impracticable details.'[3] Gallatin, with unusual self-denial, now proposed to charge the Treasury with these 'impracticable details,' and recommended detailed and specific appropriations. The records show, however, that a very slight advance in this direction was made under Jefferson and Madison; and it was not until after the War of 1812 that congressmen discovered that the useful frontier practice of 'log-rolling,' when applied to appropriations, served to create unnecessary work and direct federal money into their constituencies.

Jefferson's remark 'We are all republicans — we are all federalists' caused no little dismay in his own camp. Gallatin's father-in-law asked if enemies were to be kept 'in office to trample upon us.' William B. Giles of Virginia reminded the President that

a pretty general purgation of office, has been one of the benefits expected by the friends of the new order of things. . . . It can never be unpopular to turn a vicious man out and put a virtuous one in his room. . . . Taking it for granted, therefore, that this salutary check will be applied, I take the liberty of mentioning to you a neighbour of mine as properly qualified to fill the office of marshall for this district of Virginia, when the same shall be vacated.

No one seriously pretended that the federal civil service was inefficient or corrupt; but it was almost completely Federalist. Washington and Adams had never knowingly appointed a member of the opposition to office. Offices were already regarded as proper rewards for public service; and Jefferson's followers were eager to feed at the public crib. Yet, as he complained, functionaries seldom die, and never resign. The only thing to do, then, was to create vacancies

[3] Albert S. Bolles, *Financial History of United States* (1885), ii. 182.

by the presidential prerogative of removal. It soon became clear that, in respect of the Federalists, Jefferson 'intended to entice the flock with one hand and belabor the shepherds with the other.' There was no general purgation, but performance did not square with the bland professions of the inaugural discourse. It was a good instance of what Hamilton called Jefferson's 'ineradicable duplicity' — seeming to say one thing while meaning another.

3. A Maritime Adventure

Although foreign commerce was threatened with neglect, it was actually treated as a distinct and valuable interest until 1807. Neither Jefferson nor Congress tampered with the discriminating tonnage duties, the fishing bounties, or Jay's treaty. Theoretically the whole Republican party was hostile to the army and navy, which, according to John Taylor, would 'only serve to excite wars, squander money, and extend corruption.' Jefferson reduced the army by a 'chaste reformation,' as he called it, from four thousand to twenty-five hundred men. Yet he reduced the naval establishment no farther than an act of the last Federalist Congress permitted; and he employed the fleet, as neither Washington nor Adams had done, to protect the American carrying trade against the Barbary corsairs. The most brilliant achievements of his first administration were in war and diplomacy!

Franklin's reported maxim of the London merchants — 'If there were no Algiers, it would be worth England's while to build one' — may be only a saying of Poor Richard; but the complaisance of great powers for the Barbary corsairs, their toleration of white slavery for others so long as they were able to purchase immunity for themselves, filled Americans with disgust. Morocco, Algiers, Tunis, and Tripoli quickly discovered that the United States was independent, and preyed upon the American schooners and brigs that passed the Pillars of Hercules. Washington, unprovided with a navy, was forced to follow the European precedent and pay tribute. In ten years the United States paid almost two million dollars in tribute, ransom, and usance to these squalid barbarians.

Jefferson, the lover of peace, calculated that force in this instance would be cheaper in the long run. When the Pasha of Tripoli, discontented with his annual tribute, repudiated his treaty with the United States, Jefferson despatched a naval squadron to deal with him. Hostilities began, and continued for several years. The American navy, four thousand miles from its base, starved by a niggardly Congress and an economizing Treasury, operated under most difficult conditions. The Barbary coast, a lee shore during the winter months, could not be properly blockaded. Yet officers and men showed a gallantry and resourcefulness that earned them the esteem of the British service, and the hospitality of Malta and Gibraltar; American traders were able to go their way unmolested, and the final treaty with Tripoli (1805) was more honorable and less expensive than any European power had previously extorted. Tributes continued to be paid to other Barbary potentates until 1815, when Algiers was forced to respect the American flag.

4. *The Louisiana Purchase*

While Tripoli was being taught a lesson, the boundary of the United States advanced from the Mississippi to the Rocky Mountains.

Louisiana, which then comprised the whole of that vast territory, had been in Spanish possession since 1763. Less than one per cent of its area was settled. The Creoles, numbering with their slaves about forty thousand in 1800, were concentrated on both banks of the lower Mississippi. There were a few garrisons and trading posts on the west bank of the river between that point and St. Louis, and a few more on the Red river; the rest was in undisputed possession of the redskins. Sugar cane and cotton had recently been introduced from the West Indies, but the province was a drain on the Spanish exchequer.

We have already seen the importance of the Mississippi river commerce to the American West. The retrocession of this great province from Spain to France, by the secret treaty of San Ildefonso on 1 October 1800, completed the Western policy which the successive French governments had followed since 1792. Their main object was to establish a political and commercial base in North America. Napoleon proposed to give France a maritime and colonial empire; to make her the first power in the New World, as in the Old.

As France did not take immediate possession of Louisiana, the Treaty of San Ildefonso was kept secret for over a year. In May, 1801 Jefferson got wind of it, and another event revealed its implications. Bonaparte despatched an expeditionary force to Santo Domingo, with orders to suppress Toussaint l'Ouverture's insurrection of the blacks, and then take possession of New Orleans and Louisiana. The prospect of a veteran French army at America's back door was not pleasant. On 18 April 1802 Jefferson wrote to the American minister at Paris:

The day that France takes possession of New Orleans. . . . We must marry ourselves to the British fleet and nation. We must turn all our attentions to a maritime force [and] make the first cannon which shall be fired in Europe the signal for . . . holding the two continents of America in sequestration for the common purposes of the united British and American nations. This is not a state of things we seek or desire. It is one which this measure, if adopted by France, forces on us.

Astounding as this letter may appear, it was a logical development of Jefferson's policy for the last twelve years. Jefferson hated England not as such, but as the embodiment of monarchy, militarism, and aristocracy. With the Federalists in power he feared British influence on American social and constitutional development; with Jefferson in power that danger was obviously ended! He was an isolationist in a deeper sense even than Washington; but his experience of the Nootka crisis convinced him that so long as the mouth of the Mississippi was in foreign possession, the United States was in danger of being drawn into every European war. Isolation was not a fact but a goal; and to attain it Jefferson was ready to adopt Washington's formula of 'temporary alliances for extraordinary emergencies.'

Up to this point Jefferson's Louisiana diplomacy had been secret; but another event almost forced his hand. Late in 1802 the Spanish Intendant withdrew the 'right of deposit' from American traders. This privilege had been guaranteed only for three years by the Treaty of San Lorenzo (1795); but the inhabitants of the Ohio valley, who were annually trans-shipping a million dollars' worth of produce at New Orleans, believed they had secured it for ever. An explosion of indignation followed in the West. The Federalists, delighted at an opportunity to divide Jefferson from his western admirers, fanned the flame and clamored for war. Jefferson remained serene and imperturbable. His annual message, in December 1802, breathed platitudes of peace, friendship, and economy. In the meantime, some of his friends pushed through Congress an appropriation of two million dollars for ' expenses in relation to the intercourse between the United States and foreign nations.' And in March 1803 the President commissioned James Monroe as envoy extraordinary to France, with the following instructions to himself and to the resident minister, Robert Livingston.

First they were to offer anything up to fifty million francs for New Orleans and the Floridas, which would give the United States the whole east bank of the Mississippi, and the Gulf coast to the eastward. If France refused, three-quarters of the sum should be offered for the Island of New Orleans [4] alone; or space on the east bank should be purchased for an American port. Failing here, they must press for a perpetual guarantee of the rights of navigation and deposit. That was Jefferson's ultimatum. If the last terms were refused, Monroe and Livingston were ordered to ' open a confidential communication with ministers of the British Government,' with a view to ' a candid understanding, and a closer connection with Great Britain.' If a treaty were concluded with Britain, a mutual promise not to make a separate peace with France could not ' be deemed unreasonable.'

Livingston began the negotiation before Monroe sailed; and it made little progress at first. But Napoleon was turning back from the West towards the Orient. Troops had been poured into Santo Domingo to the number of thirty-five thousand, but yellow fever swept away those that the blacks did not massacre. Without Santo Domingo, Louisiana lost half its value to France. The renewal of war with England seemed inevitable. When war came, Louisiana would be Britain's for the plucking. Why not sell it to the United States while there was yet time?

Napoleon reached decisions quickly. On 11 April 1803 he hurled defiance at the British ambassador. The same day, when Livingston approached the Minister of Foreign Affairs to repeat his usual arguments for selling New Orleans, Talleyrand suddenly remarked, ' What will you give for the *whole* of Louisiana? ' Livingston gasped out that he supposed the United States would not object to paying twenty million francs. ' Too low! ' said Talleyrand, ' Reflect, and see me tomorrow.' On the morrow Talleyrand was evasive; but Napoleon had already determined to sell the whole. On 30 April 1803 the treaty of cession was signed. Sixty million francs were paid for

---

[4] New Orleans is on an island, made by Lakes Pontchartrain and Borgne, the River Iberville, the Mississippi, and two short bayous.

the province of Louisiana, as acquired from Spain in 1800, and the United States assumed all the claims of her citizens against France. The inhabitants of Louisiana were guaranteed the rights of American citizens, and eventual admission to the Union.

The Louisiana purchase turned out to be the greatest bargain in American history; but in 1803 it seemed quite likely that the United States was paying twelve million dollars for a scrap of paper. Her title was defective on several points. The province was still in the hands of Spain. Bonaparte had never performed his part of the agreement with Spain, which also forbade France to dispose of Louisiana to a third power. The French Constitution forbade the alienation of national territory without a vote of the legislature; and Napoleon's brothers protested against it on that ground. The boundaries were indefinite; how far north Louisiana extended, and whether it included West Florida or Texas or neither, was uncertain. Finally, the treaty was illegal under the American Constitution, by every canon of interpretation ever promulgated by the Virginia Republicans.[5] If the Federal Government, as Jefferson had always claimed, possessed no power not expressly granted, the President and Senate had no right to increase the national domain by treaty, much less to promise incorporation in the Union to persons outside its original limits. Jefferson realized this, and proposed a constitutional amendment to validate the purchase; but he dropped that like a hot potato when a warning arrived from Livingston that Napoleon might change his mind. So Jefferson decided that the purchase treaty must be ratified ' now,' and it was. On 30 November 1803 Louisiana was formally handed over by the Spanish governor to the French prefect, who promptly established the *code Napoléon,* and as many other institutions as he could. On 20 December the final transfer from France to the United States was effected.

' Never was there an administration more brilliant than that of Mr. Jefferson up to this period,' said John Randolph in after years. ' We were indeed in the " full tide of successful experiment." Taxes repealed; the public debt amply provided for, both principal and interest; sinecures abolished; Louisiana acquired; public confidence unbounded.'

---

[5] The constitutionality of the Louisiana purchase was eventually upheld in American Insurance Co. *v.* Canter, 1828.

XIX

CONSPIRACIES AND COMPLICATIONS
1803–1809

1. *Crumbling Federalism*

JEFFERSON yearned to convert New England from her perverse Federalist ways. He appreciated the danger of attempting to govern a loose-knit federal union by a sectional party, and hoped by his moderation to persuade the Yankees that their commercial and shipping interests were safe in Republican hands. Republican gains in the congressional elections of 1802–03 showed that he was succeeding; but the Federalist leaders grew bitter and desperate as their power waned.

To the clergy and party leaders of New England Jefferson's victory was the triumph of democracy, which to them was but another name for terror, atheism, and free love. It meant just what communism does to many respectable Americans today. 'The principles of democracy are everywhere what they have been in France,' wrote Fisher Ames. New England was yet pure; but the barriers to her virtue were falling. 'And must we with folded hands wait the result?' wrote Senator Pickering of Massachusetts. 'The principles of our Revolution point to the remedy — a separation.'

Thus Virginians like John Taylor had reasoned in 1798, when Virginia was hag-ridden by Hamilton. Jefferson then had calmed them with a promise of victory. No such hope could console New England Federalists for the Louisiana purchase. Their majority was dwindling, and they knew it. Ohio, admitted to the Union in 1803, looked to Virginia for guidance, although largely settled by Yankees. It was certain that the new states to be formed from French Louisiana would follow the same light; and their political weight would be increased by the federal ratio of representation. The annexation of Louisiana, upsetting the balance of power within the Union, absolved New England from allegiance to the Union; at least so the Federalists reasoned. Before 1803 was out the 'Essex Junto' of Massachusetts and the 'River Gods' of Connecticut began to plan a new confederacy, 'exempt from the corrupt and corrupting influence and oppression of the aristocratic democrats of the South': a North-ern Confederacy with New England as a nucleus, and New York as a barrier state against Virginia. New England conservatives in 1804, like Southern conservatives in 1861, assumed that a political boundary could protect them from ideas.

Knowledge of the conspiracy was confined to the high churchmen of New England federalism and the British minister at Washington. Hamilton would have none of it. Intrigue was repulsive to his character, and reasoning such as Pickering's to his intellect. The conspirators then turned to Aaron Burr.

Burr had carried New York for Jefferson in 1800, and without that state Jefferson would have lost. Yet once safe in office, Jefferson ignored Burr's wishes in distributing the patronage, and the Republi-can party dropped him from the presidential ticket in 1804. Burr then decided to contest the governorship of New York with the regular Republican candidate. We know very little for certain of what went on; it seems highly probable that, in return for Federalist aid to elect him Governor, Burr agreed, if successful, to swing New York into the Northern Confederacy, and become its president. But Hamilton advised his friends not to vote for Burr, and Burr was defeated. The Federalist conspiracy dissolved. How remote was its chance of success the presidential election of 1804 proved. Jefferson carried every state but two, Connecticut and Delaware.

Burr was now a ruined politician. He had broken irretrievably with the Republicans, and failed the Federalists. Hamilton was responsible. It was not the first time that Hamilton had crossed his path; it must be the last. On 18 June 1804, six weeks after the New York election, Burr wrote his enemy, demanding 'a prompt and unqualified acknowledgment or denial' of a slur upon his char-acter reported in the press. Hamilton refused to retract, and an-swered, 'I trust on more reflection you will see the matter in the same light with me. If not, I can only regret the circumstances, and must abide the consequences.'

According to the code of honor observed by the gentry of the South and of New York, such language was an invitation to a chal-lenge; and the challenge quickly came. Hamilton had a wife and seven children dependent upon him, and his affairs were much in-volved. Burr was a widower, and his only child was married. Hamil-ton, who had led troops through heavy fire up to the ramparts of Yorktown, did not need to prove his courage. Further, he believed it murder to kill an adversary in a duel. Yet the infirmity of a noble mind forced him to accept the challenge.

Hamilton was enmeshed in a double net of theory and ambition. He might differ from the New England Federalists as to the cure for democracy, but he judged the future by their gloomy formula. A crisis was impending. The year 1804 in America corresponded to 1791 in France. Jefferson would disappear like Mirabeau; dissolution and anarchy would follow; finally America would demand a Bonaparte. Hamilton intended to be ready at the call—but no one under suspicion of cowardice could save his country. So Hamilton went to his doom, resolved to prove his courage and yet not to kill: to reserve and throw away his first fire, in the hope that Burr would miss and honor be satisfied. Aaron Burr did not intend to miss.

At six o'clock on a bright summer morning, 11 July 1804, Hamilton and his second were ferried across the Hudson to a grove of trees under the Palisades, where Burr and his friends were engaged in clearing the duelling ground. The distance agreed upon was ten paces. When the signal *present* was given, Burr raised his arm slowly, took deliberate aim, and fired. Hamilton received the bullet just below his chest, and as he fell a convulsive movement of the fingers discharged his pistol aimlessly. Death relieved him after thirty hours of intense suffering.

So perished one of the greatest men of the age, for his little faith in the government he had formed, and in the people he had served so well.

2. *The Judicial Barrier*

Aaron Burr fled to Washington, where the President received him amiably, and conferred upon his friends the three best offices in Louisiana Territory. It was not that Jefferson wished to reward the slayer of Hamilton, but that he wanted something of Burr. For the Vice-President must preside over the United States Senate, sitting as a court of impeachment to try Justice Chase of the Supreme Court.

This trial was part of a Republican attempt to rid the federal judiciary of partisan Federalists. Under Chief Justice Jay the federal courts had exercised their constitutional powers without much opposition. They had, however, made two false steps, and others that were unseemly to Republican eyes. In a case involving land claims, the Supreme Court ordered the State of Georgia to appear before the bar as defendant, and entered judgment against it by default.

State susceptibilities, thus aroused, produced the Eleventh Amend‚ ment to the Constitution, forbidding suits against states by citizens of other states or nations. In 1798 certain federal judges, excited by the supposed Jacobin menace, enforced with excessive severity the Sedition Act (which they might well have found to be a violation of civil rights guaranteed by the First Amendment), and delivered political harangues to grand juries in the best seventeenth- (or twentieth-) century style. When Congress, in 1801, increased the number of federal courts, President Adams filled all the new places with members of his party, and conferred the chief justiceship on John Marshall, a kinsman and enemy to Jefferson. The new President came into power on the crest of a Republican wave, only to find his defeated rivals entrenched in the judiciary; and Chief Justice Marshall defied him, at the first subsequent session of the Supreme Court, by an opinion in the case of Marbury v. Madison.

Marbury was a justice of the peace for the District of Columbia, a ‘midnight appointment’ by President Adams in the last hours of his administration. Madison, the new Secretary of State, refused to deliver his commission to Marbury, who applied to the Supreme Court for a writ of mandamus, under section 13 of the Judiciary Act of 1789. Chief Justice Marshall, delivering the opinion of the court (February 1803), first considered the point whether Madison had a right to withhold the commission of a properly appointed official, and decided against the Secretary of State. ‘Is it to be contended that the heads of departments are not amenable to the laws of their country?’ Mr. Marbury's hopes were dashed by the rest of the opinion, on the point whether the Supreme Court was competent to grant him a remedy. The Federal Constitution, in defining the original jurisdiction of the Supreme Court, did not include the issue of writs to executive officers. The real question, then, was whether the Court should follow section 13 of the Judiciary Act, or the Constitution.

It was Marshall's opinion on this point that has vitally influenced the development of constitutional law in the United States.

The powers of the legislature are defined and limited; and that those limits may not be mistaken, or forgotten, the Constitution is written. To what purpose are powers limited, and to what purpose is that limitation committed to writing, if these limits may, at any time, be passed by those intended to be restrained? . . . It is a proposition too plain to be contested, that the Constitution controls any legislative act repugnant to it.

. . . A legislative act contrary to the Consitution is not law. . . . It is emphatically the province and duty of the judicial department to say what the law is. . . . The particular phraseology of the Constitution of the United States confirms and strengthens the principle, supposed to be essential to all written constitutions, that a law repugnant to the Constitution is void; and that *courts,* as well as other departments, are bound by that instrument.

Judging from the current comment, Marshall's reasoning on this point was generally acceptable; but his rebuke to Madison was strongly resented in administration circles. Jefferson promptly incited some of his henchmen in the House to move an impeachment of certain federal judges. A district judge who had become intemperate to the point of insanity was removed by impeachment; and the next victim was being prepared for the sacrifice when Aaron Burr reappeared in Washington.

Justice Chase of the Supreme Court, an American Dr. Johnson in appearance, intellect, and manners, had made himself peculiarly obnoxious to the Republicans. Before a trial for sedition in 1798, he had ordered the marshal to strike off the panel 'any of those creatures or persons called democrats.' The House of Representatives presented him to the Senate for impeachment on several counts of malfeasance and misfeasance in office. Strange to relate, after all that had been said about the danger of monarchical trappings, the Senate was fitted up in imitation of the House of Lords at the impeachment of Warren Hastings. Aaron Burr presided and the eloquent Randolph of Roanoke prosecuted for the House. There was insufficient evidence to substantiate the serious charges against Justice Chase; and those that were proved were points of manners rather than of justice. The Republicans in the Senate had the necessary two-thirds majority to convict; but when it came to a vote on 1 March 1805 the impeachment failed.

Had Chase been found guilty, there is some reason to believe that a majority of the Supreme Court would have been impeached out of office. But this trial proved to be the high-water mark of 'Jacobinism.' Federalism and conservatism rallied under the captaincy of Chief Justice Marshall, and from behind the Supreme Court barricade developed a subtle offensive of ideas — the supremacy of the nation and the sanctity of property — that in due time would leave little of Jeffersonian democracy but a memory and a tradition.

3. *Florida and the Southwest*

Jefferson, having purchased the whole of Louisiana for little more than half again as much as he had been prepared to pay for a small portion of it, was discontented with the bargain. In the matter of boundaries he believed that the United States had been cheated.

The question whether Louisiana rightfully included Texas and West Florida is a complicated one that need not concern us. Napoleon and Spain insisted that Louisiana included neither; Jefferson and Madison, after examining such maps as they could find, believed that it included both. Jefferson had never wanted the bulk of Louisiana; but he set an exaggerated value upon West Florida, which included Mobile Bay, the only good naval harbor in the Gulf, and the lower courses of the rivers that drained the Mississippi Territory and the Creek Nation. Continued possession of West Florida by Spain would enable her to play the same diplomatic game as in the eighteenth century.

Jefferson never understood the fortuitous combination of European events that procured him Louisiana. He believed it to be due to the diplomatic skill of his friend Monroe. That favorite son of the Virginia dynasty was accordingly sent to Madrid in order to see what could be done with money and threats. The Spanish government was not in a ceding mood; and the good offices of Napoleon were invoked in vain. One needed a long spoon, and a golden one, to sup with the foreign offices of Europe in the decade between Austerlitz and Waterloo.

In December 1805 the President tried another game. Informed by the American minister at Paris that Napoleon might be persuaded to extort West Florida from Spain if it were made worth his while, Jefferson in his annual message adverted to the Spanish 'aggressions' in terms that led the people to expect war. Then followed a special and secret message to Congress, hinting at his need for money. The stage was all set for another secret appropriation of two million dollars for 'diplomatic intercourse.'

This message was the signal for a schism in the Republican party. John Randolph of Roanoke, brilliant in intellect, erratic in conduct, but steadfast in the faith of ideal republicanism that had carried Jefferson into office, had for some time been chafing under the yoke of party discipline. Jefferson, he observed, had done little more in his first years of office than spell federalism backwards; he was now beginning to spell it forwards again. Randolph followed him to Louisiana, but it was time to call a halt. He now announced that he would stand for no shifting of responsibility; if the President wanted money, he must ask for it without evasion. Invited to a conference with the Secretary of State, Randolph was told by Madison that 'France wants money, and we must give it to her or have a Spanish and a French war'—a phrase that Randolph promptly published, and that the Federalists did not allow the country to forget. In the end Congress voted two million dollars, but it proved to be useless in a shifting Europe. Madison lost the support of John Taylor, high priest of Virginia Republicanism; made an enemy of John Randolph, who for the next eight years assaulted him with scorn and mockery from the floor of the House; and convinced the Federalists that he was sold to Bonaparte.

The concluding episode of this crucial year in Jefferson's fortunes was the so-called Burr conspiracy, an enterprise that still remains a mystery. Before leaving Washington at the expiration of his term as Vice-President, Burr approached the British minister with an offer to detach the Western states from the Union for half a million dollars. Probably this was a mere blind for obtaining money. Mr. Merry thought well of it and urged his government to pay, but received no reply. Downing Street was no longer interested in promoting American secession.

Burr then proceded to the headwaters of the Ohio and floated down the river in a flat-boat. The Westerners, inveterate duellers themselves, were charmed by the polished gentleman and statesman from New York. Herman Blennerhasset, a romantic Irish exile, was fascinated with a plan to conquer Mexico, to make Burr emperor, and himself a grand potentate of the court. In Tennessee Burr met and won Andrew Jackson among others, who proposed to elect him to the Senate. With General Wilkinson, who was still in Spanish pay while Governor of Upper Louisiana and ranking general of the army, Burr discussed some project yet unknown. At New Orleans he got in touch with certain creole malcontents, and with an association of American filibusters who were eager to 'liberate' Mexico. The Catholic bishop of New Orleans and the mother superior of the Ursuline convent gave Burr their support and blessing. Returning overland, he found the Westerners everywhere eager for war with Spain. Louisiana had whetted their appetite for Texas, as it had Jefferson's for Florida. In Washington again, Burr obtained ten thousand dollars from the Spanish minister, ostensibly for the purpose of defending Spanish America; and then attempted to promote an attack on Mexico. After all, war with Spain was supposed to be imminent.

In the summer of 1806 the former Vice-President pushed off once more down the Ohio, with a few flat-boats and sixty followers. The chance of war with Spain had passed; and it is probable that Burr's present object was to take up a land claim he had purchased in western Louisiana. General Wilkinson, deciding that Burr was worth more to betray than to befriend, sent a lurid letter to the President denouncing 'a deep, dark, wicked, and wide-spread conspiracy' to dismember the Union. Similar warnings came from loyal Westerners. In the late autumn of 1806 Jefferson issued a proclamation for the arrest of Burr, and put a price on his head. He was apprehended and brought to Richmond for trial, on a charge of treason against the United States.

Although it should have been obvious that a Western secession from the Union could not be performed by Burr and sixty men, Jefferson left no stone unturned to obtain a conviction. Fortunately for the prisoner, Chief Justice Marshall presided at his trial, and took care that the constitutional definition of treason, 'levying war against the United States or adhering to their enemies,' and the constitutional safeguard of 'two witnesses to the same overt act,' should be strictly observed. Burr was acquitted, and sought exile in France. Wilkinson, a traitor to every cause he embraced, retained his command and the confidence of the President.

Acquittal of Justice Chase, defection of John Randolph, frustration as to Florida, and the Burr fiasco; the turn in Jefferson's fortunes had come.

4. *Impressment*

Returned to the Presidency by an overwhelming majority, Jefferson began his second term on 4 March 1805, expecting to pursue the 'wise and frugal' policy of 1801 to its logical conclusion. Instead, his party began to break up into its constituent sections of land-hungry Westerners, New England under-dogs, Virginian Republicans who cared only for principle, and Middle-state democrats who cared little for principle but much for place. Peace in Europe had been the condition of Jefferson's earlier success; but there was to be no peace in Europe for ten years. Before the end of 1805 Napoleon was supreme on land, and Britain on sea. Each side sought to starve or strangle the other by continental or maritime blockade. It was a more difficult situation for the American government than in the wars of 1792 to 1801. Washington, Hamilton, and Adams had had to deal with but one belligerent at a time; Jefferson was confronted with both at once. A clever diplomatist might conceivably have played off one country against another, if he had possessed an armed force as a stake in the game. But neither Jefferson nor Madison could grasp the realities of Napoleonic Europe, and the President abandoned his energetic naval policy before peace was concluded with Tripoli.

During the Mediterranean hostilities American naval commanders had felt the need of small gunboats for use in shoal waters and light winds. Eight of them, only about 45 feet long and carrying but a single gun, crossed the Atlantic in 1805. Jefferson, as civilian administrators are apt to do, took this innovation for more than it was worth. Gunboats were cheap, they could be hauled out when not in use, and their construction, by numerous petty shipbuilders, made votes. Congress, instead of providing the frigates that the navy wanted, had sixty-nine gunboats built by 1807, the largest only 75 feet long and carrying two guns. When one of them, torn from her moorings by a tropical storm, was deposited in a cornfield, a Federalist declared: 'If our gunboats are no use on the water, may they at least be the best on earth!'

Until 1807 Jefferson's principal problems were connected with British sea power. As soon as the royal navy considered the renewal of war likely, it resumed the practice of impressing British subjects from American vessels on the high seas. It never claimed the right to take native-born Americans but to impress its own subjects from foreign vessels wherever found. British seamen were constantly deserting to the American merchant marine and navy. The U.S.S. *Constitution* in 1807 had 149 avowed British subjects, and only 241 who claimed American citizenship, in her crew of 419. And neither country then admitted the right of expatriation.

When a short-handed man-of-war visited an American merchantman, the boarding officer was apt to impress any likely looking lad who had the slightest trace of an Irish or British accent. Mistakes were inevitable, and difficult to rectify. Easily ninety per cent of the correspondence of American ministers at the Court of St. James's had to do with attempts to obtain the release of their compatriots.

Many were finally discharged, but probably as many more were unable to get in touch with their government, and served until they found an opportunity to desert, or were killed in action. There were enough instances of brutality and palpable injustice to create indignation, quite apart from the question of law.

With the renewal of European war in 1803, impressments increased, and men were plucked off American ships just outside New York harbor. At the same time, the old controversies over neutral rights were revived. American merchants and shipowners were making such profits out of neutral trade that they remained silent under these restrictions. But the British courts became aware that Americans were landing French colonial produce in their own ports in bond, relading it in time to escape customs duty, and then taking it to a European port under Napoleon's control. Hence the courts began to condemn such cargoes on the ground that the voyage broken in the United States was really one continuous voyage with enemy property between enemy ports. The United States found this precedent very useful in 1861–65, but it was inconvenient in 1805, and the merchants complained bitterly. The situation was not unlike that of 1793 over the British spoliations in the West Indies. Jefferson followed Washington's example to the extent of negotiation, but no farther.

The negotiations began at London in the summer of 1806, between James Monroe and William Pinkney, and Lord Holland. The American envoys soon realized that it was impossible to obtain the terms desired by Jefferson, so they followed Jay's precedent of disregarding instructions, and signed (31 December 1806) the best terms they could obtain. It was a treaty very similar in character to Jay's that Monroe had so vehemently denounced. Britain compromised on her maritime practice without abandoning impressment completely. But this treaty was lost because at the last moment the British government inserted an unnecessary and unwise reservation; Jefferson refused to submit it to the Senate. There followed an Order in Council (7 January 1807) further narrowing the scope of neutral commerce, and an impressment outrage that brought the two countries to the verge of war.

A British squadron, stationed at the capes of the Chesapeake in order to attack some French frigates when they came out, lost many men by desertion, and had reason to believe that Jenkin Ratford, the ringleader, had **enlisted on** the United States frigate *Chesa-*

peake. He had been searched for by the Navy Department, but not detected. On June 22 the *Chesapeake,* flying the broad pennant of Commodore Barron, got under way from Norfolk Roads. As she passed Lynnhaven Bay, the frigate *Leopard* detached herself from the British squadron and followed; but no one on the *Chesapeake* suspected her intent. When both vessels were about ten miles outside the capes, the *Leopard* luffed up about half a cable's length to windward, and signalled 'Dispatches.' Barron supposed that she wished him to carry mail to Europe, a common courtesy between the two navies in those days. He backed his main topsail and invited the British captain to send a boat on board. The dispatches proved to be an order from Admiral Berkeley to search for and remove deserters. Barron, ignorant of Ratford's presence, replied that the only British deserters in his crew were three Americans formerly impressed; and that he could not permit the search. The boarding officer was recalled, and eight minutes after, the *Leopard* fired her full broadside into the American, and poured in two more before Barron could reply; for the *Chesapeake's* decks were littered with stores, and few of her guns were mounted. After suffering twenty casualties, Barron struck his flag. His crew were then mustered by the *Leopard's* officers, and the three Americans and Ratford taken off. Barron offered the *Leopard's* commander his sword, which was refused; and the *Chesapeake* limped back to Norfolk.

News of this insult to the flag brought the first united expression of American feeling since 1798. Even the Federalists, who had hitherto defended every move of British sea-power, were confounded. If Jefferson had summoned Congress to a special session, he would have had war at the drop of a hat; and it would have been a far more popular and successful war than the one finally declared in 1812. But Jefferson's serenity was undisturbed. He instructed Monroe to demand apology and reparation in London, and ordered British warships out of American territorial waters. When Congress met, in late October, the President obtained an appropriation of $850,000 for building 188 more gunboats, and ordered three of the largest ships of the small sea-going navy to be laid up in ordinary.

5. *Embargo*

George Canning, the British Foreign Secretary, expressed his 'concern and sorrow' at the first news of the *Chesapeake* affair, and his intention to take all proper steps as soon as the facts could be ascertained. Jefferson, however, made reparation impossible by ordering Monroe to accept none that did not include the complete abandonment of impressing British subjects from American merchant ships. Insult was then heaped upon injury by a royal proclamation of 17 October 1807, directing the navy to impress British subjects from neutral shipping to the fullest possible extent.

By the time this order arrived in America the popular ardor for war had cooled; but Congress was ready to follow any lead from the executive. No suggestion of war, or of preparation for war, came from the President. For Jefferson imagined he had England by the throat, and could strangle her by a mere turn of the wrist. For years he had been aching for an opportunity to try commercial exclusion as a substitute for war. The moment had arrived. Jefferson sent a brief message to Congress and in one day, 22 December 1807, it passed the famous Embargo Act. American or other vessels were forbidden to clear foreign, all exports from the United States whether by sea or land were prohibited, and certain specified articles of British manufacture were refused entrance.[1] The Act went into effect immediately; and for fourteen months all the American ships that were not already abroad, and could not escape, lay in port or went coasting.

It is true that between British orders and French decrees, American vessels could visit no part of the world without rendering themselves liable to capture by one or the other belligerents. The neutrals, wrote Spencer Perceval, ' will have no trade, or they must . . . accept it through us.' But the American merchant marine throve on such treatment; shipowners wanted no protection other than that which the British navy afforded them. European restrictions merely increased the profit with the risk; and there were plenty of lines of trade open to neutral shipowners who were willing to put up with British inspection and license, which was far less rigorous than the system during the World War. At Smyrna, for instance, American ships enjoyed the privileges of the Levant Company and the protection of the British consul. In 1810 a Salem ship that forced the Dardanelles was saved from confiscation by the British ambassador. Hence the embargo was detested by the very interest it was supposed to protect. Smuggling of British goods and American products went

---

[1] The last measure was not, strictly speaking, a part of the embargo of December 1807, but the Non-importation Act of 16 April 1806, which did not go into effect until the embargo was adopted.

on over the Canadian and Florida boundaries, but unemployed seamen and shipwrights emigrated in such large numbers to the British provinces that a sarcastic loyalist called the embargo ' an act for the better encouragement of the British Colonies in America.' The greater shipowners who had a fleet abroad survived the embargo very well; but numerous small ones were ruined, and some of the lesser seaports such as New Haven never recovered their earlier prosperity. Jefferson even tried to hold up the coasting trade by executive orders, but Justice William Johnson, whom he had appointed to the Supreme Bench to counteract Marshall, stopped that by writ of mandamus. Agricultural produce fell, and the interior had to live on its own fat; but cotton, tobacco, and wheat could bear storage better than ships. Consequently the embargo bore most heavily on New England and New York; and it was there that its political effects were felt by the administration. As a successful weapon of offense, commercial retaliation requires an unusual combination of circumstances, such as actually occurred in 1812. The embargo of 1807–09 was completely futile. It caused a shortage of provisions in the French Antilles, and of colonial produce in France; but Napoleon confiscated every American vessel that arrived at a French port, on the ground that he was helping Jefferson to enforce the embargo! In the English manufacturing districts the embargo caused some distress, but the usual exports soon found their way into the United States through Canada, and a new South American market was opened. When the American minister in London offered to lift the embargo if Britain would withdraw the Orders in Council, George Canning replied that His Majesty ' would gladly have facilitated its removal as a measure of inconvenient restriction upon the American people! ' As J. Q. Adams once remarked, Canning ' had a little too much wit for a minister of state.'

Jefferson's mistake was the Federalists' opportunity. Their strength had been dwindling steadily, even in New England, where in 1807 every state government except Connecticut was Republican. Senator Pickering, the conspirator of 1804, rallied New England opinion by a public letter, roundly asserting that the embargo was dictated by Napoleon, and adopted by Jefferson in the hope of destroying the shipping interest and impoverishing New England. Northern Republicans were restive under a measure that turned their constituents Federalist; and in New York City the embargo produced a schism in the Republican party. When Madison was nominated for the presidential succession by a congressional caucus, the New York legislature placed George Clinton in nomination as an anti-embargo Republican. In Virginia John Randolph's sect of 'pure Republicans' nominated Monroe, who had been disaffected since the rejection of his treaty. If a union could have been effected between these factions and the Federalists, Madison might have been defeated; as it was, the Federalists carried little but New England, and Madison was elected President by a comfortable majority.

Jefferson intended to maintain the embargo until the British orders or the French decrees were repealed. In January 1809 Congress passed the 'Force Act,' permitting federal officials without warrant to seize goods under suspicion of foreign destination, and protecting them from legal liability for their actions. George III and Lord North had been tender in comparison. The people of New England, now in their second winter of privation and distress, began to look to their state governments for protection; and by this time all the state governments of New England were in Federalist hands. The legislatures hurled back in the teeth of Jefferson and Madison the doctrines of the Kentucky and Virginia resolves of 1798. Connecticut resolved that 'whenever our national legislature is led to overleap the prescribed bounds of their constitutional powers,' it becomes the duty of the state legislatures 'to interpose their protecting shield between the right and liberty of the people, and the assumed power of the General Government.' A proposal to summon a New England convention for nullification of the embargo was being discussed in February 1809.

By that time the embargo had been in force fourteen months. The Northern Republicans revolted; and Jefferson was shaken by a volley of protests from New England town meetings, some of them threatening secession. A bill for the repeal of the embargo was rushed through Congress, and on 1 March 1809 it was approved by Jefferson. Three days later his term ended, and he retired to Monticello.

The embargo was intended to be the crowning glory of Jefferson's second administration, as Louisiana was of his first. It failed to influence the policy of Britain or of Napoleon; it failed to protect the merchant marine. It wasted the fruit of Jefferson's first administration: the creation of a broad, country-wide party in every state of the Union. As Randolph said, the four lean kine ate up the four fat kine. It convinced many good people that the 'Virginia dynasty' was bound to that of Bonaparte; that the Republican party was a greater enemy than British sea-power to American shipping.

Yet this mistake must not efface the good that Jefferson had done during his eight years of office. He was one of the greatest of presidents, and the most tolerant of revolutionists. Few men have combined in like degree a lofty idealism with political wisdom and administrative ability. Few minority leaders have resisted when in power, as he did, the temptation to persecute their opponents. Accustomed as we have been since 1920 to the spectacle of leaders sprung from the people imposing their policies and dogmas by the most rigid tyranny and cruel oppression, we can the better appreciate a democratic leader who, in spite of an unmistakable popular mandate to rule, preferred the slow process of reason to the short way of force. By this forbearance even more than by his acts, Jefferson kept alive the flame of liberty that Napoleon had almost quenched. He was the nearest approximation in modern history to Plato's ideal of a philosopher-king.

XX

THE WAR OF 1812
1809–1815

1. *Drifting into War*

THE change in the Presidency was not for the better. Madison surpassed Jefferson in knowledge of political science, but lacked his genius for politics and administration. Slight in stature and unimpressive in personality, anxious to please but with an air of perplexity on his wizened features, James Madison was beloved by a few intimate friends, but unable to inspire loyalty in his subordinates, or enthusiasm in the nation. His talent for the marshalling of words in a contest of reason was of little use in dealing with European statesmen who took the trouble to reason only when their cause was desperate.

Madison's inaugural address (4 March 1809) was a colorless echo of Jeffersonian principles. He chose a cabinet of respectable mediocrities, excepting Gallatin, who retained the Treasury. Yet within six weeks of his inauguration Madison was being hailed as a great peacemaker. Apparently he had reached a settlement with Great Britain. With the British minister at Washington he concluded the so-called Erskine agreement, which provided that Britain would exempt American vessels from the Orders in Council in return for the United States lifting all commercial interdicts from England, and forbidding American ships to trade with France. Madison had gone the limit in concession; he had even consented to postpone the troublesome subject of impressment.

If the Erskine agreement had been ratified at London—it was in a form that needed no ratification at Washington—there might have been no second Anglo-American war. Like Jay's treaty, it would have embroiled the United States with France, and made us a silent partner of the Allies. But for reasons that no one has been able to explain, much less to justify, Canning repudiated the agreement, recalled Erskine, restored Anglo-American relations to their normal instability, and gave free play to the forces that were pushing the United States into war.

The Congress that assembled in December 1809 had no idea what to do, and received no lead from Madison. At length, on 1 May 1810, it passed the so-called Macon's Bill No. 2, which restored commercial intercourse with both Britain and France, but offered to the first power which recognized neutral rights the bait of refusing to trade with her enemy. In the event of either country exempting the United States from its edicts, the President was authorized to forbid Americans to trade with the other — provided the other did not follow suit within three months. American shipping was soon engaged in making profits under British license, and in 1811 American tonnage reached figures that were not again attained for twenty years.

Madison took advantage of the interlude in commercial warfare to take a bite of West Florida. The Republican administrations claimed this province as part of Louisiana; but forbore to enforce their claim while there was hope of inducing the Spanish government to admit it. In 1810 there were two Spanish governments, and the Spanish Empire was breaking up. Accordingly the inhabitants of that portion of West Florida bordering on the Mississippi, ' self-determined ' for the United States, seized Baton Rouge, and were incorporated by presidential proclamation into the Territory of Orleans, which two years later became the State of Louisiana.

The American minister at St. Petersburg undertook to explain this act to Alexander I. The Emperor bowed and remarked pleasantly, ' Everybody is getting a little bigger, nowadays.'

Napoleon, who had done a good deal of that sort of thing, found time enough between his campaigns and administrative problems, and divorcing and re-marrying, to cast his eye over Macon's Act, and perceive an opportunity to incorporate the United States in his continental system.

For five years Napoleon had treated American shipping arbitrarily and the American government insolently. In July 1810, the American merchantmen at Naples were seized by imperial command, and the next month Napoleon ordered the sale of all sequestrated ships and cargoes. But on the same day, the imperial government informed the American minister that ' His Majesty loves the Americans,' and as proof of his tender solicitude for their prosperity had seen fit to declare ' that the Decrees of Berlin and Milan are revoked, and that after 1 November they will cease to have effect — it being understood that the English are to revoke their Orders in Council.'

The equivocal language of this note was unaccompanied by any such pledge of good faith as the release of sequestrated American vessels. John Quincy Adams warned Madison that it was 'a trap to catch us into a war with England.' But the guileless President snapped at the bait. By a proclamation of 2 November he announced that non-intercourse would be revived against Britain, if in three months' time she did not repeal the Orders in Council.

In London William Pinkney urged repeal on the Foreign Secretary, asserting that the Berlin and Milan Decrees were actually revoked. Lord Wellesley could perceive no evidence that they were, and President Madison ignored all evidence that they were not. Every mail brought news of fresh seizures and scuttlings of American vessels by French port authorities and privateers. Yet Madison, with the obstinacy of weakness, insisted that 'the national faith was pledged to France,' and on 11 February 1811 forbade trade with Great Britain, under authority of Macon's Act. Had the United States formally adhered to Napoleon's continental system, the result would have been no different.

This was the third instance within four years that the United States government prohibited Anglo-American commerce, in order to procure repeal of the Orders in Council. On the two former occasions, when there was justice in the American complaints, commercial restriction had had no effect. In 1811-12, when the American complaint was grounded on Napoleon's falsehood and deception, circumstances brought the first and only victory for peaceful persuasion — too late to preserve the peace.

The winter of 1811-12 was a bitter one for the British people. Napoleon's continental system had reached its zenith. Practically all western Europe was closed to British goods. American non-intercourse shut the only important market yet open save Russia, which Napoleon was forcing into his cordon. A crop failure drove the price of wheat to unheard-of figures. Warehouses were crammed with goods for which there was no market, factories were closing, workmen rioting. Deputations from the manufacturing cities besought Parliament to repeal the Orders, if only to recover their American market. Various delays postponed a decision, but finally, on 16 June 1812, Lord Castlereagh announced in the House of Commons that the Orders in Council would be suspended immediately.

It was too late. On 18 June 1812 Congress declared war against Great Britain. But the fundamental reason for this act had as much to do with western lands and Indians as with maritime affairs.

2. *Tecumseh and Tippecanoe*

The reason for this abandonment of Jefferson's policy at the very point of scoring its first and only success must be sought on the American frontier. It was not that seamen wanted freedom of the seas, but that frontiersmen wanted free land, which could be obtained only at the expense of the Indians and the British Empire.

One may well gasp at the appetite of a people who had not yet settled their original limits, who had just doubled their area by the Louisiana purchase, yet hankered for more. The West felt crowded in 1812 for the same reason that England felt crowded in 1612; because population had outstripped the supporting capacity of an outgrown economic system. It always seems easier and more manly to relieve a pressure of population by conquest than by economic adjustments that will enable the land to support more people.

The American frontier was advanced by hunters and rough-and-tumble pioneer farmers, who purchased their acres from a speculator or a government land office, cleared a small part of them, cropped their fields until the fertility was exhausted, and then sold out to a more substantial class of emigrants, and moved on. Kentucky and Tennessee and part of Ohio by 1812 were in the hands of farmers who owned slaves (if south of the Ohio), produced wheat, hemp, tobacco, and cotton, planted orchards, built frame instead of log houses, founded schools, churches, and colleges, and were introducing the refinements of the East and the culture of Europe. The pioneer farmer had neither the patience, the knowledge, nor the desire for these things. He was pushed into the less fertile and mountainous regions, or, like Abraham Lincoln's shiftless father, deciding that 'old Kaintuck was no place for a pore man no more,' packed his belongings on a raft or wagon, and proceeded west or south. Even the better farmers swelled the tide of migration by their huge families; and every farmer, then as now, took up more land than he could possibly cultivate, in the hope of selling at a profit.

The pioneer of 1812 was a woodsman. He relied upon standing timber for his building, fencing, and fuel; and until the industrial revolution furnished him with substitutes, he shunned the treeless prairies of Illinios and the Far West. The prairies were remote from rivers and streams, and their tough sod was too much for the crude ploughs of the day. The greater part of the Louisiana purchase, moreover, was in the hands of powerful Indian tribes. No land office for these regions had as yet been opened by the government. Hence the land-hungry pioneer turned longingly to the forest lands still held by the redskins in Illinois and Indiana; and to a still more accessible region, the fertile, wooded peninsula of Upper Canada, between Lakes Huron, Erie, and Ontario, with its vast uncultivated crown reserves and its sparse population of loyalists.

Down to 1808 or thereabouts, the pioneers had been kept quiet by government purchases from the Northwest Indians. The Treaty of Greenville in 1795, following the Battle of the Fallen Timbers, ended a period in which the Indians had on the whole been the aggressors, and began one in which the Americans were decidedly on the offensive. Washington and Adams stood by that treaty. Jefferson professed the most benevolent principles toward the Indians, but coveted their lands in order to keep the United States an agricultural country. He hoped to induce them to abandon hunting and adopt agriculture as their sole means of livelihood, when they would require a mere fraction of the lands they still possessed. Eventually they must remove across the Mississippi. Such a policy could square with humanity and justice only by protecting the Indians from the whites during the process. Although the Indians faithfully fulfilled their treaty stipulations, white men committed the most wanton and cruel murders on them with impunity. It was impossible to persuade a pioneer jury to convict. A good Indian was a dead Indian on the frontier. From time to time a few hungry and thirsty chiefs were rounded up by government officials, and plied with oratory and whisky until they signed a treaty alienating forever the hunting grounds of their tribe. Jefferson encouraged the process; and William Henry Harrison, superintendent of the Northwest Indians and Governor of Indiana Territory,[1] pushed it so successfully that between 1795 and 1809 the Indians of that region parted with forty-eight million acres.

There came a halt in this process in 1809, owing to the efforts of Tecumseh and his brother the Prophet, two noble red men indeed. Tecumseh, son of a Shawnee brave, undertook the task of saving his people by reforming their habits, stopping the alienation of their land, keeping them apart from the whites, and welding all the virile tribes East of the Mississippi into a confederacy. It was a movement

---

[1] Indiana Territory, created in 1800, included all the Northwest Territory except Ohio, which became a state in 1802. Michigan Territory was detached from it in 1805, and Illinois Territory (including Wisconsin) in 1809.

of regeneration and defense, menacing indeed the indefinite expansion of the West, but in no sense its existence. The Indians had so decreased in the last decade that scarcely four thousand warriors were counted in the space between the Lakes, the Mississippi, and the Ohio. Opposed to them were at least two hundred thousand white men of fighting age in the Ohio valley.

The partnership of warrior and priest was for a time irresistible. The Prophet kindled a religious revival among the tribes of the Northwest, and Indians came from far and wide to listen to his teachings. He actually induced them to give up intoxicating liquor. All intercourse with white men, except for trade, ceased; rum and whisky were refused with disdain. In 1809 Tecumseh and the Prophet began a settlement at the Great Clearing, where Tippecanoe creek empties into the Wabash river. The whole frontier was alarmed. Indian prohibitionists were something new to backwoods experience.

Governor Harrison met the situation with an act that Tecumseh could only regard as a challenge. Rounding up a few score survivors of tribes whom he frankly described as ' the most depraved wretches on earth,' Harrison concluded with them a treaty which deprived Tecumseh of his remaining hunting grounds, and brought the white border within fifty miles of the Tippecanoe. Tecumseh, with justice, declared this treaty null and void. More western nations joined his confederacy; and in July 1811, again assuring Governor Harrison that his object was defensive, he journeyed south to obtain the alliance of the Creeks. Harrison then decided to force hostilities. With the tacit approval of the War Department, he collected a force of about eleven hundred men, and marched them up the Wabash valley into the Indian country. On 6 November 1811 they encamped hard by Tecumseh's village at the mouth of the Tippecanoe. Envoys from the Prophet brought a pacific message; but the presence of an armed force of white men was too much for the reckless young braves. There was a sharp two hours' fight, and the Indian village was destroyed. Harrison was hailed as victor of the battle of Tippecanoe.

Throughout the West it was believed that Britain was behind Tecumseh's confederacy. It is true that the Governor of Canada encouraged the formation of Tecumseh's confederacy; but he withheld the customary presents of ammunition early in 1812, and discouraged hostilities with the United States. Tecumseh's league would have been formed and Tippecanoe have been fought if there had not been a single Englishman in Canada. Unfortunately, however, it is not the truth, but what people believe, that makes history. The notion that every defensive move of the Indians was due to British machination not only served to cover and excuse the frontiersmen's lust for Canada, but to convince thousands of people who desired no extension of territory that the only safety for the West lay in driving British power from North America. And a new Congress in which this belief and desire became articulate met at Washington just three days before the battle of Tippecanoe.

The congressional elections of 1810–11 had been a landslide. Nearly half the members of the inept House that enacted Macon's Act failed of re-election. A new generation came into power. From Kentucky there was Henry Clay, from Tennessee came ' Citizen ' Sevier and Felix Grundy, who had had three brothers killed by Indians. From western New York came Peter B. Porter, who lived within gunshot of the Canadian border; and from the Carolina Piedmont, John C. Calhoun. These ' war-hawks,' as they were called, were far short of a majority; but they quickly combined with other new members to place Henry Clay in the speaker's chair; and the Speaker of the House has the appointment of important committees, including that of foreign relations.

These young Westerners, who had never seen the ocean in their lives, and whose communities were completely immune from the influence of Orders in Council and French Decrees, quickly learned the vocabulary of neutral rights, and catch-words of the freedom of the seas. Not content to wrap their desires in the American flag, they cursed Canadian ' scalp-buyers,' boasted that Canada could be conquered in six weeks, and elaborated upon the destiny of the United States to reach the North Pole. In vain John Randolph poured out his scorn on this ' cant of patriotism,' this ' agrarian cupidity,' this chanting ' like the whip-poor-will but one eternal monotonous tone — Canada! Canada! Canada! ' New members from North and South joined the chorus. There was an accidental engagement between the frigate *President* and the corvette *Little Belt,* under circumstances that increased the ardor of the American navy for a good stand-up fight, and enhanced the contempt of the Royal navy for American ' fir-built frigates.' A feeling was rising that the Jeffersonian system of commercial retaliation was dastardly, that America must show the world she was not too proud to fight. Since

1806 the American government had ceased publicly to complain of impressment; but the practice continued, and a tardy but generous reparation for the *Chesapeake* affair proved insufficient balm for the growing public irritation at having American seamen removed from American ships because they were conveniently mistaken for British.

Madison long held out against the clamor for war; and it is not necessary to explain his final yielding by the story that Clay exacted it as the price of his renomination to the Presidency. In the last week of May 1812 the British minister at Washington communicated a dispatch from his government which seemed to close all hope of the Orders in Council being repealed. This convinced Madison that commercial retaliation had failed. Too obstinate to see that Napoleon had duped him, and that the Berlin and Milan Decrees had never been repealed, Madison, on 1 June, sent Congress a message recommending war with England on four grounds: impressment, violations of the three-mile limit, paper blockades, and Orders in Council. On 18 June war was declared.

The vote on the declaration was 79 to 49 in the House; 19 to 13 in the Senate. The inland and Western states of Vermont, Ohio, Kentucky, and Tennessee lacked but one vote of unanimity for war. The maritime sections of New England were unanimous for peace. A majority of the congressmen from New England, New York, and New Jersey, the states which owned three-quarters of the tonnage and provided most of the seamen, voted against war; and one-quarter of the Republicans refused to vote.

Congress adjourned on 6 July without voting war taxes, or providing for any increase of the navy. It was to be a short war; a mere frontiersmen's frolic into Canada, to dictate peace at Quebec.

3. On to Canada!

The War of 1812-15, forced upon the Republican party by its fighting frontier wing, was unsuccessful and generally unpopular in the United States until it was over. From the Canadian point of view it was a defensive war, gallantly maintaining imperial integrity against overwhelming odds. The British nation, absorbed in its struggle with Napoleon, paid little attention to America until the Yankee frigates and privateers touched it in a tender spot; and it was not until Napoleon was disposed of that they made any serious effort to win this outlying conflict.

The Federalists, with a different vision of national honor from that of the party in power, believed that the great issue was Napoleon and military despotism against the Allies and nationalism. One week after America declared war, Napoleon invaded Russia with his Grand Army. Thousands of Americans deemed it immoral to hamper the Allies at that crisis. If war were required to cleanse the national honor, they argued, it should have been declared against Napoleon, who had not only deceived the administration, but by Madison's own admission had captured more American vessels since 1807 than the British. A war for 'free trade and seamen's rights,' forced by a section that had neither ships nor sailors, and accepted by a party that refused appropriations for the navy, could only be regarded with loathing in maritime New England. Robert Smith of Baltimore, Madison's first Secretary of State, issued a public address against the war. John Marshall wrote to him that as Chief Justice he could take no active part in politics, yet as an American he was mortified at his country's base submission to Napoleon; that the only party division henceforth should be between the friends of peace and the advocates of war. That was indeed the division in the presidential election of 1812. The Federalists supported DeWitt Clinton, who was nominated by a peace faction of the New York Republicans, and carried every state north of the Potomac save Pennsylvania and Vermont; but Madison was re-elected by the votes of the South and West.

The 'war-hawks' had good reason to expect a prompt victory. The population of the United States in 1810 was seven and a quarter millions, of which sixteen per cent were slaves. The population of British North America was in the neighborhood of five hundred thousand, of which a large majority were French. A considerable part of the English-speaking Canadians were isolated in the Maritime Provinces; another part, consisting of emigrants from the United States, was disaffected. There was no great difference, however, in the forces ready to meet the first shock of war. Canada contained four regiments of the line, with forty-five hundred effectives, about four thousand Canadian regulars, most of them specially raised for the occasion, and the same number of militia. Tecumseh's confederacy would provide three or four thousand Indian auxiliaries.

The United States regular army was less than seven thousand strong on 8 June 1812, and enlistments came in very slowly. Over four hundred thousand state militia were called into service during the war; but only a small part of these served on the Canadian front, where they proved the uselessness of untrained militia in offensive warfare. William Eustis, the American Secretary of War, was an amiable politician who had been a surgeon in the War of Independence. Henry Dearborn, the senior major-general, had been a deputy quartermaster-general in the same war. America did not discover Andrew Jackson until the close of the war: Canada had Isaac Brock at the start.

The United States was unprepared in strategy as in armament. The settled portions of Canada in 1812 were shaped like a tree, of which the St. Lawrence was the trunk, the Great Lakes and their tributaries the branches, and the sea lanes to England the roots. Chatham had reduced Canada in 1759–60 by grasping the roots and grappling the trunk. Madison had no proper navy to attempt the former, but he might well have attempted to hew the tree by a sharp stroke at Montreal. Instead, he attempted several feeble and unsystematic lopping at the branches.

A week before war was declared, General William Hull was placed in command of fifteen hundred troops at Urbana, Ohio, and ordered to march two hundred miles, cutting his own road through the wilderness, to Detroit, and thence to invade Upper Canada. Hull begged the government to obtain control of Lake Erie, in order to secure his communications and hamper those of Brock; but nothing was done. He led his force to Detroit, and on 12 July crossed the river into Upper Canada. Parading through that thinly settled country, he found the inhabitants so poor and unfriendly that he shortly fell back on Detroit. In the meantime, the commander of the British post at the Sault Ste. Marie forced the American garrison at Michilimackinac to surrender (17 July), which brought Tecumseh's confederacy definitely to the British side. General Brock promptly transported to Detroit all the troops he could spare from the Niagara front, and summoned Hull to surrender. A broad hint in Brock's note, that the Indians would be beyond his control the moment fighting began, completely unnerved the American general. Dreading a massacre of women and children, deserted by some of his militia, and cut off from his base, Hull surrendered on 16 August 1812. So ended the first invasion of Canada. Fort Dearborn (Chicago) was also lost, and the effective military frontier of the United States was thrown back to the Wabash and the Ohio.

One week later Brock was back at Niagara with Hull's army as prisoners of war, and eager to attack his enemy on the New York side of the Niagara river. Prevost restrained him, and the Americans took the initiative on 13 October. Captain John E. Wool led a small detachment of regulars across the river, to a gallant and successful attack on Queenston heights, where General Brock was killed. Wool should have been supported by the New York militia under General Van Rensselaer; but the militia refused to budge. They had turned out to defend their homes, not to invade Canada. General Van Rensselaer exhorted them in vain; the militia calmly watched their comrades on the other bank being enveloped, shot down, and forced to surrender.

Alexander Smyth, a regular army officer, was then given command on the Niagara front. After issuing another proclamation to the Canadians, and exhorting his soldiers to ' Be strong! Be brave! And let the ruffian power of the British king cease on this continent! ' General Smyth threw up the sponge, and refused to cross Niagara river. His men joyfully discharged their muskets in every direction, showing a preference for the general's tent as target. Smyth followed Hull and Van Rensselaer into retirement.

There still remained a considerable force at Plattsburg on Lake Champlain, under the immediate command of General Dearborn. This army should have struck the Canadian trunk at Montreal. On 20 November Dearborn marched twenty miles north of Plattsburg, when the militia refused to go farther. The general then marched them back to Plattsburg.

4. 'Fir-built Frigates'

On the ocean there is a different story to tell. At the beginning of hostilities the American navy consisted of sixteen sea-going vessels, excluding Jefferson's gunboats. The pride of the navy was its three 44's, the *Constitution, United States,* and *President* frigates, which had been designed to outclass all other frigates, and to outrun ships of the line. They threw a heavier broadside than the British frigates, and were so heavily timbered and planked as to deserve the name ' Old Ironsides '; yet with such fine, clean lines under water that they could outsail almost anything that floated. The American crews were volunteers, and the officers, tried by experience against France and Tripoli, were burning to avenge the *Chesapeake.* Such were the ' few fir-built frigates, manned by a handful of bastards and outlaws '

— a London journalist's phrase that became quite popular with the Americans.

Admiral Sir John Borlase Warren, who commanded the consolidated transatlantic station at the beginning of the war, had under him ninety-seven sail, including eleven of the line and thirty-four frigates. The conquerors at Cape St. Vincent, Trafalgar, and the Nile were the spoiled children of victory, confident of beating any vessel not more than twice their size. Hence, when the *Constitution* knocked the *Guerrière* helpless in two hours and a half (19 August 1812) and reduced the *Java* to a useless hulk (29 December); when the sloop-of-war *Wasp* mastered the *Frolic* in forty-three minutes, and the *Hornet*, after a close fight of fifteen minutes off the Demerara river, sank the *Peacock* (24 February 1813); and when the frigate *United States*, Captain Decatur, entered New London harbor with the British frigate *Macedonian* as prize (4 December 1812), there was amazement and indignation in England, and rejoicing in the United States. In four out of the five engagements the American vessel threw the heavier broadside, and deserved the victory; but the British commanders were no less ingenious in finding excuses for defeat than they had been brisk in seeking battle.

The moral value of these victories to the American people, following disaster on the Canadian border, was beyond all calculation; but the military value was slight. Most of the American men-of-war that put into harbor during the winter of 1812–13 were there blockaded during the remainder of the war. Captain Lawrence of the unlucky *Chesapeake*, with a green and mutinous crew, unwisely accepted a challenge from Captain Broke of the *Shannon*, and sailed from Boston harbor to defeat and a glorious death (1 June 1813); the *Essex*, after clearing British privateers from the South Pacific, was destroyed by the *Phoebe* and *Cherub* while seeking asylum within the three-mile limit of Chile (28 March 1814); and Decatur surrendered the *President*, fastest of the three frigates, because she grounded when trying to elude the New York blockading squadron (17 January 1815). When the war ended, only the *Constitution* and four smaller vessels of the United States navy were at sea. American privateers managed to continue their depredations, although forced by convoys and blockades to transfer their operations to European and far eastern waters.

Hostilities might have ended with the year 1812, had Lord Liverpool's government been willing to abandon impressment. There was no desire for war on the part of the British people, and the government was anxious to terminate it as soon as possible. After the Orders in Council were repealed (23 June 1812), and the news of the American declaration of war reached London, the American chargé d'affaires endeavored to negotiate an armistice, on the condition that impressment from American vessels be suspended. In return he was instructed to promise that the enlistment of British-born seamen in American ships would be forbidden. Castlereagh replied (29 August) that His Majesty could not give up his 'ancient and accustomed practice.' Discussions were then transferred to America, and Admiral Warren proposed an armistice to the Secretary of State. Monroe replied (27 October) that no armistice would be concluded without at least a suspension of impressment. 'Having gone to war,' he wrote John Taylor, 'it seemed to be our duty not to withdraw from it till the rights of our country were placed on a more secure basis.' Hence the war continued on the single ground of impressment — for the conquest of Canada had never been alleged as an official war aim.

Congress, swept off its feet by enthusiasm over the naval victories, authorized an increase in the navy in December 1812 by four ships-of-the-line and six heavy frigates. None of the new vessels got to sea during the war; but in the meantime fresh-water naval history was being made on the Great Lakes.

Hull's surrender of Detroit convinced the American government that command of the Lakes was essential. At the same time the Canadian authorities determined to retain the supremacy they already enjoyed. It was comparatively easy for the power that controlled the Lakes to bring in more guns and fresh supplies. The Americans surmounted their greater difficulties through the energy and resourcefulness of Captain Oliver H. Perry, with headquarters at Presqu'ile on Lake Erie. All the cordage, sails, ordnance, and other supplies for the Lake Erie flotilla had to be hauled over the Alleghany Mountains to Pittsburgh and thence poled up the French river to the old carrying place between Fort Le Bœuf and Presqu'ile. Nevertheless, Perry managed to construct a fleet of stout little vessels during the winter of 1812–13. As the larger units had to be helped over a harbor bar by pontoons, and receive their guns outside, the British Commodore Barclay found it easy to contain the American fleet by blockade.

General Harrison, a commander in whom the West had confidence, advanced from the Ohio toward Detroit in three divisions

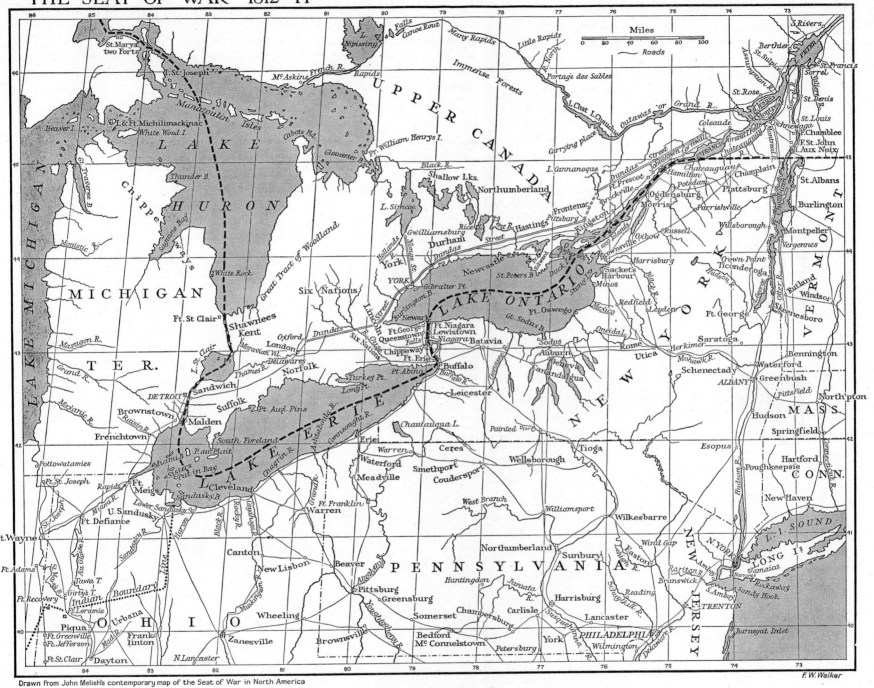

THE SEAT OF WAR 1812~14

Drawn from John Melish's contemporary map of the Seat of War in North America

F. W. Walker

The Seat of War, 1812–1814

Redrawn for The Oxford History of the United States *from* John Melish, Military and Topographical Atlas of the United States, 1815

during the winter of 1812–13. General Proctor did not wait for them to unite, but beat two of them separately in fierce wilderness fights. Harrison then decided to await the decision on Lake Erie. Owing to a temporary relaxation of Barclay's blockade, Perry was able to get his fleet over the bar on 4 August, and to seek out the British squadron. He found it on 10 September at Put-in-Bay among the islands near the western end of the lake. A strange sort of naval battle ensued, between vessels hastily built of green wood, manned largely by militiamen, negroes, frontier scouts, and Canadian *voyageurs*. Perry's plans were foiled for want of wind, and the fight was a matter of fire-away-Flannagan until one or the other went down. Superior weight of metal gave the Battle of Lake Erie to Perry. His laconic report, ' We have met the enemy, and they are ours,' was literally true.

Harrison then pursued Proctor to the center of the Ontario peninsula and defeated him at the Battle of the Thames (5 October 1813). Tecumseh was killed, Proctor saved his life only by flight, the Indian confederacy was broken up, and the American military frontier in the Northwest was re-established.

On Lake Ontario, where another fleet was improvised by Captain Isaac Chauncey, there was no such decisive result in 1813. In April 1813 Chauncey and General Dearborn raided York (later Toronto), the capital of Upper Canada. A large powder magazine exploded when the Americans were advancing upon the village, killing General Pike and about three hundred men. As a result of this incident, or of general indiscipline, the American troops got out of hand after the surrender, burnt the two brick parliament houses, the governor's residence, and other buildings as well. As the British had a considerable naval force on Lake Ontario, the Americans had to evacuate York; but Chauncey's fleet co-operated with the American forces on the Niagara front in a successful attack on Fort George.

A devastating American invasion of Upper Canada now began in earnest. General Vincent stopped it at Stony Creek, near Hamilton, and captured both American commanders (27 May 1813). Their subordinate, a militia general named McClure, burned the town of Newark and as much as he could of Queenston (19 December), turning the inhabitants out of their houses on a cold winter's night, before he retreated across the Niagara river. For this cruelty the innocent inhabitants on the American side paid dearly. On 30 December Fort Niagara was taken by surprise, the Indians were let loose on the surrounding country, and the villages of Black Rock and Buffalo were destroyed. In the meantime, two American columns were converging on Montreal: General Wilkinson, proceeding down the St. Lawrence from Sackett's Harbor, and General Wade Hampton advancing west from Plattsburg. Both allowed themselves to be turned back by mere skirmishes — at Chrysler's Farm (11 November 1813) and Chateauguay (26 October).

The second year of the war then closed with Canada cleared of American troops, and the Canadians in possession of Fort Niagara. American reoccupation of Detroit, and command of Lake Erie, ended all danger of a flanking movement from the Northwest, and made it impossible for Great Britain, at the peace conference, to annex the southern shores of the Lakes. So far, the British forces in Canada had waged defensive warfare; but the tables were turned in 1814.

5. From Chippewa to New Orleans

The Allies entered Paris on 31 March, Napoleon abdicated on 6 April 1814, and the last Napoleonic stronghold capitulated to Wellington three weeks later. At last Britain was able to provide Canada with an adequate army, to carry the war into the United States, to concentrate her navy on the American coast, and to force her own terms of peace. The plan was to invade the United States from three points successively: Niagara, Lake Champlain, and New Orleans; and simultaneously to raid the American coast, under cover of a strict blockade.

On the Niagara front the Americans were able to take the initiative before British reinforcements arrived. Their army had learned much from two years of adversity. Incompetent officers had been weeded out, and promising young men promoted; more reliance was placed on regulars, and less on militia. On 4 July General Jacob Brown got his army of five or six thousand men across the Niagara river, and forced the ill-garrisoned Fort Erie to capitulate the same day. On the 5th, his subordinate, Winfield Scott, after giving the men of his brigade a Fourth of July dinner that they had been too busy to partake of on the proper date, was marching them across a creek to hold a holiday parade on the plain beyond, when it appeared that three British regiments were there to break up the celebration. Scott deployed his brigade under fire, and the parade became the battle of Chippewa. The two lines advanced in close order, stopping alternately to load and fire; when they came in contact the British line broke. The Battle of Lundy's Lane on 25 July, hard by Niagara Falls, was the most stubbornly contested fight of the war, but inconclusive.

Very few of the reinforcements from Europe appear to have been engaged at Lundy's Lane; but by the middle of August Sir George Prevost commanded ten or eleven thousand of Wellington's veterans near Montreal, in readiness to invade the United States by Burgoyne's route of Lake Champlain and the Hudson. Prospects were very black for the United States, particularly as the War Department had lately transferred most of the regulars from Plattsburg to Niagara. Early in September, Prevost moved down the western side of Lake Champlain, synchronizing his movements with a freshwater flotilla, and forcing the Americans back to a strong position behind the river that empties into Plattsburg Bay. There they were protected by a line of forts, and by the American lake squadron, which was anchored inside the entrance to the bay in such a position as to rake enemy ships upon entering.

Prevost reached Plattsburg with his magnificent army on 6 September. Facing him were only fifteen hundred American regulars, and a few thousand militia. He has been severely criticized for not pushing home a frontal attack; but the American forts, constructed by West Point engineers, were formidable; and he wished first to secure control of the Lake. Early in the morning of 11 September the British fleet hove to off Cumberland Head. There followed a murderous engagement. Small vessels, without bulwarks to protect their crew, anchored side by side at pistol range and attempted to pound each other to pieces. The American fleet under Commodore Macdonough was the better handled and won the day. Prevost retreated to Canada; and the naval Battle of Plattsburg proved decisive in the war.

It was not, however, the last battle. Throughout the summer of 1814 the British navy had its will on the Atlantic coast. Maine was occupied to the Penobscot, and a base for the blockading fleet established at the tip of Cape Cod. During the previous year a naval squadron under Admiral Cockburn had waged inglorious warfare on the hen-houses, cow-barns, and movable property along the shores of Chesapeake Bay. In June 1814 a British expeditionary force was sent from Bordeaux in order to make a diversion in this region. The campaign that followed reflected little credit on the one side, and considerable disgrace on the other. General Ross, commander of the land forces, was instructed by Admiral Cochrane ' to destroy and lay waste such towns and districts upon the coast' as he might find assailable.

A fleet of Jeffersonian gunboats, retreating up the Patuxent river, led Ross's army from Chesapeake Bay to the back door of Washington. For five days the army marched along the banks of this river, approaching the capital of the United States without seeing an enemy or firing a shot. In the meantime, Washington was in a feverish state of preparation. About seven thousand militia, all that appeared out of ninety-five thousand summoned, were placed under an unusually incompetent general, and hurried to a strong position behind the village of Bladensburg, athwart the road over which the invaders must advance, and only five miles from the Capitol. President Madison and some of the cabinet officers came out to see the fun. After the militia had suffered only 66 casualties they broke and ran, leaving Commodore Barney with four hundred seamen and five guns of the boat squadron to dispute the field. Their gallant resistance was soon overcome, and the British army pressed on to Washington that evening (24 August). Some of the officers arrived in time to eat a dinner at the White House that had been prepared for the President and Mrs. Madison.

All the public buildings of the capital were deliberately burned. There was no looting and little destruction of private property — small consolation for the loss of the White House and Capitol.

It was a dark period for Madison's fugitive administration. Only discouraging news had arrived from the peace negotiators at Ghent. New England was disaffected, the last national war loan had failed, and all the banks south of New England had suspended specie payments. Prevost was expected to march south again; and a new British expeditionary force was expected at New Orleans.

Fortunately, the destruction of Washington only showed that invading a country like the United States is like hurling a hammer into a bin of corn. A few kernels were hurt, but the hammer had to be withdrawn quickly, or lost. On the night of 25–26 August 1814 the British army withdrew to its transports and proceeded to the next objective, Baltimore. Here the inhabitants were prepared, and the Maryland militia showed a very different spirit from that of their Virginia comrades. A naval bombardment on Fort McHenry made little impression, except on the imagination of Francis Scott Key, who celebrated its failure in 'The Star Spangled Banner.' That was the end of the Chesapeake campaign.

By the time the third British expeditionary force reached New Orleans, 18 December 1814, the West had produced a military leader. General Andrew Jackson, a frontiersman who had gone to Tennessee as a young man and grown up with the state, had been winning laurels in warfare against the Creek Indians. That nation wanted to remain neutral, but some outsiders visited their villages in 1811 and stirred up the younger warriors, who raided the frontier and captured Fort Mims above Mobile, together with some five hundred white scalps, in 1813.

This news reached Andrew Jackson in bed at Nashville, as he was recovering from a pistol shot received in a street brawl with the future Senator Benton. In a month's time he had many militia and a band of Choctaw auxiliaries in the Creek country. Nothing was accomplished that year; but after General Jackson had executed a few militiamen to encourage the others, the campaign went very well. The Creeks were beaten, their military power broken, and their territory dismembered by treaty (9 August 1814).

A few days before this, a small British force landed at Pensacola in Spanish Florida, and its leader, an impetuous Irishman named Edward Nicholls, proceeded to organize and drill Creek refugees with a view to renewing the war in that quarter. Jackson then invaded Florida on his own responsibility and captured Pensacola. Ignorant of the exact destination of the approaching British expeditionary force, he was ordered to New Orleans just in time to defend it. Mistaking the route by which the British would approach, Jackson allowed them to arrive unnoticed within a few miles of the city. Their commander, Sir Edward Pakenham, ought to have attacked New Orleans at once. Delay was fatal for anyone facing Andrew Jackson. This lank, long-haired general in his 'well-worn leather cap, a short Spanish cloak of old blue cloth, and great unpolished boots whose vast tops swayed uneasily around his bony knees,' was master of the situation the moment his enemy was in sight. Taking a strong position on the left bank of the Mississippi, between the levee and a swamp, he awaited an attack; and on the morning of 8 January 1815 the attack came. It was one of the most foolhardy events in British military annals: a frontal assault in close column formation against earthworks protected by artillery and riflemen. General Pakenham was killed, there were over two thousand casualties of all ranks; and the second and third generals in command were fatally wounded. Exactly thirteen Americans were killed before the attacking columns melted. The only surviving general officer withdrew the British army to its transports.

This Battle of New Orleans had no military value, since peace had been signed on Christmas eve; but it made a future President of the United States, and created the American tradition of the War of 1812, as a 'second War of Independence.' Although the Treaty of Ghent was a peace without a victory, and the Americans did not attain a single object for which their government had declared war, the people came to believe that they had won a just and glorious contest for free trade and seamen's rights.

6. New England and the War

New England's opposition to the war increased with its duration, although it was paradoxical that she should not be the most bellicose section of the United States. A war for free trade and seamen's rights was regarded with loathing in the maritime state of Massachusetts; a war for the conquest of Canada was resented by the section whose power in the Union would have been enhanced by the annexation of Canada. And hostilities enriched New England at the expense of the rest of the country.

The British blockade of the American coast was not extended to Massachusetts until the spring of 1814. Consequently, practically all the American imports came through New England custom houses, and most of the specie in the United States flowed into Yankee banks. And, strangest of all, Jefferson's embargo and Madison's war had the effect of diversifying the economic life of New England, as Hamilton had hoped to do for the entire country.

In 1807 there were only 15 cotton mills, with eight thousand spindles, in the United States. By 1810, after two winters of Jefferson's embargo, there were 87 mills with eighty thousand spindles; three-quarters of them located within thirty miles of Providence, R. I., and all operated by water power; Paterson, N. J., was also experiencing a revival. Madison's non-intercourse proclamation of 1811 again shut off English competition; and by the close of the War of 1812 there were half a million spindles in operation. While John Lowell, leader of the Boston Federalists, was advocating a New England Confederation as the only cure for commerce, his brother

Francis C. Lowell was picking up information in England about power looms. On his return to the United States, this Lowell invented a power loom of his own, and in 1814 at Waltham, Mass., equipped the first complete American cotton factory.

While the War of 1812 was preparing New England for a necessary transition from seafaring to manufacturing, the New England Federalists cried ruin. Blind to new economic forces, their ideas of the Republican administrations and of their own consequence became hardened and fixed. The doctrine that New England depended exclusively on shipping and commerce, the charge that ' Mr. Madison's war ' was dictated by Napoleon and designed to ruin their section, was propagated in the press, and in pamphlets of great pith and cogency. The Yankees were told again and again that they were the earth's chosen people, that the Constitution was weighted against them, and that the annexation of Louisiana absolved them from all obligation to remain in the Union.

In 1813 the Federalists controlled all the state governments of New England, and were again in a position to employ the doctrine of state rights against the administration. Up to that time, their opposition had been individual rather than corporate. Enlistments were discouraged, the President's requisitions for militia refused. Allied victories in Europe were celebrated, and a vote of thanks to a naval hero was rejected in the Massachusetts legislature as ' not becoming a moral and religious people.' However justified these stern puritans may have been in refusing to support a war of conquest against a kindred people, there was no excuse for their continuing the same policy after Napoleon had been disposed of and the character of the war had been changed. They chose the darkest moment for the American cause to agitate state rights and to summon a sectional convention.

For some years there had been talk of holding a New England convention to concert protest or action against Republican policy. Events of the summer of 1814 conspired to bring it about. Massachusetts was thrown upon her own resources for defense. Eastern Maine had been occupied by the enemy, the blockading squadron was making descents on various parts of the coast, and for all their heavy war taxes the New England States were receiving no protection from the Federal Government. That this condition existed was largely the fault of the Federalist governors in refusing to place their militia under officers of the United States army; but New England was past reasoning on these matters. On 5 October 1814 the legislature of Massachusetts summoned a New England Convention at Hartford, for the express purpose of conferring upon 'their public grievances and concerns,' upon 'defence against the enemy . . . and also to take measures, if they shall think proper, for procuring a convention of delegates from all the United States, in order to revise the Constitution thereof.'

The language of this summons showed a compromise between the moderate and the extreme Federalists. The former, led by Harrison Gray Otis, were not disunionists, but wished to improve the situation in order to obtain concessions for New England. Alarmed at the rising tide of secessionist sentiment, they hoped the Convention would act as a safety valve to let it off; and their desire to concert defensive measures against the enemy was sincere. But the violent wing of the Federalist party, led by Timothy Pickering and the 'Essex Junto,' had other objects in view. It was their belief that the British invasion of New Orleans would succeed; and the West, shut off from the ocean, would then secede. The Hartford Convention would draft a new Federal Constitution, with clauses to protect New England interests, and present it as a pistol to the original Thirteen States. If they accepted it, well and good; if not, New England would act on her own, and make a separate peace with Great Britain. These extremists desired no further union with the democratic West.

The Hartford Convention, representing mainly the states of Massachusetts, Rhode Island, and Connecticut, met in secret session on 15 December 1814. President Madison was apprehensive, and the war party feared the worst. Fortunately the moderates gained control and issued a sensible and statesmanlike report (5 January 1815). Madison's administration and the war were severely arraigned. 'But to attempt upon every abuse of power to change the Constitution, would be to perpetuate the evils of revolution.' The policy of secession was squarely faced, and ruled out as inexpedient and unnecessary, since the causes of New England's calamities were not deep and permanent, but the result of bad administration, and of partisanship in the European war. The New England states were invited to nullify the conscription bill then before Congress, if it should pass. A suggestion was thrown out that Congress might permit them to assume their own defense, applying to that purpose the federal taxes collected within their borders. A few constitutional

amendments were proposed. But there was no suggestion of a separate peace, or of leaving the West out of a new Union.

The report of the Hartford Convention was praised for its moderation by the war press, and secession agitation in New England
immediately calmed down; but presently the news from Ghent and
New Orleans put Madison's administration on stilts, and made New
England the scapegoat for government mismanagement. A stigma
of unpatriotism, from which it never recovered, was attached to the
Federalist party. Yet no stigma was attached to the doctrine of state
rights; and within five years it was revived by politicians who had
denounced the Hartford Convention as treasonable.

7. The Treaty of Ghent

Peace negotiations began as soon as the war. Even before Admiral
Warren had been able to offer an armistice, the Emperor of Russia
proposed to mediate between England and the United States. For
reasons still somewhat obscure this came to nothing, and it was not
until January 1814 that Madison received a direct offer from London
to treat. He replied favorably at once. After further delay, Ghent
was decided upon as the place of negotiation. But by the time the
American commissioners arrived there, in June 1814, the Liverpool
ministry was in no hurry to negotiate. News of decisive victories
in America was shortly expected, when Britain would be in a position to dictate, instead of negotiate.

The Americans had been instructed to insist upon the abandonment of impressment as a first condition of peace. The British commissioners were instructed not to admit impressment or neutral
rights as subjects of discussion. They further informed the Americans that the United States must abandon her rights to the Newfoundland and Labrador fisheries: a proposal that infuriated John
Quincy Adams, the head of the American delegation. The Canada-
United States boundary must be revised in the Northeast, to provide
a direct British road between St. John and Quebec; and also in the
Northwest, to give Canada access to the upper Mississippi. Finally,
the old project of a neutral Indian barrier state was revived. When
Gallatin inquired what was to be done with the hundred thousand or
so white inhabitants already settled within the proposed Indian state,
one of the British commissioners remarked that they must undoubtedly shift for themselves.

J. Q. Adams, an experienced diplomatist, thought that the negotiations would terminate on this point, and prepared to go home. His western colleague Henry Clay, untrained in diplomacy but skilled in the ways of men, was confident that the British would recede, as they did. They dropped the barrier project, and at the same time Madison withdrew his conditions of abandoning impressment.

The next obstacle was a British proposal to settle the boundary on the basis of *uti possidetis,* which would mean the cession of eastern Maine, and of any territory that Sir George Prevost might conquer. The Americans refused to entertain any other basis than *status quo ante bellum*. Again came a deadlock, which was broken by the battle of Plattsburg and the Duke of Wellington. Lord Liverpool wrote to the Duke at Paris, on 4 November, suggesting that he should take the chief command in America, 'with full powers to make peace, or to continue the war . . . with renewed vigor.' Wellington, who had studied the Battle of Plattsburg, replied to the effect that he could do nothing without a naval superiority on the Lakes and that he saw no means of acquiring that superiority; that in his opinion England had no military grounds for demanding a cession of territory.

By this time the ministry was anxious to conclude the war. The Congress of Vienna was suffering one of its recurrent crises, Englishmen were crying out against taxation, and Wellington's arguments seemed irresistible. The American principle of *status quo* was accordingly accepted for the boundary.

A third crisis occurred over the navigation of the Mississippi and the fisheries. Britain insisted that she must be secured in the one, if she conceded the other; and in so doing divided the American delegation. These five Americans of diverse origin and temperament, after living together in stuffy lodgings for several months, had got upon each other's nerves. Adams, a man of irritating virtues, would rise at five on a winter's morning to indite documents, when Henry Clay's card party was breaking up in the next room. Bayard had a feeling that some of his colleagues were not gentlemen; Jonathan Russell was a trouble-maker. This personal friction exaggerated a sectional divergence. Adams insisted on the fisheries, and was for treating the navigation of the Mississippi as of little importance. Clay declared that New England deserved to lose the fisheries for her treasonable conduct; but as a Westerner he would never admit so much as a Canadian canoe to a river that flowed from its source to its mouth through American territory. 'A dreadful day. Angry disputes,' wrote Gallatin's son in his diary on 28 November. It was Gallatin's tact, patience, and good humor that finally brought Adams and Clay to a compromise. Nothing was said in the treaty about the fisheries or the Mississippi; but the United States agreed to restore Tecumseh's Indians to the lands they possessed in 1811.

In the end, nothing very much was said about anything in the Treaty of Ghent (24 December 1814). Both sides agreed to disagree on everything important except the conclusion of hostilities, and pre-war boundaries. Yet, like Jay's treaty, it provided the machinery for disposing of present and future disputes. Four boundary commissions were created to settle the line between Canada and the United States; claims, commercial relations, the question of naval forces on the Lakes, and that of Oregon, were postponed to future negotiations; and before the next maritime war took place, impressment had been given up as a means of recruiting the British navy.

So ended a futile and unnecessary war, which might have been prevented by a little more imagination on the one side, and a broader vision on the other. A different and victorious result for either side would have been worse; but the event was bad enough. Anglophobia became a tradition in the United States, when, by a happier combination of events, it might have been exorcized. Dislike of America was never so rife in Britain as during the generation after 1815. On the relations between the two governments, however, the war had rather a happy effect. The soldiers, sailors, and diplomatists learned to respect one another; and the United States was never again refused the treatment due to an independent nation. Comparing Anglo-American relations before 1812 and after 1814, one must agree that in one respect at least the War of 1812 was a second War of American Independence.

XXI

THE ERA OF GOOD FEELINGS
1815–1822

1. *The Key to the Period*

EIGHTEEN hundred and fifteen is a turning-point in American
as in European history; and a point of divergence between them.
Up to that time the development of the United States had been
vitally affected by European forces. In spite of independence, colonial
rivalries and maritime commerce kept the contact warm between
the two worlds, and the European war had been projected into
America. With the Peace of Vienna, Europe turned to problems that
had little interest for America; and with the Peace of Ghent, America
turned her back on the Atlantic. Every serious difficulty under which
the young republic had labored since the War of Independence
dropped out of sight. With national union achieved, a balance between liberty and order secured, a trifling national debt, and a virgin
continent awaiting the plow, there opened a serene prospect of peace,
prosperity, and social progress. No one suspected that expansion
would bring its problems no less than encircling pressure, that the
'self-evident truths' of the Declaration of Independence would be
challenged anew, and that within half a century Americans would
be slaughtering one another in the valleys of Virginia, and the rolling
farmlands of Pennsylvania.

An 'era of good feelings,' as contemporaries called it, followed
a quarter-century of rivalry between Federalists and Republicans.
President Madison and his party accepted the nationalism of Washington and Hamilton as if they had been born to it; and Federalist
enmity did not long survive Republican conversion. A Congress
in which Republicans were dominant resurrected Hamilton's report
on manufactures, and passed the first American protective tariff in
1816. The same year it chartered a second Bank of the United States,
on the model of Hamilton's. Several outstanding controversies with
Great Britain, any one of which would earlier have aroused political
bitterness, were quietly settled. James Monroe, legitimate heir of the
Virginia dynasty, succeeded to the presidency in 1817 almost unop-

posed; in 1821 he obtained every electoral vote but one, and two years later, with unanimous approval, issued a momentous declaration of American foreign policy.

American politics did not long continue in this placid rhythm. No real conversion to nationalism had taken place. The United States, like Europe, had found no permanent balance. They were tired of sectional strife, as she of war and revolution. New forces were transforming the states of the Union; and while this readjustment was taking place, Americans acquiesced in the sort of nationalism represented by President and Congress, as Europeans endured the sort of internationalism represented by the Holy Alliance. That is the key to the era of good feelings. Manufacturing was becoming the dominant interest in New England and Pennsylvania; democracy was invading society and politics in New York. Virginia, slowly declining as an agricultural state, had as yet found no other main interest. King Cotton's domain was advancing from South Carolina and Georgia into the new Gulf states. The Northwest, rapidly expanding in population and influence, was acquiring new wants and aspirations. A series of sharp and bitter sectional conflicts brought out the underlying antagonism; by 1830 the sections had again become articulate, and defined the stand they were to take until the Civil War. It became the major problem of politics to form combinations and alliances between sections whose interests were complementary, in the hope of achieving their common wants through the Federal Government; and the first end of statesmen was to reconcile rival interests and sections through national party organizations.

With new interests came a change in the attitude of the different sections toward the Constitution, completely reversing the similar change that had taken place during Jefferson's administration. As nationalist legislation began to cramp the economic life of certain states and sections, their public men adopted the state rights theories which New England Federalists had taken over from Jefferson in 1807. Daniel Webster of Massachusetts, who in 1814 had warned Congress that his state would not obey conscription, in 1830 was intoning hymns to the Union; while John C. Calhoun of South Carolina, leader of the 'war-hawks' in 1812 and of nationalistic legislation after the war, began in 1828 to write textbooks of state rights. Of all the American publicists and statesmen whose careers bridged the War of 1812, only three were consistent, and all were

Virginians: Chief Justice Marshall, who refused to unlearn the nationalism he had learned from Washington; John Taylor of Caroline, who went on writing; and John Randolph of Roanoke, who went on talking, as if nothing had happened since 1798.

2. *Nationalism and the Judiciary*

Every nationalistic feature of the era of good feelings aroused bad feelings in states that were suffering from growing or dissolving pains. Calhoun, introducing the bill chartering a second Bank of the United States, declared that to discuss its constitutionality would be a useless consumption of time. The bill passed, and the B.U.S., as contemporaries abbreviated the title, began operations in 1817. It was a bank of deposit, discount, and issue, having the government as principal client and holder of one-fifth of the capital stock, differing from the Bank of England mainly in the power to establish branches in the principal towns and cities. This feature, necessary for the fiscal operations of a federal government, hampered the ordinary banks operating under state charters. The Maryland legislature levied a heavy tax upon the notes of the Baltimore branch of this 'foreign corporation.' The B.U.S. refused to pay. Maryland was sustained by the state court of appeals, whence, in accordance with the Judiciary Act of 1789, the case was carried on appeal by writ of error to the Supreme Court of the United States. This case of McCulloch *v.* Maryland became a milestone in American nationalism, and gave Chief Justice Marshall an opportunity to pronounce one of the greatest of his constitutional opinions.

There were three great issues at stake. Are the states separately, or the people of the United States collectively, sovereign? Was the Act of Congress chartering the B.U.S. constitutional? If constitutional, had a state the reserved right to tax its operation? On the first point, the counsel for Maryland followed Jefferson's Kentucky resolutions of 1798. 'The powers of the general government are delegated by the States, who alone are truly sovereign; and must be exercised in subordination to the States, who alone possess supreme dominion.' Marshall met this argument with an historical survey of the origin of the Constitution, and concluded: 'The government of the Union, then, is emphatically and truly a government of the people. In form and substance it emanates from them. Its powers are granted by them, and are to be exercised directly on them, and

for their benefit.' Here is the classic definition of national sovereignty, cutting the whole ground of the state-rights theory from
underneath.

On the second point, the defendant followed the Virginia remonstrance of 1790, and Jefferson's opinion on the bill chartering the
first Bank of the United States. The power to charter corporations
is not expressly granted to Congress by the Constitution. It cannot
be inferred from the 'necessary and proper' clause. A national bank
is not necessary, as the want of one since 1811 proved. All powers
not granted to the Federal Government are reserved to the states,
by the Tenth Amendment to the Constitution.

Marshall found little more to say on this point than Hamilton
had written in his Bank opinion of 1791; but that little was well said.

> The government of the Union, though limited in its powers, is su-
> preme within its sphere of action. . . . We admit, as all must admit,
> that the powers of the government are limited, and that its limits are
> not to be transcended. But we think the sound construction of the Con-
> stitution must allow to the national legislature that discretion, with re-
> spect to the means by which the powers it confers are to be carried into
> execution, which will enable that body to perform the high duties assigned
> to it, in the manner most beneficial to the people. Let the end be legiti-
> mate, let it be within the scope of the Constitution, and all means which
> are appropriate, which are plainly adapted to that end, which are not
> prohibited, but consist with the letter and spirit of the Constitution, are
> constitutional.

Here is the classic 'loose construction,' the doctrine of implied
powers.

Finally, may a state, by virtue of its reserved power of taxation,
levy a tax upon the operations of the B.U.S.? Marshall disposed of
this point by a bold analogy to a state tax on the United States mails,
or on custom house papers:

> The result is a conviction that the States have no power by taxation
> or otherwise, to retard, impede, burden, or in any manner control, the
> operations of the constitutional laws enacted by Congress to carry into
> execution the powers vested in the general government. This is, we think,
> the unavoidable consequence of that supremacy which the Constitution
> has declared.

'A deadly blow has been struck at the sovereignty of the states,'
declared a Baltimore newspaper in printing the opinion of the

court in McCulloch *v.* Maryland. Pennsylvania proposed a constitutional amendment prohibiting Congress from erecting a 'moneyed institution' outside the District of Columbia; and in this
amendment, Ohio, Indiana, and Illinois concurred. The legislature of South Carolina, on the contrary, declared that 'Congress is
constitutionally vested with the right to incorporate a bank,' and
'they apprehend no danger from the exercise of the powers which
the people of the United States have confided to Congress.' South
Carolina would not speak this language much longer; Pennsylvania
would shortly speak no other.

The Supreme Court was not to be deterred, however, by local
opposition, or influenced by public opinion. So long as Marshall
was Chief Justice, it went straight ahead along the lines which he
had marked out as early as 1803,[1] giving judicial sanction to the
doctrine of centralization of powers at the expense of the states,
and erecting judicial barriers against democratic attacks upon property rights. To the first category belong Martin *v.* Hunter's Lessee
(1816), Cohens *v.* Virginia (1821), McCulloch *v.* Maryland (1819),
Gibbons *v.* Ogden (1824), Martin *v.* Mott (1827), and Worcester *v.*
Georgia (1832), to mention only a few of the most important. In
Martin *v.* Hunter's Lessee the Court upheld the constitutionality of
Section 25 of the Judiciary Act of 1789 giving it the power to review
and reverse decisions of the state courts where they conflicted with
rights guaranteed under the Constitution. In Cohens *v.* Virginia
Marshall not only vigorously reasserted this principle, but partially
nullified the purpose of the Eleventh Amendment by accepting appellate jurisdiction over a suit against a state provided the state
had originally instituted the suit. In connection with this case Marshall set forth in forceful terms the doctrine of nationalism:

That the United States form, for many, and for most important purposes, a single nation, has not yet been denied. In war, we are one people.
In making peace, we are one people. In all commercial relations, we are
one and the same people. In many other respects, the American people
are one; and the government which is alone capable of controlling and
managing their interests, in all these respects, is the government of the
Union. It is their government, and in that character they have no other.
America has chosen to be, in many respects, and to many purposes, a

---

[1] So completely did Marshall dominate the court, despite numerous changes in
personnel, that in 34 years' service he dissented only 8 times. Of the 1106 opinions
handed down by the Court during this period, Marshall wrote 519.

nation; and for all these purposes her government is complete; to all these objects, it is competent. The people have declared, that in the exercise of all powers given for these objects, it is supreme. It can, then, in effecting these objects, legitimately control all individuals or governments within the American territory.

In Martin *v.* Mott the Court denied to a state the right, which New England had asserted during the War of 1812, to withhold her militia from the national service when requisitioned by the President. In Gibbons *v.* Ogden, most luminous and far-reaching of his decisions, Marshall not only smashed a state-chartered monopoly of steamboat traffic, but mapped out the course that Congress would follow for a century in regulating interstate commerce. The case involved an interpretation of the commerce clause of the Constitution. The Chief Justice, in vigorous and prophetic words, defined commerce as 'intercourse' of all kinds, and the power of Congress as complete, absolute, and exclusive. 'If the sovereignty of Congress, though limited to specified objects, is plenary as to those objects, the power over commerce with foreign nations and among the several states is vested in Congress as absolutely as it would be in a single government. . . . The power therefore is not to be confined by state lines, but acts upon its subject matter wherever it is to be found.' Under this ruling Congress has been able to control not only interstate but a large part of intrastate commerce as well; since the World War, however, the Supreme Court has limited federal regulation of labor engaged in interstate commerce. It was decisions of this nature that led Jefferson to write: 'The great object of my fear is the Federal Judiciary. That body, like gravity, ever acting with noiseless foot and unalarming advance, gaining ground step by step, and holding what it gains, is engulfing insidiously the special governments into the jaws of that which feeds them.'

To the second category of Marshall's decisions, those throwing the protective veil of the Constitution over property interests, belong, most notably, Fletcher *v.* Peck (1810), Dartmouth College *v.* Woodward (1819), and Craig *v.* Missouri (1830). In the first of these, the so-called Yazoo land fraud case, Marshall prohibited the state of Georgia from rescinding a grossly corrupt sale of western lands on the principle that such action impaired the obligation of a contract. The issue involved in the Dartmouth College case was the same. This case had to do with the right of the legislature of New Hampshire to rescind the pre-revolutionary royal charter of Dartmouth College and confer a new one that placed the College under state control. Daniel Webster defended his alma mater with characteristic eloquence and illogic. Marshall's decision that a charter to a corporation was a contract within the meaning of the Constitution, and so inviolate and beyond the control of a state, was of far-reaching importance, both for good and ill. On the one hand, it protected privately endowed colleges, schools, and the like from political interference, and encouraged endowments for education and charity. On the other, in conjunction with the Yazoo decision it gave to corporations an immunity from legislative interference that was only gradually destroyed through judicial recognition of the police power of the states.

In Craig *v.* Missouri the Court was confronted with an attempt on the part of a state to evade the constitutional prohibition against the emission of bills of credit. Marshall's decision declaring the Missouri law null and void and upholding the principle of sound money against the soft-money panaceas of the frontier states aroused deep resentment against the Court.

Marshall's opinions were the most enduring feature of the new nationalism that came in on flood tide after what has justly been called the second war of Independence. As James Bryce wrote:

> The Constitution seemed not so much to rise under his hands to full stature, as to be gradually unveiled by him till it stood revealed in the harmonious perfection of the form which its framers had designed. That admirable flexibility and capacity for growth which characterize it beyond all other rigid or supreme constitutions, is largely due to him, yet not more to his courage than to his caution.

Yet if Marshall worked with 'the spirit of the times' in fostering nationalism, he worked against it in opposing democracy and majority rule; and the passage of a century has justified not a few of Jefferson's fears.

3. The 'American System'

Henry Clay and John C. Calhoun were the nationalist leaders in Congress at this period. Both men saw and feared the growing particularism of the sections. Like Hamilton, they could imagine no stronger binding force than self-interest; and their policy was but a broader version of his reports on public credit and manufactures. Their formula, which Clay christened the 'American System,' was protection and internal improvements: a protective tariff for the manufacturers, a home market and better transportation for the farmers. 'We are greatly and rapidly — I was about to say fearfully — growing,' said Calhoun in 1817. 'This is our pride and our danger; our weakness and our strength. . . . Let us, then, bind the Republic together with a perfect system of roads and canals.' Protection 'would make the parts adhere more closely. . . . It would form a new and most powerful cement.'

It was a propitious moment to raise the customs tariff. National pride had been wounded by dependence on smuggled British goods. War industries, suffering from the dumping of British manufactures, were crying for protection, from which almost every section of the country expected to benefit. In New England few cotton mills managed to survive the fall in prices unless they had adopted improved spinning machinery and the power loom. The few experimental mills in the Carolinas were staggering. Pittsburgh, already a flourishing smelter for iron deposits of the northern Appalachians, was eager to push its iron pigs and bars into the coastal region, in place of British and Swedish iron. In Kentucky there was a new industry of weaving local hemp into cotton bagging, which was menaced by the Scotch bagging industry. All the Western states needed roads and canals. The shepherds of Vermont and Ohio wished protection against English wool; the granaries of central New York, shut out of England by the corn laws, were attracted by the home market argument. Even Jefferson, outgrowing his old prejudice against factories, wrote. 'We must now place the manufacturer by the side of the agriculturist.'[2] Congressmen from states that a generation later preferred secession to protection eagerly voted for the tariff of 1816; it was maritime New England, destined to pocket the earliest benefits of protection, which voted against it.

Textiles, in the tariff of 1816, were taxed at twenty-five per cent *ad valorem;* but no cotton cloth was to be rated at a less value than twenty-five cents a yard. As some of the India print-cloths then being imported were worth only one-quarter of that sum, this 'minimum principle' erected an insurmountable barrier about the coarse sheetings and shirtings produced by Northern cotton factories, whilst the constitutional provision of internal free trade gave them the entire home market. Apart from this cunning provision, the tariff

[2] When forced, however, to pay treble the pre-war price for suitings, Jefferson reverted to free trade.

rates of 1816 did not afford much protection against British woolens, cottons, and iron; but were high enough to whet the appetite of American manufacturers for more.

'Internal improvements' — public works at federal expense — were the complement to protection. Immediately after the War of 1812 there was a rush of emigrants to the West, eager to exploit the lands conquered from Tecumseh and from the Creek. Between 1810 and 1820 the population of the states and territories west of the Appalachians increased from 1,080,000 to 2,234,000. Four new states, Indiana (1816), Mississippi (1817), Illinois (1818), and Alabama (1819), were admitted from this region, as well as Louisiana in 1812.

Owing to the difficulty of ascending the Mississippi and Ohio rivers, Western supplies of manufactured goods came by wagon road from Atlantic seaports. After the war the increasing use of steamboats on the Western rivers threatened the Eastern cities with loss of this Western trade. In 1817 a steamboat managed to reach Cincinnati from New Orleans, and two years later there were sixty light-draught stern-wheelers plying between New Orleans and Louisville. Their freight charges to the upper Ohio were less than half the cost of wagon transport from Philadelphia and Baltimore. For local and selfish reasons the Eastern cities would not combine to further the Western desire for federal roads and canals. New England and the Carolinas feared isolation. Virginia lent state assistance to two companies which hoped to pierce the Appalachians with canals. Pennsylvania went in for road building, and New York State began in 1817 the construction of the Erie canal, which was destined to make New York City outstrip all her rival seaports.

Clay and Calhoun induced Congress to push through a national road from Cumberland on the upper Potomac to Wheeling on the Ohio.[3] Connected with Baltimore by a state road, this 'national pike' became the most important route for emigrants to the Northwest until 1840. In 1817 Congress proposed to earmark certain federal revenues for bolder projects of the same sort. President Madison so far had accepted every item in the nationalist program; but here he drew the line, and vetoed the internal improvement bill. President Monroe had similar constitutional scruples; and by the time J. Q.

---

[3] The national or Cumberland road was afterwards pushed across Ohio and Indiana to Vandalia, Illinois, by successive appropriations between 1822 and 1838; but the Federal Government relinquished each section, upon its completion, to the state within which it lay.

Adams reached the White House, with even more ambitious plans for the expenditure of federal moneys, Congress proved disappointingly stubborn. The Appalachians were destined to be crossed and tunnelled by private enterprise under state authority.

4. *The Western Panic of 1819*

Other and more serious problems than transportation were raised by the westward movement after the war. The new settlers, tempted by rising prices of cotton, cattle, and grain, purchased land far beyond their capacity to pay; for the Public Land Act of 1800 extended long credit. Much of the best land was engrossed by speculators. When cotton rose to thirty-four cents a pound in 1818, planters paid up to $150 an acre for uncleared land in the black belt of Alabama. All this led to a wide dispersal of settlers, instead of the orderly progression along a definite frontier that the Act of 1796 had planned. Until vacant spaces were settled, the scattered frontier farmers found themselves without schools, means of communication, or markets, yet deeply in debt to the Federal Government or to ' wild-cat ' Western banks. These in turn were indebted to the B.U.S. and to Eastern capitalists, who at the same time were erecting new manufacturing and other corporations far in advance of the country's needs. It was just what happened after the Civil War and the World War: the piling up of credits in a gigantic top, which could be kept whirling for some time by the lash of speculation, but was certain in the end to topple by its own weight.

The Bank of the United States, which might have put a brake on inflation, was second to none in the mad scramble for wealth. The Western branches discounted recklessly. Late in 1818 the directors took steps to curtail credits. Branches were ordered to accept no bills but their own, to present all state bank-notes for payment at once, to renew no personal notes of mortgages. The result was to hasten the inevitable panic; and in 1819 it came. State banks collapsed; and enormous amounts of Western real estate became the property of the B.U.S. At this juncture came the decision in McCulloch *v.* Maryland, forbidding the states to tax the ' Monster.' It became the Western bogy. ' All the flourishing cities of the West are mortgaged to this money power,' declared Senator Benton of Missouri. ' They may be devoured by it at any moment. They are in the jaws of the Monster. A lump of butter in the mouth of a dog — one gulp, one swallow, and all is gone!' Ohio, ignoring the Supreme Court's decision, laid a tax of fifty thousand dollars each on two local branches of the B.U.S. Ohio congressmen were shouting for 'internal improvements' at federal expense, but their state legislature declared the Kentucky and Virginia resolves of 1798 to be 'the settled construction of the Constitution.'

Would the panic and the McCulloch case, then, turn the West against nationalism, and some new Wilkinson or Burr arise to plot secession? Or would West and South shake hands, conquer the Federal Government by votes, and turn it against the money power?

When the panic came in 1819, payments due to the government for public land were in arrears many millions, most of which never were and never could be paid. It was clearly time for an alteration in the land laws. By the Public Land Act of 1820 credit was stopped, the upset price was lowered to a dollar and a quarter an acre, and the minimum unit of sale to eighty acres. This made it easier for a poor man to acquire land; but the West was not satisfied. Hard times lasted until 1824, affording an ideal culture-bed for the movement afterwards known as Jacksonian Democracy. Some of the same remedies for sectional indebtedness were tried as in 1786. Kentucky, for instance, incorporated a bank without stockholders, with state officials as directors, and no other capital than an appropriation of seven thousand dollars for printing notes, which were to be lent on mortgage security to all citizens who applied, 'for the purpose of paying his, her, or their just debts.' By this subterfuge the constitutional prohibition against the emission of paper money by states was evaded; but the courts refused to enforce acceptance of the bank-notes.

5. The Missouri Compromise

While debt, deflation, and hard times were producing these preliminary symptoms of a vertical cleavage between East and West, another Western question, that of slavery extension, threatened to cut the Union horizontally into North and South. Ever since the Federal Convention of 1787 there had been a tacit political balance between these two great sections, along the old Mason and Dixon line and the Ohio river which divided the slaveholding states and territories from those in which slavery was abolished, or in process of extinction. In 1789 North and South were approximately equal in numbers, but in 1820 the Northern or free states had a population of 5,152,000 with 105 members in the House of Representatives; while the Southern or slave states had 4,485,000 people with 81 congress-men. An even balance had been maintained in the Senate by the admission of free and slave states alternately; after the admission of Alabama in 1819 there were exactly eleven of each.

In the territory of the Louisiana Purchase, Congress had done nothing to disturb slavery as it existed by French and Spanish law. Consequently, in the westward rush after the War of 1812, several thousand slave-owners with their human property emigrated to the Territory of Upper Louisiana, establishing wheat and cotton planta-tions in the rich bottom lands of the lower Missouri river, or on the west bank of the Mississippi near the fur-trading post of St. Louis. When the people of this region decided to claim admission to the Union as the State of Missouri, slavery was naturally permitted by their proposed state constitution. In February 1819 a bill admitting Missouri as a state came before the House of Representatives. To the surprise and indignation of Southern members, James Tallmadge of New York offered an amendment prohibiting the further intro-duction of slaves into Missouri, and requiring that all children sub-sequently born therein of slave parents should be free at the age of twenty-five. Thus amended, the bill passed the House, but was lost in the Senate.

Congress dissolved in March, and the question of slavery or free-dom in Missouri went to the people. In state legislatures, in the news-papers, and in popular mass meetings it was discussed and agitated — not as a moral question but as one of sectional power and prestige, yet no less bitterly for that. Northerners had long been dissatisfied with the 'federal ratio' which gave the slave states twenty seats in Congress and twenty electoral votes, based on the enumeration of human chattels. They regarded the admission of Missouri, which lay almost wholly north of the then dividing line between freedom and slavery, as an aggressive move toward increasing the voting power of the South; and many threatened secession if slavery were not defeated. Southerners did not yet defend the rightfulness of slavery, but asserted their right to enjoy human property in the trans-Mississippi West; and threatened secession if they were denied. Sur-viving Federalist politicians, and middle-state Republicans, saw an opportunity to create a solid North; to ' snatch the sceptre from Vir-ginia for ever,' as H. G. Otis said. ' Federalism,' wrote the aged Jefferson, ' devised this decoy to draw off the weak and wicked from the Republican ranks. . . . The East is replaced in the saddle of gov-

ernment, and the Middle States are to be the cattle yoked to their car.
. . . My hope and confidence however is . . . that they will retrace
their steps back to those honester brethren of the South and West.'

Equally important with the slavery issue was the question of the
power of Congress to place qualifications upon the admission of
new states. A precedent had been established in the case of the states
created out of the Northwest Territory and Louisiana. The principle was now challenged by William Pinkney of Maryland, who
solemnly warned the West that if this power of Congress were once
definitely admitted, the older Eastern states might use it to keep new
Western states in a permanently subordinate position, and that the
Union would become one 'between giants and dwarfs, between
power and feebleness.'

Jefferson's confidence was rewarded. When the new Congress
took up the question, in January 1820, enough Northern Republicans were detached from the anti-slavery bloc by fear of a Federalist
renaissance, to get a compromise measure through House and Senate. Missouri was admitted as a slaveholding state, and slavery was
prohibited in the Louisiana territory north of latitude 36° 30'. As
part of the compromise, Maine, which had just detached itself from
Massachusetts, was admitted as a free state, making twelve of each.

This was the famous Missouri Compromise, which put the question of slavery extension at rest for almost a generation. It was a fair
enough solution. The South obtained its immediate object, with the
prospect of Arkansas and Florida entering as slave states in the near
future; the North secured the greater expanse of unsettled territory,
and maintained the principle of 1787, that Congress could keep
slavery out of the Territories if it would.

Angry passions quickly subsided, the sectional alignment dissolved, and politics resumed their delusive tranquillity. For a moment the veil had been lifted, and there were some who saw the
bloody prospect ahead. 'This momentous question, like a fire bell
in the night, awakened and filled me with terror,' wrote Jefferson.
'I considered it at once as the knell of the Union.' And J. Q. Adams
recorded in his diary: 'I take it for granted that the present question
is a mere preamble — a title-page to a great, tragic volume.'

6. Anglo-American Adjustments

Almost a century of diplomacy was required to clear up all the
questions left open between Britain and America by the Treaty of

Ghent. That diplomacy did settle them is perhaps the greatest triumph of that much abused profession during the nineteenth century. Neither the treaty, nor the situation in 1815, nor the mutual disposition of the British and American peoples, gave much ground for hope of a lasting peace. J. Q. Adams wrote before the year was out that the treaty was ' a truce rather than a peace. Neither party gave up anything; all the points of collision which had subsisted between them before the war were left open.' Canada with a long and vague boundary, rival peltry and fishing interests, and a freshwater naval force, promised so many points of friction between the two countries that Alexander Baring wished his government would give up Canada at once. It ' was fit for nothing but to breed quarrels.' No more attempts were made, as in 1783–95, to evade just debts or to stir up Indians; but there was no abatement of rival pretensions respecting the carrying trade and West India commerce that had caused so much trouble in the eighteenth century. *The Times,* in its editorial on the Treaty of Ghent, predicted ' the speedy growth of the American navy, and the recurrence of a new and more formidable American war.' A dangerous business, indeed, to give Neptune a black eye but leave him the trident!

Many Americans, and not a few Britons, were thinking of Rome and Carthage. Naval victories and New Orleans had drawn off much of the Anglophobia that had been festering in America since 1783; but there was plenty of bad humor left. As George Canning wrote to the first British minister to the United States after the war, the toughest problem for him was ' not what to do, but what to bear.' English tories no longer regarded the United States as a jest, but as a menace to British institutions; there was grave danger lest the success of republicanism and the progress of democracy might delude the weak and wicked into a belief that such things might be in England! That uneasy feeling was largely responsible for the sneering strictures upon American life, character, and letters with which the *Edinburgh* and the *Quarterly* teemed during the years following 1815; an attitude which prevented the common ties of blood and language from having their natural effect.

During the first fifteen years of peace the tories were in power. Yet it was a leader of that party who did most to bring the two nations together. Lord Castlereagh coined no phrases about Anglo-Saxon solidarity during his long career. In England his achievements were eclipsed by the plausible Canning; in America he is known chiefly through Byron's savage verses. Yet, judged by his deeds, this great and silent statesman must be placed beside Washington, Hamilton, Peel, and Bright as a promoter of Anglo-American concord. He was the first British statesman to regard friendship with America as a permanent British interest. His policy was to treat the United States in every respect as an equal, ' to smooth all asperities between the two nations, and to unite them in sentiments of good will as well as of substantial interest, with each other.' And he was met half-way by Madison and Monroe, founders of a party traditionally anti-British.

Few would assert that Castlereagh was met half-way by J. Q. Adams, who became Monroe's Secretary of State in 1817. Adams really desired peace and friendship, but the spectacle of Downing Street bearing gifts was new to his experience, and a challenge to his suspicious nature. Adams, moreover, was an aggressive nationalist. He loved his country with a bitter intensity that was not returned. To advance every American interest and defend every American right, well knowing that others would get the credit of success and he alone the blame of failure, afforded him that sort of pain which in a puritanic nature becomes pleasure. Harsh and irascible in personal intercourse, Adams made a poor diplomatist, and as Secretary of State his notes needed pruning and softening by the kindly and mellow Monroe. But his perception was abnormally keen, and almost alone of contemporaries he predicted America's future place in the world.

Disarmament on the Great Lakes was the first fruit of Anglo-American diplomacy after the war; and the most lasting. Peace found each side feverishly building ships against the other on Lake Ontario. The Canadians, apprehensive of further American aggression, frustrated in their hope of a buffer state that would give them complete control of the Lakes, looked for large outlays by the British treasury to complete this building program.

It used to be the habit of Americans to prepare for war only when war came, and when war was over to prepare for peace; and while that habit endured, the United States expanded and prospered as no other nation. In 1815, as in 1920, the initiative in disarmament came from the United States. An Act of Congress of 27 February 1815 authorized President Madison to sell or lay up all the Lake fleet not necessary for enforcement of the revenue laws; and this he promptly did. The army at the same time was reduced to ten thousand men, and in 1820 to six thousand. During the summer occurred several 'untoward incidents' on the Lakes connected with the right of search; and in the autumn came a disquieting rumor from London, that the British Admiralty had determined to carry on its building program in Canada. President Madison then made the momentous proposal of naval disarmament on the Lakes. Adams, in London, won over Castlereagh to the policy, and on 28–29 April 1817 an agreement was effected by an exchange of notes at Washington. The Rush-Bagot agreement, as it is called, provides that the naval force to be maintained upon the American lakes by the two governments shall be limited, on each side, to a single-gun vessel of one hundred tons on Lake Champlain, another on Lake Ontario, and two of the same sort on the other Great Lakes. The treaty might be denounced at six months' notice; but in spite of strong pressure at periods of Anglo-American tension, it is still in force, although modified in detail by mutual agreement in order to meet changed needs of revenue control, and newer methods of naval propulsion.

In weighing the causes of American-Canadian amity, we must not forget that the Rush-Bagot agreement, important as it was in removing causes of irritation, could have been maintained only by the United States abandoning designs on Canada, and by Canada renouncing her dream of a buffer Indian state. Without violating that agreement, the American-Canadian boundary might have been lined on both sides with forts and armed encampments. Mutual respect and good will have kept it undefended and unfortified, despite three subsequent periods of severe border tension.

With frigates rotting on the ways, it was a much easier matter to adjust this four thousand mile boundary, of which a scant two hundred miles had as yet been determined beyond dispute. Several joint commissions for this purpose were provided in the Treaty of Ghent. The first promptly settled where the eastern end of the boundary should run, between the islands of Passamaquoddy Bay. The second was quite unable to discover the whereabouts of the famous highlands between the St. Lawrence and the Atlantic Ocean, mentioned by the Treaty of 1783. This question was then referred to the arbitrament of the King of the Netherlands who, pleading similar inability, recommended a compromise which the United States refused to accept; and the matter went over to the Webster-Ashburton negotiation of 1842. The third joint commission drew the boundary from the forty-fifth parallel of latitude, through the St. Lawrence and the

Lakes, just short of the Sault Ste. Marie between Huron and Superior; Webster and Ashburton continued it as far as the Lake of the Woods. At that point the international frontier had been left hanging in mid-air by the Treaty of 1783. No line could be drawn from 'the most northwestern point' of said Lake ' on a due west course to the river Mississippi,' because that river happened to flow considerably to the eastward and southward. This and the Oregon question were dealt with in the Convention of 1818, which extended the Canadian-American boundary along the forty-ninth parallel to the ' Stony Mountains.'

West of the Rocky Mountains, between Spanish California and Russian Alaska, was the region vaguely known as Oregon. Britain had challenged Spain's exclusive claim to this territory in the Nootka Sound affair of 1790; but a Boston seaman's discovery of the Columbia river in 1792 gave the United States a claim. No settlement had yet been made, but the Hudson's Bay Company and an American fur company had established trading posts there before the war. The British company controlled the region during the War of 1812, but American rights were restored by the Treaty of Ghent. No agreement could be reached in the negotiation of 1818 as to the partition of Oregon, so the region was left open for ten years to the vessels, citizens, and subjects of the two powers. Before the decade elapsed, the claims of Russia and Spain had been eliminated, and in 1827 the agreement for joint occupation was renewed.

The Newfoundland fisheries question, on which the Ghent negotiators failed to agree, was also dealt with in the Convention of 1818. Certain privileges within the three-mile limit on parts of the Newfoundland and Labrador coasts were restored to American fishermen, but, unfortunately, the treaty was not carefully drawn, and efforts of the Newfoundland government to police the Yankee fishermen produced an almost continuous diplomatic controversy until 1910, when the Hague Tribunal gave an arbitral decision which, it is devoutly hoped, has put the question to sleep permanently.

7. Arbuthnot and Ambrister

It was on the southeastern border, between the southern tier of states and Florida, that Anglo-American amity was gravely endangered. East Florida was a Spanish province, but Spanish authority was hardly exercised beyond the three fortified posts of Pensacola,

St. Marks, and St. Augustine. The loyalist settlers of 1782 had long since left; the only breaks in the vast stretches of semi-tropical forest and morass were made by Seminole villages and a few obscure encampments of maroons, fugitive slaves from Georgia. After the battle of New Orleans, Lieutenant-Colonel Nicholls took his 'colonial marines' to Florida, built a fort on Spanish territory near the Georgian border, concluded an alliance with the Seminoles and refugee Creeks, and encouraged the latter to believe that the disastrous treaty exacted of them by Jackson in 1814 was nullified by the Treaty of Ghent. Returning to England in the summer of 1815, Nicholls was promptly disavowed by the government, which nevertheless bestowed costly presents on his Indian allies, and on one a brigadier's commission and a scarlet coat. To the Colonial Office, all this was nothing more than a graceful dismissal; the Indians and the American frontiersmen naturally did not see it that way.

About the time that Nicholls disappeared there arrived on the coast of Florida an elderly Scot named Arbuthnot, in his trading schooner *Chance*. By fair dealings he gained the Indians' friendship, but with mistaken kindness he too suggested that Jackson's Creek treaty of 1814 was void. This, too, was dangerous doctrine from the point of view of the American frontiersman. And now returns to Florida a former subaltern in Nicholls' regiment, a young adventurer named Ambrister, in search of fun and fortune. After a short time in Arbuthnot's employ, he leaves it to join a group of Seminoles on the Suwanee river, under a chief whom the whites called Billy Bowlegs. Splendid fellows Ambrister found them — best soldiers in the world if properly led and equipped. If only those damned clerks at the Colonial Office would not interfere! However, the shooting was magnificent, and the land was certain to be the garden spot of America one of these days. By a few days' march across the peninsula one could visit M'Gregor and his boys, at Amelia Island. Pirates if you like, but generous, open-handed chaps who put it in a fellow's way to make a little money.

In 1817 the Seminoles on the American side of the border defied settlers to enter upon the Creek lands which had been ceded three years before, and scalped some of those who did. General Andrew Jackson was ordered by President Monroe to raise a force of Tennessee militia, chastise the offenders, and pursue them into Spanish Florida if necessary. While Jackson was destroying Seminole villages an army detachment on the way to join him, with women and children, was ambushed by the Seminole chief Himollemico, and destroyed. Jackson burst into Florida like an avenging flame. Himollemico and Hillis Hago, he of the scarlet coat and brigadier's commission, fled to St. Marks. In the bay was a small gun-boat with the Union Jack at her peak — help at last from the Great White Father! Eagerly the two chiefs rowed out to greet their allies. With mock honors they were received, and promptly clapped into irons. It was an American gun-boat and the Union Jack was a ruse. The next day (7 April 1818) Jackson entered St. Marks against the protest of the Spanish governor, hauled down the Spanish flag and hanged the two chiefs without trial. Arbuthnot was arrested when about to leave the town. Reserving him for later attention, Jackson pushed eastward through the gloomy forest festooned with Spanish moss, to surprise Billy Bowlegs at the Suwanee. The Indians escaped to the impenetrable thickets and everglades of central Florida. Jackson, furious and baffled, learned the cause of their escape when Ambrister blundered into his camp. On one of his escort was found a letter from Arbuthnot, warning Billy of Jackson's approach, and offering him ten kegs of gunpowder.

A court martial was quickly constituted at St. Marks, Arbuthnot placed on trial for espionage and inciting the Indians against the United States, Ambrister for actively leading them in war. Arbuthnot put up a stout defense, Ambrister threw himself on the mercy of the court. Both were found guilty and sentenced to death. The verdict was reconsidered in the case of Ambrister, whose youthful recklessness appealed to the court; but General Jackson sternly set it aside. How could he spare these ' unprincipled villains ' as he deemed them, ' wretches who by false promises delude and excite an Indian tribe to all the horrid deeds of savage war ' ? Within a few hours Ambrister went before a firing squad, and Arbuthnot, protesting with the dignity of seventy years that his country would avenge him, was hanged from the topsail yard of the *Chance*.

The Seminoles were beaten, but Jackson had not finished. Another forced march through the jungle and Pensacola was taken, the Spanish governor ejected, and the fortress garrisoned with Americans. Then Jackson returned, to be acclaimed once more a hero by the West; but Easterners thought of Roman history and trembled. ' It was in the provinces that were laid the seeds of the ambitious projects that overturned the liberties of Rome,' said Clay. In Monroe's cabinet, Adams alone took the high ground that Jackson's every act was justified by the incompetence of Spanish authority to police its own territory; and Adams had his way.

When the news reached London in the autumn of 1818, Parliament fortunately was not in session. But the press rang with denunciation of America, and the 'ruffian' who had murdered two British subjects. Public opinion demanded instant disavowal, apology, reparation. Lord Castlereagh's firmness was the main cause of preventing a rupture, wrote the American minister, Richard Rush. War would have been declared ' if the ministry had but held up a finger.' Unmoved by public clamor, the Foreign Secretary calmly examined the documents from Washington, and decided, as he wrote Bagot, ' that the unfortunate sufferers, whatever were their intentions, had been engaged in unauthorized practices of such a description as to have deprived them of any claim on their own government for interference.'

There was no need to repeat the warning that the execution of Arbuthnot and Ambrister was intended to convey.

Castlereagh's life ended in August 1822. George Canning, his successor, was a man of different metal. Five new American nations had come into existence. Let them be linked up with Britain and Canada, and the United States be made to feel the cost of isolation!

XXII

MONROE AND J. Q. ADAMS
1817–1829

1. *Revolution in Latin America*

IN 1815 the United States was the only republic in a colonial hemisphere. During the next seven years almost the whole of the continental area from Canada to Cape Horn had freed itself from European control, and the greater part was republican. A status meagre in elements of stability, rich in possibilities of trouble, had been created. Armed intervention by the Holy Alliance, a new balance of power, an Anglo-American entente, or a Pan-American alliance — anything might have happened. Out of the confusion of voices came one clear note: the Monroe Doctrine, to which American foreign policy has more or less been tuned ever since.

In the eighteenth century Latin America had few points of contact with the United States, and nothing in common. An inert mass of Indian serfs, negro slaves, and mixed breeds was exploited by a small governing class of Castilians, highly intelligent in many matters, but ignorant of liberty and content to be ruled by Spanish viceroys under the laws of the Indies. The few men, such as Bolívar and Miranda, who aspired to something different and better were forced into exile; Miranda's attempt in 1806 to free his native province with British aid was a complete fiasco.

Two years later, when Napoleon invaded Spain, Spanish America had the taste of liberty that gave appetite for more. The governing classes, unwilling to obey a usurping Bonaparte, formed provisional juntas which professed to govern Spanish America in the name of Ferdinand VII until his happy restoration. By 1812 all the mainland provinces were *de facto* independent of Spain. Their commerce was thrown open to the world, their intellect to modern ideas. Congress appropriated money for the relief of sufferers from an earthquake in Venezuela, and the first newspaper in Chile was set up by newcomers from New York. So many Yankee ships resorted to South American ports that President Madison sent consuls to Buenos Aires and Carácas in the years 1810–12.

The restoration of Ferdinand VII in 1814 took by surprise the South American leaders, who rejected his peremptory demand for unconditional submission. The king, however, had an army and a fleet. By 1816 he had reduced all the *de facto* states but La Plata (the Argentine), and restored the Spanish colonial system.

José de San Martín kept the revolutionary flame alive in a remote and recently settled province of La Plata, among a population not unlike the North American frontiersmen. In January 1817 he began his epic march across the Andes with thirty-five hundred men, several thousand animals, and artillery, by a pass over half again as high as the Grand St. Bernard. At Chacabuco on the Pacific slope he defeated a royalist army. Chile was then liberated, and organized as a republic under Bernardo O'Higgins, son of an Irish soldier in the Spanish service, as supreme dictator. In the meantime, Simón de Bolívar had spread revolution up the Orinoco valley, and framed a fantastic constitution for the Republic of Venezuela.

Recognition of their independence at Washington was both sought for and expected by the three new republics. Henry Clay, in an oration describing the ' glorious spectacle of eighteen millions of people struggling to burst their chains and be free,' gave the lead to North American opinion. Yet Clay was unable to prevent Congress from passing a neutrality act in 1818; and on President Monroe his eloquence had slight effect. J. Q. Adams, the Secretary of State, never allowed sentiment to weaken his grasp of his own country's permanent interest. ' That the final issue of their present struggle would be their entire independence of Spain, I had never doubted,' he told Clay:

That it was our true policy and duty to take no part in the contest, . . . was equally clear. The principle of neutrality to *all* foreign wars was, in my opinion, fundamental to the continuance of our liberties and of our Union. So far as they were contending for independence, I wished well to their cause; but I had seen and yet see no prospect that they would establish free or liberal institutions of government. . . . Arbitrary power, military and ecclesiastical, was stamped upon their habits, and upon all their institutions. Civil dissension was infused into all their seminal principles. . . . I had little expectation of any beneficial result to this country from any future connection with them, political or commercial.

This passage reveals the policy of Monroe's administration toward the Latin Americans. Their independence was desired as an additional bulwark for American isolation; but not with sufficient ardor to risk a European war. It was a policy unadventurous and frankly selfish, as Latin-American publicists have pointed out. Yet Monroe, Adams, and Clay had no wish to obtain exclusive commercial privileges, or to organize and dominate a league of western republics against monarchical Europe. So long as Europe did not actively intervene, Monroe and Adams were content to stand aside and let Spain fight it out with her colonies; but they would certainly oppose any attempt of the Holy Alliance to interpose.

Castlereagh and Canning were torn between desire to uphold the monarchical principle in South America and ambition to preserve it as a British market. British exports to South America by 1822 surpassed British exports to the United States; Englishmen obtained mining concessions in Mexico, Brazil, Colombia, and La Plata, and London floated several loans of the revolutionary governments. Hence England endeavored to reconcile Spain with her colonies on the basis of autonomy and free trade. She was equally opposed to absolutism, which would restore the exclusive Spanish colonial system, and independence, which would mean republicanism and perhaps a Pan-American alliance.

From 1817 to 1822 Castlereagh and Monroe frequently invited each other to co-operate toward the solution they respectively desired: on the one side reconciliation; on the other independence. Each government refused the other's advance because each thought it could obtain all it wanted by waiting. Time worked for America, as Adams well knew. He anticipated that the reconciliation policy would fail, as fail it did at the Congress of Aix-la-Chapelle in 1818. Castlereagh could not induce Spain to listen to peaceful mediation; and in turn vetoed the Franco-Russian proposal of armed intervention.

The clash of British and continental views at Aix-la-Chapelle created a rift between England and the Holy Alliance, which Russia sought to increase. Alexander I, who looked to America for a counterpoise to British naval power, invited the United States to enter the Holy Alliance. Doubtless he expected a seat on the European areopagus to alter American policy: a point of view not yet altogether extinct. Adams's reply to this strange invitation foreshadows not only the Monroe Doctrine, but American foreign policy between the two World Wars:

To stand in firm and cautious independence of all entanglements in the European system has been a cardinal point of their policy under every administration of their government from the peace of 1783 to this day. . . . Yet in proportion as the importance of the United States . . . increases in the eyes of the others, the difficulties of maintaining this system, and the temptations to depart from it, increase and multiply with it. . . . A direct though unofficial application has been made by the present Russian minister here, that the United States should become formal parties to the Holy Alliance. . . . As a general declaration of principles . . . the United States not only give their hearty assent to the articles of the Holy Alliance, but will be the most earnest and conscientious in observing them. But . . . for the repose of Europe as well as of America, the European and American political systems should be kept as separate and distinct from each other as possible.

Now that England was actually if not formally detached from the Holy Alliance, Adams believed he could afford to act without risking a collision. Early in 1819 he informed Castlereagh that the United States would recognize the Argentine republic ' at no remote period, should no event occur which will justify a further postponement of that intention.' Such an event did occur, very shortly. On 22 February 1819 Adams obtained the signature of the Spanish minister at Washington to a very important treaty, by which Florida was ceded to the United States.

Since 1810 the United States had been nibbling at the Floridas. General Jackson was forced to disgorge his rather generous bites, but his invasion of the province in 1818 convinced Madrid that Florida had better be sold before it was seized. Accordingly, Spain ceded all her lands east of the Mississippi, together with her ancient rights to the Oregon country, in return for five million dollars (22 February 1819). In addition, the boundary between the United States and Mexico was determined. Reluctance of the Senate to relinquish the American claim to Texas, and a change of government at Madrid, delayed ratification of the Florida treaty for two years, during which Monroe dared not offend Spain by recognizing her revolted provinces.

Before the Florida treaty was ratified (22 February 1821), events in Spanish America had begun to move rapidly. The Argentine and Chile, having established their independence, went to the aid of Peru. Bolívar, at the same time, was rolling up the Spanish armies westward from the Orinoco, consolidating the liberated territory in the Great Colombian Republic. His subordinate, General Sucre, entered Quito in triumph in May 1821. A year later when Bolívar and San

Martín met at Guayaquil, only one Spanish army was left in the field, and that surrendered after the Battle of Ayacucho in 1824. Dom Pedro of the House of Braganza proclaimed the independence of Brazil in September 1822. A mutiny in the Spanish garrison at Vera Cruz forced the viceroy to accept a provisional treaty for the independence of Mexico, including Central America. Thus, by the autumn of 1822, America from the Great Lakes to Cape Horn was independent. European sovereignty was maintained only in Belize, the Guianas, Bolivia, and the West Indies.

Already the United States had acted. There was danger lest the Latin-American republics, if longer refused a recognition by their elder sister, might cease to be republics. The Argentine had narrowly missed getting a Bourbon prince; Mexico became a monarchy for a short time under a native emperor, Iturbide. Accordingly, in a message to Congress of 8 March 1822, President Monroe declared that the new governments of La Plata, Chile, Peru, Colombia, and Mexico were 'in the full enjoyment of their independence,' of which there was 'not the most remote prospect of their being deprived' and had 'a claim to recognition by other powers, which ought not to be resisted.' Congress, disregarding protests from the Spanish minister, appropriated money to defray the expenses of 'such missions to the independent nations on the American continent as the President might deem proper.' Formal recognition was then extended, and diplomatic relations established with the five states.

'So, Mr. Adams, you are going to make honest men of them?' said the British minister when he heard the news. 'Yes, sir!' said Adams. 'We proposed to your government to join us some time ago, but they would not, and now we shall see whether you will be content to *follow* us!' And follow us George Canning did, for all his wrigglings — in one of which he touched a switch that released the Monroe Doctrine on an astonished world.

2. Canning Proposes and Adams Disposes

France invaded Spain in 1823, with the avowed object of delivering Ferdinand VII from a constitution that had been forced upon him. Contrary to Canning's calculations, the French were received as saviors. It was a matter of common talk that a Franco-Spanish expeditionary force to South America would follow this military promenade. What possibilities did that not open up! The great work of Wolfe and Chatham undone, France once more firmly seated in America, sharing a colonial monopoly to the exclusion of England, and deriving new strength from the valley of Mexico, the mines of Peru, and the plains of the Argentine. 'If the Pyrenees had fallen, England would maintain the Atlantic,' wrote Canning. But by what means short of war?

The obvious policy for Canning was to follow Adams, recognize the independence of Latin America, and face Europe with an accomplished fact. The London *Times* urged such a course. But neither George IV nor the tory party were ready to admit rebel republican colonists to the family of nations. Recognition of O'Higgins might encourage O'Connell! On the other hand, if England did not do something, Canning feared lest Monroe and Adams would obtain exclusive commercial advantages, and a Pan-American republican alliance.

On 16 August 1823 Canning put to Richard Rush, the American minister at London, a question that started many wheels revolving in the United States. What would he say to joining England in warning France to keep her hands off South America?

It was a brilliant plan that had flashed into Canning's brain, and the more he thought it over, the more it seemed to be the only escape from his dilemma. A joint Anglo-American protest against intervention would not only thwart the Holy Alliance, but maintain England's new markets, and break up American republican solidarity. England, without endorsing the republican principle, could pose as the protector of Latin America no less than the United States; and at the same time bring America's weight into the British scale of power. On 20 August Canning followed up this conversation by a note stating certain principles of foreign policy in which he hoped that Rush might immediately and publicly concur, as the basis of a joint Anglo-American declaration to the Holy Alliance. England 'conceived the recovery of the colonies by Spain to be hopeless,' but was not disposed to impede an amicable negotiation between them, and considered that 'the question of their recognition was of time and circumstances.' 'She aimed not at the possession of any portion of the colonies for herself,' but could not permit their transfer to any other power.

Richard Rush was somewhat taken aback by Canning's overture, the most flattering ever received by an American diplomatist. In contrast to his predecessors, whose social experience at the Court

of St. James's had been somewhat pallid, Mr. Rush had been made
to feel a person of consequence in London society; but the favor of
the great and the flavor of their port had not dulled the keenness
of his scent for entangling alliances. Without positive instructions
he refused to commit the United States to anything of that nature.
Canning's object, he feared, was to check France, not to promote
American liberty.

When Canning, three days later, insisted that something must be
done at once, Rush recollected his instructions of 1818, to obtain
a concurrent Anglo-American recognition of Latin-American independence. He promised to join a British protest against intervention
in the name of his government, provided that Great Britain would
instantly recognize the new republics. Had Canning been able or
willing to give this required gage of good faith, Anglo-American
co-operation would have been an established fact before Monroe
and Adams had had an opportunity to pass a decision upon it. The
Monroe Doctrine would not then have been declared. But the tory
party was not yet ready to recognize insurgents.

Rush's dispatches embodying these conversations and notes arrived at Washington on 9 October 1823. President Monroe, on the
point of departure to his plantation of Oakhill in Virginia, sent
copies of them to his political mentors, the ex-presidents Jefferson
and Madison. The covering letter stated his own opinion that Canning's overture should be accepted.

Jefferson, then eighty years old, was in placid retirement at Monticello. Horace and Tacitus, he wrote Monroe, were so much more
interesting than the newspapers that he was quite out of touch with
public affairs. But this question of co-operation with Great Britain
was

the most momentous which has ever been offered to my contemplation
since that of Independence. . . . America, North and South, has a set
of interests distinct from those of Europe, and peculiarly her own. She
should, therefore, have a system of her own, distinct from that of Europe.
. . . One nation, most of all, could disturb us in this pursuit; she now
offers to lead, aid and accompany us in it. By acceding to her proposition
we detach her from the bands [of despotism], bring her mighty weight
into the scale of free government, and emancipate a continent at one
stroke. . . . With her then, we should most sedulously cherish a cordial
friendship; and nothing would tend more to knit our affections than to
be fighting once more, side by side, in the same cause.

Here indeed was support for Canning. Jefferson, who had helped to lay the foundations of isolation, who once had regarded the touch of England as the touch of death, was willing to accept an Anglo-American alliance! Madison, from Montpelier, gave similar advice, and even proposed an Anglo-American declaration in favor of Greek independence.

Three white-haired statesmen, each on his Virginia hill-top, pondering this great question of foreign policy: what a delightful aroma of antique republicanism! It would have amused George Canning to have known the perturbation he had caused among the patriarchs, at a time when he considered the incident closed. For on 9 October 1823, France abjured all design of acting against the Spanish-American colonies by force of arms, and disclaimed any intention to annex any part of the Spanish heritage. These were the very principles for which Canning had asked American support.

John Quincy Adams, in the meantime, was pondering the meaning of Canning's astounding offer. His information from Gallatin, who had just returned from Paris, indicated slight danger of armed intervention in Latin America; and he knew that England had both the will and the power to prevent it in any case. What then was Canning's game? The clue, he thought, was the proposed pledge, in Canning's note of 20 August, against either power acquiring a part of Spanish America — a pledge that would be inconvenient if Cuba voted herself into the United States. That was probably just what Canning was thinking of. For fifteen years the statesmen at Washington had kept anxious eyes on Cuba, although even in 1823 they were not actually fishing for her. Monroe and Adams were worrying lest France or England should seize the Pearl of the Antilles; and if Adams did express the hope that Cuba would stick to the Spanish tree until ripe for the United States basket, it was because he feared lest some other naval power might shake the trunk.

Canning's refusal to recognize the new republics seemed very significant to Adams. So long as the British government maintained that attitude, he wrote Rush, their only common ground with the United States was a casual aversion from European intervention. At the first subsequent cabinet meeting in Washington (7 November 1823) Adams declared, ' It would be more candid, as well as more dignified, to avow our principles explicitly to Great Britain and

France, than to come in as a cockboat in the wake of the British man-of-war.'

For Adams, moreover, the question was not a mere choice between accepting or declining Canning's overture. It was the larger one of future relations between the Old World and the New. While the Holy Alliance seemed to threaten South America, Russia was pushing her trading posts from Alaska southward even to San Francisco Bay. On 4/16 September 1821 the Tsar issued a ukase extending Alaska to the fifty-first parallel, well within Oregon, and declaring *mare clausum* the waters thence to Bering Strait. Adams believed that colonial establishments were immoral and destined to fall. With the North American West divided between Canada, the United States, and Mexico, and with South America independent, the New World might now be considered closed to further colonization by European powers; and on 17 July 1823 Adams told the Russian minister just that.

While the Tsar made his power felt in the Pacific, he was denouncing American principles from across the Atlantic. In October 1823 the Russian minister at Washington communicated two notes to Adams: one a rather striking refusal to receive a minister from Colombia; the other a characteristic homily on the Holy Alliance. Although inoffensive by intent, for Alexander had a strange liking for the United States, it contained remarks on 'expiring republicanism' and the like, as offensive in fact to the American government as were the Moscow manifestoes on expiring democracy a century later.

As Adams saw it, his government had been approached or challenged on four different points, all of which could be answered at once: (1) the proposal of Anglo-American co-operation, (2) rumored European intervention in Latin America, (3) Russian extension of colonial establishments, (4) the Tsar's denunciation of principles upon which every independent state in America was now based. 'I remarked,' Adams wrote of the cabinet meeting of 7 November, 'that the communications lately received from the Russian Minister . . . afforded, as I thought, a very suitable and convenient opportunity for us to take our stand against the Holy Alliance, and at the same time to decline the overture of Great Britain.' Monroe and the cabinet appeared to agree, but Adams found it difficult to keep them straight. Calhoun, the Secretary of War, wished to follow Canning, even at the cost of perpetually renouncing Cuba and Texas. He fancied that the underlying motive of European monarchs was jealousy and hatred of the United States, whose turn would come after Mexico had fallen: a very persistent American opinion. President Monroe vacillated between the extremes of doing nothing for fear of the Holy Alliance, and of carrying the war into Turkey to aid the Greeks. Their struggle for independence had aroused immense interest in the United States. One of those emotional currents that threaten to pull America out of her isolation was sweeping over the country. 'The mention of Greece fills the mind with the most exalted sentiments and arouses in our bosoms the best feelings of which our nature is susceptible,' said Monroe in his annual message of 1822. The legislature of South Carolina petitioned Congress to acknowledge Greek independence, and Albert Gallatin proposed to lend the Greek government a fleet; Bryant wrote *The Greek Partisan,* and Daniel Webster much preferred the Greeks to 'the inhabitants of the Andes, and the dwellers on the borders of the Vermilion sea.' The martyrs of Chios and the exploits of Ypsilanti were commemorated in the names of frontier hamlets. Classic colonnades were added to modest farmhouses, and Greek grammar was forced on wretched schoolboys who knew little Latin. A gentleman from western New York, desirous of aiding the Greeks, said he could furnish from his sparsely settled region 'five hundred men, six feet high, with sinewy arms and case-hardened constitutions, bold spirits and daring adventurers, who would travel upon a bushel of corn and a gallon of whisky per man from the extreme part of the world to Constantinople.'

All this struck a reminiscent chord in Monroe's kindly heart. He had never forgotten the supreme moment of his early diplomatic career: his reception as American minister by the French Convention, the sonorous speeches against tyranny, and the fraternal accolade. Time had mellowed James Monroe without changing the quality of his mind. Another great war of revolution against tyranny, so he wrote Jefferson, was about to begin; could not America take a bolder stand for liberty than in 1793? In the first draft of his epoch-making message, Monroe proposed to reprove the French invasion of Spain, to acknowledge the independence of Greece, and to ask Congress for a diplomatic mission to Athens! President Monroe would fulfil the dreams of 'Jacobin' Monroe.

Against this meddling in European affairs Adams argued for the better part of two days. 'I spoke to him again, urging him to abstain from everything in his message which the Holy Allies could make a pretext for construing into aggression upon them,' Adams notes in his diary.

If the Holy Alliance were determined to make up an issue with us, it was our policy to meet, and not to make it. . . . The ground that I wish to take is that of earnest remonstrance against the interference of the European powers by force with South America, but to disclaim all interference on our part with Europe; to make an American cause, and adhere inflexibly to that.

3. Monroe's Message

In the end Adams had his own way; except that he would have preferred to announce his doctrine in a sharp note to Russia, instead of the less offensive mode of embedding it in the President's annual message to Congress. Monroe consented to omit his proposed reproof to France, and all but a pious wish for the success of Greece; Adams was forced to delete a high-pitched exposition of republican principles. The passages on foreign relations in Monroe's annual message of 2 December 1823, although written by the President in more concise and dignified language than Adams would have used, expressed exactly the conception of his Secretary of State. We may summarize the original Monroe Doctrine in the President's own words:

1. Positive principles: (*a*) 'The American continents, by the free and independent condition which they have assumed and maintain, are henceforth not to be considered as subjects for future colonization by any European powers.' (*b*) 'The political system of the allied powers is essentially different . . . from that of America. . . . We should consider any attempt on their part to extend their system to any portion of this hemisphere as dangerous to our peace and safety.'

2. Negative principles: (*a*) 'With the existing colonies or dependencies of any European power we have not interfered and shall not interfere.' (*b*) 'In the wars of the European powers in matters relating to themselves we have never taken any part, nor does it comport with our policy so to do.'

Therein is the whole of President Monroe's doctrine, whatever later developments may be included under the name of the Monroe Doctrine.

Monroe's message was well received by public opinion; but as no one outside the cabinet knew the dramatic circumstances of its birth, few appreciated its significance. Polk was the first President to appeal to Monroe's principles by name; and it was not until after the Civil War that these principles became a doctrine, deriving its sanction no less from faith than from experience, and, like religious doctrines, assuming at times a Protean shape. Critics of Monroe have pointed out that his message was a mere declaration; that intervention had already been thwarted by the obstinacy of Ferdinand VII; that in view of the exclusive power of Congress to declare war, a mere presidential announcement could not guarantee Latin-American independence. True, but irrelevant. What Adams was trying to do, and what he accomplished, was to raise a standard of American foreign policy for all the world to see; and to plant it so firmly in the national consciousness that no later President would dare to pull it down.

4. *The Second President Adams*

In December 1823 America was much more interested in the coming presidential election than in the Holy Alliance. The Republican party was breaking up into factions, and no one knew how they would divide or blend to make the parties of the future. Monroe's second and last term would expire in March 1825, and three members of his cabinet aspired to the succession. J. Q. Adams was the most highly qualified, if faithful and efficient public service for thirty years were to be considered an asset. William H. Crawford, Secretary of the Treasury, was heir-apparent of the Virginia dynasty. By birth Henry Clay had an equal pretension; as a Westerner and advocate of the 'American system' he made a wide appeal; and his charming personality and oratorical gifts made him the second choice of everyone who did not place him first. But Clay had a Western rival, General Andrew Jackson. Quarrelsome, self-educated, and self-willed, Jackson might be regarded as a dangerous radical by bankers and a possible Caesar by old-fashioned Republicans; but to the rising democracy he appeared an apostle of equality, and to Westerners a man of their own metal.

All the candidates were Republicans and nationalists. No Federalist dared raise his head, and no state-rights partisan yet ventured to come forth. Jackson carried Pennsylvania, the Carolinas, and most of the West, with a total of 99 electoral votes. Adams carried New

England, most of New York, and a few districts elsewhere, making
84. Crawford, who had suffered a paralytic stroke during the campaign, was a poor third, and Clay last. As no candidate had a majority
of the electoral vote, the election went to the House — the only instance of that sort since the passage of the Twelfth Amendment.
There Clay asked his supporters to vote for Adams, who was accordingly elected, and took office on 4 March 1825.

John Quincy Adams was a lonely, friendless figure, unable to
express his burning love of country in any way that would touch
the popular imagination. Short, thick-set, with a massive bald head
and suspicious eyes, his port was stern and his manners unconcili-
atory. A lonely walk before dawn, or an early morning swim in
summer, fitted him for the day's toil, which was concluded by
writing his perennial diary. The uncomfortable labor of compiling
a massive report on weights and measures during a long hot summer
in Washington, when he might have been playing with his children
on the coast of Massachusetts, was a real dissipation to Adams. Even
in his own New England he was respected rather than loved, and
other sections resented his election by the House over their favorite
sons. It was, said Senator Benton, with a wild plunge into what he
believed to be Greek, a violation of the *demos krateo* principle. When
Adams defiantly gave Clay the State Department, the cry of ' corrupt
bargain ' was raised; Randolph of Roanoke called it ' the coalition
of Blifil and Black George — the combination, unheard of till then,
of the puritan with the black-leg.' There followed a duel between
Randolph and Clay; fortunately both were bad shots.

Adams was too conscientious to cultivate political arts that were
repulsive to him. He would do nothing in the way of appointments
to obtain or to retain editorial support; his concessions were un-
graceful, and his refusals were bitter to the taste. In his anxiety to be
upright he was often disagreeable; and his arguments, as British
diplomatists well know, were pushed home with stinging sarcasm.

He made the grave political error of trimming his sails to the
nationalism of 1815, after the wind had changed. A sentence in
his first annual message: ' The great object of the institution of civil
government is the improvement of those who are parties to the social
compact,' was the key-note of his domestic policy. He would tran-
scend the nationalism of Hamilton, and use the ample revenues
of the Federal Government to increase the navy, build national roads
and canals, send out scientific expeditions, and establish institutions

of learning and research. All these things came in due time; but Adams urged them in the midst of a centrifugal reaction. If, asked the cotton states, we admit federal powers of this scope, will not some future administration claim the power to interfere with our 'peculiar institution'?

Foreign affairs were the President's peculiar province, and the special aptitude of Mr. Adams. But here, at every turn, he met Mr. Canning. Castlereagh regarded the United States as a turbulent younger brother, to be conciliated by tact and justice; Canning, as a rival to be checked and thwarted. Both Adams and Canning wished to settle all outstanding questions between the two countries, but Adams had no spirit of give and take, and Canning could not resist being clever at other people's expense. The Americans, wrote Captain Basil Hall, ' are plaguey sore at the dressing he gives them in his short pithy Terentian sort of sentences. . . . The more we are in the right, the more is to be gained by not thrusting our rectitude down our opponent's throat.'

The ' no future colonization ' clause of Monroe's message irritated Canning profoundly. In spite of Monroe's assurance that it meant no interference with ' existing colonies or dependencies,' Canning thought it meant Oregon. The British and American representatives at St. Petersburg were then about to begin a joint negotiation with Russia, having for its object the abatement of the Russian claims to Oregon. Canning promptly broke it off, and was much irritated when in 1824 the Imperial government signed a treaty with the United States fixing latitude 54° 40′ as the southern boundary of Russian Alaska.

Canning's transatlantic policy was to break up the continental isolation that Adams wished to defend, as well as to prevent the United States acquiring that hegemony which erroneously he thought Adams intended to establish. Obviously, the first move for England was to recognize the Latin-American republics, without waiting until they ceased to be republics. When that was done, in January 1825, Canning wrote jubilantly, ' Spanish America is free, and if we do not mismanage our affairs sadly, she is English.'

President Adams's policy towards Latin America was transparently honest, and exceedingly cautious. He wished to obtain commercial treaties on the basis of most favored nation and ' free ships make free goods'; to encourage the new nations to observe republican principles and live at peace among themselves; and to discourage them from provoking Spain by attacking Cuba. With Brazil, Peru, Chile, and the Argentine he was fairly successful; but Canning thwarted him by slipping into Mexico and Colombia, as a counter-weight to the United States in a new balance of power.

Mexico, largest and most conservative of the new republics, having many points of possible friction with the United States and a pressing need for capital and markets that England could best supply, was the most promising ground for British influence. Joel R. Poinsett, the first United States minister to Mexico, found his British colleague serenely installed in the confidence of President Victoria, with whom he had concluded an Anglo-Mexican commercial treaty. Poinsett, an accomplished gentleman from South Carolina, appeared to have the ideal qualifications for his post: experience in public affairs, and a knowledge of the Spanish language and character, acquired by extensive travels in Europe and Latin America. But he had a superfluity of zeal, that fatal quality in diplomatists, and he was a Mason. In order to counteract Britain and the monarchists, Poinsett stood in with the *federalistas*. This party was eager to establish York rite Masonic lodges, in opposition to the Scottish rite, organized by their political enemies. Poinsett obtained charters from New York for his friends' lodges, which had a surprising and embarrassing success. All Mexico became divided into ' Escoceses ' and ' Yorkinos '; civil war broke out between them, and Poinsett's name became a rallying point for one party and the target for the other. In the end England profited, and Poinsett was recalled under a cloud. But the cloud had a scarlet lining: the *Poinsettia Pulcherrima* which the minister introduced to northern horticulture.

At the Panama Congress of 1826 Canning scored again. Bolívar the Liberator summoned this meeting of American nations, primarily in order to discuss commercial treaties, to adopt a code of international law, and to arrive at some common policy towards Spain. Jealous of Monroe and suspicious of the United States Bolívar proposed to leave them out; but to invite England in the hope that she might become leader of a Latin-American league. Mexico and Colombia, however, invited the United States, and President Adams accepted as a ' token of respect to the Southern republics.' That he hoped to win a sort of moral hegemony for the United States is probable; but neither his private writings nor his public utterances disclosed a thought of political hegemony, or entangling alliance. His practical object was to induce the Congress to keep its hands off

Cuba, and to adopt the American principles of most favored nation and freedom of the seas. Adams managed the matter very ill, and was practically defeated in the Senate. The opposition was mainly political (of which more anon), but certain Southern senators were genuinely opposed to United States' representatives sitting in the same assembly with generals of mixed blood, and others feared dangerous commitments. As the British minister at Washington wrote, the ' backwardness and the opposition ' of Congress toward the Mexican invitation could hardly be reconciled with the ' supposed anxiety of the United States to form a general Federation of America, with themselves at the head of it.' In the end the United States were not represented at Panama, and Canning had it all his own way.

Only four republics took part in the conference, which accomplished nothing; but the British representative by some clever propaganda managed to make the United States appear as an enemy to Cuban freedom, and a false friend to that of South America.

A clever policy this, and dangerous. Had it leaked out what Canning was doing, Adams would have had plenty of support for an active Pan-American policy. Central America would have become the Balkans of the New World, with England and the United States playing the rôles of Russia and Austria. Mischief was prevented by concealment, by the death of Canning in 1827, and the instability of the Latin-American states, which led Canning's successors at Downing Street to drop all efforts toward redressing the balance of the Old World with the New.

5. *The Election of 1828*

Adams's campaign for re-election began as soon as he was inaugurated President. The election of 1828 was much simpler than that of 1824, because there were only two candidates; but it was still a personal contest. Just as the Jeffersonian and Hamiltonian factions of 1791 were the nuclei of the Republican and Federalist parties, so the Jackson-Calhoun and Adams-Clay factions of 1823-28 developed into the Democratic and Whig parties that occupied the political stage until the eve of the Civil War.

National political parties in the United States are almost always of local origin, and they never quite lose their essential character as a bundle of local factions and interests. In this instance, the impulse for the defeat of Adams and the election of Jackson came largely from state politicians seeking national power. During the 'era of good feelings,' while the Republican party appeared to be united under Monroe, it was breaking up into conservative and democratic factions within the different states. The precise differences between them varied from one region to another; but, generally speaking, the democratic group wished to level down all political inequalities that still remained in the state constitutions. One result of their efforts was the abolition of property qualifications for the franchise in the Northern states, thus diluting the electorate with elements susceptible to a different sort of appeal from that of the Jeffersonian school. Another effect was to breed a new litter of professional politicians, among whom enjoyment of state office and state patronage had created appetite for the more luscious emoluments of federal power. The best of these men represented some genuine aspiration toward equality, the worst were mere tub-thumping demagogues; but at the head of them were able men of lowly origin but ingratiating form and phrase, such as Martin Van Buren of New York and James Buchanan of Pennsylvania. Their obvious strategy was to join democratic factions in other states, under some national figure who would reflect glory upon themselves, and lead all to victory and spoils. Adams, stiff and scrupulous, was no sort of leader for such as these; Calhoun, the Carolina high-brow, was little better, and Clay's lot was now cast with the President. General Jackson, the hero of New Orleans, subjugator of the Creeks and executioner of Arbuthnot, was a man who would reward his friends and punish his enemies, a heaven-sent leader for democracy.

It did not matter that there was no national issue or popular grievance; the politicians would see to that in due time, and principles could be attended to after victory. Adams must be discredited. The 'corrupt bargain' charge, engineered by Buchanan, was the opening gun of the Jackson campaign. Then, in December 1825, Adams innocently introduced the Panama Congress project, which the Jackson supporters regarded as a sort of gala performance invented by Clay to dazzle the public mind, and divert attention from the 'bargain.' That is why the President's nomination of commissioners to Panama was held up in the Senate by the Jackson men, while Calhoun, as Vice-President, tolerated the most outrageous imputations on the President's and the Secretary's motives. Calhoun was rewarded by the second place on the Jackson ticket, with the assurance of the succession after one term. We shall later

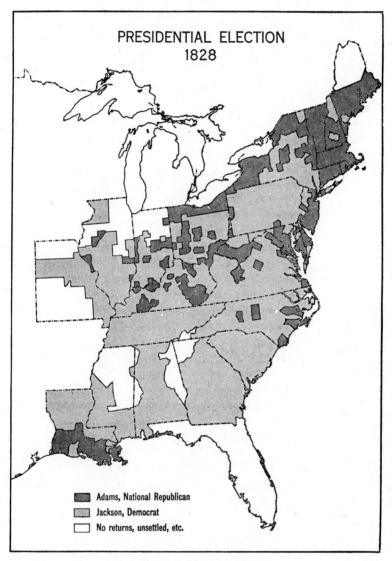

PRESIDENTIAL ELECTION
1828

■ Adams, National Republican
▨ Jackson, Democrat
☐ No returns, unsettled, etc.

Presidential Election of 1828

Based upon Charles O. Paullin, Atlas of the Historical Geography of the
United States, *Plate* 103C

see the feminine and other reasons why this assurance was not honored.

The pro-Jackson minority in Congress became a majority in the mid-term congressional elections. 'Investigations' of alleged presidential corruption were started, but not pushed home; so that the victim had no chance to clear himself. All the old prejudice against the Federalists was aroused in order to defeat the son of John Adams, reputed author of the Sedition Act of 1798. The South, now in full tide of reaction against nationalism, was assured that Jackson would defend state rights. The West's lingering loyalty to Henry Clay was destroyed by Adams's professed intention to administer the public lands on business principles, rather than squander it on shiftless squatters. The most absurdly mendacious tales were made up and broadcasted. Adams had furnished the White House at his own expense with a billiard table and a set of chessmen; in the mouth of a Jackson orator, these became 'gaming tables and gambling furniture' purchased from public funds. The newspapers that supported Adams, however, were not idle; there was a famous 'coffin hand-bill' on the shooting of six militiamen by Jackson for insubordination, and the General's frontier brawls and alleged premarital relations with Mrs. Jackson were described in detail. Altogether, it was the most unprincipled and degrading presidential election the United States had ever experienced.

The result was overwhelming. Adams's popular vote was only 44 per cent of the total; Jackson received 178 electoral votes, carried the Southern and Western states, Pennsylvania, and most of New York, winning by a large majority in the electoral college. Virginia held her aristocratic nose, and voted for Jackson, believing him the lesser evil; South Carolina voted for Jackson as a state-rights man, which she soon had reason to regret. But in the last instance it was classes rather than sections that elected Jackson: the Southern hunters and backwoods farmers whom he had led to glory; the Northern democracy, tired of respectable, gentlemanly promotions from cabinet to White House. They cared little for policies, but much for personality, and they voted for Jackson because he was their sort of man. After all, the most sophisticated among us often have no better reason for voting as we do than had the American democracy of 1828, in exalting a man of their own sort, uneducated, intolerant, yet professing the immortal principles of Thomas Jefferson. And the democracy was not disappointed.

John Quincy Adams never understood why he was spurned by the country he loved with silent passion, and rejected by the people he had served so faithfully. In the four sad months between the election and the end of his term, there kept running through his head the refrain of an old song he had first heard at the court of Versailles:

> O Richard, O mon Roi,
> L'univers t'abandonne.

Yet the noblest portion of his long career was still ahead.

XXIII

ANDREW JACKSON
1829–1837

1. *Old Hickory*

WASHINGTON had never held such crowds as assembled there on 4 March 1829 to see the people's champion installed. It was their day, without pomp or pageantry, scarcely even a uniform to be seen. General Jackson, a tall, lean figure dressed in black, with the hawk-like frontier face under a splendid crest of thick white hair, walked through the crowds and the mud up Pennsylvania Avenue, unescorted save by a few friends. At the top of a great stone stairway to the east portico of the Capitol, he took the inaugural oath and read his inaugural address. With difficulty he pushed through the shouting masses, all eager to shake his hand, to where his horse was waiting; then rode to the White House at the head of an informal procession of carriages, farm wagons, people of all ages, colors, and conditions. Since it would have seemed unbecoming for democracy's chieftain to make distinctions of persons, the White House was invaded by a mob of men, women, and boys who stood on chairs in their muddy boots, fought for the refreshments, and trod glass and porcelain underfoot. 'It would have done Mr. Wilberforce's heart good,' wrote an onlooker, ' to have seen a stout black wench eating in this free country a jelly with a gold spoon at the President's house.' Jackson was glad to escape by a window; and the mob was finally drawn off like flies to honey, by tubs of punch being placed on the lawn. Washington society thought of the Tuileries on the 10th of August, and shuddered.

One might search European history in vain for any counterpart to Andrew Jackson. He was a typical American, of a sort that is no longer typical. Born on the Carolina frontier in 1767, to immigrant parents from northern Ireland, he had all the virtues and many of the faults of the American backwoodsman; but none of the vices. Loyal, pugnacious, and honest, he was also credulous, intolerant, and unlearned, with slight conception of the complex forces that were moulding themselves under the shadow of his personality into the Democratic party. His policy was summed up in a sentence, ' The Federal Constitution must be obeyed, state rights preserved, our national debt must be paid, direct taxes and loans avoided, and the Federal Union preserved. These are the objects I have in view, and regardless of all consequences, will carry into effect.'

Jackson's frontier simplicity made him over-trusting of friends and too suspicious of opponents. An intellectual check on his emotions was wholly wanting. Yet Jackson's simplicity was his strength, for the American people looked through his eyes, and thought with his brain. Now that a century has elapsed, few will deny that his intuitive decisions were generally right; that his mistakes were fewer and less costly than those of more experienced and better educated presidents. Although quick to anger and slow to cool, rough-hewn out of native oak, and without polish, Jackson had a fine sense of honor, a deep reverence for women, and a natural, straightforward courtesy. His Talleyrand, Martin Van Buren, never had to complain that this great man had been badly brought up.

Jackson's administration opened badly. His first mistake was in the choice of a cabinet. Four places were filled by incompetent and unknown men, followers of Calhoun; but the choice of Martin Van Buren for the Department of State was excellent.

The President's first and obvious task was to ' cleanse the Augean stables.' He believed the election charges of corruption in the civil service; and his partisans took care that he did not forget, so hungry were they for the spoils of victory. Actually there was incompetence among those in office, but no corruption. The federal departments and post-offices were full of aged functionaries who had been appointed from charitable or political motives. Jackson's views of office-holding were of the eighteenth century, distorted by the democratic principle of rotation. In his first annual message he declared:

> The duties of all public offices are . . . so plain and simple that men of intelligence may readily qualify themselves for their performance; and I cannot but believe that more is lost by the long continuance of men in office than is generally to be gained by their experience. . . . No one man has any more intrinsic right to official station than another.

But Jackson's remedy was worse than the disease. He removed everyone suspected of having supported Adams, and when their places proved insufficient swept out others. Only 252 out of 612 presidential appointments, and about one in fourteen of the post-office department, were vacated; but the precedent was established for more drastic removals later in the century. Broadly speaking, Jackson introduced the spoils system from the states, where it had always existed, into the Federal Government. His appointments lowered the general tone and efficiency of the service. Aged and respectable Jeffersonians were replaced by young, often disreputable, and sometimes corrupt Jackson men. The spoils system did not noticeably increase the power of the President, for even Jackson had to please congressmen, and the Senate negatived many of his nominations; but it greatly increased the power of party and of the professional element within parties, by offering tangible rewards for faithful service.

2. *Peggy Eaton*

It was a woman who made the first and the most lasting trouble for Jackson. Eaton, the Secretary of War, a former Senator from Tennessee, was an old crony of the President. Mrs. Eaton had long been a notorious character in Washington as Peggy O'Neil, the fair, free-and-easy daughter of the leading publican. Married at an early age to a hard-drinking naval purser, she remained at the paternal tavern during her husband's tours of duty; and her flirtations with the guests, especially with Senator Eaton the 'star boarder,' were the talk of the town. When the purser committed suicide after a drunken frolic, and his widow married her senatorial lover, the gossips' tongues wagged faster than ever. But Mrs. Jackson received the wife of her husband's old friend. Thenceforth, for the gallant General, she was above reproach. Mrs. Jackson died just before her husband's inauguration. He was devoted to her memory; and the fact that many years before they had been the innocent victims of boarding-house scandal made him the more determined to champion Mrs. Eaton, and to insist that official society should receive her.

Mrs. Vice-President Calhoun was a proud Carolinian, and the other secretaries' wives were also determined to give the hussy no countenance. They refused to call, and at official receptions or White House dinners refused to speak. Neither would the ladies of the diplomatic corps, nor the wives of senators and congressmen. Van Buren, however, was a widower, and Charles Vaughan, the British minister, a bachelor. They could afford to show the lady marked attention, which was not difficult, for she had both wit and beauty.

But the dinners they gave in her honor were declined by other ladies, and at balls she was so snubbed that she soon gave up attempting social recognition. The President, however, refused to surrender. He actually held a cabinet meeting about Mrs. Eaton, where he pronounced her 'as chaste as a virgin'; but the female rebellion continued. Even Mrs. Donelson, niece of the President and mistress of the White House, would not call on the persecuted lady; and when Jackson gave her the alternative of doing so or leaving the White House, she left.

This 'Eaton malaria' was catching, and no laughing matter for the Jackson men. It was not only making a breach between the administration and respectable society, but making a fool of the President. The Adams-Clay party was jubilant; for if the American people can once be got to laugh at, instead of with, a national figure, it is all up with him. Still, there was some use to be made of the affair by Van Buren, who coveted the presidential succession. This sly fox from New York was burrowing into the heart of the old hero. It was 'little Van' who bound up the wounds of the disappointed office-seekers, who arranged the diplomatic appointments, and directed the negotiations which brought prestige to the administration. His round little figure could be seen every fair day bobbing up and down on horseback, beside the lean, easy-seated President on his daily constitutionals. Many a time they must have discussed the Eaton affair. Jackson, unable to account for the solid female phalanx against his dear departed's friend, was sure there must be politics behind it. And we may be sure that Van Buren, Oh! so gently and discreetly, would have eliminated one plotter after another until Jackson burst out, 'By the e-ter-nal! it's that proud aristocrat Calhoun' (for did not Mrs. Calhoun start the snubbing game, and were not all the recusant ministers Calhoun's friends?). And how Van Buren would protest that it could never, never be that high-souled pattern of chivalry and devoted Democrat! And how, if Jackson seemed too easily convinced, he would remind him of an ugly rumor that in Monroe's cabinet, at the time of the Arbuthnot and Ambrister affair, it was Calhoun who said General Jackson should be arrested, and tried for insubordination! Calhoun, it will be remembered, was Vice-President and heir-apparent.

Were all this merely a question of whether Martin or John should succeed Andrew, it would not be worth our attention. But the

'Eaton malaria,' as treated by Dr. Van Buren, was a mere symptom of the sectional and economic forces that presently isolated Calhoun and his adherents in a state-rights ward whence the infection escaped into the entire South.

3. The Tariff and the South

South Carolina evolved politically between 1820 and 1830 (as earlier Massachusetts) from a dominant state professing the most ardent nationalism to a semi-impoverished community, blaming her poverty on the measures of the Federal Government. English constituencies in like circumstances have turned from free trade to protection. South Carolina reversed the order. As a state in a federal union, she had a reserve weapon to use against a national majority, when votes and arguments failed.

The protective tariff of 1816 was largely the work of two South Carolinians, Lowndes and Calhoun. Although national in outlook, they expected South Carolina to share the benefits. Like New England, their native state had water-power, and unlike New England she had cotton; then why not manufactures? And was it wise for her planters to depend exclusively upon the English market? The next few years, however, proved these expectations to be hollow. Competent managers were rare in the South, and Yankee mill superintendents were unable to handle slave labor, which, after all, could be employed with more immediate profit in cotton growing. All the benefits of protection appeared to be going to the Northern manufacturers, while Southern planters bore the burden of higher prices. As the tariff schedules rose by successive acts of Congress, and the country as a whole grew richer, South Carolina remained stationary in population, and declined in prosperity. Her more enterprising planters emigrated to the black belts of Alabama and Mississippi, where their bumper crops enriched Mobile and New Orleans instead of swelling the exports of Charleston. As the cotton growing area increased, the price declined to a point below the cost of production on worn-out land.

Actually, the protective tariff only aggravated a distress for which the wasteful, land-destroying system of cotton culture was fundamentally responsible; but the South Carolina planters could hardly be expected to reason with cool logic in such a state of affairs. By 1825 there had been created among them just that atmosphere of pride, poverty, and resentment which favors the growth of fascist movements in Europe, and separatist movements in the United States. In South Carolina this took the form of a local state-rights party, propagating the doctrine that the protective tariff and 'internal improvements' were unconstitutional devices for taxing the South for the benefit of the North. The New England Federalists had taken the same line not long before, and had ended at Hartford in talk; but ten degrees of latitude separated Charleston from Boston. Climate and race relations had produced in the South Carolina aristocracy a different temper. And behind all the heat and fury of the sectional movement we are about to describe was the fear lest nationalism, in any form, lead to congressional tampering with slavery. Calhoun admitted in 1830 that ' the real cause of the present unhappy state of things ' was ' the peculiar domestic institution of the Southern States.'

Protected interests are seldom content with what they have. Northern manufacturers were not satisfied with the tariff of 1824. In 1828 the ' tariff of abominations ' was passed. It was a politicians' tariff, concerned mainly with the manufacture of a President. The pro-Jackson congressmen wished to present their candidate to the South as a free-trader, and to the North as a protectionist; they therefore introduced a bill with higher duties on raw materials than on manufactures, hoping that New England votes would help defeat it, and the onus fall on Adams. As Webster said, ' Its enemies spiced it with whatever they thought would render it distasteful; its friends took it, drugged as it was.'

At a great anti-tariff meeting in Columbia, S. C., Thomas Cooper asked, ' Is it worth our while to continue this Union of States, where the North demands to be our masters and we are required to be their tributaries? ' More and more South Carolinians became inclined to answer this question with a thumping ' No! '

4. Calhoun's Doctrine

Calhoun, aloof in the vice-presidential office, was not indifferent to this local turmoil. He had always been alive to the danger of disunion in a country so rapidly expanding. Like Hamilton, Adams, and Clay he had sought to prevent disintegration by the cement of national legislation. Now he realized his mistake. Protection, instead of a binding force, had proved an instrument of class and sectional plunder. And as Calhoun saw his beloved Carolina rushing past him down the road to secession, he revised his principles, jettisoned the Hamiltonian formula, and produced a new and dynamic version of state rights. The measure of federal power must now be determined by the vital interest of any individual state, not by a transient majority in Congress, or in the Supreme Court.

Nullification was the name of this device by which Calhoun proposed to protect the peculiar interests of his state, and preserve the Union that he loved. Set forth in a document called the South Carolina Exposition, it was approved in 1828 by the legislature of that state. Nullification was based on two postulates: the common enough assertion that the Federal Constitution was a compact between states, and the theory of indivisible, indestructible sovereignty. The Constitution was established not by the American people, but by thirteen sovereign states. Sovereign in 1787, they must still be sovereign in 1828. As sovereigns, they have severally the right to judge when their agent, the Federal Government, exceeds its powers. A state convention, the immediate organ of state sovereignty, may then determine whether a given Act of Congress be constitutional or otherwise; and, in the latter event, take measures to prevent its enforcement within the state limits. Calhoun, however, recognized one authority on the Constitution superior to the interpretation of a single state; an interpretative federal amendment, adopted by three-fourths of the states.

Such was the doctrine of nullification. It was not wholly new or original. The Kentucky and Virginia resolves of 1798 postulated the same state sovereignty; but the remedy to which they pointed against unconstitutional acts of Congress was, in the one case, a collective nullification by *all* the states; and in the other a collective ' interposition,' whatever that might mean. Nullification by a single state, disobeying the laws of the Union while claiming the privileges of the Union, was a very different matter. As the aged Madison declared, 'for this preposterous and anarchical pretension there is not a shadow of countenance in the Constitution.' It had been adumbrated, to be sure, by Massachusetts and Connecticut at the time of the embargo and the War of 1812; but neither they nor the numerous other states which had denounced this or that measure of the Federal Government as unconstitutional had done more than protest, and threaten to secede if their protests were not heeded.

Calhoun's dialectic is as tedious as his noble-Roman pose; but we must concede the power of his intellect, and his absolute sincerity. His political principles changed, but never his object. Confronted, like Jefferson and Adams in 1775, with an accepted constitutional theory that supported tyranny, he sought a new one to preserve liberty. Like them, he would preserve it within the existing body politic if possible, outside it if necessary. The South, with its growing economic particularism, could only remain in union with the more populous North, if some constitutional check were applied to majority rule. So Calhoun sought in the Federal Constitution some implicit theory that would provide that check; and discovered nullification. But, unless the other side would yield, the only possible result, as in 1776, must have been disunion.

Calhoun's authorship of the ' Exposition of 1828 ' was secret; and he advised his state to hold nullification in reserve, hoping that President Jackson would insist upon a reduction of the tariff. But Jackson was indifferent to the tariff; and Van Buren's Northern wing of the party was interested in maintaining protection. Months stretched into years, and the 'tariff of abominations' remained on the statute books. It became clear to the Southerners in the House that they could obtain no reduction without Western votes; and Western votes against nationalism could only be purchased by conceding something that the West wanted more eagerly than protection.

5. The West and the Union

The West, as we have seen, looked to Jackson to reform certain features of the national land system. The poorer public lands, unsaleable at the minimum price of $1.25 per acre, made large blocks of untaxable wilderness between the settled areas. To remedy this Senator Benton proposed the device of ' graduation ': a progressive reduction in the price of public land unsold after being offered for a given period. Frontiersmen who squatted on the public domain before it was placed on sale disliked having their illegal holdings sold to others; and often forced the man with a title to pay handsomely for their ' improvements,' before moving on. But they preferred to legalize their position by a pre-emption act, giving them an option to purchase at the minimum price the quarter-section where they had squatted, whenever it was offered for sale by the government. The first pre-emption act was passed in 1830. It was the prelude to a new public land policy.

Older communities, both North and South, were opposed to any measure likely to encourage emigration. The northeastern manufacturing states had a somewhat special attitude. Emigration tended to keep up the price of factory labor; but if the tariff schedules were to be maintained, some way must be found to get rid of the surplus revenue coming in from the public lands. In order to catch Western votes for protection, Henry Clay proposed a clever scheme of ' distribution.' The proceeds from land sales would be distributed among the states, for use in public works and education, giving a special bonus to those states wherein the lands lay.

It was all a game of balance between North, South, and West, each section offering to compromise a secondary interest, in order to get votes for a primary interest. The South would permit the West to plunder the public domain, in return for a reduction of the tariff. The North offered the tempting bait of distribution, in order to maintain protection. On the outcome of this sectional balance depended the alignment of parties in the future: even of the Civil War itself. Was it to be North and West against South, or South and West against North?

On 29 December 1829 Senator Foot of Connecticut offered a resolution to inquire into the expediency of restricting the sale of public lands to those already in the market. Senator Benton of Missouri denounced this proposal as a barefaced attempt of the manufacturers to keep their laborers from 'the blooming regions of the West.' He summoned the gallant South to the rescue of her Western brothers; and Senator Hayne of South Carolina, a recent convert to nullification, responded. One after another the giants of the upper chamber rushed into the fray, and there took place one of those classic debates that America used to love — speeches hours long, each consuming a whole day's session, yet delivered from mere scraps of notes held in the palm of the hand, and every word reported in the newspapers; one of those contests of eloquence that seemed to mobilize the whole latent manliness and shrewdness of the nation.

As the debate progressed, less was said about the public land, more on the essential sympathy of Northern or Southern ideals for the West, and most of all on constitutional theory. The acme came on 26 January 1830, when Daniel Webster of Massachusetts replied for the second time to Hayne. Webster was the most commanding figure in the Senate, a swarthy Olympian with a crag-like

face, and eyes that seemed to glow like dull coals under the precipice of brows. It has been said that no man was ever so great as
Daniel Webster looked. His magnificent presence and deep, melo-
dious voice gave distinction to the most common platitudes; but
his orations were seldom commonplace. He carried to perfection
the dramatic, rotund style of oratory that America learned from
the elder Pitt. Slumberous he was at times, even ponderous; but the
South Carolinian's attack on the patriotism of New England, no
less than his bold challenge to the Union in its own upper chamber,
called forth all Webster's immense reserve of vitality and intellectual
power. His reply is the greatest recorded American oration, thrilling
to read even today in cold print, when the issues with which it deals
are long since settled by the men who followed in 1861 the standard
that Webster raised in 1830.

Imagine, then, the small semicircular Senate chamber in the
Capitol; gallery and every bit of floor space behind the desks of the
forty-eight senators packed with visitors; Vice-President Calhoun
in the chair, his handsome, mobile face gazing into that of the
orator, and reflecting every point; Daniel Webster, in blue tailed
coat with brass buttons and buff waistcoat, getting under way
slowly and deliberately, then turning on power until he moved with
the effortless speed of a great airplane. Hour after hour the speech
flowed on, always in good taste and temper, relieving the high tone
and tension with a happy allusion or turn of phrase that provoked
laughter, thrilling his audience with rich imagery, crushing his
opponents with a barrage of facts, passing from defense of his state
and section to a devastating criticism of the 'South Carolina doctrine,' and concluding with an immortal peroration on the Union:

It is to that Union we owe our safety at home, and our consideration
and dignity abroad. It is to that Union that we are chiefly indebted for
whatever makes us most proud of our country. That Union we reached
only by the discipline of our virtues in the severe school of adversity. It
had its origin in the necessities of disordered finance, prostrate commerce, and ruined credit. Under its benign influences, these great interests immediately awoke as from the dead, and sprang forth with newness
of life. Every year of its duration has teemed with fresh proofs of its
utility and its blessings; and although our territory has stretched out wider
and wider, and our population spread farther and farther, they have not
outrun its protection or its benefits. It has been to us all a copious foun-
tain of national, social, and personal happiness.

I have not allowed myself, Sir, to look beyond the Union, to see what might lie hidden in the dark recess behind. I have not coolly weighed the chances of preserving liberty when the bonds that unite us together shall be broken asunder. I have not accustomed myself to hang over the precipice of disunion, to see whether, with my short sight, I can fathom the depth of the abyss below; nor could I regard him as a safe counsellor in the affairs of this government, whose thoughts should be mainly bent on considering, not how the Union may be best preserved, but how tolerable might be the condition of the people when it should be broken up and destroyed. While the Union lasts we have high, exciting, gratifying prospects spread out before us, for us and our children. Beyond that I seek not to penetrate the veil. God grant that in my day at least that curtain may not rise! God grant that on my vision never may be opened what lies behind! When my eyes shall be turned to behold for the last time the sun in heaven, may I not see him shining on the broken and dishonored fragments of a once glorious Union; on States dissevered, discordant, belligerent; on a land rent with civil feuds, or drenched, it may be, in fraternal blood! Let their last feeble and lingering glance rather behold the gorgeous ensign of the republic, now known and honored throughout the earth, still full high advanced, its arms and trophies streaming in their original lustre, not a stripe erased or polluted, not a single star obscured, bearing for its motto, no such miserable interrogatory as "What is all this worth?" nor those other words of delusion and folly, "Liberty first and Union afterwards"; but everywhere, spread all over in characters of living light, blazing on all its ample folds, as they float over the sea and over the land, and in every wind under the whole heavens, that other sentiment, dear to every true American heart, — Liberty *and* Union, now and forever, one and inseparable!

It was this peroration, declaimed on thousands of school platforms by the lads of the coming generation, that established in the hearts of the Northern and Western people a new semi-religious conception of the Union. One of its earliest readers was a dreamy, gangling youth on the Indiana frontier, named Abraham Lincoln.

Time only could reveal the full import of Webster's reply to Hayne; but it went home instantly to the old patriot in the White House. Jackson counted himself a state-rights man, but he never doubted the sovereignty of the nation. State rights for him was merely a formula to prevent the jobbery and corruption and consolidation toward which Adams and Clay seemed to be tending. It could never justify disobedience to the laws of the Union. Yet Calhoun and the nullification party counted upon his sympathy, as a

Carolinian born; and at an anniversary dinner that they arranged for Jefferson's birthday, 13 April 1830, they proposed to enlist him in their cause. The formal toasts and speeches were all so worded as to prove a connection between nullification and Democratic-Republican orthodoxy. Jackson sat through them outwardly impassive, inwardly fuming. When his turn came for a volunteer toast, the old chieftain arose to his full height, fixed his glaring eyes on Calhoun, and flung out a challenge:

> Our Federal Union — it must be preserved!

Calhoun took up the challenge with another:

> The Union.— next to our liberty, the most dear!

The issue was now joined between President and Vice-President; events moved fast to separate them. An authoritative letter reached the President asserting that Calhoun, who had always posed as Jackson's defender in the Arbuthnot and Ambrister affair, had been the one cabinet member to demand his arrest and trial. He enclosed it in a note to the Vice-President, inquiring if the charge were true. Calhoun replied evasively, and Jackson endorsed the letter, 'This is full evidence of the duplicity and insincerity of the man.' That form of personal disloyalty was the unforgivable sin to a man of Jackson's metal.

To complete Van Buren's triumph and Calhoun's isolation, it now remained to cure the 'Eaton malaria' which still hung over the administration like an unwholesome fog. No easy matter that; but not too difficult for little Van. On one of his daily horseback rides with Jackson, the President alluded to the cabinet discord, and wished the women would give him peace. Then Van Buren played his master stroke. 'There is but one thing can give you peace — my resignation.' 'Never, Sir!' said Jackson. But he was convinced after a few more rides; and when the matter was discussed with other cronies, Van Buren so deftly turned the argument that Eaton, as the original cause of the trouble, offered to resign with him. It was then natural for Jackson to tell the other ministers, Calhoun men all, that they must follow; and protesting they retired to the obscurity whence they came. In the summer of 1831 the cabinet was completely reorganized. Van Buren, whose apparent sacrifice assured him of the presidential succession, was nominated minister to Great Britain. His place in the cabinet was given to Edward Livingston, a statesman and jurist whose penal code for Louisiana has been universally admired. Lewis Cass, an energetic Yankee of the Northwest, replaced Eaton, and Roger B. Taney of Maryland, who later proved a worthy successor to Chief Justice Marshall, became Attorney-General. Jackson's administration was now of the North and West, and ready for the nullifiers to do their worst.

6. Nullification Attempted

For two years after the famous dinner, Calhoun and the South Carolina nullifiers were held in check by the unionists of their own state; in 1832 Henry Clay forced their hands. With the aid of Western votes, attracted by his distribution scheme, Clay pushed a new tariff bill through Congress on 14 July 1832. Some of the abominations of the 1828 tariff were removed, but the high duties on iron and textiles were maintained; and the new Act had an air of permanence which acted upon South Carolina as a challenge.

In the state election that autumn the state-rights party, the 'pinks of chivalry and fire-and-brimstone eaters,' carried all before them. The new legislature promptly summoned a state convention, which on 24 November 1832 declared in the name of the sovereign people of South Carolina that the tariff Act was 'unauthorized by the Constitution of the United States . . . null, void, and no law, nor binding upon this State, its officers or citizens.' This so-called nullification ordinance forbade federal officials to collect customs duties within the state after 1 February 1833, and threatened instant secession from the Union if the Federal Government attempted to blockade Charleston, or otherwise to use force.

President Jackson took prompt precautions to maintain the law of the land. Forts Moultrie and Sumter were reinforced, revenue cutters were ordered to collect the duties if the customs officials were resisted, and close touch was maintained with the South Carolina unionists. On 10 December the President issued a ringing proclamation to the people of South Carolina. Their nullification ordinance, he said, was founded upon no right of revolution against oppression, but on the strange position that a state might retain its place in the Union, and yet be bound only by those laws that it might choose to regard as constitutional.

I consider, then, the power to annul a law of the United States, assumed by one State, incompatible with the existence of the Union, contradicted expressly by the letter of the Constitution, unauthorized by its spirit, inconsistent with every principle on which it was founded, and destructive of the great object for which it was formed.

South Carolina was not to be conquered by proclamation. Her legislature hurled back defiance at Old Hickory, and raised a volunteer force to defend the state from 'invasion.' President Jackson, encouraged by loyal addresses that poured in from all parties and sections, wished to throw an army into South Carolina at the first show of resistance to the customs officers. But could he afford to? It was no question of suppressing a mere local insurrection, as Washington had done in 1794, but the very delicate and dangerous matter of coercing a state. Virginia regarded nullification as a caricature of her resolves of 1798, Georgia 'abhorred the doctrine,' and Alabama denounced it as 'unsound in theory and dangerous in practice'; but the majority in all the Southern states probably believed in the constitutional right of secession, and Georgia had made the very dangerous proposal of a Southern Convention.

Extremists aside, everyone wished to avoid bloodshed. Jackson's friends feared lest coercion disrupt their party; and what the nullifiers really wanted was repeal of the tariff. Within three weeks of the President's proclamation, the House committee of ways and means proposed to reduce the duties. An informal meeting at Charleston resolved on 21 January 1833 to suspend the nullification ordinance until the new tariff bill became law; and the customs officials at Charleston were not molested. In Congress compulsion and concession went hand in hand. On 2 March 1833 Jackson signed two bills — the Force Act, authorizing him to use the army and navy to collect duties if judicial process were obstructed, and Clay's compromise tariff, providing a gradual scaling down of all schedules until they should reach twenty per cent *ad valorem* in ten years' time. The South Carolina Convention then reassembled, repealed the nullification ordinance, but saved its face by declaring null and void the Force Act, for which there was no longer any need.

Each party marched from the field with colors flying, claiming victory. Both seemed to have derived new strength from the contest. Nationalism was heartened by Jackson's proclamation and the Force Act, but South Carolina had proved that a single determined state could force her will on Congress, and change the commercial policy of a country which she still denied to be a nation. Jackson would have preferred to concede nothing until Calhoun and his party had passed under the Caudine forks; for beyond nullification he saw secession. The 'next pretext,' he predicted, 'will be the negro, or slavery question.'

7. The War on the Bank

In the midst of these alarums and excursions came the presidential election of 1832, memorable in the history of political organization. Jackson men from all parts of the Union, organized as the Democratic party, sent delegates to a national party convention which renominated Old Hickory and adopted the famous two-thirds rule for the vice-presidency. The opposition organized as the National Republican party (for which the name Whig, of happy memory, was shortly substituted), and nominated Henry Clay. These were the two major parties of the future. In 1832 there was a third party in the field, the Anti-Masons.

That a party of so strange a title should contend for national power was of social rather than of political significance. Americans of the nineteenth century were so in love with the methods of democracy, that no sooner did a few earnest men capture a bit of what they took to be eternal truth, than they proceeded to organize it politically. If some local success proved the scent good, it brought politicians hot-foot to the hunt that they might join in the kill, or lead off the field in pursuit of bigger game. This Anti-Masonic party arose in 1826, out of the disappearance of a New York brick-layer named Morgan, who had divulged the secrets of his Masonic lodge. A corpse was found floating in the Niagara river. It could not be proved to be Morgan's; but, as a politician said, it was 'good enough Morgan until after election.' Both the event and the Masons' efforts to hush it up revived an old prejudice (now quite dead) against secret societies. Several young politicians, such as William H. Seward, Thurlow Weed, and Thaddeus Stevens, threw themselves into the Anti-Masonic movement, which became strong enough to elect a state governor or two. In 1831 it held a national convention and nominated presidential candidates, who took thousands of Northern votes from Clay. In a few years' time the Anti-Masons faded out; but the sort of people who were attracted by a one-idea party easily took up with the next that came along, and successively became Free-Soilers, Know-Nothings, and Republicans.

This presidential election of 1832 decided the case of Andrew Jackson *v.* the Bank of the United States. He had been elected in the first instance as a popular champion against the B.U.S. Since 1819 the Bank had been well managed, to the profit alike of the Government whose funds it handled, the business community which it served, and the stockholders; but it was still unpopular in the West. Jackson shared this prejudice, together with a profound conviction that the money power was the greatest enemy to democracy. As the Bank's charter would expire in 1836, if not sooner renewed by Congress, Jackson's opinion was of some importance.

In the Eastern states the B.U.S. had established itself as a necessary part of the business mechanism; and the Pennsylvania Democrats and Carolina state-rights people had no complaint to make of it — the figures of stock distribution show why.[1] Calhoun had no constitutional qualms on the subject, although by any consistent standard of strict construction the chartering of a national monopoly was a more palpable invasion of state rights than a mere raising of tariff schedules to a protective level.

Nicholas Biddle, President of the B.U.S., was no mean antagonist for President Jackson. Precursor of a race of energetic autocratic financiers, he had the same dislike of democracy that Jackson had of banking; but was anxious to keep the Bank out of politics, which was impossible. His social and business relations were largely with Jackson's opponents. Daniel Webster was at the same time a director of the B.U.S., its leading retained counsel, its debtor by personal notes to the sum of many thousands, and Senator from Massachusetts. Congressmen were often paid their salaries by the Bank in advance of the annual appropriation bill, without interest charges. Journalists like James Gordon Bennett, father of the yellow press, obtained loans on very favorable terms. Other newspapers were paid to insert in their columns 'real and positive information' on the patriotic services of the B.U.S.

'I do not dislike your bank more than all banks,' President Jackson informed President Biddle. 'But ever since I read the history of the South Sea Bubble, I have been afraid of banks.' What he wanted was a mere bank of deposit attached to the Treasury Department, with officials appointed under the spoils system. However,

---

[1] In January 1832 the Bank stock was distributed as follows (in round numbers): New York, 31,000; Pennsylvania, 51,000; Maryland, 34,000; South Carolina, 40,000; New England, 15,000; the West, 3,000; Europe, 84,000. Catterall, *Second B. U. S.*, p. 508. The recharter bill of 1832 was reported from a committee of which George McDuffie, Calhoun's lieutenant in the nullification movement, was chairman, and was voted for by most of Calhoun's partisans in both Houses.

the backwoodsman's axe might grow rusty in Washington. Little
favors were extended by the Bank to Jackson's friends, careful consideration was given to the Treasury's wants; and by 1830 Jackson
was speaking 'in most exalted terms' of Biddle. The octopus was
closing in on the old warrior, sucking away his prejudice. Yet no one
could induce him to say on what terms, if any, he would accept a rechartering bill.

As the election of 1832 approached, Biddle was badgered by the
opposition to allow Congress to bring forward a rechartering bill.
People warned him that such a measure would arouse Jackson's
pugnacity, and begged him to wait until after the election. But
Henry Clay, most inadvisedly, wished to make the B.U.S. an issue
in the election, and won Biddle's consent. A recharter bill passed
Congress on 3 July 1832. Jackson vetoed it, with an explanatory
message that identified the Democratic party with radicalism. The
bill, according to the President, was not only an unconstitutional invasion of state rights; it proposed to continue a monopoly and exclusive privilege, the profits of which must come 'out of the earnings of the American people,' in favor of foreign stockholders and
'a few hundred of our own citizens, chiefly of the richest class.' He
could not permit the 'prostitution of our Government to the advancement of the few at the expense of the many.'

Jackson's logic and facts may have been defective, but as an
appeal to the people his veto message was irresistible. The President was re-elected; his 'mandate' was clear. Yet Nicholas Biddle
refused to admit defeat. 'This worthy President thinks that because
he has scalped Indians and imprisoned judges, he is to have his own
way with the Bank. He is mistaken.'

Instead of waiting for the Bank to die a natural death in 1836,
Jackson decided at once to deprive it of government deposits. The
Secretary of the Treasury had to be promoted to the State Department, and another dismissed, before one could be found to obey
orders. After 1833, government receipts were deposited in local banks
— Jackson's 'pet banks,' which he believed to be safer than the expiring 'Monster.'

This financial war came in the midst of a period of unparalleled
speculative activity, coincident with improvements in transportation, a brisk demand for cotton, and increased westward migration. The decease of the B.U.S., with its wholesome if unpopular
habit of promptly presenting the notes of local banks for payment,

took off the last brake. The currency was already chaotic, when an Act of 1834 made matters worse by establishing the coinage ratio of 16 to 1 between silver and gold, which drove silver from the country. Yet the only embarrassment to the Treasury was a surplus which rapidly mounted with increased sales of public land, and the final payment of the national debt in January 1835. Henry Clay, fearing lest the administration devise some way to spend the surplus, managed to get through Congress a 'distribution' scheme in 1836. About $28,000,000 was presented by the Treasury to the state governments. Some states used the money for public works, others used it as a fund for education, one even made a *per capita* distribution; but mostly the money fed speculation. Jackson then administered a severe astringent, in the 'specie circular' of 1836, ordering that the Treasury receive no paper currency for public lands. Shortly after, the panic of 1837 burst upon the country; and the surplus disappeared almost overnight. Short-time treasury notes tided over the crisis, but the whole of the next administration (1837–41) was spent in seeking a substitute for the B.U.S.; and none was found comparable with it for service and efficiency until 1913.

Jackson's war on the Bank was not only a symptom of growing pains in America, but an aspect of that fundamental hostility to monopoly and special privilege which the colonists brought from England, and which broke out in the Boston tea-party, in Jeffersonian democracy, and in the progressive and labor movements of the present century.

8. *Indian and Foreign Affairs*

Jackson's attitude toward the Indians, like his war on the Bank, betrayed a dyed-in-the-wool Westerner. He carried out a policy suggested by Jefferson: the removal of all Indian tribes to the Far West. Between 1829 and 1837 ninety-four Indian treaties were concluded, several million acres relinquished, and many thousand redskins more or less forcibly transferred to the trans-Mississippi West.

Most of the Indian tribes were too feeble to resist the process, but at three points there was trouble. Chief Black Hawk of the Sauk and Fox endeavored to retain the ancient tribal seat at the mouth of the Rock river, Illinois. Squatters encroached on his village, enclosed the Indians' cornfields, and even ploughed up the graves of their ancestors. So in 1831 Black Hawk withdrew into Missouri territory.

There famine followed, and hostile Sioux threatened. Hoping to find a vacant prairie in which to plant a corn crop, Black Hawk returned the following year with about a thousand of the tribe. Misinterpreting this move as a hostile expedition, the Illinois militia turned out — Abraham Lincoln commanding a company — and pursued the starving Indians up the Rock river into the Wisconsin wilderness. It was a disgraceful frontier frolic, stained by a wanton massacre of Indians, including women and children, when attempting to recross the Mississippi. The only redeeming feature was the chivalrous consideration of Black Hawk by Lieutenant Jefferson Davis of the regular army, when the captured chieftain was placed in his charge.

In the South the Creek, Chickasaw, and Choctaw nations were fairly amenable, and, after some opposition and much prodding, removed to the Indian Territory (Oklahoma), where their descendants still live. Two nations, the Cherokee and Seminole, were refractory.

The Cherokee, after ceding their hunting grounds in the late eighteenth century, fell back on their mountainous lands in northwestern Georgia, guaranteed to them by solemn treaty with the United States. It had always been a grievance against the Indians that they would not settle down to civilized ways. The Cherokee, however, built themselves neat houses and good roads, preserved the peace, received Christian missionaries kindly, published books in an alphabet invented by their tribesman Sequoya, and adopted a national constitution. They had given as good evidence of worth, and made more progress in civility, than the Georgia crackers who coveted their land. In plain derogation of the Indians' treaty rights, though with some color of legalism derived from an agreement with the United States in 1802, the State of Georgia claimed the Cherokee as her subjects and tenants-at-will. An unfortunate discovery of gold in the Cherokee country about 1829 brought in a rough class of whites. It was a case of federal supremacy against state rights as clear as that of South Carolina; but President Jackson let Georgia have her way. Regulars sent in by President Adams to protect the Indians were withdrawn; and when Chief Justice Marshall decided, on a test case (Worcester *v.* Georgia), that the Cherokee nation occupied a territory within which the laws of Georgia could have no force, Jackson is said to have remarked, ' John Marshall has made his decision. Now let him enforce it.' A portion of the Cherokee were then bribed to exchange the lands of the whole for a section of the Indian

Territory, and five million dollars. The rest held out for a few years; but in 1838 they too were driven westward from the lands of their ancestors; Emerson protesting in vain: 'Such a dereliction of all faith and virtue, such a denial of justice, and such deafness to screams for mercy were never heard of in times of peace and in the dealing of a nation with its own allies and wards, since the earth was made.'

A similar controversy with the Seminoles of Florida had a more tragic solution. A treaty of removal was negotiated with a few chiefs, but repudiated by the greater portion of the tribe, led by its brave chieftain Osceola. Secure in the fastnesses of the everglades, Osceola baffled the United States army for years, and was only captured by treachery when bearing a flag of truce. His people kept up the fight until 1842, when they were all but exterminated, after costing the United States some twenty million dollars, and fifteen hundred lives.

At the end of Jackson's second term practically all the Eastern Indians had been provided for, west of a 'permanent' barrier that ran from Lake Superior through Wisconsin and Iowa Territories, and thence along the western boundaries of Missouri and Arkansas to the Red river. A chain of military posts, garrisoned by dragoons and mounted riflemen, was established to keep whites and reds apart. Jackson declared in 1835 that the nation was pledged to keep this barrier permanent. All but the southern limb of it was torn up within twenty years.

Foreign affairs in Jackson's administration are a very different story. Jackson entertained no unfriendly feelings toward the nation he had thrashed so soundly at New Orleans. There were moments of irritation and even danger over the unadjusted northeastern boundary; but Van Buren smoothed things over with Vaughan, the British minister at Washington. President Adams had clashed with Canning in Mexico and South America; Jackson recalled Poinsett, and forgot the doctrine of Monroe. Adams and Clay had been wont to prefer minor complaints in diplomatic notes; Vaughan and Van Buren settled such matters by conversation, possibly with the fair mediation of Mrs. Eaton. Adams had stood out stiffly for impossible demands in respect of American trade with the West Indies; Van Buren induced the British government to remove all restrictions from American produce and ships in the West Indies, save a moderate duty to maintain imperial preference. That question was settled permanently. In his annual message of 1830 to Congress, Jackson wrote:

It gives me unfeigned pleasure to assure you that this negotiation has been throughout characterized by the most frank and friendly spirit on the part of Great Britain, and concluded in a manner strongly indicative of a sincere desire to cultivate the best relations with the United States. To reciprocate this disposition to the fullest extent of my ability is a duty which I shall deem it a privilege to discharge.

Jackson's dealings with Great Britain were the more noteworthy in contrast with his handling of a controversy with France. There was a claim for spoliations under the Berlin and Milan Decrees, for which the government of Louis-Philippe, in a treaty of 1831, agreed to pay twenty-five million francs. The French chambers adjourned without voting the money, and a draft for the first instalment, drawn by the Secretary of the Treasury, was protested.

Jackson at once alarmed American business and offended France by ordering the navy to prepare for active service, and recommending Congress to authorize the seizure of French property (1 December 1834). Finally the French legislature voted the money, on the condition that it should not be paid until the United States offered ' satisfactory explanation ' of the President's words. Jackson refused to apologize. There matters stood until the close of 1835, when the President disclaimed any intention to insult France, though he would not apologize ' for the statement of truth and the performance of duty.' At this point the British government mediated with success. Wounded honor was satisfied, and the treaty was duly carried out.

Many of Jackson's more conservative supporters had been alienated by his breach with Calhoun, his financial vagaries, and his unfit appointments; but with the people at large he never stood higher than toward the close of his second administration: and his party allowed him to dictate the nomination of Van Buren as his successor. The Whigs were as yet so loosely organized that their strategy in 1836 was to vote by local units for ' favorite sons ' like Webster and Harrison, hoping thereby to throw the election into the House of Representatives. But Van Buren polled a majority, and was elected President.

The next 4 March marked the passing of a vital personality, and the founding of a new presidential dynasty. Up Pennsylvania Avenue wound a military procession, escorting a small phaeton (built from the wood of the *Constitution*) drawn by a team of four gray horses. The old President, feeling his seventy years and emaciated by long illness, sat erect with his fine white head bared to the

March sunshine, and the old indomitable spirit flashing this last triumph from his eyes. Beside him, and a head lower, sat Martin Van Buren, with the bland aspect of the cat who had swallowed the canary. Chief Justice Taney administered the inaugural oath to the new President; and there followed a more seemly reception at the White House than that of 1829. Andrew Jackson then returned by easy stages to his beloved Hermitage in Tennessee.

Few Presidents accomplished so much as Old Hickory, and none has made a greater appeal to popular imagination. In his person he proved that the average American of sound character and common sense could win, and was fit to administer, the most powerful elective office in the world. But democracy left the White House with the first Democrat.

XXIV

THE NORTHERN STATES
1820–1850

1. America's Awkward Age

LEAVING the 'Little Magician' safely seated in the White House, let us turn to the material and moral forces that were pulsing through the United States of his generation. Statesmen and parties had done much to shape those forces, and more could be done with foresight and courage. Without violence they had transferred power to a new class and sectional combination. They had weathered the storm of nullification, and had evolved from the political anarchy of the twenties two national parties, both pledged to preserve the Union. Yet, in spite of their efforts, social and economic forces were pulling North and South apart. Both were progressing, but divergently. Northern society was being transformed by the industrial revolution, by cheap transportation, and by educational, humanitarian, and migratory movements that touched the border slave states very little, and the lower South not at all. Southern society was readjusting itself to the cotton plantation, tilled by slaves. By 1850 two distinct civilizations had been evolved, as different in their material basis, moral ideas, and view of life, as Canada and Mexico of today.

In superficial appearance the Northern states had not changed much since 1790. Harriet Martineau in 1836, like Volney in 1797, was never out of sight of the woods, save in the prairies of Illinois; but there was a good deal less forest. The most striking new feature in the Northern landscape was not the occasional railway or canal, but the factory village, new and bright, built near some waterfall or rapid; containing from two to ten mills plainly built of wood, brick, or stone, as many pretentious mansions of the owners or superintendents, and hundreds of operatives' houses, exactly alike. New York City, as Dickens saw it in 1842, was low, flat, and straggling, enclosed by a hedge of masts; a city without baths or plumbing, lighted by gas and scavenged by pigs. Georgian architecture had given place to the neo-classic. Public buildings were being constructed of gray granite, and the wealthier farmers and country lawyers masked their wooden houses with a classic colonnade and pediment. In the Middle West the white-painted farmhouse was beginning to prevail; but in the new settlements log cabins and untidy clearings, dominated the landscape. American scenery began to be appreciated for its ' romantic' contrasts of mountain with valley, sandy beach or rocky coast with island-studded sea, and its ' stupendous' gorges and cataracts. Barrack-like hotels with long covered verandas were being put up at places like Saratoga Springs, Niagara Falls, Newport, and Nahant, in order to accommodate sight-seers, to provide for the brief vacations of business men, and the vacuous pleasures of their valetudinarian wives. Gimcrack Italian villas and Gothic cottages multiplied near the larger cities in the forties; proclaiming that wealth was being amassed faster than good taste, and portending a new class of city-bred gentleman farmer.

It was America's awkward age. The rather attractive child who had left his parent's roof, the marvellous boy who had proclaimed great truths (or perhaps delusions) to a candid world, was now a gawky hobbledehoy. He had fashioned for himself an excellent pair of skis that he called republicanism and democracy; but like pioneer skiers, he was in the stick-riding stage of development. His outrageous antics in the snow, his hair-breadth escapes, and colossal tosses were viewed with mingled amusement and disgust by devotees of the old-fashioned snowshoe. Avid of praise, he resented advice; believing that observers were really criticizing him for skiing at all.

Republicanism and democracy did work, and the resources of a new country, exploited by the inhabitants under laws of their own making and breaking, had brought a degree of comfort and security to the common man that he had not known since the days of good Queen Bess. It was not surprising that Americans were full of bounce and bluster, contemptuous of old-world monarchies. Even a frontier bully had some redeeming qualities, if only, as Emerson's grandfather remarked at the village reprobate's funeral, that he was ' useful at fires.' The American had many unpleasant habits, particularly in connection with tobacco; and no manners. Respect and deference were not to be had of him at any price; but those who addressed him as an equal discovered a natural civility and spontaneous kindness that took the place of manners. Intercourse between man and man was easy and pleasant because there was no assumption of social superiority on the one side, or acknowledged inferiority on the other. It was not so much the freedom, simplicity, and good humor of the

people that endeared them to Harriet Martineau, as the ' sweet temper . . . diffused like sunshine over the land,' and due to ' the practice of forbearance requisite in a republic.'

Forbearance the Americans carried to excess in their uncritical
attitude toward their own books, customs, institutions, and abuses.
Almost every English visitor of the period remarked the patience
of Americans under the afflictions of contemporary travel, denounced
their deference to majority opinion, and deplored their fear of expressing unpopular theories. This meant that the Americans were
becoming less independent and more gregarious; a deference to the
opinion of others being a condition of social intercourse on a democratic basis. Yet so complex was the American character that the
excess of one quality was balanced by the excess of its reverse. Intolerance appeared in the persecution of unpopular groups such as
free negroes, immigrants, abolitionists, and Catholics; and in hot
resentment of unfavorable criticism. Yet we should be mistaken in
ascribing these qualities wholly to democracy or to immaturity.
Spain, as proudly isolated beyond the Pyrenees as America once
was beyond the Atlantic, still shows many of the characteristics of
America in her awkward age.

Nor was distinction wanting in a country that produced in one
generation Calhoun, Webster, Hawthorne, and Irving; and in the
next, Emerson, Whitman, Lee, and Lincoln. There was merely a
lack of those differences in dress, manner, and mode of living by
which Europeans were accustomed to recognize the distinguished
man. Clerks dressed almost as well as their employers, factory girls
copied the latest Paris fashions. Scarcity of ' help' and total lack
of good servants — since Americans regarded domestic service as a
badge of inferiority — made it difficult for the wealthiest Northern
merchant to keep up a large establishment. Young married couples
in the cities often lived in hotels or boarding houses. Arthur Hugh
Clough, after trying to live at Harvard like an Oxford don, wisely
concluded that to enjoy America one must live roughly and simply.

It was America's busy age, or one of them. Eighteenth-century
travellers railed at the Americans for their indolence; nineteenth-
century tourists criticized their activity. ' Lazy dogs' apparently
begat ' dollar-chasers.' Each Northern community was an ant-hill,
intensely active within, and constantly exchanging ants with the
other hills. Every man worked, or at least made a semblance of it;
the few who wished to idle, and could afford idleness, fled from the

opprobrium of 'loafing' to Europe, where they swelled the chorus of complaint against democratic institutions. Nothing struck English visitors more forcibly than the total want of public parks and pleasure resorts, of games and sports, or of simple pleasures like country walking. The Northern American had not learned how to employ leisure; his pleasure came from doing things. Frontiersmen were fond of shooting and fishing, and country boys played games such as hare and hounds, prisoner's base, and rounders. But the average adult American regarded games as a waste of time. Baseball and intercollegiate rowing did not begin until just before the Civil War.

Bad cooking, an atrocious regimen, and lack of outdoor exercise made the 'females' of the period pallid and delicate; and the robust constitutions of frontiersmen were undermined by fevers and agues, particularly in the river bottoms of the Mississippi and its tributaries. 'We was sick every fall regular,' reminisced the mother of President Garfield.

Yet, with all these drawbacks, the Northern and Western states were a land where dreams of youth came true; where the majority were doing what they wished to do, without restraint by class or administration. 'We were hardly conscious of the existence of a government,' wrote a Scandinavian immigrant in New York. The fun of building, inventing, creating, in an atmosphere where one man's success did not mean another's failure, gave American life that peculiar gusto that Walt Whitman has caught in his poetry. Europeans often mistook this joyous activity for avidity: the incidental results for the object. Half the population were engaged in realizing the ambition of frustrated peasant ancestors for a farm of their very own, clear of rent and charges. The other half, having achieved the farm, had tired of it; and like the boy who loses interest in his home-made radio, had turned to some other occupation, or taken up pioneering again.

2. Transportation and the Westward Movement

The westward movement recovered its momentum after the hard times of 1837–40. New Englanders, who a generation before had settled the interior of New York and Ohio, were pressing forward into the smaller prairies of Indiana and Illinois, where the tough sod taxed their strength but repaid it in the end with bountiful crops of grain; where shoulder-high prairie-grass afforded rich pasturage for cattle, and groves of buckeye, oak, walnut, and hickory furnished wood and timber. A favorite objective for Yankee settlement was southern Michigan, a rolling country of ' oak openings,' where stately trees stood well-spaced as in a gentleman's park. As a popular song of the period put it:

> Come all ye Yankee farmers who wish to change your lot,
> Who've spunk enough to travel beyond your native spot,
> And leave behind the village where Pa and Ma do stay,
> Come follow me and settle in Michigania, —
> *Yea, yea, yea, in Michigania!*

Others were hewing farms from the forests of southern Wisconsin, and venturing across the Mississippi into land vacated by Black Hawk's redskins — to Minnesota and

> Ioway, Ioway, that's where the tall corn grows!

Yankees direct from New England, German immigrants, and the old pioneer stock from Pennsylvania and Kentucky were swelling the stream.

Improved transportation was the first condition of this quickening life. Canals, roads, and railways took people west, and connected them with a market when they got there; increased the marketing radius of cities and factory towns; made it worth while to be industrious. Only the roughest and most primitive subsistence farmers cared to settle in a region whence they could not send a cash crop to market.

In 1826, when Charles Vaughan took a trip on the newly opened Erie Canal, the country on each side of it between Utica and Rochester had been cleared to a width of not more than a mile. Yet only the next year the governor of Georgia was complaining that wheat from central New York was being sold at Savannah more cheaply than wheat from central Georgia. By bringing the Great Lakes within reach of a metropolitan market, the Erie Canal opened up the hitherto neglected northern regions of Ohio, Indiana, and Illinois. At the same time it made New York City the principal gateway to the farther West.

As soon as it became evident that little help could be expected from the Federal Government for internal improvements, other states followed New York in constructing canals, or lending their credit to canal corporations. Ohio linked the Great Lakes with the Mississippi valley by canal in 1833-34. Cleveland rose from a petty frontier village to a great lake port by 1850; Cincinnati, at the other end of the state canal system, sent pickled pork down the Ohio and Mississippi by flatboat and steamboat, shipped flour by canal boat to New York, and in 1850 had a population of 115,000 — more than that of New York City in 1815. Three hundred lake vessels arrived at Chicago in 1833, although its population was but 350. Three years later the first cargo of grain from Chicago arrived at Buffalo for transshipment by the Erie Canal. An English traveler pronounced Chicago in 1846 to be a city of ' magnificent intentions '; and predicted that after being burnt down once or twice it might amount to something. In 1856 the city was connected by railway with New York, and by 1860 it was almost as large as Cincinnati, and threatening St. Louis.

The Erie canal forced Boston, Philadelphia, and Baltimore into rival activity. Philadelphia was shocked to find that her cheapest route to Pittsburgh was by way of New York City, Albany, Buffalo, and wagon road from Lake Erie. The State of Pennsylvania then put through the great portage system to Pittsburgh, surmounting the Alleghanies at an elevation of 2,300 feet by a series of inclined planes, up which canal boats or railway cars were hauled by stationary steam-engines. Pennsylvania had almost a thousand miles of canals in operation by 1840; in twenty years' time the railways had rendered most of them unprofitable.

Baltimore's plan for cheap transit to the West was the Baltimore and Ohio Railroad. The first spadeful was turned in 1828 by the last surviving signer of the Declaration of Independence, Charles Carroll; but the project encountered unexpected difficulties, and did not reach the Ohio river until 1833. American railroads were not created to connect important cities, but to increase the distributing radius of individual cities, around which they were disposed like sticks on a fan, each system having its own gauge, lest rivals use the line. Railways were regarded merely as an improved sort of road, and one of their chief competitors down to 1850 was the plank road — a familiar feature of Civil War maps — constructed by turnpike companies as a cheap substitute for macadam. Although very few canals were constructed in the forties, while railway mileage tripled, the larger part of bulk freight still went by water. In the early fifties the completion of the Hudson River Railroad from New York to Albany (where it was connected with the New York Central for Buffalo) and of the Pennsylvania Railroad from Philadelphia to Pittsburgh, caused such

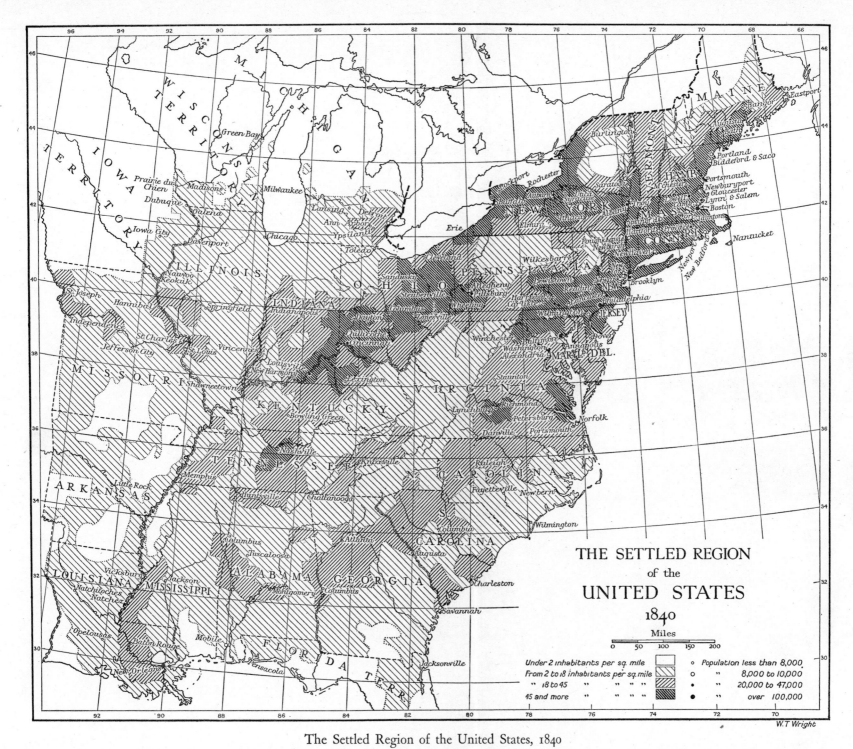

THE SETTLED REGION
of the
UNITED STATES
1840

Miles

0   50   100   150   200

Under 2 inhabitants per sq. mile   ○ Population less than 8,000
From 2 to 18 inhabitants per sq. mile   ○   "   8,000 to 10,000
  " 18 to 45   "   "   "   "   ●   "   20,000 to 47,000
  45 and more "   "   "   "   ●   "   over 100,000

W.T Wright

The Settled Region of the United States, 1840

Prepared by S. E. Morison *for* The Oxford History of the United States. *Based on* Statistical Atlas of the Twelfth Census, *Plate 7, and data in Census of* 1840.

an astounding transfer of freight from canals to railroads, particularly in the winter season, as to prove the superiority of rail for long-distance haulage, and to suggest that it was the proper instrument for penetrating the continent.

The first locomotives used in the United States were purchased at the Stephenson works in England, and iron rails were largely imported from England until the Civil War. But Americans were already experimenting in railroad equipment. The swivel or bogie truck was soon invented, as were the open one-class coach and sleeping car. In safety appliances, however, the American railroads were very backward. Collisions were frequent, strap-iron rails curled up over the wheels, and the wood-burning locomotives belched forth showers of sparks that ignited the forests, as well as the passengers' clothes.

3. The Packet-ship and Immigration

America was the first country to make practical use of the steamboat, but lagged behind England in applying steam to the deep-sea merchant marine. The wooden paddle-wheel steamboat was an ideal type for rivers, or for protected tidal waters like Long Island sound and Chesapeake bay; but the ocean steamer was born in the tempestuous waters about the British Isles. American shipbuilders concentrated their skill and energy on sailing vessels. From 1817 to 1849 the direct carrying trade between England and the United States was on the same level of competition, so far as the laws of the two countries could effect it; and until 1830 British bottoms had the exclusive privilege of the West Indies' triangular trade. Yet by 1824 the freight and passenger traffic from Liverpool to New York and Boston had been captured by the Americans. ' The reason will be evident to any one who will walk through the docks at Liverpool,' wrote an Englishman named, W. N. Blane, in 1824. ' He will see the American ships, long, sharp built, beautifully painted and rigged, and remarkable for their fine appearance and white canvas. He will see the English vessels, short, round and dirty, resembling great black tubs.' The former were the flash packets of the American marine, the famous Swallow Tail and Black Ball liners, that were driven by their dandy captains, bucko mates, and Liverpool Irish crews across the Western Ocean, winter and summer, blow high blow low, in little more than half the average time taken by British vessels. It was a proud seaman in those days who earned the right to sing:

> I served my time in the Black Ball Line,
> *To me way-aye-aye-hurrah!*
> In the Black Ball Line I served my time,
> *Hurrah for the Black Ball Line!*

As late as 1846 a British emigrants' guide advises passengers to choose an American sailing packet, rather than the new Cunard steamships, although the average passage was six weeks.

A leading motive for the repeal of the old Navigation Act in 1849 was the desire of British merchants to employ the superior American vessels. When the East India Company lost its monopoly of the China trade in 1834, the Americans still held their own against private British competitors; and in 1845 a New York shipyard produced the clipper ship *Rainbow*, first of a type carried to perfection in the next decade.

Another favorite chanty of the square-rigger days hints at the connection between packet-ships, railroads, and immigration:

> In eighteen hundred and forty-three
> I sailed away across the sea,
> I sailed away to Amerikee
> To work upon the railway,
> I'm weary of the railway,
> O! poor Paddy works upon the railway.

An era of canal and railway construction created a demand for cheap labor, and made it easier to reach the cheap western lands. England, Ireland, and Germany responded. During the decade of the twenties, less than ten thousand immigrants entered annually. Between 1830 and 1840 half a million immigrants (of which 44 per cent were Irish, 30 per cent German, and 15 per cent English) entered the United States from Europe, and in the forties over one million and a half, of which 49 per cent were Irish, and the others in the same proportion. In 1850 the total population of the United States, 23 million, included almost one million persons of Irish birth, three-quarters of them in the northern Atlantic states; and over half a million of German birth, almost equally divided between those states and the West.

Liverpool, Havre, and Hamburg were the principal ports of embarkation. European governments attempted to mitigate the hardships of the passage by requiring a minimum of space and rations, and decent treatment on the emigrant ships; but without much success. Seldom was a westward passage of the Atlantic made under a month. Neither the federal nor the state governments made any effort to protect the immigrant on his arrival. Many arrived penniless, having exhausted their savings on the journey; and the others too often fell a prey to water-front sharpers. But it must be admitted that as soon as they recovered their shore legs, the immigrants were quite able to defend themselves. As early as 1835 we hear of Irishmen driving the Whigs from the polls in New York, with showers of 'Irish confetti.' Despite the dark pictures of suffering and homesickness painted by the *Quarterly Review* and Charles Dickens, most of the immigrants prospered and sent for their friends.

All but a small fraction of the new-comers arrived in the Northern ports, and remained in the Northern states. Irish immigration reached its peak just after the great famine of 1846. Although mostly country folk, the Irish were tired of farming, and congregated in the cities, where thousands of the men were recruited for construction work, and the women for domestic service. Peasant also was a majority of the Germans, but not in like degree; among them were thousands of artisans, a sprinkling of intellectuals, and political refugees from the revolutions of 1830 and 1848, such as Carl Schurz. German colonies were formed in the cities, especially New York, Baltimore, Cincinnati, and St. Louis; and Milwaukee was a German town by 1850. But the greater number bought western land as soon as they could earn the wherewithal, especially in Wisconsin and Missouri, which Friedrich Münch hoped to make a new Germany for exiled liberals. The sloop *Restaurationen* sailed from Stavanger in 1825 with fifty-three Scandinavian pilgrims who settled in western New York, precursors of many thousands who found pine forests and lakes in Wisconsin and Minnesota similar to those of their native land.

Practically all the immigrants of the period 1820–50 belonged to the northern European races. They quickly became citizens and Jackson Democrats, and contributed greatly to the wealth and progress of their adopted country. Yet the immigrants of that era encountered bitter opposition, as did South Europeans and Asiatics in the late nineteenth century. Street fights between natives and foreigners were a common occurrence; Catholic convents and churches and German turnverein headquarters were sometimes attacked and destroyed. In part the antagonism was religious, since practically all the Irish and many of the Germans were Roman Catholics. In part it was due to emigration assisted by English and Irish authorities,

who in order to relieve the taxpayer dumped thousands of paupers
into the United States. Most of them were paupers only in a technical sense, who wanted only an opportunity to work; but many became a public charge the moment they landed. For the most part,
however, the hatred of immigrants was economic in motive. They
competed with mechanics who were trying to protect their standard
of living by labor unions. Natives refused to work with the new-
comers, who were thus forced into manual labor, whatever their
education. 'No Irish need apply' was a common sign on workshops
and counting-rooms — but not on army recruiting offices!

4. City and Factory

These new methods and instruments of transportation helped to
people the North and West, by extending the domestic market hastened the industrialization of the East, threatened the self-sufficing
farm, and brought farmers' boys into urban communities. Between
1820 and 1850 the combined population of New York, Philadelphia,
Baltimore, and Boston increased from 343,000 to 1,162,000.[1] In the
latter decade, while the population of the United States increased
thirty-six per cent, that of the towns and cities of 8,000 or more increased ninety per cent. Measured by numbers the urban movement
was more important than westward migration; and its effect on the
American character was the more lasting.

The factory system, as we have seen, became firmly established as
a result of the War of 1812. Textile machinery made America independent of foreign importations, instead of, as in England, destroying domestic hand industries; consequently the factory was introduced without violence, and with little friction. By 1840 there were
twelve hundred cotton factories in the United States, operating two

[1] POPULATION OF PRINCIPAL CITIES

	1790	1800	1810	1820	1830	1840	1850
Boston........	18,038	24,937	33,250	43,298	61,392	93,383	136,881
New York.....	33,131	60,489	96,373	123,706	202,589	312,710	515,547
Philadelphia...	42,520	69,403	91,874	112,772	161,410	220,423	340,045
Baltimore.....	13,503	26,114	35,583	62,738	80,825	102,313	169,054
Charleston.....	16,359	20,473	24,711	24,780	30,289	29,261	42,985
New Orleans...	.....	.....	17,242	27,176	46,310	102,193	116,375

and a quarter million spindles, two-thirds of them in New England. Ring or frame spinning had been invented, power looms were being manufactured in large numbers, and even exported.

Francis C. Lowell, inventor of the first American power loom, was a man of social vision. At New Lanark in Scotland he learned that it was possible to have factories without a degraded labor force. Farmers' daughters were attracted to Waltham by relatively high wages, and the scruples of their pious parents were overcome by a provision of strictly chaperoned boarding houses. The same maternal system was extended to the city of Lowell, which was founded by Boston capitalists in 1822, and to other mill towns on the Merrimac river. For a generation the Lowell factory girls, with their neat dresses, correct deportment, and literary weekly, were a wonder of America; but not typical of America. The usual effect of the factory system was simply to transfer the scene of a family's labor from the home to the factory; but on account of the wider opportunities in a new country, no permanent proletariat was created. Factory girls generally graduated from the mills in three or four years, and child laborers elsewhere usually managed to find some other occupation by the time they reached their majority.

Woolen manufactures developed more slowly, and although protected by even higher tariff schedules than those of cotton, were less successful in capturing the domestic market. Power looms and spinning-jennies were generally adopted in the twenties, and in 1840 Crompton invented a power loom for fancy woolens, just in time to produce the loud checked cassimeres favored by the beaux of the forties. Lawrence, a woolen counterpart to Lowell, was established on the same river in 1845. Already there were over fifteen hundred woolen mills in the Northern states, most of them small, individually owned establishments with a few sets of machinery, employing country people of the neighborhood, and producing blankets, flannels, or satinet. Few attempts to compete with English worsteds were made before 1860.

As a result of this factory development, which continued to advance independently of tariff fluctuations, spinning and weaving in the home had almost disappeared by the Civil War, and factory-made goods had reached all but the remoter parts of the West. The picturesque linsey, fur, and buckskin of the pioneer, and the homespun of his wife, were replaced by factory cottons and woolens, made up in the clothing shops of the Eastern cities.

In England the industrial revolution turned largely on coal and iron; but it was not so in the United States. Textile and other mills were operated largely by water power, and the iron industry developed very slowly. Suitable coal for cokeing was not found east of the Appalachians, but wood for making charcoal was abundant. Pennsylvania ironmasters were more adept in obtaining tariff protection against English iron than in improving their own methods of production. Cort's puddling process, invented in 1783, was not introduced in America until 1830, and then on a small scale. Even Pittsburgh used charcoal for smelting previous to 1840, rather than the bituminous coal which was plentiful in the neighborhood. And Pittsburgh, although it commanded the iron market of the Mississippi valley, could not sell its products in the industrialized Eastern states until it obtained through railroad connection with Philadelphia.

Eastern Pennsylvania was the principal coal- and iron-producing region until 1860. Here anthracite coal and iron were found in abundance, and a rather inferior method of smelting the one by the other was adopted about 1836. The production of pig-iron increased from 54,000 tons in 1810 to 564,000 tons in 1850; but by that time Great Britain's production was almost three million tons, and the United States was importing thence iron, steel, and the manufactures thereof to almost twice the value of its own product. Little steel was produced in America before 1870, and the engineering trades were undeveloped. Typical iron manufactures of the period were nails, iron piping, and cast-iron air-tight stoves, which caused travelers as early as 1830 to complain of overheated American houses.

Textiles and iron do not exhaust the list of factory industries in the United States at this time, nor had mass production become a necessary condition of American industrial success. ' Their washing machines, refrigerators, rocking-chairs, all articles made of India rubber, are admirable,' wrote a visiting Englishwoman in 1846. Charles Goodyear had invented the vulcanization of rubber in 1839. Connecticut, in particular, was famous for small factories and workshops where specialized articles were produced by native ingenuity. The Colt revolving pistol and Winchester rifle were the result of Eli Whitney's invention and interchangeable parts for firearms. Connecticut tinware and wooden clocks were carried by Yankee pedlars far and wide. One of the most popular exhibits at the Crystal Palace in 1851 was the array of sewing machines and other ' Yankee notions.'

Of the many American industries that were still in the domestic
stage at this period, the most important was shoemaking, for which
no machine process of any importance was invented until 1850. In
New England it was a winter occupation of farmers and fishermen,
who, when the harvest was gathered, or the vessel hauled out for
the winter, formed a 'crew' to make boots and shoes in a neighborhood workshop, from stock put out by some local merchant. Every
man was master of his own time, and had something to fall back
on when demand slackened; there was no clatter of machinery to
drown discussion. A boy was often hired to read to the workers. It
was said that 'every Lynn shoemaker was fit to be an United States
Senator'; and one Henry Wilson the 'cordwainer of Natick' became Vice-President. The shoemakers of New York and Philadelphia, more hard-pressed than their Yankee brethren by the capitalist
and the immigrant, were pioneers in the first political labor movement in America.

XXV

LABOR, EDUCATION, AND EMANCIPATION
1825–1850

1. *The First American Labor Party*

ACTIVITY, growth, and expansion are only one side of American social history in this period. Playing in and out of the material forces, like summer lightning in heavy clouds, were spiritual currents, intellectual sparks, thunderbolts of radicalism: portents of that clear flame of emancipation that split the American firmament, and set its very stars a-rocking.

Most of these forces came from Europe, and their repercussion was felt in Europe. Almost every event in the early labor history of America followed similar occurrences in the British Isles. This may have been due to the same causes producing like effects: the industrial revolution came to the Northern states a generation later than to England. But when we reflect that thousands of skilled artisans were emigrating to the United States, that religious bodies like the Friends kept up a constant intercommunication, and that reformers like Robert Owen were flitting to and fro, it is difficult to believe that there was no conscious imitation. Conversely, English radicals of such different types as William Cobbett, Major Cartwright, Gibbon Wakefield, and Joseph Sturge, were heartened and inspired by American example; the six points of the People's Charter might have been selected from the established points of American democracy. Some day, it is to be hoped, this cultural field of Anglo-American relations may be as thoroughly explored as the diplomatic; and with more detachment.

The first labor movement in America, as in England, was initiated by urban handicraftsmen rather than factory operatives; but it took a different direction. Merchant-capitalists, in order to exploit the new western markets that the canals were opening up, were organizing trades, such as tailoring and shoemaking, on a larger scale, with a system of long credits, division of labor, and wholesale marketing, that drove small establishments out of business. The old-time master workman, who employed a few journeymen and apprentices, was degraded to a foreman or boss under an entrepreneur. Minute specialization broke down the apprentice system. With the introduction of gas in the cities, the old working hours of sun to sun were lengthened in the winter, making a twelve-hour day the year round.

Unions already existed in many of the handicrafts, but they had not yet received legal recognition; and the ranks of labor were so constantly diluted by immigrants and women [1] that the artisans were alarmed over their declining status. This was an old story in England; but the American workman had the vote. Manhood suffrage was established in every Northern state save Rhode Island by 1825. Three years later a group of Philadelphia artisans organized the Workingmen's party. The platform of this pioneer labor party had nothing to do with wages, everything to do with status: free public education, mechanics' lien laws to protect wage-earners from rascally contractors, and the abolition of imprisonment for debt. This last was a crying evil. Five-sixths of the prisoners in New England and the Middle States were confined for debt, the majority of them for sums under twenty dollars.

There have always been two great obstacles to political labor parties in the United States: social democracy and federal government. Opportunity for social betterment prevented the worker from becoming class-conscious. Westward pioneering was in the back of his mind in 1825, as is the new car today. The federal form of government made it both impossible and useless for the workers to gain control of Congress, which then claimed no power to enact social legislation. It was to the state governments that labor looked for the laws they wanted. Yet no party organized for purely state purposes could hope to survive as an independent unit, since ' voting the straight ticket ' — for the same party in national, state, and municipal elections — was becoming a fixed habit.

The most that a labor party could do was to wage a vigorous state campaign, and acquire enough strength to give it bargaining power with the Democratic party, whose hostility to banks made a point of contact. The Workingmen's party, with its moderate program of social betterment, was making fast progress in the cities of

---

[1] Although women were not generally employed in shops or in offices until after the Civil War, they were to be found in over a hundred different occupations in 1835, and had even attained trades such as printing, from which the unions later excluded them.

Pennsylvania and New York, when it fell into the hands of mal-practitioners.

Robert Owen was the earliest foreign radical who imagined that because America had achieved political liberty, she would be receptive to every form of libertarianism; who came to reform, and remained to scold. In 1825 he purchased a German Rappite settlement at New Harmony, Indiana, and experimented in a form of communism. His son Robert Dale Owen, a product of Van Fellensburg's famous school at Hofwyl, took it over. In two years' time New Harmony had become new discord, and Robert Dale Owen joined forces with Frances Wright (Madame D'Arusmont), a vigorous, short-haired Scotchwoman who had founded a community in Tennessee for the purpose of emancipating slaves. When that, too, came to an untimely end, Miss Wright became a lecture-platform apostle of woman's rights, free inquiry in religion, free marital union, birth control, and a system which she called 'National, Rational, Republican Education, Free for All at the Expense of All, Conducted under the Guardianship of the State,' apart from the contaminating influence of parents.

These 'Free Enquirers' had attracted much unfavorable attention from the Northern press in 1829, when the artisans of New York City, at the end of a hard winter of unemployment, organized a Workingmen's party for that state. Grateful for intellectual leadership, they eagerly accepted the aid of George Henry Evans, a young editor imbued with the agrarian ideas of Thomas Spence, and recently arrived from England. Evans was also an ardent admirer of Owen and Miss Wright, who promptly joined the workingmen in the hope of capturing their support for 'National, Rational Education.' To the consternation of conservatives, the 'Workies' polled thirty per cent of the total New York City vote in the autumn election. A press campaign at once began, hortatory towards the workingmen, denunciatory towards Miss Wright, the 'bold blasphemer and voluptuous preacher of licentiousness.' The printers' union repudiated this 'band of choice spirits of foreign origin,' and led a secession from the party, which promptly broke up. Such was American labor's first and typical experience with intellectuals. Small groups of the party then joined the Democrats, who rewarded them by obtaining a mechanics' lien law, and the abolition of imprisonment for debt, in New York State; and these reforms led the way to similar laws in other states.

In 1833, when a period of prosperity and increasing costs began, the American labor movement adopted contemporary British methods. Politics were abandoned in favor of trade organization, the closed shop, and the strike. Unionization was pursued so rapidly and widely as to include even seamstresses and cloak-makers. Trades' unions — federations of all the organized trades in a single community — were formed in twelve Northern cities; and in 1837 delegates from these cities organized a National Trades' Union. Strikes became frequent, and on several occasions included not only the organized workers but the unskilled laborers of an entire city. The ten-hour day was established in several cities for municipal employees, and in the navy yards in 1836 by order of President Jackson. Wages were generally improved, and conditions bettered. Harriet Martineau, visiting the Northern states at that time, took note of the well-nourished and intelligent ' dandy mechanic.'

Then came the panic of 1837, bringing unemployment and misery to the landless artisans. Wages fell thirty to fifty per cent, union funds were depleted, federations collapsed, and the ' dandy mechanics' were glad to sell their ' gay watch guards and glossy hats ' for a bit of bread. Iron years followed, with long hours and lean wages, of which the workers were often mulcted by payment in kind; years of sporadic, desperate strikes. The Lowell factory girls, speeded up by improved machinery, petitioned the Massachusetts legislature in vain to reduce their twelve-hour day to ten. Immigrants took their places, and by 1850 these show workers of America, with their white gowns and literary journal, were no longer found in the cotton mills.

2. A Contest of Utopias

All this convinced the American artisan, as the panic of 1825 had taught his English brother, that mere combination was futile at a moment of widespread trade depression. He also began to question the value of his vote. Jacksonian Democracy had smashed the monster Bank, but it could not supply bread and butter. As they were searching for the root of the trouble, American laborers were approached by eager, earnest idealists, each with his peculiar vision of a new world in which men and women might lead free and happy lives, neither exploiting nor being exploited. So instead of trying to assimilate and humanize this new industrial order, both workers and thinkers dissipated their energy in efforts to escape it.

Almost every known panacea was applied, with meagre or nega-tive results. Josiah Warren, the first American anarchist, devised a system of 'time stores' and 'labor notes,' inspired by the Owenite labor bazaars. During the period of unemployment many of the unions went in for producers' co-operation, others began consumers' co-operation about 1840; and from the mistakes and failures of these early efforts the later co-operative movement has learned much. Rob-ert Owen returned in 1845, to summon a 'World Convention to Emancipate the Human Race from Ignorance, Poverty, Division, Sin, and Misery.' The typical experiment of this period was some sort of association, or community. Emerson wrote Carlyle that any one you met in the street might produce a new community project from his waistcoat pocket. Brook Farm, the transcendentalist com-munity so happily described in Hawthorne's *Blithedale Romance,* became one of forty Fourierite 'phalanxes' in the Northern states. Cabet's *Voyage en Icarie* inspired several others, and there were many 'small, sour and fierce schemes,' one of which, the Mormon Church, achieved success. Like New Harmony, the associations of the forties solved nothing; but they gave friendship and creative joy to thousands of generous and sanguine souls, before acquisitive so-ciety sucked them back into its vortex.

Horace Greeley kept the columns of the New York *Tribune* hospitable to all these movements; but his best advice to the worker was: 'Go West, young man, go West!' Here was a point of contact with national politics. Public land at $2oo the quarter-section was not for those who needed it most, but for those who had the price, or for squatters who defied all comers to dislodge them. George Henry Evans and Horace Greeley insisted that every man had the same natural right to a bit of land, as to air and sunlight. 'Equality, inalienability, indivisibility' were Evans's three points: a free home-stead from the public domain to every settler; limitation of indi-vidual holdings; no alienation of the homestead, voluntary or other-wise. 'Vote yourself a farm' was his slogan.

The first free homestead bill was introduced in Congress in 1846 by Andrew Johnson, of whom we shall hear more. Northern Whigs and Southern Democrats combined to defeat it. In 1851 a *lex agraria,* limiting inheritance of land to 320 acres, passed a second reading in the Wisconsin legislature. But the average Western farmer and lawyer was a land speculator by nature. A 'very large and respect-able meeting' at Milwaukee protested against this 'Licinian law, repudiated by Rome over 2,000 years ago.' It would 'blast the fair name' of that 'free State, where no privileged class exists, where . . . no system of agricultural tenancy can ever find its way.' The bill did not pass, but in 1930, 40 per cent of the farms in the West North Central states and 62 per cent of those in the West South Central states were operated by tenants.

Yet, for all the paucity of results, the labor movement in America, whether political, collectivist, or revolutionary, received more public sympathy than in England, and met with less violence. If American judges found criminal conspiracy in trade union activities, their sentences were in the form of fines that were easily paid by labor sympathizers. And Chief Justice Shaw of Massachusetts, in the memorable case of Commonwealth *v.* Hunt (1842), declared that a trade union was a lawful organization, the members of which were not collectively responsible for illegal acts committed by individuals; and that a strike for the closed shop was legal.[2] Jefferson had so firmly grounded his ideals of a simple agrarian society that very many Americans still regarded as alien and hideous the new industrial order, which their descendants have come to reverence as an American institution. Yet, by the same set of ideas, the American of 1840 could not use government as an instrument for social purposes. He permitted industrialism to cut deeper even than in England. Farmers could not see why factory operatives should work shorter hours than themselves; and perhaps feared that their own 'hired men' would demand the ten-hour day. The only factory acts passed by the states before the Civil War related to the hours of child labor, and were inspired largely by a desire to give all children an opportunity for education. The first state provision for factory inspection came in 1867.

3. *Education, Scholarship, and Science*

The most tangible social gain during this period of ferment was in popular education. Since the Revolution education had been left largely to private initiative and benevolence. Secondary academies and colleges had been founded, and of these the South now had more than the North. But almost all these institutions charged fees. Ele-

[2] His first point became permanently established in American law; the principle of his second has been cut into by many legal decisions since the adoption of the Fourteenth Amendment.

mentary education, in which America now excels, was then the most neglected branch. Most of the Northern states had some sort of public primary school system, but only in New England was it free and open to all. In some instances a child had to be taught his letters before he was admitted to one of these schools, and in others only those pleading poverty were exempted from fees. In addition the Quakers and other philanthropic bodies maintained charity schools for the poor. Consequently a stigma was attached to free schools. In New York City, around 1820, nearly half the children went uneducated because their parents were too poor to pay fees, and too proud to accept charity.

Opposition to free public education came from people of property, who thought it intolerable that they should be taxed to support common schools to which they would not dream of sending their children. To this argument the poor replied with votes, and reformers with the tempting argument that education was insurance against radicalism. New York City in 1832, and Philadelphia in 1836, established elementary public schools free from the taint of charity; but the growth of public schools did not keep pace with the increase of population by birth and immigration. There were half a million white adult illiterates in the country in 1840; almost a million in 1850.

In the newer states, beginning with Ohio, frontier poverty was eked out by school funds, formed from the proceeds of public land granted by the federal Government in accordance with the policy of 1785. Most of these funds were mismanaged, all proved inadequate, and the older pioneers of the Kentucky breed had a positive prejudice against book-learning. As an excellent couple of this sort remarked to a Yankee pioneer in Illinois, they 'didn't think folks was any better off for reading, an' books cost a heap and took a power of time. 'Twant so bad for men to read, for there was a heap of time when they couldn't work out and could jest set by the fire; and if a man had books and keered to read he mought; but women had no business to hurtle away their time, 'case they could allus find something to do, and there had been a heap of trouble in old Kaintuck with some rich men's gals that had learned to write.' Indiana was leavened by New Harmony. Robert Dale Owen, who remained in the state, helped to convert the Hoosier population to free schools; and established free traveling libraries, boxes of good books which made the rounds of the villages until read to pieces.

In the New England states, where interest in 'book-larnin'' had lagged but never ceased, the earliest educational periodical, *The American Journal of Education,* was founded in 1826. There, the first problem was to make efficient the old colonial system. Free elementary schools, maintained by the townships and taught by birch-wielding pedagogues or college students in their vacations, were much in need of improvement. Horace Mann, a gifted politician who preferred the uphill work of reform to the applause of the Senate, sought efficient methods in Europe, and found them in Germany. Victor Cousin's report on Prussian education was translated and widely read in the United States, and its principles adapted to American needs, when Horace Mann became chairman of the Massachusetts Board of Education (1837). He and his able coadjutors combined the enthusiasm of Owen with an intellectual balance that brought permanent results. The first American school for training teachers was established at Lexington, Mass., in 1839. After a struggle with the older teachers, who insisted that mental discipline would be lost if studies were made interesting, the elementary school ceased to be a place of terror. New England also set the example in free public high schools; but until after the Civil War the majority of American pupils following a secondary course were in the endowed academies. It should be added that the principle of freedom in education was not impaired by the adoption of Prussian pedagogy; for the educational reformers took warning from the regimentation of opinion that they observed abroad. They neither tried to suppress church and private schools, nor to impose their views of science and history on teachers in the public schools. The first battles for academic freedom were fought in the colleges.

In higher education, this period saw an amazing multiplication of small denominational colleges — and a somewhat less surprising mortality among them. In 16 Eastern and Mid-Western states (both North and South) no less than 516 colleges and universities were founded before the Civil War; but only 104 of these were still in existence in 1929. Yale alone begat 16 Congregationalist colleges before 1861, and Princeton, 25 Presbyterian ones. These institutions were all privately endowed, in some instances by funds contributed directly by the churches. It was the heyday of the small, rural college with six to a dozen professors and one to three hundred students; of six o'clock chapel, prescribed classical-mathematical course, with chemistry and physics the most popular subjects next to Greek, and a smattering of French and German; 'philosophical apparatus,' mineralogical cabınet and collection of stuffed birds; Freshman metaphysics, Saturday recitations on Paley's *Evidences of Christianity* followed by dismal Puritan Sabbath, relieved by periodic religious revivals and tremendous drinking bouts; literary and debating societies encouraged, and Greek-letter fraternities discouraged by the faculty; well selected libraries of ancient and modern classics (Voltaire locked up); botanizing and fossil-hunting excursions over the countryside, ingenious hazing and amusing pranks, but no organized sports.[3] So long as a college education meant the traditional liberal arts and three philosophies no great equipment was necessary, and a school in the country where living was cheap could attract more students than an urban college, and almost as good teachers. During a good part of this period, Amherst, Dartmouth, and Union colleges had as many or more students than Harvard, Yale, and Princeton. The average statesman and professional man of the Northern states completed his formal education at a small college, whose curriculum in many instances was not equal to that of a first-class secondary school today. Foreign visitors compared these institutions with Oxford, Cambridge, or Göttingen, and laughed or sneered. But for an integrated education, one that cultivates manliness and makes gentlemen as well as scholars, one that disciplines the social affections and trains young men to faith in God, consideration for his fellow man, and respect for learning, America has never had the equal of her little hill-top colleges.[4]

In the same period the movement for public and secular state universities, which had begun just before the Revolution, received a new impetus, in part, from the founding of the University of Virginia.[5] The earliest of the Western state universities, founded at Detroit in 1817, as the 'Catholepistemiead or University of Michigania' with a Presbyterian minister from Princeton as president and incumbent of seven professional chairs, and the pioneer Catholic missionary Fr. Gabriel Richard as vice-president and occupant of the other six chairs. Such co-operation would have been inconceivable except on the frontier, and it was not long possible there. Despite

---

[3] A few gymnasiums were established by German teachers in the 1820's; but baseball, rowing and intercollegiate contests began only in the 1850's.

[4] Oberlin in Ohio became the first co-educational college in 1833, but had very few imitators. Wesleyan College in Georgia was the first college to give degrees to women. Mary Lyon established Mount Holyoke Female Seminary in Massachusetts in 1836, but it was some years before it offered a course of college grade.

[5] See next chapter, § 4.

the high-sounding title, this foundation remained a mere secondary school until 1837, when it was rechartered by the State of Michigan, and endowed with proceeds from the educational land reserves under the Territorial Ordinances of 1785 and 1787. As in other Western states, so much of this land was lost by squatters' claims and legislative chicanery that tuition fees had to be charged in the early days, and state appropriations sought later. The University was governed by a Board of Regents, nominated by the Governor of Michigan, with full powers to dictate courses, prescribe textbooks, hire and fire professors; powers which they delighted to exercise, and not notably to the advancement of learning — the first president who endeavored to establish professional schools and to emulate the standards of a German university was dismissed by the regents. The University of Wisconsin, second of the state universities to become famous, was founded at Madison in 1848, on a wilderness site crossed by Black Hawk's warriors only sixteen years before.

Harvard was the first of the older universities after the War of 1812 to feel the new spirit of progress; and the source of her inspiration was Germany. Between the years 1815 and 1820 four young Harvard graduates — George Ticknor, Edward Everett, Joseph G. Cogswell, and George Bancroft — travelled in Europe and studied at the Universities of Göttingen and Berlin. German universities were then in the first flower of their renaissance, leading Europe in almost every branch of learning. The young Americans admired the boundless erudition, critical acumen, and unwearied diligence of German scholars, marvelled at the wealth of the university libraries, and envied the *Lernfreiheit* or academic freedom which permitted even theological professors to challenge the bases of the state church; they returned with an ambition to transform their little brick colleges into magnificently equipped universities, dedicated to the service of science, scholarship, and truth. All four upon their return received posts at Harvard. Everett gave prestige, by his graceful delivery and easily worn mantle of scholarship, to the lecture method of instruction; Bancroft (whom we shall meet in Polk's cabinet) applied German thoroughness to early American history; Cogswell, who secured in Germany a valuable collection of *Americana,* is memorable in library history; and Ticknor remained professor of belles lettres long enough to establish a worthy school of Romance and Germanic languages, and to secure the principle that undergraduates might elect them as a substitute for traditional subjects. But Ticknor's standards were too high even for the oldest American university at that period, and he was unable to obtain provision for postgraduate study. With his successor, the gentle Longfellow, came reaction; but the general level of scholarship was raised, and under these great teachers (who were first of all scholars), receptive students like Emerson, Thoreau and J. R. Lowell, J. L. Motley and F. J. Child, were encouraged to hitch their wagons to the stars. And it was in part the influence of American scholars who had caught the flame in Germany, in part the liberal tendency of Unitarianism, that made Harvard, as early as the 1830's, a steadfast defender of the scholar's freedom from political and religious pressure.

The ideal that animated these educational reformers of 1820–40 was the same republican and aristocratic ideal of Jefferson. In his famous educational bill of 1779 Jefferson wrote:

it becomes expedient for promoting the publick happiness that those persons, whom nature hath endowed with genius and virtue, should be rendered by liberal education worthy to receive, and able to guard the sacred deposit of the rights and liberties of their fellow citizens, and that they should be called to that charge without regard to wealth, birth or other accidental condition or circumstance . . .

In other words, Jefferson and the Harvard reformers proposed to train an intellectual aristocracy — one selected for ' genius and virtue,' not anyone who had the ambition — to serve the Republic. And they proposed to do this in colleges and universities free from sectarian or political control, in order to give the scholar's mind free play. Jacksonian Democracy, on the contrary, affirmed that all men were born equal, envied intellectual pre-eminence, and preached the doctrine of equal educational privileges for all. The Northern American public cared nothing for academic freedom or for scholarship as such, and suspected that a liberal education made men enemies of democracy. What it wanted was a cheap education, conducted by clerical teachers, and directed toward the acquirement of information or skills that would be directly useful in the student's future occupation. Harvard, for instance, was criticized by the Massachusetts legislature because it did not help young men to become ' better farmers, mechanics, or merchants,' and paid professors fixed salaries, instead of so much for each student who attended their instruction. They had been reading that classic in democratic educational theory, *Thoughts on the Present Collegiate System in the United States* (1842) by President Wayland of Brown University, who in one of his official reports was to proclaim the dangerously attractive principle that 'every student might study what he chose, all that he chose, and nothing but what he chose' in college. Jefferson's idea was a liberal education for those who could profit by it, and the training of a few selected scholars; Wayland and democracy demanded vocational training for everybody.

There was, of course, a crying need for engineering and technical schools in a country so fast developing industry and transportation. The earliest effort to meet this need was the Rensselaer Polytechnic Institute, founded by the eighth patroon at Troy, N. Y., in 1824. It had a very comprehensive course of practical science, with equipment that included the first laboratories designed for students' use in this, or in any country; and the first class in civil engineering graduated in 1835. Before that, the only institution in the United States to offer an engineer's training was the Military Academy at West Point; and between 1835 and the Civil War, only three or four universities established engineering departments.

While many of the colleges of mid-century had high standards in the subjects they professed to teach — few college students of today would or could read the large assignments of ancient classics required of their forbears — the university law and medical schools of the period were hardly respectable. Yet the invention of the last century that has done the most to alleviate human suffering, the application of anaesthesia to surgery, was discovered independently by three graduates of American medical schools around 1842; and sulphuric ether was first used in a surgical operation at Boston in 1846.[6] And, just as Jefferson wished to live as the founder of a university, so Dr. O. W. Holmes, author of *The Autocrat of the Breakfast Table,* considered his best title to fame the discovery in 1843 that puerperal fever could be prevented by the use of antiseptics.

Adults were not neglected in this educational awakening. In all the cities and larger towns mechanics' institutes provided vocational courses and night schools. Free public libraries were very generally established. In towns, and even villages, the Lyceums offered popular lectures, scientific demonstrations, debates, and entertainments. The Lowell Institute for public lectures on literary and scientific subjects was brilliantly inaugurated at Boston by Silliman in 1839,

[6] See *Dictionary of American Biography,* sketches of Crawford W. Long, Charles T. Jackson, W. T. G. Morton, and John C. Warren, for the discussion of priorities and claims.

and led to similar foundations in other cities. The reading habit was greatly aided by mechanical improvements in printing, which made possible the penny press, one-sixth the former price of the average daily paper. The New York *Tribune,* Baltimore *Sun,* and Philadelphia *Ledger* began as penny newspapers in the forties. They were by no means rowdy sheets like the scandalous New York *Herald,* but journals of information, including pirated English novels in serial form; and the *Tribune,* under Horace Greeley's editorship, became a liberal power of the first magnitude.

By 1850, then, there had been formulated, and to some extent established, the basic principles of American education today: (1) that free public primary and secondary schools should be available for all children; (2) that teachers should be given professional training; (3) that all children should attend school up to a certain age, but not necessarily the free public school, religious and other bodies having complete liberty to establish their own educational systems, at their own cost; (4) that a liberal higher education, and professional training schools for law, medicine, divinity, and engineering be provided, largely for paying students. Huxley's test of a national system, ' a great educational ladder with one end in the gutter and the other in the university,' was satisfied, but the research function of modern universities was hardly yet thought of. The public elementary schools of 1850 were generally superior to the private schools of 1820. Yet these reforms were in method and expansion rather than in spirit. Richard Price's exhortation to the American schoolmasters of 1785, to ' teach *how* to think rather than *what* to think,' was frankly ignored in the numerous academies and colleges under sectarian control, and imperfectly apprehended in the public schools and universities, unless by teachers who had received a spiritual rebirth from transcendentalism.

Natural science made great progress in the North in the generation after 1830. Audubon had to visit England in order to obtain subscriptions for his classic *Birds of America* (1827), but he was acclaimed a hero on his return. While Harvard shone with literary lights, Yale and Princeton were distinguished by the teaching of two great men of science, Benjamin Silliman and Joseph Henry. Silliman, appointed to a new chair of chemistry and natural history at his alma mater in 1802, at the age of 23, required many years of self-training to reach full stature. In 1818 he founded and edited the first American scientific periodical, *The American Journal of Science and Arts;* in 1830 he published *Elements of Experimental Chemistry,* one of the

first American scientific textbooks; in 1835 he delivered a series of
lectures at Boston on geology which (pious Congregationalist though
he was) made the first important dent on the Biblical theory of
creation. A year or two later the Rev. Edward Hitchcock, a science
professor of Amherst College who had already directed the geological survey of Massachusetts, discovered dinosaur tracks in the red
sandstone of the Connecticut valley: a new proof of the antiquity of
life on this planet. These men were leaders among hundreds of
science teachers and lecturers who opened up new vistas to the public
as well as to college students. But there was no American of the
period whose positive contribution to science equalled that of Joseph
Henry. The son of a Scots day-laborer, born in Albany and struggling for an education, Henry began experiments with the magnet in
1826, which led to the discovery, independent of Michael Faraday's,
of magneto-electricity, basic to the telegraph and the telephone. In
1832 Henry was called to the College of New Jersey at Princeton,
which he left in 1846 to become the first director of the Smithsonian
Institution at Washington.

This earliest American foundation for scientific research was established by a bequest of over £100,000 — greater than the then en-
dowment of any American university — from an Oxonian, a British
chemist named James Smithson, ' to the United States of America,
to found at Washington . . . an Establishment for the increase and
diffusion of knowledge among men.' Calhoun and other strict con-
structionists opposed the acceptance of the gift, but, largely owing to
the efforts of John Quincy Adams, it was accepted in 1838, the fund
invested, and the Institution organized. Congress, it appears, expected the Institution to comprise a library, art museum, and collection of scientific curiosities that would amuse congressmen and their
friends; it was at Henry's insistence, and owing to his great reputation no less than to his wise and tactful administration, that the
Smithsonian became an indispensable agency for the financing and
wide distribution of knowledge on original researches in the various
fields of natural and anthropological sciences. The American Association for the Advancement of Science, founded in 1847, was another
important step in organizing scientific teaching and research; and the
Harvard Astronomical Observatory, founded by subscription in 1843
and within three years equipped with the world's largest refracting
telescope, set a precedent for research foundations in American universities.

The very year that Henry became director of the Smithsonian,

Louis Agassiz left his native Switzerland to lecture before the Lowell Institute of Boston. From his first public appearance, it was evident that America had found a leader in natural science who was at once an original investigator, a great teacher, and one who could appeal to the popular imagination. He was promptly secured for the chair of zoölogy and geology in the new scientific school at Harvard, at once began gathering material for a museum of comparative zoölogy, organizing geological and biological exploring expeditions, corresponding with amateur naturalists in all parts of the country, writing his great *Contributions to the Natural History of the United States,* and training teachers of science. Although his Harvard colleague Jeffries Wyman did more profound work in comparative anatomy, no American, native or adopted, was Agassiz's equal in stimulating both popular and scholarly interest in that segment of natural science which stretched from biology to palaeontology.

4. *Transcendentalism and Literature*

Just as the Virginia galaxy of political theorists was flickering to a close, the same revolutionary spirit that inspired them lighted a new constellation in a higher latitude. The year 1836, when Emerson published his essay on *Nature,* may be taken as the focus of a period in American thought corresponding to 1776 in American politics.

Transcendentalism is the name generally given to this manifestation of the revolutionary spirit in the Northern states between 1820 and 1860. It may be defined as an intellectual overtone to democracy, a belief in the divinity of human nature. The new spirit appeared in some men as intense individualism, in others as a passionate sympathy for the poor and oppressed. It gave to Hawthorne his deep perception of the beauty and the tragedy of life, to Walt Whitman his robust joy in living. Transcendentalism touched the labor movement on its revolutionary side, the anti-slavery movement on its positive side; it inspired the majority of American men of letters who flourished between 1820 and 1860; and almost every aspect of it may be found in Emerson, who perfectly embodied the essential spirit, a belief in the soul's inherent power to grasp the truth. Historically speaking, transcendentalism was a movement to liberate America spiritually, as independence and democracy had liberated her politically; an attempt to make Americans worthy of their independence, and elevate them to a new stature among the mortals.

It may have been a mere accident that this outburst of intellectual activity occurred largely within a fifty-mile radius of Boston, during a single generation. Transcendentalism has been called the inevitable flowering of the puritan spirit; but puritanism does not necessarily bear blossoms, and the fruit thereof is often gnarled and bitter. In New England, however, the soil was conserved by a bed-rock of character, mellowed by two centuries of cultivation, and prepared by Unitarianism. The puritan ministers in and about Boston had by 1800 almost converted their congregations to a more liberal faith than Calvinism, when Boston Federalism checked the flow of sap, fearful lest it feed flowers of Jacobin red. There was just time for a gorgeous show of blossom and a harvest of wine-red fruit, between this late frost and the early autumn blight of industrialism.

Unitarianism and her sister Universalism took a great weight off the soul of New England. Longfellow's *Psalm of Life* which seems so trite nowadays,

> Life is real! life is earnest!
> And the grave is not its goal;
> Dust thou art, to dust returnest,
> Was not spoken of the soul.

came as a message of hope to thousands of young people reared in the fear of everlasting damnation. Yet something was lacking in mere Unitarianism. A faith in the essential goodness of human nature might be a theological counterpart to democracy; but it failed to supply the note of mysticism that democrats no less than aristocrats seek in religion.

The historical function of Unitarianism in America was to pave the way for transcendentalism, and to liberate the minds of the well-to-do; to provide a church for rationalists. That church has been prolific in men of letters and reformers. But its direct influence did not go wide of the New England settlements, or deep even within them. Holmes's 'One-Hoss Shay' was a symbol of the sudden crumbling of Calvinism; but Calvinism collapsed only in eastern Massachusetts. Congregationalists, Presbyterians, Methodists, and Baptists howled down the Unitarians as atheists, and maintained their hold on the masses. The immigrants, with some notable exceptions among the Germans, remained loyal to Catholicism or to other old-country faiths, and the Episcopal churches were of social value largely as a refuge. Harvard fell into Unitarian hands as early as 1806; but Yale clung to the five points of Calvinism, and some of the little western offshoots of Yale became centers of obscurantism, like the Presbyterian colleges of the South. Even at Harvard the odor of brimstone lingered.

Emerson in 1832, at the age of twenty-nine, laid down his pastoral office in the Unitarian church because it no longer interested him. In his next four years of reading and travel, he found God again in nature; and settled down as 'lay preacher to the world' in the placid village of Concord, typical of New England in that it contained a small group of sanguine, wide-reading men and women, exceptional in harboring during one generation Emerson, Hawthorne, Thoreau, and the Alcotts.

If Jefferson was the prophet of democracy, Emerson was its high priest. Both believed ardently in the perfectibility of mankind; but Emerson knew what Jefferson never learned, that free institutions would not liberate men who were not themselves free. His task was to induce Americans to cleanse their minds of hatred and prejudice, to make them think out the consequences of democracy instead of merely repeating its catchwords, and to seek the same eminence in spirit that they had reached in prosperity. He founded no cult and gathered no disciples, because what he said did not come from any wish to bring men to himself, but to themselves.

Of the Concord group, Henry Thoreau was the best classical scholar, and the most independent of classical modes of thought. Concord for him was not only a Selborne, but a microcosm; and his revolt was not against a dying church, but against a society so confident and vigorous that it could afford to ignore him. His genius was little appreciated in his own country until our own times, when he would not be allowed to enter as an immigrant. Hawthorne of Salem, later a sojourner in Concord, wrote tragedies of New England life that penetrate to the core of all human life.

In these three men, Emerson, Thoreau, and Hawthorne, and in Herman Melville, the New England that had slowly matured since the seventeenth century justified herself. Immigration then diluted and industrialism dissolved a society that had made such men possible. New England ceased to be a state of mind, and became a mere group of states.

In the meantime, the Dennie and Brockden Brown literary group at Philadelphia had died, and the 'Knickerbocker School' was declining in New York. Bryant's collected poems, most of them written more than a decade before, appeared in 1832, and his last spurt of poetical activity ended in 1844; during the remaining forty-six years of his life Bryant was a leading figure in American journalism as editor of the New York *Evening Post*. Washington Irving's *Sketch Book* appeared as early as 1818; seven years later he turned to Spain for inspiration, and to history for expression; returning to New York a literary hero, he visited the West for material; but his *Astoria* and *Adventures of Captain Bonneville* lack the fresh, authentic flavor of Francis Parkman's *Oregon Trail* (1849). For the rest of his long life, Irving was content with the rôles of diplomat, host, and sage. James Fenimore Cooper's Leather-stocking and sea tales appeared in the 1820's, after which he embarked on a crusade to put everybody right both in England and America, and succeeded in making himself the most unpopular person in the English-speaking world. *The Knickerbocker Magazine,* founded at New York in 1833, was the leading literary periodical in America until the *Atlantic Monthly* was born in 1857. It published the poetry and prose of budding and established writers belonging to all parts of the country; and, more than any other magazine of the age, acquainted the American people with the wealth and variety of their own literature. ' Old Knick,' as devoted readers called the magazine, did not take himself solemnly like the *North American Review,* and the reformers thought him regrettably frivolous; he went in for a little of everything except politics — poetry, science, short stories, humor, musical and dramatic criticism, western travel — so long as it was American; and in a single number could boast contributions from Irving, Cooper, Bryant, Fitz-Green Halleck, Longfellow, Whittier, and Lewis Cass.

The New England intellectuals had more to say than their New York contemporaries, but they too conveyed it in traditional forms. ' We all lean on England,' wrote Emerson. Not until 1851 did a distinctive American literature, original both in form and content, emerge with *Moby Dick*. Four years later, with Emerson's blessing, *Leaves of Grass* began to sprout. Walt Whitman, half Yankee, half New York Dutch, had grown up outside the ambit of New England respectability, in direct and intimate contact with the crude realities of American life. In the ' barbaric yawp ' that has so deeply influenced the poetry of today, Walt Whitman sang the common American and his life in seaport, farm, and frontier.

Walt Whitman was the poet of democracy, but Professor Longfellow was democracy's favorite poet. The American people, when they read poetry, wished to be lifted out of themselves by verses that rhymed or at least scanned, into a world of romance and beauty. Especially the American woman, who derived little satisfaction from the activity of her partner, and was beginning to dream dreams of her own. Mostly she took the line of competitive display, which only forced her husband to quicken his pace; but partly she turned to the old world for advice. Hence the feminine stamp to American culture.

Hawthorne and Whittier and Longfellow felt that craving themselves, and filled it for others: Hawthorne by his *Marble Faun* and *Wonder Book* of classical myths, Whittier and Longfellow by creating legends from early American history, Longfellow especially by popularizing Old World stories, and translating Dante. The music of his verse was tuned to catch the ear of a busy and unlearned people. Longfellow, ' poet of the mellow twilight of the past,' as Whitman called him, ' poet of all sympathetic gentleness — and universal poet of women and young people,' had more influence on his generation than any American man of letters save Emerson.

5. Humanitarianism and Abolition

' It was a day ' wrote John Morley ' of ideals in every camp. The general restlessness was intense among reflecting conservatives as among reflecting liberals. . . . A great wave of humanity, a great wave of social sentiment, poured itself among all who had the faculty for large and disinterested thinking.' The decades of the thirties and the forties were years of social unrest and intellectual ferment. The zeal for social and humanitarian reform left scarcely any phase of American life untouched. Emerson has described it with a quaint combination of amusement and tender sympathy in his *New England Reformers:*

But some there were, high-flying souls filled with the new wine of this idealism, to whom the reality of ideas appeared to require that immediate effect should be given to their ideas; and failing this that they should refuse all participation in an order of things which they could not approve. There was an indefinite hope, and there was an assurance that all particular mischiefs were speedily coming to an end. . . . What a fertility of projects for the salvation of the world! One apostle thought all men should go to farming; and another that no man should buy or sell; that the use of money was the cardinal evil; another that the mischief was in our diet, that we eat and drink damnation. These made unleavened bread, and were foes to the death of fermentation. . . . Others assailed particular vocations, as that of the lawyer, that of the merchant, of the clergyman, of the scholar. . . . Others devoted themselves to the worrying of churches and meetings for public worship. . . . With this din of opinions and debate, there was a keener scrutiny of institutions and domestic life than any we had yet known, and there was sincere protesting against existing evils, and there were changes of employment dictated by consciences. . . . A restless, prying, conscientious criticism broke out in unexpected quarters. Who gave me the money with which I bought my coat? Why should the professional labor and that of the counting-house be paid so disproportionately to the labor of the porter and the wood-sawyer? Am I not a too protected person? Is there not a wide disparity between the lot of me and the lot of thee, my poor brother, my poor sister?

This 'restless, prying, conscientious criticism' led to a wide variety of reforms. Throughout the Northern States, as well as Maryland and Kentucky, imprisonment for debt was abolished and the rigors of prison life were softened. Whipping was outlawed in most of the states, although by no means stamped out; flogging was abolished in the navy in 1850, owing largely to the influence of Dana's *Two Years Before the Mast*. Public and private charitable institutions multiplied. The untiring efforts of reformers like Dorothea Dix removed the insane from jails and outhouses and placed them in asylums. Samuel G. Howe, after fighting for Greek independence, returned to America with ambitious plans for the education of the blind, which were largely realized. Elihu Burritt tried to capitalize the new tenderness for his world peace movement, without much success, while William Ladd projected a plan for an international court that anticipated by eighty years the Hague Tribunal. More popular was the brisk campaign against demon rum, undertaken by certain evangelical sects. The prohibitory laws that were passed proved premature; but their educational work did considerably modify the drinking habits of the people. Agitation for woman's rights culminated in the Seneca Falls Convention of 1848 and a Declaration of Sentiments couched in the phraseology of the Declaration of Independence.

Of all these humanitarian and reform movements, the one that shook the Union to its foundation sought the abolition of slavery. An earlier anti-slavery movement, offshoot of the American Revolution, won its last victory in 1807 when Congress passed an act against the slave trade. The Quakers kept up a mild and ineffectual protest, while the cotton gin was creating a new vested interest in slavery; and in 1820, as we have seen, an effort to stay the westward advance of slavery was defeated by the admission of Missouri.

The older generation of Virginia statesmen, foreseeing the tragedy of 1861, endeavored in vain to arouse their people. Few Virginians or indeed Americans would contemplate emancipation, unless at the same time they could get rid of the colored population. Free negroes were felt to be a nuisance and a menace throughout the United States. Most of the Northern states had severe laws against their immigration; most of the Southern states allowed benevolent masters to free their slaves only on condition of removing them. Yet the cotton states gagged at emancipation, even when sweetened by compensation and deportation.

The American Colonization Society, supported largely by slave-owners of Virginia, Maryland, and Kentucky, proved that this last method was practical on a small scale. In 1827, after ten years of private effort, the Society sought a congressional appropriation towards colonizing negroes in Liberia, a part of which had already been purchased by the Society. All the northernmost tier of slave states passed favorable resolutions, but the cotton states prevented anything being done. The Georgia Legislature resolved that ' not only the retention, but the increase of the slave population ' was essential to their welfare: that the colonization project was ' wild, fanatical and destructive.' They had only remained silent hitherto under the impression that the Society's object was ' limited to the removal beyond the United States of the *then* free people of color and their descendants, and none others.' Limited in resources, and attacked by extremists from both sides, the Colonization Society could do little to solve the problem, although that little was well done. By 1831 it had returned to Africa only 1420 negroes, about as many as were born into slavery in the United States every four months.

When Jackson became President in 1829, moral suasion against slavery appeared to have spent its force. Apathy could hardly have been more complete, when on 1 January 1831, the first number of the *Liberator* appeared in Boston, printed on borrowed paper with borrowed type, by William Lloyd Garrison. On the first page he announced:

I shall strenuously contend for the immediate enfranchisement of our slave population. . . . On this subject I do not wish to think, or speak, or write, with moderation. . . . I am in earnest — I will not equivocate — I will not excuse — I will not retreat a single inch — AND I WILL BE HEARD.

Therein spoke the Old Testament, not the New. Garrison had less in common with Emerson than with Stonewall Jackson. He was all contradiction: a fighting pacifist, an aggressive non-resistant who spurned politics as a means, but employed language that made impossible the peaceful attainment of his ends. Garrison's policy was to hold up the most repulsive aspects and exceptional incidents of negro slavery to the public gaze; to castigate the slaveholders and all who defended them as man-stealers, torturers, traffickers in human flesh. He would recognize no rights of the masters, acknowledge no color problem, tolerate no delay.

Blackguarding the slaveholders would have made few converts in the South at any time, but least of all at that time. The Nat Turner slave insurrection, in which over fifty whites were murdered, occurred in August 1831. Prominent Southerners at once asserted that the *Liberator* was responsible, and demanded that the Northern States, if they valued the Union, should suppress this incendiary agitation.

Every effort short of press censorship was made in the North to satisfy the South on this point. Garrison wrote that he ' found contempt more bitter, opposition more stubborn, and apathy more frozen ' in New England than among slave-owners themselves. The workmen, especially the Irish laborers who competed with free negroes, broke up abolition meetings, with the warm approval of the respectable press. A ' broadcloth mob ' of business men forced Garrison on one occasion to seek safety in the Boston jail. One abolitionist was murdered in Illinois; few dared to cross the Ohio, or the Mason and Dixon line. Northern gentlemen like Wendell Phillips who joined the cause were black-balled at clubs and forsaken by their friends. Northern ministers who showed sympathy with them lost their pulpits. Philanthropists who established schools for colored children were hampered with lawsuits, or deterred by force. Yet the sect grew, and throve on opposition. In 1836 there were more than five hundred abolition societies in the Northern states, and by 1840 their membership was over 150,000. Whittier's pen was already consecrated to the movement: presently James Russell Lowell would lend his gift of satire.

Just as Wilberforce was called hypocrite by the English radicals, so Garrison was denounced by the American associationists and other reformers for his singleness of aim, his assumption that slavery was the great evil. What boon would freedom be to the slave, they asked, if obtained without due preparation on his part, or his master's? What use to abolish chattel slavery if wage slavery were left? To which the abolitionists replied that there could be no social reform in a nation that held one-sixth of its people in bondage, that the evils of slavery touched every one in the land, that white labor could never be secure until slave labor was abolished. It took over twenty years to induce the northern working people to see the point. The fear of black equality was stronger than a sense of slave competition.

Garrison inspired more than he led. The American abolitionists included very different sorts of people. Many Quakers of Pennsylvania, some of them old enough to remember John Woolman, recovered their antique zeal in this new cause. Denied the use of the public rooms in Philadelphia, they built themselves a hall, only to lose it by arson a week after completion. William Jay, son of Chief Justice Jay, and the Tappan brothers of New York, gave their wealth and sacrificed their social comfort to support the cause in that state, where no cause could long keep out of politics. It was they who or-organized the Liberty Party, to nominate James G. Birney, a converted Alabaman slaveholder, for the Presidency in 1840. The middle-western abolitionists founded at Oberlin one of the first American colleges that welcomed negroes; they elected Joshua R. Giddings, the first abolitionist Congressman, and did the most effective work in aiding slaves to escape from bondage. All the abolitionists saw eye-to-eye on the principle of immediate uncompensated abolition; and many received negroes as equals at their meetings and in their houses. Most of them repudiated Garrison's extreme methods, and only a few followed him in denouncing the Constitution and advocating a Northern secession. But it was the editor of the *Liberator,* mild in manner and soft of voice, yet driven by a fierce passion for righteousness to write words that cut and burned, who personified this new and dreadful force to the entire South.

Owing perhaps to their Quaker connection, the abolitionists preceded other reformers in permitting women to address their meetings and serve on committees. Lucretia Mott of Philadelphia, and the Grimké sisters, gentlewomen of South Carolina who freed their slaves and came north to obtain freedom of speech, were counted among the leaders. Frederick Douglass, an escaped slave of remarkable mental powers, was the first of several fugitives who wrote or dictated their memoirs. There was a close connection also with the English abolitionists. Garrison visited England in 1833, just in time to meet the dying Wilberforce; and twice again in the forties. But an address signed by Daniel O'Connell, Father Mathew, and seventy thousand Irishmen, enjoining their fellow countrymen in America to love liberty and hate slavery, was received with contumely by Irish-Americans who never failed to respond to anti-British appeals from that quarter. Yet this constant intercourse and mutual aid led to a sort of English-speaking union between humane and liberty-loving persons in each country.

Excepting that lonely fanatic John Brown, no abolitionist attempted to incite a slave insurrection; but every abolitionist took part in a conspiracy of evasion. The ' grape-vine telegraph ' carried news to the blacks of an ' Under Ground Railroad ' to liberty. The very few slaves who had the courage to strike out for freedom would take cover in the woods or swamps near their master's plantation until the hue and cry was over, then follow the North Star to Mason and Dixon's line, or the Ohio river. Once across, the ' U.G.' took them in charge. They were transferred from one abolitionist household to another, hidden by day in cocklofts or haystacks or shocks of Indian corn; piloted by night through the woods, or concealed in farm wagons; sometimes driven in a Friend's carriage, disguised in women's clothes and a deep Quaker bonnet. Others were smuggled north by sea, and made their way into Canada through the New England states. The total number of slaves thus rescued was not large, and their proportion to the total slave population was infinitesimal: about three one-hundredths of one per cent in 1850. Yet if measured by the stimulus it gave the abolitionist cause, and the rage it aroused in the breasts of Southern slaveholders, the ' Under Ground ' was a brilliant success.

Conducting the ' U.G.' was dangerous business. Pursuit was often hot and ruthless, the pursuers had the law on their side even where opinion was against them. In the southern, pro-slavery counties of Indiana and Illinois, men suspected of harboring runaways were apt to have their houses burned, their persons tarred and feathered. Without the manly zest and generous adventure that the ' U.G.' afforded, the cause of emancipation might well have languished for want of sap. Fugitive slaves, moreover, gave the abolitionists a handle to work both on public opinion and on the Federal government. One cringing black produced at a public meeting made more converts than hours of oratory and bushels of tracts.

By a federal statute of 1793, a master or his agent who caught a runaway in a free state, could repatriate him forcibly after swearing to his identity before a magistrate. A professional slave-catcher whom the right nigger eluded was apt to conclude that ' any nigger ' would answer. Kidnapping became so frequent that Pennsylvania (1825) and other Northern states passed ' personal liberty laws ' to protect their free colored citizens. The abolitionists cleverly turned the local resentment against kidnapping, and the Northern dislike of domineering Southerners, into a public opinion against the return of genuine fugitives. A plain duty to sister states became a shameful truckling to the ' slave power ' as Whittier presented it:

> We hunt your bondsmen, flying from Slavery's hateful hell;
> Our voices at your bidding take up the bloodhound's yell;
> We gather, at your summons, above our fathers' graves,
> From Freedom's holy altar-horns to tear your wretched slaves!

Gradually the personal liberty acts were strengthened to a degree that made a runaway's identity almost impossible to establish. The Supreme Court invalidated a Pennsylvania law of that description in 1842. But if the states had no right to obstruct, by the same token they had no obligation to assist the federal authorities; [7] and without such assistance the slave-catchers began to receive the attention of mobs, more often than abolitionists. A runaway from Virginia was forcibly rescued from his captors in Boston in 1843, and his freedom purchased by a popular collection. The abolitionists for the first time voiced a popular sentiment, when Whittier declared:

> No slave-hunt in our borders — no pirate on our strand!
> No fetters in the Bay State — no slave upon our land!

Southerners played into the abolitionists' hands by stifling criticism of slavery when they had the power, and by demanding its suppression where they had not; for Northerners who were indifferent to slavery, and disliked negroes, still valued freedom of speech, of the press, and of petition. In 1835 Abolition began to influence

---

[7] Prigg v. Pennsylvania; an important principle in American constitutional law, apart from the slave question.

national politics, when a Quaker meeting petitioned the Senate to abolish slavery and the domestic slave trade in the District of Columbia. Washington was then a point for shipping blacks from Virginia and Maryland to the cotton states. Even from the windows of the Capitol one could watch coffles of slaves marching by, to the music of clanking chains. Why, as Henry Clay inquired, should Northern members 'be outraged by a scene so inexcusable and detestable' ? Because the slave states felt that Washington was a strategic outpost of their principles, to be held at all costs. Senator Calhoun declared that any intermeddling with slavery in the federal district would be ' a foul slander on nearly one-half the states of the Union'; and all such petitions were rejected. Other abolitionist petitions, not always so limited in their scope, came pouring in on the House, which at the insistence of the Southern members passed the 'gag resolution,' a rule to the effect that all petitions having to do with slavery, whether within or without the legislative competence of Congress, be laid upon the table.

Ex-President Adams, then a member of Congress, was not an abolitionist; but the gag rule awakened in him memories of Stuart tyranny. It was a thing to be resisted in its prime, like taxation without representation. Session after session he fought for the right of petition, using his deep knowledge of parliamentary practice and rich resource in harsh and bitter eloquence. Every attempt short of personal violence was made to silence, to censure, or to expel Adams; but the tough old puritan persisted. The Northern States finally forced their representatives to support him, and in 1844 the gag rule was abandoned. It made no difference to the slaves. But on the day when the news reached South Carolina, the leading Whig newspaper of Columbia discontinued printing instalments from Washington's Farewell Address, and substituted an appeal for secession.

How, then, shall we estimate the abolitionists? Their sincerity and courage is no longer denied by friend or enemy; of their wisdom no enemy was ever convinced, and many friends are now doubtful. Channing predicted in 1835 that Garrison had only succeeded in stirring up ' bitter passions and a fierce fanaticism which have shut every ear and every heart against arguments.' Yet, as one of his followers answered Channing:

We are not to blame that wiser and better men did not espouse . . . the cause of our oppressed, colored countrymen. . . . We Abolitionists are what we are — babes, sucklings, obscure men, silly women, publicans, sinners, and we shall manage this matter just as might be expected from such persons as we are.

Certain it is that they closed every avenue to emancipation save civil war: their means almost defeated their end. Abolition came in spite of the abolitionists rather than because of them; and in the worst way. But could it have come in any other way? Garrison broke a great conspiracy of silence. His indignant pity seared the Northern conscience with the image of a slave cowering under his master's lash — but at what cost in hatred, bloodshed, and uncharitableness!

Three generations have elapsed since the thirteenth federal amendment destroyed chattel slavery on United States soil. We now know that the slavery question was but one aspect of a race and class problem that is still far from solution. The grapes of wrath have not yet yielded all their bitter vintage.

XXVI

THE COTTON KINGDOM
1820–1850

1. *The Land of Cotton*

COTTON was king in almost every aspect of Southern life from 1815 to 1861; and the principal bulwark of his throne was slavery. Almost sixty per cent of the slaves in the United States, in 1850, were employed in growing cotton. Like rice, sugar, and tobacco, it was a plantation crop, requiring continuous attention of a sort that the most ignorant negroes were well able to perform. In 1820 the cotton crop of one hundred and sixty million pounds was already the most valuable Southern interest. Meeting a constantly increasing demand, it rose to twice as much in 1830, and more than doubled in the next decade. By 1850 it had passed a thousand million pounds; and the crop of 1860 was almost twenty-three hundred million pounds in weight, and in value two-thirds of the total exports of the United States.

This enormous increase in production was brought by a rapid extension of the cotton-growing area. Like typical pioneer farmers, exploiters rather than conservers of the soil, the cotton planters advanced from South Carolina and Georgia across the 'black belts' and Indian cessions of Alabama and Mississippi, occupied the great valley up to Memphis, pushed up the Red river of Louisiana to the Indian Territory, and passed the boundary of Mexico into Texas eating the fat of the land and leaving devastation behind. On the march King Cotton acquired new subjects: moneyed immigrants from the North, ambitious yeomen who purchased a slave or two on credit, and might with good luck become magnates. But for the most part the pioneers of the Southwest disliked the planters, who in turn accused the poor-white 'crackers' and 'hill-billies' of exchanging moonshine whisky with the slaves for stolen goods. In every region fit for cotton, the richest lands were sooner or later absorbed by planters. Hunter folk moved westward, yeomen farmers were forced into the poorer lands, and a shiftless and vagabond class of 'pore white trash,' afflicted with the hookworm disease and despised alike by master and slave, closed in on pine-barren, gullied hillsides and abandoned field. Some of the best minds of the South endeavored to arrest this process by scientific methods of agriculture; but so long as good land remained plentiful and cheap, whether within the United States or adjacent under feeble sovereignty, the cotton planters preferred their own ways. Abandoned farms later became as common in New England as in the South, and in part for the same reason: western competition. Slavery merely hastened the process by the opportunity it afforded for large-scale exploitation; and there were few industries in the South to take up the slack.

Sugar planters of Louisiana and the tobacco planters of Kentucky were allies of the cotton kingdom; the border slave states were tributary provinces, supplying labor, food, and mules; and much of the plantation revenue found its way to the Northern centers of banking and manufacturing. North Carolina, a state where little cotton was grown, remained an enclave of antique republicanism in the new monarchy; western Virginia and the mountainous regions of Kentucky and Tennessee were Northern salients. Kentucky had the most varied agriculture of any of the slave states; her people were a fine blend of the old West with the older Virginia. Eastern Virginia could no longer profitably employ her dense slave population on depleted land, and many a tobacco or wheat plantation was maintained only through the sale of surplus negroes. Her economic decrepitude was a spiritual loss to the nation. The Old Dominion squirearchy, which once had led the progressive thought and statesmanship of the United States, now devoted itself to sustaining a hopeless cause.

Cotton plantations differed greatly both in size and character. Absenteeism was frequent in the lower South, although hardly the rule outside the bottom lands between Vicksburg and New Orleans. Many a show plantation of the older South, where visitors were received with lavish hospitality and impressed with the happy life of devoted blacks, was supported by latifundia in the newer South. One of the better sort in Mississippi, described by Olmsted, covered several square miles. The mansion house, which the owner had not seen for two years, was four miles distant from the nearest white neighbor. The cleared portion, about fourteen hundred acres, was tilled by a plough-gang of thirty men and a larger hoe-gang, mainly women, who were encouraged by a black driver with whip in hand. Enough corn and pork were usually raised to feed the cattle and the

135 slaves, who included three mechanics, two seamstresses, four teamsters and cattle-tenders, a midwife, and a nurse who had charge of a pickaninny crèche. The overseer maintained a pack of hounds to hunt runaways. He kept the field hands working from sun to sun, but gave them most of Saturday as well as Sunday off, except in the picking season. They cut their fuel in the master's woods, and were allowed to make boards for sale in their free time. Everywhere in the South slave families were given allotments on which they could raise vegetables and poultry to eke out the rations of corn and pork, or even cotton for sale to the master.

A 'middle-class plantation,' which did not produce enough surplus to enable the owner to travel or reside elsewhere, would have four hundred to one thousand acres under cultivation, and ten to forty slaves. A planter of this class might be a younger son, a self-made pioneer, an ex-overseer, or a professional man using his plantation to enhance his dignity in the community. In few instances did he enjoy comforts or amenities superior to those of the poorest sort of farmers in the North: a bare house without conveniences, a diet largely of 'hog and hominy,' no literature but a weekly paper, no diversion but hunting, and an occasional visit to the county seat. That sort of planter belonged to the governing class, and had things much his own way in Alabama, Mississippi, and Arkansas. Like most Americans of the time, he distrusted other parts of the country than his own, and held the rest of the world in hearty contempt. Although division of labor was most effective on plantations with fifty to one hundred slaves, virtually half the cotton crop was made by small farmers with one to half a dozen slaves. Mark Twain describes 'one of these little one-horse cotton plantations' in *Huckleberry Finn*:

A rail fence round a two-acre yard; a stile, made out of logs sawed off and up-ended, in steps, like barrels of a different length, to climb over the fence with, and for the women to stand on when they are going to jump on to a horse; some sickly grass-patches in the big yard, but mostly it was bare and smooth, like an old hat with the nap rubbed off; big double log house for the white folks — hewed logs, with the chinks stopped up with mud or mortar, and these mud-stripes had been white-washed some time or another; round-log kitchen, with a big, broad, open but roofed passage joining it to the house; log smoke-house back of the kitchen; three little log nigger-cabbins in a row t'other side the smoke-house; one little hut all by itself away down against the back fence, and some outbuildings down a piece the other side; ash-hopper, and big kettle to bile soap in, by the little hut; bench by the kitchen door, with a bucket of water and a gourd; hound [1] asleep there, in the sun; more hounds asleep, roundabout; about three shade-trees away off in a corner; some currant bushes and gooseberry bushes in one place by the fence; outside the fence a garden and a watermelon patch; then the cotton fields begin; and after the fields, the woods.

On a first-class plantation, with improved implements, healthy negroes, strong mules, and a competent overseer, ten acres of cotton and ten of corn could be cultivated per able-bodied field hand. On rich soil, with a proper division of labor, five bales (two thousand pounds) or more of cotton per field hand could be produced; but a more nearly average figure, in the Carolina and Georgia Piedmont, would be twelve hundred pounds. The average annual price of middling upland cotton at Liverpool fluctuated between 11 and 17½ cents a pound from 1820 to 1840, fell to 8 cents in 1845–48, rose to 14 in 1850, and averaged about 12 cents until the Civil War. Of course a planter was lucky to get half the Liverpool price for himself; the rest was consumed by transportation, brokerage, and interest on advance-money.

Once entangled in the meshes of the system, no planter could escape it, and few wished to. Slaves were the only available labor for large-scale production by men of capital, but their cost absorbed an inordinate amount of capital. The most expensive sort, a ' prime field hand ' 18 to 25 years old, was worth $500 in 1832, whence the price rose to $1,300 just before the panic of 1837. The same ' buck nigger ' who brought $650 in 1845 at the age of eighteen, sold readily for $1,000 when five years older; and the price of this class of slave reached $1,800 on the eve of the Civil War. Infant mortality was so high on cotton-plantations that the labor supply had to be replenished by purchase, and land was always wearing out; hence the profits that on a Northern farm would have been invested, or spent on better buildings and more comforts, in the South went into more land and more slaves. Even the planters most opulent in nominal wealth found it difficult to keep out of debt, and the poorer depended on the money-lender for maintenance between crops. That is why the system was uneconomical even for large plant-

---

[1] ' Hound ' in the Southwest means a mongrel. As the Missouri anthem has it:
It makes no difference if he is a houn',
You gotta stop kickin' my dawg aroun'.

ers in the long run; and for yeoman farmers the first cost of labor became prohibitive.

2. *The Slave*

As for Sambo, whose wrongs moved the abolitionists to wrath and tears, there is some reason to believe that he suffered less than any other class in the South from its 'peculiar institution.' The majority of slaves were adequately fed, well cared for, and apparently happy. Competent observers reported that they performed less labor than the hired man of the Northern states. Their physical wants were better supplied than those of thousands of Northern laborers, English operatives, and Irish peasants; their liberty was not much less than that enjoyed by the North of England 'hinds' or the Finnish *torpare*. Although brought to America by force, the incurably optimistic negro soon became attached to the country, and devoted to his ' white folks.' Slave insurrections were planned — usually by the free negroes — but invariably betrayed by some faithful darky; and trained obedience kept the slaves faithful throughout the Civil War.

Between a Virginian slave major-domo, whose ancestors had been American for two centuries, and a Carolina rice hand, who might have been smuggled over from Africa within a year, there was an immense gap. Topsy and Tom Sawyer's nigger Jim were nearer to the average childlike, improvident, humorous, prevaricating, and superstitious negro than the unctuous Uncle Tom. Many were quick at picking up trades, and became skilled artisans who were hired out by the month or year; nor are we much impressed by the complaint of a planter that his slave bricklayer would lay but one thousand bricks per day. Occasionally a humane owner would allow such a one to purchase his freedom out of his earnings; but the laws made this increasingly difficult. American, as contrasted with antique slavery, offered no legal escape to the talented or intellectual slave; it subjected a writer like Frederick Douglass or a born leader of men like Booker T. Washington to the caprice of a white owner. his inferior in every respect save pigment. A Virginian planter wrote in 1819 that overseers ' in these days are little respected by our intelligent negroes, many of whom are far superior in mind, morals, and manners to those who are placed in authority over them.' And one drop of African blood made anyone a negro.

While the average Englishman or American disliked the negro

as negro, Southern slave-owners understood him as slave; Southern gentlemen still love him ' in his place.' There was no physical repulsion from color in the South. White children were suckled by black mammies, and played promiscuously with the pickaninnies. In a stage-coach or railroad car, as a squeamish abolitionist observed, ' a lady makes no objection to ride next a fat negro woman, even when the thermometer is at ninety degrees; provided always that her fellow travellers understand she is her *property.*' There was a great difference between one region and another, even between one plantation and another, in the treatment of slaves; and everywhere the house servants fared better than the field hands. In central Mississippi, Olmsted passed a plantation owned by a ' very religious lady ' who worked her slaves from half-past three every weekday morning, frequently until nine at night, and alternately catechized and whipped them every Sabbath. But a few days before he had stopped with the jolly owner of twenty slaves who had not been ' licked in five year,' who taught one another to read, who swung their master's hoes to their own languid cadence, and shared his dinner ' right out of the same fryin'-pan.' In every part of the South a small slaveholder worked side by side with his men in the field, and treated them like his own children, as indeed they sometimes were. But if he rose to planter's estate, that sort of thing became undignified. Just as the apprentice sank to *proletaire* when his master became *entrepreneur,* so woolly-headed Uncle Daniel, who had learned to read the Bible in the log cabin with old massa's children, moved into slave quarters when young massa built a mansion.

Flogging with the rawhide or blacksnake whip was the usual method of punishing slaves. Imprisonment lost the master their time, and short rations their health. Although the law forbade cruelty, a master or overseer was not often brought to book for it, since a negro's testimony was not received against a white man; and the abolition agitation created a feeling in the South that the white man must always be right. A slave had rather less chance for redress at that period than a seaman against his Yankee skipper, or an enlisted man in the army against his officer. Severity pushed too far was apt to turn the slaves into runaways, if not into dead men; and a live negro was a valuable piece of property. Yet the most civilized communities need societies for the prevention of cruelty to children and animals. It was an old plantation maxim ' never to threaten a negro, or he will run.' Consequently, little time elapsed between detection

and a punishment which was not softened by reflection. Few travelers in the lower South failed to report instances of cruelty.

The feature of slavery that most outraged humane feelings was
the separation of families by private sale or auction. It was often
asserted in defense that negroes had a very slight family attachment;
that Whittier's *Farewell of a Virginia Slave Mother,* with its haunting refrain:

> Gone, gone, — sold and gone
> To the rice-swamps dank and lone,
> From Virginia's hill and waters:
> Woe is me, my stolen daughters!

was mere abolitionist cant. Yet when a young Northerner asked
John Randolph of Roanoke to name the greatest orator he had ever
heard, the old Virginian snapped out: 'A slave, Sir. She was a
mother, and her rostrum was the auction-block.'

Since colonial days there had been in the lower South a system
of night patrols to prevent slaves roaming about at night and getting
into mischief. The Denmark Vesey insurrection at Charleston (1822)
caused this system to be extended to the free negroes as well; and
the upper South organized night patrols after the Nat Turner insurrection of 1831. Abolitionist agitation caused a general tightening
up of black codes. A free negro who left his state was not allowed
to return, for fear he might bring pernicious doctrines; and for the
same reason it became a misdemeanor to teach a slave to read. As
a Carolina magistrate wrote, 'Such laws look to me as rather cowardly. It seems as if we were afraid of our slaves.' The free negroes
fared worst under this regime of fear; a Georgia law of 1859
even allowed them to be sold into slavery for a violation of city ordinances.

If we overlook the original sin of the slave trade, there was much
to be said for slavery as a transitional status between barbarism and
civilization. The negro learned his master's language, received his
religion, and accepted his moral standards. In return he contributed
much besides his labor — rhythm and humor for instance — to
American civilization. Unfortunately the South, after 1830, ceased
to regard slavery as transitional, and began to look upon it as a positive good and a permanent basis of society. That it could not be,
in a world growing more tender of human rights, without artificial
bulwarks that only the North could build; without banners and emblems of prestige which the North must respect.

3. Southern Society

Slavery and cotton preserved in the South a rural, almost feudal, society.[2] The old Anglo-Virginian contempt for merchants still prevailed. Agriculture, the army, the church, and the law were the only proper careers for a planter's son. Northern and European merchant-bankers and shipowners handled the cotton crop, and took most of the profits. Shopkeepers in the market towns were often Yankees, Germans, or Jews. There were few factories; for capital was tied up in slaves, who produced greater profits by growing than by spinning cotton. William Gregg's experiments with native white labor were successful, but few Southern capitalists were bold enough to follow his example. European immigrants, who in this era came from Northern countries, shunned a region where manual labor was regarded as 'nigger's work,' and where the warm climate made adjustment difficult. Railway development was slow, for the relatively sparse population of the uplands was largely self-sustaining, and cotton afforded freight traffic during a brief season of the year. The main roads in Kentucky, Virginia, and the Carolinas were considerably improved, and provided with decent inns; but west and south of these states one followed the usual pioneer sloughs and trails. Frontier conditions still prevailed through the greater part of the lower South in 1850, combined with a turbulence and ignorance that seldom lingered in the Northern frontier beyond the first generation.

Michigan and Arkansas were admitted to the Union together, in 1836.[3] The constitution of Michigan prohibited slavery. The consti-

---

[2] The following statistics roughly indicate the social classes in the South as a whole (including the District of Columbia), and in the cotton states (South Carolina, Georgia, Florida, Alabama, Mississippi, Louisiana, Arkansas, and Texas), in 1850:

	All Slave States	Cotton States
Number of slaveholding families	347,525	154,391
Number of families owning 1 to 9 slaves	255,258	104,956
Number of families owning 10 to 49 slaves	84,328	43,299
Number of families owning 50 or more slaves	7,939	6,144
White population	6,242,418	2,137,284
Free negro population	238,187	34,485
Slave population	3,204,077	1,808,768

Century of Population Growth, p. 136; J. D. B. De Bow, *Statistical View of the U. S.* (1854), pp. 45, 63, 82, 95, 99. Slaveholding families are counted more than once if they owned slaves in different counties.

[3] At the time they were admitted to the Union, Arkansas and Michigan had approximately the same population. The following statistics from the Census of 1850, show comparative growth.

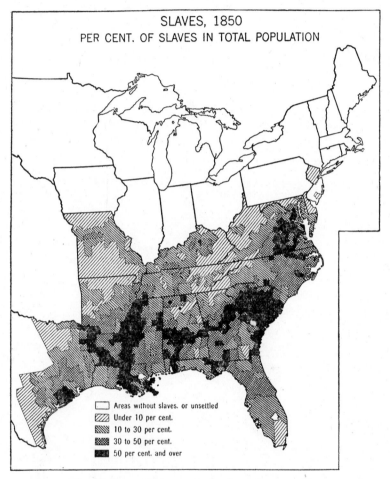

Proportion of Slaves to Total Population, 1850

From Charles O. Paullin, Atlas of the Historical Geography of the United States, *Plate* 68A

tution of Arkansas prohibited the legislature from tampering with slavery. The first Michigan legislature created a university, at Ann Arbor. The first Arkansas legislature was remembered for a fatal brawl, when the Speaker of the House came down from his chair and slew a member with his bowie-knife. This was, to be sure, only the ugly side of the rollicking, rough-and-tumble society so well described by Augustus B. Longstreet in those parts of the South where there was no gentry to set the tone. It was a society that made admirable soldiers, as the North shortly learned; but poor citizens, as the South has since learned to its cost. ' Bleaseism,' a recent brand of poor-white politics named after one of the breed that led it to power, was part of the price the South has paid for the cultivation of cotton and the neglect of men.

Theology, which had been neglected in the South when the section was liberal and anti-slavery, was much cultivated after it became conservative and pro-slavery. The influence of the evangelical sects among the planters increased in proportion as their ministers found pro-slavery arguments in the Bible. The Catholic and Episcopalian Churches remained neutral on the slavery question, and stationary in numbers. Thomas Jefferson, dying, saluted the rising sun of Unitarianism as destined to enlighten the South; but it sent only a few feeble rays beyond the Mason and Dixon line. Horace Holley, the gifted young Unitarian who had made of Transylvania Uni-

	Arkansas	Michigan
White population	162,189	395,071
Free colored population	608	2,583
Slave population	47,100	0
Number of colleges	3	3
Number of pupils in colleges	150	308
Number of public schools	353	2,714
Number of pupils in public schools	8,493	110,455
Income of public schools from taxation	$250	$88,879
Total income of public schools	$43,763	$167,806
Number of academies	90	37
Number of pupils in academies	2,407	1,619
Number of adult white illiterates	16,819	7,912
Value of farms and plantations	$15,265,245	$51,872,446
Number of newspapers and periodicals . . .	9	58
Circulation of newspapers and periodicals . . .	7,250	52,718
Number of public libraries	1	280
Volumes in public libraries	250	65,116
Number of churches	362	399
Value of church property	$89,315	$723,600

The student must beware, however, of reading too much out of these statistics. Even had slavery been abolished in 1830, conditions would probably have been approximately the same.

versity in Kentucky a southern Harvard, was driven from his post by the Presbyterians. Priestley's old friend Thomas Cooper, who had taken refuge in the South from the anti-Jacobin spirit of the North, was promised by Jefferson the first chair of chemistry in the University of Virginia; but Cooper was a Unitarian, and the Virginians raised such an outcry that he resigned. Later, in spite of his services to the state-rights cause, Cooper was ' tried ' for atheism, and ejected, at the age of seventy-five, from the presidency of the University of South Carolina.

The Presbyterian joined the Episcopalian sect as a fashionable church; Methodists and Baptists enjoyed successive revivals among the poor whites and colored folk. For a time these churches were a bond of union between North and South; but when the Northern Methodists unreasonably insisted that a Southern bishop emancipate slaves which he had inherited and could not conscientiously get rid of, the Southern members seceded and formed the Methodist Church South (1844). The Baptists followed, and doubled their membership in fifteen years. While these Southern evangelicals condoned slavery, they banned card-playing and dancing; by 1860 the bastard puritanism of the age was more prevalent in Alabama and Mississippi than in Massachusetts and Connecticut. It was in the ex-slave states that theology would make its last stand against biology, in the twentieth century.

The finest product of the plantation regime was the Southern gentleman. Numbering but few, the gentry ruled the older Southern states by virtue of personality even more than property, and governed them honorably and efficiently, although not with enlightenment. Discriminatingly hospitable, invariably gracious to women, endowed with a high sense of personal honor and civic virtue, they yet lacked the instinct for compromise that, time and again, has preserved the English aristocracy from annihilation.

Of this ruling class, only a small fraction belonged to the eighteenth-century aristocracy of Maryland, Virginia, and the Carolinas. The supreme type of colonial gentleman that Washington was appeared undiminished in his Lee kinsmen; but the old Huguenot families of Charleston were declining, and the Creoles of Louisiana were easygoing and unambitious. Apart from these three persistent types, the mass of the greater planters, in 1850, were self-made men like Jefferson Davis, whose parents had lived in log cabins. If not well educated themselves, their sons and daughters were. The South, despite poverty in elementary education, had good secondary schools, especially of the military type, and more students in college than the North.

Life on a resident plantation of the better sort was neither sordid as the abolitionists asserted, nor splendid as the novelists have depicted it. The mansion house, seated on a rising bit of ground, was generally a well-proportioned wooden building of neo-classic style, with a columned portico or veranda that gave dignity to the front elevation and afforded shade to the ground floor and first story. The rooms, seldom more than fifteen in number, were high-ceiled and simply furnished. There were plenty of flowers, although negro gardening was by no means thrifty; and masses of native flowering shrubs and creepers such as the Cherokee rose, in which the South-land was rich. Simplicity rather than ostentation was the dominant note in the planter's life. His recreations were the wholesome ones of the English country gentry, but he enjoyed little leisure. On a Virginia plantation visited by Olmsted, not ten consecutive minutes elapsed, even during dinner, when the proprietor was not importuned by his slaves. He must lock his stables every night as the alternative to finding his horses hag-ridden in the morning, and rise at dawn to unlock them. Even if an overseer were employed to direct the field force, the owner's wife must keep linen, silver, food, and household supplies under lock and key from the pilfering house-servants, must serve out supplies with economy, and admonition with tact; must bind up wounds, and nurse the sick. Mrs. Ann R. Page of Virginia devoted her life to the welfare of her slaves, ran heavily into debt to avoid selling their increase, and when, at her husband's death, the property had to be divided, she sat apart in her room praying that none might fall into alien hands. Yet even Mrs. Page had to put up with meals an hour late, with tasks undone and orders forgotten, with prevarication and sluttishness. And the hearts of Southern mothers were wrung by knowledge of the temptations to which their growing boys were exposed.

Such a life was a continuous exercise of tact, self-control, and firmness; yet the condition of unlimited power over a race with exasperating habits was a constant temptation to passion. The sort of bluster which was considered gentlemanly in the eighteenth century was accentuated by these conditions, at a time when smoother and more reticent manners had become the mark of good breeding in England and the North. The Southern gentleman had the same conflicting character as a Russian or Hungarian landlord. He would tolerate an amount of shirking and evasion that would drive any Northern employer frantic; but cross his will or question his authority, and you found the Tartar. An outburst of temper was a sign of high mettle, not a mark of poor breeding. Duelling was frequent, and not all disputes between gentlemen were settled on the 'field of honor.' Alexander H. Stephens of Georgia was unable to take part in the political campaign of 1848 because disabled by stabs received in an 'affray' with Judge Cone. Southerners in Congress made great efforts to master their passions, not always with success. When Senator Foote of Mississippi invited Senator Hale of New Hampshire to visit his good state, and promised him 'that he could not go ten miles into the interior before he would grace one of the tallest trees of the forest, with a rope around his neck, with the approbation of every virtuous and patriotic citizen; and that, if necessary, he himself would assist in the operation,' Northerners might be pardoned for wondering whether gentleman and bully were not synonymous terms in the South.

4. Education and Science

Free popular education made little progress prior to the 1850's, when Wiley of North Carolina and Yancey of Alabama inaugurated reforms which were rudely interrupted by the Civil War. Meantime, the ruling classes were well served by tutors, academies and colleges. The University of Virginia (1825), the South's greatest contribution to American education, was the last flowering of Jeffersonian liberalism rather than the seed of new growth; the partial realization of a comprehensive scheme for public education, for which Jefferson had been striving since 1779. The essence of Jefferson's experiment was a division of the curriculum into eight vertical ' schools,' some (such as law and medicine) corresponding to modern faculties, others (such as chemistry), to departments; and allowing every student to elect one or more, each school granting its own degree. Jefferson insisted that the university be non-sectarian, and proposed to import distinguished European scholars to set standards equal to those of the German universities. But his generous ambition was thwarted by factors over which he had no control — the miserably inadequate support ($15,000 a year) granted by the state, so that each ' school ' in practice became a one-man department; the jealousy of older colleges and hostility of evangelicals to a ' Godless ' university; the poor preparation of Southern students and their frolicsome manners — horsewhipping unpopular professors, and fighting bowie-knife duels among themselves. After a few years, the University of Virginia was better staffed, organized, and patronized, and for liberal education and professional training in law it became one of the leaders. But the South as a whole remained faithful to the eighteenth-century type of liberal arts college. Frederick A. P. Barnard (the future President of Columbia University) in 1854 investigating the situation at the University of Alabama, where he was then a professor, found no demand for a university of the Virginia type. The people did not want intellectual discipline for their sons; their idea of a university was a place to study whatever you liked, without any particular preparation.

In this respect the average Southerner and Northerner saw eye-to-eye; so also in the matter of natural science. It was not geology but the clash of orthodox with liberal theology that ousted liberals like Holley and Cooper, and limited Jefferson's choice of professors. In the South there was the same curiosity about natural phenomena as in the North, but lack of urban centers made for fewer lyceums, natural history societies, and popular scientific lectures. There was the same amateur botanizing and compiling of herbaria, the same fossil hunting and mineral collecting among young people; and in Charleston some of the gentry contributed to the advancement of science: men such as Edmund Ravenel the pioneer conchologist, and his cousin Henry W. Ravenel the mycologist. It was at Charleston that Audubon met the Rev. John Bachman, who collaborated with him in the *Quadrupeds of North America*. Louis LeConte, a Georgian planter, returned from education at Columbia College with a passionate enthusiasm for science; setting up a chemical laboratory and a botanical garden at his plantation, he was rewarded by two sons, John and Joseph, who became eminent in biology, medicine, and geology in the decade before the Civil War. Several Southern states began geological surveys (not all finished them), and Edmund Ruffin's work on soil chemistry, first published in Virginia in 1832, did much to bring back to fruitfulness the worn-out tobacco lands of the Tidewater. New Orleans made few scientific gestures; but despite a cultural bond with France, the country then pre-eminent in natural sciences, the intellect of New Orleans largely found vent in sprightly journalism. It was in part the strength of the genteel tradition, in part intense individualism, that made for so few scientific achievements in the Cotton Kingdom; feeble and ephemeral ' academies ' of the eighteenth-century type were founded, rather than research foundations, museums, and scientific schools.

5. *The Literature of Chivalry*

The ' Southern chivalry ' tradition was created in the generation of 1820 to 1850. In *Ivanhoe* and the flood of imitative literature that followed, the cotton lord and his lady found a romantic mirror of their life and ideals. Someone remembered what the Washingtons and Lees had forgotten, that certain Virginia planters were descended from Stuart refugees, who forthwith were adopted as ancestors by the entire South. Every owner of ten negroes, however dubious his origin or squalid his existence, became a ' cavalier,' entitled to despise the low-bred shopkeepers, artisans, and clerks of the North. We should ill begrudge this romantic compensation to an isolated, almost beleaguered people, had it not fed an unwholesome pride and dangerous insolence. What the South wanted was a Cervantes; what it got was fake romance.

To comprehend the psychology of the Southern planter, we must remember that his social system was on the defensive against the North, and indeed the civilized world. All his bluster and proud assertiveness was the sign not of confidence but of fear. It was fear, not insensibility, that made him indifferent or hostile to the new tenderness that was dissolving the harsher social relations in England and the Northern states. Just as New England in 1800 refused every quickening current from France or Virginia, for fear it might bear the seeds of Jacobinism; so the South, a generation later, rejected a literature and philosophy which might conceal abolition. At a time when Bryant, Longfellow and Whittier were redeeming Northern materialism with cheerful song, Southern silence was broken only by the gloomy and romantic notes of Edgar Allan Poe; it was a Pennsylvanian, Stephen C. Foster, who attuned the beauty and pathos of the old South to the human heart in ' Uncle Ned,' ' Old Black Joe,' and ' My Old Kentucky Home.'

The most distinguished and prolific man of letters of the Cotton Kingdom was William Gilmore Simms of Charleston, and of 'Woodlands,' Barnwell county. Bryant encouraged him and Harper's of New York published the ten romances that he wrote between 1834 and 1842, including the famous *Guy Rivers* and *The Yemassee,* one of the best American historical novels ever written. In one year he published no less than 22 magazine articles, and at all times he was grinding out better verse than any Southerner save Poe; but Charleston society could not forget that Simms was not to the manner born, and failed to support the literary quarterly that he founded. For a decade Simms deserted fiction for slavery apologetics, hack histories, and biographies glorifying South Carolina. In the 1850's he produced another cycle of romances on the Revolution in the South; yet the recognition of his fellows was always wanting. In the North letters had become a recognized road to fame and fortune; historians like Bancroft, Prescott, and Irving, novelists like Cooper and Hawthorne, poets like Whittier and Longfellow, earned consideration and applause; a philosopher at large like Emerson and a poet-journalist like Bryant achieved a warm and satisfactory contact with the educated public in the North and West. But a Southerner (as Professor Trent has written)

had to think in certain grooves, or else have his opinions smiled at as harmless eccentricities. His imagination was dwarfed because his mind was never really free, also because his love of ease rarely permitted him to exercise the faculty. . . . The models before him were those of statesmen and men of action, and he lost his chances for distinction if he proposed to himself any others. Besides, he had no critics, no audience whose applause was worth having. His easy verses were received with a smile by his friends or with extravagant praise by an editor only too glad to fill his columns. When praise was so readily obtained, he naturally took the easiest way to obtain it.[4]

In the last few years before the war, Simms played the Dr. Johnson to a young literary group in Charleston, some of whom were destined to go far: Paul Hayne and Henry Timrod the lyric poets, and Hugh Swinton Legaré, jurist and scholar. Yet in 1858 Simms could write:

All that I have [done] has been poured to waste in Charleston, which has never smiled on any of my labors, which has steadily ignored my claims, which has disparaged me to the last, has been the last place to give me its adhesion, to which I owe no favor, having never received an office, or a compliment, or a dollar at her hands; and, with the exception of some dozen of her citizens, who have been kind to me, and some scores of her young men, who have honored me with a loving sympathy and some-

---

[4] William P. Trent, *William Gilmore Simms,* pp. 147–148.

thing like reverence, which has always treated me rather as a public enemy, to be sneered at, than as a dutiful son doing her honor.[5]

The literary output of the Southern people, from 1830 to the Civil War, was permeated by pro-slavery apologetics. Newspapers and periodicals, religious and secular, were filled with articles on slavery, and almost every public question was brought to that touchstone. Sermons, lectures, speeches, and discussions in literary societies, revolved about the general theme. 'Indeed, a survey of the literature of the period produces the impression that the entire produce of the collective mind of the South was colored by this one absorbing interest.'[6] It has been claimed that the South was driven to defend slavery as a reaction against that intemperate criticism of it by the abolitionists that began in 1831. On the contrary, the 'positive good' theory was an outgrowth of the 1820's, antedating the Garrisonian propaganda.[7] Thomas Cooper, President of South Carolina College, published his first pro-slavery pamphlet in 1826. Governor Stephen D. Miller struck the keynote of the next thirty years in a message to the South Carolina legislature of 1829: 'Slavery is not a national evil; on the contrary, it is a national benefit.' The growth of this feeling, clashing with Northern agitation for abolition, resulted in the suppression of criticism of slavery in the South. Northern mails were seized upon and censored. Ministers, teachers, professional men, and politicians who would not bow down to mumbo-jumbo were eliminated. Laws were even passed against criticism outside the South of Southern institutions, and a price was placed on the heads of prominent abolitionists. Bishop Moore of Virginia ' spoke of the certainty of an abolitionist being lynched, not indeed as a thing he approved, but without any expression of moral indignation.' The 'cavalier' blood of Moncure Daniel Conway did not save him from being hustled off Virginian soil when he returned there from Harvard a Unitarian and an abolitionist.

Conviction and denial was not enough. What the ruling class wanted was some positive pro-slavery theory of society corresponding to the political doctrine of state rights. Thomas R. Dew, a bright

---

[5] Trent, Simms, p. 239.

[6] William S. Jenkins, Pro-Slavery Thought in the Old South (Chapel Hill, 1935), p. 90.

[7] The debate on slavery in the Virginia legislature of 1830–31 was at bottom a sectional struggle of Valley and Western Virginia against the slaveholding sections, and had no reference to the Liberator. C. H. Ambler, Sectionalism in Virginia (Chicago, 1910), pp. 185–200.

young Virginian who returned from study in Germany to a chair at William and Mary College, did much to lead opinion in Virginia to the position that the lower South had already reached. In a pamphlet of 1832, he proved that slavery had been the condition of classical culture, that the Hebrew prophets and St. Paul admitted its moral validity, that civilization required the many to work and the few to think. William Harper of South Carolina worked out the corollaries of these propositions, while hundreds of clergymen undertook to prove it ' God's law that fetters on black skins don't chafe.' George Fitzhugh, in a tract entitled *Cannibals All* showed the negro to be something less than man, and in his *Sociology for the South* provided a new set of principles to replace the ' glittering generalities' of a century of enlightenment. John C. Calhoun gave pro-slavery doctrine the sanction of his name and character, and so cunningly combined it with American prepossessions that slavery appeared no longer the antithesis, but the condition, of democracy.

Calhoun began with the axiom that no wealthy or civilized society could exist unless one portion of the community lived upon the labor of another. White wage-earners, class-conscious in England and enfranchised in the Northern states, were threatening property and civilization. Chartism, agrarianism, and trade-unionism proved that social stability could not be maintained where labor was free. It was too late to re-establish serfdom in Europe and the North. But to the South a mysterious providence had brought a race marked by God with mental and physical inferiority, created to be hewers of wood and drawers of water for His chosen people. In return, kind masters provided for all reasonable wants of their slaves, and saved them from the fear of misery and destitution that haunted the white proletariat. The masters themselves, relieved from manual labor and sordid competition, would reach that intellectual and spiritual eminence of which the founders of the Republic had dreamed. ' Many in the South once believed that slavery was a moral and political evil. That folly and delusion are gone. We see it now in its true light, and regard it as the most safe and stable basis for free institutions in the world.'

Such was the doctrine that most educated Southerners accepted between 1830 and 1850, because it was what they had unconsciously come to believe. It harmonized with the facts of their existence as Jeffersonian democracy had never done. Yet it is doubtful how wide or deep the new faith really went. It was never accepted by those Virginian planters who fought so valiantly for the Confederacy. There was no place in the system for poor whites, from one of whom, Hinton R. Helper, came the first prophecy of disaster. Even the planting class did not accept the logical deduction that the slave trade should be reopened. Even Calhoun, more humane than his doctrine, refused privately to condone the domestic slave trade, although he might publicly threaten that the South would secede rather than have it forbidden in Washington. The non-slaveholding and illiterate whites continued to dislike slavery, but they agreed with the planters that it would never do to emancipate the slave, for the South must be kept a ' white man's country.' It is a grave error to suppose that profits dictated all this valiant if feverish defense of slavery. The South did not view the institution in terms of economics but as a social issue. Continued enslavement of the blacks was the only possible way to maintain white supremacy. ' In the very coil of negro complications,' as Carlyle wrote, they knew no way out.

Just as the new imperialism of 1763 had created a self-conscious unity in the Thirteen Colonies, so the new abolitionism of 1831 created self-conscious unity in the thirteen slave states. In both instances there was a basic social unity, which wanted only political passion to become nationalism. Just as the Seven Years' War made England less tolerant of colonial autonomy, so industrialism, westward expansion, and humanitarianism made the Northern states less tolerant of a ' slave power ' within their democratic empire. It was not inevitable in 1850 that Southern society would take a nationalist form: but the prospect of any other result was dubious. The Southern ruling class might be brought to face facts. They might learn to diversify their economic life, and look forward to a gradual extinction of slavery. English ruling classes have done as much, again and again: but English ruling classes were never isolated, or in a position to seek a way out by secession. By 1850 the cotton kingdom, closing in on itself, had excluded every means of saving reform, and had resolved to make negro slavery, in an ever-widening radius, a permanent basis of society.

XXVII

WHIGS AND DEMOCRATS
1837–1844

1. *Party Machinery*

NATIONAL politics long concealed the growing divergence between North and South. Churches might split, social differences might deepen, and extremists revile one another; but, so long as the Whig and Democratic parties remained national in scope, the Union was safe. The nature of a political system that not only postponed disunion but survived it is a matter of some consequence to American history.

After forty years' growth party organization acquired in the Jackson era a settled character. In contrast to its British prototype, which exists normally in a single plane for electing members of Parliament, the American party became tri-dimensional, functioning not only in federal but in state and municipal elections. Analysis of the Whig and Democratic parties and their successors reveals a bundle of local, sectional, and class interests. Their cross-sections, instead of displaying a few simple colors, were a jig-saw puzzle of radicalism and conservatism, nationalism and state rights, personal loyalties and local issues. Party strategy was directed towards accumulating as many bundles as possible; and statesmanship was the art of finding some person or principle common to all the bundles that would make them forget their differences and in union find strength.

Constitutional developments in the states were quickly reflected in the national party organization, as new sectional interests, during the era of good feelings, had thwarted or transformed national party policy. State constitutional changes between 1830 and 1850 tended towards government of, for, and by the people. They continued the process which began during the War of Independence, but which, so far as the Eastern states were concerned, came to a halt about 1790. Religious tests and property qualifications for office were generally swept away, and manhood suffrage adopted. The newer state constitutions, beginning with that of Mississippi in 1832, transferred many offices from the appointive to the elective class. County officials such as sheriffs and justices of the peace, heads of executive departments such as the state treasurer and attorney-general, even judges of the higher courts, were now elected by the people; and the democratic principle of rotation limited both the number and the length of their terms. Furthermore, these constitutional changes were effected in almost every instance by the democratic method initiated by Massachusetts in 1780: a popularly elected constitutional convention, with a popular referendum on the result. The most noted statesmen were elected to the state conventions, the people took a keen interest in them, and voted intelligently on their work. Nevertheless, in the long run, the making of so many minor officials elective made the ballot too long to be intelligently studied, and decreased the responsibility of officials. As the urban movement gathered volume, new municipalities with elective mayors and bicameral councils were established. Political partisanship extended down from the federal to the state and municipal governments; a good Democrat would no more think of voting for a Whig governor or a Whig mayor than for a Whig congressman or President. Federal, state, and local politics were so closely articulated that the misconduct of a state treasurer might turn a presidential election; and the attitude of a President on the tariff or the public lands might embarrass his party's candidate for a municipal office. The state legislatures consumed much time in drafting resolutions on federal matters outside their competence, with the idea of attracting voters or of influencing Congress.

The convention method of nominating candidates for elective office was invented by the Democrats, and by 1840 had been adopted by the Whigs. Local caucuses sent delegates to county conventions for nominating candidates to county office; county conventions sent delegates to state conventions for nominating state candidates, and to district conventions for nominating congressional candidates; state conventions sent delegates to the quadrennial national conventions for nominating the presidential candidates and drafting the platform. Few but professional politicians managed to survive these successive winnowings. Every state had its captains of hundreds and captains of thousands, working for the party every day in the year, and looking for reward to the spoils of victory. Annual or biennial state and local elections kept interest from flagging in the course of a presidential term, and were regarded as portents of the next general election. Innumerable local rallies, often held on the same day with a county fair, barbecue, or anniversary, gave the leaders an occasion for inspiring the faithful, ' spellbinding' the doubtful, and confounding the enemy. Steamboats and railroads carried political orators long distances and enabled them to speak in other parts of the country than their own. In 1840, for instance, Senator Rives of Virginia addressed a great outdoor gathering at Auburn in New York for three hours and a half, after which Mr. Legaré of South Carolina carried on for two hours and a half more. The long endurance of mid-century audiences was marvellous!

It was a good system for socially democratic regions, where politics still offered the most attractive career to talented and ambitious men, and where the people, for want of other diversions, took a keen interest in their government. Men like Abraham Lincoln rose through the caucus and convention to heights that they could hardly have attained otherwise. But in the cities and manufacturing districts of the North, and wherever social inequality was the rule, property went in search of power, and power in search of property. The multiplicity of elective offices and the spoils system led to corruption. The rough-and-tumble of politics repelled many excellent men from public life, and the civil service was degraded in America at a time when it was improving in England. Yet these political methods, in so far as they aroused the active interest of the average voter and stimulated party loyalty, strengthened the Federal Union.

2. *Van Buren and Tippecanoe*

President Van Buren inherited from Jackson (4 March 1837) an organic party whose dominant note was equality, and whose common tendency was westward expansion. Eventually this Democratic party became an instrument of slaveholders, but in the thirties it was a well-balanced alliance of North, South, and West. Shortly it became identified with state rights, but in 1837 the sturdy nationalism of Andrew Jackson was dominant. ' Old Hickory' had caught the imagination or catered to the appetite of Southern yeomen and petty planters, of pioneer farmers in the Northwest, German and Irish immigrants in the Northern states, and plain country folk in New England and New York. They voted for his adopted heir in 1836, and were prepared to support him so long as he trod in Jackson's footsteps, if not longer. The ' little magician,' however, could not dispel the whirlwind that Jackson's blasts had sowed. He had been in office only a few months when the panic of 1837 broke.

The distress that followed seemed to justify the alarmist prophecies of the moneyed men, and gave the administration grave financial embarrassment. Several 'pet banks' defaulted, carrying several millions of federal deposits, and bringing to light corrupt gambling with public money by certain Jackson appointees. A government which in 1836 had been trying to get rid of a surplus was in 1837 at a loss to meet current expenses. Van Buren obtained from Congress a temporary issue of treasury notes. As a permanent fiscal policy, he proposed to lock up government funds in an 'independent treasury' at Washington and 'sub-treasuries' in the federal mints, safe from the clutches of the money power and the wild-cats.

Van Buren's Independent Treasury Bill of 1837 was a sound and statesmanlike measure; and was hailed with delight by the 'loco-foco' or radical wing of the New York Democracy. This faction (so called from having provided themselves at a party caucus with candles and the new loco-foco matches, which enabled them to carry on when the conservatives turned out the gas) was an outgrowth of the old Workingmen's party of 1829, and included many idealists and reformers who held paper money and the credit system responsible for poverty and the panic of 1837. Conversely the 'hunkers' or New York conservative Democrats, who had profited corruptly by the connection between state-chartered banks and federal deposits, viewed Van Buren's new policy with alarm. A general exodus of conservatives from the Democratic party elected William H. Seward, a brilliant young Whig of western New York, the Governor of that state. In Congress the conservative Democrats prevented the Independent Treasury bill from becoming law until 1840. Repealed by the Whigs in 1841, it was re-enacted by the Democrats in 1846 and established the federal fiscal system until the Civil War.

By Van Buren going 'loco-foco' the Democrats became the party of poverty and numbers, and the Whigs the party of property and talents. As Emerson remarked, Democrats had the best principles, Whigs the best men. In the North, where their favorite son was Daniel Webster, the Whigs carried on the nationalist and paternal tradition of Hamilton. The manufacturing interest which wanted protection, the merchants and bankers who suffered from Jackson's financial vagaries, went Whig. Earlier third-party movements, such as the Anti-Masons, the nativists, and the anti-slavery followers of J. Q. Adams, were also absorbed, introducing a radical strain that contended with the conservative element. A large number of Westerners, including young Abraham Lincoln, were attracted to the

Whig party by the personality of Henry Clay, and the hope of getting something done about the public lands. In the South the Whigs were the party of gentility and property, owning over two-thirds of all the slaves. Sugar planters of Louisiana, who wanted protection against Cuba; big cotton planters, who regretted the United States Bank, and who in state politics resisted the repudiating tendencies of their poorer fellows; antique Republicans of Virginia and North Carolina, who disliked Jackson's aggressive nationalism and 'executive tyranny' — all went Whig. Nowhere but in America could a political party have been formed from such heterogeneous elements.

South Carolina followed Calhoun out of the Democratic party in 1832, but refused to ally with the Whigs, noting with alarm the anti-slavery and nationalist tendencies in their Northern wing. It was Calhoun's policy to unite the entire South under the banner of state rights to protect slavery, while the political abolitionists endeavored to unite the North under the banner of anti-slavery. Both Whigs and Democrats very wisely endeavored to keep this dangerous issue out of national politics; but events were to force it in.

Senator Archer of Virginia wrote Sir Charles Vaughan in 1840 that the presidential election of that year was a 'contest between radicalism and the property and education of the country.' Sir Charles must have had some difficulty in distinguishing which was the conservative party, since the Whigs were too wise to appear in their true character. It was necessary to out-demagogue the Democrats, and carry the West. To this end Clay revived his 'distribution' scheme for public land; and the Whig national convention, instead of nominating Clay or Webster or a Southern planter, chose old General Harrison, the 'hero of Tippecanoe.' John Tyler, a Virginian who had sympathized with nullification, was nominated for the Vice-Presidency in order to attract Calhoun's followers. The Whig convention wisely adopted no platform. Catch phrases such as 'Tippecanoe and Tyler too,' 'Harrison, two dollars a day, and roast beef,' served better than principles.

Harrison's nomination was a milepost in the evolution of the presidency. Wise politicians realized that when sectional issues threatened the national parties, they could nominate a 'favorite son' such as Webster, or a statesman with a definite policy such as Clay, only at a risk of alienating other members of the party alliance, and losing the election. Since 1840 successful presidential candidates have not been prominent and experienced statesmen, but military heroes or relatively obscure men who have not had time to make enemies. Only by inadvertence, as in the case of Lincoln and the Roosevelts, did the President prove to be a man of outstanding ability.

The campaign of 1840 was the jolliest presidential election America has ever known. Van Buren suffered from the same buncombe that he had used against Adams in 1828; and the Whigs had plenty of money to influence the numerous unemployed. Clay happily denounced the Independent Treasury as ' The perilous union of the purse and sword, so justly dreaded by our British and Revolutionary ancestors.' A sensible reorganization of the state militia, proposed by the Secretary of War, was compared to Persian satrapies. Van Buren was pictured with cologne-scented whiskers, drinking champagne out of a crystal goblet at a table loaded with costly viands and massive plate. An unlucky sneer in a Democratic newspaper, to the effect that Harrison would be content with a log cabin and plenty of hard cider, gave opportunity for effective contrast. It became the log-cabin, hard-cider campaign. There were log-cabin badges and log-cabin songs, a *Log Cabin* newspaper and log-cabin clubs, big log cabins where the thirsty were regaled with hard cider that the jealous Democrats alleged to be spiked with whisky; little log cabins borne on floats in procession, with latch-string out, cider barrel marked ' O.K.' by the door,[1] coon-skin nailed up beside, and real smoke coming out of the chimney, while lusty voices bawled:

> Let Van from his coolers of silver drink wine,
>   And lounge on his cushioned settee.
> Our man on his buckeye bench can recline,
>   Content with hard cider is he,
>   The iron-armed soldier, the true hearted soldier,
>   The gallant old soldier of Tippecanoe!

Huge balls, supposed to represent the gathering majority, were rolled by men and boys from village to village and state to state, singing as they rolled:

> What has caused this great commotion, motion, motion,
>   Our country through?
> — It is the ball a-rolling on, for

---

[1] O.K., meaning Old Kinderhook (the home of Van Buren), was the secret name for Democratic clubs in New York in the campaign of 1840. The Whigs, unable to penetrate the meaning, invented this conversation between Kendall and Jackson. ' " Those papers, Amos, are all correct. I have marked them O.K. (oll korrect)." The Gen. never was good at spelling.' *Saturday Review of Literature*, July 19, 1941.

(*Chorus.*) TIPPECANOE and Tyler too: —
 Tippecanoe and Tyler too.
And with them we'll beat little Van, Van, Van,
 Oh! Van is a used-up man.

Tippecanoe and Tyler too rolled up 234 electoral votes, a four-to-one majority.

General Harrison, an honest, simple soldier of sixty-eight years, was expected by the Whig politicians to place himself in the hands of such men as Clay and Webster. The latter had the insolence to offer him a ready-made inaugural address of his own composition. But the General had already compiled from schoolboy memories of Plutarch and Roman history a turgid address of which he was very proud. With some difficulty he was induced to let Webster revise it. The ' god-like Daniel ' claimed to have killed seventeen Roman proconsuls ' as dead as smelts ' in one day. On 4 April 1841, a month after delivering his emasculated inaugural address, the Hero of Tippecanoe died. John Tyler succeeded to his office, and title too.

It was soon demonstrated that desire for office was the only binding force in the Whig party. Henry Clay expected to be mayor of the White House as well as leader of the Senate; but the new President was an obstinate man of commonplace mind and narrow views. Clay, like Hamilton, wished to integrate the Federal Government by catering to substantial interests; and his immediate ambition was to charter a new Bank of the United States. Tyler believed it his mission to assert Virginian state-rights ' principles of 1798,' and to strip the Federal Government of its ' usurped ' power; but he lacked both the personal magnetism and the saving common sense of Jefferson.

Tyler signed the ' log cabin ' bill which made permanent in public land policy the pre-emption principle of the Act of 1830. Any American not already an owner of 320 acres or more could now stake out 160 acres in the public domain, and pay for it later at the rate of $1.25 an acre. This Pre-emption Act of 1841 was probably the most important agrarian measure ever passed by Congress. It was a clean-cut frontier victory.

In other respects, President Tyler fulfilled Whig expectations. He took over Harrison's cabinet intact. He carried through the political purge of the civil service that Harrison had begun. He accepted an upward revision of the tariff as a necessary measure for the revenue. But he vetoed all bills for internal improvements and harbor works, and refused to accept any fiscal device that bore the remotest resemblance to the B.U.S. of detestable memory. Clay's bill for a new bank was returned with the President's veto, as was a second bill especially drafted to meet his constitutional scruples (9 September 1841).

From that moment there was open warfare between Tyler and Clay. Four days later the cabinet resigned—excepting Webster who wished to appear independent of Clay—and the President was read out of the Whig party.

Here was Calhoun's chance to count in the sectional balance of power. For three years (1841-43), while Tyler attempted to form a party with a corporal's guard of faithful Whigs, Calhoun played a waiting game, repressing a secession movement among his hot-headed followers in South Carolina, intriguing to obtain the Democratic nomination for the Presidency in 1844. Webster left the cabinet in 1843; and in March 1844 Calhoun became Tyler's Secretary of State.

The new combination was revolutionary in American politics. It meant that Tyler had gone over to the Democrats, and Calhoun returned to them. Calhoun's purpose was to 'reform' the Democratic party on the basis of state rights; to force upon it the formula which he believed to be necessary to preserve the Union. And this state-rights formula was a mere theoretic cover for the main purpose of his devoted followers, to perpetuate slavery where it existed, and extend it into regions where it existed not. Calhoun tipped the internal balance of the Democratic party very definitely southward; the loss of Tyler inclined the internal balance of the Whig party slightly, but no less definitely, northward. The important question of which side the West would take was decided when the Democrats nominated James K. Polk for the Presidency in 1844, on a platform of westward expansion. It was even more significant that in the same platform the Democrats neglected to reaffirm their faith, as had been their wont, in the principles of the Declaration of Independence.

So soon did the clean-cut division between the Democrats as the party of poverty and numbers, and the Whigs as the party of property and talents, become blurred. Only ten years more, and the main division between them would be sectional—and then woe betide the Union!

3. *The Supreme Court under Taney*

Jackson's second term concluded the first nationalizing era of the Supreme Court. One resignation and a number of deaths, including that of Chief Justice Marshall, disposed of all but two of the judges appointed by John Adams and the Virginia dynasty. Jackson was able to appoint a new Chief Justice and seven associate justices, and this new blood dominated the Court down to the Civil War.

No appointment to the supreme bench has ever been the occasion of so much anger, disgust, and apprehension as the choice of Roger B. Taney to succeed the sainted Marshall. Taney was a gentleman (even that was denied) of an old Maryland Catholic family, a lawyer and politician without judicial training, a Jackson partisan who had defended the right of his chief to hold views on the Constitution different from those of Marshall. His name had twice been rejected by the Senate: once as Secretary of the Treasury,[2] and once as associate justice of the Court over which he was destined to preside brilliantly for 28 years. Taney by 1830 had emerged completely from the Hamiltonian background; his intimate knowledge of Jackson's war on the B.U.S. taught him the arrogance and potential danger of organized finance, and his first service to the country was to provide an important limitation of Chief Justice Marshall's definition of the contract clause in the Dartmouth College case.

A corporation chartered half a century before to build and operate a toll bridge leading out of Boston sought by implication to secure a monopoly of crossing the waters of the Charles, and to invalidate a recent state law which had provided a rival and parallel bridge whose owners were pledged to throw it open free to the public as soon as reimbursed for the cost. Justice Story, following what would probably have been the opinion of his former chief, believed the state's action to be confiscatory and a breach of contract; the new Chief Justice, speaking for the majority, upheld Massachusetts, on the ground that no corporate charter could confer implied powers against the public. ' While the rights of private property are sacredly guarded,' he declared, ' we must not forget that the community also have rights, and that the happiness and well-being of every citizen depends on

---

[2] His appointment was an *ad interim* one, in a recess of the Senate; he was rejected as soon as the Senate met, as punishment for removing the deposits from the B.U.S. It was only the election of new Democratic senators in 1836 that made possible Taney's confirmation as Chief Justice in 1837.

their faithful preservation ' (Charles River Bridge *v.* Warren Bridge, 1837). Herein appears, for perhaps the first time in the Supreme Court, the modern doctrine of the social responsibilities of private property. Although denounced by conservatives as opening the floodgates to confiscation and destruction, the Charles River Bridge decision helped capital to find profitable investment by financing improved transportation, and made railroads possible without the necessity of buying up every competing stagecoach, canal, or turnpike company. In another important decision, Bank of Augusta *v.* Earle, Taney recognized the practical capacity of a corporation chartered in one state to do business in another, yet so worded his opinion as to let it be known that state legislation regulating ' foreign ' corporations would not be regarded as unconstitutional by the Court.

A second field in which Taney limited the possible consequences of a Marshall decision was in ' commerce among the several states.' Marshall in Gibbons *v.* Ogden and Brown *v.* Maryland declared, or implied, that the national power to regulate commerce was not only full but exclusive, even when not exercised by Congress, voiding state regulations even if they filled a need that the Federal Government had not yet recognized. Taney posted a different thesis in the License Cases (1847):

It appears to me to be very clear, that the mere grant of power to the general government cannot, upon any just principles of construction, be construed to be an absolute prohibition to the exercise of any power over the same subject by the states. The controlling and supreme power over commerce with foreign nations and the several states is undoubtedly conferred upon Congress. Yet, in my judgment, the state may nevertheless, for the safety or convenience of trade, or for the protection of the health of its citizens, make regulations of commerce for its own ports and harbors, and for its own territory; and such regulations are valid unless they come in conflict with a law of Congress.

In many respects, the Jackson court reflected the reaction in favor of state rights. The Bank of Augusta decision was really prompted by Taney's wish to leave the states power to shape their own economic policies. ' Because two states have adopted a particular policy in relation to the banking corporations of other states, we cannot infer that the same rule prevails in all of the other states. Each state must decide for itself.' In the Passaic Bridge case (1857), for instance, the Supreme Court declined to debate whether a railroad bridge erected under the authority of New Jersey was or was not a nuisance and a hindrance to interstate commerce on the Passaic river. 'These questions have all been ruled by the legislature of New Jersey, having (as we believe) the sole jurisdiction in the matter.' But, in general, Taney had the same views as to the relation between state and nation as his predecessor. None of the state rights hotspurs, the political challengers of federal authority, found aid or comfort from the Supreme Court in his day. Taney on one occasion went out of his way to find an act of Congress unconstitutional, as Marshall had done; and he was unfortunate in the reaction of public opinion. Yet, despite the Dred Scott opinion (which we shall consider in due course), Roger B. Taney must, for the luminous perception of his legal intellect, and for his sound grasp of those social and economic realities upon which judicial statesmanship rests, be considered one of the three or four really great Chief Justices of the United States.

4. Anglo-American Relations

From Lake Champlain to the Rocky Mountains the Canadian-United States boundary had been determined and fixed after the Peace of Ghent,[3] but the two ends of it were still hanging loose, wanting definition or compromise, when a fresh expansive movement of the American population threatened once more to involve the two countries in war.

Although war was averted through diplomacy, there was a deeper reason why the two nations remained at peace during a period when their press was provocative, and their expansive energies seemed certain to clash. Each country was bound to the other by economic ties the rupture of which would have been disastrous. In spite of tariff fluctuations the United States remained Britain's best customer, taking on the average about fifteen per cent of her total exports. At the same time England was America's best customer for raw materials, especially cotton;[4] a fact which counteracted Southern hostility towards the foremost anti-slavery nation. American products supplanted only the coarser sort of British cottons and woolens in the United States, and competed very slightly with British manufactures in South America and the Far East. At the same time the American textile industry created a market for British

---

[3] See Chapter XVIII.
[4] The percentage of the American cotton crop taken by Great Britain varied from 46.7 in 1847 to 67.3 in 1827; it was 54 per cent in 1860.

machinery, the export of which had been permitted since 1825, and provided new employment for emigrating artisans. And although each country considered its own interest when framing tariff schedules, it could not ignore the other's purchasing power. Sir Charles Vaughan, when British minister at Washington, supplied his Southern friends with free-trade statistics and arguments, which may well have influenced votes for the gradual scaling down of American tariff schedules that began in 1833; and this reduction helped the English free-traders in their drive on the Corn Laws. When the American tariff was again raised in 1842, there was a chorus of 'We told you so' from the English free-traders. Conversely, the repeal of the British Corn Laws — described by Senator McDuffie of South Carolina as 'the greatest of all the measures of modern times' — was an effective free-trade argument in the American tariff debates of 1846 against the Whig catchwords of 'home market,' 'British dumping,' and 'pauper labor.' In this Walker Tariff of 1846 the United States adopted schedules more moderate than those of the principal European countries, and with the tariff of 1857 America may be said to have joined the free-trading nations. Wheat and cotton might well have kept her in that column through the nineteenth century, had not the secession of the Southern states given the protectionists a new opportunity.

If commercial relations had a pacifying influence on the two countries, financial relations had quite the contrary effect for several years after 1837. England was then the principal source of capital for American industrial development. During the frenzy of speculation in 1835–36 millions of dollars' worth of state bonds had been floated in London in order to finance state-aided canal, railroad, and banking enterprises. The panic of 1837, and the hard times that followed, made it impossible for some of the states and corporations to meet their obligations. The collapse of the 'Cairo City & Canal Co.,' in which Charles Dickens had invested, was responsible for his western tour of 1842 and his subsequent onslaught on the American character. A suspension of interest payments on the Pennsylvania bonds, in which Sidney Smith had invested, caused his famous outburst against 'a nation with whom no contract can be made because none will be kept,' and his facetious proposal to divide the raiment of Pennsylvanian visitors in London among the creditors of their state. Pennsylvania eventually paid every penny due, with interest; but as late as 1845 the interest payments were still suspended on the bonds of seven states, and the bonds of two, Michigan and Mississippi, were repudiated. Since the non-suability of states (except by other states) was protected by the Eleventh Federal Amendment, there was no way of forcing them to pay up. These financial vagaries, and Dickens's literary exploitation of them, made the task of preserving Anglo-American peace in the early forties much more difficult.

5. Northern Boundary Controversies

Against this confused background of commercial rivalry and financial irritation occurred several ' regrettable incidents ' along the northern border. In the autumn of 1837 rebellion broke out in Upper and Lower Canada. The long constitutional controversy that preceded this outbreak bore so marked a resemblance to the history of the Thirteen Colonies that most Americans hailed the Canadian rebellion as a new American Revolution. Northern New York and Vermont, adjoining the centers of disturbance, harbored numerous smugglers and refugees from Canadian justice; and among their permanent population were thousands of active, energetic young men who were ready for any sort of row. A network of secret societies called the Hunters' Lodges, pledged to expel British dominion from North America, was formed along the border.

President Van Buren endeavored to maintain a strict neutrality; but on the long, unfortified boundary his means were few and feeble, while the state governments were weak in will, and not much stronger in means. Hence, for a period of over a year (1837-38), the Canadian rebel MacKenzie and his followers were able to recruit money, supplies, and men in the United States, and return to loot and burn in Canada. A force of regulars under General Scott was stationed at Buffalo, just after MacKenzie had recruited two or three hundred ' liberators ' among the bargees, lake sailors, and others who were suffering from winter unemployment. The rebel headquarters on Navy Island were supplied from the New York shore by a small American steamer called the *Caroline*. On the night of 29 December 1837, as she lay at her wharf in the United States, a picked band of Canadian volunteers performed the hazardous feat of rowing across the Niagara river where it rushes to the head of the falls, cutting out the *Caroline,* and setting her on fire.

It was a violation — or counter-violation — of neutrality analogous to that of Jackson in Florida; but New York was not a Spanish province, and peppery Palmerston was in Downing Street instead of calm Castlereagh.

Lord Durham, who had been sent to Canada to report on conditions there, saw the real significance of these incidents. No matter how firmly the rebellion might be suppressed, protracted discontent in Canada must lead to Anglo-American war, or to the liberal elements in Canada seeking annexation to the United States. Canada owes her grant of responsible government in 1841, in some measure at least, to the disturbing presence of her neighbor. Later, the federation movement was inspired by similar considerations; and if Canadian union assumed a more nationalist form than the union of the States, it was largely because the action of New York in 1837-41, and of the Southern states in 1860-61, had bared the weakness of American federal government. A similar repulsion from the congressional form of representative government led Canada to adopt the British parliamentary system, a guarantee against political connection with the United States.

In 1840, before the United States could obtain an admission from Palmerston that the attack on the *Caroline* had been deliberate and official, a Canadian named McLeod boasted in a New York bar-room that he had killed an American in the affray, and was promptly arrested and indicted for murder. Palmerston then admitted that the ship had been destroyed under orders as a necessary means of defense against American 'pirates,' and demanded the immediate release of McLeod. Execution of him, so he wrote the British minister at Washington, 'would produce war, war immediate and frightful in its character, because it would be a war of retaliation and vengeance.' President Tyler and Secretary Webster, anxious as Van Buren to preserve the peace, were equally hampered by the limitations of federal government. Governor Seward of New York insisted that the justice of his state should take its course, and Webster could do no more than provide counsel for the prisoner.

In other directions Anglo-American relations were dangerously strained. The Maine boundary controversy had just been rendered more acute by fresh *ex parte* surveys and reports. Palmerston was not prepared to give an inch on this point, and his temper was rising against slave-traders who claimed immunity under the American flag. In a note of 27 August 1841 he emphatically asserted the right of visit, which the United States government refused to admit, as an entering wedge for the humiliating right of search. On that day the two countries were nearer war than at any time between 1815 and 1861; but on the following day the Melbourne ministry resigned, and Sir Robert Peel formed a new one with Lord Aberdeen in the Foreign Office.

Instantly the war clouds rolled away. In England, Aberdeen appointed a special mission to Washington; in New York, McLeod sober managed to find an alibi for McLeod drunk, and was acquitted.

The northeastern boundary controversy was already sixty years old. On the merits it is difficult to avoid the conclusion that 'the British claim had no foundation of any sort or kind ' in law.[*] It had been the intention of the negotiators in 1782–83 to give the United States the territory of the old Province of Sagadahoc (eastern Maine), and the United States claimed no more. The northern part of that region was then, as much of it still is, a wilderness; hence the provincial boundaries had never been marked, and the negotiators of 1782 merely copied the terms of former grants and governors' commissions in agreeing that the international boundary should follow the ' Highlands which divide those rivers that empty themselves into the St. Lawrence from those which fall into the Atlantic Ocean.'

East of Lake Champlain, if this treaty were followed literally, the boundary would run inconveniently close to the St. Lawrence river and obstruct the natural land route between Quebec and the Maritime Provinces. Accordingly, a British case for flattening out the Maine salient was built up, largely on the quibble that the Bay of Fundy was not the Atlantic Ocean. If that interpretation were admitted, the entire valley of the St. John, which flowed into the Bay of Fundy, must be included in Canada. The War of 1812 emphasized this strategic consideration; and in course of time this interpretation became, in the minds of most British subjects, a prescriptive right, the denial of which by Americans was accounted low and grasping. The question was referred to Dutch arbitration in 1831; but the King of the Netherlands expressed his inability to locate the ' highlands,' and proposed to divide the disputed territory by an arbitrary line

---

[*] Lieut.-Col. D. H. Mills, in *United Empire*, ii. 687. New Brunswick subsequently made the United States' case her own, in demanding from Quebec such part of the disputed territory as Ashburton had obtained; and a royal commission in 1851 sustained New Brunswick's case, indirectly validating that of Maine and the United States.

which the United States refused to accept. More legal briefs were then accumulated, more surveys were made, and Maine lumber-jacks had some gorgeous fights with their rivals from New Brunswick. In 1838 British 'trespassers' along the Aroostook (a tributary to the St. John) seized a 'trespassing' official of Maine; both state and provincial governors called out their militia, and the resulting 'Aroostook War' remained bloodless only because President Van Buren was willing to arrange a *modus vivendi* until the diplomatists could try their skill again.

So matters stood early in 1842, when Aberdeen sent Lord Ashburton of the house of Baring to negotiate at Washington with Daniel Webster, sometime of the house of Biddle. Both men, and Aberdeen and Tyler too, were ardent for peace. To that end Webster stepped down from the Olympian atmosphere in which he was wont to move, conducted the negotiations informally, discarded the treaty of 1783 as inexecutable, and compromised. The negotiation, conducted wholly in private and largely by conversation, resulted in the Webster-Ashburton treaty of 9 August 1842, which established the present boundary. Great Britain obtained about five-twelfths of the disputed territory — better than the Dutch proposal of 1831, and sufficient for a connecting link between Quebec and New Brunswick. The United States with the other seven-twelfths obtained a rectification of frontier on Lake Champlain, sufficient to include a fort that had inadvertently been built on Canadian territory. The international lake and river boundary, which a joint commission under the Treaty of Ghent had completed only to the Sault Ste. Marie, was continued thence to the Lake of the Woods.

It was one thing for Webster and Ashburton to sign a treaty; quite another to get it ratified by the Senate and accepted by Parliament. This contest was won by what Webster called the 'battle of the maps.' Professor Jared Sparks had discovered in Paris, and placed in Webster's hands, an early French map with a red line sustaining the British claim. Both he and Webster assumed that this was the map referred to by Franklin in a letter to Vergennes, as a map 'marked with a Strong Red Line [representing] the Limits of the thirteen United States, as settled in the Preliminaries between the British and American plenipotentiarys.' One look at it brought the delegates of Maine to Webster's heel, and in the Senate it helped to obtain the necessary two-thirds majority. On the other side, the director of the British Museum had discovered, and the Foreign Office impounded, a map formerly belonging to George III, which showed the ' Boundary as described by Mr. Oswald ' (the British peace commissioner of 1782), along the line of the American claim! Aberdeen happily produced this map in Parliament when Palmerston attacked the treaty as the ' Ashburton capitulation.' The actual ' red-line map,' or a contemporary copy of it, has recently been found in the Spanish national archives. It shows that the United States was entitled to about five thousand square miles more than she obtained.[6]

[6] L. Martin and S. F. Bemis, ' Franklin's Red-Line Map,' *N. E. Quarterly*, X (1937), 105–111.

XXVIII

THE FAR WEST
1825–1848

1. *The Far West*

THE Webster-Ashburton treaty left only one Anglo-American controversy unadjusted; and that too was a question of the northern border. Both countries claimed the whole of Oregon,[1] while submitting to joint occupation under the treaty of 1818, until the question of sovereignty could be settled. Castlereagh in 1818, Canning in 1824 and 1826, refused the offers of J. Q. Adams to divide Oregon by latitude 49°. By the Florida treaty of 1819 the United States inherited all the Spanish claims north of latitude 42°; and Russia, by later treaties with the United States and Great Britain, withdrew the southern boundary of Alaska to latitude 54° 40′. But the rival pretensions of the Hudson's Bay Company and of American pioneers were to force an issue between England and the United States.

Since 1806, when Lewis and Clark returned from their overland exploration of a transcontinental route to the Pacific, the United States government had not taken much interest in the Far West. Major Long's expedition of 1819 reported the Great Plains 'almost wholly unfit for cultivation,' and laid down on the map of that region, which now supports a thriving population of several millions, the legend 'Great American Desert.' In 1821 the Canadian Northwest Company, which had purchased the American trading-post of Astoria on the Columbia river, amalgamated with the Hudson's Bay Company. Three years later Fort Vancouver was constructed by the Company on the north bank of the lower Columbia. It became an emporium for fur, salmon, and timber, the resort alike of native and white trappers, and the center of a small agricultural settlement. The

---

[1] Including not only the present state of Oregon, but Washington, Idaho, a part of Montana, and British Columbia. The name, derived from Jonathan Carver's *Travels,* was popularized by Bryant's *Thanatopsis* in 1817:

> The continuous woods
> Where rolls the Oregon and hears no sound
> Save his own dashings.

Hudson's Bay factor, Dr. John McLoughlin, ruled the community with wisdom and humanity, preserved the peace between whites and savages, upheld civilized standards of social life, and later received American missionaries with kindness and hospitality that he did not extend to American traders — the rivals of his company.

Distance and the Indians were the principal obstacles to an American settlement of Oregon. After two centuries of colonization, the settled frontier of the United States in 1830 was only half-way across the continent. Independence, Missouri, was its farthest point from the Atlantic. Thence the frontier line sloped away easterly, and the Pacific coast was distant fifteen hundred miles as the crow flies. North and South through Independence, near the present Kansas City, ran the Andrew Jackson Indian barrier. Transplanted Indians occupied the area where the prairies rise into the great plains.

The great plains of the United States cover an area equal to that of European Russia. Their smooth or gently rolling surface, rising gradually or by step-like escarpments from an elevation of two thousand to six thousand feet, was covered with a carpet of grass, rank and thick in the eastern portions, but giving way to tufts of short buffalo-grass and sage-brush in the parched high plains. An occasional rocky dome, butte, or mesa established a welcome landmark. The Platte and Missouri rivers, with their short tributaries, cut deep gashes in the soil and watered a thin line of willow, cottonwood, and wild plum trees. A short summer of blistering heat, with fierce thunderstorms and frequent cyclones, followed hard on a long winter of bitter northwest winds and heavy snow. Over this area roamed the Kansa, Pawnee, Sioux, Cheyenne, Blackfoot, Crow, and Arapaho tribes: the plains Indians who were to the movie of yesterday what the forest Indians were to Fenimore Cooper. Countless herds of buffalo grazed on the plains and supplied the redskins with every necessity of life: with meat for immediate use, or, dried and pounded into pemmican, for winter subsistence; with skins for clothing, shields, harness, vessels, and the cover of the tipis or tents; with sinews for thread, cordage, and bow-strings; with bone for arrow-heads and implements; with peltry to sell the traders; even with fuel. These Indians had long since domesticated the wild mustang, offspring of those set free by the Spanish *conquistadores,* and showed marvellous skill in shooting buffalo with bow and arrow while riding bareback.

The plains Indians seldom practiced agriculture, and knew little or nothing of pottery, basketry, or weaving; but they were the finest physical specimens of the race, and in warfare, once they had learned the use of the rifle, were more formidable than the eastern tribes that had yielded so slowly to the white man. Politically they were even less developed; tribe warred with tribe, and itself knew no common head or council. A highly developed sign language was the only means of intertribal communication. The effective unit was the band or village of a few hundred souls, which might be seen in the course of its wanderings encamped by some watercourse with tipis erected; or pouring over the plain, squaws and children leading the dogs and pack-horses with their trailing travois, superbly dressed braves loping gaily ahead on their wiry steeds. Like other redskins, they lived only for the day, recognized no rights of property, robbed or killed any party of whites who could not defend themselves, inflicted cruelty without a qualm, and endured torture without flinching.

The only white men who penetrated this region before 1830 were explorers, fur traders, and trappers. As soon as Lewis and Clark brought news of the untouched store of fur-bearing animals in the core of the continent, commercial companies were organized to hunt them. The plains Indians were able to supply plenty of buffalo skins, but disliked trapping; hence the trading companies organized bands of *engagés,* trappers who spent most of their time in the Rocky Mountains or Black Hills, and returned yearly to a company post on the upper Platte or Missouri, in order to turn in their furs, and enjoy a week's riotous living on the proceeds. Peltry was also obtained from free-lance trappers who managed by prowess or diplomacy to obtain a certain immunity from the Indians. Supplies and trading goods were sent up-river from St. Louis in the spring floods, as far as possible by steamboat, and farther in rough *bateaux* manned by French-Canadian *voyageurs.* Peltry and buffalo hides were sent down in the same way; or, if the year's taking surpassed the available tonnage, in ' bull-boats ' made of buffalo hides stretched on a wicker frame, bound with buffalo sinews and paid with buffalo tallow. Every river, valley, mountain, and water-hole of the Far West was known to the trappers before 1830: and without their guidance and knowledge transcontinental emigration would have been impossible. It was they who discovered the South Pass of the Rockies in Wyoming, a wide valley of rolling hills that takes one to the transcontinental divide by easy gradients. A party of trappers led by Jedediah Smith and William Sublette took the first covered wagons from the Missouri to the Rockies, in 1830. Six years later Captain Bonneville, whose ad-

The Far West, 1830–1848

Prepared by S. E. Morison and drawn by F. W. Walker for The Oxford History of the United States

ventures provided literary material for Washington Irving, took the
first loaded wagons through the South Pass, and down the Snake
valley to the Columbia.

2. *The Oregon Trail*

The methods of the fur trade, and much of the personnel, were
of French Canada. As in the Canada of Louis XIV, missionaries
followed close on the heels of traders, but the missionaries in this
instance were Protestant Yankees. In 1832 a group of Methodists
under the Rev. Jason Lee joined a fur-trading party on the long overland route, and by 1834 had established a mission in the valley of the
Willamette, which flowed into the Columbia at the site of Portland.
Two years later a band of Presbyterians, including the energetic Dr.
Marcus Whitman about whom a legend was soon built up, and the
first white woman to cross the American continent, founded mission stations in the Walla Walla country, at the junction of the Snake
and Columbia. Supply ships were sent to them round the Horn, and
Dr. McLoughlin gave them every aid and encouragement, although
he had more reason to favor the French Canadian priests who were
coming to the Bitter Root valley and the Cœur d'Alêne country, somewhat northward.

Proselytizing among the tribes of Oregon was not notably successful, but the missionaries in the Willamette valley found themselves in clover. Western Oregon has a delightfully mild and equable
climate. The country was a mixture of open prairie with magnificent
pine woods, rich soil for tillage, and natural meadows for grazing
cattle. The missionaries' widely published letters spread the notion
of Oregon as a home, while Washington Irving in his *Astoria* (1836)
and *Adventures of Captain Bonneville* (1837) stressed the wilderness theme. Settlers began to arrive from New England; not many,
to be sure, but enough to give Oregon a Yankee flavor.

In 1842 the 'Oregon fever' struck the frontier folk of Iowa and
Missouri, eager to renew their forest pioneering. Independence was
the 'jumping-off place' for the Oregon trail. Covered wagons converged there from the eastward in May, when the plains grass was
fresh and green. More supplies were taken in, since hunting was a
precarious source of food; and no help could be expected on the
two-thousand-mile hike to the Willamette, unless from fur-trading
posts that were not too well stocked themselves. Parties were organ-

ized, a captain appointed, an experienced trapper or fur trader engaged as pilot; and amid a great blowing of bugles and cracking of
long whips, the caravan, perhaps a hundred wagons strong with
thousands of cattle on the hoof, moved off up the west bank of the
Missouri. At Fort Leavenworth, one of the bastions of the Indian
frontier, the emigrants for the last time enjoyed the protection of
their flag.

Near the Council Bluffs, where the Missouri is joined by the
Platte, the Oregon trail turned west to follow the latter river over
the Great Plains.[2] Until a road had been beaten into the sod, it was
easy to lose the way. Numerous tributaries of the Platte, swollen and
turbid in the spring of the year, had to be forded or swum, to the
great damage of stores and baggage. Francis Parkman in 1846 found
ancient tables and chests of drawers which perhaps had served some
family in a dozen homes between England and the Mississippi, left
cracking in the sun where this latest wave of migration had grounded
them. Every night the caravan made a hollow square of wagons
round its fire of cottonwood or buffalo chips. Sentries stood guard
to protect the hobbled horses and grazing cattle, and the howling of
prairie wolves was drowned by the chorus of an old Appalachian
ballad:

> Then o'er the hills in legions, boys,
>   Fair freedom's star
> Points to the sunset regions, boys,
>   Ha, ha! ha, ha!

Until the forks of the Platte were reached, near the present northeastern corner of Colorado, the herbage was luxuriant, and the grades
easy. Following the north fork, the trail became hilly and then mountainous, as one turned north to avoid the Laramie spur of the Rockies.
Beyond the South Pass came the worst part of the journey — a
long, hard pull across the arid Wyoming basin, where the grass was
scanty, and alkali deposits made the water almost undrinkable. Between the Gros Ventre and Teton ranges of the Rockies the Oregon
emigrant found westward-flowing waters, and took heart; but there
were still eight hundred miles to go to the lower Columbia, following the meanderings of the Snake river. As there was no good road
in early days through the heavily forested country along the Columbia, wagons were often rafted down the stream; and with fair luck

---

[2] Later, the Oregon trail cut straight across the prairie from Independence to the
southernmost bend of the Platte, near the site of Kearney, Nebraska.

a party that left Independence in May might expect to celebrate
Thanksgiving Day in the Willamette valley. But it was a lucky
caravan indeed that arrived with the same number of souls that
started; and some of the weaker parties disappeared — whether by
starvation after losing the trail, or at the hands of Indians, no one
knows.

Up to this time there had been no law in the Oregon country
outside the Hudson's Bay settlement; and it speaks well for the character of the first emigrants that there was no crime. A group of
Willamette valley settlers who gathered to hear a Fourth of July
speech in 1843 remained to form a government by compact, as their
ancestors had done in the Appalachian valleys. The heavy immigration of 1843–45, four to five thousand strong, including pioneers
of lawless proclivities from Missouri, Arkansas, Iowa, and Illinois,
strained the provisional organization, and convinced Congress that
something must be done to provide this remote colony with government, law, and land titles. First, however, the Federal Government
wished to reach a settlement with Great Britain.

Webster and Ashburton discussed the Oregon question informally in 1842, but reached no conclusion. The next year, agitation
for annexing the whole of Oregon up to 54° 40′ was begun in the
Western states, and Democratic politicians scented a good issue to
win the Western vote in the next presidential election. A bill for
organizing Oregon as a United States Territory passed the Senate
in February 1843, but the House, fortunately ignorant of Palmerston's threat that the passage 'would be a declaration of war,' let it
drop. Secretary Calhoun opened negotiations on the subject in 1844
with the British minister at Washington, and repeated the proposal
thrice made by Adams, to divide the territory along latitude 49°.
Aberdeen, like Castlereagh and Canning, refused to retire from the
north bank of the Columbia.

If the question were to be decided by extent of actual occupation
the British claim was just; and it would be difficult to discover any
other basis of division. North of the Columbia, about Fort Vancouver and along Puget Sound, were living over seven hundred British subjects, and only half a dozen American citizens. The United
States, however, could well afford to wait. A decline in the Columbia
valley fur trade was making Fort Vancouver unprofitable, and the
menacing attitude of the latest American immigrants threatened its
security. At Dr. McLoughlin's suggestion the Company abandoned

Fort Vancouver to the Americans in 1845, and erected a new post on Vancouver Island.

By this time the expansionist James K. Polk had become President of the United States. In his inaugural address (4 March 1845) the President shouted defiance at Britain; and in December, asserting that the American title to the whole of Oregon was ' clear and unquestionable,' he asked Congress for authority to terminate the joint occupation agreement of 1818. To a timid congressman Polk remarked that ' the only way to treat John Bull was to look him straight in the eye; that he considered a bold and firm course on our part the pacific one.'

3. *The Mormons*

Before the Oregon question was finally adjusted came the hegira of the Mormons to the Great Salt Lake.

In New England, and that part of the Middle West settled by Yankees, there was a class corresponding to the ' poor white trash ' of the South; drifters unable to get on in an atmosphere of energy and thrift, resenting the pity or disdain of their successful neighbors, susceptible to religious charlatanry. The Southern under-dog was at this period a frontier individualist, who took his religion in violent revivalist doses. ' When I hear a man preach I like to see him act as if he were fighting bees,' said Abraham Lincoln. But the more social Yankee liked to merge his identity in a communal movement, preferably of a sort that gave him a definite place in a homespun theocracy, and promised him glorious compensation beyond the grave for his worldly humiliations. Further, the New England population had an excess of women. Dozens of new sects such as the Millerites competed in our period for this Yankee substratum, which was completely immune to such intellectual movements as Unitarianism. The most permanent and successful upheaval from these cultural depths was the ' Church of Jesus Christ of the Latter-day Saints.'

Joseph Smith was the offspring of a family of New England frontier drifters, who had made at least ten moves in nineteen years, ending at Palmyra, N. Y. At the age of fifteen he began to see visions and dig for buried treasure. An Angel of the Lord, so he claimed, showed him the hiding-place of a package of inscribed gold plates, together with a pair of magic spectacles which enabled him to read the ' reformed Egyptian ' characters. The resulting Book of Mormon (first printed in 1830), a tedious anthology of personal experiences, religious notions, and historical quackery, described the history of certain lost tribes of Israel (the Indians), whom the Saints were commanded to redeem from paganism. The same year Joseph Smith organized the Church of the Latter-day Saints, a co-operative theocracy in which all power emanated from Smith the Prophet, who stood at the head of a complicated hierarchy. There is no question of Smith's ability. In comparison with some of the pallid intellectuals who founded Fourierist and other communities of the time, Smith was an upstanding, jovial, out-door sort of man, who dressed like a dandy ' and at times drank like a sailor and swore like a pirate.'

The first Mormon community was at Kirtland, Ohio; but in order to approach the Lost Tribes, it moved to a spot near Independence, Missouri. The hostility of pious frontier folk forced a transfer to Nauvoo, Illinois, on the east bank of the Mississippi. At first the Mormons were welcomed in Illinois, courted by both political parties, and given a charter that made Nauvoo practically an autonomous theocracy. The settlement grew rapidly — even faster than Chicago. It was at Nauvoo that Joseph Smith received the ' revelation ' sanctioning polygamy, which he and the inner circle of ' elders ' were already practicing. Although supported by Isaiah, iv. 1, this revelation split the church. The monogamous ' schismatics ' started a paper at Nauvoo; Smith caused the press to be destroyed after the first issue; he and his brother were then arrested by the authorities for destruction of property and lodged in the county jail, where they were lynched. Brigham Young, who succeeded to the mantle of the Prophet, and to five of his twenty-seven widows, directed retaliation on the ' Gentiles ' by a corps of ' Avenging Angels '; and for two years terror reigned in western Illinois. The Mormons were a virile, fighting people, but the time had come for them to make another move, before they were hopelessly outnumbered and exterminated.

Although polygamy was the feature of Mormonism that attracted popular attention, it was little more than a recruiting device appropriate for a wandering tribe. The genius of the Mormons lay in a disciplined community life, integrated by a peculiar faith and directed by ruthless men of action.

In the meantime the Saints had made an astonishing gain in numbers. Missionaries had been raking in converts from the Northern states since 1831; and by 1840, when Brigham Young visited Liverpool, England had become one of their principal harvest fields. For in England thousands of poor laborers were allured by the prospect of a decent living, and the promise of heavenly 'thrones, kingdoms, principalities and powers.' Almost four thousand English converts reached Nauvoo between 1840 and 1846, and forty or fifty churches of Latter-day Saints in the old country contributed modest tithes to the Prophet's bulging treasury.

Under their new leader the Mormons abandoned their homes in Nauvoo, and in 1846, twelve thousand strong, began their great westward trek. After wintering near the Council Bluffs, Brigham Young pushed ahead with a pioneer band along a new 'Mormon trail' on the north bank of the Platte; and in July reached the promised land, the basin of the Great Salt Lake. Many flinched from the long journey, but by the end of 1848 five thousand had arrived in the future state of Utah. This new Canaan was a dry and inhospitable land. Young had selected it in the hope that his Saints would no longer be molested by Gentiles. Arid wastes, where salt and alkali deposits glistened among sage-brush thickets, sloped down from the Wasatch Mountains to the Great Salt Lake, desolate and repulsive as another Dead Sea. Up in the mountains lay natural reservoirs of rain and snow, the means of quickening life.

For such unfamiliar conditions the individualistic tradition of English-speaking pioneers was inadequate; the communal, theocratic customs of the Mormons were appropriate. Brigham Young, equally competent as ruler and lawgiver, priest and patriarch, caused irrigation canals and ditches to be dug, appointed committees to control the water for the public benefit, discarding the common-law doctrine of riparian rights, and adopted a system of small farms, intensively cultivated and carefully fertilized. He forbade speculation in land, but respected private property and accumulated a considerable fortune for himself. He organized home industries so that the farming surplus would not be consumed by transportation costs and Eastern capitalists. He kept the Indians quiet by a judicious mixture of firmness and justice. He repressed heresy and schism with a heavy hand, organized foreign and domestic missions, and financed the transcontinental immigration. By means of a complicated hierarchy he controlled both temporal and spiritual affairs with Yankee shrewdness, rough humor, and substantial justice, and held himself responsible only to God.

For ten years there was intermittent want and starvation in Utah, and the gold rush of '49 caused unrest. Brigham Young announced in the Tabernacle of Salt Lake City, 'If you Elders of Israel want to go to the gold mines, go and be damned! ' The wiser Saints found it more profitable to sell corn and potatoes to the Argonauts, who have left abundant testimony of their kindness and hospitality to the weak and hungry. Yearly the community grew in numbers and in wealth, a polygamous theocracy within a monogamous and democratic nation. Utah was organized as a territory of the United States in 1850, but federal control was practically suspended when President Fillmore appointed Brigham Young the territorial governor. Federal judges were driven from the territory when they refused to obey the Mormon Church; Colonel Albert Sidney Johnston and fifteen hundred regulars could obtain only a nominal submission by the Saints in 1858, and President Lincoln mostly left them alone.

The Pacific Railway brought Salt Lake City into closer touch with the outside world in 1869, but the Mormons have in general remained near to the cultural level from which they were recruited. Polygamy has died out with a rising cost of living, but the Mormon government was too autocratic for a democratic civic life. Until very recently, freedom of thought and liberty of action were narrowly restricted by the Church. Yet the Mormons brought comfort, happiness, and self-respect to thousands of humble folk; and Brigham Young must be placed among the successful empire builders of the English-speaking world.

XXIX

FROM THE RIO GRANDE TO MEXICO CITY
1820–1848

1. *The Spanish Borderlands*

WHILE one column of pioneers was deploying into the prairies of Illinois and Iowa, and another winding over the Oregon Trail, a third had crossed into Mexican territory, and taken possession of the coastal plain of Texas. Expansion in that direction was no simple matter of endurance or driving back Indians. There the English-speaking pioneer came into contact with a proud and ancient civilization, no longer upheld by a dying empire, but by the young Republic of Mexico. Who could tell whether Mexico might not develop the same expansive force as the United States, and Spain recover in the New World the moral dominion she had lost in the Old?

There was little sign of it in 1820. Upper California, New Mexico, and Texas, frontier provinces of the old viceroyalty, spread out fanwise towards the United States, and were attached to the parent trunk by the frailest of stems. Explored as early as the sixteenth century by the Spaniards, they had been thinly colonized after a long interval, and in the Roman rather than the English sense. Missions had been planted among the Indians as centers of civilization and exploitation; *presidios* or frontier garrisons established to protect the fathers in their work; and such few colonists as could be persuaded to venture so far were generously endowed by the Spanish government with lands and Indian serfs. A constant drain on the mother country, the frontier provinces had been maintained simply as a protection to Mexico against the enterprising peoples to the North and East. In 1600, all North America had been a Spanish bastion, with feeble forts and missions studding the coast as far north as Virginia. The American conquest of Texas and California was a large chapter in the volume that began with the settlement of Jamestown in 1607 and ended with the Spanish-American War of 1898.

Spain has left the stamp of her distinction on the architecture, the place-names, and the customs of these frontier provinces; but her

hold on them was slight, as their connection with Mexico was tenu·
ous. Weak, distracted, lacking expansive energy, Mexico knew not
how to use them and was too proud to dispose of them. Garrisons
were withdrawn, the missions secularized, and the Indians allowed
to relapse into barbarism. Upper California, a province the size of
Asia Minor with a mild and equable climate, forests of giant pines
and sequoias, broad valleys of marvellous fertility, and mountain
ranges abounding in mineral wealth, contained little more than six
thousand white men in 1846. The large free-handed life of these
Mexicans of California has been admirably described in *Two Years
before the Mast,* by a seaman of one of those Yankee ships which
were their principal connection with the outside world. Already in
1835 hundreds of Yankees had 'left their consciences at Cape Horn'
to live and trade in this delightful country; and about 1840 overland
emigrants began to trickle in from the Oregon trail through the
passes of the Sierra Nevada.

Between the Sierra and the Rocky Mountains was another vast
region, nominally under Mexican dominion, that did not contain a
single white settler until 1846, when Brigham Young led his Saints
into the basin of the Great Salt Lake.

Fifteen hundred miles from Vera Cruz, and over three hundred
from the Mexican border, lay Santa Fe, the capital and chief town of
New Mexico. It was the gateway to a country of marvels and enchant-
ments, shimmering plains that grew strange cacti, mesas striped with
ochre and vermilion, aboriginal cliff-dwellings, Indian *pueblos,* and
the stupendous cañon of the Colorado river. Annually an armed
caravan of American traders assembled at Independence, and followed the Santa Fe trail with pack-mule and wagon through the
country of the Osage and Comanche, to this lonely emporium of
New Mexico, returning with silver and peltry.

It was in Texas that the first compact wedge of English-speaking
people was thrust across Mexico's borders. Texas, seven hundred
and fifty miles long from the Sabine river to El Paso, and of equal
depth from the tip of the 'panhandle' to the mouth of the Rio
Grande del Norte, is a province larger than France, and almost as
varied in climate and natural resource. The pioneers found moist
gulf plains studded with cane-brakes, and cold arid plateaux; dense
forests of pine and hardwood; prairies of a deep, black, waxy loam,
perfect for cotton growing, and others of lighter soil, adapted for

grain; sage-brush and yucca deserts; and the Llano Estacado or high plains, where roamed immense herds of buffalo and mustang.

We must tread warily here; for a major controversy of American history rages round Texas and the Mexican War. One theory, invented by the abolitionists, made orthodox by the Republican party, and given literary currency by such men as James Russell Lowell, regards the American colonization of Texas, the Texan annexation to the United States, and the Mexican War, as the fruit of a gigantic conspiracy of Southern politicians to get 'bigger pens to cram with slaves.' The other theory regards the whole movement as a more or less conscious and entirely justifiable effort of high-souled pioneers to advance civilization and democracy in a region feebly held by a decadent society. Probably we shall find the truth somewhere between the two extremes.

Texas never formed part of Louisiana, and the United States' claim to it, renounced in the Florida Treaty of 1819, was based on nothing better than the fact that Napoleon was prepared to seize the province, before he decided to sell Louisiana to the United States. However, no sooner had the United States renounced Texas, and agreed upon the Sabine and the Red rivers as the American southwestern boundary, than they regretted the supposed loss. Adams was accused of abandoning American territory, and he had not been in office three weeks when he instructed Poinsett to propose the purchase of a whole or a part of Texas, with the amazingly naïve argument that 'it would have the effect of placing the City of Mexico nearer the centre of its territories.' Jackson pressed the same proposal as Adams, with more persistence and even less tact. At Washington there was 'no comprehension of the out-at-elbows pride of the average Mexican, his vanity and his fierce dreaminess.' The mere offer was an insult; its repetition aroused suspicion.

Yet, with strange inconsistency, Mexico encouraged American emigration to Texas. In 1823 the Emperor Augustín I (Iturbide) confirmed to Stephen F. Austin a concession granted to his father by the Spanish viceroy, to colonize two hundred American families in one of the most fertile regions of Texas. In 1824 the Mexican Congress offered the same *empresario* privilege, with sixty-six thousand acres free, to anyone who could persuade two hundred families to emigrate and receive each 177 acres of rich tillage, or 4,428 acres of prairie pasture and scrub-oak.

Why these terms were offered is one mystery; why they were not more fully taken advantage of is another. In 1825 Austin's colony, then four years old, included but 1,347 whites and 443 slaves, and by 1834 the white English-speaking population of Texas was probably not higher than eighteen thousand, with two thousand slaves. Every frontier community in the United States was growing more rapidly than that. Austin, son of a roving Connecticut Yankee, a grave, gentle, and persistent young man with a profound knowledge of human nature, picked the materials for his colony with care, and ruled it with autocratic power until 1829. It resembled in social structure one of the English proprietary colonies of New England or Carolina, and was more law-abiding and better governed than any American frontier of the nineteenth century except Utah.

Austin seems to have been anti-slavery by preference, but found himself confronted by the dilemma that meets all colonists with capital: the choice between log-cabin poverty and using some form of forced labor. There were no Indian peons in that part of Mexico, and the soil offered such opportunities for cotton and sugar culture that Southern planters would not come unless permitted to bring their slaves, and could not prosper without them. The Mexican Congress, the state legislature at Saltillo, and various Mexican dictators passed laws or decrees declaring the abolition of slavery throughout the Republic. But Austin was always able to obtain some 'explanation' of these decrees which allowed the Americans to hold their slaves in fact, if not by law.

Insecurity of slave property was but one of many factors pulling towards the separation of Texas from Mexico. Austin and the older American *empresarios* tried to be good Mexicans; but it was difficult to respect a government in constant turmoil and revolution. The American colonist admired the horsemanship of his Mexican neighbor, adopted his saddle and trappings — and sometimes, we fear, appropriated his horse — but his general attitude towards Mexico was one of humorous contempt for the people, and impatience at the restrictions which their government sought to impose. As time went on the contempt did not lessen, and the irritations multiplied. There was trouble about the tariff, representation, and immigration; conflicts with Mexican garrisons, whose proud officers resented the crude wit and boisterous individualism of the settlers. And in the early thirties the quiet law-abiding pioneers of Austin's first hegira began to be outnumbered by men of another type — swashbucklers like Sam Houston, once a subordinate of General Jackson, then Senator

and Governor of Tennessee, and sometime resident among the Comanche Indians; Burnet of New Jersey, who had followed Miranda
to Carácas in 1806; Archer of Virginia, who had killed his man in a
duel; the Bowie brothers of Louisiana, slave-smugglers who designed
the long and deadly knife that bears their name; Davy Crockett, a
professional backwoodsman of Tennessee; and many others of restless ambition and pungent personality, who had left their country
for their country's good.

2. *The Lone Star Republic*

The break came in 1835, when Santa Anna proclaimed a unified
constitution for Mexico that made a clean sweep of state rights. The
American settlers of Texas then established a provisional government and expelled the Mexican garrison from San Antonio de Bexar.
Over the Rio Grande came Santa Anna with three thousand men.
In the Alamo, the fortified mission at San Antonio, was a garrison
of less than two hundred Texans. They refused to retreat or to surrender. On 6 March 1836 Santa Anna assaulted the Alamo, captured
it after every Texan had been killed or wounded, and put the
wounded to death.   *also Goliad (sauve*

Already a convention elected by the American settlers had proclaimed the independent Republic of Texas, and adopted a flag with
a single star. Santa Anna quickly advanced eastward with his wiry
Mexican troops, the settlers fleeing before him, and for a few weeks
it looked as if the Lone Star Republic would be snuffed out. Gen-
eralissimo Sam Houston managed to keep a force together, acquired
volunteers from across the border, and awaited the Mexicans in an
ilex grove by the ferry of the San Jacinto river, not far from the site
of the city that bears his name. On 21 April, shouting 'Remember
the Alamo! ' the Texans and their allies burst on Santa Anna's army,
scattered it, and took the leader prisoner. And as Mexico made no
serious effort towards reconquest, the Battle of San Jacinto was
decisive. The Texans ratified their new constitution, legalized negro
slavery, elected Sam Houston their President, and sent an envoy to
Washington to demand annexation to the United States, or recognition as an independent republic.

Enthusiasm over the defense of the Alamo, and liberal land offers
by the Republic drew hundreds of American adventurers into the
Texan army. President Jackson made no attempt to prevent this un-

neutral aid, but on the questions of recognition and annexation his attitude was diplomatically correct. Only on his last day but one of office (3 March 1837), after Congress had approved, did Jackson recognize the Lone Star Republic.

Texas, unsatisfied, pressed for annexation to the United States. Unfortunately for her ambition, it was a year of agitation in Congress over the slave trade and the right of petition. On 23 May 1836 Calhoun remarked in the Senate, that ' there were powerful reasons why Texas should be a part of this Union. The Southern States, owning a slave population, were deeply interested in preventing that country from having the power to annoy them.' The same year an abolitionist named Lundy brought out a pamphlet called *The War in Texas,* which attempted to prove that the Texas revolution was a conspiracy to open new slave markets, and gain slave territory for cotton. Lundy spoke with an appearance of authority, for he had been to Texas; and with the bitterness of frustration, for he had hoped to found there an abolitionist colony. His pamphlet, describing the Texans as a gang of horse-thieves, land-jobbers, and desperadoes, appealed to that widespread Northern sentiment opposed to the political dominance of the South and the extension of the slave territory: the same sentiment that resented the admission of Missouri as a slave state in 1820. Almost in a moment the whole country realized that the annexation of Texas would affect the balance of power between North and South. On 1 November 1837 the Vermont legislature ' solemnly protested ' against the admission ' of any state whose constitution tolerates domestic slavery.' Of course that was the very way to arouse a contrary feeling in the South. Calhoun solemnly announced that any attempt to exclude a state on account of its ' peculiar institutions ' would be a virtual dissolution of the Union.

The slave states were already beginning to realize that they had got the small end of the Missouri Compromise of 1820, which prohibited slavery in the federal territory north of 36° 30'. Arkansas and Michigan had just been admitted to the Union, making thirteen free and thirteen slave states. Florida was the only slave territory left; but three free territories, Wisconsin, Iowa, and Minnesota would be demanding admission in a few years, and more might well follow if the Indian barrier to the great plains were broken. The Alabama legislature, on Christmas Day 1837, resolved: ' It needs but a glance at the map to satisfy the most superficial observer that an overbalance is produced by the extreme northeast, which as regards territory would be happily corrected and counterbalanced by the annexation of Texas.' The Lone Star Republic, greater in area than the nine free states of the northeast, might be carved into several slave states, to balance New England.

A resolution for the annexation of Texas was promptly introduced in Congress. President Van Buren, engaged at the time in some delicate negotiations with Mexico, and anxious to keep the slavery issue out of politics, used his influence against the resolution, which was finally smothered by a speech of J. Q. Adams that took three weeks to deliver (July 1838).

The politicians were content to let so explosive a question rest. In the meantime, thousands of petty planters, ruined by the panic of 1837, were glad to leave their debts at home, and start life anew across the Sabine.

Texas acquired a navy, accumulated a national debt, and received British and French recognition. The Lone Star Republic belonged to the family of nations, but for how long? Her white population was barely fifty thousand; Mexico had six or seven million. Except for a fantastic raid in 1842, Mexico made no attempt to reconquer Texas; and in 1843 the British minister to Texas negotiated a truce between the two republics. But at any turn of the political wheel in Mexico City the truce might be denounced, and hostilities renewed. Political conditions in Texas were chaotic. A Texan President who bore the conquering name of Mirabeau B. Lamar hoped to incorporate New Mexico, California, and the northern tier of Mexican states in his government, and himself led a forlorn hope against Santa Fe. Sam Houston, who succeeded him after that escapade, knew that Texas needed protection and security. He probably preferred to obtain it through annexation to the United States. But there was no hope of obtaining American consent until 1843, when Webster left Tyler's cabinet, and Upshur of Virginia became Secretary of State. Houston's second string was a dual mediation by Britain and France to obtain recognition of Texan independence by Mexico; and a dual or triple guarantee to maintain it.

Such a project was certain to appeal to European statesmen. The desire to extend the European balance of power to America, and erect a barrier to further expansion by the United States — the policy successively pursued by Talleyrand, Canning, and Napoleon III — was awakened by Texan independence. Here was a ready-made wedge between the United States and Latin America, an independent source of supply for cotton, sugar, and tobacco, a possible center of British or French influence. How Canning would have hastened to 'slip in between'! But Lord Aberdeen was now in the Foreign Office. He toyed with the idea. What sweetened it for him was the notion that in return for British guarantee and financial assistance Texas might be induced to abolish slavery. The convention of the British and Foreign Anti-Slavery Society at London, in the summer of 1843, put the proposition to Aberdeen, definitely. He would not say he would, but refused to say he might not. A year later, he went so far as to tell the Mexican minister at London that if Mexico would recognize Texan independence, and France would co-operate, England would guarantee both the independence of Texas and the boundaries of Mexico against the United States and the world. At the same time King Louis-Philippe warmly urged the same plan on the Mexican minister at Paris, pointing out the analogy to his own recognition of Belgian independence and neutrality.

That the Peel and the Guizot ministries were really prepared to set up an American Portugal or Belgium is improbable, but not impossible, given Aberdeen's propensity for assuming dangerous responsibilities. If neither government was brought to the test, it was owing to Mexican obstinacy. There was little doubt of Texan acceptance, if the offer were made in time. But no Mexican cabinet dared recognize Texan independence. A better sense of perspective at Mexico City in 1844, a disposition to recognize accomplished fact, might have changed history.

Amid the cross-currents of notes, suggestions, and conversations between London, Paris, Washington, Austin, and Mexico City, another fact stands out clearly: the fear of Southern statesmen that Texas might abolish slavery. It leaked out that Aberdeen had agreed to guarantee a Texan loan if the Lone Star Republic would abolish slavery. The prospect of Texas becoming a refuge for fugitive slaves from the Gulf States alarmed the South to the point of panic. Upshur, Tyler's new Secretary of State, at once began to negotiate a treaty of annexation with the Texan minister at Washington, and informed the Texan government that the abolition project was inadmissible. Aberdeen, as soon as he heard of the misunderstanding, denied the report of his intentions in a note imprudent in its frankness. 'Great Britain desires, and is constantly exerting herself to procure, the general abolition of slavery throughout the world. But the means which she has adopted, and will continue to adopt, for this humane and virtuous purpose, are open and undisguised.' Calhoun's reply, which he published at once, seized upon this admission to justify the annexation treaty; and proceeded to read the British Government a lesson on negro slavery. Adducing some questionable statistics, Calhoun offered to convince the noble lord that the negro race would be reduced to wretchedness and vice by his misdirected charity! In other words, Tyler's administration declared that the mere prospect of abolition in a neighboring republic was sufficient reason to absorb it; and suggested that the mission of the United States was to make the world safe for slavery.

Annexation, urged on such grounds and from that source, repelled more votes from one section than it attracted from another. Calhoun's annexation treaty failed to pass the Senate. Then came the presidential election of 1844, in which the Democratic party cleverly lifted the Texas question out of its slavery setting, and made it one of national expansion and prestige.

3. James K. Polk

In the Democratic nominating convention of 1844 there was the usual strife between Northern and Southern elements. Then James K. Polk of Tennessee, the first 'dark horse' in a presidential race, trotted out on to a platform where 'Reoccupation of Oregon and reannexation of Texas' was written large. Washington heard the result in a minute, by the new electric telegraph. Henry Clay, the Whig candidate, was expected to rally the divided forces of the Whigs, and to win the election; but he remained on the fence too long. His non-committal policy as to Texas diverted so many New York votes to Birney, the abolitionist candidate, that Polk carried the state by a trifling plurality; and the thirty-six electoral votes of New York decided the contest.

There was a deeper reason, however, why Polk carried the election over his popular and distinguished rival, and that reason had nothing to do with slavery or abolition. Another movement of westward expansion had begun, both in thought and in fact. The Oregon Trail and the Lone Star Republic appealed to a people recovering confidence after the hard times of 1837 to 1840. The 'manifest destiny' of the United States to expand westward and southward, and prove the democratic principle on a scale hitherto undreamed, became the theme of countless newspaper articles, Fourth of July orations, and political speeches. Much talk there was, too, of Anglo-Saxon genius in colonization and self-government. Parson Wilbur of the Biglow Papers might preach that 'all this big talk of our destinies is half on it ignorance, an' t'other half rum,' but no good Democrat or Westerner believed him. The slogans of 1844, 'Reoccupation of Oregon and reannexation of Texas,' 'Fifty-four forty or fight,' rallied the same sort of people who shouted 'Tippecanoe and Tyler too' in 1840; Clay tried to straddle the issue. Jeffersonian simplicity was dead, and the new note of emancipation was silenced by the war-whoops of strutting democracy.

Congress, persuaded that quick action was necessary to forestall England, voted by joint resolution on 18 February 1845 to admit Texas into the Union. And on his last day of office, President Tyler had the satisfaction of sending off a courier to inform Texas that only her consent was necessary to become the twenty-eighth United State. But the ambition of his successor soared far beyond the Lone Star Republic.

James Knox Polk had been Speaker of the House, and left Congress to become Governor of Tennessee, where he won the approval of Old Hickory. He was a stiff, angular person, with sharp gray eyes in a sad, lean face, and grizzled hair overlapping a black coat-collar. He had majored in mathematics and the classics at the University of North Carolina to train his mind, and the event proved that he succeeded. His working day in the White House was nearer eighteen than eight hours, and in four years he was absent only six weeks from Washington. His will controlled a cabinet of experienced and distinguished men. Determined and tenacious, seldom smiling and never relaxing, Polk recalls in much but intelligence that other presidential scholar and diarist, J. Q. Adams. Their domestic policies were as wide as the poles, but Polk adopted the same foreign policy as Adams, and he had a way of getting things done. He aspired to reduce the tariff, re-establish Van Buren's independent treasury, settle the Oregon boundary, and acquire California. Within four years his ambition was fulfilled.

Although Polk was a slaveholder, he did not think in terms of slavery. The 'peculiar institution' had no more influence on his expansionist ambitions than on those of Adams. Tyler robbed him at the eleventh hour of the glory of acquiring Texas, but California was still wanting to flatten out the re-entrant angle in the western boundary.

Polk's desire for California was quickened by the fear lest England or France should forestall him. Both countries were then active in the Pacific. New Zealand had been acquired in 1840 by the British who did not want it, in order to keep it from the French who did want it. In 1842 Admiral Dupetit-Thouars took the Marquesas and in 1843 bombarded Queen Pomaré out of Papeete. In the same year the Hawaiian monarch Kamehameha III, hitherto a friend to American whalemen and protector of Yankee missionaries, prepared to place the Sandwich Islands and his royal person under the protection of Queen Victoria. Rumor reached Polk that Lord Aberdeen was fishing for California. It was only his agents who were, and Mexico refused to bite; but Aberdeen would not remain Foreign Secretary forever, and circumstances might alter.

The situation in California was not unlike that in Texas a decade earlier, except that 'greaser' and 'gringo' were more evenly matched: about seven thousand of each, together with three or four thousand mission Indians. Between the two groups there was the usual antagonism. The Americans regarded the Spaniards as lazy, childlike, and cowardly; the Mexican Californians resented the newcomers as brutal, grasping, and uncivilized. As the Americans were increasing and the Mexicans were not, some sort of revolt was inevitable.

Shortly after Polk entered office, Mexico protested against the annexation of Texas, and broke diplomatic relations. From her point of view, Texas was still a rebellious province. In July 1845, when Texas had accepted annexation by a plebiscite, Polk ordered a detachment of the regular army under General Taylor to take up a position on the Nueces river, the southwestern border of Texas, to protect the new state against a possible Mexican attack. Polk's apologists make much of the sophistry that as soon as Taylor crossed the Sabine river into Texas, he was invading Mexico from the Mexican point of view; hence war was inevitable, whatever else Polk might do. This argument makes no allowance for Latin disinclination to acknowledge a disagreeable *fait accompli*. In 1845 Spain was still technically at war with most of Spanish America, although hostilities between them had long since ceased; but no Latin-American state would have thought itself thereby justified in attacking Puerto Rico, or some other region still faithful to Spain. If Polk had been content with Texas, and had not reached out for something besides, there is no reason to suppose that Mexico would have initiated hostilities; although she might long have delayed acknowledging the annexation of Texas to the United States.

On 24 June 1845 the Secretary of the Navy sent secret orders to Commodore Sloat, commanding the Pacific station, to seize San Francisco if he should 'ascertain with certainty' that Mexico had declared war on the United States. In October 1845 the Secretary of War wrote to Larkin, the American consul at Monterey (California), 'Whilst the President will make no effort and use no influence to induce California to become one of the free and independent States of the Union, yet if the people should desire to unite their destiny with ours, they would be received as brethren, whenever this can be done without affording Mexico just cause of complaint.' John C. Frémont, a young captain of United States Engineers, was also on his way to California with an exploring expedition. He had no political instructions, but they would come in time.

While Polk was priming revolt in California, he proposed to see what could be got out of Mexico in exchange for claims. Like most nations at most times, the United States had claims on Mexico for repudiated bonds, revoked concessions, and damage done to American property during the civil war that broke out every few months. Hitherto the United States had been forbearing, in comparison with the French government, which sent a squadron to bombard San Juan de Ulúa in 1839. A mixed commission awarded the United States about a million and a half dollars in 1841, since when claims to about three million more had accumulated. In 1843 the two countries ratified a convention by virtue of which Mexico was to pay the whole with accrued interest in twenty quarterly instalments. After three instalments Mexico suspended payment — as several states of the Union had done on their bonds — but did not repudiate the debt, like Michigan, Mississippi, and our associates in the World War. Torn by civil dissension and virtually bankrupt, Mexico could not pay at that time, as President Polk knew and admitted.

On 10 November 1845 the President commissioned John Slidell minister plenipotentiary to Mexico, with instructions to offer that the United States should assume the unpaid claims of its citizens against Mexico, in return for Mexican recognition of the Rio Grande as the southern boundary of Texas and of the United States. Five million additional would be paid for the cession of New Mexico as well, and 'money would be no object' if the cession of California could also be obtained. Polk's enemies doubted his sincerity in this matter, as the Mexican government, since breaking relations on account of Texas, had offered to receive an American 'commissioner,' not a 'minister.' But Polk was simply contemptuous of diplomatic procedure, and ignorant of the Mexican character. A practical man, he hoped to put through a business deal with a government that did not have a business mentality.

Slidell was refused reception by the Herrera government to which he was accredited. No Mexican minister could afford to receive an American plenipotentiary, any more than the Spanish government could afford to think of South American independence in 1824. Notwithstanding this refusal, General Paredes at once raised the standard of revolution, on the ground that Herrera was proposing a treasonable bargain with the United States. The revolution succeeded, as most Mexican revolutions do; and by New Year's day 1846 the government was in the hands of a military faction that was spoiling for a fight with the United States.

Polk did not give them long to wait. On 13 January 1846, the day after he had received word of Herrera's refusal to receive Slidell, but before he knew of the Paredes revolution, Polk ordered General Taylor to take his army across the Nueces river, and to occupy the left bank of the Rio Grande del Norte.

. Thereby the President attempted to force the solution of a boundary controversy. That is the important point. It also happens that his view of the controversy was wrong. The Nueces river had been the southern boundary of the Province and State of Texas during a century past. The territory between the Nueces and the Rio Grande, and east of longitude 100°, was a barren tract belonging to the State of Tamaulipas. Texas laid claim to the Rio Grande in her declaration of independence; but her authority as state or republic had never been exercised beyond the Nueces, where the few scattered inhabitants remained under Mexican jurisdiction. The United States, in annexing Texas, was pledged to adjust the southern boundary, but not committed to insist upon the Rio Grande.[1]

---

[1] This was also Calhoun's view. Certain writers make much of a convention that Texas concluded with General Santa Anna, when in captivity, recognizing the Rio Grande boundary. Santa Anna had no authority to conclude such a convention; he was not a free agent; and it was not ratified by the Mexican Congress.

4. 'War by Act of Mexico'

General Taylor, in obedience to orders, took up a position on the left bank of the Rio Grande, with his guns bearing across it upon the Mexican town of Matamoras (23 March 1846). The Mexican general in command of that district ordered him back to the Nueces (11 April). Taylor replied by blockading the Rio Grande in order to cut off food supplies from Matamoras (23 April). In spite of furious threats by the Mexican press, and by its own members, the Paredes government had made no military disposition threatening Texas, and had kept its forces out of the disputed territory between the two rivers. The responsibilities of office were making the new government more cautious in action than in speech; but more than Mexican caution was now needed to stop Polk.

On 12 March 1846 the Mexican foreign minister informed Slidell definitely that he could not be received, that Mexico still regarded the annexation of Texas as a just cause of war, which would be inevitable if the United States persisted in its present course of adding insult to injury. Having thus asserted his own and his country's dignity, the foreign minister 'intimated a willingness to negotiate' with a commissioner *ad hoc,* on the simple question of the annexation of Texas. This sort of distinction, which did not touch any vital issue, had a real meaning to the Latin-American mind. The government had to save its face, after so much bluster about national honor. The real obstacle to a peaceful settlement was the fact that Polk wanted much more than the Rio Grande boundary. His eyes were fixed on the Pacific, and nothing less than upper California would have satisfied his ambition for expansion.

Polk dismissed the last Mexican offer as insincere and treacherous; and on 25 April began to prepare a message to Congress urging war on the sole grounds of Slidell's rejection and the unpaid claims — which amounted to exactly $3,208,314.96 when adjudicated by a United States commission in 1851. On 8 May Slidell saw the President, and urged him to act promptly. On Saturday morning the 9th, Polk informed the cabinet that he believed it his duty to send the war message to Congress the following Tuesday. All agreed but Bancroft, who thought that war should not be declared until Mexico committed some definite act of hostility. Buchanan, the Secretary of State, said that he would feel better satisfied if that happened, but that as matters stood there was ample ground for war against Mexico.

The cabinet adjourned at two o'clock. At six, dispatches from General Taylor reached the White House. It appeared that on 25 April — two days after Taylor blockaded Matamoras — a Mexican force had crossed the Rio Grande, engaged in a cavalry skirmish with United States dragoons, killed a few of the troopers, and captured the rest. Polk called another cabinet meeting for half-past seven. The consciences of Bancroft and Buchanan were now satisfied; it was agreed unanimously that a war message, with documents proving the 'wrongs and injuries' the United States had suffered from Mexico, should be laid before Congress on Monday. All day Sunday, except for two hours spent at church, Polk labored with his secretaries preparing the war message. 'It was a day of great anxiety to me,' wrote the President in his diary, 'and I regretted the necessity which had existed to make it necessary for me to spend the Sabbath in the manner I have.'

At noon on Monday, 11 May 1846, the war message was sent to Congress. 'The cup of forbearance has been exhausted,' declared the President. 'After reiterated menaces, Mexico has passed the boundary of the United States, has invaded our territory and shed American blood upon the American soil.' In the evening the President received visits of congratulation from Senator Sam Houston of Texas, and Governor Archibald Yell of Arkansas. Two days later Congress declared that 'by the act of the Republic of Mexico, a state of war exists between that Government and the United States.'

In the Mississippi valley the war was highly popular. Mexico evoked visions of gold and glory among the men of the frontier, as in other days to the men of Drake and Hawkins. Thousands of western volunteers came forward, eager to 'revel in the halls of the Montezumas.' In the older states there was little enthusiasm and much opposition. The Mississippi valley and Texas together furnished forty-nine thousand volunteers; the original Thirteen States thirteen thousand. Most of the elder statesmen of the South were content with Texas; Calhoun's clear vision foresaw that the conquest of more territory would upset the sectional balance and revive the dangerous question of slavery in the Territories. The Whig party opposed, although with more wisdom than the Federalists of 1812 they voted for war credits and supplies, in the hope that the Democrats would be hanged if given plenty of rope. Anti-slavery men and abolitionists regarded the war as part of an expansionist conspiracy of slaveowners:

> They may talk o' Freedom's airy
> Tell they're pupple in the face;
> It's a grand gret cemetary
> Fer the barthrights of our race;
> They just want this Californy
> So's to lug new slave-states in
> To abuse ye, an' to scorn ye,
> An' to plunder ye like sin.

Thus James Russell Lowell castigated the Mexican War, in his *Biglow Papers*. And although few agreed with him that it was time to part from the slave states, the legislature of Massachusetts declared that the Mexican War was a war of conquest, a war to strengthen the ' slave power,' a war against the free states, unconstitutional, insupportable by honest men, to be concluded without delay, and to be followed by ' all constitutional efforts for the abolition of slavery within the United States.'

5. *The Oregon Compromise*

President Polk expected a quick and easy victory, for which twenty thousand volunteers, in addition to the regular army of seventy-five hundred, would suffice. In Europe many doubted whether the United States could beat Mexico. People admitted a great disparity of population and resources, but remembered American failure in offensive warfare against Canada. Mexico was confident enough. An officer boasted that his cavalry could break the ' gringo ' infantry squares with the lasso. There was wild talk of breaking into Louisiana, arming the slaves, and loosing the Comanche and Sioux on the American frontier. And the unsettled Oregon question suggested that Mexico might soon have a powerful ally.

In April 1846, after a long Senate discussion, Polk threw Oregon into hotchpot by giving notice to England that in twelve months' time the joint occupation would expire. He did not, however, shut the door on negotiation. Every previous attempt at compromise had been thwarted by a Colonial Office notion that the Columbia river was a western St. Lawrence, an essential link of communication between Hudson's Bay and China. Aberdeen now knew better. After sounding the President, he proposed to extend the boundary along latitude 49° to Puget Sound, thence to the ocean through the straits of Juan de Fuca, leaving Vancouver Island to Canada. Polk submitted this offer to his cabinet on 6 June 1846. Buchanan ' said the " fifty-four forty " men were the true friends of the administration, and he wished no backing out on the subject.' Mr. Buchanan was properly admonished; the President laid the proposition before the Senate for advice and consent, which it promptly gave in the affirmative; and on 15 June the Oregon treaty, describing the boundary between the United States and British Columbia, was signed. Another Anglo-American crisis had passed, largely by reason of the conciliatory disposition of Lord Aberdeen and the desire of Polk to be free to thrash Mexico. There can be little doubt that England gave up a just claim to territory; but so had the United States, in the Maine negotiation of 1842.

6. *Glory and Conquest*

California, the main objective, lay beyond the principal seat of war; and was the scene of minor if decisive conflicts. Frémont learned of the impending war with Mexico in May, 1846, when encamped near Klamath Lake. Moving his exploring expedition into the lower Sacramento Valley, his presence naturally encouraged settlers who wished to shake off Mexican rule. Hostilities began even before news arrived of the declaration of war; a few dozen American squatters in the Sacramento valley took possession of Sonoma with its commandant, proclaimed the 'Republic of California,' and hoisted a white flag with a bear and star painted on it (14 June 1846). On 7 July Commodore Sloat, having heard of the outbreak of hostilities on the Rio Grande, hoisted the Stars and Stripes at Monterey, and declared California a part of the United States. The Spanish-speaking Californians, not relishing these proceedings, rose in arms, reoccupied Los Angeles for a time, and had a brush with Colonel Kearny, who had led 500 troopers overland from Independence, mopping up Santa Fe on the way. But by the end of 1846 California was completely in the hands of the Americans.

General Zachary Taylor began what was intended to be a march on Mexico City by pushing across the Rio Grande before war was even declared, and winning two minor engagements; but refused to move farther from his base until properly reinforced and supplied. Polk, who had never seen northern Mexico, thought that Taylor ought to live on the country. Finally men and munitions were sent. Taylor's army then advanced and captured the town of Monterey, after a three days' battle (21–23 September 1846).

President Polk was not altogether pleased with this brilliant victory. 'Old Rough and Ready' Taylor, an outspoken, blaspheming veteran of the Jackson breed, was becoming dangerously popular, and the Whigs began to talk of nominating him for the Presidency in 1848. As a way out, Polk conceived the brilliant stroke of creating Thomas H. Benton, the aged Senator from Missouri, Lieutenant-General in command of the United States army. Unfortunately for Mexico, Congress refused to create this new grade. The President then turned to Major-General Winfield Scott of the regular army, a Whig indeed, but a dandy swashbuckler whose airs and foibles were unlikely to win golden opinions from democracy. Scott's plan to end the war by marching on Mexico City from Vera Cruz was now adopted.

In the meantime, Polk had provided Mexico with a leader. General Santa Anna was in exile at Havana when the war broke out. Although he had twice broken his word to the Texans, he was able to persuade Polk that, once in possession of the Mexican government, he would sign the sort of treaty that was wanted. By the President's command, Santa Anna was allowed to slip past the United States blockading squadron into Vera Cruz. He entered Mexico City in triumph in September 1846, and assumed the dictatorship.

> O Santy Anna gained the day
> *Hooray! Santy Anna.*
> He lost it once, but gained it twice,
> *All on the plains of Mexico.*

So runs a rousing old chanty, completely reversing the facts. For Santa Anna could not even dispose of the rival to his American benefactor. General Taylor beat him badly at Buena Vista (22–23 February 1847) — a splendid picture-book battle on a sun-soaked plain; a fight that advanced both General Taylor and his son-in-law, Colonel Jefferson Davis.

General Scott's campaign was a brilliant feat of arms. With little more than half the twenty thousand troops he wanted, hampered by insubordinate volunteer officers who had been appointed for political reasons, thwarted by the jealousy and incompetence of the administration, often forced to live off the country and to fight with captured ammunition, he yet accomplished his ends. Vera Cruz surrendered on 27 March 1847, and the American army started for Mexico City along the road Cortez had followed three centuries before. In two weeks' time it reached the pass of Cerro Gordo, which the ubiquitous Santa Anna had fortified. Captain Robert E. Lee found a way to outflank the Mexicans by a mountain slope, a brilliant operation in which Captain George B. McClellan and Lieutenant U. S. Grant took part. The army pushed on to Puebla, and remained there for three months, renewing half its numbers by replacements for the volunteers whose terms of enlistment had expired. On 7 August General Scott cut connection with the coast. Three days later his army reached the divide ten thousand feet above sea level, with the wonderful Valley of Mexico stretching before, and the towers of Mexico City rising through the mist. More good staff work carried out by the engineers, stiff fights at Contreras and Churubusco (7–20 August), and the army was ready to follow the fleeing Mexicans into the city.

Just in time to stop them, Santa Anna accepted an armistice for which Scott had already paid him ten thousand dollars, and consented to begin peace negotiations. He was promised a million more at the conclusion. Polk had attached to the American army as peace commissioner an absurd little gentleman named Trist, the chief clerk of the Department of State. Trist's instructions were to obtain the Rio Grande boundary, with New Mexico, Upper California, and a right of transit across the Isthmus of Tehuantepec, one of the proposed inter-oceanic canal routes. The Mexican politicians, unable to face reality, made such an uproar on hearing these terms that Santa Anna decided to try another throw of the dice with Scott. The American army, refreshed by a fortnight among the orchards and orange groves of the Valley of Mexico, marched forward to a blood-bath at Molino del Rey (8 September), and five days later stormed its last obstacle, the fortified hill of Chapultepec. On they pushed, taking cover under the arches of the aqueducts, Lieutenant U. S. Grant cleverly mounting a howitzer in the belfry of a suburban church. At dawn of 17 September a white flag came out from Mexico City.

The excitable Mexicans fell silent and glum, as a vanguard of battered, mudstained doughboys and hard-boiled marines, led by a brigadier general who had lost a boot in the latest fight, swung along their streets to the Plaza de la Constitución. There the conquerors gazed with wonder on the great baroque Cathedral and the lofty pink-walled palace — the Halls of the Montezumas at last. Presently a clatter of hoofs was heard on the stone-paved streets; and as the weary veterans snapped into ' Atten — *shun!* Present — *arms!* ' General Scott, splendidly uniformed and superbly mounted, escorted by a squadron of dragoons with gleaming swords, came dashing into the plaza.

Santa Anna promptly abdicated, for the third but not the last time; and two months elapsed before Scott and Trist could find a Mexican government willing to negotiate peace. In the meantime Trist had been recalled, on account of his muddling the August negotiations. Instead of obeying orders he remained, and negotiated the Treaty of Guadalupe Hidalgo (2 February 1848) in accordance with his original instructions. Mexico ceded Texas with the Rio Grande boundary, New Mexico (including Arizona), and Upper California to the United States. The victor assumed the unpaid claims, and paid fifteen million dollars to boot — three-fifths of the amount Slidell had been instructed to offer for the same territory in 1846.

In the meantime, American public opinion was beginning to demand that the whole of Mexico should be annexed. Buchanan, who more than once had been reproached by Polk for his ' contracted and sectional views ' of American destiny, chimed in with the new *vox populi,* and advised the President to repudiate both Trist and the treaty. Polk coldly reminded the Secretary of his inconsistency, and sent the treaty to the Senate, which ratified it after the usual bitter debate. It was, in fact, a more emphatic victory than the war.

The United States had rounded out her continental area substantially to the present limits. It remained only to complete the present southwestern boundary of the United States by the ' Gadsden purchase ' from Mexico (1853) of the Gila river valley, in southern Arizona. But it also remained to be seen whether these immense and valuable acquisitions would be added to ' Freedom's airy,' or provide ' bigger pens to cram with slaves.'

XXX

THE COMPROMISE OF 1850
1846–1850

1. *The Wilmot Proviso*

NO sooner were Polk's clutch of eaglets hatched, than North and South began to quarrel over them. Inspection of the nest revealed a young cuckoo whose strident squawks, despite frantic efforts of papa Democrat and mamma Whig to glut him into silence, soon drowned all other notes in the national aerie.

The slavery question was the intruder. Southern Democrats had obtained Northern support for the annexation of Texas up to the Rio Grande, even though it meant war; and then let their allies down to latitude 49° in Oregon, because 54° 40′ would have meant another war. An unforgivable sin in politics or diplomacy! So that when Polk asked Congress for two million dollars to buy more territory from Mexico (August 1846), a disgruntled Pennsylvania Democrat named David Wilmot tacked on to the bill a proviso to the effect that 'neither slavery nor involuntary servitude shall ever exist' in the territory so acquired.[1] There was no need of this prohibition. So far as anyone could foresee, the arid wastes of New Mexico and the cattle-ranches of California were unsuitable for slave labor. Once put forward, however, the Wilmot proviso was maintained as a matter of principle and sectional strategy. Every Northern legislature but one, whether Whig or Democrat, passed resolutions approving it, and acclaiming Wilmot a great statesman.

If Northern Democrats were mischievous in demanding an abstract and unnecessary slavery restriction, Southern Democrats were reckless in opposing it; and the fury of their opposition gave color to the charge that the Mexican War was being fought for slavery. The Wilmot proviso seemed to them an insulting abstraction, an attempt to put their 'peculiar institution' in the wrong. Polk proposed that latitude 36° 30′ (the old Missouri Compromise line of 1820) should divide freedom and slavery in the new territories as in the old; but there were too many extremists for this common-sense com-

---

[1] The phrase was copied from the Northwest Ordinance of 1787.

promise. Southern Whigs who voted for the proviso in the interest of peace were denounced as 'Southern traitors'; Northern Democrats who voted the other way, for the same reason, were denounced as 'dough-faces' or 'Northern men with Southern principles.' The Wilmot proviso did not pass, nor did any measure to organize the newly acquired territory. American settlers in the Far West lacked law and government, because Congress could not decide whether or not they should have slaves. Oregon was finally organized as a territorial government without slavery in 1848, but Polk's presidential term ended (4 March 1849) before anything had been done about California, New Mexico, or Utah.

Hitherto, everyone supposed that Congress could legislate slavery in or out of the territories, since the Constitution gave it the power to ' make all needful rules and regulations respecting the territory or other property belonging to the United States.' Congress had introduced slavery into some territories, such as Mississippi, and banned it from others, such as Indiana and Minnesota. From the Wilmot proviso debates new theories on the subject emerged: (a) Congress has the moral duty to prohibit slavery wheresoever its jurisdiction extends: freedom must be national, slavery sectional. In a little while the Free Soil and Republican parties will be founded to enforce this doctrine. (b) Congress has no power to prohibit slavery in the territories, but a duty to protect it there. In a little while the South will support this doctrine almost unanimously.

It was difficult to sustain this extreme Southern view, traversing as it did a constitutional practice of sixty years; but the mind of John C. Calhoun was equal to the task. The territories, he argued, belonged to the states united, not to the United States. Congress was merely the attorney of a partnership, and every partner had an equal right to protection for his property in his territories. Slaves were common-law property; Lord Mansfield's contrary dictum in the Sommersett case (1772) did not affect America, consequently the Mexican laws against slavery ceased to have effect in California and New Mexico when they were annexed to the United States. If Congress had, in 1820, prohibited slavery in the territories north of 36° 30', that act was unconstitutional and void. Slavery followed the American flag, wherever firmly planted. Calhoun's new doctrine, embodied in resolutions by the Virginia legislature in 1847, became the ' platform of the South'; and in the Dred Scott case of 1857 it was read into the Federal Constitution. Only one more step, feared many

Northerners, and slave-owning would come to be regarded as a natural right, which not even a state legislature could impair.

It is idle to debate whether Wilmot or Calhoun, North or South was the aggressor in this matter. All depends on the moral standpoint. If slavery was a positive good or a practical necessity, any attempt to restrict or to pinch it out by degrees would justify Southern indignation, if not secession. If slavery was an evil and a curse, any attempt to establish it in virgin territory, even nominally, would be an insult to the free states, and an affront to the public opinion of the Christian world. Motives on both sides were fundamentally defensive. Even when Calhoun wrote of forcing the slavery issue in the North, his motive was to protect the domestic institutions of the slave states. Even when Seward and Chase asserted that every inch of the new territory must be free soil, their object was to defend Northern farmers, wage-earners, and lovers of peace and liberty, against further wars and encroachments of the ' slave power.' Both sides were thinking in terms of principles and precedents. To yield on the purely technical issue of the territories, it was feared, would merely encourage extremists on the other side to new aggressions. It is just such matters of prestige, punctilio, and strategic advantage that bring on great wars.

The state of the American Union in 1848 may be compared with that of Europe in 1905. Political and diplomatic moves will become frequent and startling. Integrating forces will win apparent victories, but in reality grow feebler. The tension will increase, until some event that in ordinary times would have little consequence precipitates a bloody conflict.

2. *Election of 1848*

President Polk, exhausted by the labors of his eventful term, refused to stand for re-election in 1848. Lewis Cass of Michigan, an ardent expansionist, received the Democratic nomination. The Whigs again passed over Henry Clay, and nominated General Taylor, the hero of Buena Vista. A third party, the Free Soil, was formed in the North by a coalition of three hitherto separate and hostile elements — the abolitionist Liberty Party, the ' conscience' or anti-slavery Whigs of New England, and the ' Barnburner' faction of the New York Democracy, which came in to be revenged on Cass for ' stealing ' the Democratic nomination from Van Buren. ' Free soil, free speech, free labor and free men ' was the slogan; Martin Van Buren was the candidate. He carried not one state, but robbed Cass of so many votes in New York that the Whigs won its electoral vote; and as New York went, so went the nation.

Nathaniel Hawthorne in 1849 lost his place in the Salem custom house, and proceeded to write *The Scarlet Letter*. Walt Whitman the same year lost his position with an unsuccessful Democratic newspaper, and proceeded to write *Leaves of Grass*. These were the most memorable results of Zachary Taylor's election, and of the clean sweep that followed in the civil service. 'Old Zach' was a simple, honest soldier, who detested the sophistries of politicians and regarded the slavery question as the artificial abstraction that it was. He was ready to sign any sort of bill Congress might pass for organizing new territories; but before Congress could resolve the deadlock, California proposed to skip the territorial stage altogether, and to become a non-slaveholding state of the Union.

3. *The Forty-niners*

On 24 January 1848, shortly before peace was signed with Mexico, a workman in the Sacramento valley discovered gold in Sutter's mill-race. The news spread along the Pacific coast and by the end of the year all the world was repeating tales of fortunes made from the stream beds of the Sierra Nevada, merely by separating the golden grains from the sand in a common washbowl. Farmers mortgaged their farms, pioneers deserted their clearings, workmen downed tools, clerks left their desks and even ministers their pulpits, for the California gold washings. Young men organized companies with elaborate equipment and by-laws, and were 'grub-staked' by local capitalists as the Elizabethan sea-dogs had been financed by merchant adventurers. Five 'California and Mining' companies were registered in London in January 1849, with a capital of a million and a quarter pounds. Any and every route was taken by the 'forty-niners'; round the Horn in the slowest and craziest vessels, across the continent by the Oregon or more southern trails, or, if pressed for time, by the deadly Isthmus of Panama. It seemed as if all the world were chanting, to the tune of 'Oh! Susanna' —

> Oh! California,
>   That's the land for me;
> I'm off for Sacramento
>   With my washbowl on my knee.

By the end of 1849 thousands of Argonauts from every region of Europe, North America, and the antipodes, were jumping each other's claims, drinking, gambling, and fighting in ramshackle mining villages such as Red Dog, Grub Gulch, and Poker Flat. San Francisco arose in a few months from a village to a city of twenty or twenty-five thousand, where eggs laid on the other side of Cape Horn sold for ten dollars a dozen, and a drink of whisky cost a pinch of gold dust; where Englishmen and Frenchmen, Yankees and Hoosiers, Georgia crackers and Missouri pikers rubbed shoulders with Indians, Mexicans, Sydney ducks, and the 'heathen Chinee.' Fortunes were made in the gold-diggings, to be lost in a night at a 'Frisco faro palace; even more were made by speculation in goods and land. It was a state of nature that would have made Rousseau a tory. Owing to the neglect of Congress the government was still military in theory, though impotent in fact; *alcaldes* and *ayuntamientos* appointed by the military governor administered any sort of law they pleased — it might be the code of Mexico or of Napoleon, or of Judge Lynch.

If Congress would not organize California as a territory, California might make herself a state. The suggestion came from President Taylor. In August his military governor issued writs of election for a convention which met at Monterey in September 1849, and drafted a state constitution prohibiting slavery. This constitution was ratified by a popular vote of over twelve thousand ayes to eight hundred noes; and without waiting for congressional sanction, the people chose a governor and legislature which began to function in 1850. Only formal admission to the Union was wanting; but on that issue the Union almost split.

Up to this time the most extreme Southerners had admitted the right of a state to prohibit slavery — for slavery was emphatically a state matter. But if California were admitted to the Union with its 'Wilmot proviso' constitution, slavery would have lost over half the American conquests from Mexico. During 1849 the temper of the South had been steadily rising. The governor and legislature of South Carolina only hesitated from secession because they hoped to unite the entire South on that program. Calhoun wrote 'I trust we shall persist in our resistance [to the admission of California] until the restoration of all our rights, or disunion, one or the other, is the consequence. We have borne the wrongs and insults of the North long enough.' California's demand for admission, when Con-

gress was convened in December 1849, at once started a movement
for a Southern convention. Like the Hartford Convention of 1814,
this was intended by extremists to form a stepping-stone toward a
new confederacy.

It is difficult to grasp the real reason for all this sound and fury.
After all, as Henry Clay pointed out, the Southern states had an
equal vote in the Senate, a majority of the cabinet and the Supreme
Court, and a President who was Virginia born and Louisiana bred.
The South had in the end obtained from the Union what she really
wanted — low tariff, protection to slavery in the national capital and
on the high seas, vast theatres of slavery such as Louisiana, Florida,
the Creek and Cherokee lands, and Texas, which had greatly
augmented the economic and political power of the slaveholders.
Only the abolitionists were trying to interfere with slavery where it
already existed; and the Garrison abolitionists had lately come out
for a separation of North from South — secession was their game.
And although passenger traffic on the Underground Railroad was
increasing, its effect upon the security of slave property in the cotton
states was negligible. Judged by the canons of economic determinism, the Southern slave-owners were the nation's ruling class.

Even so, the South had a strong, emotional sense of insecurity.
From every side — England and New England, Jamaica and Mexico,
Ohio and the Northwest, and now California, abolition seemed to be
pointing daggers at the heart of the South. It is under circumstances
such as these that men call upon imagination to supersede thought.
The vision of a great slaveholding republic stretching from the Potomac to the Rio Grande, governed by gentlemen and affording perfect
security to their property in human beings, monopolizing the production of cotton and so dictating to the world, was beginning to lift
up Southern hearts. Slavery must expand to live; contracting its area,
or admitting that it might be contracted, would mean that the abolitionists had the South on the run.

4. The Union Preserved

The House of Representatives that met in December 1849 was so
factional that sixty-three ballots were taken before it could elect a
Speaker, and even the opinions on slavery of candidates for the post
of doorkeeper had to be made the subject of careful inquiry. President Taylor recommended the immediate admission of California

with her free constitution, and the organization of New Mexico and Utah territories without reference to slavery. To protesting senators from Georgia, the old soldier declared his determination to crush secession wherever and whenever it might appear, if he had to lead the army himself.

In the Senate, leaders of the coming struggle such as Davis, Douglas, Seward, and Chase, sat with giants of other days such as Webster, Clay, and Calhoun. It was Henry Clay who divined the high strategy of the moment. The Union was not ripe to meet the issue of secession. Concessions must be made to stop the movement now; time might be trusted to deal with it later. On 27 January 1850 he brought forward the compromise resolutions that kept the peace for ten years. The gist of them was (*a*) immediate admission of free California as her right; (*b*) the organization of territorial governments in New Mexico and Utah, without mention of slavery; (*c*) a new and stringent fugitive slave law; (*d*) abolition of the domestic slave trade in the District of Columbia; (*e*) adjustment of boundary dispute between Texas and New Mexico with assumption of the Texan national debt by the Federal Government.

These resolutions brought on one of those superb Senate debates that did so much to mold public opinion. Clay defended them in a speech that lasted the better part of two days. Haggard in aspect and faltering in voice he rose to speak, but his passionate, unwavering devotion to the Union seemed to bring back all the charm and fire of 'Young Harry of the West,' and to lift him and his audience to high issues. His appeal was to the North for concession, and to the South for peace. He asked the North to accept the substance of the Wilmot proviso without the principle, and honestly to fulfil her obligation to return fugitive slaves. He reminded the South of the great benefits she derived from the Union, and warned her against the delusion that secession was constitutional, or could be peaceful, or would be acquiesced in by the Middle West. For Clay was old enough to remember the excitement in Kentucky when Spain and France had attempted to stop her river outlet. 'My life upon it,' he offered, 'that the vast population which has already concentrated . . . on the headwaters and the tributaries of the Mississippi, will never give their consent that the mouth of that river shall be held subject to the power of any foreign State.'

Calhoun, grim and emaciated, his voice stifled by the catarrh that shortly led to his death, sat silent, glaring defiance from his hawk-like eyes, while his ultimatum was voiced for him by Senator Mason of Virginia (4 March 1850). ' I have, Senators, believed from the first that the agitation of the subject of slavery would, if not prevented by some timely and effective measure, end in disunion.' ' The cords that bind the States together' are snapping one by one. Three great evangelical churches are now divided. The Federal Union can be saved only by satisfying the South that she can remain within it in safety, that it is not 'being permanently and hopelessly converted into the means of oppressing instead of protecting' her. The Senator from Kentucky cannot save the Union with his compromise. The North must ' do justice by conceding to the South an equal right in the acquired territory' — by admitting slavery to California and New Mexico — by doing her duty as to fugitive slaves, by restoring to the South, through constitutional amendment, the equilibrium of power she once possessed in the Federal Government; [2] and she must 'cease the agitation of the slave question.' Free speech on slavery must end, even in the North.

Three days later Webster rose for his last great speech. His voice had lost its deep resonance, his massive frame was shrunk, and his face was lined with suffering and sorrow. But in his heart glowed the ancient love of country, and the spell of his personality fell on Senate and galleries with his opening words: ' I speak to-day for the preservation of the Union. " Hear me for my cause." ' Viewing the situation eye to eye with Clay, Webster merely restated in richer language the points made by his old-time rival; but the North could never have been induced to swallow a new fugitive slave law, unless Webster held the spoon. Just as his reply to Hayne in 1830 stimulated the growth of Union sentiment, so the seventh of March speech of 1850 permitted that sentiment to ripen, until it became irresistible.

Senator Seward of New York, in opposing the compromise from the opposite angle, spoke for the ' conscience' Whigs, and for the yet unborn Republican party. He admitted that Congress had the constitutional power to establish slavery in the territories. ' But there is a higher law than the Constitution which regulates our authority over the domain': the law of God, whence alone the laws of man can derive their sanction. The fugitive slave bill would endanger the Union far more than any anti-slavery measure. 'All measures which

---

[2] There seems no doubt that Calhoun's proposed amendment would have taken the form of a dual executive, one President elected by the North and one by the South, each armed with a veto.

fortify slavery or extend it, tend to the consummation of violence; all that check its extension, and abate its strength, tend to its peaceful extirpation.'

As the debate progressed compromise sentiment developed. The Southern convention at Nashville, of which the disunionists had high hopes, adjourned in June, after passing some harmless resolutions. Yet much parliamentary manœuvring, and the steady, loyal support of the Southern Whigs both in and out of Congress, were necessary to get the compromise through. In early September 1850 the essential bills passed: the admission of California; the fugitive slave law; the organization of New Mexico and Utah as territories free to enter the Union with or without slavery when sufficiently populous; abolition of the slave trade in Washington; adjustment of the Texan boundary; assumption of the Texan debt. Once more the Union was preserved by the same spirit of compromise that created it; but for the last time.

Another year elapsed before it was certain that the secession movement in the cotton states could be stopped. In the state elections Whigs and Democrats disappeared. The contest was between a Union party led by the Georgian triumvirate, Stephens, Toombs, and Cobb; and a 'Southern rights' or immediate secession party, led by Rhett, Quitman, and Yancey. The Unionists met the secessionists on their own ground, squarely denying the existence of a constitutional right of secession; although, like all Americans, they freely admitted the Lockean 'right of revolution' in case the South were really oppressed. In every cotton state the Unionists won, though in South Carolina and Mississippi the contest was close.

In the North the Democrats accepted the compromise; the Free-Soilers and abolitionists denounced it in the most frenzied terms; the Whigs, in spite of Webster's eloquence, were divided in sentiment between acquiescence and repudiation. It was the Fugitive Slave Act which stuck in Northern throats. If only the South could have realized that the one hope for slavery was to let the North forget about it, instead of perpetually rubbing it in by hunting runaways through Northern streets and countryside! Even Emerson, the serene philosopher who had advised the abolitionists to love neighbors more and black brethren less, wrote in his journal, ' This filthy enactment was made in the nineteenth century, by people who could read and write. I will not obey it, by God! '

Already two of the principal antagonists had passed away. Calhoun died on 31 March 1850. His coffin made a triumphal progress through the Southern states to Charleston, where friends and followers pledged devotion to his principles by the marble tombstone over his grave in St. Philip's churchyard. His real monument, as Walt Whitman heard a soldier say in 1865, was the ruined South, a generation of young men destroyed, society torn up by the roots, and slaves become masters.

President Taylor died on 9 July 1850. His vice-presidential successor, a colorless New York Whig named Millard Fillmore, signed the compromise bills. ' Old Bullion ' Benton was defeated for re-election to the Senate in 1851. His Andrew Jackson nationalism had grown old-fashioned in Missouri. Clay and Webster, the one denounced as traitor by Southern hotspurs, the other compared with Lucifer by New England reformers, had two years only to live; but that was time enough to teach them grave doubts whether their compromise could long be maintained. With their death the second generation of independent Americans may be said to have gone. The galaxy of 1812 that had seemed to bind the heavens together was extinguished.

XXXI

YOUNG AMERICA
1850–1854

1. *Calm before Storm*

WITH the passage of the compromise of 1850 the slavery question subsided, and other matters occupied the public prints, if not the public's mind. Higher prices for cotton restored prosperity in the South, and confidence to her sons. In the North, Jenny Lind and the Rochester spirit-rappings supplanted the compromise as a topic of conversation. Not that slavery was forgotten. *Uncle Tom's Cabin,* published in 1852, served to keep it in the back of people's minds; but everyone save Northern abolitionists and Southern 'fire-eaters' wished to let it remain there.

The period 1849 to 1857 was one of industrial development, along the lines already marked out between North and South. The railroad supplanted the canal as a freight carrier, and opened the prairies to profitable settlement. Immigration reached a new high level, and occasioned a new nativist movement in politics. Industrial expansion and westward migration allowed wages to rise evenly with prices. In the labor movement talk gave way to action. Unions of the later American type were concluding trade agreements with their employers, federating nationally on craft lines, but strictly avoiding politics. Marxian socialism came in with the German immigrants, but the 'Proletarierbund' that one of them founded quickly expired. The American workingman ignored Utopia but demanded two dollars a day and roast beef. Neal Dow won a famous victory with the Maine prohibitory law, and Arthur's *Ten Nights in a Bar-Room* spread the gospel of Temperance; Melville and Walt Whitman joined the increasing ranks of men of letters. Baseball became popular; yacht racing and intercollegiate rowing were introduced, together with vulgar luxury. In New York, Newport, and Saratoga, according to the season, could be found 'a set of exquisites — daintily arrayed men who spend half their income on their persons, and shrink from the touch of a woollen glove . . . delicate and lovely women, who wear the finest furs and roll in the most stylish equipages.'

At the same time the cotton kingdom was consolidating, and becoming more conscious of its strength. Kentucky backwoodsmen, who in the thirties had taken up land in the black belts, were now gentleman planters, who mingled on equal terms with the first families of Virginia in the thermal stations of the mountains. Their elder sons, after leading volunteers in the Mexican War, had become lawyers or planters in turn; their younger sons were patronizing the newer colleges of the lower South, or attending the University of Virginia, with hounds and hunters and black servants. Dread of abolition, with its implication of negro equality, was binding the yeoman and poor whites more closely to their slaveholding neighbors. Economically, the cotton kingdom appeared to be growing stronger. The annual cotton crop rose from a thousand million to twenty-three hundred million pounds, but never lacked purchasers. De Bow's *Review* was preaching the use of guano, conservation of soil, diversification of crops, and local manufactures. Southern society was ripening into Southern civilization. If only the South could have achieved security for her social system, or had dared to lift her ban on creative thought, the late fifties might well have brought an outburst of literary activity that would have surpassed that of New England. Instead, they brought a fierce propaganda for Southern independence.

The presidential election of 1852 proved that an overwhelming majority of Americans were disposed to regard the Compromise of 1850 as final. As such it was proclaimed by the Democratic party when nominating Franklin Pierce of New Hampshire. A winning smile and a blank (hence blameless) political record were the only apparent qualifications of this gentleman. No more were needed. The New York ' Barnburners,' starved by four lean years with the Free-Soilers, returned to their Democratic allegiance; and thousands of Southern Unionists, disgusted by the anti-slavery tendencies of Northern Whigs, went over to their opponents. General Winfield Scott, the Whig presidential candidate, made himself rather ridiculous in the campaign; and, although he was a Virginian by birth, that asset was cancelled by a nationalist career which recalled Jackson, Harrison, and Taylor. The result was a ' landslide ' for Pierce. Scott carried only four states.

The Whig party never recovered from this defeat. Wanting organic unity, they could not survive when their rivals undertook to maintain the great compromise and the great silence. The Democratic party was fast becoming a national conservative party, directed by Southern planters and maintained by Northern votes. It controlled by Federal Government for eight years, while the doting Whigs grew almost cross-eyed trying to discern the leading trends in thirty-one states.

2. *Irredentist Democracy*

For a time it seemed as if more expansion would be the thing. The revolutions of 1848 justified America no less than the victory over Mexico. France adopted a constitution which was a centralized edition of that of the United States. Republicanism and democracy appeared to be sweeping the world. A 'Young America' movement sprang up within the Democratic party, a movement devoted at first to creating ideals of service and duty, then to enlisting young America's aid for democratic movements beyond the seas — and finally to electing Stephen A. Douglas to the Presidency. Walt Whitman spoke for young America in his poem on the flag:

O hasten flag of man — O with sure and steady step, passing highest
    flag of kings,
Walk supreme to the heavens' mighty symbol — run up above them all
Flag of stars! thick-sprinkled bunting!

When the events of 1850 dashed these generous hopes Walt sounded the note of robust optimism that has heartened thousands of imprisoned and exiled patriots:

Liberty, let others despair of you — I never despair of you!

There had been wild talk in 1848 of annexing Ireland and Sicily, as certain revolutionists in those countries requested; and when the news came that Hungary had fallen, the legislatures of New York, Ohio, and Indiana called for action. In Congress most of the Western senators voted for a resolution offered by Lewis Cass, to suspend diplomatic relations with Austria; but the cautious Whigs and Southern Democrats voted it down. Even Webster indulged popular sentiment by insulting the House of Hapsburg in a diplomatic note. Louis Kossuth, brought to New York as guest of the nation in 1851, was given an overwhelming ovation; and a Harvard professor who exposed Hungarian humbug was voted out of office by state senators. 'Europe is antiquated, decrepit, tottering on the verge of dissolution,' declared Senator Douglas. 'It is a vast grave-yard.'

American diplomacy was particularly truculent when directed by Southern gentlemen who wanted new slave territory, as compensation for the 'loss' of California. Cuba, during these eventful years, was in its normal state of unrest. Certain Southern statesmen professed to fear lest the island should fall to England, or become a black republic like Hayti. Others had an eye on the large and redundant slave population there. Polk proposed to buy Cuba in 1848 for a hundred million dollars, but Spain rejected his offer with contempt. Then came filibustering expeditions, frowned upon by Taylor, tolerated by Fillmore and Pierce; and consequent interference by the Spanish authorities with Yankee traders. One such instance, the case of the *Black Warrior* (1854), seemed a good opportunity to provoke Spain into war. The Secretary of War, Jefferson Davis, urged President Pierce to take that line; but the Secretary of State, W. L. Marcy, kept his head; and Spain disappointed the annexationists by apologizing. There was a comic anticlimax when the American ministers to Spain, France, and Great Britain held a conclave at Ostend, and issued a farcical manifesto (18 October 1854). 'In the progress of human events the time has arrived,' they informed the world, ' when the vital interests of Spain are as seriously involved in the sale as those of the United States in the purchase of the island' of Cuba. With the purchase money, Spain might 'become a centre of attraction for the travelling world,' and ' her vineyards would bring forth a vastly increased quantity of choice wines.' Should she be so unreasonable as to refuse, then, 'by every law, human and divine, we shall be justified in wresting it from Spain if we possess the power.' The Ostend manifesto had no other result than to lower American prestige in Europe, and that of Pierce at home.

3. *Pacific and Caribbean Waters*

The more solid achievements of American diplomacy under Fillmore and Pierce flowed from the territorial acquisitions in 1846–48. California and Oregon together became the mainspring of American history for ten years. Desire for the one led to the Mexican War; the acquisition of both brought on the slavery dispute of 1846 to 1850. Together they inspired a remarkable diplomatic adventure in the Pacific that broke down Japanese isolation. The difficulty of communicating with California and Oregon by overland trails led (*a*) to projects of inter-oceanic canals, which raised another controversy with Great Britain; (*b*) to the perfection of the sailing ship, and a temporary ascendency of the American merchant marine; (*c*) to projects of transcontinental railways, which raised once more the question of slavery in the territories, and led directly to the Civil War.

Diplomacy lagged far behind the American merchant flag in the Pacific, until it was planted firmly on Pacific shores. In 1844 Caleb Cushing negotiated a treaty with China, in which he obtained access to the treaty ports and extra-territorial privileges for American merchants, but expressly discountenanced those who were dealing in opium. Japan had been closed for two centuries to all foreign intercourse, save a strictly regulated trade with the Dutch and Chinese at Nagasaki, when the gold rush to California brought American steamships into the Pacific. A desire for a coaling station and for trade prompted the first American mission to Japan. Commodore Matthew C. Perry, brother of the hero of Lake Erie, was entrusted with the mission. On 8 July 1853 his armed squadron, including a new steam frigate, anchored in Yedo Bay, about thirty miles from the then capital of Japan. Although forbidden to land there, Perry so impressed the Shogunate by his display of force, that, contrary to all precedent, his credentials were received and referred to the Mikado and the daimios. Perry tactfully sailed away to China, in order to give the daimios time to make up their minds; and by the time he returned (February 1854) they had decided to yield. Picturesque conferences were held at the little village of Yokohama. Gifts were exchanged: the rarest lacquers and most beautiful brocades for a set of telegraph instruments, a miniature locomotive, and an assortment of farming implements, lethal weapons, and whiskys. Such was old Japan's first taste of modern civilization. On 31 March 1854 the epoch-making Treaty of Kanagawa was signed. The United States was allowed to establish a consulate, and American vessels were permitted to visit certain Japanese ports for supplies and a limited trade. Such was the famous opening of Japan. But, as Mr. Dooley once observed, ' We didn't go in; they kim out.'

In the matter of communications between the older United States and its Pacific territories, the simplest solution appeared to be an inter-oceanic canal. Three different routes were seriously considered: the Isthmus of Tehuantepec, the Isthmus of Panama, and

Lake Nicaragua. Over the first route, which was impracticable for a canal, President Pierce obtained by the Gadsden treaty of 1853 the privilege to build a rail or plank road, with the right of transit, even in time of war. This concession, never used, was formally abrogated in 1937. Over the Isthmus of Panama, Polk obtained a right of transit by treaty with Colombia, in return for guaranteeing to that republic her sovereignty over the Isthmus, and undertaking to defend its neutrality. A Panama railway was undertaken by American capital and completed in 1855. The Nicaragua route brought on a dangerous controversy with Great Britain.

When the Monroe Doctrine was declared, the British Empire already had two bases in Central America: the old logwood establishment of Belize, and a shadowy protectorate over the Mosquito Indians on the Nicaraguan coast. Owing to the weakness of the local republics, the enterprise of British agents, and the lapse of the Monroe Doctrine at Washington, British influence and dominion sensibly increased in Central America between 1825 and 1845. A British superintendent of Belize took possession of the Bay Islands off the coast of Honduras in 1838, and at his suggestion the government stationed a British resident in 'Mosquitia,' which thus became a native Indian protectorate, with a flag incorporating the Union Jack. Lord Palmerston, who returned to the Foreign Office in 1846, believed it high time to check 'manifest destiny' in that part of the world, and in 1848 formally declared the sovereignty of 'Mosquitia' over San Juan or Greytown, the eastern terminus of the proposed Nicaragua ship canal.

Further and unauthorized activities of American and British agents in Central America then brought about a very ticklish situation, from which their two countries were only able to emerge by negotiating the Clayton-Bulwer treaty (15 April 1850). It was agreed that neither government would ever fortify, or obtain exclusive control over, the proposed Nicaragua canal. Both guaranteed its neutrality, and invited other nations to join. Later generations of Americans regarded the Clayton-Bulwer treaty as a self-denying ordinance, and condemned the Senate for ratifying it. At the time, however, it was a very fair compromise of the interests that Britain had acquired in Central America without protest from the United States, and the new special interest of the United States in Isthmian communication. Nevertheless, it marked a retreat from the foreign policy of Adams and Polk.

As American capitalists showed much less enthusiasm than the diplomatists for a ship canal, the Clayton-Bulwer treaty might have caused no embarrassment for fifty years, but for a clause on the exact meaning of which both Clayton and Bulwer agreed to disagree.[1] The United States government supposed that it meant British withdrawal from the Bay Islands, Greytown, and the Mosquito coast; although it did not object to the ancient custom of crowning some black-and-tan Sambo with an old admiral's hat as King of Mosquitia, if that gratified him and amused the authorities of Belize. The British government insisted that the treaty merely forbade future acquisition, and held on to what it had. This dispute became dangerous in 1854, when President Pierce and the Democrats were looking for an issue to distract the country from the slavery question, and their opponents were determined to prevent them from running away with it. The game of 'twisting the lion's tail' then began, the object being to produce a roar that would be grateful in the ears of native and Irish-American voters. The equally dangerous game of converting a doubtful interpretation into a prescriptive right was played by Palmerston. And the filibustering game was played in Nicaragua by William Walker, the 'grey-eyed man of destiny,' with the object of bringing it into the Union as another slave state. Fortunately both governments had the good sense to compromise. In 1859–60 Great Britain ceded the Bay Islands to Honduras and the Mosquito coast to Nicaragua — with a string to it, to be sure, but a string that was never pulled. In the end, the whole subject of Isthmian diplomacy served to clear up Anglo-American relations. America became more attached to the Monroe Doctrine, and England very definitely renounced the policy of Canning, Aberdeen, and Palmerston, of establishing a British counterweight in Latin America.

4. Reciprocity with Canada

Midway in the Isthmian negotiations there was established a landmark in North American commerce and diplomacy, the Canadian Reciprocity Treaty of 1854. The onward march of free trade in Britain had harassed Canadian feeling, and played fast and loose with Canadian interests. Preference to colonial grain and flour gave

---

[1] 'The Governments of the United States and Great Britain hereby declare that neither one nor the other will ever . . . occupy, or fortify, or colonize, or assume, or exercise any dominion over Nicaragua, Costa Rica, the Mosquito Coast, or any part of Central America.'

Canada the business of milling American wheat for the British market. Peel's repeal of the Corn Laws abolished this preference and prostrated the industry. At the request of the Canadian legislature the British government attempted to negotiate at Washington a reciprocity treaty for Canada, and Parliament passed an enabling act.

Canada could offer *quid pro quo:* the free navigation of the St. Lawrence, which the United States had been demanding as a natural right; and the fishing grounds off Labrador and the Gulf, where the sportive mackerel was wont to elude Yankee fishermen. But it was a difficult matter to effect that exchange. The Foreign Office and the State Department had no trouble in concluding a reciprocity treaty, but such a treaty required concurrent acts of Parliament, of Congress, and of four Canadian legislatures; and the Maritime Provinces were loath to admit Yankees to their shore fisheries. William L. Marcy, the New York spoilsman who became Pierce's Secretary of State, greased the way at Halifax, Fredericton, and St. John by judicious bribery; and Lord Elgin, a hard-headed but genial Scot, is said to have floated the treaty through the United States Senate on oceans of champagne. Both served their respective countries well. The treaty (5 June 1854) opened the United States market to Canadian farm produce, timber, and fish, and dealt a heavy blow to Canadian separatism, while Yankee fishermen obtained new privileges in Canadian territorial waters and the right to navigate the Great Lakes, the St. Lawrence, and their connecting canals. Thus Britain maintained her political dominion over Canada by sanctioning an economic union with the United States.

5. *The Clipper Ship*

While the diplomatists were wrangling over imaginary canals to the Pacific, the shipwrights of New York and New England were engaged in cutting down the time of ocean passage round Cape Horn. In one month of 1850 thirty-three sailing vessels from New York and Boston entered San Francisco bay after an average passage of one hundred and fifty-nine days. Then there came booming through the Golden Gate the clipper ship *Sea Witch* of New York, ninety-seven days out. At once the cry went up for clipper ships at any price.

This new type of sailing vessel — characterized by great length in proportion to breadth of beam, an enormous sail area, and long concave bows ending in a gracefully curved cutwater — had been devised for the China-New York tea trade. The voyage of the *Sea Witch* showed its possibilities. Her record was broken by the *Surprise* within a year, and in 1851 the *Flying Cloud* made 'Frisco in eighty-nine days from New York, a record never surpassed. As California then afforded no return cargo save gold dust (the export of wheat began only in 1855), the Yankee clippers proceeded in ballast to the Chinese treaty ports, where they came into competition with the British marine; and the result was more impressive than the victory of the yacht *America*. Crack East-Indiamen humbly waited for a cargo weeks on end, while one American clipper after another sailed off with a cargo of tea at double the ordinary freights. When the *Oriental* of New York appeared at London, ninety-seven days from Hong-Kong, crowds thronged the West India docks to admire her beautiful hull, lofty rig, and patent fittings; the Admiralty took off her lines in dry dock, and the *Times* came out with a leader challenging British shipbuilders to set their 'long practised skill, steady industry and dogged determination' against the 'youth, ingenuity and ardour' of the United States.

In answer to this challenge, the first British clipper ships, the *Stornoway* and *Chrysolite,* were promptly built. Yet so swiftly was the type developed that by the time British designers had caught up with the *Oriental,* their Yankee rivals had far outdistanced them. In 1852 Donald McKay of Boston launched the *Sovereign of the Seas,* the largest merchant vessel yet built, and the boldest in design: stately as a cathedral, beautiful as a terraced cloud. A young American naval officer, Lieutenant Matthew Fontaine Maury of Virginia, had just been charting trade-winds and ocean currents by the study of ships' logs. It was he who discovered that the strong and steady westerly gales were to be found in the 'roaring forties' south latitude. Following his sailing directions, the *Sovereign of the Seas* on her homeward voyage made a day's run of 411 nautical miles, a run surpassed only four or five times in the history of sailing vessels, only once by the product of another shipyard than McKay's, and that was in the State of Maine.

By this time the British Navigation Acts had been repealed, and gold had been discovered in Australia. For that destination the *Sovereign* was chartered in Liverpool, and made so successful a voyage that four clippers were ordered of Donald McKay for the Australian Black Ball Line. Two of them, the *James Baines* and

Lightning, were the fastest sailing ships that ever sailed under the red ensign. The *Baines,* with her skysail studding-sails and main moonsail, established the record transatlantic sailing passage — 12¼ days Boston to Liverpool — and then another from Liverpool to Melbourne — 63 days — that still holds good. The *Lightning* on her maiden voyage made a day's run never equalled by a sailing vessel, and not surpassed by a steamship for a generation afterward: 436 nautical miles.

Nightingale and *Witch of the Wave, Northern Light* and *Southern Cross, Young America* and *Great Republic, Golden Age* and *Herald of the Morning, Red Jacket* and *Westward Ho!, Dreadnought* and *Glory of the Seas* —

> I cannot tell their wonder nor make known
>
> . . . .
>
> These splendid ships, each with her grace, her glory,
> Her memory of old song or comrade's story,
> Still in my mind the image of life's need,
> Beauty in hardest action, beauty indeed [2]

No sailing vessel ever approached them in power, majesty, or speed. It seemed as if all the ingenuity of the Yankee race, with its latent artistic genius, had at last found perfect and harmonious expression. Yet the Yankee clipper fulfilled a very limited purpose: speed to the gold-fields at any price or risk. When that was no longer an object, no more were built; and when the panic of 1857 brought a worldwide depression in shipping, it was the clipper-shipowners who suffered first and most. British builders, leaving glory to their rivals, were quietly evolving a more useful type of medium clipper, and perfecting the iron screw steamer.

The American iron industry and engineering trades were so backward, and the extent of inland and protected waters in the United States was so great, that American steamship builders clung too long to the wooden side-wheeler, unsuitable for ocean work. The Pacific Mail did well in its own sphere, and for a few years the Collins Line, heavily subsidized by Congress, challenged the Cunard; but its vessels had an unfortunate way of foundering. By 1857 the British Empire had an ocean-going steam tonnage of almost half a million tons, as compared with ninety thousand under the American flag. England had won back her maritime supremacy in fair compe-

---

[2] John Masefield, 'Ships'; quoted by kind permission of the Poet Laureate and Messrs. Macmillan.

tition, by the skill of her engineers and the sturdy courage of her shipbuilders. Civil war turned the Yankee mind to other objects; the World War revived an ancient challenge.

6. *Prairie Settlement and Pacific Railways*

Transportation also had a vital effect on the settlement of the West, where a contest over railway routes leads us back to slavery once more.

Down to 1850 American agricultural settlement had been limited to the forests and to the smaller prairies with scattered groves of trees by the pioneer's dependence on wood and running water. The larger treeless prairies of Illinois and Iowa were devoid of shelter and remote from markets. Their earliest settlers had to live in sod cabins, and contend with wolves, prairie fires, locusts, and agues. Most emigrants preferred to take the long journey to Oregon, where they could renew the backwoods life that they loved. As late as 1849 one could look northward from a knoll near Peoria, Illinois, over an undulating plain, unbroken by a house or tree as far as the eye could reach.

After 1850 the prairie farmer instead of the backwoodsman became the typical American pioneer. In part the change was due to the new agricultural machinery, which helped to solve the labor problem; for, owing to the amazing fertility of the prairies, grain crops were often too abundant for their owner to harvest with scythe, cradle, and sickle, even when all the neighbors within thirty miles helped each other. The important principle of the modern reaper, a moving knife against a fixed finger, was the basis of the reaping machines invented independently by Obed Hussey at Cincinnati, and Cyrus H. McCormick in the Valley of Virginia, and patented respectively in 1833 and 1834. McCormick, who was the better business man and organizer of the two, was building a thousand reapers a year at his Chicago plant by 1851. Marsh's harvester, which gathered the wheat into sheaves, Appleby's self-knotting binder, and the steel-toothed cultivator followed later. An improved form of plow with a steel mold-board made it easier to break up the tough prairie sod. Steel wire solved the fencing problem. At London in 1851 and Paris in 1855, American machines beat all comers in competitive trials. Yet the greatest impetus to prairie farming came from the rising price of wheat (from $0.93 a bushel in 1851 to $2.50 in 1855 at the New

York market), and the rapid building of railroads into the prairie country, from lake and river ports like Chicago, Milwaukee, and St. Louis. In 1850 railroads had hardly penetrated the Middle West; by 1860 their network covered it. The railway mileage in Ohio, Indiana, Illinois, Michigan, and Wisconsin increased from 660 in 1847 to 7,653 in 1861; that of the United States as a whole from 9,021 to 30,365. The prairie farmer, hitherto dependent on long wagon hauls over execrable roads, was then able to market his grain, and obtain the means of comfortable living. Most important of the prairie railways was the Illinois Central, financed and managed by capitalists of New York and Boston, and endowed by Act of Congress with alternate sections of public land on each side of its right-of-way. The completion of this line from Chicago to Cairo in 1856 opened up the central prairies to profitable settlement. And it is a curious coincidence that the same year saw the foundation of a North-and-West political party which shattered the dream of a South-and-West alliance; and which, four years later, drove the South to seek safety in independence.

In the meantime a struggle over the route of a transcontinental railway was promoting the same result. Of the many different schemes projected since 1845, the four most important were (1) the northern, from the upper Mississippi to the upper Missouri, and by Lewis and Clark's trail to the Columbia river (the route of the Great Northern Railway); (2) the central, from St. Louis up the Kansas and Arkansas rivers, across the Rockies to the Great Salt Lake and by the California trail to San Francisco (followed in part by the Missouri Pacific); (3) the thirty-fifth parallel route from Memphis, up the Arkansas and Canadian rivers, across the Rockies near Santa Fé, and through the Apache and Mojave country to Los Angeles; (4) the southern, from New Orleans up the Red river and across Texas, and by the Gila valley to Yuma and San Diego. Either of the first two would follow the natural route of emigration, and bind California and Oregon to the North; but the unorganized Indian country was an obstacle. The southern route was the shortest to the coast, with the best contours, and led through states and territories already organized. It might well be the means of the South recovering all she had lost by the compromise of 1850. Congress, in March 1853, authorized surveys of these four routes under the direction of the War Department.

Jefferson Davis was Secretary of War and President Pierce's mentor. Although a state-rights man, his keen desire for a southern transcontinental railway led him to advocate its construction by the Federal Government under the war power — a policy that could only be justified by the nationalist theories of Marshall and Adams. As soon as it became clear that such a railway would have to pass through a bit of Mexican territory, Davis induced the President to buy the land for ten million dollars. In the Gadsden treaty of 30 December 1853 this purchase was effected. The stage was now set for Congress to sanction the southern route.

7. The Kansas-Nebraska Bill

Stephen A. Douglas was then senior Senator from Illinois. A sturdy five-footer, chock-full of brains, bounce, and swagger, the 'little giant' or 'steam engine in britches' was the best orator in the Northwest, and the idol of Northern Democrats. As an Illinoisian and a heavy speculator in western lands including the city site which he expected to be the eastern terminus of the road, he wished the transcontinental railway to take the central route. In order to contest the southern route on even terms, law and government must be extended over, and settlers invited into, the region through which the central route must pass. Douglas, accordingly, reported a bill to organize the great plains as the Territory of Nebraska, in January 1854. Earlier bills of that nature had been defeated by Southern opposition. So Douglas baited this one for Southern votes with a principle that he called 'popular sovereignty.' It would rest with the people of the new territory to decide whether or not they would have slavery, as soon as they obtained a territorial legislature.

Popular sovereignty (or 'squatter sovereignty' as it was contemptuously called) did not satisfy certain senators. As Nebraska would be wholly north of 36° 30', slavery therein would be prohibited by the Missouri Compromise Act of 1820. Douglas's bill would have repealed that act implicitly; but the senators from Kentucky and Missouri insisted on repealing it explicitly. Douglas consented, although, as he told Senator Dixon, it would 'raise a hell of a storm.' He also agreed to divide the new territory into Kansas and Nebraska, so that the Missourians might secure the one, and the Iowans the other. President Pierce was easily persuaded by Jefferson Davis to make it an administration measure; for Davis was glad to renounce the Southern route in return for removing a prohibition of slavery.

The fat was in the fire. At this proposal to repeal the Missouri Compromise the angry passions of anti-slavery and pro-slavery flared up; and there was no Clay to quench them. Everyone forgot about the railroad. The South had not asked for Kansas, and did not want Kansas; but 'Southern rights' were involved. No one outside Missouri proposed to take slaves farther west, and even Missouri's chief interest was not so much in promoting a transcontinental railway as in preventing an extension of the Underground Railroad; but Southern honor demanded that slavery should follow the flag. Northerners, on the other hand, were alarmed at a new proposal to extend the 'slave power,' and to break a compromise of thirty years' standing. People could hardly have been more startled at a proposition to repeal habeas corpus and trial by jury, than they were by the Kansas-Nebraska bill. Stephen Douglas, morally obtuse, could not see that a principle was involved: he simply did not realize the depth and strength of Northern sentiment against opening virgin territory to the 'peculiar institution.' The North, in Lincoln's picturesque phrase, was determined to give her pioneers 'a clean bed, with no snakes in it.'

For three months the bitter debate dragged on. President Pierce, under the influence of Jefferson Davis, tried to whip his party into line; and all but a few Northern Democrats obeyed. Old Sam Houston of Texas reminded the Senate in vain that by solemn treaties it had confirmed most of Kansas and Nebraska to the Indians 'as long as grass shall grow and water run.' No one else thought of the aborigines. Federal agents were already bullying them into renouncing their perpetual titles. The once powerful Delaware or Leni-Lenape accepted a small reservation with an annual bounty. Others, like the Shawnee and Miami, who had once terrorized the Kentucky frontier and beaten a federal army, were removed to the Indian Territory, which fortunately lay between the rival railway routes.

Democratic discipline triumphed, and on 25 May 1854 the Kansas-Nebraska bill passed the Senate by a comfortable majority. 'It is at once the worst and best Bill on which Congress ever acted,' declared Senator Sumner. The worst, inasmuch as it is a present victory for slavery. The best, for 'it annuls all past compromises with slavery, and makes all future compromises impossible. Thus it puts freedom and slavery face to face, and bids them grapple. Who can doubt the result?'

XXXII

THE IRREPRESSIBLE CONFLICT
1854–1859

1. The Know-Nothing Interlude

'IF the Nebraska bill should be passed, the Fugitive Slave Law is a dead letter throughout New England' wrote a Southerner in Boston. 'As easily could a law prohibiting the eating of codfish and pumpkin pies be enforced.' It did pass on 25 May 1854. The next day a Boston mob led by a Unitarian minister tried to rescue a fugitive slave from the courthouse where he was detained for examination. They did not succeed. Anthony Burns, the slave, was identified by his master, and escorted to the wharf by a battalion of United States artillery, four platoons of marines, and the sheriff's posse, through streets lined with hissing and groaning spectators, who were held back by twenty-two companies of state militia. It cost the United States about $100,000 to return that slave to his master; the real bill came later, and it was paid in blood.

Many people who were indignant over the Kansas-Nebraska Act felt it was time to form a new anti-slavery party. A convention held under the oaks at Jackson, Michigan, on 6 July 1854, resolved to oppose the extension of slavery, and 'be known as "Republicans" until the contest be terminated.' Many places claim the birthplace of the Republican Party, but Jackson at least made the happy suggestion of adopting Jefferson's old label, disused since the time when his Republican Party split into Democrats and Whigs. The new party, however, was slow in gathering momentum outside the Northwest. Seward sulked in his Whig tent; the 'Anti-Nebraska Democrats' were loath to cut all connection with their party; the Free-Soilers could not see why a new party was needed; and the people were distracted by a new gospel of ignorance.

Know-nothingism was the political exploitation of an instinctive dislike for foreigners. Many native-born Americans found the rising flood of Irish Catholics and Germans most unpleasant. Others regarded the catering of Democrats to the immigrant vote as a menace, and the truculent attitude of the immigrant press towards American institutions, alarming. The visit of a tactless papal nuncio appears to have convinced many Northern patriots that the Republic was in danger from Rome; and the activities of German radicals, who had begun to preach the gospel according to St. Marx, alarmed the pious South. Accordingly a secret 'Order of the Star-Spangled Banner,' with elaborate ritual and rigid discipline, was formed by native-born Protestants. Members, when questioned by outsiders, answered 'I know nothing.' Candidates nominated secretly developed surprising strength at the polls, and many politicians joined up, thinking the cat would jump that way. In the state elections of 1854 the Know-nothings almost won New York, and did win Massachusetts, electing a new legislature that spent its time largely on clownish investigations of Catholic schools and nunneries. At Baltimore they organized the 'plug-uglies,' gangs who attended the polls armed with carpenters' awls, to 'plug' voters who did not give the pass-word. In the summer of 1855 the American party, as it then called itself, held a national convention of which the Southern members obtained control, and passed pro-slavery resolutions. The Northerners then lost interest, and outside Maryland the movement collapsed. 'Anything more low, obscene, feculent,' wrote Rufus Choate, 'the manifold heavings of history have not cast up.' Mr. Choate did not live to see the Ku Klux Klan, the Black Legion, and similar manifestations of our own day.

2. Bleeding Kansas, Black Republicanism

Kansas soon diverted attention from the popish peril. Since 'popular sovereignty' was to settle the status of slavery in Kansas, pro- and anti-slavery people scrambled to get there first. The Federal Government opened a land office in the territory in July 1854, before the Indian titles were fairly extinguished; and even before that Missourians began to flock across the border and stake out claims. In the meantime, some enterprising Yankees had formed a company to finance the migration of Northerners. This effort aroused the utmost indignation among the Missourians, who proceeded to blockade the Missouri river against the Northern immigrants, and to sack their first settlement at Lawrence. Presently the Emigrant Aid Company began to arm free-state settlers with a new breech-loading weapon of precision, the Sharps rifle, or 'Beecher's Bible,' so called after the abolitionist preacher who advised its use. There were merry times in Kansas for three years. Parties of Northern 'jayhawkers' gave battle with 'Kickapoo Rangers,' 'Doniphan Tigers,' and other organizations of 'border ruffians' from Missouri and points south. 'We had at least seven thousand men in the Territory on the day of the election, and one-third of them will remain there,' wrote Senator Atchison of Missouri:

> The pro slavery ticket prevailed everywhere. . . . Now let the Southern men come on with their slaves. Ten thousand families can take possession of and hold every acre of timber in the Territory of Kansas, and this secures the prairie. . . . We are playing for a mighty stake; if we win, we carry slavery to the Pacific Ocean.

Few Southern men, however, cared to risk valuable property in such a region, and free-state settlers came pouring in with the spirit of crusaders. One of them named John Brown accounted for quite a number of 'border ruffians' at the 'Pottawatomi massacre.' Such were the workings of popular sovereignty. Kansas had become the theatre of a Western flanking movement preliminary to the Civil War.

On 19 May 1856 Senator Sumner of Massachusetts delivered a speech on 'The Crime against Kansas' which contained some unpalatable truth, much that was neither truthful nor in good taste, and some disgraceful personal invective against Senator Butler of South Carolina. Three days after, a kinsman of Butler, Preston Brooks, attacked Sumner as he was sitting at his desk in the Senate chamber, and beat him senseless with a stout cane, while Douglas and Toombs looked on. Returning to South Carolina the assailant was fêted from place to place, and presented by admirers with suitably inscribed canes.

A few days after that, the Republican party held a national nominating convention at Philadelphia. It was a mass-meeting of earnest men from all the Northern states, who were convinced that the North, in self-defense, must have a Northern party. For some strange reason the explorer John C. Frémont stampeded the convention, and obtained the first Republican presidential nomination. Their platform proclaimed it 'both the right and the duty of Congress to prohibit in the territories those twin relics of barbarism, polygamy and slavery.' James Buchanan, who had been carefully coached for several years by his bosom friend Slidell, obtained the Democratic nomination; the Know-nothings put up the pallid ex-President Fillmore.

The 'Black Republicans,' as their enemies called them, made a lively campaign. ' Free soil, free speech, and Frémont ' was the slogan. Slavery in the territories was the main issue. Most of the Northern Whigs came over, and the Northern Know-nothings as well. Maryland asserted her independence by voting for Fillmore. Buchanan carried the rest of the South, with Pennsylvania, Illinois, and Indiana; and was elected. Frémont swept the rest of the North.[1] No previous candidate had so nearly united the North and West against the South. Party lines were approaching dangerously close to the Mason and Dixon line; and Southerners, even in this campaign, made it perfectly clear that they would not remain in the Union if a purely Northern party elected its presidential candidate.

3. Dred Scott

On 6 March 1857, two days after Buchanan's inauguration, the Supreme Court published its decision on the famous case of Dred Scott *v*. Sandford. Dred was a slave who had been taken by his master to Illinois, thence to the unorganized territory north of 36° 30′, where slavery had been forbidden by the Missouri Compromise, and finally back to Missouri, where he sued for freedom on the ground of having twice been resident on free soil. Chief Justice Taney, and the four Southerners among his eight associates, welcomed this opportunity to settle the status of slavery in the territories. The opinion of the court declared against Scott's claim for freedom on three grounds: (*a*) as a negro he could not be a citizen of the United States, and therefore had no right to sue in a federal court; (*b*) as a resident of Missouri the laws of Illinois had no longer any effect on his status; (*c*) as a resident of the territory north of 36° 30′ he had not been emancipated because Congress had no right to deprive citizens of their property without ' due process of law.' The Missouri Compromise, it followed, was unconstitutional and void — as Calhoun and the extreme Southerners had claimed.

---

[1] The popular vote was:

Buchanan	1,838,169
Frémont	1,341,264
Fillmore	874,534

The figures include no popular vote for South Carolina. Note the close approximation to the popular vote of 1860.

None of the Chief Justice's opinion was *obiter dictum;* but only on the second point was it sound. As Justice Curtis proved in his vigorous dissenting opinion, negroes had been considered citizens in all the Northern states, even though they had seldom possessed the vote, and as citizens had the right to sue in United States courts. If slaves ever had been common-law property, they ceased to be such upon Lord Mansfield's decision of the Sommersett case (1772). 'Due process of law,' in the Constitution [2] referred to the method of a law's enforcement, not to the substance of a law itself. Once before, in Marbury *v.* Madison (1803), the Supreme Court had declared an act of Congress unconstitutional; but in that case the act in question directly concerned the federal judiciary, while in this it was a general law, resting on precedent, the result of sectional compromise, and enforced during a period of thirty-four years. The decision, therefore, looked like a very far-fetched and questionable attempt of the Supreme Court to sanction Calhoun's doctrine that slavery followed the flag into the territories. Nebraska and Oregon were opened to slavery, as well as Kansas. Squatter sovereignty thenceforth was no sovereignty, for the squatters would no longer overthrow slavery.

Events in Kansas pointed to the same condition. Federal troops were now keeping order, but the free-state and pro-slavery men refused to co-operate. Each group held a convention, drafted a state constitution, ratified it, and appealed to Washington for statehood. The anti-slavery Topeka constitution was rejected in the Senate in 1856. The Lecompton constitution, the most out-and-out pro-slavery charter yet drafted, was accepted by the Senate; but Stephen Douglas insisted on principle that it be re-submitted to the people of Kansas, who rejected it emphatically. In the meantime slavery was legal in Kansas, and in all the Western territories; but the overwhelming majority of Northerners in Kansas made that territory certain to become a free state, sooner or later.

4. *The Lincoln-Douglas Debates*

Until the Kansas struggle Abraham Lincoln had been distinguished from hundreds of Northwestern lawyer-politicians only by a

---

[2] The phrase is from Amendment V of the Constitution, and was a translation of *per legem terrae* in Magna Carta. Lincoln observed in his Springfield speech of 17 June 1858 that the Chief Justice's construction of 'due process' would invalidate

reputation for truthfulness and honesty, and a habit of prolonged, abstracted contemplation. He had played the usual game of Illinois politics, and not well. He had served one term in Congress as a Whig, without distinction. Mary Todd, the belle of Springfield, had married him much against his will, and made his life unhappy. Slavery he had long regarded as an evil thing; but the abolitionist agitation seemed to him mischievous in its effects: a cure worse than the disease.

About the time of the Kansas-Nebraska Act an unseen force began to work on Lincoln's soul, and to prepare him for the most arduous and distressing responsibility that has ever fallen to an American. He began to preach a new testament of anti-slavery, without malice or hatred toward slave-owners.

I surely will not blame them for not doing what I should not know how to do myself. If all earthly power were given me, I should not know what to do as to the existing institution. . . . When they remind us of their constitutional rights, I acknowledge them — not grudgingly, but fully and fairly, and I would give them any legislation for the reclaiming of their fugitives which should not in its stringency be more likely to carry a free man into slavery than our ordinary criminal laws are to hang an innocent one. . . . But all this, to my judgment, furnishes no more excuse for permitting slavery to go into our own free territory than it would for reviving the African slave-trade by law.

Slavery is founded on the selfishness of man's nature — opposition to it in his love of justice. These principles are in eternal antagonism, and when brought into collision so fiercely as slavery extension brings them, shocks and throes and convulsions must ceaselessly follow.

These quotations are from Lincoln's Peoria speech of 16 October 1854. It made him famous throughout the Northwest. Two years later he became a rival candidate to Stephen A. Douglas for election to the Senate from Illinois. The first paragraph of his opening speech in the campaign (16 June 1858) gave the ripe conclusion to his ponderings during the last four years; and struck the key-note of American history for the seven years to come:

We are now far into the fifth year since a policy was initiated with the avowed object and confident promise of putting an end to slavery agitation. Under the operation of that policy, that agitation has not only not ceased, but has constantly augmented. In my opinion it will not cease

every emancipatory act of a state; for a similar clause was in the bill of rights of every northern state constitution.

until a crisis shall have been reached and passed. "A house divided against itself cannot stand." I believe this government cannot endure permanently half slave and half free. I do not expect the Union to be dissolved — I do not expect the house to fall — but I do expect it will cease to be divided. It will become all one thing, or all the other. Either the opponents of slavery will arrest the further spread of it, and place it where the public mind shall rest in the belief that it is in the course of ultimate extinction; or its advocates will push it forward till it shall become alike lawful in all the States, old as well as new, North as well as South.

Lincoln and Douglas engaged in a series of seven joint debates, covering every section of the state, through the summer and autumn of 1858. Imagine some parched little prairie town of central Illinois, set in fields of rustling corn; a dusty courthouse square surrounded by low wooden houses and stores blistering in the August sunshine, decked with flags and party emblems; shirt-sleeved farmers and their families in wagons and buggies and on foot, brass bands blaring out ' Hail! Columbia' and 'Oh! Susanna,' wooden platform with railing, perspiring semicircle of local dignitaries in black frock coats and two-quart beaver hats. The Douglas special train (provided by George B. McClellan, superintendent of the Illinois Central) pulls into the ' deepo ' and fires a salute from the twelve-pounder cannon bolted to a flatcar at the rear. Senator Douglas, escorted by the local Democratic club in columns of fours, drives up in an open carriage, and aggressively mounts the platform. His short, stocky figure is clothed in the best that the city of Washington can produce. Every feature of his face bespeaks confidence and mastery; every gesture of his body, vigor and combativeness. Abe Lincoln, who had previously arrived by an ordinary passenger train, approaches on foot, his furrowed face and long neck conspicuous above the crowd. He shambles on to the platform, displaying a rusty frock coat the sleeves of which stop several inches short of his wrists, and well-worn trousers that show a similar reluctance to approach a pair of enormous feet. His face, as he turns to the crowd, has an air of settled melancholy. If Dickens had only visited Illinois in the summer of 1858! How he would have roared with laughter at the sight of the two champions — the frenzied gestures of Douglas, and Lincoln's awkward habit of bending his knees and then rising to his full height with a jerk, in order to enforce a point — and how he would have listened to them in the end. For no recorded debate in the English language surpassed those between Lincoln and Douglas for keen give and take, pithy Saxon language, and clear exposition of vital issues.

The Dred Scott decision was a blow to popular sovereignty; for it meant that the territories had no legal choice but to accept slavery. But Douglas stuck to his doctrine courageously, and defied Buchanan and the Southern Democrats, when they attempted to impose the Lecompton constitution on Kansas. In the debate at Freeport, Lincoln placed Douglas in a dilemma by asking whether the people of a territory could, in any lawful way, exclude slavery from their limits. Apparently, Douglas must either accept the Dred Scott decision and admit popular sovereignty to be a farce, or separate from his party by repudiating a dictum of the Supreme Court. But this clever statesman had already found a way out of the dilemma. 'Slavery cannot exist a day or an hour anywhere, unless it is supported by local police regulations,' and if a territorial legislature fail to pass a black code, they will effectually keep slavery out. Of course Douglas was right. The relation of a territorial legislature to Congress was similar to that of a colonial legislature in the British Empire to the Privy Council. Congress could invalidate a positive enactment of the territorial legislature, but not force it to pass a law against its will.

It is probable that this 'Freeport doctrine,' as it was called, won Douglas his re-election to the Senate; and he deserved it. Kansas was safe for freedom; and if theoretically slavery were legal in all the territories, there was no chance that any save New Mexico would become a slaveholding state. The only political justification for Lincoln's policy, the Republican policy of overriding the Supreme Court decision and outlawing slavery in the territories, was the extreme unlikelihood that the South could rest content with the Dred Scott principle, any more than she had rested content with the compromises of 1787, 1820, and 1850. Abolition was blowing on the South like a perpetual trade-wind. She was fated to insist on erecting barriers for slavery further and further afield until the world should cry out 'Away with this foul thing!'

Lincoln furnished an even deeper justification in his Quincy speech of 13 October 1858. This controversy over strategic positions, he pointed out, was an effort to dominate the fundamental moral issue:

the difference between the men who think slavery a wrong and those who do not think it wrong. The Republican party think it wrong —

we think it is a moral, a social, and a political wrong. We think it is a wrong not confining itself merely to the persons of the States where it exists, but that it is a wrong which in its tendency, to say the least, affects the existence of the whole nation. Because we think it wrong, we propose a course of policy that shall deal with it as a wrong. We deal with it as with any other wrong, in so far as we can prevent its growing any larger, and so deal with it that in the run of time there may be some promise of an end to it. . . .

I will add this, that if there be any man who does not believe that slavery is wrong in the three aspects which I have mentioned, or in any one of them, that man is misplaced and ought to leave us. While, on the other hand, if there be any man in the Republican party who is impatient over the necessity springing from its actual presence, and is impatient of the constitutional guarantees thrown around it, and would act in disregard of these, he too is misplaced, standing with us.

In his reply Douglas took the ground that the right and wrong of slavery was nobody's business outside the slave states. ' If each state will only agree to mind its own business, and let its neighbors alone . . . this republic can exist forever divided into free and slave states, as our fathers made it and the people of each state have decided.' Lincoln, in rejoinder, thanked his opponent for the admission that slavery must exist forever. The North, almost unconsciously, had come to a determination that this must not be.

5. Was Slavery Doomed?

Lincoln and Seward believed that the next Southern demand would be to force slavery into the free states, as it had already been forced into the free territories. A case involving the status of slaves in transit across free states was actually on its way to the Supreme Court. No responsible Southerner wished to legalize slavery in such places as New York and New England, although most vocal Southerners were becoming insistent that the Northern states should silence the abolitionists. The next desire of the slavery protagonists was for new territory to the southward, and for reopening the African slave trade.

Buchanan had been an expansionist since 1848, and his friend Slidell kept him steady on that point. In his message of 7 January 1858 the President gently chided William Walker for his filibustering activities in Nicaragua, on the ground that he was hampering ' the destiny of our race to spread themselves over the continent of North

America, and this at no distant day, should events be permitted to take their natural course.' At the end of that year he asked Congress for money to buy Cuba, and Slidell introduced an appropriation for that purpose; but the Republicans were on the alert and did not allow it to be brought to a vote. The same rising anti-slavery sentiment defeated a treaty that Buchanan negotiated with the Juarez government in Mexico, giving the United States a new railway concession, and an unlimited right of intervention to preserve order.

Unquestionably the reopening of the African slave trade was the coming demand of the South. Prime field hands were becoming so highly priced that only wealthy planters could afford to buy them. Bootlegging of blacks was on the increase. Not only picaroons of the Gulf, but respectable merchantmen of Baltimore and whalers of New Bedford were loading ' black ivory ' on the west coast of Africa, and unloading it on the sea islands of Georgia, where customs supervision was slack. The governor of South Carolina in a public message (1856) argued at length for the repeal of the federal law of 1807 that outlawed the slave trade. The governor of Florida opposed repeal, from no ' sickly sentimentality,' so he said, but because it would alienate Virginia from the cotton kingdom. Reopening the slave trade was virtually the only subject discussed by Southern business men in their annual conventions; the Vicksburg commercial convention of 1859 adopted a resolution that ' all laws, state or federal, prohibiting the African slave trade, ought to be repealed.' A senator from Florida proposed, as an entering wedge, that negroes captured on slavers by the United States navy be ' apprenticed ' to kind planters, instead of being sent to Liberia.

By most Southern gentlemen these proposals were regarded with horror. Yet it is difficult to see how the gentry could long have resisted the logic of William L. Yancey of Alabama: ' If it is right to buy slaves in Virginia and carry them to New Orleans, why is it not right to buy them in Cuba, Brazil, or Africa, and carry them there? ' If slavery was ' airth's greatest boon,' as almost every articulate Southerner was now agreed, why not indeed extend its blessings to those in darkest Africa? And, without surplus slave population to take advantage of them, the Kansas-Nebraska Act and the Dred Scott decision had been barren victories.

A rather facile assumption of a few historians that slavery was already on the decline in the South in 1860, and would have disappeared within twenty years if the South had been left alone, is rendered highly improbable by these changes in Southern opinion during the 1850's. Economics had very little to do with these opinions; slavery never profited so few people as at the period when it had the hottest advocates. Slavery was simply a social necessity for keeping the negro population in its proper place, for keeping the South ' a white man's country.' Many high-minded Southerners like Robert E. Lee still deplored slavery; but even they saw no alternative, and suggested none. Suppose Lincoln had not been elected, or that the Southern states had not seceded. The South, in the natural course of events, would have demanded new and more stringent guarantees to her peculiar institution, including most probably the reopening of the slave trade (which, even if conceded by an abject North, would have brought on war with England); and the absolute suppression of abolitionist agitation. Supposing the impossible, that the North had conceded everything, and left the South entirely free to deal with her race problem, what possible break in Southern mentality would have done away with slavery before the twentieth century?

6. John Brown

It was now the turn of the North to be the aggressor. In 1859 came two startling portents of the 'irrepressible conflict.' The Burns fugitive slave case of 1854 was followed by a new crop of state ' personal liberty laws,' which penalized their citizens for helping federal officials to perform this unwelcome duty. A certain Booth of Wisconsin, convicted in a federal court of having forcibly rescued a runaway slave, was released by the Supreme Court of his state on the ground that the Fugitive Slave Act of 1850 was unconstitutional and void. The Supreme Court of the United States reversed the state decision. The Wisconsin Legislature, quoting the Kentucky resolutions of 1798 which Southern men considered canonical, declared ' that this assumption of jurisdiction by the federal judiciary . . . is an act of undelegated power, void, and of no force.' Here was Calhoun's nullification in a new quarter. The Federal Government vindicated its power by rearresting and imprisoning Booth; but that did not minimize the effect on Southern sentiment. For us the deeper significance lies in the fact that the slavery issue had transcended constitutional theory. Janus-like, each side turned to nationalism or state rights, as best suited its purpose. Had it been the South instead of the North that was growing and gaining power, Garrison's principle of 'no union with slaveholders' might well have become the nucleus of an irresistible secession movement in the Northern states.

If the Booth case aroused scorn and bitterness, the next episode of the year brought the deeper anger that comes of fear. John Brown, perpetrator of the Pottawatomi massacre in Kansas, was a belated puritan who would have found his proper work in Cromwell's invasion of Ireland. Fanatic but no madman, he formed an audacious plan to establish a sort of abolitionist republic in the Appalachian mountains, and make war on slavery with fugitive blacks and a few determined whites. On the night of 16 October 1859, leading an army of thirteen white men and five negroes, Brown seized the federal arsenal at Harper's Ferry, and took prisoner some of the leading townspeople. Daybreak brought the neighboring militia swarming about him, while the telegraph was spreading consternation through Virginia. The irrepressible conflict at last!

Governor Wise called out the entire state militia and implored the Federal Government for aid. John Brown retreated to a locomotive round-house, knocked portholes through the brick wall, and defended himself. Lewis Washington, one of his prisoners, has left us a graphic description of the scene: 'Brown was the coolest and firmest man I ever saw in defying danger and death. With one son dead by his side, and another shot through, he felt the pulse of his dying son with one hand and held his rifle with the other, and commanded his men with the utmost composure, encouraging them to be firm and to sell their lives as dearly as they could.' In the evening, when Colonel Robert E. Lee arrived with a company of marines, there were only four of Brown's men alive and unwounded. The next day the marines forced an entrance, and captured the slender remnant alive.

Eight days after his capture the trial of John Brown began in the court house of Charles Town, Virginia. From the pallet where he lay wounded the old ironside rejected his counsel's plea of insanity. There could be no doubt of the result. On 31 October the jury brought in a verdict of murder, criminal conspiracy, and treason against the Commonwealth of Virginia. John Brown, content (as he wrote his children) 'to die for God's eternal truth on the scaffold as in any other way,' was hanged on 2 December 1859.

Southerners thought of Hayti and shuddered, although not a single slave had voluntarily joined the liberator. Keenly they watched for indications of Northern opinion. That Christian burial was with difficulty obtained for John Brown's body they did not know. That every Democratic or Republican newspaper condemned his acts they did not heed, so much as the admiration for a brave man that Northern opinion could not conceal. And the babble of shocked repudiation by politicians and public men was dimmed in Southern ears by one bell-like note from Emerson: 'That new saint, than whom nothing purer or more brave was ever led by love of men into conflict and death . . . will make the gallows glorious like the cross.'

XXXIII

LINCOLN, SECESSION, CIVIL WAR
1860–1861

1. *The Election of 1860*

THE Republican party had won the congressional elections of 1858, and had good reason to hope for victory in 1860, although the leaders of the lower South let it be clearly understood that they would not submit to the rule of a 'Black Republican' president. The four-year-old party was already more of an organic whole than the old Whigs had ever been; and the platform of its national convention, adopted at Chicago on 18 May 1860, showed that it was no longer a party of one idea, but a party of the North. On the slavery question it was as clear as in 1856, though less truculent: no more slavery in the territories; no interference with slavery in the states. So there was no place in the party for the abolitionists, who denounced new Republicanism as old Whiggery writ large. John Brown was condemned in the same breath with the border ruffians of Missouri, and secession was called plain treason. The Chicago platform also promised the settlers a free quarter-section of public land, and revived Henry Clay's old 'American system' of internal improvements and protective tariff, representing Northern desires that had been balked by Southern interests. Low tariffs and the panic of 1857 had brought distress to the iron-masters of Pennsylvania and to the wool growers of Ohio, both unable as yet to meet British competition on equal terms.

This careful construction of the platform showed that the Republican party was no longer guided by crusaders, but by seasoned politicians. It had lost the first flush of radicalism, and was beginning that evolution to the right which made it eventually the party of big business and finance. In 1860 Republicanism combined the solid policies of Hamiltonian Federalism with the hopeful and humanitarian outlook of its namesake, the party of Jefferson.

Abraham Lincoln received the presidential nomination on the third ballot; not for his transcendent merits, which no one yet suspected, but as a matter of political strategy. His humble birth, homely wit, and skill in debate would attract the same sort of Northerners who had once voted for Andrew Jackson; and no one else could carry the doubtful states of Indiana and Illinois. Seward, the most distinguished and experienced candidate, had too long and vulnerable a record; the others were little known outside their own states.

Already the Democratic convention at Charleston had split on the slavery question. Stephen A. Douglas was the logical candidate, and if he had been nominated he would undoubtedly have won. In that event not a single state, save possibly South Carolina, would have seceded. But the Buchanan administration threw its weight against Douglas, and the Southern Rights men believed that they had been duped by him. They had gone in for popular sovereignty in 1854, expecting to get Kansas; but the Kansas territorial legislature was now in the hands of anti-slavery men, encouraged by Douglas's 'Freeport doctrine' to flout the Dred Scott decision. Nothing less than active protection to slavery in every territory would satisfy the Southerners. The Democratic party must take distinctly the position 'that slavery was right,' said Yancey of Alabama. 'Gentlemen of the South,' replied Senator Pugh of Ohio, 'you mistake us — you mistake us — we will not do it.' They did not do it. A 'leave slavery in the territories to the Supreme Court' plank was adopted, but that was not enough for the 'fire-eaters' who demanded a congressional slave code for the territories. On 30 April the cotton state delegates stalked out of the Democratic national convention.

After this symbolic secession Douglas was unable to command the necessary two-thirds majority that the Democratic party required (until 1936) for a presidential nomination. The convention, therefore, adjourned to Baltimore, where with fresh delegates it made Douglas the official nominee of the Democratic party. The seceders held a separate convention, which nominated the then Vice-President, John C. Breckinridge of Kentucky, on a platform of slavery extension and annexation of Cuba.

Senator Bell of Tennessee was placed in nomination by a new party, the National Constitutional Union. Composed largely of what Lincoln called 'the nice exclusive sort' of Whigs, who hoped to persuade the American people to forget everything that had occurred since 1848, this party avowed 'no political principle other than the Constitution of the country, the union of the states, and the enforcement of the laws.'

As Minnesota and Oregon had been admitted to the Union in

1858 and 1859, there were now eighteen free and fifteen slave states. Breckinridge carried every cotton state, together with North Caro- lina, Delaware, and Maryland. Douglas, although a good second to Lincoln in the total popular vote, had a plurality only in Missouri. Virginia, Kentucky, and Tennessee went for Bell. The South, then, was divided; but Lincoln, with hardly a ballot from south of the Mason and Dixon line, carried every free state, and rolled up a large majority in the electoral college.[1]

Apart from the Democratic split, Northern labor was the decisive force in the election. The German-Americans for the most part had joined the Democratic party as soon as they became naturalized; but they had suffered too much from tyranny in the fatherland to support it in any new shape. The personality of Lincoln swept them into a new party allegiance, and in conjunction with the New Eng- land element they carried the northwestern states. Before 1854 the native American artisan had been a negro baiter. Since then he had been aroused by the frequent sneers of Southern statesmen at wage- earners, and by deadly quotations from Southern literature on the evils of free society. He had been deeply impressed by the favorite question of Republican orators: could the free laboring man ever get two dollars a day, when a black slave cost his master but ten cents a day to keep? Or, as Senator Ben Wade put it, when a Southern colleague called the Homestead bill a sop to Northern paupers, ' Is it to be lands for the landless, or niggers for the niggerless? ' And in some obscure way Northern labor had come to look upon slavery as an ally of the Northern capitalism that exploited him.

2. Secession

It was a foregone conclusion that South Carolina would secede if Lincoln were elected. Since Calhoun's death, if not before, the leaders of opinion in that state had been waiting for an occasion that would unite the South in a new confederacy. As soon as the result of the

[1] Candidates	Popular vote	Electoral vote
Lincoln	1,866,452	180
Douglas	1,376,957	12
Breckinridge	849,781	72
Bell	588,879	39

These figures include no popular vote in South Carolina, where Breckinridge electors were chosen by the legislature. In the other states that seceded the por vote was Breckinridge, 736,592; Bell, 345,919; Douglas, 72,084.

election was certain, the South Carolina legislature summoned a state convention. On 20 December 1860 the convention met at Charleston, and unanimously declared 'that the Union now subsisting between South Carolina and other states under the name of "The United States of America" is hereby dissolved.'

In the other cotton states there was a strong unionist minority. Many planters like Jefferson Davis, who had travelled in the North and maintained their sense of proportion, wished to give Lincoln's administration a fair trial; but secession was insisted upon by petty planters, provincial lawyer-politicians, and clergymen. 'The people are run mad,' wrote Alexander H. Stephens of Georgia. 'They are wild with passion and frenzy, doing they know not what.' Georgia, Alabama, Florida, Mississippi, Louisiana, and Texas (where old Sam Houston, Jackson nationalist to the last, pleaded in vain for delay) were out of the Union by 1 February 1861. Three days later, delegates from the seven seceded states met in Congress at Montgomery, Alabama, and on the 8th formed the Confederate States of America. The next day the Congress elected Jefferson Davis provisional President, and A. H. Stephens Vice-President of the Southern Confederacy.

The causes of secession, as they appeared to its protagonists, were plainly expressed by the state conventions. 'The people of the Northern states,' declared Mississippi, 'have assumed a revolutionary position towards the Southern states.' 'They have enticed our slaves from us,' and obstructed their rendition under the fugitive slave law. They claim the right 'to exclude slavery from the territories,' and from any state henceforth admitted to the Union. They have 'insulted and outraged our citizens when travelling among them . . . by taking their servants and liberating the same.' They have 'encouraged a hostile invasion of a Southern state to excite insurrection, murder and rapine.' To which South Carolina added, 'They have denounced as sinful the institution of slavery; they have permitted the open establishment among them' of abolition societies, and 'have united in the election of a man to the high office of President of the United States whose opinions and purposes are hostile to slavery.'

On their own showing, then, the states of the lower South seceded as the result of a long series of dissatisfactions respecting the Northern attitude towards slavery. There was no mention in their manifestoes or in their leaders' writings and speeches of any other cause. Protection figured as a 'cause' in the Confederate propaganda abroad and in Southern apologetics since; but there was no contemporary mention of it because most of the Southern congressmen, including the entire South Carolina delegation, had voted for the tariff act then in force. The Morrill Tariff of 20 February 1861, the first strongly protective tariff since 1832, was only passed in consequence of the withdrawal of Southern senators from Congress. Nor was any allusion made to state rights apart from slavery; on the contrary, the Northern states were reproached for sheltering themselves under state rights against the fugitive slave laws and the Dred Scott decision. A letter of Jefferson Davis to a Northern friend, written on 20 January 1861, is a fair example of what was in the Southern mind at the moment of secession: 'Many States, like Iowa, have denied our rights, disregarded their obligations, and have sacrificed their true representatives. To us it became a necessity to transfer our domestic institutions from hostile to friendly hands, and we have acted accordingly. There seems to be but little prospect that we will be permitted to do so peacefully.' All these 'rights,' 'obligations,' and 'institutions' had reference to slavery and nothing but slavery.

Nor was the secession the result of a sudden passion or political landslide. 'The discussion of disunion during the several years preceding the actual launching of the experiment left no phase of the subject untouched. Every possible angle of the question was explored.'[2] Intellectual arguments were implemented by emotion, to be sure; but the emotion too was engendered by slavery. Already a strong minority regarded Southern independence as an end in itself. Their minds were filled with the vision of a great republic ruled by themselves and their own kind, affording perfect security to their social organism. Lincoln, we must remember, appeared to the South not as we know him, but as a sort of coarse baboon, with the serpent Garrison coiled about his body. His election inspired the same fear and loathing that would arise today among conservatives if a communist were elected president.

The Southern people should have listened to Stephens when he predicted that even for the purpose of protecting slavery, secession was a colossal act of folly. Southerners and Democrats combined would have possessed a majority in both houses of Congress, at least until 1863. Lincoln could have done nothing without their consent. Republicans might outlaw slavery in the territories, but secession

[2] R. R. Russel, *Economic Aspects of Southern Sectionalism*, p. 181.

would lose the cotton states all rights of any sort in the territories. Northern states were not enforcing the fugitive slave law, but secession would make that law a dead letter. Abolitionists were disagreeable fellow-countrymen; but their propaganda could not be stopped by international boundaries. The Republicans proposed no interference with slavery in the Southern states, and were ready to pledge their sincerity by a constitutional amendment to that effect. Even had they wished, they could have freed the blacks in unwilling states only by a constitutional amendment, or as an act of war. The one way would have been impossible even today, if the slave states had stayed united,[3] the other way was courted by secession. But there was very little expectation in the South that the North would care or dare to fight for preservation of the Union; and if it should, was not one Southerner a match for five Yankees? And was not cotton king? Senator Hammond of South Carolina wrote on 19 April 1860, ' Cotton, rice, tobacco and naval stores command the world; and we have the sense to know it, and are sufficiently Teutonic to carry it out successfully. The North without us would be a motherless calf, bleating about, and die of mange and starvation.'

No people of British stock enjoy revolution for its own sake. It is necessary for their comfort and peace of mind to prove rebellion no treason. The Long Parliament applied the common law against King Charles; Thomas Jefferson discovered dominion home rule in the British Constitution; and, when the British government refused to acknowledge it, appealed to the law of nature against George III. Similarly, Calhoun laid the legal foundation for the Southern Confederacy in his masterly exposition of all that was implied in state sovereignty. So ably was the case presented that many people in the North were converted, and almost every white child in the Southern states today is brought up in the belief that secession, in a legal sense, was absolutely right. Historically, the doctrine of constitutional secession, as distinct from the Lockean right of revolution, seems to have been first enunciated by John Taylor of Caroline, and first elaborated by the New England Federalists in 1814. There had been little difference between the two sections in this respect before 1850, as we have seen; every section denounced as contrary to state sovereignty national measures which were against its interests, and with complete lack of humor denounced as treasonable similar

---

[3] Thirteen states can prevent the ratification of a constitutional amendment in 1942; there were fifteen slave states in 1860.

declarations by other sections. The humiliation of defeat and reconstruction gave the Southern people a sentimental devotion to the
principle of state rights, without affecting their practice; while in
Northern eyes the principle seemed befouled with treason. But even
these attitudes have been again reversed since 1933; state rights
are now an historical exhibit maintained by the Republican party.

The constitutional rightness or wrongness of secession, which
meant a great deal to the American people for fifty years after 1860,
is now an academic question. With few exceptions, the Americans of
1860–61 made up their minds about secession on other than constitutional grounds, and then sought arguments to prove themselves right
and the enemy wrong. The case for secession rests on the axiom
that the Federal Constitution created a confederacy, not a government, and did not impair state sovereignty. Although the history
of the United States affords the most perfect example of plural
sovereignty in history, everyone in 1860 was thinking in monistic
terms. Either the states were individually sovereign, or the people of
the whole United States were. Supporters of national sovereignty
were embarrassed in their search for the precise moment when it
came into existence, in a Union that was ratified successively by
the people of the states. Consequently, they took refuge in the historical fallacy that the Union was older than the states. Conversely,
the state sovereignty supporters found it difficult to explain how
states like Ohio and Arkansas, erected out of the national domain by
act of Congress, obtained a sovereignty superior to their creator. Just
as Rome, in arguing papal supremacy, rests her case upon authority
and origin, but scorns the excellent argument of historical growth; so
the American nationalists tried to prove their theory by the language
of the Constitution and the debates of 1788, instead of pointing to
the gradual growth of national feeling which was the real sanction
of nationalism. In 1800 the vast majority of American citizens felt
more loyal to their respective states than to the Union. In 1830 none
but Virginians, Georgians, and South Carolinians would have followed their states out of the Union, on any possible issue. After 1844,
with the growth of Southern self-consciousness, the phrase and the
idea of state rights gave place in that section to 'Southern rights.'
Leaders like Jefferson Davis spoke the language of state rights while
thinking and acting in terms of Southern nationalism, but others
like Rhett and Yancey meant what they said — a source of future
trouble in the Southern Confederacy. In the North, especially among

old Jackson Democrats, there was still considerable state loyalty in 1860; but the mobility of the Northern population made for nationalism, and recent immigrants understood no half-way loyalty between their old country and their new.

State rights is a relative term. Everyone then believed, and believes today, that the states have certain rights which the Federal Government has no lawful power to touch. State sovereignty is another matter. Admitting that the rights reserved to the states in the Federal Constitution are sovereign in their ordinary nature, they are hardly so in the condition under which they are enjoyed, since the Constitution, as interpreted by the Supreme Court, is the law of the land, and three-quarters of the states, including only a minority of the population, may deprive the other quarter of all their privileges (excepting equal representation in the Senate) by constitutional amendment. Secessionists made much of the reservation under which certain states ratified the Constitution, as if that could have had any effect on the others; and of the Kentucky and Virginian resolves of 1798, as if they were official glosses on the Constitution. The nationalists, on the other hand, could point to the fact that every presidential administration except Tyler's, and the Supreme Court under Jay, Marshall, and Taney, had acted on the assumption that a sovereign American people existed. No stronger assertions of nationalism were ever made than by three Southern Presidents: Washington, Jackson, and Polk. After all, effectiveness is the only test of sovereignty. Under the Articles of Confederation the states could and did do anything they pleased; their several wills were the court of last resort. And if the American people had not cared enough about nationalism in 1861 to maintain it by force, the sovereignty of the states would have been an accomplished fact.

3. Confusion and Attempted Compromise

Many things happened during the awkward four months' interval between the choice of presidential electors and the inauguration of a new President. Lincoln's election was assured in early November 1860. South Carolina seceded in December, and the Confederate government was formed on 8 February 1861; but Lincoln could not be inaugurated until 4 March. In the meantime James Buchanan was President, with a cabinet that included three secessionists, and only one strong nationalist after Cass resigned in disgust (12 December).

Buchanan had the same power to defend federal property and collect federal taxes within states that obstructed federal law as Jackson possessed in 1832, but was timid by nature, scrupulous of principle, and oppressed by his surroundings. Washington was a Southern city. Congress, cabinet, and all the federal departments were riddled with secession. To onlookers the Federal Government seemed to be dissolving; soon there would be nothing left to secede from. Public opinion gave the President no lead. The Northern people had grown so accustomed to Southern threats of secession that when the talk became a reality they could hardly credit the fact, and few had any notion what to do about it. Oliver Wendell Holmes wrote a pleasant little poem to 'Caroline, Caroline, child of the sun,' promising to kiss the naughty child when she came home again. Horace Greeley of the New York *Tribune* and General Winfield Scott struck the key-note of Northern sentiment in January with the phrase, 'Wayward sisters, depart in peace!'

'Why not?' we are entitled to ask, in an era that has heard much of self-determination. The answer was given in Lincoln's inaugural address: 'Physically speaking, we cannot separate.' With the best will in the world, a readjustment and redistribution of federal power would have been difficult;[4] and good will was notably wanting. Peace could not have been maintained for a year between the United States and the Southern Confederacy. Fugitive slaves, adjustments of the national debt, of each government's share in the territories, of the Mississippi outlet for the Northwest, would have raised dilemmas inescapable save by force; and there was no knowing where secession might stop. The best possible solution would have been an armed peace; the probable result would have been something like the state of Europe from 1870 to the present.

Buchanan's attorney-general advised him that secession was illegal, but that he had no right to coerce a state; so the good man, with many tears and prayers, spent his slender store of energy in promoting various schemes of compromise. There was still hope, he thought, of tempting back the seceded states, so long as Virginia and seven other slave states were within the Union. Although nothing came of these projects, they served the useful purpose of showing

[4] The matter of breaking up the federal postal service, for instance, was so difficult that the Confederacy permitted the United States mails to run their usual course through the South until 1 June 1861, six weeks after the Civil War had begun, and almost six months after South Carolina had 'resumed her separate and equal place among nations.'

Northern conservatives that there could be no compromise between separation and coercion.

The first of these compromise schemes came in the form of constitutional amendments, proposed by Senator Crittenden of Kentucky, on 18 December 1860: (a) re-establishment of the 36° 30′ division in the territories, (b) non-interference by Congress with slavery in the states and the District of Columbia, (c) compensation to owners for fugitive slaves not recovered. Lincoln, the President-elect, was willing to accept the last two, if the Southern senators would issue an appeal to their states against secession. Respecting the first proposition he had already written to a Republican congressman, ' Prevent, as far as possible, any of our friends from demoralizing themselves and our cause by entertaining propositions for compromise of any sort on " slavery extension." There is no possible compromise upon it but which puts us under again and leaves us all our work to do over again. . . . On that point hold firm, as with a chain of steel.'

The Crittenden compromise, therefore, was not supported by the Republicans; and the seceded states showed not the slightest interest in a so-called peace convention summoned by Virginia on 4 February 1861. The futility of it was thought out by an ironic amendment proposed by a Northern member:

Whenever a party shall be beaten in any election for President, such party may rebel and take up arms, and, unless the successful shall adopt as its own the principles of the defeated party, and consent to such amendments to the Constitution as the latter party shall dictate, then, in such case, the Union shall be at an end.

A few days later Lincoln agreed that ' no concession . . . short of a surrender of everything worth preserving and contending for would satisfy the South.'

And so nothing had been done toward compromise, or indeed about anything, by 4 March 1861, when Abraham Lincoln was inaugurated President of the no longer United States.

The City of Washington appeared carefree and slovenly as usual. Actually, the people were nervously expectant of trouble. It was rumored that secessionists from Virginia or ' plug-uglies ' from Baltimore would raid the capital, surrounded as it was by slave territory, and prevent the inauguration. General Scott took every possible precaution, but the soldiers at his disposal were too few even to relieve the black-coated sombreness of the crowd. The inaugural procession, as it moved up Pennsylvania Avenue under the harsh glare of a March sun, while a blustering wind blew clouds of dust roof-high, might have been a funeral procession. The Capitol, with its great uncompleted dome supporting an unkempt fringe of derricks, suggested ruination. President Buchanan, urbane and white-haired, Chief Justice Taney, stern and dignified, seemed symbols of a golden age of the Republic that was over. President Lincoln, uncouth and ill at ease, inspired no confidence until his high-pitched, determined voice was heard delivering the solemn phrases of the inaugural address. One slight incident in the ceremony alone gave promise of better days. As Lincoln, ready to speak and holding his manuscript in one hand, seemed embarrassed by his high hat in the other, Senator Douglas relieved him of it, and stood by as his ancient rival made another plea for union.

After a brief review of the constitutional issues involved in secession, Lincoln renewed the pledge of his party to respect slavery in the states, and to enforce any fugitive slave law that had proper safeguards for the colored people of the free states.

In your hands [he addressed the South] and not in mine, is the momentous issue of the civil war. The Government will not assail you. [But] I hold that, in contemplation of universal law and the Constitution, the Union of these States is perpetual. . . . No State, upon its own mere action, can lawfully get out of the Union. . . . I shall take care, as the Constitution itself expressly enjoins upon me, that the laws of the Union be faithfully executed in all the States. . . . The power confided to me will be used to hold, occupy, and possess the property and places belonging to the Government, and to collect the duties and imposts.

4. *Fort Sumter, Seward, and Virginia*

Buchanan had flinched from defending those coigns of vantage, the federal forts in the Southern states; and we shall judge him less harshly when we reflect that it took Lincoln a month to meet the issue bravely. By the time he was inaugurated, all the forts and navy yards in the seceded states, save Fort Pickens at Pensacola and Fort Sumter at Charleston, had fallen unresisting to the Confederate authorities. From the extreme Southern point of view, the jurisdiction of such places passed with secession to the states, and their retention by the Federal Government was equivalent to an act of war.

Confederate commissioners came to Washington to treat for their surrender, a few days after Lincoln's inauguration. Although Seward refused to receive the gentlemen, he assured them indirectly that no supplies or provisions would be sent to the forts without due notice, and led them to expect a speedy evacuation.

William H. Seward, as Lincoln's chief rival for the nomination, and the most experienced statesman in the Republican party, had been given the State Department, where he was playing a deep and dangerous game. Lincoln he regarded as an inexperienced small-town lawyer; and in truth Lincoln's public appearances during the crisis of the winter had been for the most part undignified, and some of his utterances, flippant. Of course Lincoln was always flippant when thinking most deeply, but Seward did not yet know that; nor did he know the Confederate leaders. Judging them in the light of New York politics, Seward doubted their sincerity and determination. In his opinion, secession was a mere humbug for obtaining concessions to Southern rights; if a collision could be avoided, the leaders would sneak back into the Union. If they did not, Seward would rally the Southern people to their old flag by a foreign war.

Major Anderson, commanding Fort Sumter, notified the War Department that his supplies were giving out, and that new Confederate batteries commanded his position. Fort Sumter had no strategic value in case of civil war. Why, then, risk war by holding it? The Confederacy made it clear that any attempt to reinforce or even to supply Sumter would be regarded as a hostile act, when Virginia was certain to join the Confederacy. If, however, the forts were tamely yielded, would not the principle of union be fatally compromised? Could a recognition of the Confederacy thereafter be avoided?

Lincoln delayed decision not from fear, but because he was watching Virginia. Jefferson Davis, too, was watching Virginia. The Old Dominion was a stake worth playing for. Although long since fallen from her primacy in wealth and statesmanship, her sons were the ablest officers in the United States army, and her soil was almost certain to be the theatre of any war between the sections. The ' panhandle' of western Virginia thrust a salient between Pennsylvania and Ohio, to within a hundred miles of Lake Erie. If Virginia seceded, she must carry North Carolina with her; and Maryland, Kentucky, Tennessee, Missouri, and Arkansas would probably follow.

Virginia showed her union sentiment in 1860 by voting for Bell rather than Breckinridge; but unionism in Virginia meant a voluntary association of sovereign states. Delegates to a Virginia state convention were elected by the people in January 1861, and met at Richmond on 13 February. A majority of the delegates were elected as Union men, the secessionist minority was united and aggressive. Delegations of unionist members visited Washington and besought Lincoln to let Fort Sumter go. Twice the President offered to do so if the Virginian unionists ' would break up their convention without any row or nonsense '; but they could not promise that. And Lincoln came to see that to yield Fort Sumter would not bring the ' wayward sisters ' back; and Virginia would join them the moment he raised his hand to strike. If Virginia would not accept the Union as it was, she must abide the consequences.

Toward the end of March Lincoln determined to face the issue squarely. Against the advice of General Scott, and of five out of seven members of the Cabinet, he ordered a relief expedition to be prepared for Fort Sumter.

Seward then showed his hand. On April Fools Day 1861, he presented Lincoln with a paper entitled ' Thoughts for the President's Consideration.' The most startling proposal in this extraordinary document was one that the United States should at once pick a quarrel with France and Spain, possibly with England and Russia as well, as a means of reuniting North and South for glory and conquest! And Lincoln was invited to appoint Seward his prime minister to execute this mad policy! Lincoln calmly replied that he saw no reason to abandon the policy outlined in his inaugural address. As for declaring war on Europe, ' I remark that if this must be done, *I* must do it.' But Seward was too intent on his scheme to catch the President's meaning. On 6 April, when the President ordered the Sumter expedition to sail, Seward by deception obtained the President's signature diverting the capital ship of the expedition to Fort Pickens.

It mattered nothing. When Lincoln's informal warning that an attempt would be made ' to supply Fort Sumter with provisions only ' arrived at Montgomery, it found Jefferson Davis in a similar state of confusion and perplexity. Southern spirits were evaporating for want of a fight; in Charleston there were murmurs of dissatisfaction with the Confederacy; only a collision could ' fire the Southern heart ' and bring in Virginia. Robert Toombs, Confederate

Secretary of State, begged for delay. To attack Fort Sumter, he predicted, would be to 'strike a hornet's nest which extends from mountain to ocean, and legions now quiet will swarm out and sting us to death.' Finally, Davis ordered General Beauregard, commanding the Charleston district, to fire on Sumter only if absolutely necessary to prevent reinforcement. On the night of 11–12 April Beauregard sent four staff officers to Fort Sumter demanding surrender. Major Anderson, a Kentuckian who loathed the idea of civil war, had no desire for the sort of fame that would come from being the occasion of it. Nothing as yet had been seen or heard of the relief expedition. So, at a quarter past three in the morning, he offered to surrender as soon as he might do so with honor — in two days' time, when the garrison's food would be exhausted. The Confederate staff officers peremptorily refused this condition, and on their own responsibility gave orders to open fire. For, as one of them admitted in later life, they feared that Davis would clasp hands with Seward, and the chance of war would slip away forever.

On 12 April 1861, at 4:30 A.M., the first gun of the Civil War was fired against Fort Sumter. The relief expedition appeared, but for lack of its capital ship was unable to pass the batteries. All day Major Anderson replied as best he could, to a concentric fire from four or five Confederate forts and batteries, while the beauty and fashion of Charleston flocked to the waterfront as to a gala. At nine the next morning, 13 April, the barracks caught fire; in the early afternoon the flagstaff was shot away, and a few hours later, although his situation was by no means desperate, Major Anderson accepted terms of surrender. On the afternoon of Sunday, 14 April, the garrison marched out with drums beating and colors flying.

Walt Whitman caught the spirit of the moment in his

Beat! beat! drums! — blow! bugles! blow!
Through the windows — through doors — burst like a ruthless force,
Into the solemn church, and scatter the congregation,
Into the school where the scholar is studying;
Leave not the bridegroom quiet — no happiness must he have now with
    his bride,
Nor the peaceful farmer any peace, ploughing his field or gathering his
    grain.
So fierce you whirr and pound you drums — so shrill you bugles blow.

Doubt and hesitation vanished in the North. Men knew instantly that the Union was what they cared for most and the flag was what they held most sacred. Advocates of letting the 'wayward sisters' depart in peace now remembered Webster's warning, and Clay's, that there could be no peaceable secession. Those who loathed the idea of a union maintained by force now knew there could be no union upon any other terms. Democrats and Republicans, state-rights men and nationalists, native-born and foreign-born, had only one word for the act of firing on their flag — treason.

5. Secession Completed

On 15 April President Lincoln issued a call for seventy-five thousand volunteers in order to put down combinations 'too powerful to be suppressed by the ordinary course of judicial proceedings,' and 'to cause the laws to be duly executed.' Virginia saw no honorable alternative between contributing her quota for coercion and taking the Southern part. Already the Virginian secessionists were organizing attacks on the Norfolk navy yard and the arsenal at Harper's Ferry, and threatening to purge the state convention. That body was in a state of high-strung emotion bordering on hysteria, when Lincoln's call precipitated matters. On 17 April it voted, 88 to 55, to submit an ordinance of secession to the people. Without waiting their certain verdict, the governor placed his state under Confederate orders.

The western part of Virginia refused to leave the Union; [5] but three more states followed her greater part into the Southern Confederacy. Arkansas seceded on 6 May; Tennessee on 7 May concluded an alliance with the Confederacy, which a month later the people approved; North Carolina, having previously voted down secession, was in the impossible position of a Union enclave until 20 May, when she ratified the Confederate constitution. The attitude of Maryland was crucial, for her secession would isolate the Federal Government at Washington. The first Northern troops on their way to the capital were mobbed as they passed through Baltimore (19 April), and Lincoln wisely permitted the rest to be marched round the city until he could spare enough troops to occupy it and enforce martial law. The Maryland legislature protested against 'coercion' of the Southern Confederacy, but refused to sum-

---

[5] West Virginia was admitted as a state in 1863, but gave comparatively little aid to the Union cause. It was dislike of the planter aristocracy rather than unionism which caused this disruption of the Old Dominion.

mon a state convention; and danger of disunion in that quarter passed. The government of Kentucky, where opinion was evenly divided, refused to obey the call for volunteers, and endeavored in vain to enforce neutrality, but by the end of the year threw in its lot with the Union. Missouri was practically under a dual régime throughout the war; Delaware never wavered in her loyalty. In California there was a fierce struggle between Southern sympathizers and the Unionists, which the latter won; but California was too remote to give the Union cause other than pecuniary aid, in which she was generous. The Indians of the Indian Territory, many of them slaveholders, threw in their lot with the South.

The motives for this second group of secessions, beginning with Virginia, were obviously very different from those of the lower South. The upper South had been willing to give the Lincoln administration a try. But it was drawn to the lower South by ties of blood, and the determination to keep that region a ' white men's country.' This emotion was rationalized by the theory of state sovereignty, which was strong and genuine in eastern Virginia and Maryland, and in western and central Tennessee. According to this theory every state had a right to secede, hence Lincoln's call for coercion was illegal. And it forced the issue: everyone had to choose between defending the Confederacy or helping to put it down.

Yet the issue was not quite so simple as we relate it. Throughout the Civil War, the lines were not strictly drawn between the states that seceded and those that did not. The majority of men went with their neighbors, as most people always do. But there were thousands who chose their side from higher motives of sentiment and opinion. It by no means follows that if Stonewall Jackson had been a Yankee he would have fought for the Union, or that Grant, if born a Virginian, would have worn the Confederate gray. The Confederate army contained men from every Northern state, who preferred the Southern type of civilization to their own; and fashionable society in Baltimore, Philadelphia, and New York was pro-Southern to the end. The United States army and navy contained loyal men from every seceded state, Americans who knew that the break-up of the Union would be the worst blow to the cause of self-government, Republicanism, and Democracy since the day that Bonaparte assumed the purple. Robert J. Walker, the most efficient Union agent in Europe, was the former senator from Mississippi; Caleb Huse, the most efficient Confederate agent in Europe, was from Massachusetts.

Samuel P. Lee commanded the Union naval forces on the James while his uncle, General Lee, was resisting Grant in the Wilderness; two sons of Commodore Porter, U.S.N., fought under Stonewall Jackson; Major-General T. L. Crittenden, U.S.A., was brother to Major-General G. B. Crittenden, C.S.A. Three brothers of Mrs. Lincoln died for the South, and the President's kinsmen on his mother's side were Southern sympathizers, while near kinsmen of Mrs. Davis were in the Union army. In a house in West Twentieth Street, New York, a little boy named Theodore Roosevelt prayed for the Union armies at the knee of his Georgia mother, whose brothers were in the Confederate navy. At the same moment, in the Presbyterian parsonage of Augusta, Georgia, another little boy named Thomas Woodrow Wilson knelt in the family circle while his Ohio-born father invoked the God of Battles for the Southern cause.

It is degrading to the memory of a man of Robert E. Lee's stature to assume that he acted on the vulgar principle of his country (or his state), right or wrong. Lee was a great and simple person, like George Washington, with a character so pure and well-rounded as to offer no flaw or protuberance for the historian's scalpel. His traditions, and those of his family, were nationalist. Lee abhorred the methods of the abolitionists, but agreed with them that slavery was wrong, and emancipated his few inherited slaves. He did not believe in the constitutional right of secession, and severely criticized the action of the cotton states. Lincoln's inaugural address seemed to him a sufficient guarantee for Virginia. On 23 January 1861 Lee wrote to his son, 'I can contemplate no greater calamity for the country than a dissolution of the Union. . . . Still, a Union that can only be maintained by swords and bayonets, and in which strife and civil war are to take the place of brotherly love and kindness, has no charm for me.' To a cousin and brother officer of the United States army, who determined to remain faithful to the flag, Lee wrote expressing sympathy and respect for his 'notions of allegiance.' But, 'I have been unable to make up my mind to raise my hand against my native state, my relatives, my children and my home.' With deep regret Colonel Lee resigned his commission in the United States army; only a sense of duty induced him to accept a ·commission in the cause of which he was to be the main prop.

Robert E. Lee might make a mistake, but he could not do wrong. He would have been right in accepting the offer of Lincoln to command the United States army, and in leading the forces of Union to victory in a year's time, as he alone might have done. He was right in choosing the part of those who were dearest to him. What anguish that decision cost him we can never know. What it cost the United States we know too well.

George H. Thomas, another great and simple Virginian in the United States army, loved his state no less than Lee; but after the guns at Sumter had spoken, 'whichever way he turned the matter over in his mind, his oath of allegiance to his government always came uppermost.'

To a third Virginian, Senator James M. Mason, we are indebted for the most accurate definition of the great struggle that was about to begin: 'I look upon it then, Sir, as a war of sentiment and opinion by one form of society against another form of society.'

XXXIV

CONDITIONS AND CONSIDERATIONS
1861–1865

1. *Conditions of Victory*

AT a distance of sixty years men wonder at the rash and hopeless gallantry of the Southern war for independence. A loose agrarian confederacy of five or six million whites and three and a half million slaves challenged a federal union of nineteen or twenty million freemen with overwhelming financial and industrial advantages.[1] Yet, futile as the effort proved and tragic as the consequences, the Southern cause was not predestined to defeat.

The Confederacy, in order to win, needed merely to defend her own territory long enough to weary the Northerners of war. The United States, in order to win, had to conquer an empire[2] and crush

---

[1] By the census of 1860 the white population of the eleven seceded states was 5,449,467; the white population of the nineteen free states, 18,936,579. Both figures leave out of account the white population (2,589,533) of the four border slave states (Delaware, Maryland, Kentucky, and Missouri), which did not secede, but which probably contributed as many men to the Confederacy as to the Union. Subtracting the loyal regions of Virginia and Tennessee would reduce the Confederacy's white population to about five million. By the census of 1860 there were 3,521,111 slaves in the Confederate states, and 429,401 in the four border states, and from those the Union recruited about 100,000 troops. For a discussion of the insoluble problem of the numbers of the two armies, see Channing, *U.S.*, vi. 430–34, and A. B. Moore, *Conscription in the Confederacy*, pp. 357–58. Both Channing and Eckenrode believe that there were about 800,000 enrolments in the Confederate army; Moore estimates from 850,000 to 900,000. T. L. Livermore, *Numbers and Losses in the Civil War*, pp. 50, 61, computes 2,900,000 enlistments in the Union army, which reduced to three-year enlistments by doubling up short terms would make 1,556,000; but his estimate for Confederate three-year enlistments, 1,082,000, is probably too high. The classic Southern estimate, accepted by most Southern historians and even inscribed on monuments, is 600,000 Confederates to 2,750,000 Union soldiers. That is certainly very far from the truth. Perhaps the most accurate basis of comparison is the census of 1890, which showed 432,020 Confederate and 1,034,073 Union veterans surviving. 'In the Union army 67,058 were killed on the field, and 43,012 died of wounds (total 110,070); 224,586 died from disease and 24,872 from accidents and other causes. The total deaths were thus 359,528. The number wounded in battle but recovered was 275,175. In the Confederate army 94,000 were killed or mortally wounded; probably 164,000 died from disease, accidents, and other causes.' J. F. Rhodes, *U.S.* v. 186–87.

[2] The area of the Confederacy at its greatest extent was equal to that of the whole of western Europe, less Scandinavia and Italy. Texas alone was the size of France, and had a greater man-power than the two Boer republics in 1899–1901.

a people. A negotiated peace, or any less emphatic result than unconditional surrender of the Southern armies and total collapse of the
Confederate government, would have meant some sort of special
privilege to the Southern states within the Union, if not independence without the Union: in either event a Southern victory. Material
advantages were not all in favor of the Union. To offset the Northern superiority in numbers, wealth, industry, and sea-power, the
Confederacy had the advantage of interior lines, and a social organization better fitted for creating an efficient fighting force. The moral
scales were heavily balanced in favor of the Confederacy. Slavery
was the cause of secession, but only indirectly a force in the war.
From their own point of view, Southerners were fighting for everything that men hold most dear: for liberty and self-government, for
hearth and home, for the supremacy of their race. They could
abandon the struggle only by sacrificing the very bases of their
society; and defeat for them involved the most bitter humiliation to
which any people has been subjected in modern times. The Northern people, on the contrary, could have stopped the war at any moment, at the mere cost of recognizing what to many seemed an
accomplished fact, and without any sacrifice of the solid and material
factors that most closely touch the life of the individual. They were
fighting merely for an idea and a sentiment, the sentiment of Union,
which, translated into action, seemed to tender souls scarcely different
from conquest. Negro emancipation, itself an ideal, came more as an
incident than as an object of the war. It was not the abolitionist
'Battle-Hymn of the Republic' that sent the blood leaping through
Northern veins in those years of trial, but the simple sentiment of:

> The Union forever, hurrah! boys, hurrah!
>   Down with the traitor, up with the star,
> While we rally round the flag, boys, rally once again,
>   Shouting the battle-cry of Freedom.

Under these circumstances there was every reason to expect that
the South would win. Europe as a whole so believed, as soon as
the news of Bull Run seemed to prove that the South was in earnest,
and that the North was not. The Thirteen Colonies, the Netherlands, and in recent memory the South American and the Italian
states had achieved their independence against greater odds; and if
Hungary had failed, it was because Russia threw her weight on the
other side. Even devoted partisans of the American Union like John

Bright hardly dared hope for its complete restoration; and among the statesmen, the military experts, the journalists, the men of letters, and leaders of public opinion in western Europe, those who before the end of 1864 doubted the permanency of separation were few and inconspicuous. For there was one imponderable and unique factor of which almost everyone in Europe was ignorant: the steadfast devotion to the Union which alone made it possible for the superior material resources of the United States to prevail.

2. The Confederate States of America

The opposing governments were nearly identical in pattern. The Constitution of the Confederate States differed only from that of the 'fathers,' said Jefferson Davis, in so far as it was ' explanatory of their well-known intent.' In making explicit those guarantees of slave property and state rights, that the South found implicit in the older document, she did not improve it as a framework of government, still less as an instrument of war. Bounties, protective tariffs, and 'internal improvements' were forbidden. Federal officials and even judges could be impeached by the legislatures of the state in which their functions were exercised. No ' law denying or impairing the right of property in negro slaves' could be passed by the Confederate Congress, and in all new territory acquired ' the institution of negro slavery, as it now exists in the Confederate States, shall be recognized and protected.' In two respects only was the Confederate Constitution an improvement over its model. Congress, unless by a two-thirds majority, could appropriate money only upon the President's transmitting the request and estimate by some head of an executive department; and these heads of departments, who constituted an informal cabinet in the new government as in the old, might be granted a seat in Congress and the privilege of discussion. The President, further, had the right to veto items of appropriation bills. Actually these provisions, which Lord Acton declared alone to be worth a revolution, remained inoperative during the short lifetime of the Confederacy. President Davis and his Congress worked less in harmony than had any President and Congress of the United States since Tyler. Davis, in four years of office, vetoed thirty-eight bills, all but one of which were passed over his veto. Lincoln in the same period vetoed only three bills.

In the view of outsiders, the Southern Confederacy seemed animated by a single will and purpose; actually it was weakened by faction and shaken by its inherent vice of localism. Davis and most of the Southern leaders had been talking state rights but thinking Southern nationalism; yet many important men, especially in Virginia and the Carolinas, loved state rights more than Southern unity, and feared a centralizing tyranny at Richmond no less than they had at Washington. No Union general ever had to write, as Lee did of Georgia and Carolina when contemplating an advance: 'If these states will give up their troops, I think it can be done.' State rights stood always at Davis's elbow; supplies could not be seized, or taxes enforced. The composition and character of the Southern people was unfavorable for united and intelligent effort. The gentry, more accustomed to direct slaves than to control themselves, full of fixed notions on politics as on slavery, could not co-operate effectively with their President, and were only happy in active army life. The Southern democracy made excellent fighting material, and up to a certain point could easily be led; but that point, as we shall see, happened to be at the crucial moment. Ignorant and provincial, this Southern democracy never even remotely realized what the Confederacy had to face, and the government did nothing to enlighten it. Slaves proved to be a material asset for war production. If Davis could have made up his mind to arm them before Lincoln decided to free them, they might well have been the decisive military factor.

3. The Two Presidents

During the war both Davis and Lincoln were regarded by their enemies as fiends incarnate; and by many of their own people were accused of everything from incompetence and corruption to tyranny and treason. At the outset few doubted that the Southerner was the abler, as he appeared the more dignified figure of the two. Successively lieutenant of dragoons, colonel of volunteers, congressman, senator, and Secretary of War, Davis brought experience such as Lincoln had never had, and talents that he never claimed, to the Southern presidency. Courage, sincerity, patience, and integrity were his; only tact, perception, and inner harmony were wanting to make him a very great man. Davis was torn between a desire to command and a taste for intellectual solitude; between nationalist instinct and state-rights faith. Isolated from the Southern democracy out of which he had sprung, he moved as to the manner born among the whispering aristocracy of Richmond; yet he had a perverse knack of infuriating the gentlemen who tried to work under him, unless they would place their minds in his keeping.

His pronounced military tastes and slight military experience led Davis to attempt to direct military operations as well as civil administration. Only a Bonaparte could successfully have played the dual rôle in the Confederacy; and even Bonaparte had a general staff and a centralized government. Davis had neither the time to exercise effective control nor the talent to choose effective instruments. Thus the Confederacy lacked the strategic unity that would have given it the full benefit of interior lines. The President's health and nerves gave away, and his state papers show an increasing querulousness and bitterness, which contrast sadly with the sustained dignity and magnanimity of all that Lincoln wrote during the war.

Davis selected his cabinet for work, not for politics. It contained only two members of the governing class, Robert Toombs and Pope Walker, both of whom soon quarrelled with the President and resigned. The others, able and devoted servants to the Confederacy, exerted no influence and inspired slight confidence. Secretary Memminger of the Treasury was German, and both Secretary Mallory of the Navy and Judah P. Benjamin, the Attorney General, were British West Indian by birth. Benjamin, ablest of the group and the closest to Davis, was a Jew, whose perpetual smile and imperturbable suavity were peculiarly irritating to the Southern gentry.

If Lincoln's cabinet carried more political weight than that of Davis, it had less cohesion. Not a single member was a personal friend or follower of the President. His choice was restricted by the need of representing every element in the Republican party, and every loyal section of the Union. Seward's appointment brought the administration confidence, and eventually strength; but not until he had almost wrecked it by his aggressive foreign policy. Simon Cameron, the Secretary of War, was a Pennsylvania manufacturer who proved to be criminally careless if not corrupt. Salmon P. Chase, an apostle of righteousness with a superiority complex, received the Treasury as a party chieftain, and a rival for the Republican nomination in 1860. He never developed more than a moderate talent for administration and finance. Gideon Welles, formerly a bureau chief in the Navy Department, latterly a newspaper editor in a small inland town, was appointed Secretary of the Navy as a New Englander and a recent convert from the Democratic party. His Biblical

name and patriarchal beard made Welles the butt of the administration; later he took appropriate revenge by writing a pungent Diary.
Edward Bates and Montgomery Blair, the Attorney-General and
Postmaster-General, were good second-rate characters who represented the loyal slave states in the cabinet.

At the beginning of Lincoln's administration the members of the
cabinet distrusted one another, and Blair alone had much respect
for the President. Seward assumed the rôle of premier — as he liked
to be called and considered. After the firing on Sumter, several
months elapsed before the President was really master in his own
house. The change of scene, the hurly-burly of war preparations,
seemed for a time to cut his contact with that unconscious, unseen
force that lifted him from the common herd. Yet his feeling for
the democratic medium in which he had to work, for its limitations,
imperfections, and possibilities, was akin to that of a great artist
for the medium of sculpture or painting. He could capture the
imagination of the common soldier and citizen; and at the same time
make the outstanding quality of an ill-balanced character, as of
McClellan and Stanton, an instrument of his great purpose. This
rail-splitter, this prairie politician with his droll stories and his few,
poor, crude social devices, had an innate tact and delicacy that carried conviction of his superiority to all but the most obtuse, and
a humanity that opened the hearts of all men to him in the end.

If Lincoln was slow to direct the conduct of the war, he never
faltered in his conception of the purpose of the war. From Sumter
to Appomattox, it was for him a war to preserve the Union. The
power that lay in that word came less from an instinct of nationality
than from the passionate desire of a youthful people to prove its
worth by the only test that all the world recognized. The Union,
which for Washington was a justification for the American Revolution, and for Hamilton a panoply of social order, had become, in the
hands of Jackson, Clay, and Webster, a symbol of popular government. Lincoln drove home this conception in his every utterance,
and gave it classical expression in the Gettysburg address. He made
the average American feel that his dignity as a citizen of a free republic was bound up with the fate of the Union, whose destruction
would be a victory for the enemies of freedom in every country.

Lincoln could not bring everyone to this conception. Many members of the Democratic party in the North still looked upon the
states as the symbol of democracy. Many believed civil war too

great a price to pay for union. The abolitionists would support him only on the condition of his serving their immediate purpose. Nor did Lincoln completely dominate his own group. Many Republicans regarded the war as a mere assertion of Northern superiority; for in 1861 they were essentially a Northern, not a Union party. Because Lincoln, ignoring all appeals to hatred, sectionalism, and humanitarianism, raised the union standard at the beginning and kept it paramount, the Union was preserved. Prominent Democrats such as Stephen Douglas promptly rallied the best elements of their party to the colors; and in a few months the entire Ohio valley, half slaveholding in fact, and largely pro-slavery in sentiment, was secure. His enemies sneered, 'Lincoln would like to have God on his side, but he must have Kentucky.' His friends doubted whether even God could preserve the Union without Kentucky. Nor did he ever forget that those whom he liked to call ' our late friends, now adversaries ' must, if his object were attained, become fellow citizens once more. Lincoln could never bring himself to contemplate the South with other feelings than sorrow and compassion.

4. *The Two Armies*

In the matter of military preparations the Confederacy had a start of several months on the United States, and secured the ablest officers of the United States army then in active service — Lee, both Johnstons, Beauregard, J. E. B. Stuart, and A. P. Hill; as well as Jackson and D. H. Hill, who were teaching in Southern military colleges. No other nation has ever had commanders of such calibre at the very beginning of a great war. The Union army found its proper leaders only through the costly method of trial and error. McClellan, Grant, Sherman, indeed most of the West Pointers who rose to prominence in the Union army, were in civil life at the beginning; and it was fortunate for the Union that they were, since the regular army of the United States — only sixteen thousand strong — was kept intact. Hence many brilliant young officers like Philip Sheridan were confined to small regular units, instead of being used as their seceding brethren to leaven the loaf.

The forty United States naval vessels in commission were scattered over the seven seas. Until mid-April no attempt was made to enlarge or even to concentrate these slender forces, for fear of offending the Virginia unionists. In the meantime the Confederate states had seized upon the United States arsenals and navy yards within their limits, had obtained munitions from the North and from Europe, had organized state armies; and on 6 March 1861 President Davis called for and quickly obtained a hundred thousand volunteers for twelve months.

Winfield Scott, General-in-Chief of the United States Army, infirm in body but robust in mind, advised the President that at least three hundred thousand men, a general of Wolfe's capacity, and two or three years' time would be required to conquer even the lower South. No one else dared place the estimate so high; and Seward believed with the man in the street that one vigorous thrust would overthrow the Confederacy within ninety days. The President, in his proclamation of 15 April 1861, called for only seventy-five thousand volunteers, for three months. Militia regiments fell over one another in their alacrity to aid the government; New York alone voted to supply thirty thousand men for three years. Within two weeks thirty-five thousand troops were in Washington or on their way thither, and twenty thousand more were waiting for transportation. Undoubtedly the government should have taken advantage of this patriotic outburst to create a really national army for the duration of the war. Instead, Lincoln on 3 May called for forty more volunteer regiments of 1050 men each, and forty thousand three-year enlistments in the regular army and navy; leaving the recruiting, organization, and equipment of all volunteer regiments to the states. Over-zealous states were coldly admonished, 'it is important to reduce rather than enlarge this number.' That Lincoln, inexperienced and bewildered, should have lost this golden opportunity is not surprising, for the War Department preferred the traditional American method of raising an army by state quotas, as in 1776, 1812, and 1846.

As a basis for the new army, every Northern state had some sort of volunteer militia force which was mobilized for an annual 'muster' and 'Cornwallis' (sham battle) — usually not much more than a drunken frolic. The company officers were elected by the men, the regimental and general officers appointed by the state governor. A few militia regiments, like the Seventh New York, were well officered and drilled. There were also a number of semi-social, military companies, such as the Fire Zouaves and Sarsfield Guards, which performed fancy evolutions in showy uniforms. Many of these volunteered *en masse,* and proceeded on the road to glory without undue delay. Walt Whitman describes how two Brooklyn companies were provided with pieces of rope, tied to their musket barrels, with which to bring back ' traitors' from the South. (Similarly the Southern volunteers armed themselves with huge bowie-knives to terrorize their presumably pallid enemies.) But for the most part, the volunteer regiments that made up the bulk of the United States army during the war were regiments created on the spot. A patriotic citizen would receive a colonel's commission from his state governor, and raise a regiment by his own efforts and of those who expected to be officers under him. When the regiment was reasonably complete and partially equipped, it was forwarded to a training camp, and placed under federal control. The Federal Government in practice had to respect state appointments until they were found wanting in action; and its own were scarcely better. Prominent politicians like Banks and Butler, without the slightest military experience, received major-generals' commissions from the President, and outranked seasoned officers of the regular army. There was something to be said for this system as a means of giving an unmilitary country a stake in the war, and utilizing community pride and competition. But something better was wanted before a year had elapsed.

By much the same system was the first Confederate army raised. The Southern respect for rank and caste gave prompt recognition to natural leaders. Indeed the earlier Southern armies were embarrassed by a plethora of officer material. J. E. B. Stuart remarked of one Virginia unit, ' They are pretty good officers now, and after a while they will make excellent soldiers too. They only need reducing to the ranks!' The Southern troops had the advantage of being accustomed to the use of arms — for every slaveholder had to keep weapons by him in case of insurrection, and the non-slaveholders were good marksmen. Both classes were lovers of horse-flesh, and it was a poor white indeed who did not own a saddle-horse. Northern troops, unless from the West, had outgrown the hunting and horseback-riding frontier, and the Northern gentry had not yet adopted field sports or fox-hunting for recreation. Discipline, from which the more primitive individualistic Southerners were averse, soon ironed out these differences. The two armies became as nearly equal in fighting capacity, man for man, as any two in history; and they took an unprecedented amount of punishment. If the Confederates won more battles, it was due to their better leadership, which gave them a 'tactical' superiority on the field of battle, against the 'strategical' superiority of their enemies on the field of operations. Again and again we find a numerically inferior Confederate army defeating its enemy in detail; or a Union commander failing to get his available forces into action in time to influence the result. As the North had the greater immigrant population, it had a larger proportion of foreign-born soldiers; but the average Northern soldier was a farmer's son rather than a clerk or factory hand. There were large numbers of Irish and Germans on both sides; Dick Taylor's Louisiana Creoles gave quite as good an account of themselves as Stonewall Jackson's dour Presbyterians.

Throughout the war the Union army was the better equipped in shoes and clothing, and more abundantly supplied with munitions; yet the red tape of War Department bureaus, and the prejudice of elderly officers, prevented the adoption of the breech-loading rifle. Both in artillery and small-arms, it was largely a war of the muzzle-loader, and to a great extent of the smooth-bore. When the blockade stopped regular shipments from Europe, which was not until the end of 1863, the Confederate ordnance service, under a resourceful Pennsylvanian named Josiah Gorgas, was able to keep the army supplied; and the Confederacy never lost a battle for want of ammunition. Richmond was one of the principal coal- and iron-producing centers in the United States, and her Tredegar Iron Works were well equipped for the manufacture of heavy castings and ordnance. It was there that the iron armor of the *Merrimac* was rolled and her rifled guns were cast, and that the first practical submarine was built. But these were the only works in the Confederacy so equipped until 1863, when a newly established plant at Selma, Alabama, began to turn out cannon. Much enterprise was also shown by the Confederate government in organizing Southern woolen mills to weave cloth for uniforms, but the Southern armies were never properly supplied with shoes. Deficiencies in clothing, equipment, artillery, and small-arms, were constantly made good from the supplies abandoned by Union armies in their frequent retreats.

5. Terrain, Tactics, and Strategy

Civil War battles were fought in a rough, forested country with occasional clearings — Antietam, Gettysburg, and Fredericksburg were the only important engagements in open country. The defending infantry is drawn up in a double line, the men firing erect or from a kneeling posture. The attacking force moves forward by brigade units of 2,000 to 2,500 men, covering a front of 800 to 1,000 yards, in double rank; captains in the front rank, the other officers and non-coms. in the rear, to discourage straggling. They are preceded by a line of skirmishers. Normally the attack moves forward in cadenced step, and is halted at intervals to fire and reload, the enemy returning fire until one or the other gives ground. Occasionally the boys in blue, more often the boys in gray, advance on the double-quick, the former shouting a deep-chested 'Hurrah!', the latter giving vent to their famous 'rebel yell,' a shrill staccato yelp. An attack of this sort generally ends in a bayonet encounter; but both sides, ill-trained in bayonet work, prefer to club their muskets. There was slight attempt at concealment, and so little entrenchment until 1864 that the moments of actual combat were more deadly to officers and men than the battles of the World War; but as soon as contact was broken the men were comparatively safe. A regular feature of the Civil War was the fraternizing of picket guards, and even whole units of men, during the intervals between fighting.

Union strategy, aggressive by the nature of the cause, took a form dictated by the geography of the Confederate States. The Appalachians and the Mississippi river divided the Confederacy into three parts, nearly equal in area: the eastern, the western, and the trans-Mississippi theatres of war. The scene of the most spectacular campaigns and battles was in that part of the eastern theatre bounded by North Carolina, the Appalachians, the Susquehanna, and Chesapeake bay. Here were the two capitals, Washington and Richmond, and between them a rough wooded country, crossed by numerous streams and rivers. Of course the enemy's army, not the enemy's capital, is the proper object in warfare, but in a civil war, especially, possession of the enemy capital is of immense moral value, and the Union spent more money and effort on trying to attain Richmond than on all its other operations combined. In the retaliating threats to Washington, the Shenandoah-Cumberland valley, pointing like a long cannon at the heart of the Union, became the scene of dashing raids and military exploits. Military operations beyond the Mississippi had little effect on the result. But the western theatre of war between the Mississippi and the Appalachians was at least of equal importance with the eastern. Lee might perform miracles in Virginia, and even carry the war into the enemy's country;

but when Grant and the gunboats had secured the Mississippi, and Sherman was ready to swing round the southern spurs of the Appalachians into Georgia, the Confederacy was doomed. Control of the sea was a priceless asset to the Union. The navy maintained communications with Europe, cut off those of the South, captured important coastal cities, and on the western rivers co-operated with the army like the other blade to a pair of shears.

A threefold task lay before the armed forces of the Union: constriction, scission, and defeat of the Southern armies. Both the nature and the magnitude of the task were imperfectly apprehended in 1861, unless by Winfield Scott, whose ' anaconda policy' of constriction was dismissed as the ravings of an old fogy.

6. The War in 1861

The Union plan of campaign for 1861 was to blockade the Southern coast, and occupy strategic points along its edge; to mobilize and train the volunteer army in regions convenient for invading the Southern states, and to capture Richmond, which, it was fondly supposed, would cause the Confederacy to collapse. Kentucky had to be nursed carefully out of neutrality during the summer and the autumn, and Confederate sympathizers in Missouri threatened the Union right flank. Hence the first forward movements were from Columbus, Ohio, St. Louis, and Washington.

Congress, convened in special session on 4 July, voted loans and taxes, and authorized the President to recruit half a million men for the duration of the war. Already there were some twenty-five thousand three-months volunteers at Washington, spoiling for a fight. The Northern press and people were vociferous for action. Against General Scott's advice, President and Cabinet yielded to the cry of ' On to Richmond.' General McDowell, with a ' grand army' of thirty thousand, crossed the Potomac in order to seek out Beauregard's army near Manassas Junction, Virginia. A throng of newspaper correspondents, sightseers on horse and foot, and congressmen in carriages came out to see the sport.

On 21 July McDowell attacked Beauregard on a plateau behind the small stream called Bull Run. The troops on both sides were so ill-trained, the officers so unused to handling large numbers, the opposing flags so similar, and the uniforms so varied that a scene of extraordinary confusion took place. For hours it was anyone's

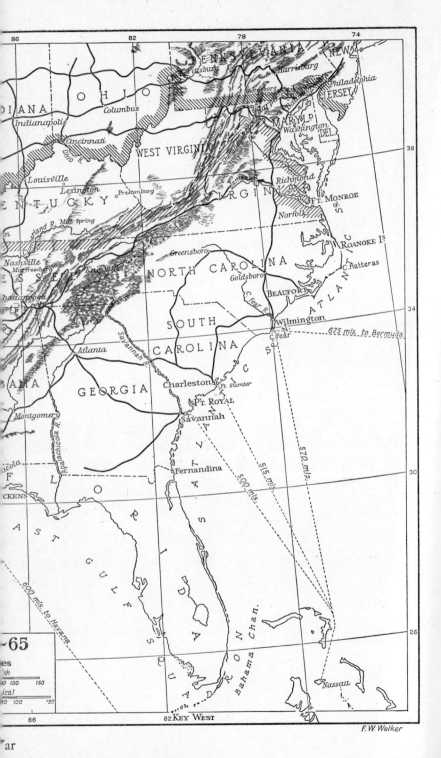

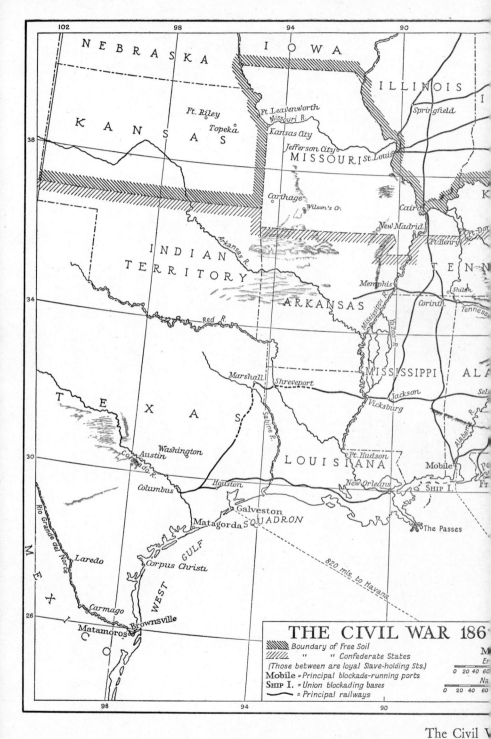

THE CIVIL WAR 186

The Civil W

Prepared by S. E. Morison and drawn by F. W. Walker

battle, although the famous stand of the Stonewall Virginia brigade probably averted a Union victory. Union retreat turned to rout. All the next day, soldiers came straggling into Washington without order or formation, dropping down to sleep in the very streets; rumors flying about that Beauregard was in hot pursuit, that the Capitol would be blown up if not abandoned; treason openly preached everywhere. But Lincoln did not flinch, and Beauregard did not pursue. ' The Confederate army was more disorganized by victory than that of the United States by defeat,' wrote General Johnston. There was no more talk of a ninety-days war. From the dregs of humiliation the Union was nerved to make adequate preparations for a long war; while the South, believing her proved superiority would dissolve the Northern ' hordes ' and procure foreign recognition, indulged in an orgy of conceit and self-applause.

At this point, on 24 July 1861, President Lincoln summoned General McClellan to Washington, and gave him command of the army in that department. George B. McClellan was only thirty-four years old. A graduate of West Point on the eve of the Mexican War, in which he performed distinguished service, his subsequent business experience accustomed him to deal with large affairs in a large way, and gave him the confidence of men of property; his personal magnetism and some easy successes in western Virginia in June 1861, made him a popular hero. The Northern states provided him with plenty of three-year volunteers. Congress was generous with money and equipment, and the President gave him the fullest support. No untried general in modern times has had such abundant means as McClellan enjoyed during the nine months that followed Bull Run; and few have been so cruelly deprived of them when the opportunity came to use them.

McClellan proved an ideal organizer. His precise, methodical mind, his appetite for detail and love of work, and above all his attractive personality and genuine interest in his men were exactly the qualities needed to form an army from a mob. But his defects in conduct and character impaired his usefulness and weakened his support when the time came for action. There was never a grain of truth in the charges against McClellan's loyalty. There can no longer be any reasonable doubt of his technical military ability. His position, however, required not only military ability, but some perception of the democratic medium in which he must work; and that perception, which was given to Grant and Lincoln, McClellan wholly lacked. Impatient democracy demanded quick results, and McClellan neither gave them nor explained in terms that people could understand why quick results could not be expected. His love of display, the Orléans princes on his staff, too frequent mention of 'my army,' a short way with politicians combined with frequent public statements as to what the politicians should do, seemed out of place in a republican soldier. The note of self-laudation and of contempt for Lincoln that runs through McClellan's confidential letters makes it difficult to do him justice today. He was the type of man who is not content merely to do well the task at hand, but must be forever dreaming of the future in terms of self: victorious McClellan, dictator McClellan, President McClellan. Yet no Union general was so beloved as 'Little Mac' by the untrained volunteers whom his genius turned into a superb instrument of war, the Army of the Potomac.

Weeks stretched into months, and the newspapers had nothing to report but drills and reviews. 'All quiet along the Potomac' appeared so often in the headlines as to become a jest. Joseph E. Johnston extended his lines along the south bank of the Potomac, and closed the river to traffic in October. McClellan estimated the enemy's number at 150,000. Actually, at that time, the Confederate army of northern Virginia was less than 50,000 strong, and wretchedly equipped. General Johnston, dogmatic in temper and choleric in disposition, had much the harder task of the two. President Davis found him recruits with some difficulty, for every section of the South wished a large home guard, and looked upon the Washington army with contempt.

Lincoln refused to let the politicians worry him into ordering an advance. When General Scott got in McClellan's way, the President on 1 November appointed McClellan General-in-Chief of all the armies of the Republic. At his instance the War Department took over all matters of recruiting, equipment, and organization from the states. Yet McClellan persistently snubbed the President, and on one occasion affronted him in a way that no other ruler would have pardoned. 'Never mind,' said Lincoln, 'I will hold McClellan's horse if he will only bring us success.' November passed with no preparations made for an offensive. December came, and the General began to play with plans for an oblique instead of a direct advance on Richmond. 'What are you waiting for, tardy George?' was the burden of a new popular song. 'If something is not done soon, the bottom will be out of the whole affair,' said the President. 'If General McClellan does not want to use the army I would like to *borrow* it.'

It was no mere temperamental caution, or illusion of the enemy's strength, that was holding McClellan back. Loving his army and his country, and loathing bloodshed, he sought 'to heal as well as to conquer.' A mere victory, he believed, would be indecisive; but one dramatic coup such as the capture of Richmond, if accompanied by satisfactory assurances as to slave property, would win back the South. 'I shall carry the thing *en grande,* and crush the rebels in one campaign,' he wrote to his young and adoring wife.

Now McClellan was not alone in this delusion that rebellion could be stamped out as suddenly as it arose. Lincoln, Seward, Grant, and the mass of the Northern public shared it, until the year 1862 ended in the horror of Fredericksburg. He differed from others only in his estimate of the preparation necessary for a fatal blow. Yet McClellan's strategy of delay was correct, as his policy of crushing was mistaken. Since 1914 we have learned to our cost that it takes time to create an army from a mob. Nothing was to be gained by stirring up Johnston prematurely. He would have fallen back, and the Confederacy would have been aroused from its fool's paradise of over-confidence, as it finally was in April 1862. The Confederacy was defeated in 1865, as Germany was in 1918, by attrition and constriction. It was the true policy of the Union to postpone offensive movements until its superior resources were organized for offensive war. It was the true policy of the Confederacy to force an issue promptly. The Union could not afford another Bull Run; the Confederacy could not afford to let another such opportunity slip. McClellan was inspired, in so far as he spent his efforts in preparation; and Lincoln was inspired, in so far as he supported McClellan's strategy. Neither could rationalize an instinct that ran counter to his reasoned policy of crushing; hence neither was able to explain himself to the other, or to his country. McClellan, from Yorktown to Antietam, thought he was 'striking at the heart of the rebellion,' while his strategy was uniformly directed by this instinct of delay and constriction. On the Confederate side, Lee certainly, and Johnston probably, had the right instinct of aggression; but they were overruled by their President's academic policy of defense and delay.

7. The Union Navy and the Blockade

In naval strategy, the policy of constriction was so obvious that it was consciously applied from the first. President Davis invited applications for letters of marque on 17 April 1861; two days later President Lincoln proclaimed a blockade of the Southern ports. The following day brought a naval counterpart to Bull Run. The navy yard at Norfolk, which the United States government had neglected to reinforce for fear of offending Virginia, was captured without a blow by the troops of that state, together with enormous stores of ordnance, munitions, and the hull of the *Merrimac* frigate.

The Navy Department then awoke, and Gideon Welles proved to be one of Lincoln's lucky finds. Painstaking and methodical as an administrator, respectful of navy traditions, his meagre knowledge of the service was supplemented by a capable assistant secretary, Gustavus V. Fox. By them the navy was much more efficiently directed than the army, because Congress did not try to help, or to make rear-admirals out of politicians. But the problem of blockading 3,550 miles of coastline from Washington to Matamoras, with the vessels and seamen available, seemed at first insoluble. The sixty sailing vessels proved as obsolete as medieval galleys. Congress had begun to build a new steam navy in 1850; but as yet only twenty-four steamers had been placed in commission, and only twelve of these were in the home squadron. The American merchant marine had a very small supply of screw steamers suitable for conversion, and the number of machine shops capable of turning out good engines was small. Although American inventors had for some years been planning ironclads, whose value had been suggested by the Crimean War and proved by Napoleon III; and although the Navy Department was eager to experiment, Congress had refused to appropriate money for that purpose, or even, latterly, for proper upkeep of the existing fleet. There was no naval reserve. Without waiting for Congress to assemble, a large construction program was undertaken, and side-wheelers, screw steamers, clipper ships, tug-boats, and even ferry-boats were purchased in wholesale quantities, at retail prices. Time and legislation were required to build ironclads, to retire aged officers, and to establish promotion by merit. Throughout the war old-fashioned seamen were placed in command of steamers, where they were apt to be more anxious about their boilers than eager to engage the enemy.

It was a paper blockade for two or three months after 19 April, but by the end of July four blockading squadrons were stationed off the seven or eight enemy ports that were commercially important. About eight hundred vessels entered and cleared from the ports of the Confederacy during the first year of the blockade; but the corresponding figures for the last year of peace had been in excess of six thousand. It was impossible to close the Confederate ports completely. From the Chesapeake to Wilmington the coast proper is protected by long barrier beaches, jutting out in Cape Hatteras, Cape Lookout, and Cape Fear, and pierced by numerous inlets. Again, from Georgetown, S. C., to Fernandina, the littoral is protected by the 'sea islands' which make an intricate network of channels. Small vessels clearing from a Carolinian port could sneak along an inside passage until they reached an outlet to a clear horizon, and then make a dash for the high seas. It was about six hundred miles from Mobile to Havana, and even less distance from the South Atlantic ports to protected waters in the Bahamas, where Nassau quickly acquired an importance it had not known since the days of the buccaneers, and a prosperity it did not recover until the days of the bootleggers. Until 1862 the Confederacy had no naval vessels that could even challenge the blockading squadrons; but the more important Southern harbors had been provided by the United States with excellent fortifications, which served to keep hostile ships at a respectful distance.

During the summer of 1861 the Navy Department began to establish bases on the Southern coast. Cape Hatteras, Ship Island in the Gulf of Mexico near New Orleans, and Hilton Head on the sea islands off Port Royal, S. C., were captured between August and November 1861. This last was the only important Union victory of that year. And in February-March 1862, General Burnside, at the head of a joint naval-military expedition, captured Roanoke Island, Newbern, and Beaufort, N. C., giving the Union control of Albemarle and Pamlico Sounds. But Wilmington, N. C., remained a major leak in the blockade until nearly the end of the war. For want of military co-operation these successes were not followed up by raids into the interior; but they kept thousands of Southern troops out of Lee's army.

8. *The Attitude of Europe*

From the very start the British and French people were deeply interested in the Civil War. Their opinion divided along lines of political thought. Europe in general saw the issue eye-to-eye with Lincoln. Restoration of the Union would mean a new triumph for democracy; destruction of the Union a mortal wound to democracy. The United States had long been obnoxious to European ruling classes for the encouragement that its success afforded to European radicals. ' An involuntary instinct, all-powerful and unconquerable,' wrote the Comte de Montalembert, ' at once arrayed on the side of the pro-slavery people all the open or secret partisans of the fanaticism and absolutism of Europe.' Many Englishmen outside that category favored the South, for, as Henry Adams wrote, ' the English mind took naturally to rebellion — when foreign.' Most liberals could see no difference between the Southern struggle for independence and the nationalist movements in Europe with which they had always sympathized. Dissenters and humanitarians, who would have welcomed a war against slavery, were put off by the repeated declarations of Lincoln and Seward that slavery was not an issue. The commercial classes marked the return of the United States to a high protective policy, which the Confederate constitution forbade; and Southern propaganda made much of the contrast. Shipping interests hoped for the ruin of their most formidable competitor, and approved a new cotton kingdom for which they might do the carrying trade. Indeed it is not surprising that the Union had few articulate partisans in the England of 1861. In such an atmosphere there was grave danger lest some untoward incident should precipitate hostilities between the Union and the Empire. Fortunately there were no outstanding disputes between the two countries in 1860; but with England in the unusual rôle of neutral sea-power, they were certain to arise.

Southern expectations of victory were based on three delusions: that ' cavaliers' were invincible, that the Ohio valley would not fight, and that England would break the blockade to get cotton. The theory that inspired the Association of 1774 and Jefferson's embargo, the old delusion that American staples ran the wheels of industry in Europe, had gathered strength with the growing export of cotton to Great Britain and France. British and French industry did depend on American cotton to a surprising extent; but in April 1861 there was a fifty per cent over-supply both of cotton and of cottons in the English market. So instead of demanding intervention to get more cotton, the big textile interests of England and France welcomed the opportunity to work off surplus stocks. A second factor ignored by the South was the British doctrine of naval warfare. As Lord John Russell wrote, the American blockade satisfied the British standard; and in view of England's sea-power, it would be highly imprudent for her to insist on a higher standard which would hamper her offensive strength in the future. The reiterated Southern complaints of the ineffectiveness of the blockade, Russell shrewdly suspected to be indications to the contrary.

International complications first arose from the fact that the United States officially regarded the war as a domestic insurrection, yet tacitly accorded belligerent status to the Confederacy by declaring a public blockade. Lincoln might simply have declared rebel ports closed to foreign commerce, as any government would do under similar circumstances today. But the world was not then prepared to respect a blockade unless the word were pronounced, and the fact proclaimed; nor would neutral vessels on any other terms submit to visit and search.

Lord Palmerston's government, alarmed by the probable consequences of the war to British commerce, hastened to define its attitude in the Queen's Proclamation of 13 May 1861, declaring her ' Royal determination to maintain a strict and impartial neutrality in the contest . . . between the Government of the United States of America and certain states styling themselves the Confederate States of America,' and her intention to enforce the Foreign Enlistment Act against unneutral aid. This proclamation was greatly to the advantage of the Union. A Foreign Office circular of 1 June, forbidding British and Imperial port authorities to admit prize ships, was decidedly to the disadvantage of the Confederacy. But the very promptitude and explicitness of the neutrality proclamation and its unprecedented mention of a rebel government by its chosen name, seemed unfriendly to the Northern people, and raised false expectations of recognition in the South. Seward at once drafted an aggressive protest which Lincoln carefully toned down, and which he instructed the American minister at London to communicate in substance only. Otherwise diplomatic relations between the two countries would have been severed at the outset. France and the other continental countries soon issued neutrality proclamations of their own.

The first positive danger of European intervention came over the *Trent* affair. The British mail steamer of that name was conveying to Southampton two Confederate diplomatic agents, J. M. Mason and John Slidell, when on 8 November 1861 she was boarded from the U.S.S. *San Jacinto,* Captain Wilkes commanding, deprived of her two distinguished passengers, and allowed to proceed. Of course Captain Wilkes should have sent in the *Trent* for adjudication, when she would have been condemned for performing unneutral service. When the news reached England the press rang the tocsin of war, the government sent reinforcements to Canada, and Russell drafted a demand for apology and reparation, in terms which resembled those of the famous Austrian ultimatum to Serbia.

Fortunately Prince Albert toned down Russell's dispatch; and by a notable dispensation of Providence the Atlantic cable had ceased to function. Yet the minatory tone of the British press made it difficult for the United States government to give way, and the glorification of Wilkes in the American press made it impossible for the British government to recede. Seward from the first saw that Mason and Slidell must be surrendered; but Lincoln feared the political effect of yielding to British menace. Not until Charles Sumner, armed with admonitory letters from Bright and Cobden, had argued before the cabinet during a four-hour session on Christmas Day, could the President be persuaded to yield. Seward's note to Lyons, designed more to placate the American than the British public, contained no apology; but Mason and Slidell were promtply released and forwarded to their uncomfortable posts.

In the end the *Trent* episode cleared the air. Seward now appeared in the new rôle of conciliator; an Anglo-American war had been faced and found disagreeable to both governments; and the British cabinet was stiffened in its policy of neutrality. The Northern people even forgot their resentment in laughing over the London *Times'* warning to Mason and Slidell that they, personally, were nothing to the English people, who would ' have done just as much to rescue two of their own negroes.'

XXXV

THE WAR IN 1862

1. *Plans and Personalities*

ALMOST half a year had elapsed since Bull Run, and nothing had happened. In the North, McClellan's inaction increased day by day the political difficulties that were gathering about Lincoln. The united spirit formed by the guns that fired on Fort Sumter was evaporating; and from the Republican party a faction emerged to challenge Lincoln's leadership. This was the radical group, led by 'Bluff Ben' Wade and 'Zach' Chandler, Middle-Western senators of coarse fibre but fine talent for politics. From their point of view the war was one of revenge on the insolent slave power; and abolitionist doctrine gave moral sanction to their hatred. The policy they wished to force upon the President was immediate emancipation and arming of the slaves — a policy which, if adopted in 1861, would have driven the border slave states into secession, alienated the Northern Democrats, and narrowed the war party to a faction.

Lincoln's statement in his first annual message to Congress (3 December 1861): 'I have been anxious and careful that the inevitable conflict . . . shall not degenerate into a violent and remorseless revolutionary struggle,' seemed to the radicals a challenge and a sign of weakness. McClellan, a Democrat, and even more conservative than Lincoln on the slavery question, was the particular object of their jealousy and suspicion, while General Frémont's pretense to free the slaves in Missouri by proclamation, an act which Lincoln sternly rebuked, received their hearty approbation.

'A new temper was forming throughout the land, . . . a blend of all those elements of violent feeling which war inevitably releases, . . . the resurrection of that primitive bloodlust which lies dormant in every peaceful nation like a sleeping beast.'[1] To this temper the radicals appealed by voice and pen, during the recess of Congress (August–December 1861). To their standard surged the hundred-per-cent unconditional-surrender sort of patriots, sincere in their desire to win the war, yet certain to lose it for any government that yielded to their misguided zeal. The first product of this complex

---

[1] N. Stephenson, *Lincoln*, p. 195.

of hatred and zeal, suspicion and patriotism, was the appointment by Congress of a joint committee on the conduct of the war (20 December 1861). Radical Republicans were the dominant spirits of this committee. Throughout the war their inquisitorial activities, *ex parte* investigations, and missions to the front, hampered the executive, undermined army discipline, and discouraged the more competent generals. Frémont, Butler, and Hooker were, in the opinion of this committee, the three peerless leaders who could do no wrong.

Owing to the efforts of another House committee, corruption on a gigantic scale was uncovered in the War Department, and the scandal smirched Secretary Cameron. Lincoln sent him on a foreign mission and appointed a 'War Democrat,' Edwin M. Stanton, Secretary of War. Gloomy, ill-mannered, and vituperative, Stanton was another cross for Lincoln to bear. Ignorant of military matters and contemptuous of military science, intolerant of delay and harsh to subordinates, he was hated by almost every officer with whom he came in contact; and on several he did cruel injustice. Yet for all that, Stanton's determination, thoroughness, and system proved him a fit instrument for Lincoln's purpose. He stood for discipline against the President's desire to pardon all deserters. He browbeat politicians and got things done. As Lincoln remarked at a dark period for the Union cause, 'Folks come up here and tell me that there are a great many men in the country who have all Stanton's excellent qualities without his defects. All I have to say is, I haven't met 'em! I don't know 'em! I wish I did!'

When Stanton took office (15 January 1862), McClellan had already prepared, and the President approved, the general outlines of a plan of operations for 1862, which we can mention bit by bit as we take it up. In brief, it was to capture and hold the line of the Mississippi; to occupy Kentucky and Tennessee and cut the Memphis and Charleston railway; and to catch Richmond between two nippers, one operating from Albemarle Sound, and the other from Washington. The blockade, of course, was to be pressed home by the occupation of more bases on the Southern coast.

Lincoln was so pathetically eager to have something to show for all these elaborate preparations, that he issued 'War Order No. 1,' designating Washington's Birthday as the date for a general forward movement of all the sea and land forces of the Republic. Needless to say, 22 February passed without any forward move from McClellan, at whom the order was aimed. But already the first substantial victory for the Union had come in an unsuspected quarter, from an unknown general.

2. Grant and Farragut

Ulysses S. Grant, an officer who disliked war and loathed army routine, had fallen on evil days since the proud moment before Mexico City. After promotion to a captaincy he was forced to resign from the army in order to avoid a court-martial for drunkenness. Unable to extract a living from 'Hardscrabble Farm' near St. Louis, he attempted to sell real estate, and failed again. His father bestowed a clerkship in the family leather store at Galena, Illinois. Brothers condescended, fellow townsmen sneered. Only his wife had faith; and the meanest horses were obedient to his voice and hands.

Fort Sumter fell two weeks before Grant's thirty-ninth birthday. His love of the Union blazed forth and kindled a new faith in himself. After many rebuffs he obtained a colonelcy of volunteers. His regiment, the 21st Illinois, was promptly ordered into Missouri, to dislodge a Confederate regiment under a Colonel Harris. Approaching the reported position, so Grant relates, fear gripped his heart; but he had not the moral courage to halt and consider what to do. Suddenly there opened a view of the enemy's encampment — abandoned! 'It occurred to me at once that Harris had been as much afraid of me as I had been of him. This was a new view of the question I had never taken before; but it was one I never forgot afterwards.' [2]

In August 1861 Grant received a brigadier's commission. 'Be careful, Ulyss,' said his father, 'you are a general now — it's a good job, don't lose it!' In the late autumn he was assigned to Halleck's department, and stationed at Cairo, Illinois, at the junction of the Ohio with the Mississippi. In the summer of 1861 the Confederates began to throw up earthworks at strategic points along the Mississippi where the old Spanish forts used to choke down-river trade. In order to force a passage past them, J. B. Eads of St. Louis undertook to construct a fleet of river gunboats, each with a partially armored casemate shaped like a mansard roof, resting on a flat-bottomed hull.

Less than fifty miles up the Ohio from Cairo the Tennessee and

---

[2] *Personal Memoirs*, i. 250. Throughout the Civil War there was partisan fighting of the most bitter and ferocious nature in Missouri, between Union and Confederate partisans. It had little influence on the outcome of the war elsewhere.

Cumberland rivers offered parallel routes into Tennessee, Alabama, and Mississippi. Grant observed that Fort Henry and Fort Donelson, the two Confederate earthworks which closed these rivers, were the twin keys to the Confederate West. Their capture would open a navigable waterway into the enemy's center, and drive in his flanks. On 11 January Grant obtained Halleck's reluctant consent to try, and was furnished with the necessary transports and gunboats. On 7 February Fort Henry was reduced by the gunboat flotilla before Grant's army arrived.

Fifteen miles across country, on the high left bank of the Cumberland, was the strong, entrenched camp called Fort Donelson. There Albert Sidney Johnston, the Confederate commander in that department, had stationed half his army of 30,000, and thither the Fort Henry garrison retired. Grant disposed his troops in a semicircle about Fort Donelson on the land side, while the gunboats steamed down the Tennessee and up the Cumberland. On 13 February they attacked the fort at a range of 400 yards, but were driven back disabled. It seemed that a siege would be necessary. Two days later the Union right, occupying dense woods on either side of the road to Nashville, was surprised by a sortie. Grant, who was then conferring with the gunboat commander, arrived in the thick of the battle to find his right in disorder and his center in danger. With the utmost coolness he thought out the situation. Deducing from the three-days' rations in a captured Confederate's haversack that the enemy was trying to cut his way out, and perceiving a certain confusion in his movements, Grant made exactly the right tactical disposition to drive the Confederates back into their entrenchments. It was a fierce, blind battle in the forest, but the result justified Grant in asking and the Confederate generals in granting unconditional surrender of army and fortress.

The results of this Battle of Fort Donelson (15 February 1862) were unexpected, even to Grant. Nashville was no longer tenable by the enemy, and A. S. Johnston retreated to the Memphis-Chattanooga railway. Grant had practically restored Tennessee to the Union; and, if his victory were followed up, the Mississippi would be open. Equally important was the moral gain to the then dispirited North. The prairie boys of the new Northwest had tried their mettle with the rangy foresters of the old Southwest; and the legend of Southern invincibility collapsed.

'Unconditional Surrender' Grant had still an old army reputation to live down. His jealous and pedantic superior, General Halleck, instead of allowing him to pursue A. S. Johnston, held up his advance and withdrew his troops to attack the northernmost Confederate strongholds on the Mississippi. In consequence Johnston found time to concentrate at Corinth with gallant Beauregard and that notable man of God, Bishop and General Leonidas Polk.

These caught Grant napping, on 6 April. His army, encamped in an ill-chosen position at Pittsburg Landing, with its rear to the swollen Tennessee river and its front unprotected by entrenchments, had forced upon it the Battle of Shiloh. For twelve hours there was confused fighting between detached portions of the Union lines and the dashing Confederates, superbly led. If the Union army was not routed it was due less to Grant's steadfast coolness than to the fiery valor of divisional commanders like William Tecumseh Sherman, and to the pluck of individual soldiers. By the end of the day the Confederates had captured the key position at Shiloh church, the Union lines were dangerously near the river, and thousands of stragglers were cowering under the bluffs at Pittsburg Landing. But the South had lost her most gallant leader. Albert Sidney Johnston, leading a charge, was mortally wounded. All night a torrential rain drenched both armies, and the Union gunboats dropped shells on the Confederates. When the battle reopened at dawn on 7 April Grant had been strengthened by Lew Wallace's division, and the van of General Don Carlos Buell's Army of the Ohio. After ten hours more of desperate fighting Beauregard withdrew the Confederate army to Corinth. Grant's army was too exhausted to pursue.

Shiloh was a Union victory at a dreadful price. Out of 63,000 Union troops engaged, the loss was 13,000; the Confederate loss was 11,000 out of 40,000. One could walk on corpses across some of the clearings on the battlefield. A storm of controversy arose. Pressure was put upon the President to remove Grant. Lincoln replied, 'I can't spare this man; he fights.' But General Halleck thought he could spare Grant, and did so by taking command of his army in person, in consequence of which, little more was accomplished by the army during 1862 in this western theatre of the war. But the river gunboats continued their advance down the Mississippi, defeating a Confederate flotilla off Memphis, running up the White river into the heart of Arkansas, forcing the enemy to evacuate Missouri, and on 1 July 1862 joining Farragut's fleet above Vicksburg.

Captain Farragut had to force his way up the Mississippi from the Gulf without a single ironclad; but his old wooden walls were manned by stout hearts. At Plaquemines Bend, twenty miles from the head of the Passes and ninety miles below New Orleans, the river was protected by Forts Jackson and St. Philip, by sunken hulls supporting a boom, by a fleet of rams and armed steamers, and by a current of three- to four-knot strength. In the small hours of 24 April Farragut's fleet of eight steam sloops-of-war and fifteen wooden gunboats, with chain cables secured as a coat of mail abreast the engines, crashed through the boom single line ahead, and ran the gauntlet of armored rams, fire-rafts, river defense fleet, and the two forts.

In the gay creole city of New Orleans, largest and wealthiest of the Confederacy, there had been no business since the blockade closed down, and little laughter since the news of Shiloh. When Farragut's fleet anchored off the levee on 25 April, New Orleans was already abandoned by the Confederacy, and the following day the United States forces took possession. New Orleans was a rough city, and the troops of occupation were commanded by a tough character, General B. F. Butler. Repeated insults to his men by the creole wenches were put a stop to by his famous order rendering such a person ' liable to be treated as a woman of the town plying her avocation,' or in other words to be lodged in the common jail. Butler was declared a felon and an outlaw by President Davis, denounced in the British Parliament, and finally removed from his post in consequence of diplomatic protest.

After landing the army Farragut proceeded up-river, receiving the surrender of Baton Rouge and Natchez, and running past Vicksburg to join the up-river gunboat fleet. But as Halleck could not be induced to provide troops for a joint attack on Vicksburg, that ' Gibraltar of the Mississippi' held out for a year longer, enabling Richmond to maintain communication with Arkansas, Missouri, and Texas.

The Confederacy was tightly pinched along its waistline; but the blood could still circulate. The Union offensive in the West had failed in its great purpose, yet accomplished much of value. That was more than could be said of the grand campaigns of this year in the eastern theatre of war.

3. The Peninsular Campaign Begins

' In ten days I shall be in Richmond,' declared General McClellan on 13 February 1862. It was one of those rash boasts that belied his sound instinct, and made men doubt his sincerity. He was planning to outflank J. E. Johnston — then stationed at Manassas — by the Rappahannock, and race him for Richmond. A glance at the map will show the extreme unlikelihood of his success; and Johnston countered by moving to Fredericksburg (7 March). McClellan promptly emulated the famous King of France by marching a portion of his army to the deserted Confederate headquarters at Manassas, and back again to Washington. For Lincoln this was the last straw.

Throughout the winter Lincoln had stood between McClellan and a rising tide of popular impatience, radical suspicion, and denunciation by the committee on the conduct of the war. His patience was now exhausted, his confidence impaired, his resistance worn down. Stanton was even beginning to suspect the General's loyalty. Lincoln offered McClellan the choice between an immediate frontal attack on Richmond, covering Washington as he advanced, and a wide flanking movement by the York peninsula. McClellan chose the peninsular campaign. The President then (11 March) stripped McClellan of his superior command, leaving him only the Army of the Potomac; and within the next few weeks detached Blenker's division and McDowell's corps from that army, gave Stanton supreme control of military operations, created a new department in western Virginia for Frémont with more troops than he knew how to handle, and, just as the campaign was beginning, allowed Stanton to stop recruiting, and to dismantle the new federal recruiting machinery established at McClellan's instance in December. McClellan received these distressing orders as a soldier and a gentleman should, and went forward gallantly to do his best with his means in hand. But his hands were tied. There were three independent commands besides his in Virginia alone, and at sundry points the War Department dictated his movements. There was no peninsular campaign of McClellan. It was the campaign of Lincoln and Stanton.

The peninsular plan, at least, was McClellan's, and it was a good one, enabling the Union army to be supplied and reinforced by sea. Fortress Monroe, at the tip of the York peninsula, was in federal possession. The navy could protect the army's right flank as it advanced up the peninsula as far as White House on the Pamunkey river. On its left flank the James, with deep water up to the suburbs of Richmond, was a better line of approach; but the *Virginia* (ex *Merrimac*) closed it to the Union navy during the first few weeks of the campaign. The *Virginia* — a more powerful edition of the armored gunboats already being used on the Mississippi — met her equal in the *Monitor* in Hampton Roads on 8 March 1862. A new principle of naval armament, the revolving turret, thereupon obtained the sanction of success. But so long as the *Virginia* was afloat she protected the mouth of the James, and held the North Atlantic Squadron in Hampton Roads.

The Army of the Potomac, well armed, trained, and equipped, and 100,000 strong, was the most formidable military force yet seen on American soil. The men were eager for action, their discipline was at top notch, their devotion to their young commander absolute; and now that they were finally in motion, popular confidence rallied to them. In the York peninsula they were on a classic ground of American history. Here were the ruins of Jamestown, the Chickahominy river, arising north of Richmond in the old hunting grounds of Powhatan, the colonial capital of Williamsburg, and Yorktown where the War of Independence was concluded. A few mansions of the eighteenth century still lined the York and James, but the greater part of the peninsula had reverted to its savage state. Even the environs of Richmond were a wilderness, broken by occasional farms and clearing; Lee speaks of impassable swamps, dense forests, and even unknown country, in his report on the Seven Days.

McClellan intended and expected to take Richmond, and crush the rebellion that summer. His sense of injury at the hands of the administration, his suspicion that they did not really wish him to win, only made him the more ardent of success. Splendid visions were in his brain. Himself, on prancing charger, entering Richmond in triumph, the Comte de Paris and Duc de Chartres conspicuous among his glittering staff, Davis, Stephens, and Toombs playing the rôle of suppliants. Magnanimous terms to the gallant enemy: civil rights restored, slave property guaranteed. Discomfited administration not daring to refuse ratification. Grand review at Washington. Modest savior of his country resigns sword to Congress and returns to wife and baby at Cincinnati. Nominated by acclamation for President in 1864.

Yet McClellan did not employ the only methods that had the slightest chance of realizing these dreams: audacity, mobility, dash. His strategy throughout the campaign was determined not by his ambition, but by his inner perception of the true Union policy of cautious constriction. This first appeared in his allowing the Con-

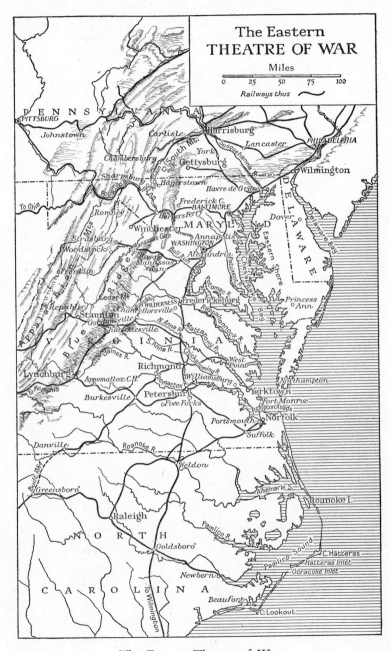

The Eastern Theatre of War

Prepared by S. E. Morison for The Oxford History of the United States

federate field-works that crossed the peninsula from Yorktown to hold up his advance for the entire month of April. For, as the Comte de Paris wrote, 'Thinking that the national cause could endure delays and slow movements, but not such another disaster as that of Bull Run, he preferred to rely upon the superiority of his artillery in order to dislodge the enemy from his lines.' 'Spades are trumps,' sneered the critics.

4. Lee and Jackson

The Confederate government had been shaken out of its lethargy by Grant's capture of Fort Donelson. Its military organization had been improved by the President's appointment of Lee as his military adviser (13 March). Yet it was difficult to see how Richmond could be saved, certainly not by the theory of the bigger battalions. No men could be spared from the West, and at least 50,000 were held in the lower South by the thrusts and threats of Union expeditionary forces. Looking out from Richmond along the roads and waterways that led to the Union periphery, McClellan with over 100,000 men would soon be advancing up the York peninsula, and J. E. Johnston had less than 60,000 to oppose him. McDowell's corps of 40,000 was before Fredericksburg (21 April) with only 11,000 Confederates between him and McClellan's right flank. Banks with 20,000, having defeated Stonewall Jackson's 10,000 near Winchester, had apparently corked up the Shenandoah valley. Frémont with 15,000 was approaching the upper valley through the Appalachian passes, and only 3,000 Confederates faced him. Ewell's shuttle division of 8,000 Confederates was just east of the Blue Ridge. Upon Lee's advice President Davis on 16 April adopted the strategy of delaying McClellan before Yorktown until Jackson could confuse the Union forces in the Valley, threaten Harper's Ferry, and thus frighten the Union government into recalling McDowell's corps from its advanced position. On the same day the Confederate Congress adopted conscription. Of doubtful constitutionality, this courageous act drove a wedge between Davis and his state-rights critics, who feared that their precious theory was being done to death in the house of its friends. But conscription retained in the ranks the men who saved Richmond.

On 14 May McClellan, at last free from the Yorktown lines and within three days' march of Richmond, wired 'for every man the War Department can send, by water.' But Secretary Stanton ordered McDowell's corps to join the Army of the Potomac by land. It was destined never to reach him, and it made just the difference between victory and a drawn campaign. Lee, instead of recalling the scattered legions of the Confederacy to her capital, had the glorious audacity to use Jackson to neutralize three Union units, and to break up McClellan's plans by threatening Washington.

Stonewall Jackson, a stern and bearded puritan, brought to the Southern cause a mastery of the principles of strategy and a religious faith that enabled him to perform what seemed miracles to his enemies. The nucleus of his division was the 'Stonewall brigade' recruited in the Shenandoah Valley, whose population, Unionist in the spring of 1861, as Jackson himself then had been, was now whole-hearted for the Southern cause. The Valley itself, a long, rolling plateau of copses and cornfields, white wooden farmhouses and great red barns, was enclosed by the wooded ridges of the Appalachians and the Blue Ridge, through which numerous 'gaps' or passes offered innumerable combinations to the clever strategist; and Jackson knew every hole and corner of it. Although greatly outnumbered, he was faced by inferior generals: by Nathaniel P. Banks, promoted from the speakership of the House to a major-generalcy, and Frémont, the abolitionists' darling. Nor were the military deficiencies of these gentlemen made good by the efforts of Stanton to move them as upon a chess-board, from Washington.

Having neutralized Frémont on 8 May (Battle of McDowell), Jackson returned to the upper Valley, got around behind Banks, crushed his outposts, almost cut his communications with Washington, administered a stinging defeat at Winchester, and sent him whirling north to the safe side of the Potomac (26 May). Washington was panic-stricken by Jackson's rapid advance, although shielded by double his numbers. Stanton, in a blue funk, telegraphed the governors of the loyal states, 'Enemy in great force advancing on Washington'; and Lincoln did exactly what Lee intended him to do: on 25 May he recalled McDowell's corps, on the point of marching to join McClellan.

Jackson, after a feint at Harper's Ferry, doubled on his tracks, passed between his enemies' converging columns, and on two successive days, 8 and 9 June, whipped Frémont at Cross Keys and one of Banks's divisions at Port Republic. He was then ready to transfer his army to the York peninsula, while large Union forces remained immobile in the Valley to protect Washington from another attack of nerves. In a few days McClellan would be on the defensive.

If McClellan had had the ordering of his campaign, he would have made his base on the James river (controlled by the Union navy since the *Monitor's* victory), instead of the Pamunkey. But in order to reach out to McDowell, he had to extend his army well to the north, and divide it. And after all, McDowell never came. On 31 May, when abnormal rainfall had flooded the sluggish Chickahominy to a zone of swirling waters, J. E. Johnston fell upon McClellan's two corps on the south bank. The pious Army of Northern Virginia doubtless expected that the Lord had delivered up the heathen to be stubble to their swords. But Johnston's orders were not well executed, he was severely wounded, and a part of Sumner's corps managed to cross the Chickahominy by swaying bridges and save the day.

After this Battle of Fair Oaks (or Seven Pines), McClellan, true to his instinctive strategy of caution and constriction, dug himself into a stronger position, and waited for good weather to advance on Richmond under cover of his superior artillery. By the testimony of his enemies this strategy was sound. ' We are engaged in a species of warfare at which we can never win,' Johnston had written Lee. ' It is plain that General McClellan will adhere to the system adopted by him last summer, and depend for success upon artillery and engineering.'

Lee, who succeeded the wounded Johnston as commander of the Army of Northern Virginia on 1 June, saw that McClellan must win Richmond if he were permitted to choose his own ' species of warfare.' The closing cordon must be broken. Accordingly, on 11 June, he ordered Jackson to sweep down from the Shenandoah upon McClellan's right flank while the Army of Northern Virginia attacked him in front. McClellan, warned by an untimely cavalry raid by J. E. B. Stuart, prepared a new base on the James river, and studied with his usual thoroughness the intervening terrain.

5. *The Seven Days' Battles*

McClellan's advance on Richmond, by positions, was timed for 25 June. The next day Lee took the initiative, and the great Seven Days' battles [3] began. Lee planned to crumple up McClellan's right, north of the Chickahominy, with A. P. Hill's and Jackson's divisions, to cut his communications with White House, harass his army front

---

[3] Mechanicsville (26 June), Gaines's Mill or first Battle of Cold Harbor (27th), Savage Station (29th), Frayser's Farm or Glendale (30th), Malvern Hill (1 July).

and rear, and force him either to retreat down the peninsula or to surrender. Superb strategy, but too ambitious for his army to execute. Neither his staff nor his commanders were yet equal to the task of executing an exact combination of several columns in a thickly wooded country. And the Jackson of the Seven Days was not the Jackson of the Valley. His delay in arriving at Mechanicsville (26 June) was probably due to a Sabbath halt to propitiate the God of Battles; but his failure to cross White Oak Swamp on the 30th is still a mystery.

After beating off the first attack on his extreme right at Mechanicsville (26 June), McClellan withdrew Fitz John Porter's corps, which occupied that wing of his army, to a much stronger position near Gaines's Mill. There the Union troops threw up hasty field entrenchments that mark a stage in modern tactics; if spades were not yet trumps, they would be shortly. Against them, on the 27th, Lee developed his plan. The massed commands of Jackson, both Hills, and Longstreet (57,000) were hurled in line after line against the Union defenders (34,000), and at nightfall broke through.

Towards midnight McClellan made his great decision: to move his army by the left to the newly prepared base on the James. It was either that or retreat down the peninsula (which would have fitted Lee's plans exactly), or march around Lee's right toward Richmond. During the evening McClellan considered the possibility of this 'swing into Richmond,' and promptly dismissed it as offering not even a sporting chance of success. Richmond was not an open town that a hostile army could stroll into at will. The Army of the Potomac would have been placed in an impossible position, cut off by Lee from its base; and unless Lee made some colossal error, would have been surrounded and captured.[4] Again McClellan's instinct for cautious constriction won over his ardent desire to 'crush the rebellion at one blow'; and again his instinct was inspired. The distress that decision cost him, after the slaughter of Gaines's Mill, found vent in an unforgivable dispatch to Stanton: ' If I save this army now, I tell you plainly that I owe no thanks to you or to any other persons in Washington.' To which Lincoln replied:

Save your army, at all events. . . . I feel any misfortune to you and your army quite as keenly as you feel it yourself. If you have had a drawn

---

[4] An unaccountable thing in Civil War literature is the persistent criticism of McClellan for not doing in 1862 what Grant, with infinitely superior means, was unable to do in 1864, after a battle on the identical ground of Gaines's Mill.

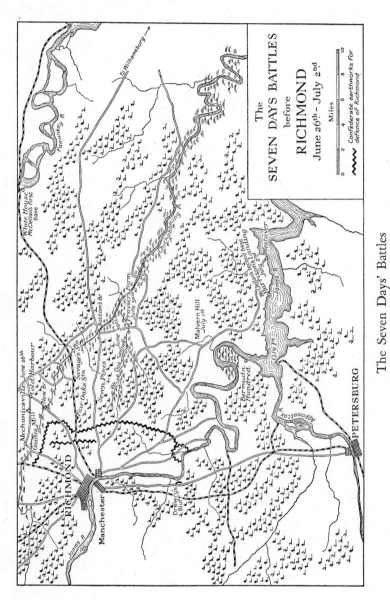

The Seven Days' Battles

Prepared by S. E. Morison for The Oxford History of the United States

battle, or a repulse, it is the price we pay for the enemy not being in Washington. We protected Washington, and the enemy concentrated on you . . . neither you nor the government is to blame.

On the night of 27–28 June McClellan withdrew his right across the Chickahominy, and began to move by the left, southward, to the James. Lee was completely baffled. His cavalry was sent sweeping eastward, to cut communications that were no longer there. During thirty precious hours the Confederate leader lost all touch and knowledge of an army of 90,000 men, whose rear-guard was only a few hundred yards from his pickets, and whose van was within a few miles of his capital. Only at sunrise on the 29th did Lee discover that he had concentrated on empty camps and deserted entrenchments. Promptly he drafted another brilliant plan of concentration, but again his staff and his divisional commanders were unequal to the task. McClellan's manœuvre was conducted with the precision of a grand review. 'Throughout this campaign we attacked just when and where the enemy wished us to attack,' wrote D. H. Hill. The Army of the Potomac, 90,000 strong, with its trains of artillery, 5,000 wagons, and 2,500 beeves, marched by two narrow country roads crossing the highways that led from Richmond, defending itself flank and rear in fierce bayonet encounters at Savage Station and Frayser's Farm (29–30 June) against Lee's pursuing army. On Malvern Hill (1 July), in a position carefully chosen by its commander, the Union army stood at bay, while Lee hurled his divisions without order or unity over cannon-swept wheatfields, in a last desperate attempt to trap the host he had hoped to destroy. By the close of the second day of July, while Lee was withdrawing his decimated legions towards Richmond, the Army of the Potomac, with trains intact and morale unimpaired, was safe within its fortified base at Harrison's Landing on the James.

It was magnificent, and it was not a retreat. McClellan, outnumbered in effective force at the beginning of the Seven Days, had inflicted a superior loss on his adversaries.[5] His army was still full of fight, and ready to resume the advance on Richmond if properly reinforced. The summer was still young. McClellan entreated Lincoln, who visited Harrison's Landing on 9 July, to give him an opportunity to attack Richmond via Petersburg. But General Halleck

[5] Union effectives engaged, 91,169; Union loss (killed, wounded, and missing), 15,849. Confederate effectives engaged, 95,481; Confederate loss, 20,614. T. L. Livermore, *Numbers and Losses*, p. 86.

(who had replaced Stanton in control of operations) pronounced this plan, by which Grant brought the war to an end, to be impracticable; and Lincoln feared that the Administration could no longer carry McClellan. The country had lost confidence in him, if the army had not. Politicians and public could see nothing save that Richmond was still in rebel hands after a costly campaign. Accordingly, on 3 August, Halleck ordered the Army of the Potomac back to the river that gave it birth; and all the gains of the Peninsular Campaign were thrown away. Not for over two years did another Union army approach so near Richmond.

So ended the first grand campaign of the war. Lee by audacious strategy, Jackson by brilliant execution of Lee's orders, had taken full advantage of the enemy's mistakes, and saved Richmond. But Richmond alone was hardly worth the loss of 20,000 men; only the capture or destruction of the Army of the Potomac could have won Southern independence. McClellan too had been wanting; but he missed no such opportunity as that. Asked to do the impossible, he had saved his army, and with it the Union. Intuitively, almost unconsciously, he had adapted his strategy to the true Union policy of attrition. For all that, the Peninsular Campaign, so interesting a study from the point of view of military strategy and tactics, is one of the most beautiful illustrations of the ' great illusion ' that is modern warfare. By August 1862, the Union after immense effort and over a year's preparation was not an inch nearer its goal in this theatre of the war. And on the Southern side, if Lee and Jackson could have foreseen future events and acted upon them (which being men of honor they could not possibly have done) their best policy for their people would have been to have surrendered to McClellan their entire army and Richmond as well — especially if it could have been arranged to include all the Confederate ' fire-eaters ' in the bag. If the war had ended that summer, the horrors of reconstruction could not have occurred, slavery would not have been abolished by violence, or Southern society gutted, and the South would have had some voice in whatever means of gradual emancipation might subsequently have been adopted. In a little while, President Lincoln would feel that he had more need of the moral forces represented by abolition, than of the border slave states: that God, after all, had a higher fighting value than Kentucky.

6. *Weighing Imponderables*

The eight weeks that followed the Seven Days were pure sunshine for the Confederacy. Davis and Lee were masters of the situation. Although New Orleans was gone, Vicksburg kept in touch with the Far West; delegates from Arizona and the Indian Territory sat in the Confederate Congress. Morgan's brilliant cavalry raid through Kentucky, in July, seemed to prove that state ripe for Southern picking. With Chattanooga in Confederate hands railway communications were maintained with all parts of the Republic, and thousands of replacements for Lee's army came pouring into Richmond. If the blockade was tightening, the Confederate cruiser *Florida,* built at Liverpool and armed at Nassau, was beginning to embarrass the blockaders; and on 28 July the *Alabama* left Liverpool for a cruise that proved costly for the American merchant marine and somewhat more so for the British taxpayer.

' There is an all but unanimous belief that you *cannot* subject the South to the Union,' Cobden wrote Senator Sumner on 11 July, when news of the Seven Days' battles reached England. ' I feel quite convinced that unless cotton comes in considerable quantities before the end of the year, the governments of Europe will be knocking at your door.' The same day W. S. Lindsay, M.P., the largest shipowner and most active Southern partisan in Great Britain, introduced a motion for Franco-British mediation in the Civil War. On 16 July, at Vichy, Napoleon III listened graciously to John Slidell's offer of one hundred thousand bales of cotton if France would denounce the blockade. The Emperor telegraphed to his foreign minister: ' Ask the English government if it does not think the moment has arrived to recognize the South.' Palmerston was still against recognition; but the cotton shortage was becoming acute, and Lee's army was preparing to break through. ' The pinch has again passed by for the moment and we breathe more freely,' wrote Henry Adams from the London legation. In his opinion only victory, or a prompt and definite stand on the slavery question, could prevent interference.

For Lincoln the slavery question was somewhat more complicated than for a young Bostonian in the London legation. Lincoln always remembered what it seemed all the world had forgotten, that he was President of the United States — not of the Northern states.

His policy in that respect was stated in the famous letter to Horace Greeley, of 22 August 1862:

As to the policy I 'seem to be pursuing,' as you say, I have not meant to leave any one in doubt. I would save the Union. I would save it the shortest way under the Constitution. The sooner the national authority can be restored, the nearer the Union will be 'the Union as it was.' If there be those who would not save the Union unless they could at the same time save slavery, I do not agree with them. If there be those who would not save the Union unless they could at the same time destroy slavery, I do not agree with them. My paramount object in this struggle is to save the Union, and is not either to save or to destroy slavery. If I could save the Union without freeing any slave, I would do it; and if I could save it by freeing all the slaves I would do it; and if I could save it by freeing some and leaving others alone, I would also do that. What I do about slavery, and the colored race, I do because I believe it helps to save the Union; and what I forbear, I forbear because I do not believe it would help to save the Union. I shall do less whenever I shall believe what I am doing hurts the cause, and I shall do more whenever I shall believe doing more will help the cause. I shall try to correct errors when shown to be errors, and I shall adopt new views so fast as they shall appear to be true views. I have here stated my purpose according to my view of official duty; and I intend no modification of my oft-expressed personal wish that all men everywhere could be free.

From the first advance into Southern territory, slaves of rebel owners had flocked into the Union lines, embarrassing both government and commanders, until the irrepressible Benjamin F. Butler declared them 'contraband of war.' The 'contrabands' were organized in labor battalions, and school teachers were provided to look after their welfare. Emancipation was not really a practical question, for wherever the Union armies penetrated, slavery dissolved; beyond their reach slavery would thrive whatever the United States might decide. But it was a burning question of politics, sentiment, and constitutional law.

On one hand the border states, sensitive on the subject of slavery, blocked proposals for compensated emancipation on which the President had set his heart. Little Delaware lost a chance to start the ball a-rolling in defeating by a single vote a bill for gradual emancipation of her eighteen hundred slaves, with compensation to their owners from the Federal Government. In April and June 1862 Congress finally carried out a party pledge by abolishing slavery in the District of Columbia and the territories. This failed to satisfy abolitionists who since the summer of 1861 had been trying to free all the slaves without compensation, and recruit them for the Union army.

An even larger question intruded: of what avail to restore the Union if slavery, the original cause of disruption, remained? James Russell Lowell expressed this admirably in his 'Biglow Paper' that appeared in the *Atlantic Monthly* of June 1862. Hosea is conversing with the shade of his 'gret-gret-gret-gran'ther,' sometime colonel in the New Model Army:

> 'Hosee,' sez he, 'I think you're goin' to fail:
> The rettlesnake ain't dangerous in the tail;
> This 'ere rebellion's nothin' but the rettle, —
> You'll stomp on thet an' think you've won the bettle;
> It's Slavery thet's the fangs an' thinkin' head,
> An' ef you want selvation, cresh it dead, —
> An' cresh it suddin, or you'll larn by waitin'
> That Chance wun't stop to listen to debatin'.'
> 'God's truth!' sez I, — 'An' ef *I* held the club,
> An' knowed jes' where to strike — but there's the rub!'

'The moment came,' said Lincoln, 'when I felt that slavery must die that the nation might live.' In the cabinet meeting on 22 July he proposed to declare that on the next New Year's Day all slaves in rebel territory would be free. Seward pointed out that such a proclamation at such a time would be interpreted as 'our last shriek on the retreat' from Richmond. Emancipation was then put aside to be a crown to the first victory.

Victory seemed well within reach that summer, if one merely counted the battalions; but Northern morale had been gravely impaired by McClellan's failure to take Richmond. There was a panic in Wall Street; and the gold dollar reached a seventeen per cent premium over paper, in mid-July, when Congress authorized a new issue of $150,000,000 in paper money. Lincoln called upon the states for 300,000 volunteers for nine months, but less than 90,000 volunteered, and they were organized in new nine-month regiments instead of being used like the Confederate conscripts as permanent replacements.

Yet, if the situation had changed for the worse, Lincoln had attained new stature. Resolute in purpose and sure of vision he had always been; but often vacillating and uncertain in performance. From those anxious vigils at the White House during the Seven

Days the perplexed, over-advised, and humble Lincoln emerged humble only before God, but the master of men. He seemed to have captured all the greater qualities of the great Americans who preceded him, without their defects: the poise of Washington without his aloofness, the mental audacity of Hamilton without his insolence, the astuteness of Jefferson without his indirection, the conscience of J. Q. Adams without his harshness, the democracy of Jackson without his ignorance, the magnetism of Clay without his vanity, the lucidity of Webster without his ponderousness; and fused them with a magnanimity peculiarly his own.

7. The Second Bull Run

From the Peninsular Campaign Lincoln had learned the folly of divided command and civilian direction; but the instruments of victory he had not yet found. On 11 July he relegated Stanton to his proper place as war minister, and summoned Halleck from the West to become General-in-Chief in control of operations. 'Old Brains' Halleck, as the army called him, wrote excellent treatises on military science, but seemed helpless before actual problems.

McClellan was still at Harrison's Landing, begging for reinforcements to attack Richmond by way of Petersburg; but Halleck withdrew his army by driblets to reinforce the War Department's favorite plan of an overland march on Richmond, covering Washington. To lead this advance, he summoned General John Pope, who had won some trifling successes on the Mississippi, but had the confidence of a Napoleon. Now was Lee's most precious opportunity to break the wall of steel that was closing about the Confederacy, to carry the war into the free states, and win peace and recognition on Northern soil. Again with Jackson's close co-operation in an audacious manœuvre, he got behind Pope, drew the Army of the Potomac into the spot he wanted, and badly defeated it in the second Battle of Bull Run, or Manassas (29–30 August 1862). It was the neatest, cleanest bit of work that Lee and Jackson ever performed. Their irresistible combination of bold strategy and perfect tactics had undone the Union gains of an entire year in the Virginia theatre of war.

General Halleck, confounded by the rapid movements of the last few days, sat in the War Department, perpetually rubbing his elbows and gazing with watery eyes at a mounting pile of dispatches. One bright thought came, to summon McClellan, then a general without command at Alexandria. On 1 September, as the news from the front became more and more alarming, McClellan conferred with Halleck and the President. Early the next morning Lincoln, without consulting Halleck or his cabinet, placed McClellan in 'command of the fortifications of Washington, and of all the troops for the defence of the capital.' The General at once rode out to meet Pope's retreating army, and to receive the enthusiastic acclaim of his troops.

In the meantime Lincoln faced his cabinet meeting. Stanton and Chase were vehement in their opposition to McClellan, and all their colleagues but Seward and Blair concurred. Lincoln admitted most of their allegations — but pointed out that no one else had the confidence of officers and men, or the ability to cope with so desperate a situation. As Gideon Welles wrote:

In stating what he had done, the President was deliberate, but firm and decisive. His language and manner were kind and affectionate, especially toward two of the members who were greatly disturbed; but every person present felt that he was truly the chief, and every one knew his decision, though mildly expressed, was as fixed and unalterable as if given out with the imperious command and determined will of Andrew Jackson.

When, three days later (5 September), news came that Lee was crossing the Potomac above Washington into Maryland, Lincoln verbally gave McClellan 'command of the forces in the field.'

Of many crises for the Union this was the most acute. With Virginia clear of invaders Lee was about to break through into the heart of the Union. In the West a Confederate offensive was undoing the work of Grant and Buell; [6] in England the sentiment for intervention was coming to a head.

Lee expected to win Maryland for the Confederacy; but his prime objective was the railway bridge over the Susquehanna at Harrisburg, Pennsylvania. Possession of that bridge and of the line of approach would come perilously near cutting the Union in two. It would leave Washington connected with the West only by the roundabout Hudson river and Great Lakes route. The victorious Southern army would be in a central position to attack Washington, Baltimore, or Philadelphia. President Davis, on Northern soil, would

[6] Kirby Smith had taken Lexington and was threatening Cincinnati; Braxton Bragg, Davis's favorite general, was racing Buell for Louisville; if he won, Kentucky might be secured for the Confederacy, and a Southern invasion of Ohio might follow.

propose peace on the basis of Southern independence; and if Lincoln's government refused they would have to reckon with the people in the November election, and face the likelihood of foreign intervention. On 7 September the French minister at Washington informed Seward that in his opinion it was time to recognize the independence of the Confederacy. Napoleon III was only waiting for English approval to do so; and the private correspondence of the English cabinet suggests that they might be ready after the next Confederate victory.

8. Antietam

As they splashed through the fords of the Potomac the regimental bands of Lee's army played the stirring air in which an ardent citizen of Maryland implored his state to ' clothe her beauteous limbs with steel ' and ' be the battle-queen of yore.'

> Come, for thy shield is bright and strong,
>   Maryland! My Maryland!
> Come, for thy dalliance does thee wrong,
>   Maryland! My Maryland!

But she did not come. Southern influence in Maryland extended little beyond the Tidewater. The prudent farmers of the western counties were more impressed by the ragged uniforms of Lee's barefooted veterans than by his invitation to throw off their ' foreign yoke.' It was the harvest season in that rich Maryland Piedmont. Orchards heavily fruited, well-stocked piggeries, and ripe ' roastin' ears ' refreshed the foot-weary boys in gray, but tempted many to remain. Lee lost more men by desertion than he gained by recruiting.

Lee counted on McClellan taking weeks to reorganize; but McClellan's energy and personality worked miracles with Pope's defeated army. Within a week of Manassas he was marching on Frederick Town with 70,000 men, followed by frantic telegrams from Halleck to the effect that Lee's move was a mere feint to draw him from Washington. But McClellan kept on, ' with a halter around his neck ' — and the committee on the conduct of the war at the other end of the rope — for he had no formal written order to command the army in the field. But he had something better, a copy of Lee's order disclosing the exact scheme of his march.

South Mountain, as the Blue Ridge is called where it crosses Maryland, separated the hostile armies. Sending his van to force the passes, McClellan sat his horse as in review by the roadside, pointing to where clouds of smoke showed that the Battle of South Mountain had begun. Men and officers as they passed cheered themselves hoarse, falling out of ranks to touch his charger. That day (14 September) South Mountain was carried. 'I thought I knew McClellan, but this movement of his puzzles me,' exclaimed his West Point classmate, Stonewall Jackson. Lee knew what it meant, and hastened south from Hagerstown just in time to prevent the Union army interposing between his great lieutenant and himself. An over-careful reconnaissance by the Union commander gave Jackson time to cross the Potomac and join Lee on the 16th; but the reunited Army of Northern Virginia was fairly caught in a cramped position between Antietam Creek and the Potomac, where Lee had no room to perform those brilliant manœuvres that were his delight and the enemy's confusion. He had no alternative but to fight or to retreat, and he chose to fight.

The Battle of the Antietam or Sharpsburg (17 September) was a series of desperate unco-ordinated attacks and equally desperate but skillful counter-attacks, that exhausted Lee's army but did not drive it from position. Although fresh reserves were available, McClellan refused to renew the battle the next day, as Grant or Sherman would certainly have done under like circumstances. Without further pressure from him, Lee recrossed the Potomac into Virginia on the night of 18 September. The crisis was ended.

Antietam was the most nearly decisive battle of the Civil War. It might have been really decisive if McClellan had attacked more promptly, combined his attacks properly, and held on persistently. Two years and a half more elapsed before the war closed, but the Confederacy was never so near independence as on that bloody day in the Maryland hills. Thereafter, if the Northern will to victory could be maintained, Union victory was inevitable. A better general might have destroyed Lee's army; but McClellan by restoring morale to the army, by assuming responsibility in the absence of precise orders, and through the lucky break of the lost order, had frustrated Lee's campaign and parried the most serious thrust at his country's heart. Antietam averted all danger of foreign recognition of the Confederacy; and by giving Lincoln the opportunity he sought to issue the Emancipation Proclamation, it brought the liberal opinion of the world to his side.

9. *Forever Free*

It was on 22 September 1862, five days after Antietam, that Lincoln opened a momentous cabinet meeting by reading Artemus Ward's 'High-handed Outrage in Uticy.' The President had not summoned his cabinet for their advice, so he told them. He had made a covenant with God to free the slaves as soon as the rebels were driven out of Maryland; God had decided on the field of Antietam. His mind was fixed, his decision made. Blair and Bates, both from border slave states, thought the moment inopportune; the President reminded them that for months he had urged their states to take the initiative in emancipation. He must now take the forward movement. In the Preliminary Emancipation Proclamation the President, by virtue of his power as commander-in-chief of the army and navy, declared that upon the first day of January 1863 all slaves within any state or district then in rebellion against the United States 'shall be then, thenceforward, and forever free.'

This proclamation, potentially more revolutionary in human relationships than any event in American history since 1776, lifted the Civil War to the dignity of a crusade. But it was very slow to influence public opinion; and only a complete Union victory could give it practical effect. The South, indignant at what she considered an invitation to the slaves to cut their masters' throats, was nerved to greater effort. The Northern armies received from it no new impetus. The Democratic party, presenting it to the Northern people as proof that abolitionists were responsible for the duration of the war, obtained signal gains in the autumn elections. Julia Ward Howe saw in it the glory of the coming of the Lord; but many radicals and abolitionists received it as a tardy surrender to themselves. In England and Europe the proclamation was greeted by liberals and radicals with joy, but by most people with contempt, as a flat political manœuvre. Only by degrees did public opinion at home and abroad perceive that the cause of American Union had been definitely fused with that of human liberty.

Antietam did not alter the opinion held by almost every member of Palmerston's ministry that the Union could never conquer the South; but it did convince every member of the cabinet save Gladstone that the moment was inopportune for intervention. Joint mediation between North and South, which Lord John Russell began to advocate after the second Bull Run, died in the hands of his colleagues by the end of October. A more concrete proposal from Napoleon III, that England, France, and Russia should join in proposing an armistice and lifting the blockade for six months, was definitely rejected by the British cabinet on 11 November. So passed the second and great crisis in foreign relations.

10. *Fredericksburg*

Lee's Army of Northern Virginia retreated up the Shenandoah valley in a demoralized condition. 'The absent are scattered broadcast over the land,' Lee wrote the Secretary of War, on 23 September. 'There is great dereliction of duty among the regimental and company officers, and unless something is done the army will melt away.' And the invasion of Kentucky had proved as disappointing as that of Maryland; the spirit of Henry Clay was too strong. 'Unless a change occurs soon, we must abandon the garden spot of Kentucky to its cupidity,' wrote Braxton Bragg on 25 September. On 8 October Buell won a western Antietam, at Perryville; and Bragg retreated to central Tennessee.

Public opinion in the North was less grateful to McClellan for what he had done than indignant because he had let Lee escape. On 6 October Lincoln ordered McClellan to 'cross the Potomac and give battle to the enemy, or drive him South.' Instead of moving at once, McClellan began to clamor for supplies and clothing and to bandy words with the President. The prospect of another winter of bickering and procrastination was more than Lincoln could bear; and the fall elections had begun. Towards the end of October Lincoln decided that if McClellan permitted Lee to get between him and Richmond, McClellan must go. Lee did just that; and on 7 November the President relieved McClellan of command of the Army of the Potomac, and appointed Burnside in his place.

That ended forever the military career of the Union general of whom Lee afterwards said that he was the ablest of his opponents 'by all odds.' The reasons for Lincoln's action are clear; the consequences are no less certain. It was one of the most costly mistakes Lincoln ever made. On the morrow of victory the Army of the Potomac was deprived of its beloved commander, then fast learning the art of offensive strategy, and sent to useless sacrifice under a general distinguished for fine manners and flowing side-whiskers, who had already proved his incompetence as a corps commander at the Antietam. And Halleck was still General-in-Chief.

Burnside reverted to the old plan of a 'covering advance' on Richmond, from a base behind the Rappahannock opposite Fredericksburg. As Johnston had done in March, so Lee and Jackson now hastened across northern Virginia, and before Burnside had obtained the means of crossing, were posted on the south bank of the Rappahannock, on the wooded heights above Fredericksburg. There, on 13 December, they met an attack by Burnside that presented the most inspiring spectacle and the most useless slaughter of the Civil War. Six times the Union infantry — long double lines of blue, bright national and regimental colors, bayonets gleaming in the sun — pressed on across an open plain, completely covered by the Confederate artillery and entrenched riflemen, to the stone wall at the foot of Marye's Heights. Six times the survivors were hurled back, leaving seven thousand killed and wounded lying literally in heaps. 'Your soldier's heart almost stood still as he watched those sons of Erin fearlessly rush to their death,' General Pickett wrote his wife. 'The brilliant assault on Marye's Heights of their Irish Brigade was beyond description. Why, my darling, we forgot they were fighting us, and cheer after cheer at their fearlessness went up all along our lines.' 'It is well this is so terrible!' said Lee, as he watched the battle; 'we should grow too fond of it.'

11. Political Intrigue

The South hoped that this battle would end the war; but the Fredericksburg position was not one from which Lee could pursue the enemy with profit. Yet to many loyal men in the North it must have seemed, as it did to an English war correspondent, that the day of Fredericksburg would be a memorable one to the historian of the decline and fall of the American Republic. Elections in October and November to the new House of Representatives had increased the Democratic delegation from 44 to 75 members. New York elected a Democratic governor by 10,000 majority; Pennsylvania, Republican by 60,000 in 1860, went Democratic by 4,000 in 1862. Ohio, Indiana, and Illinois — Lincoln's own state — together returned 33 Democrats and only 11 Republicans to the new House; and among the Democrats were several of the so-called 'copperheads,' the pro-Southern defeatists. Only in New England and the trans-Mississippi West did the Emancipation Proclamation seem to strike a responsive note; those regions and (strangely enough) the border slave states saved the Republican majority.

Instead of being drawn more closely to the President by emancipation and misfortune, the radicals were still his bitterest enemies. A few days after Fredericksburg, the Republican members of Congress held a caucus, and on Senator Sumner's proposal appointed a committee of seven radicals to call on the President and demand a change of men and measures. Seward must go, for Seward was the friend of McClellan; and the jealous Chase, angling for the Presidency in 1864, had convinced his friends in Congress that Seward was the cause of all the nation's woes. That night the President confided his distress to an intimate friend, Senator Browning, 'We are now on the brink of destruction. It appears to me the Almighty is against us, and I can hardly see a ray of hope.'

Apparently, Lincoln must choose between yielding to the radicals by sacrificing the indispensable Seward, and defying the Republican party by expelling Chase. He must, in derogation of established constitutional practice, allow Congress to choose his cabinet, or separate himself wholly from Congress. Either horn of the dilemma would entail disaster. Browning told him that the game was to surround him by a radical cabinet. ' The President said with a good deal of emphasis that he was master, and that they should not do that.'

Seward promptly offered his resignation. Holding it in his pocket, Lincoln confronted the visiting committee with all his cabinet but Seward. Questions were asked. Chase, who had been the tale-bearer, wriggled and squirmed, but in the presence of his colleagues said that the cabinet was harmonious. The committee retired convinced that Chase had lied; still they would have Seward's scalp. In the hope of recovering their confidence and support, Chase proffered his resignation to the President. Lincoln, his eye lighting up, almost snatched the paper from his secretary's hesitating hand. Laughing, he exclaimed with a graphic frontier metaphor, 'Now I can ride! I have got a pumpkin in each end of my bag.' He wrote identical letters to both secretaries, refusing to accept their resignations; and both resumed their duties. Lincoln was master indeed.

To crown this eventful year there only remained for Lincoln to issue the definite Emancipation Proclamation, which faint-hearted Union men had urged him to postpone indefinitely. In anticipation, on New Year's eve, pro-Union meetings were held in several English cities, and stout resolves were passed that heartened the President and his people. ' The erasure of that foul blot upon civilization and Christianity — chattel slavery — during your Presidency will cause the name of Abraham Lincoln to be honored and revered by posterity,' declared a meeting of six thousand working men at Manchester, the city which suffered most from the Union blockade. To which Lincoln replied on 19 January 1863:

I know and deeply deplore the sufferings which the working men at Manchester, and in all Europe are called to endure in this crisis. . . . Under the circumstances, I cannot but regard your decisive utterances upon the question as an instance of sublime Christian heroism which has not been surpassed in any age or in any country. It is indeed an energetic and reinspiring assurance of the inherent power of truth and of the ultimate and universal triumph of justice, humanity and freedom. I do not doubt that the sentiments you have expressed will be sustained by your great nation; and, on the other hand, I have no hesitation in assuring you that they will excite admiration, esteem and the most reciprocal feeling of friendship among the American people. I hail this interchange of sentiment, therefore, as an augury that whatever else may happen, whatever misfortune may befall your country or my own, the peace and friendship which now exist between the two nations will be, as it shall be my desire to make them, perpetual.

XXXVI

BEHIND THE LINES
1861–1865

1. *Liberty in War Time*

IN the cabinet crisis of December 1862, only Lincoln's astuteness saved him from becoming a mere premier, instead of a President. As it happened, Lincoln wielded a greater power throughout the war than any other chief magistrate, not excepting Wilson; a wider authority than any English-speaking ruler between Cromwell and Lloyd George. Contemporary accusations against him of tyranny and depotism are strange reading to those who know his character, but not to students of his administration. If Lincoln was the ideal tyrant of whom Plato dreamed, he was none the less a dictator from the standpoint of American constitutional law and practice; and even the safety of the Republic cannot justify certain acts committed under his authority. President Davis is open to the same charge. In the Confederacy, as in the United States, there were many men of high standing and character who preferred to risk defeat at the hands of the enemy rather than submit to an arbitrary government by their own President.

The war power of the President as Commander-in-Chief of the army and navy is, in practice, limited only by public opinion and the courts. At the very beginning of the war, Lincoln of his own authority called for enlistments not yet sanctioned by Congress, declared the blockade, and suspended the writ of habeas corpus in parts of Maryland. The first assumption of power was shortly legalized by Congress, the second by the Supreme Court; but Chief Justice Taney protested in vain against executive suspension of the famous writ (*ex parte* Merryman). At the same time military officers, acting under orders from the State or the War Department, began to arrest persons suspected of disloyalty or espionage, and to confine them without trial in military prisons, for indefinite terms. Lincoln could not afford to indulge a meticulous reverence for the Constitution when the Union was crumbling; but the power he asserted was grossly abused. A loyal mayor of Baltimore, suspected of Southern sympathies, was arrested and confined in a fortress for over a year; a Maryland judge who had charged a grand jury to inquire into illegal acts of government officials was set upon by soldiers when his court was in session, beaten and dragged bleeding from his bench, and imprisoned for six months; a former congressman from Ohio, seventy years old, was arrested in his home by military authority, for alleged 'discouragement of enlistments.' His constituents elected him to the state legislature while in prison.

Simultaneously with the Emancipation Proclamation, the President issued an order that seemed to deny to white citizens the liberty he proposed to accord to negro slaves. He proclaimed that all persons resisting the draft, discouraging enlistment, or 'guilty of any disloyal practice affording aid and comfort to rebels' would be subject to martial law, tried by court-martial, and denied the writ of habeas corpus. Under this proclamation, over thirteen thousand persons were arrested and confined by military authority, for offenses ranging from the theft of government property to treason. Earlier in 1862 — only a few days after he had scathingly denounced Lincoln's tyranny — President Davis obtained from his Congress the power to suspend the writ of habeas corpus, and promptly did so in Richmond and other places, where equally arbitrary and unjust proceedings occurred.

Undoubtedly the provocation was great, especially in the North, where opposition to the war was open, organized, and active in almost every state. One of the most delicate and difficult subjects with which both Lincoln and Davis had to deal was the peace movement. On both sides it included doctrinaire pacifists and defeatists; but the great body was composed of sincere persons who, if Northerners, believed that the Union could be restored, or if Southerners, that independence could be established, by negotiation: that only the obstinacy of Lincoln, or the ambition of Davis, prevented peace. The 'copperheads,' as the Northern opponents to the war were called, held a great mass-meeting in Lincoln's home town, on 17 June 1863. They resolved 'that a further offensive prosecution of this war tends to subvert the Constitution and the Government,' and proposed 'a national Convention to settle upon terms of peace, which should have in view the restoration of the Union as it was.' In North Carolina over one hundred peace meetings were held within two months after Gettysburg, in order to promote negotiations for reunion. On both sides the defeatists organized secret societies. In the North the 'Knights of the Golden Circle' harassed loyal households by midnight raids and barn-burnings; in the South the ' Heroes of America ' gave aid and comfort to the enemy.

Neither the Union nor the Confederate government made any systematic effort to suppress these organizations: they were too formidable. In Ohio, Indiana, and Illinois, where treason flourished side by side with the most stalwart loyalty, General Burnside attempted repression in 1863 with slight success. In a general order he declared, ' The habit of declaring sympathy for the enemy will not be allowed in this department.' For violation of this order, in a campaign speech, a prominent copperhead named Vallandigham was arrested, tried by a military commission, and sentenced to confinement for the duration of the war. Lincoln humorously altered the sentence to banishment, and Vallandigham was escorted within the military lines of the Confederacy. He received *in absentia* the Democratic nomination for governor of Ohio, and conducted a campaign for peace and reunion from Canadian soil, although his unwilling Confederate hosts had made it perfectly clear that they would accept peace only with independence. In 1867 the Supreme Court took cognizance of a very similar case (*ex parte* Milligan), and declared in unmistakable terms that neither the Constitution nor any usage of war would sanction the military trial of a civilian in districts where the civil courts were open.

This was after the war was over, and helped nobody. Because of the unchecked acts of military officers, personal liberty, freedom of speech and of the press were subject to a more arbitrary control during the Civil War than during the World War. During both conflicts the courts failed to protect civil rights. Yet one who has studied the administration of Lincoln, and lived through the second administration of Wilson, believes that pacifists, conscientious objectors, the outspoken press, and critics of the government fared better under the earlier régime. There was no single act in the World War so outrageous to decency, right, and justice as the trial of the conspirators in the assassination of Lincoln; but the Espionage Act of 1917, administered by a Department of Justice with a corps of paid spies and volunteer informers, enforced by judges and juries often maddened with war propaganda, was much more drastic in its effect and unjust in its operation than the court-martial of 1861-65. Throughout the Civil War active disloyalty was effectively dealt with wherever it raised its head; but there was no censorship of the press (although Burnside for a time stopped the circulation of the New

York *World* and the Cincinnati *Inquirer* in his Department), and discussion of war aims and peace terms was seldom hindered. Hardly a Northern community lacked a few ' unterrified Democrats ' who maintained with impunity that Jeff Davis was a better man than Abe Lincoln, that secession was legitimate, and the Union forever dissolved. Sentences of the court-martial were comparatively mild, and offenders were pardoned promptly with the coming of peace; but sentences of twenty years and over were common during the World War, and pardons were difficult to obtain after it was over.

2. Northern Industry and Westward Expansion

It was an article of faith among subjects of King Cotton that Northern industry, cut off from its Southern markets and its supply of fibre, would collapse. On the contrary, Northern industry grew fat and saucy during the war. Union sea power maintained the routes to foreign markets; the waste of war stimulated production. In Philadelphia alone 180 new factories were built during the years 1862–64. The government, generous in its contracts and lavish in expenditure, helped to create a new ' shoddy aristocracy ' of profiteers, who became masters of capital after the war. Paper money and the high protective tariff that Congress imposed as a counterweight to internal taxation brought a sharp rise of prices, which the government made no effort to control. Owing to the relatively slight development of labor unions, wages did not rise in the same proportion,[1] and the salaried classes suffered considerably. After the middle of 1862 enough cotton was obtained from the occupied parts of the South, and even from Liverpool, to reopen many of the cotton mills. Indeed the only essential Northern industry that suffered from the war was the carrying trade. Only 257 American merchantmen were destroyed by Confederate cruisers, but many more took foreign registry to escape capture; and with the diversion of the better ships into government service, the share of foreign bottoms in American trade greatly increased.

In many ways the drain of men into the army and navy was compensated. Immigration for the five war years amounted to almost eight hundred thousand. Labor-saving devices, invented before the war, were now generally applied. The Howe sewing-machine proved a boon to the clothing manufacturer, and a curse to the poor seam-

[1] Average prices rose 117 per cent, 1860–65; average wages 43 per cent.

stress, whose wage dropped to eight cents an hour in 1864. The Gordon McKay machine for sewing uppers to shoe-soles actually speeded up that process one hundred-fold, and revolutionized the industry. Petroleum, discovered in Pennsylvania in 1859, was so rapidly extracted that the production increased from 84,000 to 128,000,000 gallons in three years; and refining methods were so rapidly improved that kerosene in cheap glass lamps had begun to replace candles and whale oil by 1865.

Like causes speeded up the revolution in American agriculture. The mechanical reaper, hitherto confined to the better prairie farms, came into general use, giving every harvest hand five-fold his former capacity with scythe and cradle. The annual pork pack almost doubled, the annual wool clip more than tripled between 1860 and 1865. Westward migration and the opening up of new prairie wheatfields were greatly stimulated by the passage of the Homestead Act in 1862, which supplemented the Pre-emption Act of 1841 by offering a settler title to one hundred and sixty acres of public land after five years' residence and use, for a nominal fee. Some fifteen thousand homesteads were thus pre-empted during the war. Every autumn brought bumper crops of wheat and corn, while Europe suffered a succession of poor harvests. England imported fifty-fold the amount of wheat and flour in 1862 that she had in 1859. Although the lack of cotton threw many English factory operatives out of work, it was evident that any attempt to break the blockade, and consequently fight the United States, would bring the British Isles face to face with starvation. 'Old King Cotton's dead and buried, brave young Corn is King,' went the refrain of a popular song.

Apart from this westward extension of prairie farming, the normal development of the Far West continued during the Civil War. Colorado, the goal of the 'Pike's Peak or Bust' gold rush in 1859, was organized as a territory in 1861; and with the reorganization of Dakota and Nevada territories the same year, no part of the United States, on paper at least, was any longer outside the dominion of law. Kansas became a state as soon as Congress lost its Southern delegation in 1861; and Nevada was admitted prematurely in 1864, because the Republicans thought they needed its electoral vote. At least three hundred thousand emigrants crossed the plains to California, Oregon, and the new territories during the war — some to farm, others to seek gold, and many to escape the draft.

In general, the normal growth and activity of a civilized community continued in the North, without abatement. The cities increased in wealth and population. Enrollment in the universities hardly decreased beyond the loss of Southern students, although in some of the Western colleges the undergraduates enlisted in a body for short tours of service. Fifteen new institutions of higher learning, including Cornell University, Swarthmore College, and the Massachusetts Institute of Technology, were founded in war time, and numerous bequests and new buildings were obtained by the older colleges. The Harvard-Yale boat-races, interrupted in 1861, were resumed in 1864 while Grant was besieging Petersburg, and not a single member of either crew enlisted.

The Union was more conspicuous for organized service than for individual sacrifice. Following the experience of Florence Nightingale and the British Sanitary Commission in the Crimean War, a number of public-spirited citizens organized the United States Sanitary Commission at the beginning of the Civil War. As an auxiliary to the Army Medical Corps, the Sanitary Commission fitted up hospital ships, organized hospital units and kept them supplied; taught company officers how to care for their men, sent men and women to nurse the wounded at the front, supplied the soldiers with clothing, comforts, and welcome additions to their abundant but unvaried army rations of bread, beef, and coffee. Clara Barton, later the founder of the American Red Cross, and Dorothea Dix were active in this work. There was also a United States Christian Commission which deluged the army with Bibles, tracts, and patriotic song-books, and supplied a certain number of coffee bars and reading rooms. If the boys in blue and the boys in gray obtained less aid and attention than the combatants of the World War, they expected less; and their standard of comfort was lower. Compared with any earlier conflict the amount and variety of volunteer organized non-combatant service was unprecedented.[2]

3. Conscription, North and South

Lincoln, having allowed Stanton to dismantle the new federal recruiting service before the Peninsular Campaign, had to appeal to the states to raise 'three hundred thousand more' on 2 July 1862;

[2] Most of the army nurses in the Civil War were men; Walt Whitman has related his nursing experiences in his *Specimen Days* and other writings.

and the states, even by drafting from their own militia, produced but eighty-eight thousand men, organized in new regiments and enlisted for nine months. Replacements for veteran regiments could not be obtained. Yet Congress flinched from a national conscription. During the winter of 1862–63 it became evident that unless these scruples were surmounted, the game was up; and Congress on 3 March 1863 passed the first United States Conscription Act.

It was a most imperfect law, a travesty of a conscription act. All men between the ages of 20 and 45 were declared liable to military service, and had to be registered. As men were needed, the number was divided among the loyal states in proportion to their total population, and subdivided among districts, giving credit for previous enlistments. In the first draft (1863) these credits wiped out the liability of most of the Western states, which had been most forward in volunteering. Between each subsequent call and the actual draft, every state and district had fifty days' grace to furnish its revised quota by volunteering, after which the balance was obtained by drafting names on the registered lists. No attempt was made to levy first on the younger men or bachelors, and instead of exempting specified classes such as ministers and supporters of families, money payment was made the basis of exemption. You could commute service in a particular draft upon payment of three hundred dollars; or evade service during the entire war by procuring a substitute to enlist for three years — no matter if the substitute died the next month, or deserted the next day.[3] The system was inequitable to the poor, and in the working-class quarters of New York the first drawing of names in 1863 was the signal for terrible riots.

Apparently the Irish-Americans of New York, always hostile to the negro, were disaffected by the Emancipation Proclamation, and inflamed by the importation of ' contrabands' to break a stevedores' strike. On 13 July, while the names were being drawn, the provost

[3] The system was so complicated that certain exceptions to these broad statements must be noted. (a) The basis of the quota was changed from total population to population registered for service, after the first draft. (b) Naval enlistments were not credited in the first draft. (c) In the first draft the married men over thirty-five were not to be drafted until all others had been called out; but there was no such distinction in later drafts. (d) From all the drafts exemption was granted to sole supporters of aged parents and eldest brothers in large families of young children, but not to supporters of families as such. Physical disability was the principal cause for exemption. (e) The commutation privilege was abolished for all but religious conscientious objectors by Act of 24 February 1864, but such objectors had to serve in some non-combatant branch.

marshal was driven from his office by a mob. Men, women, and boys paraded the streets during the better part of four days and nights, sacking shops, gutting saloons, burning mansions, lynching and torturing every negro who fell into their clutches. The police — who also for the most part were Irish-Americans — did their best, but it was not until troops were poured into the city that order was restored, after the loss of hundreds of lives. This was equivalent to a Confederate victory, for Meade's army was so weakened by detachments for guard duty in northern cities, that he was unable to take the offensive against Lee after Gettysburg. In fact, although there were three more drafts after the first, a very small proportion of the Union army was furnished by direct conscription, as the subjoined table shows.[4] Every fresh draft began an ignoble competition between districts to reduce their quotas by fictitious credits, and to fill the residue by bounty-bought volunteers. As recruits were credited to the district where they enlisted, and not to that of their residence, several wealthy communities escaped the draft altogether by purchasing cannon-fodder in the poorer country districts. These were left with only fathers of families and physical rejects to fill subsequent drafts — which, therefore, were not filled at all. Professional bounty-brokers so covered the country with their network that it was difficult for anyone to get into service without passing through their clutches; and as the state bounties or individual substitution

[4] The following table is compiled from the final report of the Provost-Marshal-General (1866), 39th Cong., 1st Sess., House Exec. Docs., iv, part i, pp. 43–213 and 3 rev. Official Records of the Rebellion, v. 732–39.

Draft of {	1863 July	1864 14 Mar.	1864 18 July	1864 19 Dec.
Number called for	700,000		500,000	300,000
Reduced by credits to	407,092		234,327	300,000
Names drawn	292,441	113,446	231,918	139,024
Failed to report	39,415	27,193	66,159	28,477
Examined	252,566	84,957	138,536	46,128
Exempted for physical disability, etc.	164,855	39,952	82,531	28,631
Exempted by paying commutation	52,288	32,678	1,298	460
Substitutes furnished by registered men	84,733		29,584	12,997
Substitutes furnished by draftees	26,002	8,911	28,502	10,192
Draftees held to personal service	9,881	3,416	26,205	6,845
Voluntary enlistments	489,462		188,172	157,058
Total number obtained	537,672 *		272,463	187,092

* The excess, 130,579, credited to call of 18 July 1864.

fees were paid cash down, the brokers often induced the recruits they furnished to desert at the first opportunity, and re-enlist elsewhere. 'Bounty jumpers' enlisted and deserted, ten, twenty, even thirty times, before being apprehended.[5] Brokers had their crimps in Canada, offering fabulous bounties that were never paid, kidnapping civilians, and tempting soldiers of the British garrison to desert — there were almost 50,000 Canadian enlistments in the Union army. State agents scoured occupied portions of the South for negroes, and obtained shiploads of men from the poorhouses of Belgium and Germany, all of whom were credited to their state quotas. Federal officials were bribed to admit cripples, idiots, and criminals as recruits. One can easily imagine the effect on the morale of a veteran regiment which received replacements of this nature.

The success of the Union conscription, however, is not to be measured by the very small number of actual draftees obtained, or the large proportion of deserters, but by the enormous number of volunteers obtained under pressure. Unquestionably the average quality of both armies deteriorated as the war dragged on; but the men who followed Grant through the Wilderness and Sherman to Atlanta will compare well with any soldiers of modern times for courage, discipline, and tenacity.

Compared with the Union, the Confederacy was a nation in arms. During four years, war was its only business. Fighting for independence and race supremacy, the Southerners gave their government more, and asked of it less, than did the Northern people. Yet the glamour of a lost cause and the reticence of Southern writers have until recently obscured the part that selfishness, indifference, and defeatism played in losing it. Not that there was any Union party in the Confederacy, outside the mountainous regions — where no Confederate conscription officer dared show his face — but there was inveterate provincialism and widespread ignorance, and withal a certain shrewd instinct on the part of the poor whites that it was ' a rich man's war and a poor man's fight.'

The Union system of conscription was simply a series of requisitions on the states, differing from that of the War of Independence because it was administered and enforced by national authority. The Confederate system was, in theory, a mass levy of Southern

---

[5] The United States Provost-General Fry, estimated total desertions from the Union army at 201,397 — approximately one to every seven enlistments. Desertions from the Confederate army totalled 104,428, or one to every nine enlistments.

manhood between the ages of 18 and 35. Yet, instead of promoting solidarity, it fomented class antagonism. Originally adopted (April 1862) in order to obtain replacements, and retain in the ranks all men whose terms of enlistment were expiring, it was generally regarded as a mere temporary expedient of doubtful constitutionality. There was no answer to Senator Foote's question, ' If agents of the Confederate Government had the right to go into any state and take therefrom the men belonging to that state, how were state rights and state sovereignty to be maintained? ' Most state courts supported the law, even quoting decisions of Chief Justice Marshall. But others did not. The Chief Justice of North Carolina even discharged two deserters who killed a man when resisting capture, on the ground that a state had nothing to do with enforcing Confederate conscription! Although the law granted exemptions to ministers, conscientious objectors, railway employees, postmen, apothecaries, teachers, and the like, South Carolina of her own sovereign authority proceeded to extend the privilege, and to assert the right of nullification in 1862 as roundly as in 1832. Congress was persuaded to add millers, blacksmiths, editors, printers, and plantation overseers, at the rate of one to every twenty slaves, to the exempted classes; whereupon there arose a mighty clamor from the democracy, especially against the ' twenty-nigger' provision, and the privilege of substitution. So much fraud and skulking developed that Congress swung in the other direction until the Confederate War Department had to supply labor for essential industries by details from the army. Substitution was stopped towards the close of 1863, when the price of a substitute had reached six thousand paper dollars. Early in 1864 the Confederate Congress cut down exemptions and extended the age of military service to seventeen and fifty.

No Southern city was disgraced by draft riots like that of New York, but fraud and evasion were widespread, and many of the remoter districts of the South were terrorized by armed bands of deserters and draft-dodgers, who waged a successful guerrilla warfare against the troops sent to apprehend them. President Lincoln on 10 March 1863 proclaimed amnesty to all absentees without leave who would return to the colors within the month. In June, when the percentage of absentees in the Confederate army was approaching thirty per cent, President Davis extended a similar invitation to them. So few came in that the offer of twenty days' grace was repeated shortly after Gettysburg, Davis declaring the South to be invincible if every man liable to service would do his duty. There is no doubt that he was right.

4. *The South in War Time*

In 1863 Southerners began to feel the pinch of poverty, and as the war dragged on many came face to face with starvation. Yet the South was an agricultural country, and the production of food steadily rose as an increasing proportion of the cotton fields were planted with corn and wheat. There was no lack of labor, for the slaves remained loyal and at work, unless a Union army appeared in the neighborhood. Only transportation was wanting.

Railway transportation was the weak point in the Confederate economic organization. Numerous local lines of varying gauges converged on market towns and seaports. Through traffic, which hardly existed in the South before the war, encountered many 'bottle-necks' and breaks — as in Petersburg, Lynchburg, Knoxville, Chattanooga, and Raleigh — where freight had to be carted from one station to another. The government was slow to assert control over railroads, and although Congress appropriated money to construct missing links, little was done. The few rolling mills and foundries were too busy with government work to replace outworn equipment. Main lines could be kept going only by using the rolling-stock and tearing up the rails of branch lines; junctions became congested with supplies, and breakdowns were frequent. That is why there were bread-riots in Richmond when the barns of the valley were bursting with wheat; why government clerks had to pay fifteen dollars a bushel for corn that was bringing the farmer only a dollar in southwestern Georgia.

The ruling class in the South, which had most at stake, gave all it had to the cause. In the North able-bodied young men of means and position could buy substitutes without incurring social stigma; in the South the women saw to it that there were no gentlemen slackers. The patriotism of the Southern women was only equalled by their devotion. Left in charge of plantations they had to direct the necessary changes from cotton-raising to the production of food, to revive obsolete household industries such as spinning, weaving, and dyeing, to extract nitrates from the earth of cellars and smoke-houses, to care for wounded soldiers, and to feed passing armies. It was the Southern women who

Made courage from terror and bread from bran
And propped the South on a swansdown fan
Through four long years of ruin and stress,
The pride — and the deadly bitterness.[6]

5. *War Finance*

Both governments attempted to finance the war by loans and taxes; both resorted to indirect taxation by paper money. Neither Secretary Chase nor Secretary Memminger rose above mediocrity as ministers of war finance. Chase's earliest expedient of importance was an issue of 7.3 per cent three-year gold notes, to which the Northern banks subscribed liberally. The Treasury then sucked away their specie reserves to such an extent that they were forced to suspend specie payments at the end of 1861. Congress was able to devise nothing better, although William P. Fessenden, chairman of the Senate committee on finance, learned enough to make him a competent successor to Chase. The customs duties were raised; an income tax, with rates varying between three and ten per cent, was levied; bonds were issued in small denominations, and eagerly subscribed; and in July 1862 a comprehensive scheme of internal taxation was imposed. 'No other nation,' said the London *Economist,* 'would have endured a system of excise duties so searching, so effective or troublesome.' System, however, there was none, since Chase was unable to guide Congress, and Congress could not force Chase. During the fiscal year between 1 July 1862 and 30 June 1863 the government received 111 million dollars from taxation, and 175 million from bonds; but spent 715 million; it was not until 1864 that taxation even met one-third of the government's expenditure. That it did reach this proportion was a matter of astonishment to foreign governments, and a tribute to the strength of American democracy.

The deficiency was made up chiefly by inflation. Legal tender notes, known as greenbacks, were authorized by Congress against the wishes of Chase and of Wall Street, in February 1862.[7] Gold

---

[6] Stephen Vincent Benét, *John Brown's Body* (Doubleday, Doran Co., 1929), book iv, p. 163.

[7] These were the first issued by Congress that were legal tender for all debts and payments, public and private. Previous and later issues of interest-bearing 'treasury notes' were receivable only for federal dues. The customs duties, however, were by special act collected in gold or the equivalent, throughout the Civil War. The Supreme Court decided in 1869 that the Legal Tender Act was unconstitutional and void in respect of debts contracted before its passage; but upon the filling of two vacancies in the Court, it promptly reversed its decision.

had already disappeared; silver and copper followed as the green-backs depreciated to thirty-five cents on the gold dollar. 'Shin-plasters' — fractional paper currency, in denominations as low as three cents — were then issued. The greenbacks rallied to seventy-eight cents after Lee's surrender, but did not reach parity with gold until 1879.

As legal tender for all debts and payments the greenbacks were fiat money like our present currency. Their influence on the financial standards of the nation was deep and pernicious, and they need not have been issued so early in the war. The banking side of Chase's financial policy was more creditable. He recommended the National Bank Act of February 1863, which allowed banks to issue notes up to ninety per cent of their holdings in government bonds. Al-though comparatively few banks took advantage of this law during the war, it subsequently became the basis of the federal currency system, until its inelasticity and other defects caused it to be super-seded by the Federal Reserve system in 1913.

Inflation was almost the exclusive method of Confederate war finance. Jefferson Davis had to obtain supply from a people even less used to heavy taxation than those of the North, and much less able to bear it; and the blockade precluded any considerable income from customs duties. In four years the receipts of the Confederate government did not exceed $27,000,000 in specie value. Its expendi-tures ran to a couple of billions in treasury notes, payable in gold upon 'ratification of a treaty of peace between the Confederate States and the United States.' Prices, measured by this currency, rose to levels that seemed fantastic until after the World War. The Confederate dollar did not fall below 33 cents until 1863 when it began to slide, and was worth only 1.6 cents in gold at the time of Lee's surrender. But the Davis government was never at a loss for money. Inflation tempted Southerners to hoard food, to speculate in other essential supplies, and to exchange any profits that they made into United States dollars or sterling. The government fixed maxi-mum prices, but had no authority to enforce them; and blockade runners imported luxuries for the profiteers rather than necessities for the army. As the stringency of the blockade increased, Southern economic life diverged more widely from the normal; but economic revolution came only with defeat and reconstruction.

After noticing these many instances of selfishness, indifference, and defeatism on both sides, we must remember that, after all, both the Union and the Confederate governments were sustained by popular suffrage in 1862 and 1864, and that no earlier war in modern history drew out so much sacrifice, energy, and heroism. Vice-President Stephens divined the situation at the beginning of 1863, when he wrote, ' The great majority of the masses both North and South are true to the cause of their side. . . . A large majority on both sides are tired of the war; want peace. . . . But as we do not want peace without independence, so they do not want peace without union.' Similarly it might be said that the European peoples in 1916 and 1917 were tired of the World War; but none desired peace without victory. The very numerous elements that wanted peace at any price were either silenced by a repression such as Lincoln and Davis could not exert, or converted by a war propaganda in comparison with which the efforts of North and South were amateurish and unconvincing. Outwardly, at least, the American people in 1918 were more whole-heartedly in the war against Germany than their grandfathers had been in the war against each other; but in comparison with the heart-breaking struggle of 1861–65, the World War, so far as the American people were concerned, was a brief and happy adventure.

XXXVII

FROM VICKSBURG TO APPOMATTOX
January 1863 — April 1865

1. *The Diplomatic Front*

MILITARY operations became simpler as the war progressed. In 1863 both sides concentrated upon the objectives they had failed to attain the year before: the Union on strengthening the blockade, and pressing out such obstacles to military constriction as Vicksburg, Chattanooga, and Lee's army; the Confederacy on defense, and breaking through into Kentucky, Pennsylvania, and the high seas. The year was a brilliant one for the Confederate navy. Two improvised 'cotton-clads' recaptured Galveston; the guns of Fort Sumter repelled three separate attacks on Charleston; the *Alabama* and *Florida* were at large, destroying United States shipping; and orders were placed in England and France for some powerful armored rams, which might well have broken the Union blockade.

The interventionist forces in Europe, encouraged by Fredericksburg, began to make trouble again in 1863. Of these forces, Napoleon III was the most dangerous, because the least calculable. Napoleon's American policy was determined by his Mexican adventure, which began in 1861 and became a purely French enterprise the next year; in June 1863, a French army took Mexico City, and the next year the unfortunate Maximilian of Austria accepted the imperial crown of Mexico from France. Thus the Civil War gave Napoleon III an opportunity to perform the feat of which Talleyrand, Canning, and Aberdeen had dreamed: to bring the New World into the balance of power, to re-establish European influence in North America. Slidell, the Southern agent in Paris, offered Confederate support to the Emperor in Mexico; a practical demonstration that American disunion was playing the European game. In January 1863, Napoleon III proposed a peace conference between North and South, with the object of establishing the Confederacy. Seward refused the offer very definitely.

Spain in a small way was pursuing the same policy. At the invitation of the conservative faction in Santo Domingo she was endeavoring to convert that unstable republic into a Spanish colony. France in Mexico, Spain in Santo Domingo, meant a counter-stroke of monarchial Europe against republican America; an after-clap of the Holy Alliance. ' A little audacity,' wrote a Spanish historian, 'and France was assured of her possessions, England of Canada, . . . ourselves of the treasure of our Antilles, and the future of the Spanish race. Mexico and the Southern States . . . were the two advanced redoubts which Europe in its own interest should have thrown up against the American colossus.'[1]

Impressive was the rally of liberal sentiment to the Union in England, France, and Spain, as the meaning of the Emancipation Proclamation sank in. A Confederate agent reported of France, 'With the exception of the Emperor and his nearest personal adherents, all the intelligence, the science, the social respectability, is leagued with the ignorance and the radicalism in a deep-rooted antipathy . . . against us.' Emilio Castelar, the Spanish liberal leader, declared ' An empire in Mexico is nothing else at bottom than an aid to the slaveholders of the South.' In England, the Emancipation Proclamation brought about such an upheaval of evangelical, radical, and working-class opinion in favor of the Union, that no ministry could, if it would, give aid and comfort to the slave power. Bright, Forster, and Goldwin Smith were now believed when they asserted that the cause of the Union was the cause of liberty. There were many enthusiastic pro-Union meetings like that of Manchester in 1862. Karl Marx organized a gathering of three thousand representatives of the London trades unions on 26 March 1863, which was addressed by Bright, and resolved 'that the success of free institutions in America was a political question of deep consequence in England, and that they would not tolerate any interference unfavorable to the North.' Henry Adams, who reported the meeting for his father, wrote, 'I never quite appreciated the moral influence of American democracy, nor the cause that the privileged classes in Europe have to fear us, until I saw directly how it works.'

Yet the Confederate partisans did not give up hope. Just one week before the trades union meeting the Confederacy launched its first foreign loan, precursor of a new diplomatic offensive. Bonds to the amount of £3,000,000, redeemable in cotton at a rate of exchange that promised fabulous profits, were issued at 90 and

[1] Navarro y Rodrigo, *O'Donnell y su Tiempo* (1869), p. 195.

promptly rose to 95. Slidell deemed this success 'a financial recognition of our independence'; Mason wrote, 'Cotton is king at last.'

The *Alabama* and *Florida* were active; another English-built commerce-destroyer, the *Alexandria,* was almost ready for sea; and the Lairds were building two armored rams to break the Union blockade. On 4 April Lord Russell ordered the detention of the *Alexandria.* At once King Cotton began to tremble on his new financial throne. The bonds fell to 87, and only by using the subscription money to bull the market were Mason and Slidell able to arrest their decline.

2. *The Vicksburg Campaign*

It is a relief to turn from this diplomatic front to the western theatre of war, to Union armies composed of stout fellows of the Middle West ('reg'lar great big hellsnorters, same breed as ourselves,' said an admiring enemy), officers who for the most part had risen from the ranks by merit, generals who never knew they were beaten and seldom were.

Although both sides of the Mississippi below Memphis were Confederate territory, there was nothing on the river to oppose the passage of a hostile fleet and army until it reached Vicksburg. At that point the line of bluffs that borders the valley touches the river itself, and follows close beside its eastern bank for over a hundred miles to Port Hudson, Louisiana. At both points the Confederates had strongly fortified the bluffs, and between them troops and supplies reached the heart of the Confederacy from Arkansas, Louisiana, and Texas. General Banks, who had learned something of war by this time, had 15,000 troops at New Orleans, mostly nine-months men and negroes, with which to reduce Port Hudson. He and Grant were the first generals to make any considerable use of negro troops, and it was during the Vicksburg Campaign that the famous ballad of the 'contrabands' was heard:

> Say, darkeys, hab you seen de massa,
>   Wid de muffstash on he face,
> Go long de road some time dis mornin',
>   Like he gwine leabe de place?
> He see de smoke way up de ribber
>   Whar de Lincum gunboats lay;
> He took he hat an' leff berry sudden,
>   And I spose he's runned away.

De massa run, ha, ha!
De darkey stay, ho, ho!
It mus' be now de kingdum comin',
An' de yar ob jubilo.

Vicksburg was a difficult nut to crack. Strongly fortified and held by General Pemberton, its front was impregnable to assault from the river, its rear was two hundred miles from Grant's base at Memphis, and its right was protected by the densely wooded and water-logged valley of the Yazoo, intersected with countless backwaters and bayous. After one check, in December 1862, Grant concentrated his army on the west bank of the Mississippi north of the fortress, and spent the cold wet months of the new year in fruitless attempts to outflank Pemberton in the slimy jungle of the lower Yazoo. But he was not discouraged, as McClellan would have been. 'There was nothing left to be done but to go forward to a decisive victory.' In order to advance he must cut loose from his base of supplies, march his army below Vicksburg along the west bank of the Mississippi, cross over to the dry ground, and attack the fortress from the rear.

'I don't know what to make of Grant, he's such a quiet little fellow,' said Lincoln, whose experience had been mainly with generals who let their presence be known to the eye and ear. 'The only way I know he's around is by the way he makes things *git!*' Grant's Army of the Tennessee worked in perfect concert with the freshwater navy. 'Grant and Sherman are on board almost every day. Dine and tea with me often; we agree in everything,' wrote Flag-Officer Porter.

Grant's plan was as audacious as any campaign by Lee; and he had difficulties that Lee never encountered. The Army of the Tennessee marched along the west bank of the Mississippi to a point south of Grand Gulf, where there was an easy crossing. The fleet had to run the gauntlet of Vicksburg on the night of 16–17 April 1863. With lights dowsed and engines stopped, it floated down stream until discovered by a Confederate sentry. Then, what a torrent of shot and shell from the fortress, and what a cracking-on of steam in the fleet, and what a magnificent spectacle, lighted by flashing guns and burning cotton-bales, as the casemated gunboats, turtle-backed rams, and river steamboats with tall flaring funnels, dashed by the batteries! 'Their heavy shot walked right through us,' wrote Porter; but all save one transport got by safely.

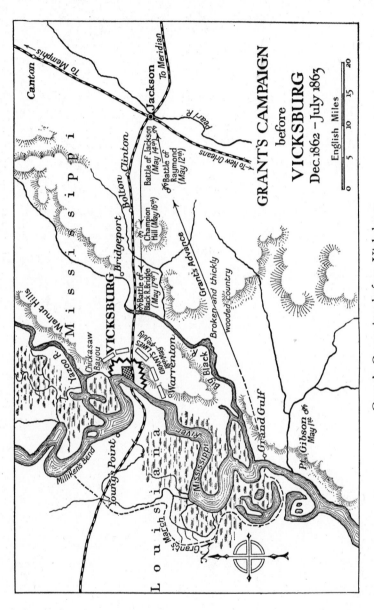

Grant's Campaign before Vicksburg

Prepared by S. E. Morison for The Oxford History of the United States

A part of Grant's army crossed the river south of Grand Gulf unopposed (30 April). Without waiting for Sherman, or for a line of communications to be established, Grant struck out for the rear of Vicksburg with 20,000 men, subsisting on the country. Pemberton came out to meet him; and Joe Johnston was moving south from Chattanooga with another army. By a series of masterly combinations and rapid marches, fighting as he progressed, Grant captured the important railway junction at Jackson, Mississippi, before Johnston could occupy it (14 May), then turned on Pemberton in quick pursuit. 'In eighteen days he marched two hundred miles, won five pitched battles, took eight thousand prisoners and eighty cannon, scattered a hostile army larger than his own fighting on its chosen ground, and had the rebel army penned in Vicksburg.' [2] It was as good as Stonewall Jackson's best; and Stonewall never campaigned in enemy country.

On 22 May, the siege of Vicksburg began. Civilians were living in bomb-proofs and the Confederate defenders were on the point of mutiny when Pemberton, on 3 July, sent out a flag of truce, asking for a parley. The next day he surrendered his army, and the 'Confederate Gibraltar.' Port Hudson surrendered to Banks on the 9th. Within a week a steamboat arrived at New Orleans from St. Louis, having passed the entire course of the Mississippi undisturbed by hostile shot or challenge.

3. Chancellorsville

In the eastern theatre of war 'Fighting Joe' Hooker, brave, vain, and unreliable, replaced Burnside after the Fredericksburg disaster, as head of the Army of the Potomac. He did much to restore their morale, but his first move in the direction of Richmond, on 27 April, brought on Chancellorsville, one of the bloodiest battles of the war. Again, as at the second Manassas, Lee divided his army in the face of superior numbers, and sent Jackson by a wood road through the Wilderness round the Union right, whose commander refused to change front in spite of ample warnings from his picket line (2 May). Earlier in the war, so complete a surprise as Jackson then sprung would have meant disaster. Only individual valor saved it then, for Hooker seemed to forget the very rudiments of generalship, while Lee, with half his man-power, chose time and place of attack, always

[2] L. A. Coolidge, *U. S. Grant*, p. 118.

outnumbering him at the point of contact. Three days of this and Hooker, dazed and bewildered, retired across the Rappahannock (5 May). A well-earned Southern victory was too dearly won by the loss of Stonewall Jackson, mortally wounded by his own men when reconnoitering between the lines.

Lee's army was soon ready for another spring at the enemy's throat, and on enemy soil. Such a victory might knock out Northern morale, already staggering from Chancellorsville, and trembling in prospect of the first draft; French and perhaps British recognition would follow. It was a bold game for the highest stake, but President Davis was not a bold player. He could not make up his mind to weaken the other Confederate forces to push this invasion home. So Lee moved northward (3 June 1863) into Pennsylvania with only 73,000 men, while 190,000 Confederate field troops were scattered between the Mississippi and the Rappahannock.

Keeping time with Lee's marching men, the Confederacy launched a diplomatic drive. Confederate bonds rose from 87 to 91 upon news of Chancellorsville, but something more than financial recognition was wanted. Accordingly, Mason and Slidell planned with J. A. Roebuck and Lindsay, the two principal pro-Southern members of Parliament, to place the ministry in a dilemma between recognition and resignation. Their plans went astray. Debate on Roebuck's motion to recognize the Confederacy was adjourned from day to day by pro-Southern members in the hope that the next mail would bring news of a crushing victory by Lee on Northern soil. The news they finally received was of Gettysburg and Vicksburg.

4. The Gettysburg Campaign

General Lee, on 3 June, began to move his left towards the Shenandoah valley, having selected that well-screened highway to Pennsylvania. Ewell cleared the way for him by smashing the Union garrison at Winchester. One corps only, A. P. Hill's, remained on the Rappahannock to watch the Army of the Potomac. Hooker was eager to make a counter-stroke at the Confederate capital, but Lincoln advised him, 'Lee's army, and not Richmond, is your true objective point. If he comes toward the upper Potomac, follow on his flank and on his inside track, shortening your lines while he lengthens his.' Hooker took this excellent bit of advice. On 17 June a part of Ewell's corps was across the Potomac; on the 23rd it was near Chambersburg in the Cumberland valley of Pennsylvania. The same day Lee sent J. E. B. Stuart on a cavalry raid, with orders not sufficiently precise to restrain that gallant horseman. ' Jeb ' and his men enjoyed themselves as usual, and cut out a wagon train within four miles of Washington; but Hooker, by crossing the Potomac on the 25th, separated them from Lee, and deprived the Confederate army of its 'eyes' during the most critical days of the campaign.

On 27 June Lee's entire army was in Pennsylvania; his headquarters at Chambersburg. Ewell had reached Carlisle, within twenty miles of the state capital at Harrisburg, and the next day Jubal A. Early's division laid York under contribution of dollars and shoes. Hooker, on the 28th, having concentrated the Army of the Potomac about Frederick Town, resigned the command on a squabble with Halleck. Lincoln turned it over to one of his corps commanders, General George Gordon Meade. For once, swapping horses in the middle of the stream was justified. There was no counting on ' Fighting Joe,' but Meade was safe and sane, certain to do nothing foolish if unlikely to perform any brilliant feat of arms.

Lee hoped that the mere presence of his army in Pennsylvania would strengthen the copperheads, and would force Lincoln to receive Vice-President Stephens, then proceeding towards Washington under flag of truce to open peace negotiations on the basis of independence. Yet the North showed no sign of flinching. Democratic governors were not behind their Republican colleagues in offering volunteers. Militia and civilians turned out in large numbers to protect the Pennsylvania cities. Grave anxiety was felt, but no panic; and Lincoln did not recall a single unit from the West.

On 29 June, when Ewell's cavalry had reached the Confederacy's farthest north — a point within ten miles of Harrisburg — Lee ordered his entire army to concentrate along the eastern slope of South Mountain, near Cashtown. There, in a strong defensive position, he proposed to await attack. Meade intended to take position behind Pipe Creek, and let Lee attack him. But chance placed the great battle where neither Lee nor Meade wanted it; because neither knew exactly where the other was. On 30 June a part of A. P. Hill's corps, which was covering Lee's concentration, strayed into Gettysburg in search of new boots. Boots and saddles were there — on Buford's cavalry division, masking the Army of the Potomac. Gettysburg commanded some important roads; and each army was so eager for action that this chance contact drew both into the quiet little market town, as to a magnet. There, on 1 July, the great three-day battle began, each unit joining in the fray as it arrived. Hill's zeal for footwear changed the battle from a defensive one near Cashtown to an offensive one at Gettysburg.

The first day (1 July) went ill for the Union. Hill and Ewell drove the First Corps through the town. In the nick of time, Winfield Scott Hancock, the greatest fighting general in the Army of the Potomac, rallied the fugitives on Cemetery Ridge. The position so fortunately chosen proved to be admirable for defense: a limestone outcrop shaped like a fish-hook, with the convex side turned west and north, towards the Confederates. Along it the Union army was placed as rapidly as it arrived from the south and east, while the Confederates took up an encircling position, their right on the partially wooded Seminary Ridge, parallel to Cemetery Ridge. Lee decided to attack the following day. Ignorant of the whereabouts of the rest of Meade's army, he dared not retreat to the Cumberland valley, or attempt the flanking movement that Longstreet advocated.

Lee's great opportunity came on the evening of 2 July when Early broke the Union defenses on Cemetery Ridge and Ewell stormed up the slope of Culp's Hill on the Union right — the barb of the hook. But reinforcements failed to appear. Early was hurled back within an hour, and the next morning a withering fire drove back Ewell's veterans. Meantime Longstreet had driven in Sickles's corps which had occupied the peach orchard in advance of Cemetery Ridge, but failed to take Little Round Top — the eye of the hook — which would have enabled his artillery to enfilade the entire Union position. Meade's army lost heavily, but he determined to fight it out.

The third day of the battle and of July opened with a desperate struggle for Culp's Hill, from which Ewell's corps was finally dislodged. Silence fell on the field at noon. Meade guessed what was coming, and reinforced his center. At one o'clock there came a deafening artillery fire from the Confederate lines. Deep silence again. Lee, against Longstreet's protest, had ordered a direct attack on the strongest part of the Union center with Pickett's, Pettigrew's, and Trimble's divisions, 15,000 strong. The time had come. Pickett rode up to Longstreet and asked, 'General, shall I advance?' Longstreet, unwilling to give the word, bowed his head. 'Sir, I shall lead my division forward," said Pickett.

From Cemetery Ridge, the Union troops saw three gray lines of battle issue from the wooded ridge three-quarters of a mile away,

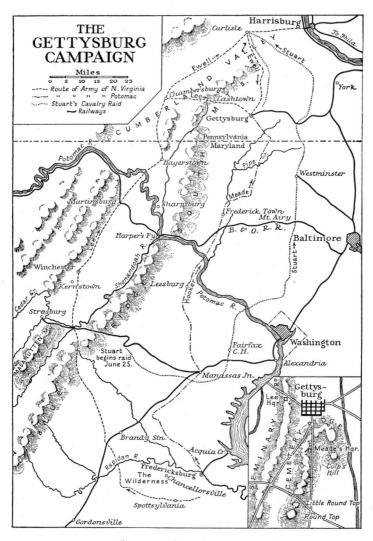

The Gettysburg Campaign

Prepared by S. E. Morison for The Oxford History of the United States

and march with colors flying and bayonets glittering into the valley before them. Less than half-way across, the Union artillery opened fire upon them; a little nearer they came under a raking fire from the batteries on Round Top. The flank divisions melted away; but the Northern troops, peering through the smoke, could see Pickett's division still coming on, merged in one crowding, rushing line. Lost for a moment in a swale, they emerged so near that the expression on their faces could be seen. Then the boys in blue let them have it. Two of Pickett's brigadiers were killed. Fifteen of his regimental commanders were killed, and the other five wounded. General Armistead, with cap raised on point of sword, leaped the stone wall into the Union lines, a hundred men followed him, and for a brief moment the battle cross of the Confederacy floated on the crest of Cemetery Ridge. The Union lines closed in relentlessly, and Armistead's men were shot down or captured.

All the next day — 4 July — Lee remained defiantly in position. That evening his army, with baggage and prisoners, retired to a position west of Sharpsburg. There the flooded Potomac stopped his retreat, and gave Meade an opportunity that Lincoln begged him to seize. 'Act upon your own judgment and make your generals execute your orders,' telegraphed Halleck. 'Call no council of war. . . . Do not let the enemy escape.' Meade called a council of war, the Potomac fell, and the enemy escaped.

Lee was too candid to congratulate himself for having escaped. He had seen the flower of his army wither under the Union fire. He knew that all hope for peace that summer was gone, and he must have felt that slight hope for Southern independence remained. Yet after the battle, as before, his soldiers gathered only confidence and resolution from the placid countenance of their beloved 'Marse Robert.' With justice Lee might have blamed Longstreet, where failure to obey orders probably led to the disaster, but no word of censure escaped him. To President Davis he wrote, 'No blame can be attached to the army for its failure to accomplish what was projected by me, nor should it be censured for the unreasonable expectations of the public. I am alone to blame.'

Lincoln was deeply mortified by the escape of Lee's army. 'Our army held the war in the hollow of their hand, and they would not close it,' he said. 'Still, I am very grateful to Meade for the great service he did at Gettysburg.' 'General Meade has my confidence, as a brave and skilful officer and a true man.' Unpopular with his men, placed in command of an army thrice whipped within a twelve-month, on the eve of battle with an enemy hitherto invincible, he fairly won the greatest battle of the war. And from the Wilderness to Appomattox he was the right arm of Grant.

Four months later, when a national cemetery was dedicated on the battle-field of Gettysburg, Lincoln delivered his immortal address:

Fourscore and seven years ago our fathers brought forth on this con-tinent a new nation, conceived in liberty, and dedicated to the proposition that all men are created equal.

Now we are engaged in a great civil war, testing whether that nation, or any nation so conceived and so dedicated, can long endure. We are met on a great battle-field of that war. We have come to dedicate a portion of that field as a final resting-place for those who here gave their lives that the nation might live. It is altogether fitting and proper that we should do this.

But, in a larger sense, we cannot dedicate — we cannot consecrate — we cannot hallow — this ground. The brave men, living and dead, who struggled here, have consecrated it far above our poor power to add or detract. The world will little note nor long remember what we say here, but it can never forget what they did here. It is for us, the living, rather, to be dedicated here to the unfinished work which they who fought here have thus far so nobly advanced. It is rather for us to be here dedicated to the great task remaining before us — that from these honored dead we take increased devotion to that cause for which they gave the last full measure of devotion; that we here highly resolve that these dead shall not have died in vain; that this nation, under God, shall have a new birth of freedom; and that government of the people, by the people, for the people, shall not perish from the earth.

*   *   *   *

After Gettysburg, nothing of consequence occurred in the eastern theatre of war until the spring of 1864; and after Vicksburg, Grant's Army of the Tennessee was dispersed from Memphis to Matamoras, by orders from Washington.

On the diplomatic front Gettysburg and Vicksburg bore fruit. Roebuck's motion to recognize the Confederacy was already with-drawn, but the Laird armored rams, from which the Confederacy hoped much, were being rushed to completion. Lord John Russell was most anxious to prevent another *Alabama* from swelling the tide of American resentment; but the destination of the vessels was so cleverly covered by a fictitious sale that he could find no evidence to warrant detention. Fortunately he decided to stretch a point, and keep the peace. On 3 September he gave orders to prevent the departure of the rams, and a month later both were seized.[3]

John Bigelow, the American consul-general at Paris, obtained evidence in the same month that four steam corvettes and two armored rams were being constructed for the Confederacy at Nantes and Bordeaux. Napoleon III had practically invited Slidell to place the contracts, although he was careful to insist that their destination should be concealed. Now that the secret was out, he ordered the vessels to be sold to foreign governments; but only the utmost vigilance by the American authorities prevented their falling into Confederate hands. The ram *Stonewall* eventually did, but too late to help the Southern cause.

5. *From Chickamauga to Atlanta and the Sea*

The advance of the Army of the Cumberland under Rosecrans from Murfreesborough to the neighborhood of Chattanooga, in July 1863, began a campaign that ended only with Sherman's march to the sea, and a subdivision of the Confederacy. Chattanooga, after Richmond and Vicksburg, was the most vital point in the Confederacy: a junction on the important Richmond-Knoxville-Memphis railway for lines running southwest and southeast. The Tennessee river, after flowing southward through the continuation of the Shenandoah valley, there breaks through the parallel ridges of the southern Appalachians. So long as the Confederates held Chattanooga, they could make counter-stroke towards the Ohio, and the Union armies could not hope to penetrate far into the lower South, however firmly they might press its periphery. Once in possession of Chattanooga, the Union armies might swing round the Great Smoky mountains and attack Savannah, Charleston, or even Richmond, from the rear. Rosecrans outmanœuvred the Confederates, and, without fighting a battle, marched into Chattanooga on 9 September 1863.

At first the Chattanooga campaign was conducted by third-rate generals: our old friend Burnside; General Rosecrans, who had most of McClellan's faults without his ability; and President Davis's favorite, Braxton Bragg, a dyspeptic martinet. From the first battle

---

[3] Charles Francis Adams's famous note to Russell on the rams, 'It would be superfluous in me to point out to your lordship that this is war,' was written two days after Russell had decided to detain them.

of the campaign, at Chickamauga (19 September), there emerged a great commander, the loyal Virginian George H. Thomas. After Bragg had swept the Union right and center into Chattanooga, George H. Thomas, for six hours that afternoon, held the left against repeated assaults by the whole Confederate army; and, when night-fall found him stripped of ammunition, retired unmolested to a safe position. 'The *élan* of the Southern soldier was never seen after Chickamauga,' wrote D. H. Hill. 'That brilliant dash which had distinguished him was gone forever.' It broke against the lines of Thomas, 'the rock of Chickamauga.' Owing to the fact that no congressmen were pushing him, Thomas never had a command equal to his ability; but no military critic today would deny him a place among the immortals; and there are many who believe that, if given the opportunity, he could have proved himself peer to Lee or Jackson.

Next, Rosecrans allowed his army to be penned up and besieged in Chattanooga. He was approaching a state of imbecility when Lincoln sent Grant to the rescue, as supreme commander in the West. Grant placed Thomas in command of the Army of the Cumberland, and ordered him to hold Chattanooga at all hazards. 'I will hold the town till we starve,' was Thomas's reply.

Grant's manner of rescuing the Army of the Cumberland from its embarrassing situation was to resume the offensive. On 24 November he began the great Battle of Chattanooga. Simultaneous attacks de-livered by Hooker, Sherman, and Thomas drove the enemy from the steep wooded ridges across the river. The capture of Missionary Ridge was perhaps the most gallant action of the war. Thomas's men, after driving the Confederates from the rifle-pits at the foot, were ordered to halt. Refusing to obey, they kept straight on up the steep rocky slope, overrunning a second and a third line of defense, rushed the Confederate guns from the crest, and turned them on the enemy; then, with Phil Sheridan leading, pursued the fleeing gray-coats down the eastern slope.

This Battle of Chattanooga placed the combined armies of the Tennessee and the Cumberland (Sherman and Thomas) in a posi-tion to advance into Georgia in the early spring. The West had proved her valor in two brilliant campaigns. One portion of the Confederacy had been severed along the Mississippi, and a deep salient, resting upon the Appalachians and the great river, had been thrust into the rest. It remained to prolong that salient to the sea, somewhere between Charleston and Savannah; and to deal with Lee and the Army of Northern Virginia.

When Grant became General-in-Chief, Sherman was left in command of 100,000 men in Chattanooga to continue that campaign. Sherman's objective was Joe Johnston's (late Bragg's) army, 65,000 strong, which lay between him and Atlanta, Georgia. In early May, 1864, he began the campaign, with an army stripped to the barest essentials in baggage and equipment. Johnston divined the needs of the situation when he adopted Fabian strategy. The only hope for the Confederacy lay in fretting, fighting only at a decided advantage, and wearying the Northern people of the war. Sherman restrained his natural eagerness and aggressiveness, to beat Johnston 'at his own game of patience.' His advance and Johnston's retreat to Atlanta was a pretty game of thrust and parry, with a constant development in the arts of field entrenchment, bridge-building, and railway reconstruction. On 17 July Sherman moved across the Chattahoochee river, eight miles from Atlanta, and began to besiege the capital of Georgia. With a line of communications 140 miles longer than at Chattanooga, his situation was perilous; and the appointment of J. B. Hood in Johnston's place meant that the Confederates would speedily take the offensive.

Hood, however, merely wasted lives by gallant thrusts at Sherman, whose troops had acquired the instinct of victory. On 2 September Hood evacuated Atlanta, and Sherman occupied the capital of Georgia.

President Davis assured the people of Georgia that Sherman must sooner or later retreat from Atlanta. 'And when that day comes the fate that befell the army of the French Empire in its retreat from Moscow will be re-acted.' Hood proposed to do this by striking high into Tennessee at the long, thin line of Union communications. The imperturbable Sherman sent Thomas back to Nashville to cope with him, and cut loose from Atlanta in the opposite direction, toward the sea (17 October 1864), marching 62,000 men without supplies into the 'garden spot of the Confederacy.'

The march to the sea, like Sheridan's campaign in the Valley, was one of deliberate and disciplined destruction. Sherman's army cut a swath sixty miles wide through central Georgia, destroying stores of provisions, standing crops and cattle, cotton-gins and mills, railways beyond all possibility of repair, in fact everything that could be useful to the Confederacy and much that was not. The looting of houses, although forbidden by orders, could not altogether be prevented, and many a Georgia family was stripped of its possessions; but outrages on persons were surprisingly few; on white women, none. ' No army ever enjoyed such freedom and kept within such bounds.' It was the sort of campaign that soldiers really love — maximum of looting and destruction, minimum of discipline and fighting: splendid weather, few impedimenta: broiled turkey for breakfast, roast lamb for dinner, and fried chicken for supper.

> How the darkeys shouted when they heard the joyful sound,
> How the turkeys gobbled which our commissary found,
> How the sweet potatoes even started from the ground,
>   While we were marching through Georgia.

>> Hurrah! Hurrah! we bring the jubilee!
>> Hurrah! Hurrah! the flag that makes you free!
>> So we sang the chorus from Atlanta to the sea,
>>   While we were marching through Georgia.

For a month the North completely lost sight of Sherman. He emerged at Savannah on 10 December 1864, and was able to offer Lincoln the city as a Christmas present.

The North had a bad turn in December when Schofield's corps, overwhelmed by Hood at Franklin (Tennessee) on 30 November, fell back on Nashville. It looked like another Confederate breakthrough to the Ohio. But the Rock of Chickamauga was in command at Nashville. Despite frantic telegrams from Stanton and Grant to attack at once, he bided his time. Finally on 27 December, when the order for his supersession had already been given, Thomas inflicted on Hood at Nashville the most smashing defeat of the war. Grant made prompt amends to Thomas for his impatience; but this great Virginian, who had forsaken home and kindred for loyalty to the Union, was neglected in the distribution of post-war honors.

6. The Wilderness

While Sherman and Thomas were carrying on this brilliant and uniformly successful scission of the Confederacy, General Grant was having a rather unhappy time of it with Lee, whose prowess very nearly conquered the Northern will to victory in the summer of 1864.

On 9 March 1864 Grant was appointed Lieutenant-General and

General-in-Chief of the armies of the United States. Summoned to Washington, where he had never been, to confer with Lincoln, whom he had never seen, this slightly seedy and very ordinary looking individual, perpetually smoking or chewing a cigar, caused some misgivings among those who were used to the glittering generals of the Army of the Potomac. For perhaps the only occasion in history, an American hotel clerk lost countenance, when the inconspicuous officer and boy to whom he assigned a top-floor room registered ' U. S. Grant and son, Galena, Ill.' Keener observers were impressed with Grant's rough dignity, simplicity, and calm confidence. He was the first of all the commanders in the East who never doubted the greatness of his President; and Lincoln knew that he had a general at last ' who would take the responsibility and act.'

Grant assumed personal direction of the Virginia campaign against Lee. It appeared to be as inexorable as a nutcracker. Grant himself, leading the Army of the Potomac under Meade and an unattached corps under Burnside, was to move by the left flank towards Richmond, forcing the Confederate leader to give battle or abandon· his capital. Sigel was to rush up the Shenandoah valley, with Lynchburg as his destination. B. F. Butler, worst of the political generals, was given command of the Army of the James, apparently in order to keep him out of politics. His task was to march up the south bank of the James and cut Lee's communications with the lower South. Both these movements miscarried. Sigel, checked half-way up the Valley, was superseded by Hunter; and Lee, after Cold Harbor, detached Early's corps which drove Hunter across the Appalachians. Butler was ' bottled up in Bermuda Hundred ' at a loop of the James, by Beauregard. Upon Grant fell the entire burden of the offensive. ' He habitually wears an expression as if he had determined to drive his head through a brick wall, and was about to do it,' wrote one of his officers. ' I determined,' wrote Grant himself, ' to hammer continuously against the armed force of the enemy and his resources, until by mere attrition, if in no other way, there should be nothing left to him but an equal submission with the loyal section of our common country to the constitution and laws of the land.'

On 4 May 1864 Grant crossed the Rapidan without opposition, and began to march his army of 102,000 men through the same tangled Wilderness from which Jackson had fallen upon Hooker at Chancellorsville. When half-way through, Lee repeated Jackson's manœuvre. Grant accepted battle and changed his front, but his enormous army corps manœuvred with great difficulty in that dense under-growth, and in two days' fierce fighting he lost 17,700 men. This Battle of the Wilderness (5–7 May) was a draw. Grant now knew that he had to deal with a general of different metal from Johnston or Bragg; and Lee learned that the Army of the Potomac had ob-tained a leader worthy of it.

Grant then tried to outflank the enemy; but clouds of dust from his marching columns warned Lee of his intention, and by the time his van had reached the cross-roads at Spottsylvania Court House, Lee was there to check him. Both armies threw up field entrench-ments, and the five-day battle that followed (Spottsylvania, 8–12 May) was the first of modern trench warfare.

Again and again we read in the story of these assaults that the attack-ing troops were thrown by their very success into confusion, and so fell easy victims to reserves who had escaped the rough and tumble of captur-ing trenches; again and again we read that the turmoil of the battle-field prevented the arrival of supports in time to enable the assaulting troops to make good their success, or, as the jargon of the Great War had it, ' to consolidate their position.' [4]

Having lost 31,000 more men, Grant declared, ' I . . . propose to fight it out on this line if it takes all summer.' Again he moved by his left in the hope of outflanking Lee's right. Again the Army of Northern Virginia was there to welcome him, and in a position so well chosen and entrenched that Grant needed all his adroitness to withdraw in safety, and continue his flanking march (26 May). Lee swung with him to McClellan's old battlefield of Gaines's Mill. Both armies entrenched. The lines were six or eight miles long. On 1–3 June came the Battle of Cold Harbor, costliest and most futile in the entire war — an assault upon the entire line of Lee's trenches with no adeqate preparations to improve any success. Before going over the top, the Union soldiers pinned papers on their backs, giving their names and addresses to identify their corpses. Eight or nine thousand men fell in two or three hours, but hardly a dent was made on the Confederate lines.

During ten more days the armies faced one another. War had now acquired most of its modern horrors. The wounded, unat-tended between the lines, died of thirst, starvation, and loss of blood.

---

[4] Maurice, *Lee, the Soldier*, p. 233. There are excellent descriptions of the methods of entrenching in *Cycle of Adams Letters*, ii. 138, and *Meade's Headquarters*.

Corpses rotted on the ground. Sharpshooters kept up their deadly work. Officers and men fought mechanically without hope. The war had begun so long ago that one could hardly remember anything else. It would continue until everyone on both sides was killed.

In one month Grant had advanced from the Rapidan to the Chickahominy, the exact spot where McClellan had stood two years before; and he had lost about 55,000 men to Lee's 30,000 — less in proportion, to be sure. On 12 June Grant followed McClellan's exact plan — a change of base to the James, and an attempt to cut the communications of Richmond at Petersburg. The manœuvre was skillfully executed, and, unlike that of 1862, was unmolested by Lee. But an opportunity to push into undefended Petersburg was lost. Lee slipped in by the interior lines, entrenched in time, and three general assaults cost the Union 8,000 more men (15–18 June). Grant's army sat down to besiege Petersburg, and remained there for nine months. A war of position had arrived.

Grant never had enough men or artillery to carry the Petersburg lines by assault, as the fiasco of the ' crater ' affair (27 July 1864) proved. He was right in holding Lee in position while Sherman reduced the effective area of the Confederacy, for Lee, unable to manœuvre, was not dangerous.

Such, in brief, was the most desperately fought campaign of the war. Lee, with an army that despised digging as ' nigger's work,' and hated fighting from entrenchments, had developed the technique of trench warfare to a point that Europe only reached in 1916. He had saved his army, and saved Richmond. Grant, after making mistakes and suffering losses that would have broken any of his predecessors, was still indomitable. But how long would the country suffer such stupendous losses, with no apparent result? The country could not then appreciate what we now know, that the end was near, and that Grant's efforts, however costly in men, were justified because they forced the Confederate government to concentrate its best efforts on supporting Lee, and prevented Joseph Johnston from receiving the necessary reinforcements to stop Sherman's march to the sea.[5]

Jubal A. Early, having qualified for the rôle of Stonewall Jackson's successor by driving the Union forces from the Shenandoah valley,

---

[5] J. I. C. Fuller, *Grant and Lee*, p. 272. See the figures on pp. 273–74, which disprove the myth that Grant's losses were abnormally high. Lee's losses at Gettysburg were proportionally greater than Grant's in the Wilderness, his most costly battle.

now had an opportunity to repeat the drama of 1862. On 2 July 1864 his 15,000 veterans were at Winchester, marching north by the classic route. A few days later he was laying Hagerstown and Frederick under contribution, and at noon on 11 July he was at Fort Stevens in the District of Columbia, only five miles from the capital. Almost at the same moment two Union divisions, which Grant had hurriedly detached from the Army of the Potomac, disembarked at Washington. The General rode out to Fort Stevens, whose commander pointed out the enemy's pickets only a few yards away, and remarked by way of greeting, 'Well, Wright, there they are; I've nothing here but quartermaster's men and hospital bummers, the enemy can walk right in if he only tries. Let's go below and get some lager beer.' What a contrast with 1862! But Early had lost his chance. Wright's men marched forth from Fort Stevens, President Lincoln watching the engagement, as the bullets whistled past his high hat. Early was driven back a mile, and on 13 July made good his escape to the valley, with loot and provisions. Three days later, Lincoln made one of his greatest speeches:

We accepted this war for an object, a worthy object, and the war will end when that object is attained. Under God, I hope it never will end until that time. Speaking of the present campaign, General Grant is reported to have said, 'I am going through on this line if it takes all summer.' This war has taken three years; it was begun or accepted upon the line of restoring the national authority over the whole national domain, and for the American people, as far as my knowledge enables me to speak, I say we are going through on this line if it takes three years more.

On 18 July the President called for half a million more volunteers, any deficiency to be filled by draft on 6 September.

As usual, the country was not up to Lincoln's stature. The appalling toll of casualties seemed to have brought the war no nearer conclusion. It looked as if Grant could never beat Lee, or Sherman take Atlanta. Paper dollars fell to their lowest point, 33 cents in gold, on the day that Early appeared before Washington. And the cost of living had soared far beyond the rise of wages or salaries. Unable to look beyond their own troubles to the far greater ills of their enemy, the Northern people began to ask whether a further prosecution of the war would profit anyone but the profiteers. This undercurrent of doubt and despair induced some strange developments in the presidential campaign that was already under way.

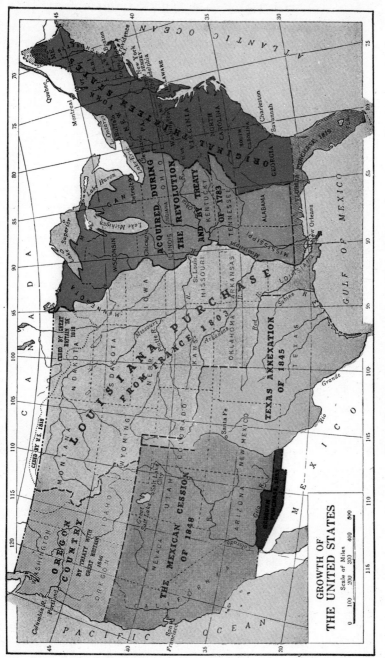

The Territorial Growth of the United States

7. *The Presidential Election*

Alone of modern governments since manhood suffrage was adopted, the United States faced a general election in war time. For, as Lincoln said, ' We cannot have free government without elections; and if the rebellion could force us to forego or postpone a national election, it might fairly claim to have already conquered and ruined us.' Lincoln was renominated for the Presidency by acclamation on 7 June in the National Union convention, representing both Republicans and War Democrats; but in early August, before the Democrats had held their convention, there developed an amazing movement against Lincoln within his own party.

Horace Greeley of the New York *Tribune* was seized in early July by another delusion: a belief that the Union could be restored through negotiation. In answer to his passionate appeal to take notice of an alleged Confederate peace mission in Canada, Lincoln ordered Greeley to go and investigate, with these credentials: ' If you can find any person, anywhere, professing to have any proposition of Jefferson Davis, in writing, for peace, embracing the restoration of the Union and abandonment of slavery, whatever else it embraces, say to him he may come to me with you.' Greeley went to Niagara Falls, and ascertained that the Southern emissaries had no authority and nothing to offer. Instead of acknowledging his error, he lent the columns of the *Tribune* to accusations that Lincoln for his own reasons wished unnecessarily to prolong the war. One can easily imagine the effect of such hints upon public opinion, at that juncture.

Greeley now thrust himself into a new breach that had developed between the President and the radicals over the manner and method of reconstructing the Union after the war. When Lincoln, on 4 July 1864, pocket-vetoed a bill embodying the radical views, Senators Wade and Henry Winter Davis issued a public manifesto accusing the President of perpetrating a ' studied outrage on the legislative authority of the people' from the basest motives of personal ambition. Greeley published this Wade-Davis manifesto in the *Tribune* on 5 August; and on the 18th he and the radicals began to circulate among the politicians a call for a new Republican convention, to reconsider the candidature of Lincoln. The pacifist had slipped into bed with the hundred-percenters.

It was an alarming situation. Lincoln received letters from some of his staunchest supporters, declaring the election already lost. The executive committee of the Republican party implored him to make a peace move. Lincoln sent them away satisfied that he cared nothing for himself, but that so palpable a confession of weakness as an overture to Jefferson Davis, at that juncture, would be equivalent to surrender. What Lincoln really thought of the situation is clear from the paper he wrote and sealed on 23 August.

It seems exceedingly probable that this administration will not be re-elected. Then it will be my duty to so co-operate with the President-elect as to save the Union between the election and the inauguration, as he will have secured his election on such ground that he cannot possibly save it afterward.

If Jefferson Davis had been adroit or dishonest he could have completed the distraction of Union councils by proposing an armistice or a peace conference on any terms; for once the fighting had stopped, it would have been impossible to get it started again. Had he been a supremely wise man he would have accepted the President's condition of peace: restoration of the Union without slavery. But President Davis still believed his cause invincible. Another and more adroit amateur diplomatist than Greeley published on 29 August the result of an interview with Davis himself. ' Say to Mr. Lincoln from me, that I shall at any time be pleased to receive proposals for peace on the basis of our Independence. It will be useless to approach me with any other.'

In the face of this plain and honest statement from the Confederate President, the Democratic national convention on 29 August adopted a resolution drafted by Vallandigham:

After four years of failure to restore the Union by the experiment of war . . . justice, humanity, liberty, and the public welfare demand that immediate efforts be made for a cessation of hostilities . . . to the end that at the earliest practicable moment, peace may be restored on the basis of the Federal Union of the States.

General McClellan received and accepted the Democratic nomination for President. He repudiated the peace plank in the platform, but was willing to ride into the White House on a wave of defeatism.

Jefferson Davis by his frankness, the Democrats by their shameless defeatism, and Sherman by capturing Atlanta on 1 September, knocked the bottom out of the Wade-Davis-Greeley conspiracy.

Nothing more was heard of the call for a new nominating convention. On 6 September the new draft went quietly into effect, the New England radicals held a ringing Lincoln rally in Faneuil Hall, and, marvellous to relate, Ben Wade announced he would take the stump for the President! Lincoln's election, so doubtful in August, was conceded on every side in October. After Sheridan had beaten Early at Cedar Creek (19 October), and devastated the Shenandoah valley so completely 'that a crow flying over it would have to carry his own rations,' the Northern people, on 8 November, chose 212 Lincoln electors, and only 21 for McClellan.

'The election,' said Lincoln two days later, 'has demonstrated that a people's government can sustain a national election in the midst of a great civil war.'

8. *The Collapse of the Confederacy*

Sherman had now planted another army in the heart of the Confederacy; and with the capture of Wilmington in January 1865 the Union blockade became very nearly absolute. Yet, in a military sense, the Confederacy was by no means doomed to defeat. On paper there was no reason why the fight should not be kept up almost indefinitely. Communication of a sort could be maintained between the Atlantic and the Gulf states, across Sherman's swath of destruction. There were some 35,000 men under arms in the Carolinas to oppose his march northward; and Lee, emulating Napoleon's strategy of 1814, might break loose from Grant and unite with them. There were enough white men of fighting age in the Confederacy to provide its armies with half a million men, (174,223 surrendered in April and May), and enrollment of the blacks might have provided two hundred thousand more. The Confederate munitions service was independent of outside supplies, and the great munition-producing center at Selma, Alabama, was not captured until 2 April 1865. There was plenty of corn and cattle in the country south of Virginia. The starving condition of Lee's troops at Appomattox was not symptomatic, but caused by failure of the government to send ahead supplies. Every material factor justified a protracted resistance; only morale was wanting. The re-election of Lincoln, the failure to obtain foreign recognition, Sherman's march to the sea, and the increasing pinch of the blockade, took the heart out of the South. 'Two-thirds of our men are absent . . . most of them absent without leave,' admitted President Davis in September 1864. Senator Hill of Georgia, who wrote the President on 25 March 1865, 'We shall conquer all enemies yet,' admitted, nine years later, 'All physical advantages are insufficient to account for our failure. The truth is, we failed because too many of our people were not determined to win.'

Davis could see only the outer reality — so many men and rifles and cannon, so much food and gunpowder. To the deeper reality in the hearts of his people he was insensible as any old-world autocrat. His last political manœuvre was to obtain from Lincoln a clear statement of Union peace terms, in the hope of 'firing the Southern heart.' On 3 February 1865 came this strange conference on a steamer in Hampton Roads, between the President of the United States and the Vice-President of the Confederacy, who had been his friend and mentor in Congress sixteen years before. Stephens had credentials to negotiate peace as the envoy of an independent republic. Lincoln patiently repeated his refusal to negotiate on that basis. Senator Hunter, who accompanied Stephens, alleged as precedent the negotiations during the English Civil War. Lincoln replied, 'I do not profess to be posted in history. On all such matters I will turn you over to Seward. All I distinctly recollect about the case of Charles I is that he lost his head.' But 'the war will cease on the part of the Government, whenever it shall have ceased on the part of those who began it.' Offered a lifeboat, Stephens clutched at a straw, the very straw that Seward set afloat on April Fool Day 1861 — Union and Confederacy might ally to expel Maximilian from Mexico.

It was as Lincoln had predicted — 'Davis cannot voluntarily re-accept the Union; we cannot voluntarily yield it.' Lee might with honor surrender his army to irresistible force; Davis could not with honor surrender his nation. The inherent dignity of his refusal was marred by his frantic boast at a public meeting in Richmond that he would compel the Yankees in less than twelve months to petition him for peace on his own terms.

*   *   *   *

It was now February 1865. The Confederacy was sinking fast. Even slavery was jettisoned — in principle. President Davis sent an envoy to Europe, in January, to offer abolition in exchange for recognition, and on 25 March the Richmond Congress authorized arming the slaves. Sherman, as he marched northward, was proving his sulphurous synonym for war. 'Columbia! — pretty much all burned; and burned *good.*' Yet the doughty Sherman passed some anxious hours, when he learned that Lee and his grim veterans were on the loose again.

For nine months the armies of Grant and Lee had faced one another across long lines of entrenchment running through the suburbs of Petersburg. At the beginning of the siege their forces were not disparate; but by the middle of March 1865 Grant had 115,000 effectives to Lee's 54,000. If Lee did not move out of his trenches Grant would soon envelop him; but if Petersburg were abandoned, Richmond must fall. Lee first tried an assault on the Union left — a costly failure. Sheridan, having marched across Virginia from the Valley, thrust back Lee's right at the Battle of Five Forks (1 April); and on the next day Grant penetrated the center of the Confederate defenses. Lee's only hope was to retreat by the line of the Danville railway, and unite with Johnston, who now commanded the remnants of his former army in North Carolina.

On the night of 2–3 April Lee's army slipped out of the Petersburg lines; and the next evening the Union forces entered Richmond. Without pause Grant pursued. Sheridan entered the important railway junction of Burkesville before the Confederates, preventing their escape southward. Rations failed Lee through some mistake at Richmond; his thirty thousand men had to live on a thinly populated country in springtime. On 9 April Sheridan closed the only avenue of escape westward. Whether Lee could have cut his way through to the mountains and continued guerrilla warfare indefinitely may well be doubted; but it is certain that, as he wrote himself, he had only to ride along the lines and all would be over. 'But it is our duty to live, for what will become of the women and children of the South, if we are not here to support and protect them?'

Lee ordered a white flag to be displayed, and requested an interview with his opponent. The scene that followed, in a house of the little village of Appomattox Court House, has become a part of American folk-lore. Lee, in the new full-dress uniform with jewel-studded sword that he had saved in the flight, Grant in his favorite private's blouse, unbuttoned, and without a sword, 'his feelings sad and depressed at the downfall of a foe who had fought so long and valiantly.'

Formal greetings. Small talk of other days, in the old army . . .

Grant writes the terms of surrender in his own hand. . . . Officers and men paroled . . . arms and *matériel* surrendered . . . not to include the officers' side-arms, and —

'Let all the men who claim to own a horse or mule take the animals home with them to work their little farms.'

'This will do much toward conciliating our people.'

The conference is over. Lee pauses a moment in the doorway, looking out over a field blossoming with the stars and stripes. Thrice, and slowly, he strikes a fist into the palm of his gauntleted hand. He mounts his horse Traveller and is gone.

A sound of cheering spreads along the Union lines.

Grant orders it to cease:

'The war is over; the rebels are our countrymen again.'

> Bury the bygone South.
> Bury the minstrel with the honey-mouth,
> Bury the broadsword virtues of the clan,
> Bury the unmachined, the planters' pride,
> The courtesy and the bitter arrogance,
> The pistol-hearted horsemen who could ride
> Like jolly centaurs under the hot stars.
> Bury the whip, bury the branding-bars,
> Bury the unjust thing
> That some tamed into mercy, being wise,
> But could not starve the tiger from its eyes
> Or make it feed where beasts of mercy feed.
> Bury the fiddle-music and the dance,
> The sick magnolias of the false romance
> And all the chivalry that went to seed
> Before its ripening.
>
> And with these things, bury the purple dream
> Of the America we have not been,
> The tropic empire, seeking the warm sea,
> The last foray of aristocracy
> Based not on dollars or initiative
> Or any blood for what blood was worth
> But on a certain code, a manner of birth,
> A certain manner of knowing how to live,
> The pastoral rebellion of the earth
> Against machines, against the Age of Steam,

The Hamiltonian extremes against the Franklin mean,
The genius of the land
Against the metal hand,
The great, slave-driven bark,
Full-oared upon the dark,
With gilded figurehead,
With fetters for the crew
And spices for the few,
The passion that is dead,
The pomp we never knew,
Bury this, too.[6]

9. The Last Days of Lincoln

. . . With malice toward none; with charity for all; with firmness in the right, as God gives us to see the right, let us strive on to finish the work we are in; to bind up the nation's wounds; to care for him who shall have borne the battle, and for his widow, and his orphan — to do all which may achieve and cherish a just and lasting peace among ourselves, and with all nations.

Thus closed the second inaugural address of President Lincoln on 4 March 1865. The struggle over reconstruction was already on. Ben Wade with his truculent vigor and fierce hatred of the slaveholders, the Democrats, eager for revenge on the President, Charles Sumner, with his passionate conviction that right and justice required the South to pass under the Caudine forks, were certain to oppose the terms with which Lincoln proposed to bind up the nation's wounds. But Congress would not meet until December. It might be confronted with the established fact of a restored nation, if the South were wise, and nothing happened to Lincoln.

On 11 April, two days after Lee's surrender, Lincoln delivered his last public address. After a brief allusion to Appomattox and the hope of a speedy peace, he unfolded his reconstruction policy — the most magnanimous terms towards a helpless opponent ever offered by a victor. For Lincoln did not consider himself a conqueror. He was, and had been since 1861, President of the United States. The rebellion must be forgotten; and every Southern state readmitted to her full privilege in the Union as soon as ten per cent of the whites had taken the oath of allegiance, and organized a state government.

[6] Stephen Vincent Benét, *John Brown's Body* (Doubleday, Doran Co., 1929), book viii, pp. 374-75.

On Thursday night, 13 April, Washington was illuminated on account of Lee's surrender, and crowds paraded the streets. A general light-heartedness was in the air; everyone knew that the war was practically over. On Good Friday, the 14th, the President held his last cabinet meeting. It was decided to lift the blockade. He urged his ministers to turn their thoughts to peace. There must be no more bloodshed, no persecution. General Grant, who attended the meeting, was asked for late news from Sherman, but had none. Lincoln remarked that it would come soon, and be favorable,[7] for last night he had dreamed a familiar dream. In a strange indescribable ship he seemed to be moving with great rapidity towards a dark and undefined shore. He had had this same dream before Sumter, Bull Run, Antietam, Murfreesborough, Vicksburg, and Wilmington. Matter-of-fact Grant remarked that Murfreesborough was no victory — 'a few such fights would have ruined us.' Lincoln looked at him curiously and said, however that might be, his dream preceded that battle.

Secretary Welles, who records this incident, may be our guide to the fearful events of that night. He had gone to bed early, and was just falling asleep when someone shouted from the street that the President had been shot, and the Secretary of State and his son assassinated. He dressed, and crossed Lafayette Square to Seward's house on 15th Street. The lower hall was full of excited people. Welles went upstairs to the room where Seward was lying on a bed soaked with blood, his lower jaw sagging as if in death. In the next room lay the son, unconscious from the injuries he had received in defending his father.

Leaving the Quartermaster-General in charge of the house, Welles, who by this time had been joined by Stanton, hurried down to 10th Street in a carriage. The President had been carried across that street from Ford's Theatre to a poor lodging-house, where he was laid on a bed in a narrow back room. He never recovered consciousness. 'The giant sufferer,' writes Welles, 'lay extended diagonally across the bed, which was not long enough for him. . . . His slow, full respiration lifted the clothes with each breath that he took. His features were calm and striking.' The room and the house were uncomfortably crowded. It was a dark and gloomy night, and rain fell at dawn. Crowds remained in the street, looking in vain for hope from the

[7] Johnston surrendered his army to Sherman 26 April. Jefferson Davis was captured 10 May. The last Confederate force surrendered 26 May.

watchers who came out for a breath of air. 'About once an hour Mrs. Lincoln would repair to the bedside of her dying husband and with lamentation and tears remain until overcome by emotion.'

A little before half-past seven the great heart ceased to beat.

Welles continues, 'I went after breakfast to the Executive Mansion. There was a cheerless cold rain and everything seemed gloomy. On the Avenue in front of the White House were several hundred colored people, mostly women and children, weeping and wailing their loss. This crowd did not appear to diminish through the whole of that cold, wet day; they seemed not to know what was to be their fate since their great benefactor was dead, and their hopeless grief affected me more than almost anything else, though strong and brave men wept when I met them.'

BIBLIOGRAPHY

GENERAL

1. HISTORIES OF THE UNITED STATES.

Edward Channing, *History of the United States* (6 vols. and General Index) is the best work from a single pen covering the whole period from the beginning to 1865. Written mainly for students and teachers, it is original in treatment, objective in point of view, sparing of interpretation, and economical in style; with excellent critical and bibliographical apparatus.

John B.McMaster, *History of the People of the United States from the Revolution to the Civil War* (8 vols. covering the period 1784–1861) is a valuable collection of facts and records, largely from contemporary newspapers, giving a moving picture of the American people in their social and economic, rather than their political relationship; but not easy to read consecutively.

Albert Bushnell Hart (ed.), *The American Nation: A History* (28 vols.). A co-operative history, representing the results of the first generation of American scientific historiography. Excellent bibliographies and maps.

Allen Johnson (ed.), *The Chronicles of America* (50 vols.). Written for the general public; eminently readable but uneven in merit.

A.M.Schlesinger and D.R.Fox (eds.), *History of American Life* (12 vols.). The latest co-operative history of the United States, shortly to be completed, and covering the entire period to 1928. Social development is stressed, and history viewed as the sum total of human activity. The single volumes will be mentioned in § 2 of this bibliography.

The Pageant of America (15 vols.) is the best pictorial history of the United States.

Allen Johnson and Dumas Malone (eds.), *The Dictionary of American Biography* (20 vols.) maintains a high level of scholarship and literary style, and is indispensable to students. Many of the sketches in it are superior to published biographies. J.T.Adams (ed.) *The Dictionary of American History* (6 vols.) is accurate and surprisingly thorough, far more useful than the older *Harper's Encyclopaedia of American History*.

2. ECONOMIC AND SOCIAL HISTORY.

GENERAL. See Schlesinger and Fox (eds.), *History of American Life* (12 vols.), in § 1. F.J.Turner, *The Frontier in American History* is a collection of essays that are the best introduction to the most characteristic feature of American life. F.L.Paxson, *History of the American Frontier, 1763–1893* is a synthesis of the enormous monographic material that was stimulated by Turner's first essay. C.W.Wright, *Economic History of the United States,* Fred A. Shannon, *America's Economic Growth,* H.U.Faulkner, *American Economic History,* and E.C.Kirkland, *A History of American Economic Life* are the best brief surveys. Guy S.Callender, *Selections from the Economic History of the U.S., 1765–1860* is a book of well-chosen source selections with luminous notes by the editor, H.U.Faulkner and F.Flugel, *Readings in American Economic History,* covers the whole ground.

LABOR. J.R.Commons *et al., History of Labor in the United States* (4 vols.) is the standard authority. Professor Commons's *Documentary History of American Industrial Society* (10 vols.) is a most valuable collection of material on the labor movement to 1880. H.Harris, *American Labor* and S.Perlman, *History of Trade Unionism in the United States* are the best brief surveys. A.M.Simons, *Social Forces in American History* presents the Marxian point of view.

SPECIAL PHASES. The ' Contributions to American Economic History,' published by the Carnegie Institute of Washington, although disappointingly inadequate, are still best in their respective fields: E.R.Johnson *et al., History of Domestic and Foreign Commerce of the U.S.* (2 vols.), B.H.Meyer *et al., History of Transportation in the U.S. before 1860,* V.S. Clark, *History of Manufactures, 1607–1860* (2 vols.), P.W.Bidwell *et al., History of Agriculture in the Northern U.S., 1620–1860,* and L.C.Gray, *History of Agriculture in the Southern States to 1860* (2 vols.). Joseph Schafer, *The Social History of American Agriculture* is brief but thoughtful. On public land see especially Roy M.Robbins, *Our Landed Heritage: The Public Domain, 1776–1936.* F.W.Taussig, *Tariff History of the U.S.* is the best compendium of that subject, by a free trader. Edward Stanwood, *American Tariff Controversies in the 19th Century* (2 vols.) is by a high protectionist. D.R.Dewey, *Financial History of the U.S.* is the best general history of banking and public finance, but the more recent W.J.Schultz and M.R.Caine, *Financial Development of the United States* should not be neglected. Sidney Ratner, *American Taxation* is valuable, especially for the more recent period. More popular presentations of aspects of American social history are F.R.Dulles, *America Learns to Play: A History of Popular Recreation 1607–1940;* A.Train, *The Story of Everyday Things;* W.C.Langdon, *Everyday Things in American Life* (2 vols.); and Dixon Wecter, *The Saga of American Society.*

IMMIGRATION. John R.Commons, *Races and Immigrants in America* is a classic account. Henry P.Fairchild, *Immigration;* George M.Stephenson, *History of American Immigration, 1820–1924,* and Lawrence G.Brown, *Immigration: Cultural conflicts and social adjustments* are more recent treatments. Maurice R.Davie, *World Immigration* is valuable for comparative material. Edith Abbott, *Immigration: Select documents and case records,* and *Historical Aspects of the Immigration Problem,* contain source material not elsewhere available.

STATISTICS. The volumes of the decennial censuses of the United States are supplied only to libraries, by the Census Bureau, Washington. The current *Statistical Abstract of the U.S., Abstract of the Census of Manufactures,* and the *Abstract of the Fifteenth Census,* which may be purchased from the Superintendent of Documents, are most useful compendia.

PERIODICALS, ETC. *The Quarterly Journal of Economics* (1865–   ), *American Economic Review* (1911–   ), *The Journal of Economic History* (1941–   ), and *Agricultural History* (1927–   ) are the principal journals of economic history, *The American Journal of Sociology,* and *Social Forces,* of social history. E.R.A.Seligman and Alvin Johnson, *The Encyclopaedia of Social Sciences* (15 vols.) contains many invaluable articles on social and economic history.

3. FOREIGN RELATIONS.

There is no comprehensive history of American foreign policy. S.F.Bemis, *The Diplomatic History of the United States* and T.A.Bailey, *A Diplomatic History of the American People* are the best and most recent one-volume surveys. Dr. Bemis also edited *The American Secretaries of State and Their Diplomacy* (10 vols.), a series of biographies by different authors. J.T.Shotwell is editing a voluminous and highly important series of volumes on the relations of Canada and the United States. The best collection of treaties is W.M.Malloy (ed.), *Treaties . . . between the U.S. and Other Powers, 1778–1909* (2 vols.), with supplements. The documentary history of foreign relations may be found in the following compilations: *Diplomatic Correspondence of the U.S., 1783–1789* (7 vols.); *American State Papers, Foreign Relations, 1789–1828* (6 vols.). From 1828 to 1860 the published papers on foreign relations must be sought in the general series of Congressional documents. From 1861 to the present, the Government has published one or more annual volumes under various titles, especially (since 1870), *Papers relating to the Foreign Relations of the U.S.* Important extracts from these collections, and from Department of State mss., were published with valuable notes in J.Bassett Moore, *History and Digest of the International Arbitrations to which the U.S. has been a party* (6 vols., 1898), and *Digest of International Law* (8 vols., 1906).

4. TRAVEL.

Contemporary books of travel for the entire period will be listed in the *Harvard Guide* (see § 11). J.L.Mesick, *The English Traveler in America,*

1785–1835, A.Nevins, *American Social Life as Seen by British Travelers,* and H.Tuckerman, *America and her Commentators* (3 vols.), have pregnant extracts. Frank Monaghan, *French Travelers in the U.S., 1765–1932,* is something more than a bibliography. Some of the more rare and important works of western travel are reprinted, with valuable notes by R.G.Thwaites, in *Early Western Travels* (32 vols.).

5. GOVERNMENT AND CONSTITUTIONAL HISTORY.

A. de Tocqueville, *Democracy in America* (2 vols.) is a classic still worth reading; see G.W.Pierson, *Tocqueville and Beaumont in America.* Lord Bryce's *American Commonwealth,* best in the early unrevised edition of 1888, is an incomparable description of the Federal and state governments during that decade. The following generation brought many changes, which are well described in Charles A.Beard, *American Government and Politics* and *The American Leviathan;* P.Odegard and E.A.Helms, *American Politics;* Pendleton Herring, *The Politics of Democracy.* On government departments see G.E.Haynes, *The Senate of the United States* (2 vols.); C.Warren, *The Supreme Court in United States History* (2 vols.); and the erudite and penetrating study by E.C.Corwin, *The President, Office and Powers.* A.N.Holcomb, *State Government in the U.S.* A complete constitutional history of the United States is much wanted but A.C.McLaughlin, *Constitutional History of the United States* is the best one-volume survey, and H.Hockett, *Constitutional History of the United States* (3 vols.) the most simple and lucid. There is a great deal of valuable material in C.Read (ed.), *The Constitution Reconsidered,* and many thoughtful essays in Max Lerner's *Ideas are Weapons.* On the Supreme Court see Charles Warren, *The Supreme Court in U.S. History* (2 vols.). His *Supreme Court and the Constitution* is more controversial. Louis Boudin, *Government by Judiciary* (2 vols.) is indispensable for all periods of Supreme Court history and contains material not found elsewhere. Of the one-volume surveys that came out of the 1936–37 recent crisis, Irving Brant, *Storm Over the Constitution* is the best. W.W.Willoughby, *The American Constitutional System* and *Constitutional Law in the United States* emphasize the constitutional side at the expense of historical background. B.F.Wright, *The Growth of American Constitutional Law* is a wonderfully condensed little volume. R.G.Gettell, *History of American Political Theories,* and C.E.Merriam, *American Political Theories* and *American Political Ideals, 1865–1917,* are general histories of political theory. E.R.Lewis, *History of American Political Thought from the Civil War to the World War* is thoughtful and critical. H.W. Horwill, *The Usages of the American Constitution* is a study of the unwritten constitution. Woodrow Wilson, *Constitutional Government in the United States* is a brilliant interpretation, though incomplete in many respects. F.J.Goodnow, *Politics and Administration* treats of the relation of party politics to government. Source material may be found in H.S. Commager, *Documents of American History;* J.B.Thayer, *Cases on Constitutional Law,* Allen Johnson, *Readings in American Constitutional History, 1776–1876,* A.Johnson and W.A.Robinson, *Readings in Recent American Constitutional History, 1876–1926* and J.M.Jacobson, *The Development of American Political Thought. The American Political Science Review* and the *Political Science Quarterly* are indispensable to the student of American government, as are A.B.Hart and A.C.McLaughlin (eds.), *Cyclopaedia of American Government* (3 vols.), and the articles on political science in *The Encyclopaedia of Social Sciences.*

6. HISTORICAL PERIODICALS AND PUBLICATIONS OF HISTORICAL SOCIETIES.

The American Historical Review (1895–   ) has reviews of new historical literature, and contains important articles and documents. There are three general indexes to it. The annual *Reports* of the American Historical Association (1889–   overlapped by 5 vols. of *Papers,* 1886–91. General Index, 1884–1914) include many other articles, monographs, and source material. The best of many regional historical quarterlies are the *Mississippi Valley Historical Review* (1915–   ), *The New England Quarterly* (1928–   ), and the *Journal of Southern History* (1935–   ). *Proceedings* and *Collections* of the *Massachusetts Historical Society,* the *Proceedings* of the American Antiquarian Society, the *Annals of the American Academy of Political and Social Science,* the Johns Hopkins University *Studies in Historical and Political Science,* and the Columbia University *Studies in History, Economics, and Public Law* contain monographic material essential to the student. A remarkably comprehensive guide to this material to 1905 was published as the *Report* of the Amer. Hist.Assn. for that year, vol.ii.

7. SOURCE COLLECTIONS.

H.S.Commager, *Documents of American History* (1492–1940) runs parallel to this work and contains extensive bibliographies. William Macdonald, *Documentary Source Book of American History, 1606–1926* is a compendium of the same editor's *Select Charters, 1606–1775, Select Documents, 1776–1861,* and *Select Statutes, 1861–1898.* For published sources on special periods, see Part II.

8. GEOGRAPHY

C.O.Paullin, *Atlas of Historical Geography of the U.S.,* published by the Carnegie Institution of Washington, is disappointingly inadequate, as are most collections of maps illustrating United States history. The works that have the best historical maps are A.B.Hart (ed.), *The American Nation: A History* (28 vols.), and E.M.Avery, *History of the U.S.*

(7 vols., to 1806 only). Those in the former are handily republished as Harper's *Atlas of American History.*

Isaiah Bowman, *Forest Physiography* is the best descriptive geography of the United States; his *The New World,* and N.S.Shaler (ed.), *United States of America* (2 vols.) emphasize the relation of geography to economics and history. A.P.Brigham, *Geographic Influences in American History,* and E.C.Semple, *American History and its Geographic Conditions* are the standard works on that subject. A.B.Hulbert, *Soil,* traces its influence on American History; his *Historic Highways of America* (16 vols.) is a collection of monographs on the great rivers and roadways of our history. Constance L.Skinner (ed.), *The Rivers of America* (in progress) interprets history against the geographical background.

9. LITERATURE, PHILOSOPHY, AND RELIGION.

The Cambridge History of American Literature (4 vols.) is a co-operative work, particularly strong on the colonial and early national periods. V.L.Parrington, *Main Currents of American Thought* (3 vols.) is a brilliant interpretation, but not always reliable as to facts. Other brief interpretations are L.Lewisohn, *The Story of American Literature;* P.H.Boynton, *Literature and American Life;* and John Macy, *Spirit of American Literature.* W.Blair, *Native American Humor* is interesting and Constance Rourke, *American Humor* brilliant. Of the briefer general histories that of Percy Boynton is the most useful. The 5th ed. of H.L.Mencken, *The American Language* is good. F.L.Mott, *History of American Magazines, 1741–1885* (3 vols.) covers the periodical literature, and his *American Journalism, 1690–1940* supplants the earlier works of W.G.Bleyer, *Main Currents in the History of American Journalism,* and J.M.Lee, *History of American Journalism.* J.F.Jameson, *Historical Writing in America,* J.S. Bassett, *The Middle Group of American Historians,* and Michael Kraus, *History of American Historiography* are the best available studies of historiography. A.Nevins, *The Gateway to History* has much of value on American historiography. W.T.Hutchinson (ed.), *Essays* in honor of Marcus Wilson Jernegan contains biographical studies of historians.

On Philosophy and Religion, Woodbridge Riley, *American Thought from Puritanism to Pragmatism,* and H.G.Townsend, *Philosophical Ideas in the United States* will do as starters in a deep subject but the absence of a substantial study of American philosophy remains one of the scandals of American scholarship. W.W.Sweet, *Story of Religions in America* is a short survey; T.C.Hall, *Religious Background of American Culture* is more interpretative; G.J.Garraghan, *The Jesuits of the Middle United States* (3 vols.) covers broad ground. Peter Mode, *Source Book and Bibliographical Guide for American Church History* is admirably full and W.W.Sweet has published three volumes of source material covering Religion on the American Frontier.

10. THE FINE ARTS AND MUSIC.

Lewis Mumford, *Sticks and Stones* is an interpretative account of American architecture; T.E.Tallmadge, *The Story of Architecture in America* is systematic; C.S.Caffin, *The Story of American Painting;* E.Neuhaus, *History and Ideals of American Art;* S.Isham and R.Cortissoz, *History of American Painting;* R.Cortissoz, *American Artists;* S.LaFollette, *Art in America;* H.St.Gaudens, *The American Artist and His Times;* and Alan Burroughs, *Limners and Likenesses: Three Centuries of American Painting* are helpful on painting. There is much of interest in William Dunlap's *History of the Rise and Progress of the Arts of Design in the United States* (3 vols.). Frank Weitenkampf, *American Graphic Art* is useful and William Murrell, *History of American Graphic Humor* (2 vols.) fascinating. Lorado Taft, *The History of American Sculpture* is almost a classic, but an up-to-date history of sculpture is badly needed. L.C.Elson, *The History of American Music,* and J.T.Howard, *Our American Music* are useful surveys.

11. MILITARY AND NAVAL HISTORY

These vital aspects of American history have been scandalously neglected for over fifty years. Three recent one-volume surveys, based on original research, mark the dawn of a better day: Colonel O.H.Spaulding, *The U.S.Army in War and Peace;* Captain D.W.Knox, *A History of the U.S.Navy;* and Lieut.Colonel C.H.Metcalf, *A History of the U.S.Marine Corps.*

12. BIBLIOGRAPHY

Writings on American History, compiled by Grace G.Griffin since 1906 and now published among the *Reports* of the American Historical Association, includes periodical articles as well as books, and is mildly critical. Special bibliographies of value are S.F.Bemis and G.G.Griffin, *Guide to the Diplomatic History of the United States,* and E.E.Edwards, *Bibliography of the History of Agriculture in the United States.*

AUTHORITIES FOR EACH CHAPTER

I. *ISOLATED AMERICA, ?*-1492

RECESSION OF THE ICE–SHEET, and ORIGIN OF MAN IN AMERICA. Reginald A.Daly, *The Changing World of the Ice Age,* Edgar B.Howard, 'Early Man in America,' *Proceedings* American Philosophical Society, lxxvi(I).327–33, Diamond Jenness (ed.), *The American Aborigines,* Ales Hrdlicka, in *Bulletins* 33 and 66 of the Bureau of American Ethnology, Smithsonian Institution, and E.B.Howard, 'Evidence of Early Man in North America,' *Museum Journal* of the University of Pennsylvania, xxiv.61–151.

THE INDIANS. For those of North America the best popular works are Clark Wissler, *Indians of the United States;* P.Radin, *Story of the American Indian;* F.R.Eggan, *Social Anthropology of North American Tribes;* and G.P.Murdock, *Our Primitive Contemporaries.* F.W.Hodge, *Handbook of American Indians North of Mexico* (2 vols.) is an indispensable aid; L.Pericot y García, *América Indígena* is an excellent survey that covers South America as well.

THE MAYAS AND ANCIENT CIVILIZATIONS OF MEXICO, and NEW MEXICO AND GUATEMALA. A.V.Kidder, *Introduction to the Study of Southwestern Archaeology* and Alfred M. Tozzer, 'Chronological Aspects of American Archaeology,' *Proceedings* Massachusetts Historical Society, lix.283–92, are good introductions. The papers in *The Maya and Their Neighbors,* dedicated to Tozzer, offer a wealth of information and a key to the latest literature. J. Eric Thompson, *Civilization of the Maya,* H.J.Spinden, *A Study of Maya Art* and *Ancient Civilizations of Mexico and Central America,* G.C.Vaillant, *Aztecs of Mexico* and Franz Blom, *The Conquest of Yucatan* are the best in their respective fields. Differing interpretations of the Maya calendar are those by S.G.Morley in *Bulletin* No.57 of the Bureau of American Ethnology, and H.J.Spinden in *Papers,* vi.No.4 of the Peabody Museum of Archaeology, Cambridge.

THE NORSE DISCOVERY OF AMERICA. Halldór Hermannsson, *The Problem of Wineland* is the best short survey; W.Hovgaard, *Voyages of the Norsemen to America* is good for the ships; the relevant sagas and other documents are translated in A.M.Reeves, *Finding of Wineland the Good,* and reprinted in J.E.Olson & E.G.Bourne, *Northmen, Columbus and Cabot.* For summaries of excavations in Greenland, see *Geographical Review,* xv.605–15 and *Am. Scandinavian Review,* xi.547–53. P.Gaffarel, *Les Irlandais en Amérique avant Colomb* puts the Irish first.

Of the various so-called Irish or Norse relics found in North America, some, like the round tower at Newport, R.I., various glacial scratches on rocks, the alleged relics near Boston, and the so-called Irish village in New Hampshire (see Hugh Hencken in *New England Quarterly*, xii.429–42) are of English colonial or geological origin. Others, like the so-called Beardmore (Ontario) sword and shield, are genuine Norse relics smuggled into this country recently (see *Canadian Historical Review*, xxii.254–79). The 'Kensington Rune Stone,' which purports to record the adventures of a Scandinavian expedition to Minnesota in A.D. 1363, we believe to be a modern forgery; for although we do not question the sincerity of Mr.H.R.Holand, who has written many ingenious arguments in its favor (e.g. *Westward from Vinland*) we regard it more significant that the few Scandinavian runologists who have thought it worth while to comment on the inscription have declared the lettering to be impossible for that era.

II. *THE ERA OF DISCOVERY*, 1492–1600

THE CENTURY OF DISCOVERY. E.G.Bourne, *Spain in America*, is still the best single volume that covers the Spanish conquest and all the early voyages. John Fiske's *Discovery of America* (2 vols.), though old, is charmingly written and valuable. Charles R.Beazley has written several important works — *The Dawn of Modern Geography, John and Sebastian Cabot*, and *Prince Henry the Navigator*. J.B.Brebner, *The Explorers of North America* covers the whole ground in a masterly fashion. H.I. Priestley, *The Coming of the White Man* is best on the cultural aspects. Dr. Diego Luis Molinari's chapters in *Historia de la Nación Argentina*, vol.ii, republished with additional matter but without notes as *El Nacimiento del Nuevo Mundo*, are the best works in any language on the controversial questions connected with Columbus, and on the discovery of South America. S.E.Morison, *Admiral of the Ocean Sea* (2 vols., or one-volume edition without notes) is the latest biography of Columbus, and a volume of *Journals of Columbus and Other Documents* is in preparation. For the conquests of Mexico and Peru, there are the classic narratives of William H.Prescott, still fresh and vivid after a century; for the exploits of Quesada and the conquest of Chile, R.B.Cunninghame Graham's *The Conquest of New Granada* and *Pedro de Valdivia* are foremost. The noble memoir of the Conquest of Mexico by Bernal Díaz del Castillo is to be found in many editions and translations. Herbert E.Bolton of Berkeley is the historian of the Spanish Southwest of the United States; his *Spanish Borderlands* in *The Chronicles of America* is a neat summary of the early explorations in that region and in Florida. He edited for the Original Narratives Series, *Spanish Exploration in the*

Southwest, which includes the narratives of the Cabrillo and Oñate expeditions; an earlier volume in that series, *Spanish Explorers in the Southern United States,* includes the narratives of Cabeza de Vaca and of the
De Soto and Coronado expeditions.

The best edition of Antonio Pigafetta's *Narrative of Magellan's Voyage* is that of James A.Robertson (3 vols.).

ENGLISH AND FRENCH BEGINNINGS. The works of James
A.Williamson, *Voyages of the Cabots* (including all the sources), *Sir
John Hawkins, Age of Drake,* and chap.ii of *The Cambridge History of
the British Empire,* 1 (of which A.P.Newton's chap.iii is also valuable)
afford the best introduction to English overseas activities in the sixteenth
century: Arthur P.Newton, *The European Nations in the West Indies*
is learned and thorough. H.R.Wagner, *Sir Francis Drake's Voyage
around the World,* Sir William Foster, *England's Quest of Eastern Trade,*
D.B.Quinn, *Voyages of Sir Humphrey Gilbert* (2 vols.), and E.G.R.Tay-
lor, *Writings & Correspondence of the Two Richard Hakluyts* are also
important. Hakluyt's famous collection, *The Principall Navigations,
Voiages, and Discoyeries of the English Nation* has been frequently reprinted and abridged; the most important of his voyages for the U.S.A.,
together with translations from Cartier's voyages, are in H.S.Burrage,
Early English and French Voyages of the Original Narratives Series.
Francis Parkman, *Pioneers of France in the New World* is still the best
general account of the founding of Canada, although H.P.Biggar, *Precursors of Cartier* and *Early Trading Companies of New France* add
fresh material; and George Wrong, *The Rise and Fall of New France,*
vol.i, provides a succinct summary. The primary works for the development of English capitalism as applied overseas are W.E.Lingelbach, *The
Merchant Adventurers of England;* W.R.Scott, *Constitution and Finance
of Joint Stock Companies* (3 vols.); R.H.Tawney, *Religion and the Rise
of Capitalism.* M.Oppenheim, *History of the Administration of the Royal
Navy* is the best account of English shipping. George L.Beer, *Origins of
the British Colonial System, 1578–1660* is a classic.

SOURCE SELECTIONS. H.S.Commager, *Documents of American
History,* Nos.1–5.

III. *THE FIRST FOUNDATIONS,* 1600–60

For the history of the English colonies in the period 1606–1775, four
general histories are of primary importance: Edward Channing, *History
of the United States,* vols.i–iii; Charles M.Andrews, *The Colonial Period
of American History* (4 vols.); and H.L.Osgood, *The American Colonies
in the Seventeenth Century* (3 vols.); the best single-volume survey, especially on the economic side, is Curtis P.Nettels, *The Roots of American*

Civilization. T.J.Wertenbacker, *The First Americans* is a social-history survey of the seventeenth century.

VIRGINIA AND MARYLAND. The chapters in Andrews, Channing and Osgood; G.L.Beer, *Origins of the British Colonial System;* P.A. Bruce's great works, the *Economic History* (2 vols.) and *Institutional History of Virginia in the Seventeenth Century* (2 vols.); W.F.Craven, *Dissolution of the Virginia Company;* J.W.Wertenbaker, *Virginia under the Stuarts* and *Planters of Colonial Virginia,* and his *Founders of American Civilization — the Southern Colonies;* B.C.Steiner's *Beginnings of Maryland* and other works on early Maryland history; Matthew P.Andrews, *Founding of Maryland,* cover this field. Narratives of Virginia and Maryland have each a volume in the Original Narratives Series. S.M. Kingsbury (ed.), *Records of the Virginia Company of London* (4 vols.); E.Arber's various editions of *The Writings of Captain John Smith;* Alexander Brown, *Genesis of the United States* (2 vols.) are collections of Virginian sources. Our quoted ballads are from C.H.Firth, *An American Garland.* For early housing both here and in New England, see H.R. Shurtleff, *The Log Cabin Myth,* and S.Fiske Kimball, *Domestic Architecture of the American Colonies.* Louis B.Wright, *First Gentlemen of Virginia* is an admirable cultural study.

BERMUDA AND THE WEST INDIES. C.M.Andrews and A.P. Newton, *European Nations in the West Indies* are comprehensive. See also Henry Wilkinson, *Adventurers of Bermuda;* V.T.Harlow, *History of Barbados, 1625–85;* J.A.Williamson, *The Caribbee Islands under Proprietary Patents.*

THE PURITAN COLONIES. Andrews, Channing, and Osgood are all excellent; J.Truslow Adams, *Founding of New England* is sprightly but unsympathetic. J.G.Palfrey, *History of New England* (5 vols.) covers the whole colonial period in great detail. For Puritanism, the best starting points are Perry Miller, *Orthodoxy in Massachusetts* and *The New England Mind,* R.G.Usher, *Reconstruction of the English Church* (2 vols.), and M.M.Knappen (ed.), *Two Elizabethan Puritan Diaries.* The Plymouth Colony may best be studied in William Bradford's *History of Plimmoth Plantation;* Massachusetts Bay in *The Winthrop Papers* published by the Massachusetts Historical Society, in John Winthrop's *Journal,* and Edward Johnson's *Wonder-Working Providence* (both in Original Narratives Series). S.E.Morison, *Builders of the Bay Colony* is a series of biographical sketches; his *Founding of Harvard College, Harvard College in the Seventeenth Century,* and *Puritan Pronaos* supplement V.L.Parrington, *The Colonial Mind,* 1, for cultural history. H.S.Burrage, *The Beginnings of Colonial Maine* untangles the complicated history of that province. S.H.Brockunier, *The Irrepressible Democrat: Roger Williams* is the best account of that founder. Williams's works are reprinted in the Narragansett Club *Publications,* vols.1–6. C.M.Andrews, *Beginnings of Connecticut,* and I.M.Calder, *The New Haven Colony* are best for southern New England. M.W.Jernegan, *Laboring and Dependent Classes* is largely devoted to education. G.F.Dow, *Every-Day Life in the Massachusetts Bay Colony* is excellent, and Oliver Wendell Holmes's chapter on early medicine and physicians, in a volume of Lowell Institute Lectures entitled *Early History of Mass.,* is a classic.

NEW NETHERLAND is well covered by the appropriate chapters in Channing and in Andrews, vol.iii; in A.C.Flick (ed.), *History of the State of New York,* i; the Swedish section in Amandus Johnson, *Swedish Settlements on the Delaware* (2 vols.), and social history in T.J. Wertenbaker, *The Founding of American Civilization: The Middle Colonies,* and Mrs.S.Van Rensselaer, *History of the City of New York in the Seventeenth Century* (2 vols.). There is interesting material in Dixon R.Fox, *Yankees and Yorkers,* written with humor and charm. J.F.Jameson edited *Narratives of New Netherland* for the Original Narratives Series. For maps and prints, in which Dutch history is unusually rich, see I.N.P.Stokes, *Iconography of Manhattan Island* (6 vols.). Commager, *Documents,* Nos.6–22 furnishes source material.

IV. *THE EMPIRE COMES OF AGE,* 1600–73

Appropriate chapters of Andrews and Osgood; L.A.Harper, *The English Navigation Laws;* G.L.Beer, *The Commercial Policy of England toward the American Colonies, The Old Colonial System* (2 vols.); E.Lipson, *Economic History of England,* ii and iii; and C.P.Nettels, 'Menace of Colonial Manufacturing, 1690–1720,' and 'The Place of Markets in the Old Colonial System,' *New England Quarterly,* iv.230–66, vi.491–512, cover the Acts of Trade and Navigation. Ralph P.Bieber, *The Lords of Trade and Plantations, 1675–96* is a useful monograph.

THE CAROLINAS. Andrews and Channing; Louise F.Brown, *The First Earl of Shaftesbury;* E.McCrady, *History of South Carolina under the Proprietary Government;* Archibald Henderson, *History of North Carolina* (2 vols.); Charles L. Raper, *North Carolina, A Study in English Colonial Government;* and *Narratives of Early Carolina* in the Original Narratives Series.

NEW YORK, THE JERSEYS AND PENNSYLVANIA. A.C.Flick (ed.), *History of the State of New York,* ii; J. R. Brodhead, *History of New York,* i and ii; E.P.Tanner, *Province of New Jersey, 1664–1738;* John H.Kennedy, *Thomas Dongan;* W.I.Hull, *William Penn, A Topical Biography;* A.C.Myers, *Immigration of Irish Quakers;* S.G.Fisher, *The Making of Pennsylvania;* M.D.Learned, *Life of Francis Daniel Pastorius;* A.C.Myers (ed.), *Narratives of Early Pennsylvania, West New Jersey and Delaware* in the Original Narratives Series.

VIRGINIA AND NEW ENGLAND, 1660–1713. T.J.Wertenbaker, *Torch-bearer of the Revolution, the story of Bacon's Rebellion;* V.F. Barnes, *The Dominion of New England;* K.B.Murdock, *Increase Mather* and T.J.Holmes's Mather super-bibliographies; in the Original Narratives Series, the volumes on *The Indian Wars, The Insurrections, Witchcraft,* and *Journal of Jasper Danckaerts;* L.B.Wright (ed.), *The Secret Diary of William Byrd of Westover, 1709–1712,* and the various editions of Byrd's *Writings* begin in this period and lap over into the next; Samuel Sewall's *Diary* is a New England classic.

COLONIAL REORGANIZATION AND WAR. G.H.Guttridge, *Colonial Policy of William III;* L.W.Labaree, *Royal Government in America;* O.M.Dickerson, *American Colonial Government, 1696–1765;* E.B.Russell, *Review of American Colonial Legislation by King in Council;* W.T.Root, *Relations of Pennsylvania with the British Government, 1696–1765;* L.Dodson, *Alexander Spotswood, Governor of Virginia;* L.W. Labaree (ed.), *Royal Instructions to British Colonial Governors, 1670–1776.* Francis Parkman, *Frontenac and New France, La Salle and the Discovery of the Great West,* and *Half-Century of Conflict* are the classic accounts of the wars on the Northern border and the exploration of the South and West. For Southern border wars, see V.W.Crane, *The Southern Frontier, 1670–1732;* H.E.Bolton, *Spain's Title to Georgia;* W.E. Dunn, *Spanish and French Rivalry in the Gulf Region of the United States, 1678–1702;* J.A.Morfi, *History of Texas, 1673–1779;* Alcée Fortier, *History of Louisiana;* P.J.Hamilton, *Colonial Mobile.* William T.Morgan's widely scattered articles on the colonial wars are most valuable, as are F.R.Hart, *The Disaster of Darien,* S.L.Mims, *Colbert's West India Policy,* and C.H.Haring, *The Buccaneers in the West Indies,* for the Caribbean. H.E.Bolton's volume of sources, *Spanish Exploration in the Southwest* contains translations of five expeditions into Texas and of Fr. Kino's *Historical Memoir of Pimería Alta;* his *Rim of Christendom* is a study of the career of Father Kino; these are supplemented by A.B. Thomas (ed.), *After Coronado, 1696–1727, Documents.*

SOURCE SELECTIONS. Commager, *Documents,* Nos.23–29.

V. *A HALF-CENTURY OF EXPANSION,* 1713–63

SOCIAL AND ECONOMIC DEVELOPMENT. The masterful survey by L.H.Gipson, *The British Empire before the American Revolution* (4 vols. out) is indispensable; H.L.Osgood, *American Colonies in the Eighteenth Century,* vols.ii, iii, and iv, has chapters on immigration, currency, and Indian relations; but the best chapters on economic and social development in a general history are those in Channing, vol.ii; and the best short account of money problems is in C.P.Nettels, *Roots of Amer-*

ican Civilization. J.T.Adams, *Provincial Society* is interesting but far from thorough. Among the more valuable monographs are R.B.Morris, *Studies in the History of American Law;* L.C.Wroth, *The Colonial Printer;* O.G.Sonneck, *Early Concert-Life in America, 1731–1800;* A.H. Quinn, *History of the American Drama,* vol.i; H.W.Foote, *Robert Feke, Colonial Portrait Painter;* J.J.Walsh, *Education of the Founding Fathers;* H.D.Eberlein, *Architecture of Colonial America* (see also Fiske Kimball's work, above); C.H.McIlwain (ed.), Wraxall's *Abridgment of Indian Affairs;* R.H.Akagi, *Town Proprietors of the New England Colonies;* H.J.Ford, *The Scotch-Irish in America;* A.B.Faust, *The German Element in the United States;* F.R.Diffenderffer, *German Immigration into Penna. through the Port of Philadelphia;* J.F.Sachse, *German Sectarians* and *German Pietists of Pennsylvania;* C.Henry Smith, *Mennonite Immigration to Pennsylvania;* A.C.Bining, *British Regulation of the Colonial Iron Industry;* R.G.Albion, *Forests and Sea Power;* C.H. Ambler, *Sectionalism in Virginia;* L.K.Koontz, *The Virginia Frontier, 1754–63;* and S.Kercheval, *History of the Valley of Virginia.*

THE GREAT AWAKENING. C.H.Maxson, *The Great Awakening in the Middle Colonies;* W.M.Gewehr, *The Great Awakening in Virginia, 1740–90;* biographies of Edwards by A.V.G.Allen and H.B.Parkes.

GEORGIA AND NOVA SCOTIA are well covered in Osgood's *Eighteenth Century,* iii and iv, and Gipson's *British Empire,* ii; V.W. Crane, *Promotion Literature of Georgia;* J.D.Wade, *John Wesley;* C.C. Jones, *History of Georgia* (2 vols.); P.S.Flippin, *Royal Government in Georgia* (running through vols.viii–xiii of the *Georgia Historical Quarterly*); H.B.Fant's articles on the trustees' activities (in vols.xv, xvi, and xx of the same periodical); and J.R.McCain, *Georgia as a Proprietary Province.* A.A.Ettinger's *Oglethorpe* is one of the best colonial biographies. W.B.Kerr, *The Maritime Provinces of British North America and the American Revolution;* W.O.Raymond, articles on Nova Scotia running through *Transactions* of the Royal Society of Canada, 3d ser., vols.iv–vi; A.G.Doughty, *The Acadian Exiles;* J.B.Brebner, *New England's Outpost* and *The Neutral Yankees of Nova Scotia.*

POLITICS AND WARS. See references to Colonial Reorganization under Chapter IV. L.W.Labaree, *Royal Government in America* is the best single volume for the politics of this period. C.A.Barker, *Background of the Revolution in Maryland,* G.A.Wood, *William Shirley,* E.McCrady, *History of South Carolina in the Revolution,* C.L.Becker, *History of Political Parties in New York, 1760–1776,* and D.R.Fox, *The Decline of Aristocracy in the Politics of New York* are among the better monographs on local politics. Francis Parkman's *Half-Century of Conflict* (2 vols.), *Montcalm and Wolfe* (2 vols.), and *Conspiracy of Pontiac* are supplemented on the naval side by J.S.Corbett, *England in the Seven Years' War* (2 vols.). See also T.P.Abernethy, *Western*

Lands and the American Revolution; J.S.McLennan, *Louisbourg;* G.M. Wrong, *The Fall of Canada;* E.I.McCormac, *Colonial Opposition . . . during French and Indian War;* L.K.Koontz, *The Virginia Frontier, 1754–63;* J.C.Long, *Mr. Pitt and Lord Jeffrey Amherst;* F.E.Whitton, *Wolfe and North America;* F.R.Hart, *The Siege of Havana;* S.Pargellis, *Lord Loudoun in North America,* ' Braddock's Defeat,' *American Hist. Rev.,* xli.253–69, and *Military Affairs in North America, 1748–65* (the Cumberland Papers); G.W.Kimball (ed.), *Correspondence of William Pitt with Colonial Governors* (2 vols.); J.Sullivan and A.C.Flick (eds.), *Papers of Sir William Johnson* (9 vols.); John Knox, *Historical Journals of Campaign in North America;* J.C.Webster (ed.), *Journal of Jeffrey Amherst.* For Washington's part in the war see his early *Diaries* and *Writings,* J.Fitzpatrick (ed.), and S.E.Morison, *The Young Man Washington.* For the Southern frontier and war, the literature is much less abundant: *The Cambridge History of the British Empire,* i.336–44, and chap.xii; Marc de Villiers, *Histoire de la fondation de la Nouvelle-Orléans;* J.T.Lanning, *Diplomatic History of Georgia;* H.W.Richmond, *The Navy in the War of 1739–48* (3 vols.); R.Pares, *War and Trade in West Indies, 1739–63; A Voyage around the World in the Years 1740–44 by George Anson, Esq.*

SOURCE SELECTIONS. Commager, *Documents,* Nos.30–32.

VI. *LIBERTY AND EMPIRE*

IMPERIAL POLICY. *The Cambridge History of the British Empire,* vol.i, is scholarly and detailed, but lacks synthesis and completeness. Some of the chapters on trade, government and law are admirable. An excellent brief survey of the empire is J.A.Williamson, *History of British Expansion* (2 vols.). Two works that furnish an adequate survey of imperial policy in the seventeenth and eighteenth centuries are G.L.Beer, *The Old Colonial System, 1660–1754* (2 vols.), and *British Colonial Policy, 1754–1765.* On the Imperial administration L.W.Labaree, *Royal Government in America* is best for certain phases; O.M.Dickerson, *American Colonial Government* for others. Labaree has edited *Royal Instructions to British Colonial Governors, 1676–1776* (2 vols.). The best biographies of imperially minded Englishmen are Albert von Ruville, *William Pitt* (3 vols.) and Lord Fitzmaurice, *Life of William Earl of Shelburne* (3 vols.).

ALBANY PLAN AND SEVEN YEARS' WAR. Benjamin Franklin, *Complete Works,* Bigelow or Smyth eds. (use index); R.Frothingham, *Rise of the Republic of the United States;* L.K.Mathews, ' Benjamin Franklin's Plans for Colonial Union,' *Amer.Pol.Sci.Rev.,* vol.viii. Francis Parkman, *Half Century of Conflict* (2 vols.) and *Montcalm and Wolfe* (2 vols.) are high-water marks of American historical literature; his

Conspiracy of Pontiac is still the classic narrative of that episode. A more recent treatment of the struggle for a continent is George M.Wrong, *Rise and Fall of New France* (2 vols.). Two essays of capital importance are W.L.Grant, ' Canada versus Guadeloupe,' *Amer.Hist.Rev.,* xvii.735 and H.Hall, ' Chatham's American Policy,' ibid., v.659.

EIGHTEENTH–CENTURY ENGLAND. The literature is enormous, but there is a fine study of the social and economic background in L.H.Gipson, *The British Empire before the American Revolution,* vol.i, and of the political background in L.B.Namier, *The Structure of British Politics at the Accession of George III* (2 vols.), and *England in the Age of the American Revolution.* W.E.H.Lecky, *History of England in the Eighteenth Century* (8 vols.) and G.O.Trevelyan, *History of the American Revolution* (6 vols.) effectively present the whig-liberal point of view, the latter with consummate literary charm. On public opinion, see W.T.Laprade, *Public Opinion and Policies in Eighteenth Century England,* and Dora M.Clark, *British Opinion and the American Revolution.* Indispensable for the royal personality and policy is Sir John W.Fortescue (ed.), *The Correspondence of King George III* (6 vols.). V.W.Crane, *Benjamin Franklin, Englishman and American* and D.D. Wallace, *Henry Laurens* illuminate the attitude of typical Americans toward the mother country. Sir Leslie Stephen, *English Thought in the Eighteenth Century* (2 vols.) is one of the most penetrating interpretations in English literature.

RENEWAL OF SPANISH ACTIVITY. Herbert E.Bolton, the Pacific Prescott, is the chief authority, and his introductory volume to *Anza's California Expeditions* (5 vols.), the best account of Alta California at this period. His *De Mézières and the Louisiana-Texas Frontier, 1768–80,* supplements the account of the O'Reilly régime in Gayarré. *Hist. of Louisiana,* vols.ii and iii, and in J.A.Robertson, *Louisiana under Spain, France and the U.S.,* vol.i. In *New Spain and the West,* vol.i (the Bolton Festschrift) there are important articles on this period by C.W.Hackett, D.K.Bjork, and others; and a few others will be found in the volume edited by H.E.Bolton and H.Morse Stephens, *The Pacific Ocean in History.* Verner Crane, *The Southern Frontier,* contains valuable material on economic rivalry and Indian policy in the Southeast.

HISTORIES OF THE THIRTEEN COLONIES. C.M.Andrews, *The Colonial Period of American History* (4 vols. out and more coming), is the latest and the most comprehensive on imperial relations; E.Channing, *United States,* vols.i,ii, makes a more balanced history; H.L.Osgood, *American Colonies in Seventeenth Century* (3 vols.) and *American Colonies in Eighteenth Century* (4 vols.) is the most detailed on internal history. C.M.Andrews, *Colonial Background of the American Revolution* is a series of four essays on imperial problems of the 1760's.

SOURCE SELECTIONS. Commager, *Documents,* Nos.31–32.

VII. *IMPERIAL REORGANIZATION,* 1764–74

GENERAL. C.M.Andrews, *Colonial Background* and C.H.Van Tyne, *Causes of the War of Independence* are useful surveys. G.L.Beer, *British Colonial Policy, 1754–1765* analyzes the reasons behind the new English policy. The march of events is ably traced in Channing's *History,* vol.iii. C.W.Alvord, *The Mississippi Valley in British Politics* (2 vols.) opens up the Western problem, and J.P.Boyd prints much material in *Susquehanna Papers.* Many of the chapters in the *Cambridge History of the British Empire,* v.i are invaluable.

PARTICULAR PROBLEMS. W.T.Laprade, 'The Stamp Act in British Politics,' *Amer.Hist.Rev.,* xxxv.735, and W.T.Root, *Relations of Pennsylvania with the British Government.* An excellent study of the Quartering Act and British military policy is S.M.Pargellis, *Lord Loudoun and North America.* On the Quebec Act see V.Coffin, *Province of Quebec and the American Revolution;* R.Coupland, *The Quebec Act;* C.H.Metzger, *The Quebec Act;* and A.L.Burt, *The Old Province of Quebec.* An important economic phase is exhaustively treated by A.M. Schlesinger, in *The Colonial Merchants and the American Revolution, 1763–76,* and more briefly in his *New Viewpoints in American History,* ch.vii. Another is sketched in R.B.Morris, *Studies in the History of American Law.* A useful monograph of a highly specialized nature is M.M.Spector, *The American Department of the British Government, 1768–1782.* The pamphlet warfare of the period is summed up in M.C.Tyler, *Literary History of the American Revolution* (2 vols.). The growth of constitutional theory is described in R.G.Adams, *Political Ideas of the American Revolution;* C.H.McIlwain, *The American Revolution,* and the counter-argument by R.L.Schuyler, *Parliament and the British Empire;* C.F. Mullett, *Fundamental Law and the American Revolution;* A.C.McLaughlin, 'The Background of American Federalism,' *Amer.Polit.Science Rev.,* xii.215; and B.F.Wright, *American Interpretations of Natural Law.* The propaganda methods of the time are studied in P.G.Davidson, *Propaganda and the American Revolution,* and J.C.Miller, *Sam Adams;* articles by A.M.Schlesinger in *N.E.Quarterly,* viii.63 and *Publications Colonial Soc. of Mass.,* xxxii.396. For BIOGRAPHIES, see § VIII.

SOURCE SELECTIONS. Commager, *Documents,* Nos.33, 35–46, 48–54, Morison, *Sources and Documents illustrating the American Revolution,* pp.1–115; G.S.Callender, *Selections from Economic History of the United States,* pp.85–140. For further source study, Force's *American Archives,* the collected works of Franklin, Jefferson, and John and Samuel Adams are recommended. Hezekiah Niles, *Principles and Acts of the Revolution* is still a most useful collection of patriotic resolves.

VIII. *SECTIONAL AND CLASS DIVISIONS,* 1760–75

GENERAL. The most penetrating treatment of sectionalism during the colonial period is to be found in the first three chapters of F.J.Turner's *Frontier in American History.* The best general survey of the colonies is L.H.Gipson, *The British Empire before the American Revolution.* A.Nevins, *American States During and After the Revolution* has a good deal of background material.

SPECIAL STUDIES of particular importance are H.J.Eckenrode, *Revolution in Virginia;* J.S.Bassett, *Regulators of North Carolina* (Amer. Hist.Assoc.*Reports,* 1894); W.A.Schaper, *Sectionalism in South Carolina* (Amer.Hist.Assoc.*Reports,* 1901); C.H.Lincoln, *Revolutionary Movement in Pennsylvania;* W.R.Shepherd, *Proprietary Government in Pennsylvania;* G.A.Cribb, *Frontier Policy of Pennsylvania;* D.K.Kemmerer, *The Path to Freedom: The Struggle for Self-Government in New Jersey, 1703–1776;* Beverly Bond, *Quit Rents in the American Colonies;* H.E. McKinley, *Suffrage Franchise in the English Colonies;* A.C.Bining, *Colonial Iron Industry;* C.L.Becker, *History of Political Parties in the Province of New York;* Irving Mark, *Agrarian Conflicts in New York, 1711–1775;* M.B.Jones, *Vermont in the Making, 1750–1777;* R.F.Upton, *Revolutionary New Hampshire;* C.D.Barker, *The Background of the Revolution in Maryland;* N.D.Mereness, *Maryland as a Proprietary Colony;* J.T.Adams, *Revolutionary New England;* E.A.Bailey, *Influences Toward Radicalism in Connecticut, 1754–1775;* P.Davidson, 'Southern Backcountry on Eve of Revolution,' in *Essays in Honor of W.E.Dodd;* A.O.Craven, *Soil Exhaustion in Virginia.* A.L.Cross, *The Anglican Episcopate in the American Colonies* is the standard authority on that subject, and Alice Baldwin, *New England Clergy and the American Revolution* important from another angle. For non-English elements, A.B.Faust, *German Element in the United States;* C.A.Hanna, *The Scotch-Irish* (2 vols.); A.J.Ford, *The Scotch-Irish in America.*

BIOGRAPHY AND REMINISCENCES (see also § I). Esther Forbes, *Paul Revere and the World he Lived In* depicts eighteenth-century Boston with charm and understanding. C.J.Stillé, *Life and Times of John Dickinson* (2 vols.); A.T.Volweiler, *George Croghan;* I.Sharpless, *Political Leaders of Provincial Pennsylvania;* J.C.Miller, *Sam Adams;* L.S. Mayo, *John Wentworth;* M.C.Tyler, *Patrick Henry;* D.D.Wallace, *Henry Laurens;* and W.C.Bruce, *Benjamin Franklin Self-Revealed* (2 vols.); Arthur Pound, *Johnson of the Mohawks.* Something of the social life of the time may be gleaned from Alexander Graydon, *Memoirs of a Life Passed Principally in Philadelphia;* Anne Grant, *Memoirs of an American Lady;* Philip Fithian, *Diary;* and Benjamin Franklin's inimitable *Autobiography.*

SOURCE SELECTIONS. Commager, *Documents,* Nos.34, 37; Morison, *Sources and Documents*, pp.9–14, 83–87; H.M.Jones and E.E.Leisy, *Major American Writers*, pp.59–120, 130–47 (Franklin and Crèvecoeur). Callender, *Selections from Economic History*, pp.6–84.

IX. THE REVOLUTION PRECIPITATED, 1774–76

GENERAL. C.H.Van Tyne, *The War of Independence*, and Richard Frothingham, *Rise of the Republic of the United States* cover the history of the period in some detail. S.G.Fisher, *The Struggle for American Independence* (2 vols.) is vivacious and suggestive but unreliable. M.C. Tyler, *Literary History of the American Revolution* is a masterly survey of the controversial literature of the period. E.C.Burnett, *The Continental Congress* is one of the most valuable monographs in our historical literature, thorough, critical, and brilliantly written. In addition to the sources mentioned in ch.II important collections of material are E.C.Burnett (ed.), *Letters of Members of the Continental Congress* (8 vols. to 1788), and W.C.Ford (ed.), *Journals of the Continental Congress* (33 vols.).

OPENING OF HOSTILITIES. Allen French, *The Day of Concord and Lexington, General Gage's Informers*, and *The First Year of the American Revolution;* J.Codman, *Arnold's Expedition to Quebec;* C.E. Carter, *Correspondence of General Thomas Gage* (2 vols.). The first of A.C.McLaughlin *et al., Source Problems in American History* deals with Lexington and is an excellent introduction to the problem of historical truth. On the beginnings of the Revolution in the South see W.E.Dodd, 'Virginia Takes the Road to Revolution' in *The Spirit of Seventy-Six and other Essays*.

DECLARATION OF INDEPENDENCE. Carl Becker's *Declaration of Independence* is in a class by itself. H.Friedenwald, *Declaration of Independence* discusses the grievances in some detail, and T.V.Smith, *American Philosophy of Equality* is useful from other points of view. The best edition of Thomas Paine's Works is that of M.D.Conway (4 vols.), who also wrote the standard biography. *The Writings of Thomas Paine*, ed. Carl Van Doren, is a useful one-volume edition. The best critical appreciation of Paine is in V.L.Parrington, *Main Currents of American Thought*, vol.i.

LOYALISTS. M.C.Tyler, *Literary History* (see ch.13) is the best introduction; Lorenzo Sabine, *Biographical Sketches of Loyalists* (2 vols.) the best biographical compendium; there is a good essay in C.Becker, *Spirit of Seventy-Six;* C.H.Van Tyne, *Loyalists in the American Revolution* well covers the whole field; Lewis Einstein, *Divided Loyalties* takes in spies as well as refugees. Among the monographs are Isaac Harrell, *Loyalism in Virginia*, A.C.Flick, *Loyalism in New York*, R. O. De Mond, *The Loyalists in North Carolina during the Revolution*, L.H.Gipson,

Jared Ingersoll: A Study of American Loyalism, Carl Van Doren, *Secret History of the American Revolution,* E.Alfred Jones, *The Loyalists of Massachusetts.* The Loyalist point of view is well expressed in *The Diary and Letters of Thomas Hutchinson; The Journal and Letters of Samuel Curwen; Lieut. James Moody's Narrative of his Exertions and Sufferings.* G.E.Ellis, *Memoir of Sir Benjamin Thompson, Count Rumford* (also in vol.i of Rumford's *Works*), and J.A.Thompson, *Count Rumford* are biographies of the most distinguished American loyalist. W.C.Abbott, *New York in the American Revolution* includes a lively account of the city under British and tory rule. Important sources are Alexander Fraser's report on United Empire loyalists in Second *Report of Bureau of Archives for Province of Ontario* (2 vols.), and D.P.Coke's notes, edited by H.E.Egerton and published by the Roxburghe Club as *The Royal Commission on the Losses and Services of the American Loyalists.* The best studies on the dispersion of the Loyalists are by W.H. Siebert, in the *Miss.Val.Hist.Rev.,* vols.i, ii, vii, *Ohio State Univ.Bulletin,* vols.xvii–xxvi, and elsewhere.

SOURCE SELECTIONS. Morison, *Sources and Documents,* pp.97–161, and Commager, *Documents,* Nos.49–67; Jones and Leisy, *Major American Writers,* pp.151–68 (Paine); Callender, *Selections from Economic History,* pp.142–63.

X. *THE WAR OF INDEPENDENCE,* 1775–83

MILITARY HISTORY. There is no first-class military history of the War of Independence, nor any body of printed sources, excepting Henri Doniol, *Histoire de la France à l'établissement des Etats-Unis d'Amérique* (5 vols.), and the rare *Stevens Facsimiles.* Carrington, *Battles of the Revolution* and *Washington the General,* Col.F.Vinton Greene, *The Revolutionary War,* and Sir John W.Fortescue, *History of the British Army,* vol.iii, are by military men with strong prejudices. G.H.Guttridge has said all that can be said for Lord George Germain in *Amer.Hist.Rev.,* xxxiii.23–43. Rupert Hughes's *George Washington,* vol.iii, covers the period 1777–81, and is a great improvement over the earlier volumes, though still somewhat marred by the 'debunking' spirit. T.G.Frothingham, *Washington, Commander-in-Chief,* is the best brief survey of the Revolutionary years. Bernard Knollenberg, *Washington and the Revolution, a Reappraisal* is critical of Washington and sympathetic towards Gates. S.W.Patterson, *Horatio Gates, Defender of American Liberties* is an apology for that much abused general. J.M.Palmer, *General von Steuben* illuminates the problem of discipline and training in the American army. Henry Lee, *Memoirs of the War in the Southern Department* is a classic. C.Hatch, *Administration of the American Revolutionary Army* is the unique study of that important subject; cf.E.Curtis *The Organiza-tion of the British Army in the American Revolution.* Col.J.W.Wright's 'Notes on the Continental Army' in *William and Mary Quarterly,* xi.81–105, 185–209, is the best account of organization, strategy, and tactics. T.S.Anderson, *The Command of the Howe Brothers* settles one con-troversy. Good monographs on campaigns: Howard Swiggett, *War Out of Niagara;* Hoffman Nickerson, *The Turning Point of the Revolution, or Burgoyne in America* (cf.Jane Clark's article compiled from the Clin-ton Papers, in *Amer.Hist.Rev.,* xxxv.542); W.S.Stryker, *The Battle of Monmouth;* James A.James, *The Life of George Rogers Clark.* Good en-emy soldiers' narratives are *The Diary of Frederick Mackenzie* (2 vols.), Thomas Anburey, *Travels through America* (2 vols.), R.W.Pettingill (ed.), *Letters from America . . . of Brunswick, Hessian, and Waldeck Officers,* which supplements the classic *Letters and Journals of the Bar-oness Riedesel.* There is still nothing to equal B.J.Lossing's old *Field-Book of the Revolution* (3 vols.) as a guide to the battlefields.

FINANCE. C.J.Bullock, *Finances of the United States, 1775–1789* is the most scholarly treatment. William G.Sumner, *The Financier and Finances of the American Revolution* (2 vols.); E.P.Oberholtzer, *Robert Morris* (2 vols.); the early chapters of D.R.Dewey, *Financial History of the United States;* and R.V.Harlow, 'Aspects of Revolutionary Finance,' *Amer.Hist.Rev.,* xxxv.46, are recommended.

NAVAL HISTORY AND YORKTOWN. Admiral A.T.Mahan, *The Influence of Sea-Power in History* takes a world-wide view; his *Major Operations of the War of Independence* is more detailed. Gardner W.Allen, *Naval History of the American Revolution* (2 vols.) is the standard history of the continental navy, E.S.Maclay, *History of Ameri-can Privateers,* of the private armed vessels. William M.James, *The British Navy in Adversity* tells that side. Mrs.R.DeKoven has written the stand-ard *Life of John Paul Jones.* J.L.Howard, *Seth Harding, Mariner* is a vivacious sea journal of a lesser figure. The best account of the naval ves-sels and conditions of the time, of D'Estaing's fiasco and the Battle off the Capes, is in Admiral F.E.Chadwick's introduction to *The Graves Papers.* Col.H.F.Landers, *Virginia Campaign and Blockade and Siege of York-town* (71st Cong.3d.session, Sen.Doc.273) covers the land campaign; Capt. D.W.Knox, *The Naval Genius of Washington,* is significant.

DIPLOMACY. S.F.Bemis, *The Diplomacy of the American Revolu-tion* is the best survey and most accurate history of the peace negotiations. Of the secondary authorities, consult C.Van Doren, *Secret History of the American Revolution,* and Weldon A.Brown, *Empire or Independ-ence: A Study of the Failure of Reconciliation;* E.S.Corwin, *French Policy and the American Alliance;* P.C.Phillips, *The West in the Di-plomacy of the American Revolution* for the Spanish attempt at ex-pansion; T.P.Abernethy, 'Silas Deane' in *Amer.Hist.Rev.,* xxxix.477, and B.J.Hendrick, *The Lees of Virginia* for Arthur Lee; J.B.Perkins, *France in the American Revolution* for French aid in general. On the Canadian aspect see G.M.Wrong, *Canada and the American Revolution;* V.F.Barnes, ' Gov.Francis Legge of Nova Scotia,' *N.E.Quarterly,* iv.420. Essential documents will be found in Doniol (see § V); in Francis Wharton, *The Diplomatic Correspondence of the American Revolution* (6 vols.); Juan F.Yela Utrilla, *España ante la independencia de los Estados Unidos* (2 vols.); and *Correspondence of George III,* vols.iv, v. British peace proposals of 1778 are printed in Morison, *Sources and Documents,* and analyzed in G.H.Guttridge, *David Hartley.* Other source selections in Callender, *Selections from Economic History,* pp. 159–67, and Commager, *Documents,* Nos.59, 69, 74. Kenneth Roberts has edited a fascinating collection, *March to Quebec; Journals of the Members of Arnold's Expedition.*

XI. *FROM COLONY TO COMMONWEALTH,* 1775–92

GENERAL. Channing, *History of U.S.,* vol.iii; Allan Nevins, *American States During and After the Revolution.* Johann D. Schoepf, *Travels in the Confederation* (trans.by A.J.Morrison), and Joseph Hadfield, *An Englishman in America, 1785* are among the most useful travels.

STATE CONSTITUTIONS. Nevins, op.cit.; W.F.Dodd, *Revision and Amendment of State Constitutions;* W.C.Morey, *The First State Constitutions,* in *Annals* of the American Academy, vol.iv. The constitutions themselves are most readily available in F.N.Thorpe, *American Charters, Constitutions and Organic Laws* (7 vols.). A good brief history of state constitutions is J.Q.Dealey, *Growth of American State Constitutions.* Special studies: J.P.Selsam, *Pennsylvania Constitution of 1776;* Leonard Lundin, *Cockpit of the Revolution: The War for Independence in New Jersey;* B.A.Konkle, *George Bryan and the Const.of Penna.;* J.C.Meyer, *Church and State in Massachusetts;* S.E.Morison, ' Struggle over Adoption of the Const.of Mass.,' *Proceedings Mass.Hist.Soc.,* l.353. T.F.Moran, *Rise and Development of the Bicameral System in America* (Johns Hopkins *Studies,* series XIII.); H.B.Grigsby, *The Virginia Convention of 1776;* A.Jellinek, *Declaration of the Rights of Man.*

POLITICAL AND SOCIAL REFORM. Nevins, op.cit., J.F.Jameson, *American Revolution Considered as a Social Movement;* J.T.Adams, *New England in the Republic;* R.J.Purcell, *Connecticut in Transition;* Edward McCrady, *South Carolina in the Revolution* (2 vols.). Richard F.Upton, *Revolutionary New Hampshire;* J.C.Ballagh, *White Servitude in Virginia;* E.T.McCormac, *White Servitude in Maryland.*

RELIGION. H.J.Eckenrode, *Separation of Church and State in Virginia,* R.B.Semple, *Rise and Progress of Baptists in Virginia,* S.B.Weeks,

Church and State in North Carolina, and R.C.Strickland, *Religion and the State in Georgia in the Eighteenth Century* are adequate for Southern disestablishment. W.M.Gewehr, *The Great Awakening in Virginia* gives the background and Kate Rowland's biography of *George Mason* gives additional data. W.W.Sweet, *The Story of Religion,* and W.P. Trent, 'Constitution-Making in American Churches,' in J.F.Jameson, *Essays in Const.History,* describe the reorganization. Peter Guilday, *Life and Times of John Carroll* (2 vols.) is a fascinating story of the Catholic Church. For the free-thinking movement, freemasonry, etc., consult G.A. Koch, *Republican Religion,* and B.Faÿ, *The Revolutionary Spirit in France and America.*

SLAVERY. M.S.Locke, *Anti-Slavery in America, 1619–1808* has the most comprehensive account of slavery and emancipation at the Revolutionary period. In the Johns Hopkins *Studies* are a series of monographs on slavery in the different states: B.C.Steiner, *Conn.,* J.R.Brackett, *Maryland,* J.S.Bassett, *North Carolina,* H.S.Cooley, *New Jersey;* to which add G.H.Moore, *Slavery in Mass.,* and J.C.Ballagh, *History of Slavery in Virginia.* Elizabeth Donnan, *Documents Illustrative of the Slave Trade in America* (4 vols.) is comprehensive, and her 'New England Slave Trade after the Revolution,' *N.E.Quarterly,* iii.251, shows that there was more than met the eye of W.E.B.DuBois, *Suppression of the African Slave Trade.* There is a vast mass of material in Helen T.Catterall (ed.), *Judicial Cases Concerning American Slavery* (5 vols., use index).

ARTS, LETTERS, AND EDUCATION. H.R.Warfel, *Noah Webster, Schoolmaster;* E.C.Shoemaker, *Noah Webster, Pioneer of Learning;* Nathan Goodman, *Benjamin Rush;* B.A.Konkle, *Joseph Hopkinson;* T.A.Zunder, *Early Days of Joel Barlow;* Solon J. Buck, *The Planting of Civilization in Western Pennsylvania;* H.B.Adams, *The College of William and Mary;* J.H.Easterby, *History of the College of Charleston;* T.H.Montgomery, *History of the University of Pennsylvania;* S.E.Morison, *Three Centuries of Harvard.* See the sketches of the various persons mentioned in the text in *Dictionary of American Biography.*

THE WEST AND VERMONT. John Pell, *Ethan Allen,* J.B.Wilbur, *Ira Allen,* and M.B.Jones, *Vermont in the Making* cover Vermont politics and separatism. Stewart Holbrook has a popular biography of *Ethan Allen.* Theodore Roosevelt, *The Winning of the West* (4 vols.), written in a tone of red-blooded morality and weak on economic factors, is the most readable narrative history of the early Northwest. Justin Winsor, *The Westward Movement* is more valuable but excessively dull. A part of the ground has been covered in both scholarly and readable fashion in Louise P.Kellogg, *The British Régime in Wisconsin and the Northwest.* Archibald Henderson, *Winning of the Old Southwest* is written in a spirited style, but over-emphasizes Judge Henderson and the Transylvania Company, which are somewhat deflated in W.S.Lester, *The Tran-*

sylvania Company. For constitutional history, H.G.Alden, *New Governments West of the Alleghanies,* and F.J.Turner, 'Western State Making
in the Revolutionary Era,' in his *Significance of Sections in American History* are particularly valuable. On the Wilderness Road see A.B.Hulbert,
Boone's Wilderness Road and C.A.Hanna, *The Wilderness Trail,* which
relate to Pennsylvania and the Northwest. There are a few good biographies for this period, but C.S.Driver, *John Sevier;* Edna Kenton, *Simon
Kenton;* J.A.James, *George Rogers Clark* and *Oliver Pollak;* and R.G.
Thwaites, *Daniel Boone* can be recommended.

SOURCE SELECTIONS. Morison, *Sources and Documents,* pp. 149–
204; Commager, *Documents,* Nos.67, 68, 70, 73, 75–81; Jones and Leisy,
Major American Writers, pp. 181–99 (Freneau).

XII. *THE CONFEDERATION,* 1777–89

GENERAL. A.C.McLaughlin, *Confederation and Constitution* is still
the best general account. John Fiske, *The Critical Period in American
History* is a charmingly written classic, based largely on secondary works,
which paints too dark a picture of the Confederation. J.B.McMaster, *History of the People of the United States,* vol.i, gives a detailed survey of the
social and economic life of the time. There is a mass of material in Burn-
ett's *Continental Congress.* Merrill Jensen, *The Articles of Confederation*
emphasizes the economic influences in the Confederation Congresses.
Robert A. East, *Business Enterprise in the American Revolutionary Era*
illuminates the forces making for a revision of the articles. David Ram-
say, *History of the American Revolution* is a contemporary account that
contains a wealth of material. For Finances, see § V.

FOREIGN AFFAIRS. S.F.Bemis, *Jay's Treaty* is an exhaustive and
impartial examination of Anglo-American relations beginning with this
period. E.Channing's *History,* vol.iii, contains excellent chapters on commercial relations. A.B.Whitaker, *The Spanish-American Frontier* is a
study of the relations of Spain and the United States in the West. Frank
Monaghan, *John Jay* is the best life of the Secretary of Foreign Affairs.

LAND POLICY AND THE ORDINANCES. Thomas P.Abernethy,
Western Lands and the American Revolution is the most recent and the
best work on the subject. A.B.Hinsdale, *The Old Northwest;* J.A.Barrett,
Evolution of the Ordinance of 1787; and J.Winsor, *The Westward Move-
ment, 1763–1789* are also valuable. On special aspects see K.P.Bailey, *The
Ohio Company of Virginia and the Westward Movement;* P.J.Treat,
National Land System, 1785–1820; C.W.Alvord, *The Illinois Country;*
and H.B.Adams, *Maryland's influence upon land cessions to the United
States* (J.H.U.Studies, ser.III).

The best study of Shays's Rebellion is in J.T.Adams, *New England in the Republic.* Cf.R.E.Moody, ' Samuel Ely, Forerunner of Shays,' *N.E. Quarterly,* v.105; J.P.Warren, ' The Confederation and the Shays Rebellion,' *Am.Hist.Rev.,* vol.xi; and A.E.Morse, *The Federalist Party in Massachusetts.* For special phases of Confederation see E.Wilder Spaulding, *New York in the Critical Period;* Thomas Cochran, *New York and the Confederation;* R.J.Upton, *Revolutionary New Hampshire.*

SOURCE SELECTIONS. Callender, *Selections from Economic History,* pp. 180–235; Morison, *Sources and Documents,* pp. 204–33; Commager, *Documents,* Nos.72, 75–78, 82.

XIII. *THE FEDERAL CONSTITUTION*

GENERAL. For a survey of the movement, A.C.McLaughlin, *Confederation and Constitution,* R.L.Schuyler, *The Constitution of the United States,* Max Farrand, *Framing of the Constitution* and *Fathers of the Constitution* are to be preferred. A day-by-day summary of the Federal Convention is Charles Warren, *The Making of the Constitution.* A.T. Prescott, *Drafting the Federal Constitution* is useful. The secondary literature on the Convention and the Constitution is enormous, but a great deal of it has been inspired by patriotic enthusiasm rather than by historical zeal. Highly important is Charles A.Beard, *Economic Interpretation of the Constitution,* a stimulating and scholarly piece of work; and, of a more general nature, A.C.McLaughlin, *Foundations of American Constitutionalism* and *Constitutional History of the United States.* Biographies of the framers are illuminating: see references in the *Dictionary of American Biography,* and such studies as L.S.Mayo, *John Langdon of New Hampshire,* George C.Groce, *William Samuel Johnson,* and T.Roosevelt, *Gouverneur Morris.* There are numerous biographies of Madison, but Irving Brandt, *James Madison* promises to supplant earlier studies by Gaillard Hunt, S.H.Gay, and Abbott Smith. Two of the critics of the Constitution are ably sketched in E.W.Spaulding, *His Excellency George Clinton,* and Helen Hull, *George Mason, Constitutionalist.*

JUDICIAL REVIEW. C.G.Haines, *The American Doctrines of Judicial Supremacy;* C.Beard, *The Supreme Court and the Constitution;* Charles Warren, *The Making of the Constitution;* Louis Boudin, *Government by Judiciary* (2 vols.); R.K.Carr, *The Supreme Court and Judicial Review;* C.Warren, *Congress, The Constitution, and the Supreme Court;* E.S.Corwin, *The Doctrine of Judicial Review;* and the selection of cases and documents in Commager, *Documents,* Nos.73, 89, 91, 109. J.B. Thayer's essay ' The Origin and Scope of the American Doctrine of Constitutional Law ' in his collected *Legal Essays* is still the most profound and penetrating thing written on the subject.

RATIFICATION. A.J.Beveridge, *Life of John Marshall*, vol.i, con. tains a lively account of the struggle for ratification in the state conventions, whose proceedings are printed in full in J.Elliot, *Debates in the Several State Conventions* (5 vols.); those of Virginia are selected in Morison, *Sources and Documents*, pp.307–62. Important monographs on ratification are O.G.Libby, *The Geographical Distribution of the Vote on the Federal Constitution* (for criticism, see C.A.Beard, *Economic Origins of Jeffersonian Democracy*). J.B.McMaster and F.D.Stone, *Pennsylvania and the Federal Convention, 1787–1788;* S.B.Harding, *Contest over Ratification in Massachusetts;* C.E.Miner, *Ratification of the Federal Constitution in the State of New York;* L.I.Trenholme, *Ratification of the Federal Constitution in North Carolina;* B.C.Steiner, *Maryland's Adoption* (*Am.Hist.Rev.*, v.22, 207); F.G.Bates, *Rhode Island and the Union;* and H.G.Grisby, *History of the Virginia Federal Convention of 1788.*

SOURCES. Fundamental to any study of the Constitution are the *Records of the Federal Convention* (4 vols.), ed. by Max Farrand, or *Documents Illustrative of the Formation of the Union*, ed. by Charles C. Tansill and published by the U.S.Government. Selections are in Morison, *Sources and Documents*, pp.233–92, Commager, *Documents*, Nos.83–88. The classic contemporary analysis of the Constitution is *The Federalist*, written by Madison, Hamilton, and Jay.

XIV. *THE UNITED STATES IN* 1790

A Century of Population Growth, 1790–1900, tabulates the results of the Census of 1790, with maps and useful descriptive matter. It is supplemented by E.B.Greene and V.D.Harrington, *American Population before the Census of 1790*. Among the more useful contemporary works are Jedidiah Morse, *American Geography;* Jefferson's *Notes on Virginia;* W.S.Robertson (ed.), *The Diary of Francisco de Miranda . . . 1783–84;* Thomas Anburey, *Travels through the Interior Parts of America in 1776–81* (2 vols.); Francis Baily, *Journal of a Tour in Unsettled Parts of North America in 1796 and 1797; The Cazenove Journal, 1794;* Marquis de Chastellux, *Travels in North America in 1780–82* (2 vols.); La Rochefoucauld-Liancourt, *Travels through the U.S., 1795–97* (2 vols.); C.F. Volney, *View of the Climate and Soil of the U.S.A.* The three last are translated from the French. The reader should be warned against romantic travellers such as Jonathan Carver, Bartram, Chateaubriand, and land-jobbers such as Brissot and Imlay. Henry Adams, *History of the United States*, vol.i, ch.i–vi is a brilliant analysis and interpretation of America in 1800. Turgot's *Letter to Dr.Price* is printed in the later editions of Price's *Observations on the Importance of the American Revolu-*

tion; cf.Roland Thomas, *Richard Price,* chap.v. There is abundant material, too, in J.B.McMaster, *History,* vols.i and ii. Allan Nevins, *American Social History as seen by British Travelers* has an extensive bibliography.

XV. *WASHINGTON, HAMILTON, AND JEFFERSON,* 1789–92

GENERAL. Claude G.Bowers, *Jefferson and Hamilton* is a vivacious but somewhat partisan history of the period. Beveridge's *Marshall,* vols.i and ii is equally prejudiced on the Federalist side. Of the general history, Channing's vol.iv and McMaster's i and ii may be supplemented by the more detailed R.Hildreth, *History of the United States,* vol.iii.

BIOGRAPHIES. We are still awaiting 'definite' biographies of Washington, Hamilton, and Jefferson. Worthington C.Ford's *Washington* (2 vols.) may be supplemented by N.W.Stephenson and Waldo H. Dunne, *George Washington* (2 vols.); P.L.Ford, *The True George Washington;* P.L.Haworth, *George Washington: Farmer;* John Corbin, *The Unknown Washington;* and Charles H.Ambler, *George Washington and the West.* Shelby Little, *George Washington* is perhaps the most adequate, one-volume biography but John C.Fitzpatrick, *George Washington* is built upon a broad basis of source material. Hamilton and Jefferson have suffered not only from each other's biographers, but from the zeal of their own. Readers of Senator Lodge's artistic *Alexander Hamilton* should remember that the author was a lifelong opponent of almost everything dear to Jefferson. A.McL.Hamilton, *Intimate Life of Alex. Hamilton* is an excellent personal study. W.G.Sumner's *Hamilton* is the most comprehending biography of him, written by an economist who as a dogmatic free-trader could not be quite fair. W.S.Culbertson, *Hamilton: An Essay* is useful on the economic side. The analysis of Hamilton in Parrington's *Main Currents,* vol.i. is penetrating and brilliant though strongly partisan. H.S.Randall, *Life of Thomas Jefferson* (3 vols.) is a classic partisan biography; James Parton's old biography is more readable. Gilbert Chinard, *Jefferson, Apostle of Americanism* (1929) is the best one-volume biography, but Francis W.Hirst's brilliant *Life and Letters of Thomas Jefferson* is somewhat better on the personal and cultural side. Saul K.Padover, *Thomas Jefferson* presents him as a precursor of the New Deal. Gaillard Hunt, *Life of James Madison* is sound and adequate. Irving Brandt, *James Madison,* in progress, promises to be the most thorough and understanding of all Madison biographies. Henry Adams, *Albert Gallatin* is one of the great political biographies of our literature. Lewis Leary, *That Rascal Freneau* tells the story of the poet and penman of the Jeffersonian party. *The Dictionary of American Biography* contains full bibliographical data.

WRITINGS OF STATESMEN of this period, especially their letters, are in general more useful than the biographies. John C.Fitzpatrick, *Writings of Washington* (in progress) is the most complete for him. H.C.Lodge, *Works of Hamilton* (12 vols.); P.L.Ford, *Writings of Jefferson* (10 vols.), and Gaillard Hunt, *Writings of Madison* (9 vols.) are to be preferred for these three statesmen, but A.E.Bergh (ed.), *The Writings of Thomas Jefferson* (20 vols.) has material not to be found in the Ford edition. J.T.Adams (ed.), *Jeffersonian Ideals* and *Hamiltonian Ideals* are excellent brief selections. J.G.deR.Hamilton (ed.), *The Best Letters of Jefferson* is revealing. C.F.Adams (ed.), *Works of John Adams with a Life* (10 vols.) is the only edition of Adams's writings. A new edition of the *Writings* of John Jay, ed. by Frank Monaghan, is promised. *The Works of Fisher Ames* (2 vols.) is important for Federalist ideas (cf.S.E.Morison, in *N.E.Quarterly,* vol.i), as are those of John Taylor for the Republicans. The last have never been reprinted, but are well summarized by C.A.Beard, with other material that sustains his thesis, in his *Economic Origins of Jeffersonian Democracy.*

ORGANIZATION OF THE FEDERAL GOVERNMENT. R.V.Harlow, *History of Legislative Methods before 1825;* H.B.Learned, *The President's Cabinet;* Gaillard Hunt, *The Department of State;* G.E. Haynes, *The Senate of the United States* (2 vols.); E.C.Corwin, *The President, Office and Powers;* Charles Warren, *Supreme Court in United States History* (2 vols.) and his ' First Decade of the Supreme Court' in *Univ. of Chicago Law Rev.,* vol.vii. These may be supplemented by the articles of G.Hunt on ' Office-Seeking' in the *Amer.Hist.Rev.,* vols.i and ii. *The Journal of William Maclay* gives an intimate picture of the Congress, by an Anti-federalist senator.

SOURCE SELECTIONS. Commager, *Documents,* Nos.90–95, 97.

XVI. *FRENCH REVOLUTION AND SECOND WASHINGTON ADMINISTRATION,* 1789-97

FRENCH REVOLUTION AND NEUTRALITY. C.D.Hazen, *Contemporary American Opinion of the French Revolution;* Bernard Faÿ, *The Revolutionary Spirit in France and the United States* is a spirited history of cultural relations which may be supplemented by H.M.Jones, *America and French Culture, 1750–1848.* F.J.Turner has published a wealth of material on Genet in Amer.Hist.Assoc.*Reports,* 1896, vol.i and 1897, and summarized them in the *Amer.Hist.Rev.,* vol.iii. There is an account of the Genet episode in McMaster, *The United States,* vol.ii. M. Minnigerode, *Jefferson, Friend of France* is bitterly prejudiced, but has an extended account of Genet. The impact of the Revolution on the United States is analyzed in Parrington's *Main Currents,* vol.i, and his lengthy introduction to *The Hartford Wits*. S.E.Forman, *The Political Activities of Philip Freneau* is a capital study of Jefferson's literary lieutenant.

FOREIGN RELATIONS are so interwoven with the history of this period that most of the works listed in § XV may be consulted with profit. A good general account is Arthur B.Darling, *Our Rising Empire, 1763–1803*. The *Correspondence of French Ministers to the U.S., 1791–1797; Letters of William Vans Murray to J.Q.Adams, 1797–1803;* and *Papers of James A.Bayard, 1796–1815* are printed in the *Reports* of the American Historical Association for 1903 (vol.ii), 1912, and 1913 (vol.ii) respectively; other correspondence in the *Reports* for 1896 (i), 1897 (ii), and 1898. W.R.Manning, *Nootka Sound Controversy* is in the *Reports* for 1904. The dispatches of Rufus King, American Minister to Great Britain, 1796–1803, are in C.R.King, *Life and Correspondence of Rufus King* (6 vols.), B.C.Davenport (ed.), *Diary of Gouverneur Morris* (2 vols.), H.P.Johnston, *Correspondence and Public Papers of John Jay* (4 vols.), Monaghan, *John Jay*, the *Writings of J.Q.Adams*, vols.i, ii, and the *Reports* of the Canadian Archives for 1889–1891 and 1894 contain additional material. F.J.Turner, 'Origin of Genet's Projected Attack' in his *Significance of Sections;* B.W.Bond, *The Monroe Mission to France*. S.F.Bemis, *Jay's Treaty* is an exhaustive examination of Anglo-American relations, beginning with this period. His bibliography lists all the important monographs and printed sources. On neutrality see C.M.Thomas, *American Neutrality in 1793*. Important articles on the Navigation Acts by J.H.Clapham in *Engl.Hist.Rev.*, vol.xxv, and D.O. McGovney in *Amer.Hist.Rev.*, vol.ix, should not be overlooked.

THE WEST AND INDIAN AFFAIRS. C.W.Alvord, *The Illinois Country* (vol.i of *Centennial History of Illinois*); M.M.Quaife, *Chicago and the Old Northwest*, and B.W.Bond, *Civilization of the Old Northwest* are the best accounts of government and settlement. C.E.Slocum, *The Ohio Country between 1783 and 1815* is ponderous but useful, as is Louise P.Kellogg, *The British Regime in Wisconsin and the Northwest*. On military affairs see Emerson Wildes *Anthony Wayne* and T.Boyd, *Mad Anthony Wayne*. A.P.Whitaker, *Spanish-American Frontier, 1783– 1795*, and S.F.Bemis, *Pinckney's Treaty* are important works on this period in Spanish-Indian-American relations. See also references in § V. Other articles and documents will be found in *Amer.Hist.Rev.*, vii.706; viii.78; ix.490, 533, 748; xi.794; *Miss.Val.Hist.Rev.*, iii.462; xii.155; *Proceedings Miss.Val.Hist.Assoc.*, xi.260.

The Whisky Rebellion may be studied in H.Adams, *Life of Albert Gallatin*, and in Leland Baldwin's racy *Whisky Rebels: The Story of a Frontier Uprising*. V.H.Paltsits, *Washington's Farewell Address* is the final word on that subject.

SOURCE SELECTIONS. Commager, *Documents*, Nos.96, 98–100.

XVII. *ADAMS'S ADMINISTRATION*, 1797–1801

GENERAL. C.F.Adams, *Works of J.Adams with a Life* (10 vols.). The only recent biography of the President is G.Chinard, *Honest John Adams*. B.C.Steiner, *Life and Correspondence of James McHenry* throws light on Adams's relations with his cabinet. J.S.Bassett, *The Federalist System*, and Claude G.Bowers, *Jefferson and Hamilton* are the most recent general treatments, and there is a great deal of material in A.J.Beveridge, *John Marshall*. Most of the biographies listed in § XV will be found useful. A.E.Morse, *Federalist Party in Massachusetts to the Year 1800*, Richard Purcell, *Connecticut in Transition*, and W.A.Robinson, *Jeffersonian Democracy in New England* describe the political background in that section.

FOREIGN RELATIONS. G.W.Allen, *Our Naval War with France*. C.L.Lokke, ' The Trumbull Episode,' *N.E.Quarterly*, vii.101; Morison, ' Elbridge Gerry,' *id.*, ii.6; Morison, *H.G.Otis*, i.59–198; Beveridge, *Marshall*, ii.214–373. F.J.Turner, ' Policy of France toward the Mississippi Valley,' in his *Significance of Sections*. A.P.Whitaker, *The Mississippi Question, 1795–1803*. See also § XVI.

ALIEN AND SEDITION ACTS, ETC. For the ' red ' scare, see G.A.Koch, *Republican Religion*, and V.Stauffer, *New England and the Bavarian Illuminati*. F.M.Anderson, ' Enforcement of the Alien and Sedition Acts,' Amer.Hist.Assoc. *Report*, 1912, and ' Contemporary Opinion of Virginia and Kentucky Resolutions,' *Amer.Hist.Rev.*, v.45, 225. P.G. Davidson, ' Virginia and Alien and Sedition Laws,' *ibid.*, xxxvi.336. E.D. Warfield, *The Kentucky Resolutions;* J.F.McLaughlin, *Matthew Lyon*. Dumas Malone, *Thomas Cooper;* A.C.McLaughlin, *Courts, Constitutions and Parties*, ch.iv; and E.P.Powell, *Nullification and Secession in the United States*.

SOURCE SELECTIONS. Commager, *Documents*, Nos.101–104.

XVIII–XIX. *JEFFERSON'S ADMINISTRATIONS*, 1801–09

GENERAL. Most of the works mentioned in the previous section are useful for this period as well; but the pre-eminent authority is Henry Adams, *History of the United States, 1801–1817* (9 vols.). Adams has the best style of any historian who has treated this period, and his work has been superseded on very few points. His attitude toward Jefferson is detached and mildly ironical; his descriptive chapters in the first and the last volumes are incomparable. His *Life of Gallatin* is one of the best Republican biographies, and W.E.Dodd, *Life of Nathaniel Macon* a valuable study of one of Jefferson's most trusted disciples. William B. Hatcher, *Edward Livingston* is critical of Jefferson. C.M.Wiltse, *The*

Jeffersonian Tradition in American Politics is the most thoughtful book on that subject. Claude Bowers, *Jefferson in Power* is partisan but vigorous and interesting. Alfred T.Mahan, *Sea Power in its Relations to the French Revolution* (2 vols.) is indispensable for the diplomacy of the period, but was written to prove a thesis, and to influence naval policy. For the actual ships of the navy, see Howard I.Chapelle, *History of American Sailing Ships,* chap.ii. For the social and political background of Washington, G.Hunt (ed.), *First Forty Years of Washington Society portrayed by the family letters of Mrs.Samuel H.Smith,* and E.S.Brown (ed.), *William Plumer's Memorandum, 1803–1807* are excellent.

LOUISIANA PURCHASE, AND CONSPIRACIES. Henry Adams is detailed and scholarly. J.A.Robertson, *Louisiana under Spain, France and the United States* (2 vols.) contains a mass of source material. E.Brown, *Constitutional History of the Louisiana Purchase* covers that phase adequately; I.J.Cox, *The West Florida Controversy* is exhaustive. See also E.Wilson Lyon, *Louisiana in French Diplomacy* and his ' Closing the Port of New Orleans,' *Amer.Hist.Rev.,* xxxvii.280. The principal documents for the Federalist plot of 1804 are printed in H.Adams (ed.), *Documents relating to New England Federalism,* and the intrigues are analyzed in Morison, *H.G.Otis,* ch.xv. The Hamilton-Burr duel is best described in A.McL.Hamilton, *Intimate Life of Hamilton.* There is no adequate life of Aaron Burr, whose conspiracy is best dealt with in W.F. McCaleb, *Burr Conspiracy;* James Parton, *Life and Times of Aaron Burr* is still fascinating reading. Holmes Alexander, *Aaron Burr* and Nathan Schachner, *Aaron Burr* are more recent but less satisfactory, and James R.Jacobs, *Tarnished Warrior: Major-General James Wilkinson* is definitive. Beveridge's *Marshall* and W.C.Bruce, *John Randolph of Roanoke* are valuable for the case of Marbury *v.* Madison, and the Chase impeachment. For the question of judicial review see § XIII.

CORSAIRS AND NEUTRAL RIGHTS. The Tripolitan War is described in G.W.Allen, *Our Navy and the Barbary Corsairs;* cf.R.H.Irwin, *Diplomatic Relations of U.S. with Barbary Powers, 1776–1816.* There are convenient summaries of the Orders in Council, French Decrees, and American Retaliatory Acts in Channing's *History,* vol.iv. Allen Johnson, *Jefferson and his Colleagues* has an excellent discussion of the Barbary Corsairs. L.M.Sears, *Jefferson and the Embargo* is the best study of that experiment. Consult also W.W.Jennings, *The American Embargo, 1807–1809.* F.E.Melvin, *Napoleon's Navigation System* is an important monograph. Morison, *Maritime Hist. of Mass.* describes the actual trading at this period, and is supplemented by an article in *N.E.Quarterly,* i.208–25.

SOURCE SELECTIONS. Commager, *Documents,* Nos.106–113.

XX. *THE WAR OF* 1812

GENERAL. For the West, the Indians, and the origin of the war, see J.W.Pratt, *Expansionists of 1812,* and M.M.Quaife, *Chicago and the Old Northwest.* A.L.Burt, *The United States, Great Britain and British North America from the Revolution to the Peace after the War of 1812* challenges some of the conclusions of Pratt, and is immensely valuable on all aspects of Canadian-American relations. The best histories from the three national points of view are Henry Adams, *History,* vols.vii-ix; J.W.Fortescue, *History of the British Army,* vol.viii and C.P.Lucas, *The Canadian War of 1812.* A.T.Mahan, *Sea Power in its Relations to the War of 1812* (2 vols.) is the best naval history; for a description of the American navy of that era see the old but fascinating G.Coggeshall, *History of American Privateers and Letters of Marque,* and H.I.Chapelle, *History of American Sailing Ships,* ch.ii. Good monographs: L.L.Babcock, *War of 1812 on the Niagara Frontier,* J.W.Pratt, 'Fur Trade and the Left Flank, 1812,' *Amer.Hist.Rev.,* xl.246, and the last chapters of Louise Kellogg, *British Régime in Wisconsin.* On Madison and the war, T.C.Smith, 'War Guilt in 1812.' *Proceedings Mass.Hist.Soc.,* vol.lxiv is conclusive.

PEACE OF GHENT AND HARTFORD CONVENTION. C.E.Hill, *Leading American Treaties* and *Diary of James Gallatin, Peace Maker* are good introductions. F.A.Updike, *Diplomacy of the War of 1812* is the principal monograph. Important documents are in Wellington's *Supplementary Despatches,* vol.ix; Castlereagh's *Correspondence,* vol.x; J.Q.Adams's *Writings,* vol.v, and *Memoirs,* vols.ii, iii; Gallatin's *Writings* (2 vols.). The Hartford Convention is treated at length in S.E.Morison, *H.G.Otis,* vol.ii; supplementary facts and documents are in *Proceedings Miss.Val.Hist.Assoc.,* vi.176; *Proceedings Mass.Hist.Soc.,* xlviii.343; lx.24; *N.E.Quarterly,* iii.316.

SOURCE SELECTIONS. H.V.Ames, *State Documents on Federal Relations,* pp.45-88; Commager, *Documents,* Nos.114-117; William Wood, *Select British Documents of the Canadian War of 1812* (3 vols.); H.Adams, *Documents Relating to N.E. Federalism.*

XXI. *ERA OF GOOD FEELINGS,* 1815-22

GENERAL. F.J.Turner, *Rise of the New West* (*American Nation,* xiv) is the best single volume covering this period. Adams's diary, published as the *Memoirs of J.Q.Adams, 1795-1848* (12 vols., or one volume of selections edited by Allan Nevins), W.C.Ford (ed.), *Writings of J.Q. Adams* (7 vols.), and S.M.Hamilton (ed.), *Writings of Monroe* (7 vols.) are important sources. Carl Schurz, *Henry Clay* (2 vols.) is one of the best American biographies. There is no adequate biography of Monroe; that by G.Morgan is amusing. Material for an appreciation of J.Q.Adams may be found in Brooks Adams's introduction to Henry Adams, *The Degradation of the Democratic Dogma*, B.C.Clark, *J.Q.Adams*, and J.T. Adams, *The Adams Family*. For other biographies pertaining to the period see § XXIII. S.Rezneck describes the depression of 1819–21 in *Amer.Hist.Rev.*, xxxix.28.

MARSHALL AND THE COURTS. Consult especially the biography of Marshall by A.J.Beveridge, and Charles Warren, *The Supreme Court in United States History*. B.F.Wright, *Growth of American Constitutional Law* is useful. Correctives to Beveridge are E.S.Corwin, *John Marshall and the Constitution*, Louis Boudin, *Government by Judiciary*, and F.Frankfurter, *The Commerce Clause under Marshall, Taney and Waite*. The leading decisions can be found in John M.Dillon (ed.), *John Marshall; Complete Constitutional Decisions*, and P.Cotton, *Constitutional Decisions of John Marshall*. Contemporary criticism by Justice Spence Roane is reprinted in *John P.Branch Historical Papers*, 1905. Joseph Story's famous *Commentaries on the Constitution of the United States* (2 vols.), one of the formative influences on American law, should not be neglected. There is no satisfactory biography of Justice Story, but see W.W.Story's filiopietistic biography, and Roscoe Pound, *Formative Era of American Law*. An admirable study of another great moulder of American law is John T.Horton, *James Kent*. There is some interesting material in Elizabeth Baker, *Henry Wheaton*.

MISSOURI COMPROMISE. J.A.Woodburn, *The Historical Significance of the Missouri Compromise* (Amer.Hist.Assoc.*Report*, 1893), H.A.Trexler, *Slavery in Missouri, 1804–1865*, F.C.Shoemaker, *Missouri's Struggle for Statehood, 1804–1821*, and F.H.Hodder, *Side Lights on the Missouri Compromise* (*id.*, 1909) will be found suggestive. The accounts in F.J.Turner, *Rise of the New West*, and J.B.McMaster, *History* are satisfactory; the treatment in Von Holst's *Constitutional History* violently partisan. Timothy Flint, *Recollections of the Last Ten Years* is excellent for cultural background.

ANGLO–AMERICAN RELATIONS. W.A.Dunning, *The British Empire and the U.S.* writes from sound knowledge and with good humor. C.K.Webster, *Foreign Policy of Castlereagh, 1815–22* is fair and discriminating in his treatment of Anglo-American policy. H.Temperley, *Foreign Policy of Canning, 1822–27* gives a British point of view. J.Fred Rippy, *Rivalry of the U.S. and Great Britain for Latin America*, C.H.Levermore, *Disarmament on the Great Lakes* (World Peace Foundation pamphlets), F.L.Benns, *American Struggle for British West-India Carrying Trade, 1815–30*, and W.E.B.DuBois, *Suppression of African Slave Trade* are important monographs. There is a useful study of the Canadian boundary in the appendix to C.P.Lucas, *History of Canada.*

1763–1812, and a general account in J.M.Callahan, *American Foreign Policy in Canadian Relations.* Richard Rush published two volumes of extracts from his diary, with reminiscences for the years 1817–25, under various titles such as *The Court of London.*

SOURCE SELECTIONS. Commager, *Documents,* Nos.109, 117–123, 129, 137; H.V.Ames, *State Documents on Federal Relations,* pp.89–132.

XXII. *MONROE AND J. Q. ADAMS,* 1817–29

MONROE DOCTRINE. The above-mentioned works of Webster, Temperley, J.Q.Adams, and Rush are indispensable. J.Reuben Clark, *Memorandum on the Monroe Doctrine* (Government Printing Office, 1930) is a brief official history and interpretation. Dexter Perkins, *Hands Off; A History of the Monroe Doctrine* is incomparably the best general account, but his three-volume history should be consulted by the student. D.Y.Thomas, *One Hundred Years of the Monroe Doctrine,* and A.Alvarez, *The Monroe Doctrine,* with appendix including interpretations by American statesmen, are general surveys. The authorship of the doctrine is discussed by W.C.Ford in *Amer.Hist.Rev.,* vols.vii, viii. Edward H.Tatum, *The United States and Europe, 1815–1823;* C.C.Griffin, *The United States and the Disruption of the Spanish Empire, 1810–1822;* Whitaker, *The U.S. and the Independence of the Latin-American States;* F.L.Paxson, *The Independence of the South American Republics;* W.S.Robertson, *Rise of the Spanish-American Republics, as told in the lives of their Liberators,* and *Hispanic-American Relations with the United States* are the best works in English on those subjects; and their bibliographies list the many important studies in French and Spanish touching the Monroe Doctrine. F.A.Golder, *Russian Expansion on the Pacific, 1641–1850* and the works on Oregon and California listed below deal with the Pacific aspect of the question. For the Anglo-American rivalry in Mexico, the Cuban question, and the Panama Congress see W.R.Manning, *Early Diplomatic Relations between the U.S. and Mexico,* J.M.Callahan, *Cuba and International Relations.* These works are, however, written largely from American sources, and should be checked by dispatches and letters from British agents in Latin America, some of which are printed in the *Amer.Hist.Rev.,* vii.304, 500 and in J.Fred Rippy's works.

ADAMS'S ADMINISTRATION. See ch.XXIII.

SOURCE SELECTIONS. Commager, *Documents,* Nos.126–27, 130–31. W.R.Manning (ed.), *Diplomatic Correspondence of the U.S. concerning the Independence of the Latin American Nations,* 3 vols.

XXIII. *ANDREW JACKSON*, 1829–37

GENERAL. F.T.Turner, *Rise of the New West*, and *The United States, 1830–50*, and W.Macdonald, *Jacksonian Democracy* cover the Jacksonian era. T.P.Abernethy, *From Frontier to Plantation in Tennessee*, and Marquis James, *Andrew Jackson, The Border Captain* explain the Jacksonian background. J.S.Bassett, *Life of Andrew Jackson* is based on the Jackson MSS., and an excellent political history of the period; Bassett also edited the *Correspondence of Andrew Jackson* (7 vols.). James Parton, *Life of Jackson* (3 vols.) is a colorful old partisan biography; Marquis James, *Andrew Jackson: Portrait of a President* is one of the liveliest political biographies in our literature and C.G.Bowers, *Party Battles of the Jackson Period* one of the best political histories. E.C.Smith, *The Blair Family in Politics* (2 vols.) throws considerable light on party history of this and the following period. Gaillard Hunt, *John C. Calhoun* is the best life of the South Carolinian; the two-volume one by W.M.Meigs is more detailed, but partisan; the essay by W.E.Dodd in his *Statesmen of the Old South* is suggestive and stimulating. Calhoun's formal *Works* are in 6 vols.; selections from his correspondence are printed in *Amer. Hist.Rev.*, xl.82, 287, and *Report* of the Amer.Hist.Assoc. for 1899, ii. H.C. Lodge, *Daniel Webster*, and C.M.Fuess, *Daniel Webster* (2 vols.) are the best biographies of that statesman. C.H.Van Tyne (ed.), *Letters of Webster* are not included in the *Writings of Webster* (18 vols.), which are mostly speeches. Bernard Mayo, *Henry Clay* (in progress) is a scholarly and beautifully written biography; Carl Schurz's *Henry Clay* (2 vols.) is a literary classic, but partisan. *The Autobiography of Martin Van Buren* (*Report* of the Amer.Hist.Assoc. for 1918, vol.ii), and *The Autobiography of Amos Kendall* should be used with caution. Holmes Alexander, *Martin Van Buren* is a recent biography. G.Hunt, *The First Forty Years of Washington Society* and Josiah Quincy, *Figures of the Past* describe Washington in the Jackson era, and Allan Nevins (ed.), *The Diary of Philip Hone* (2 vols.) describes New York. Charles A.Davis, *The Letters of Major J.Downing,* is political satire in Yankee dialect.

POLITICAL CONDITIONS AND CONSTITUTIONAL CHANGES. Alexis de Tocqueville, *Democracy in America* is a classic contemporary account, and should be read with G.W.Pierson's learned and entertaining *Tocqueville and Beaumont in America*, which analyzes the sources of Tocqueville's information. J.B.McMaster, *The Acquisition of the Rights of Man in America* assembles a wealth of material in brief compass; M.Ostrogorski, *Democracy and the Party System* is a penetrating analysis; cf.A.C.McLaughlin, 'The Significance of Political Parties' in *The Courts, the Constitution and Parties*. Special studies of value are A.B.Darling, *Political Changes in Massachusetts, 1824–1848;* C.R.Fish, *Civil Service and Patronage;* D.R.Fox, *Decline of Aristocracy in the Pol-*

itics of New York; A.C.Cole, *Whig Party in the South;* E.Malcolm Carroll, *Origins of the Whig Party;* F.M.Green, *Constitutional Changes in the South Atlantic States, 1776–1860;* Jarvis M.Morse, *A Neglected Phase of Connecticut History, 1818–1850;* George Poage, *Henry Clay and the Whig Party;* T.P.Abernethy, *Frontier to Plantation in Tennessee;* and H.L.McBain, *De Witt Clinton and the Origin of the Spoils System.*

NULLIFICATION AND INDIAN REMOVAL. D.F.Houston, *Critical Study of Nullification in South Carolina,* C.S.Boucher, *Nullification Controversy in S.C.,* and J.G.Van Deusen, *Economic Bases of Disunion in S.C.* are the three best works. Dumas Malone, *Public Life of Thomas Cooper* is a notable biography. Grant Foreman, *Indians and Pioneers,* and *Indian Removal: The Emigration of the Five Civilized Tribes,* W.Lumpkin, *Removal of the Cherokee Indians from Georgia* (2 vols.), A.Abel, ' History of the Events Resulting in Indian Consolidation West of the Mississippi River ' in Am.Hist.Assoc. *Reports,* 1906, vol.I, cover that subject. The best account of the Black Hawk War is by T.C.Pease, in *The Centennial History of Illinois,* ii. There are good maps of these Indian wars and cessions in A.B.Hart, *The American Nation,* vols.xiv, xv.

BANK OF THE UNITED STATES AND PUBLIC LANDS. R.C.H.Catterall, *Second Bank of the U.S.* is the standard work. R.C. McGrane (ed.), *Correspondence of Nicholas Biddle, 1807–44* is illuminating. R.G.Wellington, *Political Influence of the Public Lands, 1828–42,* and G.M.Stephenson, *Political History of the Public Lands, 1840–62,* S.Sato, *History of the Land Question in the United States,* B.H.Hibbard, *History of Public Land Policies* are valuable monographs and Roy M. Robbins, *Our Landed Heritage* is a general account. An important subject is disposed of in R.C.McGrane, *Foreign Bondholders and American Debts.*

SOURCE SELECTIONS. A.C.McLaughlin (ed.), *Source Problems in U.S.History,* problem v; Commager, *Documents,* Nos.124, 128, 135, 138–48, 152–54; H.V.Ames, *State Documents on Federal Relations,* pp. 132–92.

XXIV. *THE NORTHERN STATES,* 1820–50

GENERAL. A large part of Channing's *History,* vol.v and of McMaster's *United States,* vols.v-vii is devoted to the subjects treated in this chapter. A rather careless survey is Carl R.Fish, *The Rise of the Common Man;* F.J.Turner, *The United States, 1830–50,* chaps.iii, iv, vii, is better. Meade Minnigerode, *The Fabulous Forties* is a lively, popular account of that decade, as is E.D.Branch, *The Sentimental Years* of the next. There is interesting material in A.Nevins, *American Social History as Seen by British Travelers,* and in Thomas Low Nichols, *Forty Years of*

American Life, 1821–1861, Josiah Quincy, *Figures of the Past,* E.E.Hale, *A New England Boyhood* and Lucy Larcom, *New England Girlhood.* Harriet Martineau, *Society in America,* and A.B.Benson (ed.), *America of the Fifties: Letters of Fredrika Bremer* (a selection from her *Homes of the New World,* 2 vols.) contain observations on American life by two gifted women. J.Fenimore Cooper, *The American Democrat* contains mordant comments by an American man of letters just returned from Europe. Horace Greeley, *Recollections of a Varied Life* is entertaining and illuminating.

WESTWARD MOVEMENT. F.J.Turner, *Rise of the New West;* F.L.Paxson, *History of the American Frontier.* C.H.Ambler, *History of Transportation in the Ohio Valley,* and A.B.Hulbert, *Paths of Inland Commerce* may be supplemented by Seymour Dunbar, *History of Travel in America* (4 vols.); A.F.Harlow, *Old Towpaths;* C.F.Carter, *When Railroads Were New.* K.W.Porter, *John Jacob Astor* is a definitive biography of the greatest American fur trader. On agriculture and public lands see P.W.Bidwell and J.I.Falconer, *History of Agriculture in the Northern States,* and G.M.Stephenson, *The Political History of the Public Lands, 1840–62.* Henry C.Hubbart, *The Older Middle West, 1840–1880* is a highly valuable study emphasizing economic and social aspects. William H.Venable, *The Beginnings of Literary Culture in the Ohio Valley* has material not to be found elsewhere; a more recent study is James C. Miller, *The Genesis of Western Culture: The Upper Ohio Valley, 1800–1825.* H.C.Brown, *Grandmother Brown's Hundred Years,* Louis Bromfield's *The Farm,* and William Dean Howells' *Years of My Youth* and *The Leatherwood God* are autobiographical or semi-fictional accounts of early Ohio.

IMMIGRATION. H.P.Fairchild, *Immigration,* chap.ii; J.R.Commons, *Races and Immigrants;* Edith Abbott, *Historical Aspects of the Emigration Problem;* G.M.Stephenson, *American Immigration,* chaps.x, xi; W.F. Adams, *Ireland and Irish Emigration, 1815 to Famine;* A.H.Clark, *Clipper Ship Era,* chap.iii (Packet-ships); Marcus Hansen, 'The Second Colonization of New England,' *N.E.Quarterly,* ii.539; A.B.Faust, *The German Element in the United States;* R.B.Anderson, *Norwegian Immigration to 1848.* Stanley C.Johnson, *History of Emigration from the United Kingdom to North America;* Edward F.Roberts, *Ireland in America;* Kendric C.Babcock, *Scandinavian Element in the United States;* Theodore C.Blegen, *Norwegian Migration to America,* and *Norwegian Emigrant Songs and Ballads;* John S.Lindberg, *Background of Swedish Emigration to the United States;* Florence E.Janson, *Background of Swedish Immigration, 1840–1930.* Marcus Hansen, *Atlantic Migration* explains the background and the impact of immigration on American life during the pre-Civil War period. David B.Tyler, *Steam Conquers the Atlantic* throws light on the Atlantic passage.

MANUFACTURES. Consult the works listed in General list and R.M. Tryon, *Household Manufactures in the U.S.*, A.H.Cole, *The American Wool Manufacture* (2 vols.), J.M.Swank, *History of Manufacturing of Iron*, R.G.Wood, *History of Lumbering in Maine, 1820–61*. Kenneth W. Porter, *The Jacksons and the Lees: Two Generations of Massachusetts Merchants* (2 vols.) illuminates New England commerce, and Robert T. Thompson, *Colonel James Neilson: A Businessman of the Early Machine Age in New Jersey* illustrates the diversity of early business activity. Robert Albion, *The Rise of New York Port, 1815–1860* and his *Square-Riggers on Schedule* should be read in connection with S.E.Morison, *Maritime History of Massachusetts*.

SOURCE SELECTIONS. H.M.Jones and E.E.Leisy, *Major American Writers*, pp.321–29 (Bryant), 671–76 (Whittier).

XXV. *LABOR, EDUCATION AND EMANCIPATION*

LABOR AND UTOPIAS. See General list. Edith Abbott, *Women in Industry*, and Norman Ware, *The Industrial Worker, 1840–60* are fresh and interesting studies from a wide range of material; T.F.Currier, ' Whittier and the Amesbury Strike,' *N.E.Quarterly*, viii.105 is suggestive. W.R.Waterman, *Frances Wright*, and W.Bailie, *Josiah Warren the first American Anarchist* are good biographies. A useful compilation of legislation is in S.M.Kingsbury (ed.), *Labor Laws and their Enforcement*. G.B.Lockwood, *New Harmony Movement* and R.W.Leopold, *Robert Owen* contain the best account of Robert Owen in America. Morris Hillquit, *Socialism*, J.H.Noyes, *History of American Socialisms*, C.Nordhoff, *The Communistic Societies of United States*, and W.A.Hinds, *American Communities and Co-operative Colonies* include all the early communistic experiments. V.F.Calverton, *Where Angels Fear to Tread* and Gilbert Seldes, *The Stammering Century* deal with Utopian experiments in a popular way; Pierrepont B.Noyes, *My Father's House* is a memoir of the Oneida community by one brought up there. E.C.Sears, *Days of Delusion* deals with the Millerites and her *Bronson Alcott's Fruitlands* with the most ephemeral of Utopian communities. Lindsay Swift, *Brook Farm* is penetrating and comprehensive.

EDUCATION AND SCIENCE. E.Channing, *United States*, vol.v, chap.viii; articles by H.D.Mayo and others in the *Annual Reports* of the U.S. Commissioner of Education for 1896–1901; Merle Curti, *Social Ideas of American Educators;* F.T.Carlton, *Economic Influences upon Educational Progress, 1820–50;* B.A.Hinsdale, *Horace Mann and the Common School Revival*. For the impact of the German University, J.A. Walz, *German Influence in American Education;* C.F.Thwing, *The American and the German University; Life, Letters, and Journals of*

George Ticknor (2 vols.); M.A.D.Howe, *Life and Letters of George Bancroft* (2 vols.); P.R.Frothingham, *Edward Everett;* A.E.Ticknor, *Life of J.G.Cogswell.* Higher education: D.G.Tewkesbury, *Founding of American Colleges before the Civil War:* M.A.D.Howe, *Classic Shades* (Williams, Mt.Holyoke, and Yale); S.E.Morison, *Three Centuries of Harvard,* chaps.x-xii; Wilfred Shaw, *Univ.of Michigan;* L.B.Richardson, *Dartmouth College;* C.M.Fuess, *Amherst;* W.C.Bronson, *Hist.of Brown Univ.;* Francis Wayland, *Thoughts on the Present Collegiate System in the U.S.* (1842). Science and the Scientists: P.C.Ricketts, *Hist.of Rensselaer Polytechnic Institute;* G.P.Fisher, *Life of Benjamin Silliman* (2 vols.); G.B.Goode, *The Smithsonian Institution;* E.C.Agassiz, *Louis Agassiz: His Life and Correspondence* (2 vols.).

LITERATURE AND TRANSCENDENTALISM. Van Wyck Brooks, *The Flowering of New England, 1850–65* is an ideal introduction to the intellectual movement; Lewis Mumford, *The Golden Day* is briefer and less comprehensive; F.O.Matthiessen, *The American Renaissance* is particularly good on the transcendentalists. P.L.Boynton, *Literature and American Life* has some penetrating chapters; V.L.Parrington, *The Romantic Revolution, 1800–60* (vol.ii of his *Main Currents*), books ii and iii, covers the Western and Middle States as well as New England and the approach is social rather than aesthetic. R.W.Emerson's *Journals* (10 vols.), *Letters* (6 vols.), and *Works* (12 vols.) are vitally important for the intellectual life and some of his addresses and lectures such as the 'Divinity School Address,' 'The American Scholar,' 'New England Reformers,' and 'Life and Letters in New England' were dynamic to the intellectual movement or record it. A useful selection is Bliss Perry (ed.), *The Heart of Emerson's Journals.* Thoreau's *Journals* (13 vols.) and *Writings* (6 vols.), and Randall Stewart (ed.), *American Notebooks of Nathaniel Hawthorne* are almost equally important. Odell Shepard, who edited *The Heart of Thoreau's Journals* and *The Journals of Bronson Alcott,* has written one of the best New England biographies of the period, *Pedlar's Progress, the Life of Bronson Alcott;* others to be recommended are Lewis Mumford, *Herman Melville;* Newton Arvin, *Nathaniel Hawthorne;* Forrest Wilson, *Harriet Beecher Stowe;* M.B.Stern, *The Life of Margaret Fuller,* and Margaret Wade, *Margaret Fuller.* O.B.Frothingham, *Transcendentalism in New England* is a good general survey; Bliss Perry, *The Spirit of American Literature* an excellent introduction. For the 'Knickerbocker School,' see Parrington, *op.cit.,* and Stanley Williams, *Life of Washington Irving;* Hervey Allen's *Israfel* is the best on Edgar Allan Poe. For the Unitarian movement see G.W.Cooke, *Unitarianism in America,* the collected *Works* of William Ellery Channing, and R.E.Spiller, 'Case for W.E.Channing,' *N.E. Quarterly,* vol.iii. H.S.Commager, *Theodore Parker* is equally important for Unitarianism and Reform. See also his 'Blasphemy of Abner Kneeland,' *N.E.Quarterly,* viii. 29. For the Shakers see Marguerite F. Melcher, *The Shaker Adventure.*

HUMANITARIAN MOVEMENT. Parrington has the best general account. L.E.Richards (ed.), *Letters and Journals of S.G.Howe* (2 vols.), and Helen Marshall, *Dorothea Dix* are good biographies. On the early temperance movement see J.A.Krout, *The Origins of Prohibition,* and J.B.Gough, *Sunlight and Shadow.* On pacifism see the works of M.E. Curti: *The American Peace Crusade, 1815–60; Peace or War; The Learned Blacksmith* (Elihu Burritt). On the Nativist movement Roy A. Billington, *The Protestant Crusade, 1800–1860* is thorough and impartial. David Ludlum, *Social Ferment in Vermont, 1791–1850* is an excellent case study of reform in one of the most interesting of American states.

ABOLITION. G.H.Barnes, *The Antislavery Impulse, 1830–44* is an excellent introduction, emphasizing the Middle West, but harsh toward Garrison. Dwight L.Dumond, *Antislavery Origins of the Civil War* likewise emphasizes the importance of the Middle West at the expense of New England. A.B.Hart, *Slavery and Abolition* is comprehensive. Of the many lives of Garrison, the one by his sons (4 vols.) is monumental; J.H. Chapman's is exhilarating, but not quite history; Lindsay Swift's brief and judicious. Other useful biographies are W.Birney, *J.G.Birney,* T.W. Higginson, *Wendell Phillips,* and O.B.Frothingham, *Gerrit Smith,* H.S. Commager, *Theodore Parker* has material on fugitive slave rescues, and contains a useful bibliography of anti-slavery in New England. Helen Buckmaster, *Let My People Go* is a dramatic history of the underground and of fugitive slaves. Philip Van Doren Stern, *The Drums of Morning* is a novel which faithfully records the excitement of anti-slavery days and of fugitive slave rescues. B.C.Clark, *J.Q.Adams* gives a good account of the fight against the ' gag rule.' E.L.Fox, *The American Colonization Society, 1817–1840* covers that movement. W.H.Siebert supplements his *The Underground Railroad* by an article in *N.E.Quarterly,* ix.447. J.C. Hurd, *The Law of Freedom and Bondage* (2 vols.) has material not elsewhere available, but so badly organized as to be all but useless.

SOURCE SELECTIONS. Commager, *Documents,* Nos.133, 136, 149–50, 158–60, 162–63, 172–73; Jones and Leisy, *Major American Writers,* pp.346–55 (Bryant), 379–468 (Emerson), 636–44 (Whittier), 833, 861–85 (Holmes), 899–915, 934–48 (Thoreau), 969–82 (Lowell's ' Fable for Critics ').

XXVI. *THE COTTON KINGDOM*

PLANTATION ECONOMY. W.E.Dodd, *The Cotton Kingdom* is a brilliant essay. The chapters in Avery Craven, *The Coming of the Civil*

War are the best yet written on slavery and the plantation system. U.B. Phillips, *American Negro Slavery,* and *Life and Labor in the Old South* are the standard works by the greatest Southern historian. R.S.Cotterill, *The Old South* is briefer. Frederic Bancroft, *Slave-Trading in the Old South* covers that subject effectively and should be supplemented by W.H. Stephenson, *Isaac Franklin, Slave Trader and Planter of the Old South.* T.D.Jervey, *The Slave Trade* is a Carolinian view. E.V.Elliot (ed.), *The Pro-Slavery Argument* contains the contemporary arguments. H.T.Catterall, *Judicial Cases concerning American Slaves and the Negro* (4 vols., more coming) presents most valuable source material. C.S.Sydner, *Slavery in Mississippi,* and Ralph Flanders, *Plantation Slavery in Georgia* are good beginnings for much wanted sectional studies of slavery. J.W.Coleman, *Slavery Times in Kentucky* is sentimental. M.B.Hammond, *The Cotton Industry;* V.A.Moody, *Slavery on Louisiana Sugar Plantations;* L.C.Gray, *Hist. of Agriculture in the Southern States* are all valuable. U.B.Phillips, *Robert Toombs;* Avery Craven, *Edmund Ruffin, Southerner;* J.W.DuBose, *Life and Times of William L. Yancey;* Laura White, *Robert Barnwell Rhett;* Percy Flippen, *Herschel V.Johnson;* J.Fred Rippy, *Joel Poinsett* are good biographies of planter-statesmen.

SOCIETY. Susan D.Smedes, *Memorials of a Southern Planter* gives a picture of the planter at his best, and Frances A.Kemble, *Journal of Residence on a Georgian Plantation,* at its worst. R.Q.Mallard, *Plantation Life before Emancipation,* and T.Nelson Page, *Social Life in Old Virginia before the War* are somewhat roseate; but if you want romance, consult the works of Stark Young. Of the many books of travel in the South, F.L.Olmsted, *The Seaboard Slave States* (2 vols.), *Journey in the Back Country,* and *Texas Journey* record the careful observations of a northern farmer who has justly been compared to Arthur Young (see B.Mitchell, *F.L.Olmsted*); Joseph H.Ingraham, *South-West by a Yankee* (2 vols.) is almost as good. J.D.Wade, *Augustus B.Longstreet* is a study of the interesting society of middle Georgia, and should be read in connection with Longstreet's *Georgia Scenes.* M.C.Boyd, *Alabama in the Fifties* and G.G. Johnson, *Ante-Bellum North Carolina* are useful description. Joseph G. Baldwin, *Flush Times in Alabama and Mississippi* is a lively and colorful description of those states, from the authentic school of frontier literature. S.V.Benet, *John Brown's Body* catches the spirit of the Southern aristocracy better than any scholarly study.

INTELLECTUAL MOVEMENT. Parrington's *Main Currents,* vol. ii has a brilliant section on the ' Mind of the South,' and may be supplemented by Clement Eaton, *Free Thought in the Old South;* W.J.Cash, *The Mind of the South;* Virginius Dabney, *Liberalism in the South;* W.P. Trent, *William Gilmore Simms;* T.C.Johnson, *Scientific Interests in the Old South;* F.P.Gaines, *The Southern Plantation, a Tradition.* C.H. Ambler, *Thomas Ritchie* is a biography of a Virginia journalist; Lindo

Rhea, *Hugh S.Legaré* of one of the most learned southern scholars. W.S. Jenkins, *Pro-Slavery Thought in the Old South,* and C.Eaton, ' Resistance of the South to Northern Radicalism,' *N.E.Quarterly,* viii.215 show important movements of opinion. On education: E.W.Knight, *Public Education in the South;* C.G.Woodson, *Education of the Negro prior to 1861;* P.A.Bruce, *Hist. of the Univ. of Virginia* (5 vols.); F.A.P.Barnard, *Report on Collegiate Education* (1854); R. and J.Peter, *Transylvania University.*

INDUSTRY, ETC. J.D.B.DeBow, *Industrial Resources of the Southern and Western States* (4 vols.) is a useful compendium of information and propaganda. Archibald Henderson, *North Carolina* (2 vols.) is the most recent history of that much written of state. Gerald M.Capers presents valuable economic history in his *Biography of a River Town: Memphis.* Kathleen Bruce, *Virginia Iron Manufacture in the Slave Era,* T.D.Clark, *A Pioneer Southern Railroad,* and T.J.Wertenbaker, *Norfolk, Historic Southern Port* are monographs that show regional (not sectional) variations from the plantation norm. Broadus Mitchell, *William Gregg* is a biography of a southern industrialist.

SOURCE SELECTIONS. U.B.Phillips, *Plantation and Frontier* (Commons, *Documentary History,* vol.ii); Commager, *Documents,* No. 178; H.V.Ames, *State Documents on Federal Relations,* pp.193–240.

XXVII. *WHIGS AND DEMOCRATS*

VAN BUREN ADMINISTRATION. F.J.Turner, *The United States, 1830–50,* chaps.x, xi, is the best short survey, and H.R.Fraser, *Democracy in the Making, The Jackson-Tyler Era* the most interesting. *The Autobiography of Martin Van Buren,* Amer.Hist.Assoc. *Report,* 1918, vol.ii, is really a diffuse and rambling memoir and has little of value on his administration. E.M.Shepard, *Van Buren,* and Holmes Alexander, *Martin Van Buren* are the best biographies. Freeman Cleaves, *Old Tippecanoe, William Henry Harrison and his Times,* and D.B.Goebel, *William Henry Harrison* do justice to the hero of Tippecanoe; Tyler too gets more than justice in L.G.Tyler, *Letters and Times of the Tylers* (3 vols.), while Oliver P.Chitwood, *John Tyler, Champion of the Old South* is dull but thorough. R.C.McGrane, *The Panic of 1837* is thorough; cf.S.Reznick, ' Social Hist. of Depression of 1837–43,' *Amer.Hist.Rev.,* xl.612. Thomas H.Benton's *Thirty Years' View* must be used with caution. There is a good monograph on *The Barnburners* by H.D.A.Donovan, and T.C.Smith has written the history of *The Liberty and Free Soil Parties.*

C.J.TANEY AND THE SUPREME COURT. C.B.Swisher, *Roger B.Taney* is the best life of the Chief Justice; see also F.Frankfurter, *Commerce Clause under Marshall, Taney. and Waite,* and Charles Warren,

The Supreme Court in U.S. History (2 vol.ed.). Francis P.Weisenburger, *The Life of John McLean* is scarcely adequate for that Justice.

ANGLO–AMERICAN RELATIONS. D.A.Mills, 'British Diplomacy in Canada,' *United Empire*, vol.ii, is the best account of the Maine boundary controversy, but see also H.S.Burrage, *Maine in the North-eastern Boundary Controversy*, and W.F.Ganong, *Boundaries of New Brunswick*. There is an important article by E.D.Adams on Lord Ashburton in *Amer.Hist.Rev.*, vol.xvii. R.B.Mowat, *The Diplomatic Relations of Great Britain and the United States* is a general account, and H.Keenleyside, *Canada and the United States* is from the Canadian point of view. J.B.McMaster, *The United States*, vol.vi, and W.Kingsford, *History of Canada*, vol.x, contain details of the border incidents. O.E.Tiffany, 'Relations of the United States to the Rebellion of 1837,' *Publications of the Buffalo Historical Society*, vol.viii, is an elaborate discussion of the subject. Commager, *Documents*, Nos.155–58.

XXVIII. *THE FAR WEST*, 1826-48

GENERAL. Katherine Coman, *Economic Beginnings of the Far West* (2 vols.), W.J.Ghent, *Early History of the Far West*, Cardinal Goodwin, *The Trans-Mississippi West, 1803–53*, LeRoy R.Hafen, *Western America: The Exploration, Settlement, and Development of the Region beyond the Mississippi*, Dan E.Clark, *The West in American History*. H.M.Chittenden, *The American Fur Trade of the Far West* (3 vols.) includes the best map of the Far West in 1840. Everett Dick, *Vanguards of the Frontier* is an anecdotal social and economic history of the fur traders, the mountain men, the explorers, the railroad builders, and the cattlemen. G.D.Lyman, *John Marsh, Pioneer: the Life Story of a Trail-blazer on Six Frontiers* is admirable. A.B.Hulbert has edited eight volumes of source material not readily accessible elsewhere, in *Overland to the Pacific*.

OREGON, GREAT PLAINS, AND ROCKIES. W.P.Webb, *The Great Plains*, and F.Merk, *Fur Trade and Empire* are good introductions to these two sections. Francis Parkman, *The Oregon Trail* is the best contemporary description of the Great Plains and their Indians, but contains nothing on the actual settlement of Oregon, of which the best compendium is Joseph Schafer, *History of the Pacific Northwest*. W.J.Ghent, *The Road to Oregon* gives the history of the trail, and W.Hastings, *The Emigrants' Guide to Oregon and California* (1845, reprinted 1932) is full of practical information. J.C.Bell, *Opening a Highway to the Pacific, 1838–46* is the best study of the actual migration, while M.C.Jacobs, *Winning Oregon* is a study of the expansionist movement in the East. Jesse Applegate, 'A Day with the Cow Column,' *Oregon Hist.Soc.Quarterly*, 1900, is a classic narrative of the trail. Effie M.Mack, *Nevada* is one of the best of state histories. On the Santa Fé Trail, see Henry Inman, *The Old Santa Fé Trail*, and R.L.Duffus, *The Santa Fé Trail*. George Catlin, *Letters and Notes on the North American Indians* (2 vols.) was famous in its time and deserves better knowledge now. Allan Nevins, *Frémont, The West's Greatest Adventurer* has considerable material in Western exploration. B.De Voto: *1846, The Year of Decision* touches on many aspects of the westward migrations. Important contemporary narratives of exploration, fur trading, and emigrant trains, by Edwin James, J.B.Wyeth, Edmund Flagg, J.K.Townsend, Fr.P.J.de Smet, Prince Maximilian of Wied, Lord Palmer, and Alexander Ross are reprinted in Thwaites, *Early Western Travels*. Josiah Gregg, *Commerce of the Prairies* is available in several reprints. A biography, with some additional source material, has recently been prepared by Paul Horgan. To these may be added H.C.Dale, *The Ashley-Smith Explorations, 1822–29*. On British opinion and diplomacy in Oregon see articles by F.Merk in *Amer.Hist. Rev.*, vii.653, xl.38, and by H.S.Commager in *Oregon Hist.Quart.*, xxviii. 18. On the Oregon Treaty see J.S.Reeves, *American Diplomacy under Tyler and Polk*, and E.I.McCormac, *James K.Polk*.

THE MORMONS. Bernard De Voto, ' Centennial of Mormonism,' *Forays and Rebuttals* is a stimulating review; B.H.Roberts, *History of the Church of J.C. of Latter-Day Saints* (4 vols.), and J.H.Evans, *Joseph Smith* and *Charles Coulson Rich* are official; I.W.Riley, *The Founder of Mormonism* is hostile; and M.R.Werner, *Life of Brigham Young* is entertaining and not unduly inaccurate. W.A.Linn, *The Story of the Mormons* is the nearest one can expect to come to an impartial account. F.A. Golder, *The March of the Mormon Battalion* chronicles the participation of the Mormons in the Mexican War. Milo M.Quaife (ed.), *The Kingdom of St.James* is the biography of a Mormon leader. G.F.Partridge, ' The Death of a Mormon Dictator,' *N.E.Quarterly*, ix.583, is a vivid contemporary account of the Nauvoo episode. C.A.Brough, *Irrigation in Utah*, and G.Thomas, *The Development of Institutions under Irrigation* are valuable accounts of the early social and economic history of Deseret.

SOURCE SELECTIONS. Commager, *Documents*, Nos.166, 167, 169.

XXIX. TEXAS AND MEXICAN WAR, 1820–48

GENERAL. N.W.Stephenson, *Texas and the Mexican War* (*Chronicles of America*, vol.xxiv) is a brief, well-written, and judicious summary. The ' slave conspiracy ' theory is most effectively presented in Hermann von Holst, *Constitutional Hist. of the U.S.*, vii, and refuted in C.S.Boucher, ' *In re* that aggressive slavocracy,' *Miss.Val.Hist.Rev.*, viii. E.I.McCormac, *James K.Polk* is an unprejudiced and comprehensive biography. The important *Diary of James K.Polk* (4 vols.) may be had in a one-volume abridgment by Allan Nevins. J.S.Reeves, *American Diplomacy under Tyler and Polk*, and E.D.Adams, *British Interests and Activities in Texas* are important monographs, the one based largely on the State Department and the other on the Foreign Office archives. Justin H.Smith, *The Annexation of Texas* and *The War with Mexico* (2 vols.) are the most comprehensive works on either subject, based on the archives of Great Britain, France, Mexico, Texas, and the United States. But they must be used with caution. The author is deductive in his reasoning, and, to quote N.W.Stephenson, 'as artful in his silences as he is effective in his utterances.' On Guadalupe Hidalgo see J.S.Reeves, in *Amer.Hist.Rev.*, v, and Louis Sears, 'Nicholas Trist,' *Miss.Valley Hist.Rev.*, xi. J.Fred Rippy takes up the story after 1848 in his *United States and Mexico*. Madame Calderon de la Barca's *Life in Mexico* (1843, and many later editions) is the classic contemporary description. For the Oregon Treaty see § XXVIII.

TEXAS. Eugene C.Barker, the great authority, has written *Mexico and Texas, 1821–35*, an excellent *Life of Stephen F.Austin*, and edited *The Austin Papers* (*Reports* of Amer.Hist.Assoc. for 1919 and 1922) and *The Writings of Sam Houston* (in progress, probably 10 vols.). *The Diplomatic Correspondence of the Republic of Texas* is printed in these *Reports* for 1907 and 1908. Marquis James, *The Raven*, is a vivid life of Sam Houston.

THE WAR. The volumes of Justin H.Smith constitute the best military history; R.S.Ripley, *The War with Mexico* (2 vols.) is also useful. Two first-rate military biographies are Charles W.Elliott, *Winfield Scott*, and H.Hamilton, *Zachary Taylor*. These may be supplemented by W.H. Samson (ed.), *Letters of Zachary Taylor from the Battlefields;* Douglas S.Freeman, *R.E.Lee*, vol.i; and D.Rowland, *Jefferson Davis, His Letters*, etc., vols.ii, iii. Good soldiers' narratives are U.S.Grant, *Memoirs*, vol.i; Winfield Scott, *Memoirs*, vol.i; and E.K.Smith, *To Mexico with Scott*. Interesting material can be found in W.P.Webb, *The Texas Rangers*. Some excellent monographs are in the *Papers of the Military Historical Society of Massachusetts*, vol.xiii.

CALIFORNIA. The two best surveys are I.B.Richman, *California under Spain and Mexico*, and C.E.Chapman, *History of California, the Spanish Period*. C.Goodwin, *Establishment of a State Government in California, 1846–1850* gives the complete political history. R.G.Cleland, *Cattle on a Thousand Hills* is a picture of California before the coming of the Americans. Nevins, *Frémont*, covers the war period. C.E.Chapman, 'The Literature of California History,' *Southwestern Hist.Quarterly*, xxii, is a good bibliography.

SOURCE SELECTIONS. E.C.Barker, *Readings in Texas History;* Commager, *Documents*, Nos.164–71; Jones and Leisy, *Major American Writers*, pp.960–68 (Biglow Papers).

XXX–XXXII. *PERIOD* 1848–59

GENERAL AND POLITICAL. James Ford Rhodes, *History of the United States from the Compromise of 1850 to 1877* (7 vols.) is still the best detailed history of that period although shot full of holes by the research of the last forty years. Perhaps the best account of the intricate political, economic, and psychological background to secession is Avery Craven, *The Coming of the Civil War.* Channing's *History,* vi, is a good corrective to Rhodes, and A.C.Cole, *The Irrepressible Conflict, 1850–65* supplements Channing. H. Von Holst, *History,* iii, and J.Schouler, *History,* v, are still useful. To the biographies and works of Calhoun, Clay, Webster, Polk, and Frémont add Roy F.Nichols, *Franklin Pierce,* and Frederic Bancroft, *William H.Seward* (2 vols.). G.F.Milton, *The Eve of Conflict* (the best life of Stephen A. Douglas) with R.F. Nichols, *The Democratic Machine, 1850–54* give the political detail and manœuvring. Carl Sandburg, *Lincoln, The Prairie Years* (2 vols.) is an artistic and inaccurate description; Albert J.Beveridge, *Lincoln* (2 vols.) a meticulously detailed account of Lincoln's life to 1858. For other biographies of Lincoln see § XXXIII. U.B.Phillips, *Robert Toombs,* and L.Pendleton, *A.H.Stephens* are the best biographies of Southern Whigs. A.C. Cole, *Whig Party in the South* is also good on the Know-Nothings. Besides R.A.Billington's *Protestant Crusade,* we have monographs on the Know-Nothings in New York by L.D.Scisco, in Maryland by L.F. Schmeckebier, and in Rhode Island by E.Stickney, and excellent chapters in T.C.Smith, *Parties and Slavery.* C.B.Going, *David Wilmot, Free-Soiler* is a careful and elaborate biography; cf.T.C.Smith, *Liberty and Free Soil Parties in the Northwest.* Indispensable sources are the *Correspondence of Toombs, Stephens and Cobb,* and the *Correspondence of R.M.T. Hunter* in the *Reports* of the Amer.Hist.Assoc. for 1911 and 1916. R.R. Russel, *Economic Aspects of Southern Sectionalism, 1840–61,* and F.M. Green, *Constitutional Change in the South Atlantic States, 1776–1860* are capital studies of the background of secession, and may be supplemented by Hugh M.Wagstaff, *State Rights and Political Parties in North Carolina, 1776–1861;* P.M.Hamer, *Secession Movement in South Carolina, 1847–52;* M.J.White, *Secession Movement in the United States, 1847–52;* and R.H.Shryock, *Georgia and the Union in 1850.* There is useful material in the biographies of Rhett, Yancey, Toombs, Ritchie, Cobb, Ruffin, Stephens, and others, cited previously.

CALIFORNIA AND CLIPPER SHIPS. R.G.Cleland, *History of California, the American Period* is the best general account. On the Vigilantes, H.H.Bancroft, *Popular Tribunals* is still valuable; M.F.Williams, *History of the San Francisco Vigilance Committee* is more recent. The records of the trials by the Vigilante Committee of 1856 are in *American State Trials,* vol.xv. James P.Zollinger, *Sutter, The Man and His*

Empire is a critical biography; Blaise Cendras, *Sutter's Gold* is romantic, and good reading. It seems that every Forty-Niner kept a diary. Among the best in print are Charles E.Pancoast, *Diary of a Quaker Forty-Niner;* Chauncey Canfield, *Diary of a Forty-Niner;* O.T.Howe, *Argonauts of '49,* telling the story of the emigrant companies from New England. A.B.Hulbert, *Forty-Niners* is a reconstruction of many of these narratives. On early attempts to span the continent see L.R.Hafen, *The Overland Mail, 1849–1860,* and G.D.Bradley, *The Pony Express.* A.H. Clark, *The Clipper Ship Era* is a classic; Carl C.Cutler, *Greyhounds of the Sea* is more complete; O.T.Howe and F.C.Matthews, *American Clipper Ships* is a catalogue. H.I.Chapelle, in his *History of American Sailing Ships,* maintains that the clippers were no good; Morison, in *Maritime History of Mass.,* thinks well of them. C.L.Lewis, *Matthew Fontaine Maury,* and E.LeRoy Pond, *Junius Smith, the Father of the Atlantic Liner* are important biographies. For river transportation the best account is C.H.Ambler, *History of Transportation in the Ohio Valley;* and the most readable, A.B.Hulbert, *Paths of Inland Waters.*

FOREIGN RELATIONS. M.W.Williams, *Anglo-American Isthmian Diplomacy, 1815–1915* is the capital work, based on British and American archives; Miss Williams has also written on Clayton, and H.B. Learned on W.L.Marcy, in the *American Secretaries of State* series, vol. vi. J.F.Rippy, *Joel R.Poinsett, Versatile American* has a good deal on the diplomacy of this period. Additional material can be found in I.D.Travis, *History of the Clayton-Bulwer Treaty;* C.H.Huberich, *The Trans-Isthmian Canal, 1825–1904;* L.M.Keasby, *The Nicaragua Canal and the Monroe Doctrine;* and Dexter Perkins, *The Monroe Doctrine, 1826–1867.* Merle E.Curti, *Austria and the U.S., 1848–52* tells of the favorite target of ' Young America.' J.W.Foster, *American Diplomacy in the Orient* is a standard and popular work, by an experienced American diplomatist. Tyler Dennett, *Americans in Eastern Asia,* and F.R.Dulles, *The Old China Trade* cover early trading and treaty relations with China and Japan. P.J.Treat, *Dipl.Rels.between U.S. and Japan, 1853–95* (2 vols.) is comprehensive and interesting. Townsend Harris's journal has now been printed in full, *The Complete Journal of Townsend Harris.* Extracts from Commodore Perry's *Narrative* are reprinted in W.E.Griffis, *M.C. Perry.* Inazo Nitobe, *Intercourse between the U.S. and Japan* gives the other side. The Canadian reciprocity negotiations may be studied in C.G.Tansill, *Canadian Reciprocity Treaty of 1854,* and C.D.Allin, *Annexation, Preferential Trade, and Reciprocity.* Laurence Oliphant's genial account of the negotiations is in his *Episodes of a Life of Adventure.* Rhodes, *United States,* i.516–50, has a full account of Cuban episodes; cf. A.A.Ettinger, *Mission to Spain of Pierre Soulé.*

PRAIRIE SETTLEMENT, KANSAS AND NEBRASKA. Everett Dick, *Vanguards of the Frontier* and *The Sod House Frontier;*

C.A.Dawson and E.R.Younge, *Pioneering in the Prairie Provinces;* H.C. Hubbart, *The Older Middle West, 1840–1880;* W.T.Hutchinson, *Cyrus H.McCormick* (2 vols.); P.W.Gates, *Illinois Central R.R. and Colonization* are all good for prairie settlement. For the Kansas-Nebraska Act see Rhodes, *United States,* ii; G.F.Milton, *Eve of Conflict;* F.H.Hodder in *Miss.Val.Hist.Rev.,* ix.10, xii.3; P.O.Ray, *Repeal of the Missouri Compromise;* H.A.Trexler, *Slavery in Missouri.* The Lincoln-Douglas debates are printed in Lincoln's *Complete Works,* and in several separate editions. A.C.Cole, *The Era of the Civil War* gives the background. Most accounts of the struggle for Kansas are grossly partisan; Channing, *History,* vol.vi, and Beveridge, *Lincoln,* vol.ii, are exceptions. F.W.Blakmar, *Charles Robinson* is a biography of one of the Free-State leaders. For the New England Emigrant Aid Society see articles in *N.E.Quarterly,* iii.95–122, iv.148–55, and *Amer.Hist.Rev.,* xli.1. On the constitutional aspects, see Milo M.Quaife, *The Doctrine of Non-Intervention with Slavery in the Territories,* and the still valuable J.Hurd, *Law of Freedom and Bondage.*

DRED SCOTT AND JOHN BROWN. The opinions in the Dred Scott case are published at length in the *U.S. Reports* (sometimes cited as *Howard's Reports*), xix.393; extracts are in all collections of constitutional cases, and a lengthy discussion in C.Warren, *Supreme Court,* Carl Swisher, *R.B.Taney,* and A.J.Beveridge, *Abraham Lincoln.* The articles by E.E.Corwin and H.T.Cotterall in *Amer.Hist.Rev.,* xvii.52, and xxx. 56, and by F.H.Hodder in *Miss.Val.Hist.Rev.,* xvl.3 are indispensable. O.G.Villard, *John Brown* is the best biography; W.E.B.DuBois, *John Brown* is by a noted colored author. H.P.Wilson, *John Brown, Soldier of Fortune* is hostile; R.V.Harlow's article in *Amer.Hist.Rev.,* xxxviii.32 is important. The record of the John Brown trial is in *American State Trials,* vol.vi.

SOURCE SELECTIONS. Commager, *Documents,* Nos.174–88; W. Macdonald, *Documentary Source Book,* pp.397–405, gives a documentary history of the Kansas-Nebraska Act. Jones and Leisy, *Major American Writers,* pp.1120–58.

XXXIII–XXXVII. *THE CIVIL WAR,* 1861–65

GENERAL. E.Channing, *History of the U.S.,* vol.vi, and J.G.Randall, *Civil War and Reconstruction* are the best single volumes on the Civil War period. Their candid accounts of the civil and economic history of the decade are valuable antidotes for the heroic view of the Civil War that one gets by reading military history. Randall's bibliography is unusually full. C.R.Fish, *The American Civil War* is a brief interpretation no student should miss. G.F.Milton, *Conflict: The American Civil War* is well-balanced and succinct. J.T.Adams, *America's Tragedy* is a thoughtful interpretative account.

SECESSION. D.L.Dumond, *The Secession Movement* and E.M.Coulter (ed.), *The Course of the South to Secession,* essays by U.B.Phillips. For background, G.F.Milton, *The Eve of Conflict,* and R.R.Russel, *Economic Aspects of Southern Sectionalism* are indispensable. The chapters in Randall (above) are critical and comprehensive. Gerald Johnson, *The Secession of the Southern States* is a popular account. E.D.Fite, *The Presidential Campaign of 1860* is still the best study of the subject. For special phases, see William Barringer, *Lincoln's Rise to Power;* Mary Scrugham, *The Peaceable Americans, 1860–61;* E.C.Smith, *Borderland in the Civil War;* P.G.Auchampaugh, *Buchanan and his Cabinet on the Eve of Secession;* J.G.van Deusen, *Economic Basis of Disunion in South Carolina;* C.P.Denman, *Secession Movement in Alabama;* H.T.Shanks, *Secession Movement in Virginia;* W.M.Caskey, *Secession and Restoration of Louisiana;* B.B.Munford, *Virginia's Attitude toward Slavery and Secession;* articles by P.L.Rainwater in *Mississippi Law Journal,* vi; H.C.Hubbart, *The Older Middle West, 1850–1880;* George H.Porter, *Ohio Politics during the Civil War Period;* W.W.Ryle, *Missouri, Union or Secession.* The attitude of northern — especially New York — businessmen is admirably analyzed in Philip S.Foner, *Business and Slavery.* Valuable material can be found in the following biographies: L.A.White, *Rhett;* E.Merritt, *James Henry Hammond;* H.D.Capers, *C.G.Memminger;* J.F. H.Claiborne, *John A.Quitman;* C.Coleman, *Life of John J.Crittenden;* H.J.Pearce, *Benjamin H.Hill;* U.B.Phillips, *Robert Toombs;* P.S.Flippin, *Herschel V.Johnson;* J.W.DuBose, *Yancey,* and A.Craven, *Ruffin.* Two highly important articles are A.C.Cole and J.G.deR.Hamilton, 'Lincoln's Election an Immediate Menace to Slavery in the States,' *Amer.Hist.Rev.,* xxxvi.740, xxxvii.700. Two invaluable source collections are D.L.Dumond (ed.), *Southern Editorials on Secession,* and H.C.Perkins (ed.), *Northern Editorials on Secession* (2 vols.)

MILITARY. J.G.Nicolay and John Hay, *Abraham Lincoln* (10 vols.) is the most extensive military history; J.G.Randall, *Civil War and Reconstruction* the best integrated. John C.Ropes and W.R.Livermore, *The Story of the Civil War* (3 vols.) carries the story to 1863. Comte de Paris, *The Civil War in America* (4 vols.) is particularly useful for the Peninsular Campaign. The best brief account of the Confederate army is Robert S.Henry, *Story of the Confederacy.* Mathew F.Steele, *American Campaigns* (2 vols.) is by a military expert. *Battles and Leaders of the Civil War* (4 vols.), a well-illustrated symposium by Union and Confederate officers, is highly vivid, but like all post-war historical works by participants must be used with caution. *The Papers of the Military Historical Society of Massachusetts* include much material of the same sort, and much of great scientific value. Sir Frederick Maurice, *Statesmen and Soldiers of the Civil War* is a series of essays by an English expert. J.F.Rhodes, *History of the Civil War, 1861–65* is a one-volume condensation of his larger work; the maps are excellent. For particular campaigns see John Bigelow, *The Campaign of Chancellorsville;* Jacob D.Cox, *The March to the Sea;* Alexander Kearsey, *The Shenandoah Valley Campaign;* A.A.Humphreys, *The Virginia Campaign of 1864 and 1865;* Newton M.Curtis, *From Bull Run to Chancellorsville;* Morris Schaff, *The Sunset of the Confederacy;* T.R.Hay, *Hood's Tennessee Campaign;* Stanley Horn's admirable *The Army of the Tennessee;* and Alfred H.Burne, *Lee, Grant and Sherman,* which emphasizes the military abilities of General Hood. See, too, Hood's own *Advance and Retreat.* No military history deserves serious consideration unless the author has used the remarkably complete *War of the Rebellion, Official Records of the Union and Confederate Armies* (130 vols.), and *Official Records of the Union and Confederate Navies* (30 vols.). T.L.Livermore, *Numbers and Losses in the Civil War,* and W.L.Fox, *Regimental Losses in the American Civil War* are authoritative compilations from the records.

NAVAL. A.T.Mahan, *Farragut,* and *The Gulf and Inland Waters;* J.P.Baxter, *Introduction of the Ironclad Warships;* R.M.Thompson and R.Wainwright (eds.), *Confidential Correspondence of Gustavus V.Fox* (3 vols.); and M.Robinson, *The Confederate Privateers* are the most important volumes. The famous *Diary* of Secretary of the Navy Welles is of course invaluable. Pleasant essays on naval commanders are in Jim D.Hill, *Sea Dogs of the Sixties.* J.T.Scharf, *History of the Confederate Navy,* and James R.Soley, *The Blockade and the Cruisers* are still useful. Colyer Meriwether, *Raphael Semmes* is an adequate biography.

PRINCIPAL BIOGRAPHIES. Gamaliel Bradford, *Union Portraits* and *Confederate Portraits* are character sketches of leading generals and statesmen on both sides. J.B.Hendrick, *Statesmen of the Lost Cause* is valuable for lesser-known members of the Confederate Cabinet. The printed works relating to Lincoln already run to several thousand titles. J.G.Nicolay and John Hay, *Abraham Lincoln* (10 vols.) is largely a history of the Civil War by strong Union partisans. Carl Sandburg's magnificent *Lincoln: The War Years* (4 vols.) is easily the most understanding biography; J.G.Randall's *Lincoln the President: Springfield to Gettysburg* (2 vols.) the most scholarly and critical; Dennett (ed.), *Lincoln and the Civil War in the Diaries and Letters of John Hay,* has new material. Stephenson's *Lincoln,* with a volume of *Selections* from his writings, is the best one-volume life. Alonzo Rothschild, *Lincoln, Master of Men* is a useful study of his relations with generals and cabinet ministers; W.E.Barton's *Life of Lincoln* (2 vols.) is worth reading; C.R.Ballard, *The Military Genius of Lincoln* is by a British general. Nicolay and Hay (eds.), *Abraham Lincoln's Complete Works* (2 vols.) and Philip Van Doren Stern (ed.), *The Life and Writings of Abraham Lincoln* are the handiest editions of Lincoln's writings. Mrs.V.J.Davis, *Memoirs of Jefferson Davis* (2 vols.) is sentimental, but contains some revealing letters. Of several brief biographies, W.E.Dodd, *Davis* is the most valuable, Robert McElroy, *Jefferson Davis* the most thorough; H.J.Eckenrode, *Jefferson Davis* is somewhat marred by the author's conception of Davis as a conquering Nordic; Allen Tate's *Jefferson Davis, his Rise and Fall* has the best style. Davis's own *Rise and Fall of the Confederate Government* (2 vols.), and A.H.Stephens, *War between the States* (2 vols.) are typical post-war defenses, most valuable if their point of view is understood. Dunbar Rowland (ed.), *Jefferson Davis, Constitutionalist* (10 vols.) is the title of Davis's collected writings; only vols.v and vi are of much value for the Civil War. No one should condemn President Buchanan before reading his *Mr. Buchanan's Administration on the Eve of the Rebellion*. Douglas S.Freeman, *R.E.Lee* (4 vols.) supersedes all other biographies of the Southern hero. Sentimentalism characterizes most of the others; Sir F.Maurice, *Lee the Soldier* is an exception. D.S.Freeman (ed.), *Lee's Dispatches to Davis* is a good selection. Maj.-Gen.J.F.C.Fuller, *Grant and Lee* is a reappraisal of the two generals by a World War veteran. Grant's *Personal Memoirs* (2 vols.) is a classic of military reminiscence. It should be supplemented by A.L.Conger, *The Rise of U.S.Grant;* the old but still valuable Adam Badeau, *Military History of U.S.Grant* (3 vols.); J.C.Cramer (ed.), *Letters of U.S.Grant to his Father;* Gen.Horace Porter, *Campaigning with Grant;* James H.Wilson, *Under the Old Flag* and *Life of John A.Rawlins.* Lieut.-Col.G.F.R.Henderson, *Stonewall Jackson* (2 vols.) has literary and artistic qualities of the highest order, but the author is romantic, and on many points unreliable. General McClellan stands self-revealed in *McClellan's Own Story* (cf.W.S.Myers, *McClellan: a Study in Personality*); General Sherman in the *Memoirs of General W.T.Sherman* (2 vols.), and R.S. Thorndike (ed.), *The Sherman Letters, 1837–1891.* Capt.B.H.Liddell Hart, *Sherman: Soldier, Realist, American* is by a British military expert. Other valuable military biographies are Don C.Seitz, *Braxton Bragg;* John Wyeth, *Nathan Bedford Forrest* and Eric W.Sheppard, *Bedford Forrest;* John Pemberton, *General Pemberton, Defender of Vicksburg;* A.M.Stickles, *Simon Bolivar Buckner;* Joseph Hergeshiemer's somewhat romantic *Sheridan;* Alfred Roman, *General Beauregard* (2 vols.) and H.Basso, *Beauregard, The Great Creole;* H.J.Eckenrode and Bryan Conrad, *James Longstreet;* and John W.Thomason, *Jeb Stuart.* Critical biographies of General Joseph E.Johnston and General Thomas are badly needed.

Valuable political biographies are J.A.Woodburn, *Thaddeus Stevens;* G.H.Haynes, *Charles Sumner;* Pierce Butler, *Judah P.Benjamin;* L. Pendleton, *Alexander H.Stephens;* Henry G.Pearson, *Life of John A. Andrew* (2 vols.); William E.Smith, *The Francis Preston Blair Family in Politics* (2 vols.); A.B.Hart, *Salmon P.Chase;* J.H.Pearce, *Benjamin H.Hill;* Charles H.Ambler, *Francis Pierpont;* Wirt A.Cate, *L.C.Q.Lamar;*

William D.Foulke, *Oliver P.Morton;* Claude M.Fuess, *Carl Schurz;* Frederic Bancroft, *William H.Seward;* and George C.Gorham, *Life and Public Services of Edwin M.Stanton* (2 vols.).

MEMOIRS AND AUTOBIOGRAPHIES, other than those already listed. Gen.E.P.Alexander, *Military Memoirs of a Confederate* is by a participant, who has corrected battlefield impressions by the official records. Gen.J.E.Johnston, *Narrative of Military Operations,* and Gen. James Longstreet, *From Manassas to Appomattox* are defensive and controversial. E.A.Moore, *A Cannoneer under Stonewall Jackson,* Gen. Richard Taylor, *Destruction and Reconstruction,* Gen.G.H.Gordon, *Brook Farm to Cedar Mountain,* Capt.R.G.Carter, *Four Brothers in Blue,* Heros von Borcke, *Memoirs of the Confederate War* (2 vols.), Henry Hitchcock, *Marching with Sherman,* Henry K.Douglas, *I Rode with Stonewall,* John B.Gordon, *Reminiscences of the Civil War,* John B.Hood *Advance and Retreat,* Robert Stiles, *Four Years under Marse Robert,* Abner R.Small, *The Road to Richmond,* J.K.Hosmer, *The Color-Guard,* and Col.Theodore Lyman, *Meade's Headquarters* give vivid pictures of campaigning. The last has considerable literary merit. Raphael Semmes, *Memoirs of Service Afloat* is by the captain of the *Alabama;* J.M.Morgan, *Recollections of a Rebel Reefer* is more entertaining. The so-called *Diary of Gideon Welles* (3 vols.) is really a post-war memoir giving a vivid though often distorted picture of Lincoln's cabinet. Charles A.Dana, *Recollections of the Civil War* is by the Assistant Secretary of War who accompanied Grant, and gives an intimate view of military events by an intelligent civilian. J.G.Randall (ed.), *Diary of O.H.Browning* (2 vols.) is indispensable for Republican politics.

FOREIGN RELATIONS. Frederic Bancroft, *W.H.Seward* (2 vols.) is the best life of the American Secretary of State. E.D.Adams, *Great Britain and the American Civil War* (2 vols.) should be supplemented by J.P.Baxter, 3rd, ' The British Government and Neutral Rights,' *Amer. Hist.Rev.,* xxxiv.9, 77; F.L.Owsley in *Essays in Honor of W.E.Dodd.* Vivid accounts of the London legation may be found in *The Education of Henry Adams* and *A Cycle of Adams Letters, 1861–65* (2 vols.). H.D. Jordan and E.J.Pratt, *European Opinion on the American Civil War* covers England and the continent. As the French foreign archives for this period are still closed, the views of French relations in John Bigelow's *France and the Confederate Navy* and *Retrospect of an Active Life* (5 vols.) are necessarily incomplete. J.M.Callahan, *Diplomatic History of the Southern Confederacy* is a well-rounded monograph; F.L.Owsley, *King Cotton Diplomacy* more lively and more controversial. M.L.Bonham, *British Consuls in the Confederacy,* and J.D.Bulloch, *Secret Service of the Confederate States in Europe* (2 vols.) contain inside information. Printed documents of the period will be found in the *British and Foreign State Papers* and the annual *U.S. Diplomatic Correspondence, Papers relating to Foreign Affairs;* Confederate diplomatic correspondence has been published in *Official Records of the Navies,* 2nd series, vol.iii.

NORTH AND SOUTH DURING THE WAR. A.C.Cole, *The Irrepressible Conflict* is a general study of the social and economic background. Margaret Leech, *Reveille in Washington* is a lively picture of life in the capital city during the war. Bell I.Wiley, *Southern Negroes, 1861– 1865* traces the progress of emancipation during the war and illuminates the role of the slaves in the Confederacy. J.G.Randall, *Constitutional Problems under Lincoln;* and E.D.Fite, *Social and Industrial Conditions in the North during the Civil War* are the best books on these subjects. J.C.Schwab, *The Confederate States of America* is an account of Confederate economies and finance. Jefferson Davis's *Rise and Fall* gives the Confederate and U.S. Constitutions in parallel columns. Contemporary reports of debates in the Confederate Congress are in course of publication in the *Southern Hist.Soc.Papers,* beginning with No.44; official policies may also be followed in J.D.Richardson (ed.), *Messages and Papers of the Confederacy* (2 vols.). F.L.Owsley, *States' Rights in the Confederacy* is an illuminating study of Confederate constitutional problems; it may be supplemented by G.L.Tatum, *Disloyalty in the Confederacy* and the immensely erudite W.M.Robinson, *Justice in Grey, a History of the Judicial System of the Confederate States of America.* E.C.Kirkland, *The Peace Makers of 1864* is the only study of that aspect, on both sides. A.B.Moore, *Conscription and Conflict in the Confederacy* is a revelation on both those subjects, and one of the first products of the new realistic school of Southern historians. Ella Lonn, *Foreigners in the Confederacy* covers broad ground and contains one of the most complete bibliographies of the Confederacy to be found anywhere. For the Union draft, F.A.Shannon, *Organization and Administration of the Union Army* (2 vols.) is indispensable; and A.H.Meneely, *The War Department: 1861* a useful supplement. Ella Lonn, *Desertion during the Civil War* may be supplemented by Bessie Martin, *Desertion of Alabama Troops from the Confederate Army.* Miss Lonn's *Salt as a Factor* calls attention to a little-known matter of importance. Other valuable monographs are August Dietz, *Postal Service of the Confederate States;* W.W. Sweet, *The Methodist Church and the Civil War;* Curtis H.Morrow, *Politico-Military Secret Societies (Social Science,* iv and v); Edward N.Wright, *Conscientious Objectors in the Civil War;* W.B.Hesseltine, *Civil War Prisons;* and William B.Weeden, *War Government, Federal and State, 1861–1865.* George F.Milton, *Lincoln and the Fifth Column* and Wood Gray, *The Hidden War* tell the story of Northern opposition to the war and to Lincoln. The articles of C.W.Ramsdall on Southern railroads and factories in *Amer.Hist.Rev.,* xxii.794, and *Miss.Val.Hist. Rev.,* viii.231, break new ground.

Contemporary diaries and journals valuable for social background are

Eliza F.Andrews, *War Time Journal of a Georgia Girl;* John S.Wise, *The End of an Era;* J.B.Jones, *A Rebel War Clerk's Diary;* Mary B. Chestnut, *A Diary from Dixie;* Charlotte R.Holmes (ed.), *The Brock-myer Letters, 1863–65;* G.W.Bacon and E.W.Howland (eds.), *Letters of a Family during the War for the Union* (2 vols.); T.C.DeLeon, *Four Years in the Rebel Capitals;* Sarah M.Dawson, *A Confederate Girl's Diary;* Judith B.McGuire, *Diary of a Refugee;* George C.Eggleston, *A Rebel's Recollections;* Sarah A.Pryor, *Reminiscences;* and Elizabeth W. Pringle, *Chronicles of Chicora Wood.*

Of the numerous travel books, W.H.Russell, *My Diary North and South* is by the London *Times'* best war correspondent. Edward Dicey, *Six Months in the Federal States* (2 vols.), Anthony Trollope, *North America,* Lieut.-Col.A.J.Fremantle, *Three Months in the Southern States,* and Catherine C.Hopley, *Life in the South by a Blockaded British Sub-ject* (2 vols.) are by accurate English observers.

In conclusion, everyone should read the gorgeous epic poem by Stephen Vincent Benét, *John Brown's Body,* which shows more insight into the Civil War than most of the historians we have mentioned; and Walt Whitman's *Drum Taps* and *Specimen Days,* the finest contemporary literature that the war evoked.

SOURCE SELECTIONS. Frank Moore (ed.), *The Rebellion Record* (12 vols.) contains a mass of material culled from newspapers, official reports, letters, and so forth. Edward McPherson, *Political History of the Great Rebellion* contains source material, badly organized. Com-mager, *Documents,* Nos.189–244.

INDEX

INDEX

THE
CONSTITUTION
OF THE
UNITED STATES
OF
AMERICA

WE,
THE PEOPLE OF THE UNITED STATES,
IN ORDER TO
FORM A MORE PERFECT UNION,
ESTABLISH JUSTICE,
INSURE DOMESTIC TRANQUILLITY,
PROVIDE FOR
THE COMMON DEFENCE,
PROMOTE THE GENERAL WELFARE,
AND SECURE
THE BLESSINGS OF LIBERTY
TO OURSELVES
AND OUR POSTERITY,
DO ORDAIN AND ESTABLISH THIS
CONSTITUTION
FOR THE UNITED STATES OF
AMERICA.

ARTICLE I

All legislative Powers herein granted shall be vested in a Congress of
the United States, which shall consist of a Senate and a House of
Representatives.

The House of Representatives shall be composed of Members chosen
every second Year by the People of the several States, and the Electors in each State shall have the Qualifications requisite for Electors
of the most numerous Branch of the State Legislature.

No Person shall be a Representative who shall not have attained to the
Age of twenty-five Years, and been seven Years a Citizen of the
United States, and who shall not, when elected, be an Inhabitant of
that State in which he shall be chosen.

Representatives and direct Taxes shall be apportioned among the several States which may be included within this Union, according to
their respective Numbers, which shall be determined by adding to
the whole Number of free Persons, including those bound to Service for a Term of Years, and excluding Indians not taxed, three
fifths of all other Persons. The actual Enumeration shall be made
within three Years after the first Meeting of the Congress of the
United States, and within every subsequent Term of ten Years, in
such Manner as they shall by Law direct. The Number of Representatives shall not exceed one for every thirty Thousand, but each
State shall have at Least one Representative; and until such enumeration shall be made, the State of New Hampshire shall be entitled to chuse three, Massachusetts eight, Rhode-Island and Providence Plantations one, Connecticut five, New-York six, New Jersey
four, Pennsylvania eight, Delaware one, Maryland six, Virginia
ten, North Carolina five, South Carolina five, and Georgia three.

When vacancies happen in the Representation from any State, the
Executive Authority thereof shall issue Writs of Election to fill such
Vacancies.

The House of Representatives shall chuse their Speaker and other
Officers; and shall have the sole Power of Impeachment.

The Senate of the United States shall be composed of two Senators
from each State, chosen by the Legislature thereof, for six Years;
and each Senator shall have one Vote.

Immediately after they shall be assembled in Consequence of the first Election, they shall be divided as equally as may be into three Classes. The Seats of the Senators of the first Class shall be vacated at the Expiration of the second Year, of the second Class at the Expiration of the fourth Year, and of the third Class at the Expiration of the sixth Year, so that one-third may be chosen every second Year; and if Vacancies happen by Resignation, or otherwise, during the Recess of the Legislature of any State, the Executive thereof may make temporary Appointments until the next Meeting of the Legislature, which shall then fill such Vacancies.

No Person shall be a Senator who shall not have attained to the Age of thirty Years, and been nine Years a Citizen of the United States, and who shall not, when elected, be an Inhabitant of that State for which he shall be chosen.

The Vice President of the United States shall be President of the Senate, but shall have no Vote, unless they be equally divided.

The Senate shall chuse their other Officers, and also a President pro tempore, in the Absence of the Vice President, or when he shall exercise the Office of President of the United States.

The Senate shall have the sole Power to try all Impeachments. When sitting for that Purpose, they shall be on Oath or Affirmation. When the President of the United States is tried, the Chief Justice shall preside: And no Person shall be convicted without the Concurrence of two thirds of the Members present.

Judgment in Cases of Impeachment shall not extend further than to removal from Office, and disqualification to hold and enjoy any Office of honor, Trust or Profit under the United States: but the Party convicted shall nevertheless be liable and subject to Indictment, Trial, Judgment and Punishment, according to Law.

Section 4

The Times, Places and Manner of holding Elections for Senators and Representatives, shall be prescribed in each State by the Legislature thereof; but the Congress may at any time by Law make or alter such Regulations, except as to the Places of chusing Senators.

The Congress shall assemble at least once in every Year, and such Meeting shall be on the first Monday in December, unless they shall by Law appoint a different Day.

Section 5

Each House shall be the Judge of the Elections, Returns and Qualifications of its own Members, and a Majority of each shall constitute a Quorum to do Business; but a smaller Number may adjourn from day to day, and may be authorized to compel the Attendance of absent Members, in such Manner, and under such Penalties as each House may provide.

Each House may determine the Rules of its Proceedings, punish its Members for disorderly Behavior, and, with the Concurrence of two thirds, expel a Member.

Each House shall keep a Journal of its Proceedings, and from time to time publish the same, excepting such Parts as may in their Judgment require Secrecy; and the Yeas and Nays of the Members of either House on any question shall, at the Desire of one fifth of those present, be entered on the Journal.

Neither House, during the Session of Congress, shall, without the Consent of the other, adjourn for more than three days, nor to any other Place than that in which the two Houses shall be sitting.

Section 6

The Senators and Representatives shall receive a Compensation for their Services, to be ascertained by Law, and paid out of the Treasury of the United States. They shall in all Cases, except Treason, Felony and Breach of the Peace, be privileged from Arrest during their Attendance at the Session of their respective Houses, and in going to and returning from the same; and for any Speech or Debate in either House, they shall not be questioned in any other Place.

No Senator or Representative shall, during the Time for which he was elected, be appointed to any civil Office under the Authority of the United States, which shall have been created, or the Emoluments whereof shall have been encreased during such time; and no Person holding any Office under the United States, shall be a Member of either House during his Continuance in Office.

Section 7

All Bills for raising Revenue shall originate in the House of Representatives; but the Senate may propose or concur with Amendments as on other Bills.

Every Bill which shall have passed the House of Representatives and the Senate, shall, before it become a Law, be presented to the President of the United States; If he approve he shall sign it, but if not he shall return it, with his Objections to that House in which it shall have originated, who shall enter the Objections at large on their Journal, and proceed to reconsider it. If after such Reconsideration two thirds of that House shall agree to pass the Bill, it shall be sent, together with the Objections, to the other House, by which it shall likewise be reconsidered, and if approved by two thirds of that House, it shall become a Law. But in all such Cases the Votes of both Houses shall be determined by Yeas and Nays, and the Names of the Persons voting for and against the Bill shall be entered on the Journal of each House respectively. If any Bill shall not be returned by the President within ten Days (Sundays excepted) after it shall have been presented to him, the Same shall be a Law, in like Manner as if he had signed it, unless the Congress by their Adjournment prevent its Return, in which Case it shall not be a Law.

Every Order, Resolution, or Vote to which the Concurrence of the Senate and House of Representatives may be necessary (except on a question of Adjournment) shall be presented to the President of the United States; and before the Same shall take Effect, shall be approved by him, or being disapproved by him, shall be repassed by two thirds of the Senate and House of Representatives, according to the Rules and Limitations prescribed in the Case of a Bill.

Section 8

The Congress shall have Power To lay and collect Taxes, Duties, Imposts and Excises, to pay the Debts and provide for the common Defence and general Welfare of the United States; but all Duties, Imposts and Excises shall be uniform throughout the United States;

To borrow Money on the credit of the United States:

To regulate Commerce with foreign Nations, and among the several States, and with the Indian Tribes;

To establish an uniform Rule of Naturalization, and uniform Laws on the subject of Bankruptcies throughout the United States;

To coin Money, regulate the Value thereof, and of foreign Coin, and fix the Standard of Weights and Measures;

To provide for the Punishment of counterfeiting the Securities and current Coin of the United States;

To establish Post Offices and post Roads;

To promote the Progress of Science and useful Arts, by securing for limited Times to Authors and Inventors the exclusive Right to their respective Writings and Discoveries;

To constitute Tribunals inferior to the supreme Court;

To define and punish Piracies and Felonies committed on the high Seas, and Offences against the Law of Nations;

To declare War, grant Letters of Marque and Reprisal, and make Rules concerning Captures on Land and Water;

To raise and support Armies, but no Appropriation of Money to that Use shall be for a longer Term than two Years;

To provide and maintain a Navy;

To make Rules for the Government and Regulation of the land and naval Forces;

To provide for calling forth the Militia to execute the Laws of the Union, suppress Insurrections and repel Invasions;

To provide for organizing, arming, and disciplining the Militia, and for governing such Part of them as may be employed in the Service of the United States, reserving to the States respectively, the Appointment of the Officers, and the Authority of training the Militia according to the discipline prescribed by Congress;

To exercise exclusive Legislation in all Cases whatsoever, over such District (not exceeding ten Miles square) as may, by Cession of particular States, and the Acceptance of Congress, become the Seat of the Government of the United States, and to exercise like Authority over all Places purchased by the Consent of the Legislature of the State in which the Same shall be, for the Erection of Forts, Magazines, Arsenals, dock-Yards, and other needful Buildings; — And

To make all Laws which shall be necessary and proper for carrying into Execution the foregoing Powers, and all other Powers vested by this Constitution in the Government of the United States, or in any Department or Officer thereof.

SECTION 9

The Migration or Importation of such Persons as any of the States now existing shall think proper to admit, shall not be prohibited by the Congress prior to the Year one thousand eight hundred and eight, but a Tax or duty may be imposed on such Importation, not exceeding ten dollars for each Person.

The Privilege of the Writ of Habeas Corpus shall not be suspended, unless when in Cases of Rebellion or Invasion the public Safety may require it.

No Bill of Attainder or ex post facto Law shall be passed.

No Capitation, or other direct, tax shall be laid, unless in Proportion to the Census or Enumeration herein before directed to be taken.

No Tax or Duty shall be laid on Articles exported from any State.

No Preference shall be given by any Regulation of Commerce or Revenue to the Ports of one State over those of another: nor shall Vessels bound to, or from, one State, be obliged to enter, clear, or pay Duties in another.

No Money shall be drawn from the Treasury, but in Consequence of Appropriations made by Law; and a regular Statement and Account of the Receipts and Expenditures of all public Money shall be published from time to time.

No Title of Nobility shall be granted by the United States: And no Person holding any Office of Profit or Trust under them, shall, without the Consent of the Congress, accept of any present, Emolument, Office, or Title, of any kind whatever, from any King, Prince, or foreign State.

Section 10

No State shall enter into any Treaty, Alliance, or Confederation; grant Letters of Marque and Reprisal; coin Money; emit Bills of Credit; make any Thing but gold and silver Coin a Tender in Payment of Debts; pass any Bill of Attainder, ex post facto Law, or Law impairing the Obligation of Contracts, or grant any Title of Nobility.

No State shall, without the Consent of the Congress, lay any Imposts or Duties on Imports or Exports, except what may be absolutely necessary for executing it's inspection Laws: and the net Produce of all Duties and Imposts, laid by any State on Imports or Exports, shall be for the Use of the Treasury of the United States; and all such Laws shall be subject to the Revision and Controul of the Congress.

No State shall, without the Consent of Congress, lay any Duty of Tonnage, keep Troops, or Ships of War in time of Peace, enter into any Agreement or Compact with another State, or with a foreign Power, or engage in War, unless actually invaded, or in such imminent Danger as will not admit of delay.

ARTICLE II
Section 1

The executive Power shall be vested in a President of the United States of America. He shall hold his Office during the Term of four Years, and, together with the Vice President, chosen for the same Term, be elected, as follows

Each State shall appoint, in such Manner as the Legislature thereof may direct, a Number of Electors, equal to the whole Number of Senators and Representatives to which the State may be entitled in the Congress: but no Senator or Representative, or Person holding an Office of Trust or Profit under the United States, shall be appointed an Elector.

The electors shall meet in their respective States, and vote by ballot for two Persons, of whom one at least shall not be an Inhabitant of the same State with themselves. And they shall make a List of all the Persons voted for, and of the Number of Votes for each; which List they shall sign and certify, and transmit sealed to the Seat of the Government of the United States, directed to the President of the Senate. The President of the Senate shall, in the Presence of the Senate and House of Representatives, open all the Certificates, and the Votes shall then be counted. The Person having the greatest Number of Votes shall be the President, if such Number be a Majority of the whole Number of Electors appointed; and if there be more than one who have such Majority, and have an equal Number of Votes, then the House of Representatives shall immediately chuse by Ballot one of them for President; and if no Person have a Majority, then from the five highest on the List the said House shall in like Manner chuse the President. But in chusing the President, the Votes shall be taken by States, the Representation from each State having one Vote; A quorum for this Purpose shall consist of a Member or Members from two thirds of the States, and a Majority of all the States shall be necessary to a Choice. In every Case, after the Choice of the President, the Person having the greatest Number of Votes of the Electors shall be the Vice President. But if there should remain two or more who have equal Votes, the Senate shall chuse from them by Ballot the Vice President.

The Congress may determine the Time of chusing the Electors, and the Day on which they shall give their Votes; which Day shall be the same throughout the United States.

No Person except a natural born Citizen, or a Citizen of the United States, at the time of the Adoption of this Constitution, shall be eligible to the Office of President; neither shall any Person be eligible to that Office who shall not have attained to the Age of thirty five Years, and been fourteen Years a Resident within the United States.

In Case of the Removal of the President from Office, or of his Death, Resignation or Inability to discharge the Powers and Duties of the said Office, the same shall devolve on the Vice President, and the Congress may by Law provide for the Case of Removal, Death, Resignation or Inability, both of the President and Vice President, declaring what Officer shall then act as President. and such Officer shall act accordingly, until the Disability be removed, or a President shall be elected.

The President shall, at stated Times, receive for his Services, a Compensation, which shall neither be encreased nor diminished during the Period for which he shall have been elected, and he shall not receive within that Period any other Emolument from the United States, or any of them.

Before he enter on the Execution of his Office, he shall take the following Oath or Affirmation: — " I do solemnly swear (or affirm) that I will faithfully execute the Office of President of the United States, and will to the best of my Ability, preserve, protect and defend the Constitution of the United States."

SECTION 2

The President shall be Commander in Chief of the Army and Navy of the United States, and of the Militia of the several States, when called into the actual Service of the United States; he may require the Opinion, in writing, of the principal Officer in each of the executive Departments, upon any Subject relating to the Duties of their respective Offices, and he shall have Power to grant Reprieves and Pardons for Offences against the United States, except in Cases of Impeachment.

He shall have Power, by and with the Advice and Consent of the Senate, to make Treaties, provided two thirds of the Senators present concur; and he shall nominate, and by and with the Advice and Consent of the Senate, shall appoint Ambassadors, other public Ministers and Consuls, Judges of the supreme Court, and all other Officers of the United States, whose Appointments are not herein otherwise provided for, and which shall be established by Law: but the Congress may by Law vest the Appointment of such inferior Officers, as they think proper, in the President alone, in the Courts of Law, or in the Heads of Departments.

The President shall have Power to fill up all Vacancies that may happen during the Recess of the Senate, by granting Commissions which shall expire at the End of their next Session.

SECTION 3

He shall from time to time give to the Congress Information of the State of the Union, and recommend to their Consideration such Measures as he shall judge necessary and expedient; he may, on extraordinary Occasions, convene both Houses, or either of them, and, in Case of Disagreement between them, with Respect to the Time of Adjournment, he may adjourn them to such Time as he shall think proper; he shall receive Ambassadors and other public Ministers; he shall take Care that the Laws be faithfully executed, and shall Commission all the Officers of the United States.

SECTION 4

The President, Vice President and all civil Officers of the United States, shall be removed from Office on Impeachment for, and Conviction of, Treason, Bribery, or other high Crimes and Misdemeanors.

ARTICLE III

SECTION 1

The judicial Power of the United States, shall be vested in one supreme Court, and in such inferior Courts as the Congress may from time to time ordain and establish. The Judges, both of the supreme and inferior Courts, shall hold their Offices during good Behaviour, and shall, at stated Times, receive for their Services, a Compensation, which shall not be diminished during their Continuance in Office.

SECTION 2

The judicial Power shall extend to all Cases, in Law and Equity, arising under this Constitution, the Laws of the United States, and Treaties made, or which shall be made, under their Authority; — to all Cases affecting Ambassadors, other public Ministers and Consuls; — to all Cases of admiralty and maritime Jurisdiction; — to Controversies to which the United States shall be a Party; — to Controversies between two or more States; — between a State and Citizens of another State; — between Citizens of different States, — between Citizens of the same State claiming Lands under Grants of different States, and between a State, or the Citizens thereof, and foreign States, Citizens or Subjects.

In all Cases affecting Ambassadors, other public Ministers and Consuls, and those in which a State shall be Party, the supreme Court shall have original Jurisdiction. In all the other Cases before mentioned, the supreme Court shall have appellate Jurisdiction, both as to Law and Fact, with such Exceptions, and under such Regulations as the Congress shall make.

The Trial of all Crimes, except in Cases of Impeachment, shall be by Jury; and such Trial shall be held in the State where the said Crimes shall have been committed; but when not committed within any State, the Trial shall be at such Place or Places as the Congress may by Law have directed.

Section 3

Treason against the United States, shall consist only in levying War against them, or in adhering to their Enemies, giving them Aid and Comfort. No Person shall be convicted of Treason unless on the Testimony of two Witnesses to the same overt Act, or on Confession in open Court.

The Congress shall have Power to declare the Punishment of Treason, but no Attainder of Treason shall work Corruption of Blood, or Forfeiture except during the Life of the Person attainted.

ARTICLE IV
Section 1

Full Faith and Credit shall be given in each State to the public Acts, Records, and judicial Proceedings of every other State. And the Congress may by general Laws prescribe the Manner in which such Acts, Records and Proceedings shall be proved, and the Effect thereof.

Section 2

The Citizens of each State shall be entitled to all Privileges and Immunities of Citizens in the several States.

A person charged in any State with Treason, Felony, or other Crime, who shall flee from Justice, and be found in another State, shall on Demand of the executive Authority of the State from which he fled, be delivered up, to be removed to the State having Jurisdiction of the Crime.

No Person held to Service or Labour in one State, under the Laws thereof, escaping into another, shall, in Consequence of any Law or Regulation therein, be discharged from such Service or Labour, but shall be delivered up on Claim of the Party to whom such Service or Labour may be due.

Section 3

New States may be admitted by the Congress into this Union; but no new State shall be formed or erected within the Jurisdiction of any other State; nor any State be formed by the Junction of two or more States, or Parts of States, without the Consent of the Legislatures of the States concerned as well as of the Congress.

The Congress shall have Power to dispose of and make all needful Rules and Regulations respecting the Territory or other Property belonging to the United States; and nothing in this Constitution shall be so construed as to Prejudice any Claims of the United States, or of any particular State.

SECTION 4

The United States shall guarantee to every State in this Union a Republican Form of Government, and shall protect each of them against Invasion; and on Application of the Legislature, or of the Executive (when the Legislature cannot be convened) against domestic Violence.

ARTICLE V

The Congress, whenever two thirds of both Houses shall deem it necessary, shall propose Amendments to this Constitution, or, on the Application of the Legislatures of two thirds of the several States, shall call a Convention for proposing Amendments, which, in either Case, shall be valid to all Intents and Purposes, as Part of this Constitution, when ratified by the Legislatures of three fourths of the several States, or by Conventions in three fourths thereof, as the one or the other Mode of Ratification may be proposed by the Congress; Provided that no Amendment which may be made prior to the Year One thousand eight hundred and eight shall in any Manner affect the first and fourth Clauses in the Ninth Section of the first Article; and that no State, without its Consent, shall be deprived of its equal Suffrage in the Senate.

ARTICLE VI

All Debts contracted and Engagements entered into, before the Adoption of this Constitution, shall be as valid against the United States under this Constitution, as under the Confederation.

This Constitution, and the Laws of the United States which shall be made in Pursuance thereof; and all Treaties made, or which shall be made, under the Authority of the United States, shall be the supreme Law of the Land; and the Judges in every State shall be bound thereby, any Thing in the Constitution or Laws of any State to the Contrary notwithstanding.

The Senators and Representatives before mentioned, and the Members of the several State Legislatures, and all executive and judicial Officers, both of the United States and of the several States, shall be bound by Oath or Affirmation, to support this Constitution; but no religious Test shall ever be required as a Qualification to any Office or public Trust under the United States.

ARTICLE VII

The Ratification of the Conventions of nine States, shall be sufficient for the Establishment of this Constitution between the States so ratifying the Same.

DONE in Convention by the Unanimous Consent of the States present the Seventeenth Day of September in the Year of our Lord one thousand seven hundred and Eighty seven and of the Independence of the United States of America the Twelfth. IN WITNESS whereof We have hereunto subscribed our Names.

G° WASHINGTON
Presid^t and deputy from Virginia

NEW HAMPSHIRE	John Langdon Nicholas Gilman
MASSACHUSETTS	Nathaniel Gorham Rufus King
CONNECTICUT	Wm. Saml. Johnson Roger Sherman
NEW YORK	Alexander Hamilton
NEW JERSEY	Wil: Livingston David Brearley Wm. Paterson Jona: Dayton
PENNSYLVANIA	B Franklin Thomas Mifflin Robt. Morris Geo. Clymer Thos. FitzSimons Jared Ingersoll James Wilson Gouv Morris
DELAWARE	Geo: Read Gunning Bedford jun John Dickinson Richard Bassett Jaco: Broom
MARYLAND	James McHenry Dan of St. Thos. Jenifer Danl. Carroll
VIRGINIA	John Blair — James Madison Jr.

NORTH
CAROLINA
{ WM. BLOUNT
RICHD. DOBBS SPAIGHT
HU WILLIAMSON

SOUTH
CAROLINA
{ J. RUTLEDGE
CHARLES COTESWORTH PINCKNEY
CHARLES PINCKNEY
PIERCE BUTLER

GEORGIA
{ WILLIAM FEW
ABR BALDWIN

Attest WILLIAM JACKSON *Secretary*

AMENDMENTS
ARTICLE I

[THE FIRST TEN ARTICLES PROPOSED 25 SEPTEMBER 1789; DECLARED IN FORCE 15 DECEMBER 1791]

Congress shall make no law respecting an establishment of religion, or prohibiting the free exercise thereof; or abridging the freedom of speech, or of the press; or the right of the people peaceably to assemble, and to petition the Government for a redress of grievances.

ARTICLE II

A well regulated Militia, being necessary to the security of a free State, the right of the people to keep and bear Arms, shall not be infringed.

ARTICLE III

No Soldier shall, in time of peace, be quartered in any house, without the consent of the Owner, nor in time of war, but in a manner to be prescribed by law.

ARTICLE IV

The right of the people to be secure in their persons, houses, papers, and effects, against unreasonable searches and seizures, shall not be violated, and no Warrants shall issue, but upon probable cause, supported by Oath or affirmation, and particularly describing the place to be searched, and the persons or things to be seized.

ARTICLE V

No person shall be held to answer for a capital, or otherwise infamous crime, unless on a presentment or indictment of a Grand Jury, except in cases arising in the land or naval forces, or in the Militia, when in actual service in time of War or public danger; nor shall any person be subject for the same offence to be twice put in jeopardy of life or limb; nor shall be compelled in any Criminal Case to be a witness against himself, nor be deprived of life, liberty, or property, without due process of law; nor shall private property be taken for public use, without just compensation.

ARTICLE VI

In all criminal prosecutions, the accused shall enjoy the right to a speedy and public trial, by an impartial jury of the State and district wherein the crime shall have been committed, which district shall have been previously ascertained by law, and to be informed of the

nature and cause of the accusation; to be confronted with the witnesses against him; to have compulsory process for obtaining Witnesses in his favor, and to have the Assistance of Counsel for his
defence.

ARTICLE VII

In suits at common law, where the value in controversy shall exceed
twenty dollars, the right of trial by jury shall be preserved, and no
fact tried by a jury shall be otherwise re-examined in any Court of
the United States, than according to the rules of the common law.

ARTICLE VIII

Excessive bail shall not be required, nor excessive fines imposed, nor
cruel and unusual punishments inflicted.

ARTICLE IX

The enumeration in the Constitution, of certain rights, shall not be
construed to deny or disparage others retained by the people.

ARTICLE X

The powers not delegated to the United States by the Constitution,
nor prohibited by it to the States, are reserved to the States respectively, or to the people.

ARTICLE XI

[PROPOSED 5 MARCH 1794; DECLARED RATIFIED 8 JANUARY 1798]
The Judicial power of the United States shall not be construed to extend to any suit in law or equity, commenced or prosecuted against
one of the United States by Citizens of another State, or by Citizens or Subjects of any Foreign State.

ARTICLE XII

[PROPOSED 12 DECEMBER 1803; DECLARED RATIFIED 25 SEPTEMBER 1804]
The Electors shall meet in their respective states, and vote by ballot
for President and Vice-President, one of whom, at least, shall not
be an inhabitant of the same state with themselves; they shall name
in their ballots the person voted for as President, and in distinct ballots the person voted for as Vice-President, and they shall make distinct lists of all persons voted for as President, and of all persons
voted for as Vice-President, and of the number of votes for each,
which lists they shall sign and certify, and transmit sealed to the
seat of the Government of the United States, directed to the President of the Senate; — The President of the Senate shall, in the presence of the Senate and House of Representatives, open all the certificates and the votes shall then be counted; — The person having
the greatest number of votes for President, shall be the President,

if such number be a majority of the whole number of Electors appointed; and if no person have such majority, then from the persons having the highest numbers not exceeding three on the list of those voted for as President, the House of Representatives shall choose immediately, by ballot, the President. But in choosing the President, the votes shall be taken by states, the representation from each state having one vote; a quorum for this purpose shall consist of a member or members from two-thirds of the states, and a majority of all the states shall be necessary to a choice. And if the House of Representatives shall not choose a President whenever the right of choice shall devolve upon them, before the fourth day of March next following, then the Vice-President shall act as President, as in the case of the death or other constitutional disability of the President. The person having the greatest number of votes as Vice-President, shall be the Vice-President, if such number be a majority of the whole number of Electors appointed, and if no person have a majority, then from the two highest numbers on the list, the Senate shall choose the Vice-President; a quorum for the purpose shall consist of two-thirds of the whole number of Senators, and a majority of the whole number shall be necessary to a choice. But no person constitutionally ineligible to the office of President shall be eligible to that of Vice-President of the United States.

ARTICLE XIII

[PROPOSED 1 FEBRUARY 1865; DECLARED RATIFIED 18 DECEMBER 1865]

SECTION 1

Neither slavery nor involuntary servitude, except as a punishment for crime whereof the party shall have been duly convicted, shall exist within the United States, or any place subject to their jurisdiction.

SECTION 2

Congress shall have power to enforce this article by appropriate legislation.

ARTICLE XIV

[PROPOSED 16 JUNE 1866; DECLARED RATIFIED 28 JULY 1868]

SECTION 1

All persons born or naturalized in the United States, and subject to the jurisdiction thereof, are citizens of the United States and of the State wherein they reside. No State shall make or enforce any law which shall abridge the privileges or immunities of citizens of the United States; nor shall any State deprive any person of life, liberty, or property, without due process of law; nor deny to any person within its jurisdiction the equal protection of the laws.

SECTION 2

Representatives shall be apportioned among the several States according to their respective numbers, counting the whole number of persons in each State, excluding Indians not taxed. But when the right to vote at any election for the choice of electors for President and Vice President of the United States, Representatives in Congress, the Executive and Judicial officers of a State, or the members of the Legislature thereof, is denied to any of the male inhabitants of such State, being twenty-one years of age, and citizens of the United States, or in any way abridged, except for participation in rebellion, or other crime, the basis of representation therein shall be reduced in the proportion which the number of such male citizens shall bear to the whole number of male citizens twenty-one years of age in such State.

SECTION 3

No person shall be a Senator or Representative in Congress, or elector of President and Vice President, or hold any office, civil, or military, under the United States, or under any State, who, having previously taken an oath, as a member of Congress, or as an officer of the United States, or as a member of any State legislature, or as an executive or judicial officer of any State, to support the Constitution of the United States, shall have engaged in insurrection or rebellion against the same, or given aid or comfort to the enemies thereof. But Congress may by a vote of two-thirds of each House, remove such disability.

SECTION 4

The validity of the public debt of the United States, authorized by law, including debts incurred for payment of pensions and bounties for services in suppressing insurrection or rebellion, shall not be questioned. But neither the United States nor any State shall assume or pay any debt or obligation incurred in aid of insurrection or rebellion against the United States, or any claim for the loss or emancipation of any slave; but all such debts, obligations and claims shall be held illegal and void.

SECTION 5

The Congress shall have power to enforce, by appropriate legislation, the provisions of this article.

ARTICLE XV

[PROPOSED 27 FEBRUARY 1869; DECLARED RATIFIED 30 MARCH 1870]

SECTION 1

The right of citizens of the United States to vote shall not be denied or abridged by the United States or by any State on account of race color, or previous condition of servitude.

SECTION 2

The Congress shall have power to enforce this article by appropriate legislation.

ARTICLE XVI

[PROPOSED 12 JULY 1909; DECLARED RATIFIED 25 FEBRUARY 1913]

The Congress shall have power to lay and collect taxes on incomes, from whatever source derived, without apportionment among the several States, and without regard to any census or enumeration.

ARTICLE XVII

[PROPOSED 16 MAY 1912; DECLARED RATIFIED 31 MAY 1913]

The Senate of the United States shall be composed of two senators from each State, elected by the people thereof, for six years; and each Senator shall have one vote. The electors in each State shall have the qualifications requisite for electors of the most numerous branch of the State legislature.

When vacancies happen in the representation of any State in the Senate, the executive authority of such State shall issue writs of election to fill such vacancies: PROVIDED, That the legislature of any State may empower the executive thereof to make temporary appointments until the people fill the vacancies by election as the legislature may direct.

This amendment shall not be so construed as to affect the election or term of any senator chosen before it becomes valid as part of the Constitution.

ARTICLE XVIII

[PROPOSED 18 DECEMBER 1917; DECLARED RATIFIED 29 JANUARY 1919]

After one year from the ratification of this article, the manufacture, sale, or transportation of intoxicating liquors within, the importation thereof into, or the exportation thereof from the United States and all territory subject to the jurisdiction thereof for beverage purposes is hereby prohibited.

The Congress and the several States shall have concurrent power to enforce this article by appropriate legislation.

This article shall be inoperative unless it shall have been ratified as an amendment to the Constitution by the legislatures of the several States, as provided in the Constitution, within seven years from the date of the submission hereof to the States by the Congress.

ARTICLE XIX

[PROPOSED 4 JUNE 1919; DECLARED RATIFIED 26 AUGUST 1920]

The right of citizens of the United States to vote shall not be denied or abridged by the United States or by any States on account of sex.

The Congress shall have power, by appropriate legislation, to enforce the provisions of this article.

ARTICLE XX

[PROPOSED 2 MARCH 1932; DECLARED RATIFIED 6 FEBRUARY 1933]

SECTION 1

The terms of the President and Vice-President shall end at noon on the twentieth day of January, and the terms of Senators and Representatives at noon on the third day of January, of the years in which such terms would have ended if this article had not been ratified; and the terms of their successors shall then begin.

SECTION 2

The Congress shall assemble at least once in every year, and such meeting shall begin at noon on the third day of January, unless they shall by law appoint a different day.

SECTION 3

If, at the time fixed for the beginning of the term of the President, the President-elect shall have died, the Vice-President-elect shall become President. If a President shall not have been chosen before the time fixed for the beginning of his term, or if the President-elect shall have failed to qualify, then the Vice-President-elect shall act as President until a President shall have qualified; and the Congress may by law provide for the case wherein neither a President-elect nor a Vice-President-elect shall have qualified, declaring who shall then act as President, or the manner in which one who is to act shall be selected, and such person shall act accordingly until a President or Vice-President shall have qualified.

SECTION 4

The Congress may by law provide for the case of the death of any of the persons from whom the House of Representatives may choose a President whenever the right of choice shall have devolved upon them, and for the case of the death of any of the persons from whom the Senate may choose a Vice-President whenever the right of choice shall have devolved upon them.

SECTION 5

Sections 1 and 2 shall take effect on the 15th day of October following the ratification of this article.

SECTION 6

This article shall be inoperative unless it shall have been ratified as an amendment to the Constitution by the legislatures of three-fourths of the several States within seven years from the date of its submission.

ARTICLE XXI

[PROPOSED 20 FEBRUARY 1933; ADOPTED 5 DECEMBER 1933]

SECTION 1

The eighteenth article of amendment to the Constitution of the United States is hereby repealed.

SECTION 2

The transportation or importation into any State, Territory or possession of the United States for delivery or use therein of intoxicating liquors, in violation of the laws thereof, is hereby prohibited.

SECTION 3

This article shall be inoperative unless it shall have been ratified as an amendment to the Constitution by convention in the several States, as provided in the Constitution, within seven years from the date of the submission hereof to the States by the Congress.

ARTICLE XXII

[PROPOSED 2 JUNE 1924; RATIFICATION PENDING]

SECTION 1

The Congress shall have power to limit, regulate, and prohibit the labor of persons under eighteen years of age.

SECTION 2

The power of the several States is unimpaired by this article except that the operation of State laws shall be suspended to the extent necessary to give effect to legislation enacted by the Congress.